The Journal of Thomas Moore

Group photograph taken by W. H. Fox Talbot in 1841. Others in the picture with Moore are Talbot's mother, Lady Elizabeth Fielding (on left); Talbot's wife; and their children. *Reproduced by permission of Mr. Gaisford St. Lawrence, Howth Castle, Howth, Co. Dublin.*

The Journal of Thomas Moore

VOLUME 5
1836–1842

Edited by
WILFRED S. DOWDEN

Associate Editors
BARBARA G. BARTHOLOMEW   JOY L. LINSLEY

DELAWARE

Newark: University of Delaware Press
London and Toronto: Associated University Presses

92
M824 ma
V. 5

Associated University Presses
440 Forsgate Drive
Cranbury, NJ 08512

Associated University Presses
25 Sicilian Avenue
London WC1A 2QH, England

Associated University Presses
P.O. Box 488, Port Credit
Mississauga, Ontario
Canada L5G 4M2

Library of Congress Cataloging-in-Publication Data
(Revised for vol. 5)

Moore, Thomas, 1779–1852.
  The journal of Thomas Moore.

AL   Vol. 1 lacks special title.
  Vol. 2. has imprint: Newark : University of Delaware Press; v.
3 : Newark : University of Delaware Press; London : Associated University
Presses.
  Includes bibliographies and indexes.
  Contents: —v. 2. 1821–1825—v. 3. 1826–
1830—   —v. 5. 1836–1842.
  1. Moore, Thomas, 1779–1852—Diaries. 2. Poets,
Irish—19th century—Diaries. I. Dowden, Wilfred S.
II. Bartholomew, Barbara, 1941–   . III. Linsley,
Joy L. IV. Title.
PR5056.A5   1983   828'.703   79-13541
ISBN 0-87413-145-6 (v. 1)
ISBN 0-87413-257-6 (v. 5)

Printed in the United States of America

Contents

Acknowledgments

My main debt of gratitude is to the firm of Longman, particularly the late M. F. K. Longman, J. F. G. Chapple, J. A. E. Higham, and Robert Welham, for permission to publish the Journal, and for their hospitality and assistance. I am especially grateful for the decision to make the manuscript of the Journal available by permitting me to bring it to the United States on a loan.

Had it not been for the invaluable work of the two associate editors, Barbara Bartholomew and Joy L. Linsley, the completion of the edition would have been considerably delayed and the text, annotation, and other matters of editorial practice much less polished than they are. Special thanks are due each of them.

Much more than common thanks are due those who have worked on the project from time to time as editorial assistants: Judy Craig, Ann Eutsler, Andrew Kappel, Kathryn Nall, Judy Nelson, Dale Priest, Kay Pope, Alan Rister, and Richard Schell.

I am also grateful for the assistance of O. C. Bartholomew and John Freeman.

The fine working facilities of the Fondren Library, Rice University, have made my task much easier, and I am grateful for the assistance of certain members of the staff: Samuel M. Carrington, Jr., Ralph Holibaugh, Ferne Hyman, Ola Moore, Richard O'Keefe, Nancy Parker, and Beth Wray.

For advice on the restoration of portions of the manuscript I owe thanks to Carolyn Horton, Win Phelan, and Peter Waters.

I am grateful to the Board and Administration of Rice University for financial support and released time from regular duties. Special thanks are due Allen Matusow, Dean of Humanities.

For advice, assistance, and encouragement I am grateful to my colleagues Edward O. Doughtie, Helen Eaker, Alan Grob, Priscilla Jane Huston, Walter Isle, David Minter, Jane C. Nitzsche, the late John Parish, Robert Patten, William B. Piper, Ann Schnoebelen, J. D. Thomas, George Williams, Joseph B. Wilson, and Geoffrey Winningham.

Scholars in this and related fields have been most helpful. I wish to thank Leslie A. Marchand for answering questions concerning Byron and for supporting my efforts with advice and encouragement. Special thanks are due Hoover H. Jordan, whose knowledge of Moore saved me effort and time on more than one occasion. I am grateful to others who have given assistance of various kinds: Betty T. Bennett, Mary Dix, and Linda Crist (of the Jefferson Davis Association, Rice University), David V. Erdman, Paula Feldman, the late Howard Mumford Jones, Donald A. Low, Jerome J. McGann, the late Eoin MacWhite, Doris Langley Moore, Charles E. Robinson, Lord Russell, the Earl of Shelburne, Terence DeVere White, and Carl Woodring.

My gratitude is also extended to the National Endowment for the Humanities and the American Philosophical Society for grants that enabled me to carry on this extensive and expensive project.

Finally, I wish to thank my wife, Sumarie, and my daughter, Lorel, for understanding and encouragement during the preparation of this edition.

Note on Editorial Policy

Insofar as is possible, I have tried to reproduce Moore's Journal as it was written. His own spelling, capitalization, and punctuation are transcribed as they appear in the manuscript.

Moore was not always consistent in spelling. Sometimes, for example, he spelled his friend Lord John Russell's name with one *l*, and reversed the *i* and *e* in Fielding and other words. He used the dash as his all-purpose mark of punctuation at the end of sentences and even at times in the middle of the sentence where a semicolon would now appear. He was casual about capitalization, often beginning a sentence following a dash with a small letter. At other times words within a sentence were capitalized, apparently for emphasis. A bracketed *sic* is used on the rare instances where ambiguity might result from a misspelling or syntactical lapse. Superior letters such as M^r. or 3rd. have been lowered to Mr. and 3rd. Moore's practice of using & and &*c (et cetera)* has been followed throughout.

Boldface ornamental brackets { } have been used to enclose material omitted in the Lord John Russell edition. Square brackets [ ] enclose

1. words and phrases that could not be recovered from the manuscript and are supplied from the context.

2. fragments of sentences that seem significant but are deleted in the manuscript. These passages are always designated in the text as deleted. Example: 29–31 August 1818, [the "et incarnatus est" of].

3. afterthoughts that Moore placed at the end of the manuscript page with asterisks marking their locations in the text. A note is always added to explain why the passage is in square brackets.

Moore was careless about the spelling of, and the placing of diacritical marks on, foreign words. Insofar as is possible, his method of writing foreign languages has been followed verbatim.

Moore seldom broke for a paragraph and used "run-on" sentences at will. Russell supplied paragraphs and punctuation in order to make the text more coherent. I have chosen to reproduce Moore's text as accurately as possible in this respect, and often one finds that he ran two or more sentences together without any attempt to separate them for clarity by any punctuation other than the dash.

Notes have been supplied as the text demanded them. Most, though not all, quotations have been identified, but only on rare occasions have the sources of foreign quotations been cited. Books, dramas, and operas that Moore read or saw have been identified by author, title, and date. For opera the date is that of the first performance; for drama, the date of publication or of the first performance.

Moore's penchant for naming all of the people he met at dinner parties or elsewhere has made comprehensive identification impossible. Hence identification is made, usually in a note, only when it is necessary to clarify the text. Otherwise, people whose names recur most persistently in the text are identified in a glossary of proper names at the end of the last volume.

Notes have been supplied to clarify political events mentioned by Moore, but no attempt has been made to explain fully the ramifications of these events.

The notes are numbered consecutively for each entry. There are a few cross-references, but, for the most part, the reader should consult the index for names of people or works identified in earlier notes.

Rice University
Houston, Texas

List of Scholarly Works
Most Frequently
Consulted

Byron, George Gordon, Lord. *Byron's Letters and Journals*. Edited by Leslie A. Marchand. 12 vols. Cambridge, Mass: Harvard University Press, Belknap Press, 1973–82.

———. *Complete Poetical Works*. Edited by Jerome J. McGann. 4 vols. Oxford: Clarendon Press, 1980–86.

———. *Lord Byron's Correspondence*. Edited by John Murray. 2 vols. London: John Murray, 1922.

———. *The Works of Lord Byron: A New, Revised and Enlarged Edition. Letters and Journals*. Edited by Rowland E. Prothero. 6 vols. London: John Murray, 1901–4.

———. *The Works of Lord Byron. A New, Revised and Enlarged Edition. Poetry*. Edited by Ernest Hartley Coleridge. 7 vols. London: John Murray, 1898–1905.

Gibbs, Lewis. *Sheridan*. London: J. M. Dent and Sons, 1947.

Greville, Charles C. F. *The Greville Memoirs*. Edited by Henry Reeve. 6 vols. London: Longmans, Green, and Co., 1875 and 1885.

Halévy, Élie. *A History of the English People in the Nineteenth Century*. Translated by E. I. Watkin and D. A. Barker. 2d ed., rev. 4 vols. London: Ernest Benn, 1949.

Hansard Parliamentry Debates, 1st series (1803–20); 2d series (1820–30); 3d series (1830–91).

Jones, Howard Mumford. *The Harp that Once—*. New York: Henry Holt and Company, 1937.

Jordan, Hoover H. *Bolt Upright: The Life of Thomas Moore*. 2 vols. Salzburg Studies in English Literature. Salzburg: Institut für Englische Sprache und Literatur, 1975.

Longford, Elizabeth Pakenham, Countess of. *Wellington*. 1st U.S. ed. 2 vols. New York: Harper and Row, 1969–72.

Marchand, Leslie A. *Byron, a Biography*. 3 vols. New York: Alfred A. Knopf, 1957.

Moore, Thomas. *The Letters of Thomas Moore*. Edited by Wilfred S. Dowden. 2 vols. Oxford: The Clarendon Press, 1964.

———. *Memoirs, Journal, and Correspondence of Thomas Moore*. Edited by Lord John Russell. 8 vols. London: Longman, Brown, Green, and Longmans, 1853–56.

———. *The Poetical Works of Thomas Moore*. 10 vols. London: Longman, Brown, Green, and Longmans, 1853.

O'Connell, Daniel. *Correspondence of Daniel O'Connell*. Edited by W. J. Fitzpatrick. 2 vols. New York: Longman, Green, 1888.

———. *The Correspondence of Daniel O'Connell*. Edited by Maurice R. O'Connell. 2 vols. Dublin: Irish University Press, 1973.

Russell, Lord John, *Early Correspondence of Lord John Russell 1805–40.* Edited by Rollo Russell. 2 vols. London: T. Fisher Unwin, 1913.

Sheridan, Richard Brinsley. *The Plays and Poems of Richard Brinsley Sheridan.* Edited by R. Compton Rhodes. 3 vols. New York: Russell and Russell, 1962.

Sichel, Walter. *Sheridan.* 2 vols. Boston: Houghton Mifflin Company, 1909.

The Journal of Thomas Moore

1836

January {1, 1836. [Friday]—To Bowood, Mulvany & I.—The party at dinner Lord & Lady Howick, Lord & Lady Barrington, Lord Radnor & his second son, Miss Fox &c. Singing in the evening with Lady Barrington— Lady Howick most marvellously improved since I last met her, as Miss Copley—having been then that worst of social monstrosities, a female wag, but being now as it struck me refined into a gentle & intelligent woman of fashion—It turns out that the scrap of MS. which Lord Compton supposed to be mine and has carried off as such was, after all my son Tom's, who being put to sleep in my room the night he went with Lord Kerry to the Ball amused himself with scribbling rhymes before he went to bed, and wrote something, as he told me about "dreaming a dream" and the "stars shining *merrily* & *bright*"—so that this scrap, with its glorious confusion of adjective & adverb will now, I dare say, go down to posterity as mine.—All very much amused when I told them this.

2 [Saturday]—After breakfast returned to Sloperton with Mulvany.

3, 4, 5, 6 [Sunday–Wednesday]—At home.

7 [Thursday]—To Bowood to dinner, Tom & I—Bessy having been asked, but thinking it too much for her, as having to go to Farleigh next day— Company chiefly natives, Mr. & Mrs. Walter Long, Mr. Methuen & daughter, the Phipps's, and Brabant.—Sung a good deal in the evening.

8 [Friday]—Tom & I off soon after breakfast to Sloperton, and from thence started all for Farleigh—Company, the Boodés & Miss Avenill, Sir Henry Bayntun & son, & Sir Courtenay Boyle, the brother of Lord Cork—Music

in the evening—Singing from Mrs. Boodé, Miss Avenil and young Bayntun (all good) and abundance from myself, with which they seemed much pleased.

9 [Saturday]—The Boodés &c. off—none left but ourselves—Had received from the Longmans before I left home the sheets of a small work they are about to publish on "Etiquette," which they begged me to look over & correct such mistakes as my "knowledge of the world" might enable me to detect in it—Amused the company at breakfast a good deal by reading to them some extracts from it, the thing being itself full of the very vulgarisms & cockneyisms which it professes to cure. Looked over Houlton's books & wrote a few sentences of my History—None but the family at dinner.

10 [Sunday]—After breakfast walked over to Freshford to call on the Napiers—Found him in full vigour of rage and *row* on the subject of the *démêlé* he has got into in Bath with Borthwick, Captn. Vorstum & God knows how many others—Read me all the correspondence, paragraphs &c. relating to it. Never was man more formed for warfare, *petty* as well as *great*. Had a snowy and blowy walk back to Farleigh—Family party again. All very anxious (except myself) that we should stay over tomorrow, our intention originally having been to return home on that day.

11 [Monday]—Gave way to the wishes of the boys &c. and consented to remain to-day.—deep snow on the ground—Company to dinner, Mrs. White, Miss Nield, Mrs. Joy, and another lady, Nield being prevented from coming by a party at home—Singing in the evening—managed, in the absence of Catherine, to get through a duett of Asioli's with Flora, very nicely—had practised "Per valli, per boschi" with her in the morning, but she was not quite equal to it—

12 [Tuesday]—Started for home, in the Houlton's carriage, after breakfast, bringing away with me a folio from the Library—Rer. Britann. Scriptores (Commelin's Edition)[1]—took a Fly at Melksham, and got well & safe home. On my arrival found a note from Lord Lansdowne saying that he was going in a day or two to town and begging me to come, if disengaged & take a family dinner with him—Though but little prepared to be routed up again so soon, was unwilling to refuse so kind an invitation, and went. My walk down the green drive, half way up the legs in snow, not at all agreeable— The only addition to their family party, young Lord Crewe.—Slept there.— In talking of Made. de Stael's Delphine,[2] and its being supposed that in the

character of the heroine she meant to draw her own, I mentioned one trait which looked like this (as no romance-writer would be likely to *invent* it for a heroine) namely, Delphine's insisting upon having the obligations she conferred *acknowledged* by those who were the objects of them. This sort of *quid pro quo* feeling, which is clearly a deduction from the grace & generosity of kind actions was most probably Made. de Stael's own.—Lord L. mentioned Made. de Staels crying at something of Goldsmith's, I think, which Sir Samuel Romilly read aloud at Bowood—[Must try & remember to ask Lord L. *what* work or writing of Goldsmith's it was that produced this effect.][3]

13 [Wednesday]—On my return home, after breakfast, found that the boys, by some mistake about the Fly had missed of the places secured for them to town—wrote to Mr. Saunders to explain.

14 [Thursday]—Most severe weather—Bessy went with the boys to Devizes for the chance of places—Tom got one on the outside, but Russell none & was left at Devizes to go tomorrow—In the leading article of the Examiner last Sunday it was said (in reference to the late call of the *Times* upon the Tories to be more attentive to their Parliamentary duties in the approaching session, to give up their frivolous pursuits, their criminal indulgences &c. &c.) "Oh that Moore would throw the gathering of the Tories into his *piquant* verse!"[1] This invocation of the Times has brought upon me several notes of which the following are extracts & specimens.

"Bowood, Jany. 12

"* * * * There is a capital article in the last Examiner, and in it there is an appeal from Fonblanque to you which I cannot help hoping you will respond to to describe the Gathering of the Conservative *roués* described in some articles of the Times last week. Would not "Come from the Stews &c &c" do very well as a Parody upon "Come from the Hills where &c. &c."***,

**Ever yours
Kerry"
"Belgrave Square

Jany. 11h.

Extract from Examiner given.
"Will not the Cottage be in a blaze at this? Will not the pen be instantly seized and the ink flow in *Piquant* verse against those *damnable* Tories? Oh, do take the hint, or I will never frank another letter for Sloperton, eat salt with you or *sauce piquante,* unless we have the verses. I will vote against all Irish questions, swear that Roden, Lorton, Eniskillen &c. are the true

Saviours that Ireland must look to;—in short, it must be, my dear Moore—step forth, and throw your *gigantic pen* at their heads.

Yrs *2 a *friend* or a *determined*
enemy Essex"

The third note on the subject was given me by Lord Lansdowne, having been enclosed to him by Taylor, (the author of the History of Mohammedism),[3] and left open for Lord L. to read.

"Dear Sir—In the Sheikh Al Mohdi's Arabian Tales, Morad, the possessor of a magic ring, annoyed by a huge serpent whose death had been produced by his spell summons, by a second charm, the vultures, crows, ravens, kites, &c. to his aid, and is all but destroyed by the clouds of obscene birds that obey the summons. In the Examiner of Saturday last are words to the following effect. Oh that the unrivalled Muse of Moore would describe the Tories obeying the summons of the Times, coming from stews and Hells, from Cumberland's & Crockford's to save the Irish Church, or, as the phrase goes, to rescue our holy religion. You will find a translation of the Tale of Morad & the Magic Ring in the Court Magazine for September &c. &c. &c.

W. C. Taylor."

15. 16. [Friday–Saturday]—A very civil letter from Lord Cork inviting Bessy & myself to come to Marston to meet the Houltons next week.— Enquired, in a note I was writing to Lady Lansdowne what was the distance, easiest approach &c. to Marston, and in her answer she says "I never was there, but have always heard it was a very comfortable pleasant house to visit at; so I hope Mrs. Moore will go. She will like Lady Cork and Lady C. will appreciate her."—Answered Lord Cork, saying that Mrs. Moore had rather over-fatigued herself lately by society and would not be able to come, but that, taking for granted the coach to Frome would set me down at his house in time for dinner, I should myself have great pleasure in coming.

17 [Sunday]—Received an immense letter, 3s. postage, and filling (to the very rims,) eight pages of the largest sized writing paper, from some she-saint, who signs herself "Your Unknown Friend." Never was there a much larger or duller dose of abuse, my "Travels of an Irish Gentleman" being her chief text, but the vituperation extending pretty impartially to every thing that I have ever done, said, or written. Poor woman! she seems in a sad taking about me and my soul—and with all her horror & alarm on the subject it is amusing to see how deeply versed she is in the whole farrago of my writings, profane as well as sacred. I shall here give a few extracts from her huge Epistle, before I consign it to its proper place.

"You did not seek for a religion, but you went in search of any thing which could throw a false light and an unprincipled veil over a religion which you hate, but have not the justice to try whether it is according to the word of God or not, one which you vilify, insult & throw into as ridiculous a point of view as your severe pen and jaundiced mind is capable of."

"If you think such a power could belong to the Priests, why have you not, in mercy to your poor soul become one before this; surely every man should become a priest, and then there would be no occasion for the mercy of God, but for the poor females."

After accusing me of want of charity, she says of the Papists "that their Master (meaning, I suppose, Judas or the Devil) was a liar and a murderer from the beginning and they too will copy him to deny that they are his true and willing subjects at all times."

In another place, she gives a Parody of those lines of mine in Mokanna's dying speech, beginning

> But faith, fanatic faith, once wedded fast
> To some dear falshood, hugs it to the last.[1]

These she turns against Popery, and adds "Well, Sir, do you know these lines, altered & disfigured as they are, since they left your hands, by a poor ignorant female to serve her purposes and learn from this what a clever prejudiced mind, like yours can do to distort the truth &c. &c."—But I shall not waste any more of my precious eye-sight (which is at present I am sorry to say none of the best) with this saintly damsel's effusions. I cannot help mentioning, however, as a curious coincidence or rather contrast that on the very same day when her letter reached me I received one also from the Revd. F. C. Husenbeth (the opponent of Faber in what is called the Strasburg Controversy) wherein, after mentioning his intention to present to me a copy of a new theological work he has published[2] he adds "The best, and indeed only mode in my power of expressing my deep respect for your character & talents, as well as my sense of the benefit which you have rendered to religion by your incomparable works of late is to present you, in my present volume, with a slight testimony of great feeling."—

18 [Monday]—The carriage from Bowood, with Miss Fox & Lady Louisa, to take Bessy to see Lady Kerry's baby, which has just arrived from Ireland.— Went with them. Miss Fox mentioned some striking instances of Lord Holland's great sweetness of temper—The baby charming, and when in the arms of its fair, high-bred Mamma, with Lady Lansdowne's handsome face looking over the latter's shoulder, it forms as good a picture as need be. Lunched there, and having found some books I wanted, walked home (accompanied part of the way by Kerry) and left Bessy to return in the

carriage. Forget whether I have mentioned that Lord Kerry is employing himself upon a Life of his great ancestor Sir Wm. Petty,[1] some papers of the latter having lately come into the possession of Lord Lansdowne—Encouraged him by all means to go on with the task.

22 [Friday] Bessy and I dined & slept at Spye-Park—company at dinner, two sisters of Mrs. Starkey, Mr. & Mrs. Money & William ditto.—Am always glad to meet Money, notwithstanding his great superfluity of prose—he is a good man and a gentleman. Sung a good deal in the evening and all said they never heard me sing so well.

23 [Saturday]—Walked home after breakfast—Bessy nearly thrown down on the way, by the wind.}

24, 25 &c [Sunday–Monday]—Barbara Godfrey (the niece of one of the best & dearest friends I have ever had, Lady Donegall) being about to be married and I trust happily, Bessy, with her usual generosity sent her, as a nuptial gift, the beautiful tabinet gown Philip Crampton made her a present of, when I was last in Ireland. A note from Mary Godfrey to Bessy acknowledging this gift says as follows:—"Lest you should think your magnificent present for Barbara did not arrive safe I hasten to acknowledge it & to scold you, my dear friend, for having deprived yourself of so beautiful [a] gown, when you had already sent her so pretty a souvenir by Mr. Corry & had already gratified her by your kind & affectionate remembrance of her upon this eventful moment of her life. Moore's pencil & kind words added to this would have been delightful to her feelings—and why, dear Bessy, would you do so much more than you ought to have done? Why did you not keep your own handsome gown for your own handsome self?—The fact is, you and Moore ought to have just ten thousand a year, and how two such noble souls can get on in this world without it I can't conceive. My sister will take these beautiful things to her &c. &c. &c."

{26 &c. [Tuesday] A visit from Miss Fox on her way from Freshford where she had been for a few days with the Napiers.

28, 29 &c. [Thursday–Friday]

31. [Sunday]—Having received a letter from Dublin from the Committee for a Subscription to Reynolds, on whom such an unjust sentence was lately

passed sent through Milliken three pounds as my contribution.[1]—A note from Miss Fox of whom I had begged that she would ascertain for me what has been the fate of Gesenius (the great German scholar) at Holland House, as I had given him an introduction to Allen, and have never since heard what was the result. Incloses me, (with an apology from Lady Holland for not answering sooner) a memorandum from Allen of his two interviews with Gesenius which shows all to have been *comme il faut.*

Feby. 1, 2 &c. [Monday–Tuesday] Have had a correspondence lately (begun on *his* part) with Edward Moore relative to the proposal of Mr. Easthope long pending that I should become a contributor to the Morning Chronicle. Moore's last note on the subject will best explain the present state of the negociation—"I communicated to Mr. Easthope the contents of your letter & his answer was every thing that I could desire for you. He wishes that your connexion with the Chronicle should be on the same footing that you found so easy & agreeable with the Times," [I had mentioned in a general way, the very liberal and considerate manner in which I had always been treated, during my connexion with the Times][1] "and as to the *substantial* part, I may almost say that he gives me *carte blanche* to say what I think right. On this head, if you think proper to do so, I wish you would give me some notion of your ideas. I should think the most agreeable to you would be some annual arrangement, leaving it to you to write when & what you please."

3, 4, 5, 6. [Wednesday–Saturday]—at work—have not been beyond my garden, I am glad to say, for this fortnight past—. Miss Fox called one day, on her [*incomplete*]

7 [Sunday]—Wrote to Easthope, saying, among other things, that I expect to come to town in a short time, and that we shall then make some arrangement.

8 [Monday]—A letter from Brabant inviting me most earnestly to attend the Dinner to be given to Dundas, on his election, next Wednesday. But I have made up my mind to keep clear of the narrow circle of Devizes politics. The highest gain is, God knows, bad enough, but for such "small deer" as the Devizes politicians—in short, I shall keep clear of them.

9, 10, 11 [Tuesday–Thursday]—The anxiety of people for my squibs makes me almost nervous & fearful in again trying my hand at them—so much seems expected from me. In a note received to day from Lord Essex he says "Easthope is most anxious to have something on the subject you alluded to. He is ready to do every thing you can wish. Will you make me the vehicle of communicating any *Secret Articles* you may entrust to my care to deliver to him? They shall be so & no questions asked or seals broken; but do not withhold from the Public what you know is one of its first gratifications" "Yrs. Essex"—By the way, I saw quoted in a newspaper the other day, under the designation of "the quaint Law Epigram" (as if it had been as old as Methusalim) the two following lines from one of my Squibs

> If the Parson *in esse* submits to loss, he
> Inflicts the same on the Parson *in posse*.[1]

12, 13, 14 &c [Friday–Sunday]—Nothing very particular—my subscription of three pounds to the fund raising for Reynolds (on whom such an unjust sentence was lately passed in Dublin) has been received with Io Paeans by my friends of the Freemans's Journal & Evening Post.—Got down a copy of Cambrensis Eversus,[1] which the Longmans have long been in search of for me—the book being scarce & enormously dear. This copy which is lent for a short time by Smith & Hodges of Dublin is priced at near forty pounds.

15, 16 &C. [Monday–Tuesday]

17 [Wednesday]—While we were sitting after dinner John Scully (whom we have long expected) arrived—last from London.

18 [Thursday]—Got very agreeably through the day, John apparently well pleased with us & our little establishment—walked with him in the morning to Spye Park.

19 [Friday]—Took John to show him Bowood—the day very fine & our walk agreeable—much pleased with the house & grounds.

20 [Saturday]—Scully left us at eight o'clock in the morning to take the Waterford packet at Bristol.

21, 22 [Sunday–Monday]—Preparing for my trip to town.}

23 [Tuesday]—Set off in a Fly for Devizes, having taken my place in the White Hart for town—nearly an hour before my time. {A good Parsonic tract of Phipps's (the Devizes Rector) who came to the Reading Room while I was waiting there. In looking over the newspaper which announced the approaching death of the Bishop of Durham, he said "I see there's a Bishopric going."—thinking not of the man, but the place, the rich prize—not of the "vile corpus," but the "corporation sole."—Found a letter from Tom at the Post-Office, giving an account of another breeze between him and Saunders, and asking or rather gravely advising! (poor silly boy) that he should be taken away immediately from the Charter House.—Alone in the Coach most of the way, but joined by an out-sider when approaching town—a Parson of another description, a Radical, who hoped to live to see the day when there would not be a single Protestant clergyman (i.e. Established) in Ireland.—} Drove, on my arrival to Edward Moore's, according to promise, and found him & More OFerral just seated down to dinner. Dined very comfortably with them {& then} off to Paternoster Row, where I took up my abode till I should find other lodgings & was most hospitably received by Partners Rees & Brown.

24 [Wednesday]—After breakfast to Brooks's—found there a note from Lord Essex (whom I had written to before I came up) asking me to dine with him to-day. Called upon Rogers, and staid some time with him—most agreeable & cordial. Told me some amusing things, one of which was Theodore Hook's saying to some man with whom {Murray} (Biblipol.) dined the other day, and got as usual extremely drunk—"Why, you appear to me to have emptied your *wine*-cellar into your *book*-seller." {In talking of Bulwer & his wonderful reputation, R. said "For my part all I can say is that my acquaintances are divided into two parties, on the subject, one of which know the man & dislike him so much they won't read his books, and the other have read his books & dislike them so much they won't know the man." This, to be sure, settles both man & author most comfortably.—Went to call upon Lord John, but recollecting, when near Hyde Park corner, that I ought to be at the Charter House at one, took an Omnibus, and rattled down to Paternoster Row. From thence went to the Charter-House, and after a long conversation with Saunders, had Tom up, and gave him a lecture on his idleness & want of punctuality—the two points which Saunders most complained of in him, and which had led him to fear that he would not be sufficiently prepared for the examination he is to undergo at Easter for his exhibition. Settled now with Saunders (without of course communicating it to Tom) that Tom is to go on working as if for the Exhibition; but that when the time comes, if it should appear that he is at all likely to fail, Saunders is to save him the discredit of such failure, by not entering him as a candidate. Called upon the Doctor (whom I had not

before made acquaintance with) to request his attention to Russell's health, and to beg he would instantly let us know if any thing should be the matter with him [The part of this day's proceedings which refers to Tom and Saunders is placed under a wrong date, as it did not take place till the following day, Feby. 25th][1]—Took another omnibus to Barnes's (who was not yet up) and then off again to the West End. When about to proceed on my search for lodgings in the morning, luckily called at Talbots' in Sackville St, and was invited by them to take up my quarters there, which I did most willingly, and was in the course of the day installed in Feilding's room, to my no small delight & comfort. In passing through Bury St. afterwards, saw a Bill on my old lodgings (my lodgings, I mean, of nearly thirty years ago— No. 27 now, I think 28 then) and knocked at the door for the purpose of taking a view of the old gîte. Found my two-pair-stair rooms but little altered; the only important change being the introduction of a water-closet in the little dressing-room off the bed-room. In the parlour floor of that house Strangford used to be hard at work at his Camoens, while I was at the same time scribbling away at—I forget what—up stairs; and Carlo Doyle (now a grave retired officer)—was racketting up & down between both. All this came freshly back to my memory, as I followed the landlady up stairs. Called for by Rogers to go to Lord Essex's, company Lord Carlisle, Sydney Smith, Warburton & Watson—Lord E. again at me to do something against "those d——d orangemen." Nothing very remarkable from Sydney, which is, in itself, remarkable.}

25 [Thursday]—Part of to-days proceedings have been included by mistake in those of yesterday, though God knows, quite sufficient to the day is the bustle thereof.[1] Went to the British Museum & read for some time—{called upon Mulvany & saw him—}Dined at Brooks's, an old acquaintance of mine, Bob Smith (Lord Carrington's son) dining at a table near me, and had a good deal of conversation with him. Dressed & went *first* to the play to join the Byngs & Lord Russell, in the D. of Bedford's box and then to the Hollands, where I found, among others, Palgrave & Tytler (the Scotch historian)—Introduced to Palgrave who thanked me for the flattering terms in which I had mentioned him in my history—Suggested my introducing an ancient Map (such as was done by Crofton Croker for the Irish State Papers) showing the countries of the old Irish Septs, as also a map of the Pale as far as it could be ascertained. In telling him how much I had profited by his Book,[2] in my first Volume, I added that I should have to draw further upon it, in touching on Danish matters, and he said that any assistance he could himself personally give me, on those points, I might readily command. Had some talk also with Tytler, who spoke of the expedition of Bruce to Ireland as a future part of my task peculiarly interesting— Asked by my Lady to dine on Tuesday next, but told her I feared I had

some dinner engagement for that day which I could not now immediately recollect. Remembered afterwards that it was to Sir Benjamin Brodie, a dinner concocted for me by Hume. In the course of this day I was in no less than 4 omnibuses, and three hackney coaches. {Heard to-day not a bad thing which was said of Bickersteth's late marriage by Lady Charlotte Lindsay—referring to his close connexion with Lady Oxford's family, "that he had given birth to one daughter, life to another, and had now married a third." A full dress party at the Lansdowne's this evening which I was at first inclined to go to, Lady L. having written to me to say I might go in every day suit, but not having done my duty in attending the Levee yesterday, thought I had better not.

26 [Friday]—The very perfection of disagreeable weather—went to the British Museum—poked away at old musty books for some time.—Called at Mulvany's—Had written a note to Hume yesterday evening, asking him to meet me at his College of Physicians to-day at three o'clock—was there at the hour, and was shown up to the Reading Room, which happened to be quite empty—I enjoyed a whole hour there of perfect solitude and repose, and have seldom felt any thing more refreshing—At four, Hume not having made his appearance, I flew off to fresh bustle. Called at the Hollands to mention my engagement for Tuesday, and to offer myself for to-day, should there be a vacancy at their table, but found it had already overflowed.—To Brooks's, where on my mentioning this, the Duke of Norfolk said "You had better then come & fast, like a good Papist with me"—(this being Friday)—agreed to do so—Company at dinner only Sir Thomas Gage, Blount & his son. The maigre fare excellent.—Went afterwards to the Hollands, where I found Pozzo di Borgo, and some other foreign diplomatist, besides Lord Seaforth & one or two more. Pozzo referred to the time of our meeting in Paris—"Il y a douze ans," I said—"Ah" he answered "vous pouver compter—I have long given that up."—Forgot to mention that I had breakfasted in the morning with the Lansdownes, and heard all about their gay party last night.}

27 [Saturday]—To British Museum in the morning—Dined with Bryan, Company, Shiel, Wyse, and a Mr. Finlay—Talked of an infinity of subjects—Shiel giving some good mimickeries of Dan, and having evidently no vast respect for his great Coryphée.—Was astonished on removing to the drawing-room to find we had sat so late, it being then within twenty minutes of one o'clock.—quite a *séance* of the old times. Received a letter this morning sent up to me from Sloperton franked by OConnell and coming from a Mr. Quin, inclosing me a prospectus of a new Quarterly Review about to be set up, under the announced auspices of Dr. Wiseman,

OConnell & Mr. Quin himself[1]—In the course of this letter is the following passage—"On my mentioning in the hearing of Mr. OConnell that I was about to write to you, he said "Oh let me frank the letter to Moore"—after stating which Mr. Quin proceeds to add (evidently not without OConnell's sanction) what pleasure it would give him to see two such men shake hands & be friends &c. &c." This opening, thus made by OConnell himself, being all that I wanted (he being the offended party) I was resolved to lose no time in availing myself of it. In the course of the morning was called out of Brooks's by a visit from Mr. Quin himself who had just heard I was in town, and had some conversation with him, but his anxiety being all centered upon the one point of inducing me to become a cooperator in the projected Review, I had no opportunity nor indeed ever once thought of alluding, during our conversation, to what he had said on the subject of OConnell. This, though it turned out afterwards to be fortunate, I regretted at the time, as capable of being interpreted into an ungracious backwardness on my part.

28 [Sunday]—Breakfasted at home with my very kind host and hostess, and went afterwards to the Warwick St. Chapel, where I was, as usual, much affected by the music—though not a very striking Mass. Found from Tom Cooke (who said if he had known I was coming that he would have had something better for me) that it was the composition of the organist. Went to Rogers's, and while there, Lord & Lady Seymour called, she looking in great beauty. {After sitting for some time, all walked out together through the Park. Parted with Rogers at Hyde Park Corner, and posted away to Beaufort Buildings, where I found Mrs. D. at home and sat for a short time with her. Called afterwards at Shee's—he not at home, but she full of kindness & talking with tears in her eyes, of my pension.} [Being anxious to settle as soon as I could my affair with OConnell, and being convinced, on a little consideration, that to employ any intermediate person would do much more harm than good (such persons being in general more likely to make difficulties than to remove them) I resolved, now that the advance had been so far made by OConnell, to do the rest without further machinery myself. Knowing that he, in general, passed a great part of the day at Brooks's on a Sunday, I proceeded thither after returning from Shee's, and there found him at a table reading a newspaper. Walking direct up to him, with my hand held out, I said, smiling "That *frank* proceeding of yours has settled everything." He instantly rose, looking rather embarrassed and nervous, when I said, in the same cheerful tone, "You remember the frank?"—"Yes," he answered (having now recovered his self-possession and shaking my hand cordially) I *do* remember, and you have answered it exactly as I expected you would." This is *verbatim* what passed.][1] Dined at Lansdowne House—large party, Lords Melbourne, Carlisle, Morpeth, the Hollands,

Mintos, Langdales &c—got seated between Lord Minto & Lord Langdale, and found my position very agreeable {*except* for the being situated within one of my Lady Holland, who was in one of those hoity-toity moods, when she is any thing but *safe* company.} Some talk with my noble neighbors about Napier, during which a question arose as to the justifiableness of his using the Private Diary of Sir John Moore which James Moore had confided to him for the purpose of his Military history—using this same document *against* James Moore himself in the bitter article which he (Napier) wrote in the Edinburgh.[2] After giving my opinion on the subject to Lord Minto, found, on putting the case to Lord Langdale that his view of it exactly coincided with my own—namely that, this document having been given to Napier by James Moore for the express purpose of defending his brother, Sir John Moore's character, Napier was not diverting it from this purpose, nor in any degree betraying his trust, by employing it against the very worst attack of all that had been made upon Sir John—that which came under the imposing authority of his own brother.—{Notwithstanding, however all this, & that I think the above to be a very *tenable* view of the case, I confess that I doubt very much whether if I had been placed in Napier's situation, I could have brought myself so to act upon it. Forgot to mention among the guests Taylor (Von-Arteveldt) whom I thought I heard talk (for he was at some distance from me) talking rather sillily—Some conversation with Allen in the evening about Ireland. Mentioned to him a passage relating to the Irish in the Saxon Poem on the battle of Brunanburh,[3] which I find very differently translated by Dr. OConnor & Ingram—Begged him to look at it, and to give me *his* opinion as to the proper version of the passage.}

29 [Monday]—Breakfasted with Rogers to meet Taylor and young Villars— Conversation on various topics—referred to Shakspeare's Sonnets for one that Taylor had, on some former occasion praised to Rogers. It begins "That time of year thou mayst in me behold" (Sonnet 73) and is full of sweet thoughts and language throughout. The first four lines are exquisite:

> That time of year thou may'st in me behold,
> When yellow leaves, or none, or few, do hang
> Upon those boughs which shake against the cold,
> Bare, ruin'd choirs where late the sweet birds sang.

A good deal of conversation about Southey who is a great friend of Taylor's—the immense correspondence of Southey who, like myself, makes a point of answering all who write to him, but, unlike me, devotes the better & fresher part of his day (the morning) to this task—whereas I minute myself during the last hour before dinner, to despatch as many of my answers to correspondents as I can scribble through in that interval. {Taylor himself has been in the habit of receiving two letters a week from

Southey for many years past. Talked about Carlisle, the author of the clever but strange articles in the Edinburgh on German Metaphysics[1]—is rarely now employed by any of the Periodicals (Taylor said) on account of his unintelligibility—Called upon Lady Macdonald, on the subject of Tom, who still continues to prefer the army, as a profession, to any thing else—had some talk with her on the subject during which she repeated what Miss Macdonald said near two years since, that General Macdonald would be most glad to do all he could; but added that the mere insertion of Tom's name on the list where already there are thousands, would be a mere nothing towards his advancement; and that therefore I must endeavor to get him on Lord Hill's select List, which would be easily effected by a line from Lord Lansdowne or any other of my high official friends—I asked her whether some distinguished military man would not be better, and she said, if Sir Ronald Ferguson would undertake it, nobody possessed greater influence.—

March 1st. [Tuesday][1] Dined at Sir B. Brodie's, Hume having called for me between six & seven—Company, Rogers, Chauntrey & his wife, Wilkie, Sir H. Ellis of the British Museum, and one or two more.—Reminded by Chantrey of my having asked him when we were on our way from Italy together, "which of all the great painters whose works he had there seen he would most wish to have been," and his answering "Tintoret." He himself, as he now mentioned, put the same question to Turner, after *his* return from Italy (without at all communicating what had passed between him and me) and his answer, curiously enough, was exactly the same. Chantrey, in relating the above, seemed to think that, if he himself could have given the matter a little more consideration, at the time when I put the question to him, his answer would have been "Titian." Told me of a groupe which he had just executed for the King, of Mrs. Jordan and some of their children,[2] and described the strong feeling which the King evinced when he first proposed the task to him, saying that it had been for many years his intention to have such a memorial executed, as soon as he should be in a situation to afford it. Much pressed to sing in the evening, and twice sat down to the Piano-forte to try for a voice—but the wretched weather & night air have kept me so constantly coughing, wheezing & sneezing, that all singing is out of the question—Meant to have gone afterwards to the Lockharts, where I had been asked to dine, to meet Lord & Lady Ashburton, but the night was so dreadful, and the same work about singing was so sure to occur there, that I gave it up and went home—Forgot to mention that I had, in the morning called upon the Ashburtons & sat with him & her for some time—nothing could be more kind than they were and Baring himself, as I have always found him, most agreeable—In two or three anecdotes which he told he made allusions amusingly enough to the change of his politics—"It was in the days of my Whiggism"—"at that time, you know, I was a flaming Whig"& c.} Dined at Miss Rogers's {(Feby. 29th)}— Company, Rogers, Hallam, & the Smiths (Sydney & Bobus)—Some talk after dinner with Hallam, about my History, which he seemed to think very favourably of—begged of him to mention any thing that had occurred to him in it, wrong or incorrect, as I should have the power of remedying all such errors in a Preface to the Second Volume, but he said that no such objections occurred to him. Was glad to hear that he himself is about to bring out a new work, embracing the Literary History of a most important period.[3]—Came away with Rogers & Sydney and left them at the Hollands' door, not feeling well enough to go in.

March 1st. [Tuesday]—Went to take my chance of finding Lord John before breakfast—did so, and breakfasted with him. His late conduct & speech on the subject of the Orangemen has gained him great glory, and "statesmanlike" is the epithet in every one's mouth in speaking of him.[4] I do most thoroughly rejoice in his success. Found him very well and, as usual, most kind. {His official boxes from the King arrived while we were at breakfast—read me the King's remarks on the late business which were in a tone of warm approval; also some curious instructions from his Majesty, one of which was that he (Lord John) should attend watchfully to the movements of the Duke of Brunswick during his intended visit to this country. On my return home found the following kind note from Lady Lansdowne—"Dear Mr. Moore—I hope you may be able to dine with us on Friday next, as I hardly spoke to you on Sunday. Pray do not be engaged, and I will get you as pleasant a dinner as I possibly can."—Unfortunately engaged for that day.—} Found Sir Ronald Ferguson at Brooks's and spoke to him about Tom; but he told me that already his hands were full, and that, at this very moment, there were no less than five or six recommendations of his on the List, which he was engaged in pressing on the attention of the Commander in Chief. He added, however, that if I would get Lord Lansdowne to make an application to Lord Hill, he himself would most willingly back it with his interest. Went to the British Museum, and poked through folios for an hour or two—Dined at Sir B. Brodies {&c (See the preceding page, where by mistake I have substituted the dinner of *this* day (as well as part of the morning) for that of Feby. 29th.)}

2nd [Wednesday]—Having met Wilkinson (the author of the late work on Egypt)[1] one of these mornings felt a great wish to visit the Panorama of Thebes under his guidance, and the Talbots being also anxious for the same, fixed this morning for the purpose—Went together (Hume also being of the party) after breakfast. Nothing could be more intelligent, satisfactory, and at the same time unaffected than his manner of explaining to us all the localities, antiquities &c. of the place, which he has every reason to be familiar with, having remained no less than twelve years in Egypt.] {Hume afterwards took us to the British Institution to see three pictures (by different artists) taken from Lalla Rookh & the Epicurean—none of them very good. Had written to Lady Lansdowne to say I would stay over Monday, if she could fix her dinner for that day, but Lord L's engagements being such as to render it impossible before Thursday I could not stay so long.—Dined with Douglas (my old friend, the Admiral)—company, an old acquaintance of mine Mrs. Bouverie, as she used to be, I think (Lady Asgill's sister), Colonel Duffy, one or two more. Col. D. towards the end of our séance, gave a long & rather prosy detail of the circumstances attending Byron's visit to Cephalonia[2]—The night being furiously wet, Sir Pulteney (whom I found very agreeable) offered me a seat in his hackney coach & set me down at Brooks's. In talking of Lady Frances Webster and her having had the glory of captivating two such men as Lord Byron & the D. of Wellington, Sir Pulteney said that the Duke found time every day (I suppose while at Paris) to write some pages to Lady Frances. Told of himself (Sir P.) having sat next Webster at the Duke's table, without knowing who he was, and talked pretty freely to him about the liaison between his wife and the Duke, she sitting opposite to them. His horror, afterwards, on finding out who it was he had been speaking to[3]—This morning drove about a good deal with Mrs. Talbot, and borrowed her carriage for a visit to Mrs. Lockhart whom I found at home. Spoke of Willis's book in which Lockhart (or rather his friend Wilson in *reference* to him) had been treated as scurvily as myself. Spoke also of Lockhart's Life of her father and the probability that it would before long, be completed[4]—hinted at the difficulties he has to encounter from "the sensitiveness" of people—but assuredly Lockhart must be much changed if he feels any squeamishness on this point. Among this morning's operation I called also upon Sir Henry Ellis, at the British Museum, he having offered very kindly yesterday to show me the part of the Library where Irish books are chiefly to be found, as also some Irish Mss.—After he left me, read for an hour or two, looking through Abbé Geoghegan's History (which I afterwards ordered of the Longmans) and making some extracts from Peter Lombard, de Reg. Hib. Sanct.][5]

3 [Thursday]—Breakfasted at home—then to the Longmans and from thence to the British Museum, where I made some further extracts and memorandums—dined at home with the Talbots, company, the two Strangways, and a Mrs., Miss and young Mr. Chambers. and from thence, most of us, went to an assembly at Lansdowne House.—Saw a number of old town acquaintances that I have not met for ages—among the rest Lady Har-

rowby, who was very civil & kind, & expressed regret on finding that I was so soon about to leave town. The beauties of the night were Miss Erskine, just come from abroad with her father Lord Erskine, and Sir Hussey Vivians young wife who is I believe, Irish—{Home pretty early.}

4 [Friday]—{Went to breakfast with the Lansdownes, chiefly for the purpose of asking him to mention Tom's name to Lord Hill which he promised to do.—Called afterwards on Edward Moore & sat some time with him—Thence to Rogers's (not at home) and to Burdett whom I was glad to find better after the effects of his late accident—asked me to dine with him to-day, saying "I suppose it is in vain to expect that you can be disengaged."—and true enough it was, as I had already three or four other dinner-tables placed at my disposal—Rogers's among the rest, to meet Lord Aberdeen &c. &c.—Went from thence to call upon Lady Francis Egerton whom I found at home and with her, Bobus Smith & Mrs. Sullivan—Asked me to dine tomorrow, but I was obliged to refuse, having already more than a week since, pledged myself to a dinner with Easthope, out of town!} I have omitted, by the by, among my scattered records of this visit to town to give some account of the arrangement I have at last entered into with Easthope for occasional contribution of Squibs to the Chronicle. Nothing could be more prompt & liberal than his whole proceedings on the subject, and, as I had more than once expressed to him my satisfaction at the terms on which I had contributed to the Times, he requested that the same might be the nature of my connexion with the Chronicle. Accordingly I commenced by receiving an advance from him of £100, a day or two after my arrival in town.—On my return home, found a letter from Lady Macdonald saying it was the opinion of the General that an application from *myself* at the Horse-Guards would have far more weight than any other, that no time should be lost in making it, and that he himself would be very happy to accompany me to the office at the Horse Guards for the purpose. Her note contained also an invitation to dinner tomorrow to meet Lord Morpeth & some others—but that {abominable *Cockney*} dinner at Hampstead! {I give it this epithet purely in compliment to Mr. Easthope's *H*s—or rather his *want* of *H*s.} Dined with Byng, Company, Lord De Roos, Charles Greville, young Cowper (Lord Cowper's son) & Stanley, the Under-Secretary of the Treasury—The man I most wanted to meet, Fonblanque, not there, being ill—In his note, which Byng showed me, expressed much regret, adding that "it was always a treat to him to meet Mr. Moore." Charles Greville, however, (whom *I* always like to meet) consoled me a little for the loss. Staid talking, with but few *memorabilia*, till near half past eleven, when (forgetting that I had promised Lady Minto to come to her ball) I walked home. {Called, this morning at the Charter-House to take leave of the youngsters.}

5. [Saturday]—Went to breakfast with Lord John—As he sat at the table there lay his official papers on one side and a long bill of fare (for a Cabinet dinner he gives tomorrow) on the other. Lady John not well enough to see me, but after breakfast he took me up to look at the new baby asleep, that I might report to Mrs. Moore (whom he knew to be a great baby-fancier) on my return—{Lady Lansdowne had told me it was remarkably small, but as far as I could judge from the face, as it lay, it seemed rather large for its age—am bound to stand up for the credit of little men's productions. Went from thence to the Horse-Guards, but General Macdonald not there—walked to Rogers's who was not at home and took a coach back when I found Macdonald in his office. After looking in vain for Lord Hill, he took me to Lord Fitzroy Somerset who, as he himself reminded me, used to know me very well, of yore, at Lady Jersey's. Asked Tom's age, and was sorry to find he was so old, as he might have a considerable time to wait, but assured me that Lord Hill would do every thing in his power for him.—Wrote a note to Easthope to try and get off the dinner—but without success. Called upon me in his carriage at five, and took me three mortal miles to his house near Hampstead, where I had to wait till seven for dinner. Company, besides the wife and two or three daughters (one of them a very intelligent & nice-mannered girl) Doctor Black, Mr. McGillivray (one of the proprietors and an old acquaintance of mine as far back as my visit to Montreal) Pettigrew, the surgeon, and one or two others. Had ordered a carriage between nine & ten when I got away to Lady Macdonald's—found there only the diners Lord Morpeth & Lord Adolphus Fitzclarence—Lord Morpeth showing some portraits of well-known people in Dublin done for him by Miss Clarke—most of them very like, and cleverly executed—Went from thence to Lady Mary Fox's,[1] where there were a number of the *élite,* as well as some odd people besides. In the middle of the room stood together, for a considerable time, in very earnest talk on *her* part, and the usual preternatural laugh, on his, Lord Melbourne & Mrs. Norton, all eagerness, she apparently, to avail herself of the opportunity of speaking with him and he, not less evidently (in his good-humoured & slap-dash way) wishing her at the d——l. After talking a little to Mrs. Ellis & others, took my departure.}

6 [Sunday]—{Breakfasted with Rogers, who has very amiably repeated his often expressed wish for Bessy to come up & pay him a week's visit—From thence to Warwick St. Chapel, and was as usual charmed with the Music, though the Mass was again one of the Organist's own (Cooke having, I dare say, forgot his promise) and I was disappointed at not hearing something of Mozart or Beethoven. Met Mulvany there, and went with him to his lodgings to give him a few minutes sitting for my *hand*. The day deluging rain,—Set off in an omnibus to pay my visits at the Duke of Sussex's & the

Duchess of Kent's—Saw Sir John Conway, at the latter's and sat some time with him—Expressed a hope that I should be in town for the Duchess's next party—"You'll see the Princess" he said "grown up a fine young woman." The Duchess, he added, often mentioned me and always expressed a strong wish to see me again. This all very civil and adroit, whatever may be the truth of it. The Duke of Sussex not visible—Called upon Bryan, and promised, if I could, to come & dine with him tomorrow—Has received a requisition numerously signed requesting him to stand for Kilkenny and has returned an answer assenting thereto—Went from thence to Brooks's, where I found OConnell, now quite certain of being unseated for Dublin— "But you will not be kept long" I said, "without another seat"—"Oh no," he answered "there's Kilkenny."—Poor Bryan! Called upon Mrs. Lenox Conyngham and upon Sydney Smith, who showed me over his new house—} Dined at Miss Rogers's, R. & I and Sydney going there together—Company, the Hollands, the Langdales, Lady Davy, Surgeon Travers, & Rogers's nephew—Sydney highly amusing in the evening, {after Lady Holland had departed—her constantly interfering spirit being a sad obstruction in the way of conversation—She said, however, some very kind words in the course of the evening, in praise of Bessy, which incline me to forgive her a little. On her doing so, Sydney (who has never seen Mrs. Moore, often as he has been in this neighbourhood) exclaimed "*I* always maintain there's no such woman"—}His description of the *dining* process by which people in London extract all they can from new literary lions was irresistibly comic— "Here's a new man of genius arrived—put on the stew-pan—fry away— we'll soon get it all out of him"—on this & one or two other topics he set off in a style that kept us all in roars of laughter.

{7 [Monday]—Breakfasted with Rogers & Miss Rogers—went with them to the Rehearsal of Ancient Music but could only stay a short time, having to prepare for my departure on the morrow—Dined with Bryan—only himself & Madame.}

8 [Tuesday]—Off in the Regulator for home—{My companions in the Coach a young man who had been a Lieutenant in the Navy—had visited Mexico and other interesting regions and was full of agreeable information concerning them—also another person, an ordinary & plebeian looking man, in whose features, however, when he began to speak, I thought I could discover traces of something familiar to me, and who showed himself acquainted not only with the principal countries of Europe, by having visited them, but with Mexico, and other parts of the New World by having read of them—Spoke a good deal of Lord Kingsborough's late magnificent work[1]—at last recognized him to be Lord Mountcashel, and after the

Lieutenant left us (for Lord M. signified that he did not wish to be *proclaimed*) passed the rest of our way together in conversation about old friends, the Granards, Lady E. Rawdon &c.—He spoke with warm praise of my Epicurean, which he seemed to set above most other works of fiction. When I told him that its success had been greater, I thought, abroad than in England, where Lalla Rookh appeared to me to have enjoyed more popularity, he said that Lalla Rookh was indeed "a beautiful flower, or rather collection of flowers," but the Epicurean was, in his opinion, a much higher order of production. There is another class of my productions which he seemed fortunately to know nothing about, namely, my Squibs—where he would have found himself thus profanely alluded to—

> What living creature, except his nurse,
> For Lord M——ntc——l cares a curse?[2]

the fact being, as I have always understood, that his Lordship married his own nurse.—Glad to get home.

8, 9, 10 &c. [Tuesday, 8 March–Tuesday, 22 March]—Buckled to business as well as the various cares & occupations I have on my mind would let me.— While in town had given to the Morning Chronicle a squib which I wrote before I went up "Police Reports. Nos. 1 & 2," and now sent him another entitled "Thoughts on the late destructive propositions of the Tories, by a Common Councilman"[1]—Worked away at my history.

23 [Wednesday]—Bessy & I to Bath to attend the Winsor's Concert & pass a day or two with the Crawfords. Took back with us Bessy Prowse who had been staying with Bessy during my absence. Called at Prior Park & saw Dr. Baines, who was full of courtesy & kindness—Brought away with me some books I wished to consult—Muratori, Ceillier and some Volumes of the Histoire Literaire de la France.[1]—Called upon the Windsors, with the hope of their inviting Mrs. Crawford to the Concert—which they did. Dined at Crawfords—nobody but themselves, and in the evening to the Concert, where I had to stand a considerable volley of staring from some rather *brazen* artillery—two young ladies, in particular, who turned their backs completely to the orchestra, and stood for some time in a state of immoveable gaze at me, to the no small amusement of Bessy and Mrs. Crawford. The music pretty good, but Miss Windsor herself rather gone off both in looks & singing—

24 [Thursday]—Set to making extracts from the books, and then drove in Crawford's carriage to Prior Park to take them back—was introduced

yesterday by Baines to Miss Crewe (Lord Crewe's sister) of whom he has made a convert. Saw her again to-day. He has also lately it seems hauled into his holy net, a very pretty Yorkshire girl, Miss Fairfax. Baines evidently a superficial man, as regards learning & talent, but with good manners and no doubt a great portion of worldly tact. Spoke to him of Wiseman, the Catholic writer, whose Letter to Poynder I had found lying for me at Crawford's, accompanied by a very civil note from the Author.[1] Baines thought him a Lawyer, though it turns out he is a Doctor of Divinity, and Professor of oriental languages in a College at Rome.—Dined With Miss Crawford, the Doctor & Mrs. C. having been engaged to a dinner before we announced our coming & Bessy & I went snugly together to the play—got a small box to ourselves and were both fools enough to cry over a sort of melodrama with which the entertainments concluded.

25 [Friday]—Home to Sloperton in a Fly.

26, 27 &c. [Saturday–Sunday] A note from Lord Kerry reminding me that I had promised to fix a day for dining with him, before his departure for town.}

29 [Tuesday]—Went to dine with the Kerrys—only themselves—Lady Louisa having gone to visit the Ricardos—A very nice quiet evening. Kerry seriously employed with his Life of Sir W. Petty, and likely I think to perform his task creditably, as he aims at little more than being Editor of such materials on the subject as he has been able to collect. Showed me a characteristic passage in one of Sir William's letters written in answer to somebody who was desirous of obtaining a peerage, and had applied to Petty for advice or aid. "I would rather be a copper farthing of intrinsic value than a brass half crown." {Slept there.

30 [Wednesday]—Walked home after breakfast, the weather most tremendous.}

31 [Thursday]—Sent up some verses to the Chronicle, "Erasmus on earth to Cicero in the Shades"[1] which I thought not bad, though, as usual, not having the most distant idea as to what *others* may think of them. A few lines which I omitted, as being too serious for the general cast of this trifle are perhaps worthy of being preserved here—In speaking of the supposed idols in St. Paul's, I went on thus:—

But tis really too sad;—in this once pious land,
Where the form of some Saint, touched by Painting's slow hand
Into grace more than human and looks half divine,
Was all the heart look'd for, on Piety's shrine,
To exalt its own picturings, high oer this sphere,
To a world where the clouds from around us will clear,
And such bright things shall *be* what they now but appear.

{April 1, 2, 3 [Friday–Sunday]—Received one of these days a letter from the Physician of the Charter-House, informing us that our dear Russell had had an attack of Scarlatina, but the symptoms very mild—The letter having been delayed a day, a postscript was added to say that he was now convalescent, and recommending that he should come home for a few days country air—Wrote to have him sent down.

6 [Wednesday]—Our sweet Bussy arrived, looking thin & pale, but in high spirits at getting home.—Brought a letter from Saunders from which it appeared that my presence in town would be necessary sooner than I expected, as Tom's examination is to come on the 14th & 15th. and Saunders wishes to consult with me previously to its taking place.}

11 [Monday] A visit from Bowles who is in a most amusing rage against the Bishops, on account of the transfer into their hands by the new Church Reform of the preferment & patronage hitherto vested in the Dean & Chapter—No Radical could be more furious on the subject than was this comical Canon in his own odd way;—on driving off from the door, he exclaimed to Mrs. Moore, "I say, Down with the Bishops!"

{12 [Tuesday]—Started with Russell, (who was all the better for his few days of rustication) in the White Hart Coach for town.—went on with Russell to the Charter House, and had a long conversation with Saunders about Tom, during which he repeated all he had said in his letter of the perfect satisfaction Tom had given him of late by his diligence, obedience, & good-humour—With respect to the Exhibition had great doubts of his obtaining it—thought that the Examiners would send him back for another year, both from his state of preparation and from its being now a year before his regular time that Tom went in as a candidate—Had great hopes, however, (almost a certainty) that they would bestow him the award called "an apprentice Fee" amounting to £60, which would give a degree of eclat to Tom's close at the school, and make him remember it through life with a pleasurable feeling, which he seemed to consider (and I think justly) to be a most desirable object. Having ascertained from me that it was my bona fide intention to take Tom away, in pursuance of his own wish, he then recommended that it should be done immediately after the Examination, as he should not like unnecessarily any interruption of the perfect good understanding there was now between them. Altogether, nothing could be more kind and considerate than [*MS damaged*] view of the whole matter.— Stopped on my way back to leave a squib I had brought with me at the Chronicle office, "Thoughts on Soap" or "Knowledge and Soap,"[1] I forget which—Found Isaack & had some talk with him. Went to Morley's Coffee House and got something to eat and then to my *gîte* in Sackville St. Had written up to Fanny, the Housemaid to ask for a bed for a few nights, not thinking there was any one in the house but found there Talbot & George Montgomery—}

13 [Wednesday]—Breakfasted at Brooks's—and from thence to Rogers's, where I found (as one is *always* sure to find the best things going with him) Lord Jeffrey whom I have not seen for a length of time, and was most glad to find so well & prosperous, with the honours of his new Judgeship about him. They say there *cannot* be a better or more satisfactory Judge, which I rejoice at exceedingly, not only for *his* sake but as an answer to your dull prose-men, who conceit that none but themselves are fit for grave occupations, and look down upon men of lively fancy as little better than (what the Law used to call Actors) "diverting vagabonds." Jeffrey's wife and daughter were also of the party, as well as old Wishaw, who mentioned an amusing instance of Dr. Parr's stilted phraseology—In addressing a well known lawyer (whose name I forget) after some great forensic display he had made, Parr said "Sir, you are incapable of doing justice to your own argument—you weaken it by diffusion, and perplex it by reiteration." Jeffrey, in allusion to my healthy looks said I was the only "vernal thing" he had yet seen.—Went down to the Charter House, and saw Tom, who was hard at work for his examination—in order to encourage him, mentioned what Saunders had spoken of him (& how pleased he was with his late way of going on). Went for a short time to the B. Museum.—Dined at Brookes's, and from thence to Drury Lane to see the Jewess[1]—my only chance of seeing any thing, before I plunged into engagements.

14 [Thursday]—{Breakfasted with Rogers, who had proposed our going together to the opera in the evening. The tickets for the stalls, he said, were a guinea & a half each—but no matter, he would pay for two, if we could get them. When I expostulated, he said it would be money well laid out—"I buy *you*," he said "for the evening." The difficulty then arose to our getting two stalls next each other, and we left the matter undecided, any further

than that I was at all events to dine with him. As I had set my heart upon hearing the opera, I had told him, on coming to breakfast, that a friend of mine had half promised to give me a Stall Ticket. Went, on leaving him, to Sam's to *buy* one, wishing, in the first place, not to be paid for by him, and in the second, not to lose my chance of hearing the opera. Found that there were but two stalls left, and those, by a rare accident, *next* each other—just the thing Rogers wished. Thought it a pity he should not know it & accordingly ran back to tell him, when he instantly issued forth with me for Sam's, and bought both tickets at a cheaper rate, too, than he expected, being only a guinea each. Was in some fear lest Sams should betray me as to my pretended *friend's ticket*—but all turned out rightly. Went to the British Museum, and read for some time.—}Dinner with R.—none but ourselves—Opera—the Gazza Ladra[1]—perfect, in every way—with four such singers as Grisi, Lablache, Tamburini & Rubini all doing their best, it could not be otherwise. By the omission of the part of Peppo the piece was in some degree *estropié*, but altogether the feat was complete and delicious— Very pretty dancing afterwards by Grisi's sister, her first appearance— Called, in the course of to-day at Lansdowne House—saw Lady L. whose looks and manner, in speaking of poor Lady Louisa (who daily, I fear, gets worse) affected me so much that I hurried away lest she should see how deeply I felt it—another minute, and I should have burst out a-crying.

15. [Friday] {Went to Lansdowne House, at ten o'clock, in order to breakfast with them, but found that they had already (on account of some early business of Lord Ls.) breakfasted—was obliged to pretend that I had also [*MS damaged*] that operation in order to prevent Lady L. from ordering breakfast for me—Went, for that purpose, to Brookes's where Hume caught me in the fact—Walked about with him afterwards a good deal— called at Lord John's, but he had rushed [*MS damaged*] on horse-back with Lord Lansdowne to Lady Louisa—Went for a few minutes to Lady John (leaving Hume waiting for me) and fixed to come to breakfast next morning—Was much struck with her prettiness—far more so than at Bowood.} Went with Hume to be introduced to his friend Marshall at the Horse-Guards—told him, of course, about Tom and the successful result of his late application to his studies which pleased him very much. Called for a short time at the Merewethers—Had left word at Bryan's, in passing, that I would dine with him to-day—Off to the Charter-House to learn how Tom's examinations had gone on—Saw the dear fellow himself, and found to my great delight that he had succeeded in getting the Exhibition (contrary evidently to Saunders's expectation) and with great credit & praise from the examiners—Saw Saunders afterwards, who confirmed all this to me, and said that Tom's papers were very good indeed—{These papers are drawn up in answer to questions connected with Scriptural History, which the Candi-

dates are obliged to compose at the moment when the questions are propounded and without any references to books, no small trial both of the stores of their memory and their promptness in bringing those stores to bear. Saunders added that he would send me those papers of Tom, and was quite sure I should be pleased with the historical information they displayed. He told me that, as Tom was not to avail himself of the Exhibition he would receive the 60 [*unrecovered*] fee—All this delightful news for Mamma—Had taken Tom's place for home tomorrow morning, but finding there a [*MS damaged*] public proceeding to be gone through, at which Saunders wished him to attend, went to the Coach Office, and exchanged [*MS damaged*] place for one by an Evening Coach—Forgot to mention that while walking with Hume to-day, I met Lord Anglesea & had some conversation with him—Now is seldom seen a sadder wretch—is still suffering, as he told me from the tic, and was seized with a short attack while speaking with me.} After my return from the Charter-House, met Lord Grey in Pall Mall—had seen him a day or two before, immediately after my arrival in town, and was passing him without perceiving who it was, when he of himself stopped & shook my hand very cordially.—I now begged of him to tell me at what hour of the day I should be most likely to find Lady Grey at home & he told me at two o'clock, any day, & added that she would be most happy to see me. After parting with him, it occurred to me that I ought to have mentioned Tom's success to him, and I accordingly ran back after him for the purpose—as his kindness, I said, had been the means of putting Tom in the Charter-House, it was right he should know that his patronage had not been thrown away—I then told him briefly the particulars, at which he seemed much gratified & congratulated me with much warmth. On my adding that I was just about to pack off my boy, with all his honour fresh about him, to his happy Mamma, I could see that tears almost came into his eyes, as he cordially shook my hand. Nothing indeed could be more amiable than his whole manner.—Called at the Hollands', and found Lord Holland writing letters from which, however, he turned away with his usual good-humour and conversed for some time as disengaged as if he had nothing whatever to do, though I found afterwards that one of the letters he was employed upon was to Lord Sligo of Jamaica, giving him an account of the state of things at home, and that there was some danger of its being too late for the Packet. Another of his letters from which he read me some sentences was on the subject of the new Bishops—his own wish being strongly that Shuttleworth should be among the number. Speaking of Arnold, I remarked that it would be certainly a strong step to make him a Bishop after his very Latitudinarian pamphlet on Church Reform, in which he was for widening the portals of the Church so liberally as to admit, if I recollect right, even Jews.[1] "Aye"—he said—"you call that Latitudinarian—but observe that the *principle* of Intolerance is still preserved even in that apparently liberal plan—as *after* he has widened his pale to the extent which he thought proper he then drew his line as rigorously as any of the rest and says, like them, "here we take our stand"; or, in other words, "here exclusion and intolerance begin"—{asked me to name a day for dining with them, which I was unable to do, and then told me I *must* go away, or he should be too late with his letters—A kind note from Lady Grey, asking me to dine tomorrow but can't—Dined with the Bryans—None but themselves. In returning home at night met a stream of carriages going to the Devonshire House Assembly, for which I had received an invitation but mistook the night—went to Brooks's—found Byng there on his way to D. House—pressed me to go with him, but I felt tired & went home to bed. Forgot to mention that I called upon Lady Grey this morning. [*One line unrecovered*] Went a little before two o'clock—found Lady Grey alone and had conversations with her which show how painfully sensitive her mind is on the subject of Lord Grey's present position—complained that his past services are entirely forgotten, and that others now reap the credit of what was really begun & effected by him—contrasted the enthusiasm felt towards him in Scotland with the cold appreciation of his merits here. I took pains to assure her that her view of the matter, though proceeding from the noblest & warmest feelings was, in my opinion, an entirely mistaken one; that, in fact, Lord Grey now stood higher & purer than perhaps any other public man, in the eyes of politicians of all parties; his peculiar good-fortune having been that he was enabled to withdraw from the perilous post which he occupied with all the light of his past career fresh about him, and before the arrival of any of those difficulties and failures which, in the natural course of affairs *must*, at no distant time, involve those he left behind him. All this I urged most anxiously upon her seeing how painfully the contrary impression was upon her mind, and she expressed herself grateful to find that I, at least, took this view of his position, adding that the confidence which my manner inspired had induced her to say much more to me on the subject than she had to any one else since she came to town.}

16 [Saturday]—{To breakfast with Lord & Lady John—he looking jaded, but in excellent spirits—walked with them afterwards to the Pantechnicon and passed a good deal of time sauntering among the various articles—Set off then to meet Tom, whom I found with his friend Boothby waiting for me near Brooks's—Took them to two or three different shows of wax-work—Called on Mrs. Montgomery, where I went in for a little while & found a newly arrived Italian singer, whom they made sit down and sing a Barcarolle for me. From thence to call at Cramer & Co's, where I lighted upon Balse, the new singer and composer, who sung for me his music to two of my late ballads. Gave Tom & his companion luncheon at Table's Hole in Leicester Square, where Tom had himself dined once or twice and recommended as good & cheap. Had taken his place for him in an Evening

Coach. Made some other calls, and then went to Piccadilly to meet Tom & see him off. Some talk with Byng while we were waiting [*MS damaged.*]} To dinner at Lord Essex's—Company, Rogers (who took me) Luttrell, Byng, Rich, and one or two more whom I forget. Conversation agreeable— particularly Lord Essex's stories about the Prince and old Travis—Off from thence to Lady John's where I found only the remains of her dinner-party, the Lysters, and among the rest, Sergeant Talfourd now radiant with the recent fame of his "Ion."[1] Introduced to him—home, [*MS damaged*] {by the bye, mentioned Tom to me this evening, and remarked how "good-look- ing" [*MS damaged*] was very much so while the likeness to his Mamma remained; but that is, I [*MS damaged*]

[17 Sunday]—Breakfasted with [Sydney] Smith—the morning darker and the air more thoroughly impregnated with dampness than I ever re- member it in the worst London November. Were obliged, during breakfast, to have candles lighted & close the shutters—None besides but Mrs. Sydney & the son—no lack of sunshine in Sydney himself. Sat for some time with him after breakfast. Among other things [*MS damaged*] looking gravely "Now, Moore, as I have a little time on my hands I can give you an hour by the watch, to convert me to the Catholic religion." This led to a little conversation on the subject—but, of course very much of the "touch and go" designation, Sydney having no very great store either of patience or learning for such a discussion. In speaking of the Fathers, I said that perhaps Gibbon's opinion came nearest the truth when he pronounced that they were *neither* Protestants nor Catholics; but that certainly, of the two, they were far more Catholic than they were Protestant. I was then proceed- ing to touch on Middleton's previous view of primitive founders of Chris- tianity, but seeing that he neither knew nor cared much about the matter, and it being rather a ticklish subject for a Sunday morning's confab with a Canon of St. Paul's (even with a Canon) I changed the discourse to some- thing else—From him went to eat at Jeffrey's, where I found the remains of a breakfast-party, viz—Empson, Sergeant Talfourd, and I forget who else Rogers having just gone.—Talked of Rogers—the freshness of mind he still preserves, and his exceeding acuteness as well as condensation of remark upon all subjects—agreed with me that what he will leave behind him, will [*MS damaged*] inadequate notion to future times of the man he is—con- versation & the miniature painting of daily life being his true sphere & strength—Went to Rogers's—found him at home and from there accom- panied by him to Mr. Grenville's [*MS damaged*] Mr. G. however, not able to see me—On our way thither we met the Speaker [*MS damaged*] Talfourd had just been with him, and had spoken with great pleasure of having met me at breakfast—"That's very good"—exclaimed Rogers—"Moore did not breakfast with him & I *did*—but it shows (he added, laughing) how ready he was to remember the greater man." This, though very civil of Sam, by no means his real opinion—nor ought it, indeed, to be so—Forget what else I did during the day—Dined at Lansdowne House—a large party—too large, indeed. Got next to Mr. Vale, the American Minister, and was rather interested by our conversation. Another American in the party, who is Minister at Petersburgh—Among the rest of the company was [*MS damaged*] Chancellor & his Lady, Sydney & Mrs. Smith, young Howard (Lord Suffolk's son) &c.

18. [Monday] After breakfast called upon Mr. Grenville with whom I sat for some time [*MS damaged*] collection of books on such subjects which he had several times before told me were always at my disposal and now repeated his kind offer but, as far as I could judge, there were no books in his Library I was, as yet, in want of. Went down to the Charter House and saw our dear Russell looking thin, but apparently well. Called on Mrs. Story & sat some time with her—Dined at the Longmans', Company chiefly Co. with the [addition] of good honest sensible Peter McCulloch, whom I always like to meet and a Reverend Barham, a Canon of St. Paul's, whom I never want to meet again.—a dealer in second-hand facts who lives much with Theodore Hook and *shows* it. The Partners all very hearty & hospitable. On returning home found Talbot as I have done most nights,—ready for conversation, and, as usual, intelligent and agreeable—Just now full of the idea of writing a Review on Arago's book about Meteors[1] (I think) but there is unluckily little chance of his ever turning his knowledge to account in any way whatsoever—Forgot to mention that I went down with Lord Essex to-day to the House of Lords, about five o'clock, with the hope of getting in—but found there was no chance.}

19 [Tuesday]—{Forget where I breakfasted—Met Lord Francis Egerton in the course of the day and walked with him a little way. Told me that Lady Francis was about to [*MS damaged*] *Proverbs*, like her Xarifa, some time since, and hoped I should be in town to attend them—Dined at Rogers's, Company, the Sydney Smiths, Lady Charlotte Lyndsay [*MS damaged*] Grenville, Luttrell, &c. In the evening came Lady Stanhope, Lady John Russell & the Milmans, Mrs. Millman looking very handsome, and invited me most *invitingly* to dine with them tomorrow—but I was already provided with dinners, half a dozen deep, one of the invitations being to the Greys, which I was most sorry to be obliged to refuse—} Went from Rogers's to Devonshire House—a large assembly, where I met with a number of old acquaintances—Had a good deal of talk with Lady Caroline Murray, and also with {poor} Lady King who {looked more dead than alive, and who} added another to my tantalizing list for tomorrow, by asking me to meet

her daughter-in-law, Ada, at dinner. By the bye, Mr. Vale the American minister the other day, in remarking on the cool and easy way in which the English take their own celebrated people, said that even he himself, though so long accustomed to this *poco-curante-ism* of theirs, was quite surprized at the little sensation made by Lady King, the other day, on her first appearance at Levee. Nobody, he said, even looked at her—whereas to an American the opportunity of seeing Lord Byron's daughter would be a sort of era in his life.[1] I own I should like to see her myself, though I am not sure that her {learned} Mamma may not have prepossessed her mind with her prejudices about me, which might possibly render our meeting not very agreeable. {By the way [*MS damaged*] told me last year (about the time of the marriage) that Lady Byron [*MS damaged*] Lord King's proposal for her daughter just in the same cold, matter-of-fact [*MS damaged*] which she has gone through every proceeding of her extraordinary} [*MS damaged*] As I was coming away from Devonshire House, there was that gay young gentleman about town, Rogers, just arrived, having got rid of his own party and still so "up to every thing" as to think it worth his while to come out at this late hour between 12 & one o'clock to attend a Ducal Assembly! Long may he be able & willing to do so, say I. {N. B. Sydney Smith in discussing the musical slang with which his Sunday diners the Canons treat him— "Curse the fellow—he can't sing Rogers in D."}

20 [Wednesday]—It was past one when I got to bed last night, and this morning saw me at half-past nine walking with Lord Lansdowne in his garden—congratulated him heartily (and *from* the heart) on the success of his speech the night before last which has made really a very great sensation[1]—[*MS damaged*] {was talked of at Brookes's yesterday. Saw Lady L. also—pressed me to breakfast with them, but I was engaged at Rogers's, [*several words unrecovered*] This day, being my last, full of bustle and racket—} dined at Stanley's (the Sub. Sec. of the Treasury) being called for & taken by Luttrell—Company, Sydney Smith (Jeffrey was also to have been of the party, but had been called off suddenly to Edinburgh by the death of a particular friend) Labouchere, Lord Clements, Lady Emmeline Wortley, Miss Dillon &c. &c.—In saying something about OConnell (I forget what) Luttrell applied the line "Through all the compass of the notes he ran" and then added, after a short pause "The diapason closing full in Dan."[2] {The dinner not very agreeable—On coming in to the drawing room to the ladies we found a strong odour of pastilles or incense, and were told *poetically* by Lady Emmeline "We have been trying to *unstinkify* ourselves"—It appeared that one of the lamps had gone out and had been offensive—but hardly more so, I should conceive, than this fine lady's description of it. The last time I met the said Lady Emmeline at dinner (it was at Lord Worcester's, I think) on being asked what she would have to eat, she answered, pointing to

a dish near her, "I'll have some of *that stuff.*" Luttrell, who, like Rogers, is at all in the ring, went off (with his lame leg, poor fellow) to a Ball given in the City by the Goldsmiths' Company, and I got home as well as I could, through the rain to bed, having to pack first with the help of Talbot's servant.}

21 [Thursday]—Off in the Regulator at nine o'clock for Calne—an intelligent gentleman in the Coach, with whom "sicut meus est mos" I became intimately acquainted on the journey, and had a good deal of interesting conversation. For a great part of the way, I supposed myself to be incog. but found then that he had been told at the Coach Office who he was to have for companion. We had been talking, at the time, about politics, (he, a red-hot Conservative) when struck by the mere fairness, I suppose, with which I had conceded some point to him, he said "This is the first time, Sir, I have ever had the honour of being in your society, but allow me to ask you, do you continue quite as much of Liberal in your politics as you formerly were?"—I answered "Quite as much as ever—I, of course, see the dangers that lie in our path as clearly as you do, and could have wished that the necessary changes which we are undergoing could have been brought about in a more gradual and skilful manner—but still the time had come for change, and we must now only take the rough with the smooth. This average quantity of public happiness will, I have little doubt be increased by the process." Found all well at home, thank God.—Among the invitations to dinner which I received this time in town and regretted not being able to accept, here were (besides the Greys' & Lady King's) the Milmans, Lord Hatherton's, Lord John's, Dr. Holland's Lord Holland's and one or two more. {Forgot to mention that I called one day on Mrs. Shelley, [*MS damaged*] some curious conversation with her about the Melbourne & Norton affair—It seems that Trelawney (the famous gentleman who married Miss Ulysses [*MS damaged*] &c.) was the person against whom Norton chiefly directed his suspicion, and Rogers told me that on his mentioning this to Trelawney, the latter said "Yes—Norton will look any where but the right quarter"—meaning Melbourne. In talking now of Lord [*MS damaged*] supposed intrigue with Mrs. N. Mrs. Shelley said significantly [*three lines deleted and unrecovered*] Rogers told me that Mrs. N. was one night lately at the theatre seated between Melbourne & Trelawney.}

25 [Monday]—Visit from Bowles—{Gave to} me a new pamphlet of his {(the superfoetation of his pen being endless)} to ask my opinion as to the title "Popish & Protestant Intolerance—the latter the least excuseable of the two." Cried, of course, "Bravo" at this—nothing in the world being truer—the people who appeal to reason are the very last who should find fault with others for making free use of it.

27 [Wednesday]—{Had a dinner at home—the two young Moneys & Mr. & Mrs. Starkey—got on very sociably—By the bye, when at Bryan's new house, the other day (the rooms of which are covered with looking glass—reflecting from Bryan's protuberances in every direction)—it brought to my mind Sydney Smith's description once of a room of this kind where he saw himself repeated on every side. "I fancied myself," he said "at a meeting of the clergy."—} Forgot to mention my having met Woolriche while in town & walked some time with him—In talking of old times the severe illness through which he (& Bailey) attended me, now thirty years ago formed one of our subjects, and he gave me a much stronger notion of my danger, at that time, than I had before entertained. Said that he had often mentioned the case since to brother surgeons, and with surprize at his own courage in taking the step he did. From some cause or other (it did not seem certain what) there came a large abcess in my right side which increased to suppuration, and my life or death it seems, depended upon whether it broke outwardly or inwardly—The step taken by Woolriche was to apply caustic to the tumour which succeeded in determining the discharge outwardly and, according to him, saved my life. {There came a full pint of matter from the abcess—} Reminded him that on the morning of that painful day having been confined, of course, to my bed, I repeated to him some gay Epicurean verses which I had composed during the eating of the caustic into the inflamed tumour. I should not be up to such a feat now—but seven & twenty & seven & fifty make all the difference. I rather think, however, that I was no more than six & twenty as it must be now one & thirty years since I had that illness,[1] and during the whole interval since, I have never (thanks be to God for such a blessing) been confined for one single day to my bed by any illness whatsoever! Ὑγιαίνειν μεν αριστον ανδρι θνητω

{29 [Friday]—To Bowles's—Walked & found it rather too much, particularly as Tom & I missed our way in going though the fields from Hughes's—Bessy remained at Buckhill—no one at dinner [*MS damaged*] & Bowles's Curate. Slept there.

[30] [Saturday]—Returned home—}

May 1 &c. [Sunday, 1 May–Monday, 13 May] Turned to work as well as I could, having been sadly thrown back by all these interruptions. Received among other odd letters one from Mr. Bailey, the Master of the Grammar School at Cambridge, who had before applied to me for permission to insert some of my translations of Anacreon in a new Edition he is about to publish of Dalzel's Analecta Graeca Minora.[1] In his present letter he has sent me—what I have been much amused and even flattered by—namely a corrected Edition of the Greek Anacreontic I ventured to write and prefix to my translation. It was a hazardous step for a boy educated in such an unprosodian school as Dublin College then was to venture upon—but it never was much criticized, and the only two occasions I afterwards heard of it was once when I paid a visit to the Historical Society of Trinity Coll. and found among the compositions read on that evening a translation of this same Greek Ode by Dr. Croly, [the present High-Priest of Toryism,] and another time when no less a Grecian than Charles Burney talked to me about it and though (if I recollect right his words) he said that some of the metre of it was "not legitimate," yet, on the whole his opinion left rather a flattering impression on my mind. But I own I little expected at this distance of time, to find a learned Greek of Cambridge sitting down gravely to annotate me and correct my *cake-lology.* The following is his very civil strain in which he speaks of my juvenile performance. "At the head of your volume is a Greek Ode in allusion to the frontispiece,—in which I noticed some metrical peccadillos; and straightway, by way of amusement, set about working them out. The *Matériel* of the Ode, the felicity of expression which pervades it and the general harmony of the lines are such that it is paying you no compliment whatever to say that, had you been of this University you would have been found nowhere but in the foremost ranks of those who have made Greek verse and the writing of it their study. I will transcribe it throughout, with the alterations I have ventured upon, distinguishing by the common metrical marks the syllables which, in the original copy, seem to militate against the rules of Greek Prosody, supporting the proposed alterations by adequate reference which I will do, for briefness' sake, in Latin." All this he has done and a most learned affair it looks. As I told him, in my answer to his letter "The school-boy was never so honoured by the Scholiast before."

{14, 15 &c. &c. [Saturday–Sunday]—Bowles called upon us one of these days to propose a trip to Clifton before the fine weather departed—agreed that Tom & myself should go with him, Russell, who is at home for the holidays, remaining as the protector of Mamma at home.

19 [Thursday]—Called for Bowles in his chariot & long-tails, the object being to reach Bristol in time for a Concert which was to take place to-day, but Bowles had not ascertained whether it was a morning or evening one— Could learn nothing on the subject at Bath, from whence we started (wondrous to say, for the honour of Bowles's courage) in a one horse Fly— the Long-tails not being able to proceed farther without rest. Found on arriving at Bristol that the music was not to be till evening—Put up at the Glocester, and had a most [*unrecovered*] drive before dinner to Lord

Clifford's—the day splendid & the view (which I never had before seen) magnificent. Our dinner very good & [*MS damaged*] being in high feather. The concert no great things nor the company very [*MS damaged*] Came away in the middle of the Second Act and was rather taken by surprize [as I] was leaving the room, on hearing an immense burst of clapping, there being nobody at the time performing, but which was soon explained by shouts of "Moore—Moore" accompanying it [*MS damaged*] acknowledge-ment to those around [*MS damaged*] bowing—one young man stretching forth his hands, begging that I would shake [hands] with him, and said "You would have [had this] long before, Sir, had the company known who you were"

[20] [Friday]—Had to breakfast with us Miller the [*MS damaged*] intelligent young man, Mr. Tripp, an architect residing at Bristol—After breakfast went to see the Cathedral—sat & listened to the [*MS damaged*] which as usual touched me to the very soul. The several voices of the unseen (for they were not *within* the place where they sung) boys and the rolling sounds of the organ through that now empty space was at once touching & sublime. Went to the Literary Institution, & wrote down our names—thence to the Studio of Mr. Tripp's brother, a very promising artist and then set out on our return to Bath—Remained there for a few hours, after which Bowles departed for Bremhill, and Tom & I in a Fly for Sloperton. In our way from Bristol, we had stopped at the house of a primitive old Clergyman a great friend of Bowles's, whose reception of me was full of originality as well as of kindness. Holding my hand in his for a few seconds and looking earnestly in my face he said "You must forgive me for thus staring at you—but this being the first time I have ever been in the presence of a gentleman with most of whose books I am well acquainted, you cannot wonder &c. &c."—Showed Bowles, on the way, my Cambridge friend's letter about my Greek Anacreontic—Bowles delighted with the music of the Ode, and preferred much (at least, for the sweetness and flow) my own original to the corrected reading of the Cambridge scholar. This led to a long conversation between us about Prosody which I have not leisure now to report—Got home to Sloperton, Tom & I (neither of us having eaten since we left Bristol) at nine o'clock—

21, 22 &c. &c. [Saturday, 21 May–Tuesday, 31 May] Nothing else of any importance for the remainder of this month—}

June, 1, 2, 3 &c [Wednesday–Friday]—At work on my history—finishing also some Sacred Songs for Cramer & Co. and sending things occasionally to the Chronicle. Since I returned home have sent them a Parody on "The Unfortunate Miss Bailey," "Oh Lord Lyndhurst," and "The Lofty Lords"[1] {—In copying the former of these the Freeman's Journal says, "The keen satire and refined wit of the following little Poem which we extract from the Morning Chronicle satisfactorily proves the author—there is only one man living that could have written it."}

5, 6, 7, 8 &c. [Sunday–Wednesday] Sent another thing to the Chronicle— "Epistle from Captain Rock to Lord Lyndhurst,"[1] {which has had great success—}The Globe, in extracting it says as follows—"There can be no mistake about the author of the following lines: there is but one to whom the world will at once ascribe their paternity—we hope to have more of the same sort from the same witty writer." The Courier in its leading article says "There is, alas, too much truth in the following lines addressed by Captain Rock to his friend Lord L——dh——t in an Epistle the whole of which we transfer to our columns from the M. Chronicle of this morning." {This, then adding "The brilliant [*MS damaged*] of the greatest poet of the age now appear, we are glad to observe in their [*MS damaged*] in the Morning Chronicle &c. &c."—The Spectator also, in copying the [*MS damaged*] "We are informed by the Courier that Mr. Ts. Moore, whose gems of wit and [*MS damaged*] illustrated the columns of the Times in the better days of that paper now tunes his lyre to the Chronicle. The following is &c." [*MS damaged*] Received a letter from Easthope, mentioning [the] great sensation that had been excited by the verses & expressing a hope that I would [*MS damaged*] them whenever it suited my [*MS damaged*] & leisure. Forgot to mention the [*MS damaged*] I received this [week] the sort of [*MS damaged*] that had been made of my name once before to [*MS damaged*] & the pieces of [*MS damaged*] that some of the papers on my own side had made [*MS damaged*] disturbed than pleased me, as I did not feel quite sure that it was not a got-up sensation by way of a puff for the Chronicle. So much was this my impression that (having now written, the whole number of things necessary to cover Easthope's advance of £100) I had nearly resolved not to contribute any more. In Easthope's letter, however, now received, he says "You will see, from the Times of to-day, how much you have served & may still continue to serve the good cause." What he alluded to was a pretended letter from a "Correspondent of the Times" (an old trick of theirs) noticing the "alacrity" with which the Radical papers were all attributing to my pen a scurrilous lampoon upon Lord Lyndhurst which had appeared in the Chronicle, and affecting to disbelieve the imputation, both on account of the badness of the verses and even more from their conviction that Mr. Moore who was, at this moment, receiving a pension from this nation, would feel that he was peculiarly bound not to employ his pen in attacking characters," for the gratification of "the faction" to which he belonged. This, at once, determined me to go on, both because it convinced me that my squibs *were* making an impression, and because, if I ceased now, it would be very naturally taken for granted that Barnes had silenced my small battery—Wrote to Easthope to tell him my determination and promising more in the same strain, whenever a good subject presented itself. I also mentioned to him the impression under which I had been, respecting the proclamation of my connexion with the Chronicle—Received from him an answer, by return of post, in which he most earnestly assured me that the agreement between us (as to the not proclaiming me, in any manner whatever) had been most faithfully observed on the part of the Chronicle.

12 [Sunday]—Sent up to the Chronicle "Epistle from Captain Rock to Terry Alt Esqr."[1]

15 [Wednesday]—Received from Easthope £100 advance on the renewal of our agreement.

16 [Thursday]—A letter from Corry one of these days to say that he would take us in his way back from London on Friday.

17 [Friday]—Driven into Devizes by Bessy, with her new poney which I was disappointed to find rather dangerously given to shying—She returned home in the evening (driven by Tom) while I remained for Scott's dinner—Company (besides jovial old Corry whom I was delighted to see looking so well) the Oliviers, Salmon & [*MS damaged*] & his son. In the evening came Dr. & Mrs. Seagrim & Lady Stewart, the latter a very nice musician, but evidently not caring much for any performance at which she herself is not engaged. Sung some things with her & Mrs. Seagrim & afterwards a good deal by myself—my audience not being much inclined to cry out "Basta"—Some waltzes beautifully played by Lady Seagrim—Slept at Scott's—

18 [Saturday]—Corry to breakfast—A paragraph among the leaders of the Times this morning, returning to the attack upon me, in pretty much the same strain, only a little perhaps less civil—evidently supposes that the articles in my defence which have appeared in the Globe are sanctioned or prompted [*MS damaged*] Must not let him remain under this impression— After breakfast, Scott, Corry & I walked into Devizes and from there Corry & I proceeded in a Fly to Sloperton—Dined with us at four & then set off for Bath. In the Times of this morning they say "With respect to the connexion between Mr. Moore & us to which the Globe alludes, whatever

honour we may have derived from it, we neither solicited its commencement nor importuned its continuance." Neither of these assertions is true.
My connexion with the Times began (as I have recorded, I believe, in this
Journal) by my volunteering a squib, as any other correspondent might, on
the subject of Fred. Robinson (Lord Ripon's) dealings with the Bank; and
by return of post I received a bank-note for £100 from Barnes with thanks
for my communication. [This is incorrect. I had sent at least 3 or 4 squibs
before the 100 pounds came.][1] If this was not a pretty strong solicitation of
connexion, there is no virtue then in £100 Bank Notes. Then as to the
"importuning of continuance," I have more than one letter from him,
written at the time of the [*MS damaged*] of the paper, asking very earnestly
whether I could not still continue to contribute [squibs *MS damaged*] uncon-
nected with politics—

19, 20 [Sunday–Monday]—Thought it safe and right, for both our sakes, to
write Barnes respecting my defender in the Globe, whoever he may be—
Moran most likely—accordingly wrote him a letter as follows—
    "Dear Barnes—It is merely for the purpose of setting you right, upon a
point of some importance to us both that I am induced to trouble you with
these few lines. From some expressions in a paragraph relating to myself
which appeared in the Times of Friday last, I am led to suspect you may be
under the impression that the articles which the Globe has good-naturedly
put forward in my defence have been written at my suggestion. I beg to
assure you that I have not had the slightest share either in the writing or the
prompting of them; and, moreover, that, whatever you may henceforward
think it your duty to say of me or my writings (within those bounds, of
course, which your own feelings would, I am sure, dictate) you shall never
be troubled with any reply, rejoinder or animadversion, on my part, as,
with all my publicity, I am not, thank God, so much of a merely public
writer as to lose sight of private associations and ties.
    I will not *quite* promise (seeing that the subject is a tempting one & *might*
be made memorable) that there shall not be found among my papers, when
I die, an Ode to "my Pensioned Muse," reminding her of the good behavior
she is bound to observe towards such & such Tory personages, after having
received "hush-money" from the Crown.
    In short, my dear Barnes, however your correspondents may lose their
temper towards me, I am determined, if possible, not to lose mine towards
you, but to continue, as usual,
                                                        Yours truly, T. Moore"

21, 22 [Tuesday–Wednesday]—Received the following answer from Barnes
    "Dear Moore—You may rely upon my entertaining the same friendly

feeling towards you which you have so handsomely expressed towards myself. An occasional notice may perhaps appear, but you need not apprehend any uncourteous or unfriendly attack. Private friendship is too valuable to be sacrificed on the altar of politics. I hope we shall see you before long; we will forget that there are such publications as the Times & Chronicle.

Yours ever T. Barnes"

22 [Wednesday]—In expectation of our dear Nell's arrival, who had written to say she would sail for Bristol yesterday—the weather very unsettled & occasionally stormy—were therefore in hopes she had not sailed—}

23 [Thursday]—Had given up all thoughts of seeing Ellen, till the next packet, when, to our joy she arrived, having had a very rough passage not arriving at Bristol till 12 o'clock last night. Quite well however—Bessy all delight to have her here once more. Brought, among other Irish reminiscences, some pretty lines entrusted to her by Miss Ferrall, in a note beginning thus "My dear Miss Moore—I send you the promised lines & beg of you to tell Mr. Moore that if he could have communicated to me a single spark of his own genius, I should have sent him some more brilliant tribute of my own—for as we say in Ireland "It is not my heart that would hinder me." The verses are by a Miss Scriven, and as follows

Lines addressed to the Swan's quill, with which Mr.
Moore wrote his name in Miss OFerrall's
Scrap Book

"How little didst thou think
Oh fair and lovely plume
While resting by the water's brink
That thou shouldst e'er presume

To give thy gentle form
To that high hand of fame,
And thus, with feelings warm,
Inscribe so bright a name.

Were I a plume like thee,
I'd with my sires have vied,
And, uttering such sweet melody,
Have closed my wing and died—"

{24, 25 &c. [Friday–Saturday] Forgot to mention, I think, that I have lately, among my other episodes been employed upon some Sacred Songs (or

Songs of the Scriptures, as they are to be called) for Cramer's House. Have already done four. [*Unrecovered*] occasions with Tom, who, I am glad to say, shows good disposition towards improving himself. Was glad to find, in my own particular case, that I have recovered my Greek sufficient to be able to master pretty well (without reference to [*unrecovered*] or Dictionary) the Speeches in Herodotus, as I found the other day, in looking over them, with Tom.

26 &c. [Sunday] That "long since forgotten Romance, Lalla Rookh" (as a scribbler in one of the Tory Magazines lately styled it) within this week has formed the subject of entertainments at two very different sorts of places, Astley's and Bridgewater House. I should like much to have witnessed the latter. Lady Francis herself, I hope, the heroine.}

July 1, 2, &c. [Friday–Saturday]—Notwithstanding Barnes's *friendly* letter he has been shabby enough to insert some wretched poetry in which I am attacked.[1] If the poetry was even middling, I should have forgiven him, but your journalists! your journalists! Poor Perry must still hold his place as the Phoenix of all newspaper men that *I*, at least, have ever known.

{4 [Monday]—To Houlton's for a few days, Bessy, Tom, Ellen & myself—In a Fly to Melksham, where Houlton's carriage met us—weather tremendously hot—Mr. Rowe at dinner.

5 [Tuesday]—Not able to stir abroad for the heat—Looked over Spied & made some extracts—also from various works on architecture—Whittington, Milner, Sydney Hawkins &c—a Mr. ———— a clergyman and his wife and Mr. Horner another clergyman at dinner—The Vivians in the house & both very agreeable—guittar, in the evening, charming.

6 [Wednesday]—Had the loan of Mrs. Day's poney-chair & went over to Freshford to see Napier—staid with him about two hours and heard all the details of his late lawsuits and duel-cases—the former having been three or four in number and the latter six, including Peter Borthwick's the five other *incipient* duels having sprung out of statements in his history, and being all of them very shy & distant approaches towards the *ultimatum*. Indeed the only one of the six that seems *really* to have wanted to fight was Peter Borthwick and him Napier wouldn't fight, because he wasn't a gentleman—I suppose a very sufficient reason,—at least with a man of Napier's reputa-

tion,—for it wouldn't do with men in general to be over particular as to whom they fight. The only one of these threatening appeals to him that appears to have had any pith or substance about it, or to have come (as he himself said) from a real gentleman was on the subject of a very savage attack made by Napier on the conduct of Lord Cathcart at Walcheren, the appellant being a Captain ——— (I forget his name) nearly related to the nobleman in question and whose letter, rather too sentimentally, was declared to have been written from Lord Cathcart's grave, or at least, immediately after the writer's return from a visit to it. Napier's conduct in the affair appears to have been both considerate and manly, showing every disposition to make amends for the rather harsh language he had employed he wrote to this gentleman to say that the tone of the letter he had addressed to him stood completely in the way of any reparation he might be inclined to make but if Captain ——— would withdraw it, and write him such a letter as was not objectionable, on this score, he would find him (Col. N.) readily disposed to do all that justice required of him. This suggestion Captain ——— immediately acted upon, and the consequence is that the passage will *all* be expunged in the forth-coming edition of the Volume. Got back pretty early, and had rather a hot stroll afterwards through the pretty fields toward Freshford. A new clergyman & his wife at dinner—Sung a good deal in the evening (as I did, indeed, yesterday evening) and had afterwards the Siguidilla from Isabella, and some things of Baltini from Flora and the pretty Catherine.

7 [Thursday]—After breakfast off for home, in Houlton's carriage—Poor Houlton himself too unwell, all the time of our visit, to dine with us—Took a Fly at Melksham & got home very snugly.

8, 9, 10 &c. [Friday–Sunday] Received a very curious letter from *Missouri*, transmitted through Sir Martin Archer Shee, (which I have not now time to give an account of) on the subject of my "Irish Gentleman"—well & pithily written. Must find a moment to give some extracts from it.}

14 [Thursday]—Dined at Money's—Company, Mrs. Money's brother-in-law, Mr. Sutton with rather a nice daughter, the Bowless & the Starkeys. Got Bowles to tell the story of the bottle-green coat he bought at Monmouth St.—Told us also that he never lets a tailor measure him, thinking it "horrible"—the fellow must merely *look* at his shapes & make the best he can of it. The new coat he then had on was concocted, he told us, in this manner, and from a *very* hasty glance, evidently—as rough guess-work as need be.

{15, 16, 17, 18. [Friday–Monday] Dined on this last day, at Starkey's— company the Moneys, Guthrie, the Clutterbucks, & Frank Locke—Sung in the evening—the fine spacious room drew out my voice, as it always has done, most effectively—[I] even pleased myself.

19, 20 &c [Tuesday–Wednesday] Nothing note-able. Shall therefore transcribe here, to save time, the American letter mentioned above.

"St. Louis, 22nd, May
    Sir—As you have written a Book, whose object (prima facie) is to establish truth and dissipate error, on a subject which is considered of very high importance in Christendom—to wit, the divine origin and nature of the Roman Catholic faith, I trust you will excuse me for requesting your reply to a question which the reading of your able and most worthy work has suggested not only to me, but to many other of my fellow-citizens in this part of the world. The question which I would take the liberty of putting is this, whether we are to consider your work entitled "The Irish Gentleman in search of a Religion" as a *serious* defence of the Roman Catholic doctrines and of their intrinsic divinity, or whether we are to look upon it as a mere demonstration of the existence of the Roman Cat. faith (as it is at present taught) in the earliest apostolic age, without connecting it directly with the Creator of the Universe—including in the idea "Universe" not only the Solar but every other system of central stars—revolving planets & satellites, which since the Christian era, science has revealed to mankind. That you have succeeded in demonstrating its early Christian origin is admitted by most persons who have read your book—that you have refuted the objections so often urged against the doctrines of the Trinity and Transubsantiation, on the ground of their modern origin, is also admitted—that you have shown the innovations of Protestantism, and its total want of title to the name of Primitive Christianity is also conceded, but, while they admit all this, there are many who insist that you by no means prove, or *intend* to prove the intrinsic divinity as a special revelation of Roman Catholic doctrine, or even of Christianity itself in its broader Protestant signification— that, on the contrary, you *Gibbonize* (excuse the neologism) and, through your most solemn observations, a tone of irony is discoverable which, in your supposed prototype's hands, as you know, is the most unparryable (here again a "novus hostis") weapon ever directed against the vitals of Holy Mother Church. If this suspicion of Gibbonism be unfounded, permit me to recommend that you specifically disclaim any such insidious irony. If you are really sincere in defence of the Roman Catholic dogmata (particularly the dogma of transubstantiation) you are bound to say so. By so doing, you will the better attain the object which I am willing to hope you had really in view. By omitting to do so, I verily believe that object will run the risk of

being defeated. In conclusion, I beg to assure you that, whatever may have been your object, whether to sustain the Church of St. Peter, or to precipitate its fall, my opinion of your transcendant talents, and the use you have made of them in aid of the land in which I ate my first potatoe cannot be changed and I have therefore the honour to tender you the assurance of the esteem and respect of your very obt. servant, A Missourian."

21, 22 &c [Thursday–Friday]—A kind letter from Lord Lansdowne respecting a book which I had asked him to send me (a Vol. of the Irish State Papers) when last in town, and which had till now escaped his memory. In answering him inclosed the above letter for his perusal, and in sending it back he made the following [*MS damaged*] & apt remark "I return the amusing letter from your American reader. I think [you] might answer him as Talleyrand did his creditor's abrupt question as to date of payment—"Il paroit que vous êtes bien curieux, Monsieur."

25 [Monday]—Went to the Archery Meeting at night—Bess, Tom & myself—The day fine, the party small and all intimate—so that, on the whole, I found it more tolerable than usual.

26 [Tuesday]—In consequence of pressure (as it appears) from an old & stiff boot I wore yesterday, an inflammation & swelling appeared on the joint of my great toe. Had some fears it was gout.

27 [Wednesday]—Sent for Mr. Karreck at Melksham, who has announced it decidedly not gout, but merely an injury from the tight and hard boot—

28, 29 &c.} [Thursday–Friday]

31 [Sunday]—Received a letter from M{oran,} of the Globe, containing a proposal of a plan from Macrone to publish a new Edition of all my work on the following terms—"One thousand pounds for an edition of your works, prose & poetical Complete to be published by him—say 8000 copies in monthly numbers commencing with the ensuing year. If they go to 15 volumes, he makes his offer 2000 guineas. Turner to embellish the volumes with his best style of illustrations, going, if necessary, to Ireland for the purpose. If you accede to his proposal he will lay out immediately—ie between this & January £500 in advertisements and he adds that he will

devote himself exclusively to its publication so as to render it in every way worthy of your fame and the Collection &c." M{oran} adds that, if I accede to the proposal, he will himself come down next Sunday to make arrangements with me, on the subject—Wrote an answer saying that the plan proposed of a complete Edition of my Works (at least of the poetical part of them) had long been a desired object with me and that the Messrs. Longman had some time since entered with eagerness into the project—that of late, however, it had rather slumbered in their hands, owing to some difficulties as I understood, raised by Power, whose concurrence, as proprietor of the copy-right of most of my songs, would be indispensable towards our plan. I added, however, that I would lose no time in acquainting the Longmans with his proposal, and should certainly not hesitate in entering into terms with him should I find *them* not so promptly disposed toward the undertaking as I could wish.[1] Wrote accordingly to Rees.

August, 1, 2 [Monday–Tuesday]—An answer from Rees to say that he had seen Power on the subject, and would himself call upon me, on his way to Wales, tomorrow.

3 [Wednesday]—Rees arrived—a good deal of conversation between us, from the whole of which I could collect that, though he assured me they had never lost sight of the projected edition of my works, the fact was that they *had* set it aside, and that but for this proposition of Macrone's, it would have been allowed still to slumber on. It is evident that, immediately on receiving my letter they had sent off for Power, and instead of being an obstacle in the way of our plan, it appears he is quite ready to join it. From something which Rees said, as to our deferring any steps toward an Edition till my Irish History is completed, I have no doubts that their anxiety for the termination of this work was the cause of their laying on the shelf the projected Edition—{Had luncheon with us, and set off on his way to Wales.}

4–5 [Thursday–Friday]—Informed Mr. Macrone of the result of my interview with Rees, and said that while I regretted being disappointed in a speculation which he did me the honour to consider so promising still I could not but feel that he had had a lucky escape in being saved the enormous difficulty & expence he would have had to encounter in getting possession of all the copy-rights.

6, 7, 8 &c [Saturday–Monday]—Have not been able to keep notes of much of this time, but except some strange letters from strange people, nothing worth recording has occurred. As the time approaches for the departure of our dear little Nell, we begin to feel more & more the loss we shall have of her. Among my letters was one from a R. C. clergyman proposing the erection of a Round Tower, on the model of the ancient ones, at *Blarney*. Thought it at first a hoax, more particularly as he is pleased to say that *I* have done more to elucidate the history of those structures than any other antiquarian, whereas the real truth is I have but left them where I found them.

9, 10, 11 &c. [Tuesday–Thursday] The accounts of poor Lord Kerry's state of health very alarming {—Have forgot to mention the return lately of our most agreeable friends and (again) neighbours, the Feildings, who have once more taken up their quarters at Lacock.}

15, 16 &c. [Monday–Tuesday] Went over to dine with the Feildings— company only Sir David Brewster with whose good sense & simplicity of manner I was much pleased. Spoke of Sir W. Hamilton as one of the first, if not the first, among the men of Science of this day. {On my saying inter- rogatively "Robinson is a clever fellow?"—"I don't think so," he answered. Recollected then that there had been some difference between him & Robinson. In talking of my reception in Ireland last year, at the Theatre in Barrow, and elsewhere, he said Sir Walter Scott might have gone from one end of Scotland to the other without receiving even a hundredth part of such attention. At this we all marvelled, particularly among a people so national as the Scotch—but he declared that such was the fact and at- tributed it partly to the unpopular character of Scott's politics. Mentioned how sorely & almost weakly Scott felt his own unpopularity, at one time— imagining it far beyond what was the fact. His persisting in saying that the people actually "spat upon him," in coming out of some public meeting, though, as Brewster said, no sign whatever of disrespect was shown to him on that occasion. It was in vain, however, to tell Scott this—he still kept exclaiming "They spat upon me."}

17 [Wednesday]—Returned home—some more of the Savans expected at Lacock—viz. Whewel, Babbage, Dr. Roget &c.—Have had some letters lately from Lord Lansdowne, on the subject of poor Kerry's illness, and the approaching meeting at Bristol, of which Lord L. is to be the President, and to which he has asked me to accompany him. The state of Kerry however renders it most unlikely that he will be able to go there.

{19 [Friday]—A letter from Lord L.—still more disheartening about poor Kerry—says "if I could but once hear the word "safe" pronounced by the physicians"—alas, that *word*, or *thought* of safety is, I fear, wholly out of the question—but Lord L's is a sanguineness that never fails. What desolation for poor Lady L.!}

20 [Saturday]—A visit from Babbage, Dr. Roget & Brewster who are staying at Lacock, full of anxiety as to the chances of Lord Ls. being able to come—Told them that from his letter of yesterday I had scarcely a hope that it would be possible, and under all the circumstances most anxiously wished that they would relieve his mind from even *thinking* of it. They agreed that it would be right to do so, and accordingly at their request I wrote a letter to Lord L. expressing their wish that he would prevail on either Lord Minto or Lord Northampton to undertake the Presidency in his stead. To this I added my own most anxious request that he would not *think* of coming.

{21, 22 [Sunday–Monday]—On this latter day started for Bristol—Bessy and [the] rest meaning to join me there tomorrow—Had taken my [place in] the Devizes Coach to Bristol, and was driven by Tom, in the poney carriage [to] meet it at Melksham but somebody else had usurped my place & I was sent on in a Fly to Bath, from whence I got in the Coach to Bristol— Went to Moultree's, where Lord Lansdowne had provided lodgings, and where I meant to take my bed for the night, he having in one of his last letters begged me to occupy them during my stay. Went to look for Bowles at the Mall Hotel, and was most smilingly received by the pretty Bar-Maid who as he tells me, is so well read in Lalla Rookh—Found that Bowles had just gone out to look for the Bishop of Bath & Wells whom the waiter gave me a long account of, always calling him the Bath of Bishop & Wells— should like much to know what sort of aqueous divinity he conceived him to be. Called upon Strong the bookseller—found Bowles at last, and agreed we should dine at the Ordinary together—a most mobbish affair—no less than between five & six hundred diners—the Provost of Trin. Coll. Dub. in the chair, supported by Lord Northampton Ld. Nugent Ld. Cole &c. &c.— Bowles & I separated far asunder. Went afterwards to the Theatre, where the evening exhibitions of the Savans were held—the crowd & pressure enormous, and women, as usual, "the first in the throng," alternately pushing & screaming—Hovered on the outer skirts of the crowd, and even lingered so long outside as to awaken the suspicion of one of the policemen, who questioned me as to my reasons for not going in, and seemed half inclined to take me into custody. On his adopting, however, a more civil tone, I showed him my ticket as a Member of the Association, and all was right. When I *did* enter, however, I was as little the wiser for any thing that was going on as I should have been in the street, and owed, at last, my getting a seat on the platform to the kindness of one of the under strappers of the concern, who happened to know who I was and took me under his protection—So far the contrast between Bristol and Dublin was stark staring enough. After sitting some time among the Savans took to the audience part of the house, and found myself already pretty generally known and pointed out—One *cool* thing that occurred is worth mentioning—I was standing for a short time at the door of one of the boxes, looking in, when a gentleman came out of it, and said "Sir, as the ladies inside wish this door shut, you had better, I think, come in." Not perceiving at first his object, I withdrew instantly from the door, begging "a thousand pardons," when he said, smiling, "The fact is the ladies wish you to come in, as they are all anxious to have a sight of you." I of course laughed & did *not* go in— Saunders told me of a rumour that poor Kerry died yesterday

23 [Tuesday]—Breakfasted with Mr. Saunders (a friend that Lord John's Dinner has added to my list, and whom I find a very good-natured & gentlemanlike person)—a good many people at breakfast—Duncan (of Oxford) Mr. Hall, [*unrecovered*] &c. &c. The news of Kerry's death confirmed. Went to meet Tom who arrived between two & three in the Devizes Coach—his Mamma & Ellen & Russell having stopped on their way at Bath, for shopping. Shifted my quarters from Moultree's to the Gloucester Hotel, where we have not very good & comfortable apartments. On my asking Mrs. Moultree what I was in her debt for the wine and water I had on coming home last night, the wax lights &c. &c. she said "Oh dear, Sir, do not mention such trifles," and then, placing an Album before me requested, as a great favour, that I would write my name in it for her. Did so—a cheap, and poetical mode of paying one's board & lodging. Bessy, Nell &c. arrived at five, and the evening being too wet for our intended Promenade at the Gardens Tom & I dined at Saunders's—Company Mr. Hall, Duncan & some nameless (at least to *me*) young lady. Home early—}

24 [Wednesday]—{After breakfast drove with Tom into Bristol—Tom, who went to visit the different sections, having received his ticket as a Member of the Association yesterday, while I went to Strong's to look over some books—Joined by Bessy, Tom &c. afterwards, and all drove in a Fly to the Downs to see the Car driven by Kites—amused to find Lord Nugent, of all sizeable animals, in the Kite-Car, which did not do much, the wind being light and its freight heavy. Walked down the zig-zag walk to the river, the day delicious and the scenery in highest beauty—Had Peter Leigh, Nell's friend, to dine with us, and having in the morning secured places in a private box at the Theatre for Bessy and Ellen, all proceeded thither—Full of anxiety, during the evening about them as the heat was excessive, and

their box (as I saw, in putting them in) most densely filled—At last, had a summons from them to say that Ellen was taken ill—found her & Bess removed to a room behind the scenes where she soon got better & they resumed their seats—but I succeeded in persuading them to leave the Theatre early, and was glad to get the whole party safe home again.} It is gratifying to see how general is the sympathy with the Lansdownes, on their late severe loss—and it is a most trying loss. Poor Kerry had at last surmounted all the folly and idleness of his youth, and having been most lucky in his marriage, was giving every promise of a manhood of usefulness and honour when he was thus (not unexpectedly, however, to many) snatched away. It is too sad.[1]

{25. [Thursday] Having fixed with Dr. Lardner that I would attend his Lecture this morning on Steam Communication with America, started after breakfast with Tom, and found a seat reserved for me next the President of the Section, Davies Giddy. On my entering and passing to my seat, there was a very general applause through the room. Lardner's lecture excellent—exactly what such lectures should be—clear and business-like, but at the same time attracting attention by the style and manner. Walked with Saunders, and made some calls—viz, upon Dr. Pritchard, Logan the young Priest &c.—Met Bessy &c. in Bristol and walked about with them a little, after which Tom & I went to dine at the Ordinary—dull enough—home to dress for the Gardens, whither we all went—very full, but neither illuminations nor music—a most manqué concern, except in the amusement afforded to all our party by the sensation which *my* presence excited. It was really hardly less than that at the Gardens in Dublin last year, which Ellen witnessed, but Bessy did not, and therefore to her the bustle had the additional charm of novelty. She pronounced the women, however, "exceedingly impudent," with the exception only of some pretty young Quakers, who were certainly not the least forward in the train of followers and starers, but whom she forgave on account of their prettiness and neatness. One lady, rather elderly, as she passed me, said, looking earnestly in my face, "Here's a health to thee, Tom Moore."—After the Gardens, went with Tom to a soiré at Doctor Pritchard's and found a large party assembled—Was introduced to Du Pin, and afterward took Tom to present him to him, when he said, holding his hand "You possess a glorious name, and I trust you will prove yourself worthy of it." There is something interesting, but still rather too theatrical in Du Pin's look and manner. Met an old Kilkenny acquaintance—Miss Lovat (that *was*, but now God knows what) still looking very handsome. Got enough and whisked Tom away, who had not of course got half enough—in passing the end of the street near Pritchard's, heard some beautiful singing, in parts (male voices) from one of the houses and stopped to listen to it—rather think it was from the Catholic establishment in that quarter. Had been asked to a party at Miles's, where we should have seen the fine pictures lighted up, but it was much too far to go and return at night. Some talk with Babbage at Pritchard's—evidently discontented with the proceedings of his brother Savans—spoke of the immense quantity of the *ridiculous* that is mixed up with their transactions and which must be got rid of, he said, before they can take their proper station—Observing me to smile at this remark, he added "Do you know that, in talking the matter over with a friend of mine, the other night, we both agreed that *you* were the only person who could properly administer the sort of gentle instigation we require—but both agreed also that you were too good-natured, knowing so many of the men, to undertake it"—I acknowledged to him that the temptation had frequently come over me, both at the Dublin meeting and this—as I agreed with him that there could hardly be engaged a subject more *appétisant* to a quizzing Muse—but that I had resisted the call and should do so still.

26 [Friday]—Tickets sent early in the morning for the great boating expedition that was to take place that day—Called up Tom, who was most ready "& willing" to join in it, but did not go myself—breakfasted at home, and sauntered about during the day but nothing very remarkable—Dined at home, and in the evening went to the Theatre—Tom had dined at Dr. Riley's—joined Mrs. Riley in her box—

27. [Saturday] Our dear Nell's departure being fixed for this morning, in the Dublin Packet, we were all up at half past five, to see her off—Her friends, the Finlays, who have been staying in the same Hotel with us were also to be her companions in the packet. When we left her, the vessel was just putting away from the pier, and Russell was still on board, which caused us not a little fright, as he was obliged to be almost *thrown* to us from the side of the packet—On our return, too, Bessy & I for some time lost the dear little dog in the crowd that was just then collecting for the grand business of the day (the laying of the first stone of the suspension Bridge and, having already been made nervous by what happened at the packet, we both got exceedingly frightened about him—At last, we agreed to separate in our search—Bessy going back to the Hotel, where she thought it possible he might have returned, and I continuing on with the course of the crowd. I had not proceeded very far when I saw a group of young ladies approaching me, one of whom held out her hand very cordially, and said—"Do let me have the honour of being able to say that I have shaken hands with Mr. Moore." Hardly knowing what I did, I seized her hand as if she

had been my dearest friend, and said "You see me rather under painful circumstances, for I have just lost my little boy in the crowd, and cannot think what has become of him."—"There he is!" she exclaimed eagerly, pointing on a little distance before us, and there was indeed Russell himself, on his way back to look for his mamma and me. Thanked the young lady hastily (who I suppose knew him from having before noticed him with us) and hurried back to the Hotel with my prize. Bessy forgave *this* "impudence." Had three breakfasts before me, Miss Lee's, Mrs. Claxton's, and a large Dejeuner given at the Hotel—managed the two first but having been placed near a very pretty woman at the second was too late for the third. Lord Bathurst among the party at Claxton's—The spectacle of the morning was [MS damaged] those grand rocks actually swarming up to their summit with living creatures, the number of boats [MS damaged] down the river, the gay groups along the banks on both sides—all was most striking—. Sauntered a good while by myself, and found I was recognized pretty generally. When I was standing to look at a balloon that had been sent up, a man, having the appearance of [a] respectable tradesman, left his family with whom he had been walking along & coming up to me said very timidly & respectfully, "Mr. Moore, I would consider myself a most ungrateful person, if seeing you thus for the first time, I did not take the opportunity of thanking you for all the gratification you have afforded me by your writings."—On my expressing my acknowledgments for this very flattering tribute, he added, "There were a few young men, of my own station in life, with whom I once lived a good deal. Being all fond of reading, we used to meet regularly once a week to talk over what we had read, and your books were, if I may so say, the cement of our friendship." Having said thus much, and shaken hands with me he returned to his wife & children. Bessy not wishing to remain any longer in Bristol, it was settled that she & the boys should return home to-day, and that I should stay till Monday. They accordingly set off—and I dined with the Saunders's—none but themselves—To the Theatre in the evening—a sort of wind-up of the whole proceedings. Several resolutions of thanks to different persons and public bodies moved during the evening, bringing forward new parties before the public—viz. Hallam, the Revd. Mr. Stanley (who made a very good & amusing speech) Mr. Pinney &c. While this was going on Sir William Hamilton came to me with a request from the Committee that *I* would move one of the Resolutions—that of thanks to some of the artists (if I recollect right) who had contributed their services, during the meeting— but I declined notwithstanding his very urgent request that I would comply with their wishes. On thinking over the matter, however, I plucked up a little courage, and sent to Mr. Pinney to the Committee to say that, if they had not in the mean time selected some one else for the purpose, I should be very glad to undertake the moving of the Resolution. It was accordingly fixed that I should, and it was really worth while making the effort for the sake of the enthusiastic greeting with which I was received, on presenting myself, by the audience. Nothing, indeed, could be more cordial, and the speech I made was applauded most warmly throughout. Regretted exceedingly that Bessy & the boys were not present to witness my reception.

28 [Sunday]—Breakfasted with the Saunders's—no one else but Duncan, who was very agreeable—After breakfast wrote out, as well as I could, a report of my speech of last night for the Bristol papers, in order to rescue any little meaning there may be in it from the tender mercies of the Reporters.—Went afterwards to the Roman Catholic chapel to try what sort of music they could muster up there, having yesterday (though I omitted recording it) sat for near two hours in the aisle of the Cathedral waiting for & then listening to the Anthem. The Congregation at the Chapel but scanty and mean-looking, which, in such a place as Bristol, surprized me—Some of the music, however, touching. Walked about afterwards and made calls—upon Hallam, Miss Gun &c. Hallam said that he had had it in contemplation to introduce some notice of poor Kerry's death during the proceedings of the week, and then afterwards thought of asking me to undertake it—But I could as soon have flown as attempted such a task. It is strange how few people feel the sacredness of such subjects. The ornaments of Poetry and oratory are all very well on the ordinary topics of life— but there are feelings and sorrows which it is desecration to apply them to. Dined at Mr. Bengough's, the local treasurer of the Association—Company, Dupin, Colonel Sykes, Professor Hare (the American) a Scotch gentleman (whose name I forget, but a very intelligent person) and three or four more. Both the American & Colonel Sykes far more *verbose* than was agreeable—but had some conversation with the Scotchman in the evening which was very interesting—gave me an account of a mission of his to France, connected with the affairs of the Ex-Royal family, in which there was much I should like to have remembered better than I do—particularly his conversations with the Holyrood House people after his return—their enquiries respecting the furniture of the rooms of the Palaces, whether such and such pictures &c. were still in their old places and many other such natural touches.—On my return to the Gloucester, one of my rather importunate land-ladies, waylaid me as usual on the stairs (there are two of them, sisters) but rather repaid me for my patient listening by the following anecdote. Two young gentlemen, she told me, had called at the Hotel that morning, and enquired whether Mr. Moore was not staying there. On her answering in the affirmative, one of them asked "Could you manage to get us a sight of him?" to which she replied, according to her own account— "Why, Sir, we cannot at present give any answer to that question—not

having as yet *fixed the Exhibition price."* May as well add another anecdote of the *Bar,* as I am about it. Bowles asked *his* bar-maid (at the Mall) whether she meant to go see the grand doings at the Suspension Bridge—"Oh Sir" she answered "don't talk to me about bridges and sights—I have seen Mr. Moore." She then pointed to Lalla Rookh which lay, I suppose, among the cream-jugs at the Bar) and which Bowles took up and read to her in his most pathetic manner the passage at which the leaves opened—"I never loved a dear gazelle."[1] All this I heard from Tom to whom Bowles told it & the scene altogether would have been worth witnessing.

29 [Monday]—Started in the Coach for home at half past two, taking with me one of the Volumes of Seyer's Memoirs of Bristol which Strong lent me[1]—Found all pretty well at home, and glad to rejoin them—}

September {1, 2 &c. &c. [Thursday–Friday]—}Lord & Lady Lansdowne arrived at Bowood about the 10th—Bessy had written to Miss Fox to enquire about them, saying what is most true, "as you are the person whom all fly to for kindness, on such occasions, I write &c. &c."—Her answer most kind, and (as could be expected under the circumstances) satisfactory.[1]

{8, or 9th [Thursday–Friday] Wrote to Lord L. merely saying that I rejoiced to find he was so much better in health and should be glad to come to him, whenever he feels disposed to see me.—Received that evening the following answer—"My dear Moore—I shall be happy to see *you* any time you can make it convenient to come over—in the afternoons, I generally get out for airing in some way. I need not tell you how severe a trial I have had; but, tho it has been a hard struggle, I trust I have now recovered my fortitude, and, thank God, Lady L. and Lou. have borne up against it wonderfully."}

9th [Friday] Walked over to Bowood—found Miss Fox and afterwards Lord L. looking a good deal worn & still suffering from the attack of gout which came most seasonably in the midst of his mental agony—such a relief was this *contre-coup* to him, that he assured me, notwithstanding the violence of the pain, he actually slept soundly with it. A good deal of conversation on various subjects—staid luncheon—Poor Lady L. herself looking calm, and even occasionally smiling, but marked indelibly with the loss she has suffered. Felt it difficult to repress my own feeling while looking at her, but did so, and came away full of admiration & sympathy for them all—that amiable Miss Fox included.

{10, 11, 12 &c. [Saturday–Monday]

14 [Wednesday]—Received a note from Lord L. asking me to come to dinner tomorrow to meet Lady E. Feilding, but if I should be engaged tomorrow to come either Friday or Saturday, as they leave Bowood next week.

15 [Thursday]—Walked over to Bowood to dinner—Lady Elisabeth & Miss Fox the only persons besides themselves—Lord Lansdowne's mind quite restored to all its usual play & elasticity & we talked, as usual, over all sorts of subjects—but he *looks* much shaken and she will long feel the blow. It was after twelve before we separated.—slept there.

16 [Friday]—After breakfast walked home.

17 [Saturday]—Drove into Devizes to meet Brabant, who has just returned from his four months visit to Germany—Dined at Hughes's, the Brabants only & Mr. [?Markie] of the party—Told me he had heard my History quoted by a learned German Professor, in a Lecture relating to the Celts, Druids &c. &c.—A translation of all the answers to my "Irish Gentleman" has been published there in one volume.[1] Remarked on the tendency there was in the task of *historical* writing to render a man sceptical—almost all the great writers of history sceptics

18 [Sunday]—After breakfast repeated to them my late Squib in the Chronicle—"Anticipated Meeting of the British Association" which seemed to amuse them exceedingly[1]—By the bye, when I was mentioning yesterday at Bowood what Babbage had said to me at Bristol as to my being too good-natured to attack the Association, Lord L. exclaimed "But you *have* though" while Miss Fox said to me aside "Oh how good that was!"—I answered laughingly that I did not plead guilty to any thing of the sort, but even supposing that squib to *be* mine, it was not levelled at the Association— "No," answered Lord L. "but you made the Savants *subservient* to your other object—the attack upon the poor Peers."—Walked home—

21 [Wednesday]—A most kind & touching note from Lady L. to Bessy, explaining why she did not call upon her, and sending her some pretty handkerchiefs she had brought from abroad. They leave Bowood on their

way to Germany (to meet Henry) tomorrow—In one of dear Ellen's letters to us, since her return, she says that Mrs. Finlay had remarked of us that we seemed quite a "Family of Love"—and so we are, thank God, and may we, during our short stay together in this world, continue so, I pray.

22, 3, 4 &c [Thursday–Saturday] engaged in making memorandums of the different books I have to consult at the British Museum—a formidable list.

27. [Tuesday] Packing up for my departure tomorrow—engaged to dinner at Bowles's to-day.}

October 1st. [Saturday][1] *** Disappointed of having Russell out. A note from Saunders, saying that the rule is against it, and that he could not make an exception in his favour. This I ought to have recollected, the first Saturday after the return to school being a forbidden day. Hume, too, whom I had written to, never made his appearance, so that I was thrown on my own resources. Accordingly dined alone at Brookes's, being reminded, both by the weather and the dinner, of Swift's well-turned lines,—

> "On rainy days alone I dine,
> Upon a chick and pint of wine:
> On rainy days I dine alone,
> And pick my chicken to the bone."[2]

3rd. [Monday] Went out to dine with the Longmans at Hampstead; Rees, myself, and M'Culloch having clubbed in a hackney coach for the occasion. Talk with M'Culloch about Sir William Petty; told him of poor Lord Kerry's having been employed in preparing some papers of Petty's for publication, to be accompanied with a memoir of Petty's life, in which Kerry had made some progress, and that it was my intention (as soon as the family were sufficiently recovered from their grief to bear such a proposal) to offer to take up this project where Kerry left it, and avail myself of the opportunity it would afford for paying a tribute to his memory. M'Culloch strongly recommended that I should make it a durable monument at once, by publishing (as he had often suggested before) a complete edition of all Sir W. Petty's works, with a full account of his life. Mentioned his various accomplishments, his dancing and gymnastic tricks described by Evelyn, &c. &c. Company at dinner, besides our hackney-coach party, Chief Justice Tindal and his Lady, Charles Phillipps, Taylor (Van Artevelde), and one or two others.

4th. [Tuesday] Went with Hume and Dr. Travers (a young Irishman who, it seems, is preparing an answer to Mason's attack upon the *religious* part of my Irish "History,")[1] to the Zoological Gardens, to see the giraffes. Hume's account of his meeting with Sterling (of "The Times") the other day. Sterling (who had somebody walking with him when they met) said banteringly, and, at the same time opening Hume's waistcoat, "Let us see if you have the regular Whig *badge* or the death's-head & crossbones upon your breast." Hume without appearing to notice what he had said, quietly took up the skirt of Sterling's coat, and after examining it for a little while, looked up into Sterling's face, and said with a sort of dry surprize "Why, you've turned your coat!" {This, given in Hume's odd manner, must have been most effective—and (to the apostate) disconcerting—Got to the Museum for an hour or two—dined at Bryan's—none but himself & Madame—His imitation of a Foreign Baron (I forget of what name) arguing upon the cruelty of the supposition that wretched savages who had never had opportunities of even *hearing* of the existence of the Bible should be damned for not believing in it and becoming Christian—"Oh for *me* to be damned is all very right—I know of de Bible—I not believe, I am damned—dat is all quite right—but de poor man in de *wood*, who know nothing at all bout it &c. &c."—Home.

5th. [Wednesday] Breakfasted with Dr. Holland—found only himself & *Saba*, but were joined afterwards by Dr. Erasmus Darwin.—Conversation agreeable—talked of phrenology, Sydney Smith &c. Called at Lord Fitzroy Somerset's, at whose door I had been two or three times before, to enquire about his levees & whether it is necessary for Tom to attend them—A note from Lady Holland asking me to meet Lord John at dinner to-day, but again prevented from doing so, by an engagement to Sir Edd. Codrington—A note from Russell "Dear *Pa*" to say that he can come out next Saturday if I should like it—To British Museum. Find it hard to get even there some of the old antediluvian works I want to look at—Dinner at Codrington's, a strange one but amusing—Creevey and his *bull* (or rather *barrel*) Lord Kensington forming the chief treat of the day.—"Come, Kensington, tell us that story—you recollect—about what your father said on his death-bed to your mother when he spoke of "the evil weed" (meaning *you*) that he left behind him." Kensington for some time sulky & resisting— "By God, Creevey, you're drunk—you've got damned old, and have lost by God any little mind you once had." After a while, however, when Creevey had ceased for some time poking at him he came out of himself, with one of his tremendous bounces upon which Creevey very conveniently exclaimed "He is himself again!"—A Naval Captain of the party, however, beat even Kensington at this figure of speech, having told us of a man he had in the

West Indies who drank, for his daily allowance, eight bottles of port and two of brandy.

6 [Thursday]—Breakfasted at home—called at Lord Fitzroy Somerset's, for the second or third time having wished to ascertain first whether he would hold any more Levees at the Horse-Guards, and secondly whether (as some officious people have been bothering me about) there is any necessity for Tom's coming up to attend them. Hume had also written me word that, after all, Tom's name is not yet down on Lord Hill's List—Was lucky enough to meet Lord Fitzroy just coming in to town—had some talk with him, and learned that so far from Tom's name not being yet down, it has been inscribed on the list ever since the day we first talked together on the subject; and the Levees he said there was not the least occasion for Tom's attending—Called at the Home Office, and had a few minutes conversation with Lord John, who had heard of Lady Holland's little bit of *malice* about the dinner—from herself, I believe—told him I had had some thoughts of running down to Tunbridge to see him—begged that [I] should do so—Off to the British Museum and had my two or three hours of rummaging among the old Books—Out to Holland House, having picked up Charles Fox at Brookes's and given him a lift towards his own home in my hackney-coach, the rain pouring in torrents—Company at dinner, Lord Ebrington and one or two more—Lord Palmerston in the evening—(Charles Fox's story of the Naval Captain ? with the King—"A [?Cabous] Sir.") Talked with Allen about a passage in the Saxon Poem on the Battle of Brunaburg—whether relating to the Scots of Ireland? the passage "the bold in battle & the ancient in genius" being supposed by Dr. OConnor to apply to the Irish—said he would make enquiries on the point for me, but felt almost sure that the passage could not bear Dr. OConnor's interpretation of it—Thinks that the wars of the Heptarchy of which we have such an indistinct account were all religious wars. Looked at some of the pictures in Holland House which I had not before noticed—Most struck with the vulgar men-acingness of Lord Palmerston's manner, not having met him for many years, and the last time being at a dinner at Croker's, when he left, I recollect, a very disagreeable impression on my mind—Slept at Holland House, having fixed with Lord Ebrington to start early with him for town in the morning.}

7 [Friday]—{Off with Lord Ebrington before nine.}—Walked to Kensington & there took to an Omnibus—Went to Thorpe's the bookseller, and looked over some of his curious old books relating to Ireland—made several extracts—from thence to the British Museum, where I worked for some hours, and returned to Holland House to dinner—Company, Lord &

Lady Lilford (just arrived from Paris, she looking prettier than ever)—Lord Radnor and his son Lord Folkstone, Lord Ebrington, Charles Fox and Lady Mary—Day agreeable. In talking of the Russian bands of music, where each performer has his own single note to produce, Lord Holland said that there was always a man walking about with a cane, who hit each fellow, at the proper moment, to make him bring out his note. This notion of Lord H's. produced a good deal of diversion, and I mentioned as a case in point, the *pig* instrument invented by some Abbé for the amusement of Louis 15th (I believe) wherein pigs of different ages (the young ones performing the treble and the old—according to their respective years—the bass) constituted the musical scale—there being keys provided as in a harpsichord, with a spike at the end of each, which on this key being struck touched the pig & made him utter his note, while at the same time there were muzzles contrived (in the manner of dampers, for stopping vibration) which seized the pig's mouth the moment he had given out his note and prevented his further intonation till again wanted. Thus, as Pope says of asses,

> pig intoned to pig
> Harmonic twang[1]

and the whole living instrument being covered over & disguised, in the manner of an organ, the Abbé performed upon it to the no small delight of the King & his Court. This story amused Lord Holland a good deal—[I forget where I read it.—On quoting Harry Greville's famous couplet (at least one that Wm. Spencer used to attribute to him)

> My heart is glowing with desire
> For my lovely sweet Maria (r)

on my quoting this in the evening to Charles Fox & Lady Mary and telling them that, according to Spencer's account, he was never able to convince Greville that these were not most accordant symphonious rhymes, I was surprized to find them both honestly avowing the same thing, and confessing that to *them* also there appeared no difference whatever in the terminating syllables of "desire" and "Maria"—so inborn and unconquerable, in some people, is the Cockney ear. I had always before thought this story a calumny on poor Greville.—An agreeable scheme started for Tuesday next, Charles having proposed to Lord & Lady H. to come and drive with him on next day & asked me to meet them—Slept, having fixed with Lord Ebrington to start with him in the morning

8. [Saturday] In to town before breakfast—had written to Saunders to let Russell come out to me for the day, and fixed with Hume to join us.

Breakfasted with Hume at his new Club, the Parthenon—went to the British Museum & from there to C.H. for Bussy, & he & I & Hume set off for the Zoological gardens (Regent's Park)—more walking than I had bargained for, and in galoches, which was hard work for the toe—Ordered a chop and some beer for Russell at Sackville St, and went to Brooks's to write letters & have some dinner for myself. Then rattled away to Astley's, where unluckily Lalla Rookh (which has been going on most of the season) was not acted, but Mazeppa was, and the dear little ladies enjoyed it all prodigiously[1]—Walked home to Sackville St. where the housemaid gave Russell a bed.}

9 [Sunday]—{Employed myself after breakfast looking over & making extracts from the Hibernian Domenican and a few other books which Boone of Bond St. had lent me. Sent Russell to Holland House, by omnibus, for my clock which I had left there—Walked out with him and} left a card at a Lady Rawson's who had written to me some days before, and sent me a copy of a French translation of the Loves of the Angels by a Pole named Ostrowski.[1] The translation gives me a title of which I am not a little flattered, calling me "the National Poet of all oppressed countries." But he also makes a Fallen Angel of me, addressing my Bardship thus, in what he calls an Allocution

> D'ou te vient la splendeur de ce front etoilé,
> O Moore! n'es tu pas un archange exilé?

His appealing to myself for the confirmation of this suspicion of his is not a little comical. On our way to Lady Rawson's in passing through George St, Portman Square, I pointed out to Russell, as I had done once before to Tom, the house, No. 44 where I first lodged when I came to London. Seeing a Bill of Lodging to let on the house, I had the advantage of it to have a peep at my own old two-pair stair quarters, and found that the two rooms were to be let for sixteen shillings a week, which shows they have not gone down in the world since I occupied them as I paid for the two but half a guinea a week—having for some time inhabited the front room alone at seven shillings a week and it was in that room that the first proof sheet I ever received (i.e. of my Anacreon) was put into my hands by Tom Hume. {Gave Bussy luncheon at Ibbetson's, and, as the rain came on heavily, and he appeared to have caught a little cold at Astley's last night, took him home myself, in a hackney coach, to the Charter House & deposited him with the Matron—Dined at Quintin Dick's, being tempted thereto by Luttrell's being of the party. But *such* a party! chiefly broken down Dandies and quizzes beginning with Sir George Warrener & ending in Chin Grant! There was one man there—Sir Willoughby Cotton—who relieved me from a puzzle I have long been in, as to whether he was the Willoughby Cotton I used to know in old times, a flirt of Mrs. Walpole's &c. &c. and it turns out to be the very same. He said to me "I see you wear far better than I do" and thought to myself, "I *hope* so," for he looks strangely and oddly old. Warrener too, said to me during dinner "Moore you keep by far the youngest of us old ones" Got seated next the only good and agreeable fellow there— Armstrong (the Colonel)—excepting, of course, Poor Luttrell who between the dulness of the party & the uneasiness of his leg (which, as I found afterwards had been bandaged up by Scott of Bromley in the morning) spoke scarcely a word during dinner & then fell asleep—The *materials* of the repast all very good & splendid. Forgot to mention that I had an opportunity the other day of questioning Creevey as to the facts of his memory [in] connection with the Duke of Wellington, at Brussels, imme- diately after the Battle of Waterloo. In the way I have always heard it told, though very interesting it appeared to me hardly credible—the alleged time of the conversation being the night of the Duke's arrival from [the] field of Waterloo, at Brussels, when, unable to sleep from his state of excitement, as he was taking a saunter through the streets, and finding himself under Creevey's windows (Creevey being an old friend of his) stopped and called out to him on which Creevey appeared at the window and the conversation alluded to took place. There was in all this a natu- ralness of familiar life which, coupled with the glory that had then just descended upon the man himself rendered this scene in the street at night not a little thrilling and interesting—Found now, however, from Creevey, that the romantic part of the story had no foundation whatsoever in truth— he had gone with the rest of the crowd that had assembled about mid-day opposite the Duke's House, in Brussells, and the Duke, seeing him from the window beckoned to him to come up. The officer in waiting, on Creevey's coming to the House told him the Duke was just then too busy to see him, but, on Creevey's mentioning that he had beckoned to him, allowed him to go up and it was then & there that his conversation with the Duke took place. As to what the Duke said, the most remarkable part of it was his repeating frequently how devilish well the French fought, and that "it was a damned close run thing"[2]

10 [Monday]—British Museum, where I nearly completed my references— went to the Charter-House to enquire after Buss and found he was well enough to be in school—[Went from thence to the Longmans, and found Longman himself & Rees—talked about Macrone's new edition, which they still boggled at a good deal, but said they would consider a little more about it.][1] A Message from Lord John through Gore to say that both he & Lady

John were looking for my promised visit—made up my head to go down to them—dined with Lord Nugent—no one besides themselves but the Dowager Lady Arundel (whom I was very glad to meet again) and the present Lord whom I shall never want to meet again. Day however agreeable, Nugent's account of Greece & the Greeks being interesting and clever—Their pronunciation of their language he thinks likely to be the same as in ancient times—turning the *u* into *b* for instance—the favourite epithet for rivers ευρος, still traceable in the Ebrus, the Ebro &c.—their use of aspirates—*autos* they call aphthos. Mentioned a proof of the Roman pronunciation which has escaped my memory—but the words on which the fact turns were "cave ne eas," and this may so far furnish me with a clue when I have leisure to enquire about it—though asking him when we again meet would be the most ready way. Lady Arundel full of praise for my Irish Gentleman and of the "impossibility of an answer in it." Lord Nugent mentioned as illustrative of the classical discoveries of travellers an ancient seat which Sir W. Gell discovered at Ithaca and pronounced to be Homer's Seat but it turned out to be seggia d'omer instead of d'omero.

11 [Tuesday]—Breakfasted at home, and got to the British Museum early—had received an invitation from Codrington (one of many from the same quarter) asking me to a family dinner to-day but already engaged. Dinner at Charles Fox's—the Lilfords' carriage came, according to promise, to take me, but not being ready, sent it away & went in my own hackney coach—Company, besides the Hollands & Lilfords—Colonel Mitchell & a young officer of the Guards—all very hearty & agreeable, though Lady Mary at first evidently very nervous under the responsibility of having to play hostess to Lady Holland. In the evening I sung and with most *éclatant* success, my Lord & Lady and even Allen being all loud in lauding me—a truly *Orphic* triumph. Went with the Lilfords as far as Holland House, from whence their carriage took me home.

The dinners of these two past days are misplaced. It was on the 9th (Sunday) that I dined with Lord Nugent and on the 10th at Charles Fox's—(Quintin Dick's dinner not having taken place till the end of this week)—On the 11th. I dined at Holland House—my Lady being full of delight and eulogy about my singing—Lord Seaforth, who was of the party at dinner brought me home at night—Talk with Lord Holland about Porson's controversy with Travers[1]—Porson's saying that he would not deign to answer people "qui sensu communi carent," which sounds a little like English Latin. But the "sensus communis" is in Juvenal—"Rarus enim ferme sensus communis in illa fortuna"[2]—It is the word "carent," I think, that gives it so much the appearance of Anglicism. Lord H. remarked that Parr was very fond of startling people with these apparent anglicisms in his Latin and then coming down upon them with his authorities when they objected—}

12 [Wednesday]—Got out early and performed some of my home commissions, besides rooting away for a couple of hours at the British Museum. Had written to Lord John to say that I would be with him to-day, and, having secured a luncheon at Brooks's, knowing I should be too late for his dinner, started for Tunbridge at a quarter before three—A young Frenchman, part of the way, inside, with whom I was rather amused.— Tremendous storm and rain as we approached Tunbridge—Stopped at the (I forget the name) Inn, Lord John having apprized me that, from the smallness of his house, he could not *bed* me—Found a servant with a note from him to say that I must come on to dinner at his house immediately on my arrival. {Ordered a Fly and went—his house on the hill, in the Park— got there about eight o'clock, and was most cordially received both by Johnny himself and Lady Johnny, who had a nice dinner ready for me, after dispatching which, I joined them in the drawing-room.}

13 [Thursday]—Joined them at breakfast. {Had been teazed by Hume to apply to Lord John again on the subject of making him a magistrate, and took my opportunity now of mentioning it—but he interrupted me *in limine*—wouldn't hear of it, and I really *could* not in candour, say that he was wrong, for, with all my regard for Hume, he is one of the very last men I myself would make a Magistrate of—a good deal of conversation &} some curious particulars about the King. {His strong Anti-Gallic feelings, and the unfortunate manner in which he sometimes let them out—At some dinner lately gave a loud "The land we live in," and followed it up by asking that whenever again there should be war with France, &c Englishmen would show &c. &c. Said in the course of an interview either with Lord John himself or some other of the present Ministers and on some point connected with the policy of France, "My Lord, in England the King & his ministers know very well that, even when they do not agree in opinion, yet both speak what they mean, and both have the country's good at heart—but in France it is altogether different—The King is, in the first place not an honest man &c. &c." Had lately caused the Institution of the Order of St. Patrick to be held in England instead of in Ireland—was jealous, Lord J. thinks, of the Lord Lieutenant—Told me that in the case of the appointment of Frank Stanhope by Lord Mulgrave, to be ——— of the order (I forget what) Sir W. Betham bunglingly served an order on the King which made his Majesty very angry—Altogether the impression left upon me by the different things Lord John mentioned was that there is a great portion of *caractère* in the King—that though self-willed, like all of his breed, he is considerate and fair, and that there is an openness about him which makes it *safe* to have dealings with him—in this respect differing very materially from his "Sainted father," as our Curate lately called George the Third.—} Went out to drive with Lady John, meaning to go to Penshurst, Lord John

joining us on horseback—but the weather was so stormy that we did not go on to the House but merely stopped to take a view of the place from the hill—Lady John very agreeable, and a nicer little pair than the two, in their several ways, it would not be easy to find—None but themselves at dinner—Sung a little for them in the evening and left to my inn at night. In talking of Lord Stanley and the boyishness of his character and conduct, Lord John, looking inquiringly at me said "I thought that very good in the Chronicle about the Boy Statesman—didn't you?" This was my own Squib founded on Mathews's "That boy'll be the death of me."[1] I, of course, laughed and acknowledged what I saw he was already pretty sure of.

14. [Friday] Started for town per coach at nine o'clock and got to my own quarters before three—{Found a note from Lord Essex who had just arrived in town asking me to dine with him on Sunday. This, with some other reasons, induced me to change my day of departure from Sunday to Monday—A note also from Lady Holland, asking me for to-day & Sunday, but sent an excuse for both—Dined with Bryan—day as usual, except that poor Mary Bryan, alias Mrs. Brown, alias Madame Manson made one of the family party—

15 [Saturday]—To the British Museum after breakfast & worked for four hours, which pretty nearly got me through all the references I had noted down—Dined at Quintin Dick's—(See preceding page, under date 9th. where, from a misplacement of my memorandums I have noted down Dick's dinner instead of for to day.)

16 [Sunday]—Luttrell having asked me to accompany him to the Listowels of whom he had to make request respecting some trees of theirs which hang over the wall of his garden & spoil it by their dripping, I set off after breakfast to wait upon him—Found him much better than he appeared to me at Dick's yesterday. Walked with him to Lord Ls. and found Lady Listowel at home, with whom we sat for some time—remarkably nice person. During our walk there was a drunken fellow reeling from one side of the path to the other before us, apropos of whom Luttrell quoted a good definition of a drunken man—namely that he was a man who had business on both sides of the way. Mentioned in Charades "Why is Courtship like the Great Herring Fishery?" "Because it cannot go on without smacks and busses."—F.R.S., he said, meant "Fellow, remarkably stupid."—By the way, Stevenson (Lady Mary's husband) told me not a bad story at Brookes's, the other morning—The old Lord Cholmondely was a great eater or rather devourer of game, and used to gulp down shot and all, as was visible

frequently afterwards—one day, Dudley North, who was with him looking earnestly at the valet who was standing beside Lord Cs. chair, said, in his comical stammering way "Do you know, my good fellow, you are in great danger standing there so close behind your master—for if he f——ts, you'll be sure to be shot."—Dinner at Lord Essex's—Company, Mrs. Ford (her daughter) Miss Stephens & her niece, Captain Sherrif and Panizzi of the British Museum—Lord E. very well & cheerful, doing the honours of his table, (and also doing justice to its contents) most gallantly though tomorrow (as he told me) he was to enter into his 80th. year—Had singing in the evening. Miss S. & Miss Johnson sung some beautiful things together and I was also, of course, put in requisition for several songs with which I was delighted to see that Miss Stephens was *really* pleased—indeed *all* seemed very much pleased. Home.

17 [Monday]—Off for town by Emerald, most glad to get there—Have forgot to mention one of the most important events of my visit. Not having heard any thing more from the Longmans on the subject of Macrone's proposal, I wrote them to say that I concluded from the silence they were averse to my entering into the arrangement with him, and should therefore give up all further thoughts of it; but still could not help lamenting that such was their view of the matter, as, in my opinion, the publication of such an edition as M. proposes, would not injure the sale of the book in the cheap form which we meditated; while it would afford me not only the convenient supplies of whatever sum he might give me for the edition, but also the gratification of seeing the work brought out in a splendid, illustrated form. This, as far as I can recollect was the substance of my note, to which I received an answer thanking me for the kind manner in which I had expressed myself towards them, and recommending me to ascertain from Macrone what sum he would give me for the edition—In consequence of this I called upon him, and, judging from the Longmans' letter, that I might now give him reason to expect I would come to an agreement with him, *did* so. We then came to the important point of the sum he would give me for the edition, and after some very courteous parleying, during which he pressed me to name a sum, and I professed my inability to do so from my total ignorance as to what the speculation might be worth to him, he said at last, "Should you think £500 sufficient?" to which I answered laughing "most abundantly so—and I only marvel at your courage in risking so much." The fact is, £300 was the utmost I had raised my own expectations to. On this we parted, and in the course of the next day—my last in town—(Sunday—for all this happened on Saturday the 16th.) I wrote to tell the Longmans what he had offered, meaning to put my note to them into the post before I started—but forgot to do so and accordingly did not put it in till I reached home.

18 19 20 &c [Tuesday, 18 October–Thursday, 27 October]—Received an answer from the Longmans, all kindness & congratulation, saying they were "delighted" to hear of Macrone's offer[1] and advising me by all means to accept of it—only suggesting that, to avoid future disputes, I should have the number of copies he would require to print of the edition expressly stated & stipulated—From this time on, I must only *journalize en masse,* without attending much to dates or particulars, as what with my History, my visitors, and all my other various interruptions, I have no time for regular chronicling—A correspondence on the subject of our proposed agreement took place between Mr. Macrone and myself in consequence of which it was arranged he should come down to Sloperton.}

28 [Friday]—Macrone arrived in the evening—

29 [Saturday]—Found our visitor a very agreeable, clever, dashing young fellow, knowing a great deal of the general literature of the day, and having seen and known something of most of the eminent men of the time, particularly his own countrymen viz. Sir Walter Scott, Jeffry, Hogg &c.— His knowledge of Scott's life & habits chiefly derived from his intimacy with Laidlaw (Sir Walter's bailiff (?) or man of business) whom I recollect seeing at Abbotsford, and who, like Single-Speech Hamilton might be called Single-Song Laidlaw as he was the author of one very pretty Scotch Ballad, called Lucy's Flitting (which I remember Scott giving me to read) and never wrote any thing else. Was delighted to learn from Macrone that Laidlaw said he never saw Scott so pleased or happy with any visitor as he was during the few days I passed at Abbotsford, nor ever knew him to *work* so little as he did during that time. "There was no one else in the house," said Laidlaw (according to Macrone's report)—"he had Moore all to himself, and seemed to enjoy it thoroughly." This, (which I am willing to believe true, as it tallies indeed very much with what I myself observed at the time) gave me of course great pleasure to hear. {Tom took Macrone to see Bowood—

30 [Sunday]—On coming to talk business with Macrone, a difficulty arose which to a great degree "took the shine out of" his first gallant proposal to me. He had, on more closely considering the matter found that the Epicurean was a work of much smaller compass than he had at first imagined, and, that it would not therefore make a book large enough to warrant the outlay he originally intended. His proposal accordingly was that I should throw "The Loves of the Angels" in, as a make-weight. This—though I

could perceive clearly from his statement that his first offer had been an "impetus in tenebris"—completely altered, as I told him, the state of the business, as respected myself. I likewise represented to him that the alliance of the two works might prove to be an injury rather than an advantage to his speculation. The Loves of the Angels, though one of the most popular of my works abroad, was in England rather at a discount, both from the nature of the subject itself, and still more from the alarm caused at first by the title. Besides, as a matter of taste, I suggested, it would spoil the effect & character of both works thus to unite them. To this argument he answered unanswerably by referring to my own original intention (as stated in the Preface or Notes to the Epicurean) to connect the two works together. This I had entirely forgotten.

30 [Sunday][1]—Worked as much as I could well manage with so active and enthusiastic visitor in the house—Tom walked with him yesterday to Bowood, and to-day after Church took him to Laycock. Besides his other accomplishments Macrone draws well and has been employing himself in taking a likeness of Tom for his Mamma.—Returned constantly and anxiously to the subject of the Epicurean, and my objection to throwing in the Angels, as a make-weight, being of course insurmountable, there appeared little chance of ever coming to any agreement—At last, on considering the matter and taking into account the *great* convenience that a few hundred pounds would be to me just now I made up my mind to suggest (for he left the whole decision of the matter very handsomely to myself) that, if he thought he could make any thing of the Epicurean by itself, he must only reduce his payment to me, in proportion, and make it £300 instead of £500—This he most joyfully jumped at, and our agreement was so arranged.—Tried to get John Starkey to meet him at dinner but without success.—

31 [Monday]—Signed our agreement, and after dinner Macrone started for Devizes to take the night coach to town.

November 1st 2 &c [Tuesday–Wednesday] In correspondence with Ward the Engraver who is employed upon Mulvany's picture of me[1]—Called upon him while in town, and he then expressed great anxiety for an opportunity of touching the print from the original, if I could give him a sitting or two—but there not being any time then he proposed coming down to Sloperton which I acceded to.—Fixed Friday next, the 4th for his coming

3 [Thursday]—Went in, all of us, to Devizes to dine with the Hughes's—
Left word at the Bear Inn for Mr. Ward, who was to come by the night
coach.

4 [Friday]—Ward arrived, and accompanied us to Sloperton—Sat to him—
had brought with him to show us a copy in miniature by himself, of
Lawrence's full length picture of the Duchess of Richmond—a most beautiful thing, in every respect—Talking of Chauntry and poor Jackson the
painter who married a sister of Ward's wife, or rather I believe Ward's wife
was sister to Jackson—Chauntrey who was rolling in wealth, and singularly
enough has not a creature connected with either himself or his wife to leave
it to, was long the intimate friend of Jackson, and having requested that one
of Jackson's boys should be called after him and always shown, I believe, a
fondness for the boy, it naturally created a hope in the parents that he
meant to do something for him. But though Chauntrey's apparent regard
for the father continued up to the day of his death, from that time he has
never entered the house, nor taken any notice of the family—Such was
Ward's account, who agreed also entirely with the remarks I made upon
Chauntrey's frequently offensive manner—a vulgar affectation of saying
blunt things which is any thing but agreeable. This bad habit too is fostered
& encouraged in him by a set of hangers-on he has always about him—In
other respects he is a good honest man, as well as a clever one, and the
manner in which he has risen by his talent is honourable both to himself
and to the country. John Starkey to dinner—

5 [Saturday]—Sat to Ward for an hour or two—Find that he has been much
employed in the line of picture-copying—Has copied Lawrence's portrait
of the Duke of Wellington—the Duke very particular about his likenesses—
this I think I heard before from Hayter—or whether it was Hayter told me,
and not Ward, I am not quite sure. Hughes to dinner, having ordered a Fly
from Calne to come for Ward in the evening—Left us in time to catch the
night-coach to town—All much pleased with our visitor, who appears to be
a very modest, sensible, and kind-hearted man.

6–7 &c [Sunday, 6 November–Tuesday, 15 November] Hard at work again
to make up for lost time—The announcement of the Epicurean by Macrone having circulated a notion among the trade that I am in the market &
to be had, some splendid offers have in the course of the month been made
to me— and first & foremost Mr. Bentley, who had put out his feelers
before Macrone's visit to me now came to the point, and first through
Moran (of the Globe)[1] and afterwards from himself proposed to me to

write three Volumes of an Eastern Tale for which he would give me £1400 (a cheque for £500 of the sum to be paid down upon the nail) and a share in the copy-right (to the amount I think of two thirds) after the first Edition. This very dashing offer I am of course obliged to refuse—

16, 17, 18 &c. [Wednesday, 16 November–Wednesday, 23 November] Another proposal on the part of Mr. Charles Heath that I should write one volume consisting of an Eastern or other Tale, for which he would give me £1000 a volume, as he specifies in Royal Octavo, pages about 350 of 27 or 28 lines in each—and here have I been employed on a Volume for nearly two years, of nearly double the compass, and get but £750 for it, while for the volume that follows, of the same dimensions I am to receive but £500— this is sad work. Wrote of course to decline Heath's offer—

24, 25, 26 &c. &c. [Thursday–Saturday]—Another offer from Mr. Ackerman proposing to me to write 12 short poems illustrative of 12 drawings of females to be entitled "Flowers of Loveliness," and requesting me to name my own terms. This of course I also declined. Here is work, which could I have undertaken it (and Bentley professed himself willing to meet my own terms) would have brought me without much labour near 3000 pounds—

December 1, 2, 3 &c [Thursday–Saturday]

5th [Monday] To Lacock, Bessy, Tom & myself—No company, besides ourselves, but Henry Fitzmaurice, who is growing a very nice & agreeable young fellow

6 [Tuesday]—Drove with Lady Elisabeth to call upon the Methuens—Did not find them at home. The same family party at dinner.

7 [Wednesday]—Returned to Sloperton

8 [Thursday]—To Bowood, all of us, to dinner the carriage having been sent to take us. It was poor Lady Lansdowne's first meeting with Bessy since her loss, and she came up to the bed-room to her, that it might not be before witnesses, throwing her arms round Bessy's neck when she entered, while I withdrew into my own room.—She then passed on (as Bessy told

me) to ordinary subjects, and kissed her on going away.—No one at dinner but the Feildings, and Mr. Julian Young.

9 [Friday]—Returned home—Received The first proofs of The Second Volume of my History about the beginning [*incomplete*]

10, 11, 12, &c. [Saturday, 10 December–Tuesday, 20 December] At work.— A large portion of the MS. of my Second Volume in the Printer's hands—

21 [Wednesday]—To Bowood—Company, the Valletorts, Lady Minto and her daughters, Miss Fox and one or two more.

22. [Thursday] Remained at Bowood—Lord Minto expected, but did not arrive—same party at dinner

23. [Friday] Came away after breakfast, promising to return again tomorrow—}

24 [Saturday]—{To Bowood—an addition to the party of Lord Minto, Senior & the Fazakerleys—Senior somewhat improved in manner, but still an incurable coxcomb. Talk with Ld. Valletort about De Roos's affair—his propensity to cheat at cards long known it seems—any slight mark with the thumb-nail or otherwise on the ace enables the dealer to know it, and he contrives to give it either to himself or his partner. This it appears is the sort of trick the Premier Baron has been in the habit of playing. Query, whether some of the men who have been in the habit of living with him have not long known this trick of his, and even sometimes tacitly profited by it?} Anecdotes of Alvanley—Story told by {George Dawson}, who was his second in the Duel with Maurice O'Connell—Alvanley's silence as they proceeded in the carriage to the place of meeting—{Dawson} thinking to himself, "Well, I see Alvanley is for once made serious" and then, to break the silence, saying, "Let what will come of it, Alvanley, the world is extremely indebted to you for calling out this bullying fellow as you have done." "The world is debted to me, my dear fellow?"—answered Alvanley "I am devilish glad to hear it, for then the world and I are quits." Mentioned also that at some country-house where they were getting up a dramatic piece founded upon Scott's Rebecca, they wanted Alvanley to take the part of the Jew, but he declined, saying "Never could *do* a Jew, in my

life."[1]—{In the evening joined in a sort of play, which consists in guessing a line of poetry from the answers given to questions put to the company by the guesser—the verses used all taken from my songs which, being familiar to the party (consisting of Lady Louisa, the Lady Elliots, & Henry Fitzmaurice) rendered the luck of guessing more easy. Sung afterwards a good deal, as did also Lord & Lady Valletort a duett or two—

25 }[Sunday]—Returned home, glad to get back to work, and not meaning to go Bowood again till the arrival of Rogers, who is expected—Had two letters from him, one a particularly kind one chiding me for not having taken up my quarters at his house when I was last in town and when he himself was in Paris. "But why (he says) did not you the other day come at once to my house and ask for a bed there? Have not I told you to do so again and again, you varlet you?"

{26, 27, 28 &c. [Monday–Wednesday]—Tremendous fall of snow, through the whole country, interrupting communication every where, and of course shutting me up securely in my work-shop which I was not at all sorry for. My little Russell (who is home for the holidays) cut me a path through the snow, in my own walks, & I got out most days for three-quarters of an hour or so—Had written to Rogers who is expected at Bowood to know how soon he is likely to come down in order that I may reserve as much of my spare time for him as I can manage.—Received an answer saying that he had not yet fixed the day but would let me know at the same time when he apprized Lord Lansdowne, and charging me good humouredly not to squander a minute on any one else—}

Notes to 1836 Entries

12 January

1. Hieronymus Commelinus, *Rerum Britannicarum* . . . (1587).
2. Made. de Staël, *Delphine*, 3 vols. (1803).
3. Moore added the passage in square brackets at the end of the MS page, with asterisks to indicate its proper location in the text.

14 January

1. See the *Examiner*, no. 1458, 10 January 1836, p. 17.
2. Moore glosses his asterisk with the notation "Illegible" at the end of the MS page.
3. William Cooke Taylor, *The History of Mohammedanism and its sects* . . . (1834).

17 January

1. *Lalla Rookh, Works*, 6:123.
2. See entry for 19 January 1834 and its n. 1. The work Moore refers to is probably Husenbeth's *Faberism exposed and refuted* . . . (1836).

18 January

1. Never published; Kerry died in August 1836.

31 January

1. Thomas Reynolds, who was convicted of assault and riot for his participation in a disturbance at a political meeting in Dublin in 1835. He was sentenced to nine months in jail and fined £400. For an account of his trial see the *Times*, 3 November 1835.

1–2 February

1. Moore placed the passage in square brackets at the end of the MS page, with asterisks indicating its location in the text.

9–11 February

1. "Late Tithe Case," ll. 40–41, *Works*, 9:141.

12–14 February

1. John Lynch, *Cambrensis Eversus* . . . (1662).

24 February

1. The passage in square brackets appears at the bottom of the MS page, with asterisks indicating its location in the text.

25 February

1. Cf. Matt. 6:34.
2. Sir Francis Palgrave, *History of England: Anglo Saxon Period* (1831).

27 February

1. The *Dublin Review,* founded in May 1836 by O'Connell, Nicholas Patrick Stephen Wiseman (1802–65), and Michael Joseph Quin (1796–1843).

28 February

1. The passage in square brackets appears at the end of the MS page, with asterisks indicating its location in the text.
2. See entry for 1 March 1834 and its n. 1.
3. See "The Battle of Brunanburh," ll. 53–56.

29 February

1. Thomas Carlyle, "State of German Literature," *Edinburgh Review* 46 (1827): 304–51; "Taylor's History Survey of German Poetry," *Edinburgh Review* 53 (1831): 151–80.

1 March

1. This date, "March 1st," is inserted at the end of the line ending with "greater influence" and is written in darker ink than that of the rest of the text, as if it were an afterthought. Furthermore the entire passage, beginning with "Dined at Sir B. Brodie's" and ending with "I was a flaming Whig," is encircled and a line drawn to the margin of the second entry for 1 March.
2. Dorothea Jordan (1762–1816), actress, was the mistress of King William IV, by whom she had ten children, the Fitzclarences.
3. Henry Hallam, *Introduction to the Literature of Europe, in the Fifteenth, Sixteenth, and Seventeenth Centuries,* 4 vols. (1837–39).
4. During the debate on 23 February 1836 on the "Orange Lodges," secret associations of Irish Protestants, Russell introduced a resolution urging the King to suppress these and other such organizations. See *Parlia. Debates,* ser. 3, 31 (1836): 820–32.

2 March

1. Sir John Gardner Wilkinson, *Topography of Thebes, and General View of Egypt . . .* (1835).
2. See Marchand, *Byron: A Biography,* 3:1091–1146.
3. For an account of Wellington's relations with Lady Frances Webster see Elizabeth Longford, *Wellington: Pillar of State* (New York, 1972), pp. 19–24.
4. John Gibson Lockhart, *Memoirs of the Life of Sir Walter Scott, Bart.* (1837–38). For Willis' *Pencillings by the Way,* see entry for 9 November 1835 and its n.1. Comments on Moore appear in Letters LXXIV and LXXV of the 1852 American edition.
5. James MacGeoghegan, *Histoire de l'Irlande, ancienne et moderne,* 3 vols. (1758–63), trans. English 1831–32. Peter Lombard, *De Regno Hiberniae Sanctorum Insula commentarius* (1632).

5 March

1. Lady Mary Fitzclarence (d. 1864), illegitimate daughter of William IV, married Charles Richard Fox in 1824.

8 March

1. *Antiquities of Mexico; comprising fac-similes of ancient Mexican paintings and hieroglyphics . . .*, ed. Edward King, Viscount Kingsborough, 9 vols. (1830–48).
2. "The Brunswick Club," ll. 21–22. *Works,* 9:75.

8–10 March

1. "Police Reports Nos. 1 & 2" appeared in the *Morning Chronicle* for 8 March 1836. No. 1, "Breach of Peace," is not included in the *Works.* For "Case of Imposture" (No. 2), see *Works,* 9:229–31. For "Thoughts on the Late Destructive Proposition," which appeared in the *Morning Chronicle* for 17 March 1836, see *Works,* 9:212–14.

23 March

1. Ludovici Antonio Muratori (1672–1750), historian, theologian, and antiquarian. He was best known as the discoverer of the "Muratorian Canon," an eighty-five-line fragment of early Christian literature that he found in 1740. The document is part of an eighth-century compendium of theological tracts.
For Cellier see entry for 21 May 1834 and its n.1.
Histoire Literaire de la France. . . . By the Benedictines of S. Maur. A multi-volume work appearing in Paris from 1733–.

24 March

1. Nicholas Patrick Stephen Wiseman, *Letters to John Poynder, Esq., upon his work entitled "Popery in alliance with Heathenism"* (1836).

31 March

1. Published in the *Morning Chronicle,* 2 April 1836. *Works,* 9:161–65.

12 April

1. "Thoughts on Soap" appeared in the *Morning Chronicle,* 13 June 1836.

13 April

1. A drama by J. R. La Planché, adapted from Jacques François Halévy's opera *La Juive* (1835).

14 April

1. Rossini, *La Gazza Ladra* (1817).

15 April

1. Thomas Arnold, *Principles of Church Reform* (1833). "Not Jews." (Russell's note.)

16 April

1. Sir Thomas Noon Talfourd, *Ion*, privately printed in 1835, performed 1836.

18 April

1. Dominique François Jean Arago (1786–1853), French physicist and astronomer. His *Treatise on Comets* was published in London in 1833.

19 April

1. Byron's daughter, Augusta Ada, married William King-Noel, Earl of Lovelace, in 1835. At that time he was the 8th Baron King, later acquiring other honors by letters patent in 1838.

20 April

1. Lansdowne's speech in support of the Irish Corporation Reform Bill, 18 April 1836. See *Parlia. Debates*, ser. 3, 32 (1836): 1142–52.
2. Cf. John Dryden, "A Song for St. Cecilia's Day, 1687," ll. 14–15.

27 April

1. Moore's illness occurred in March 1806. See Dowden, *Letters*, 1:95 and note, and entry for 29 July 1840. Though the Moore biographies date the incident in 1800, the evidence they cite is one letter in the Russell edition (1:103), probably incorrectly dated by Russell.

1 May

1. James Bailey (d. 1864), who published in 1835 an annotated edition of Andrew Dalzel's *Analecta graeca minora*. . . .

1–3 June

1. "A Ghost Story. To the Air of 'Unfortunate Miss Bailey,'" which has the refrain "Oh Lord L-ndh-rst," appeared in the *Morning Chronicle* for 5 May 1836; see *Works*, 9:210–11. "The Lofty Lords" appeared in the *Morning Chronicle* for 9 May 1836; see Moore's *Prose and Verse*, ed. Richard Henry Shepherd (1878) pp. 20–21.

5–8 June

1. "Epistle from Captain Rock to Lord L-ndh-rst," published in the *Morning Chronicle*, 2 June 1836. *Works*, 9:284–87.

12 June

1. "Captain Rock in London; Letter from the Captain to Terry Alt, Esq.," appeared in the *Morning Chronicle*, 15 June 1836. *Works*, 9 :288–90.

18 June

1. Moore placed the passage in square brackets at the end of the MS page, with asterisks indicating its location in the text.

1–2 July

1. The *Times*, 29 June 1836, published a satirical poem on Lord John Russell entitled "Little John," in which Moore is described as a mercenary hack who "Barter'd his talents for a paltry mess / Of thin Whig pottage. . . ."

31 July

1. See Dowden, *Letters*, 2:802–3 and note.

24 August

1. "Lord Kerry died on the 21st of this month." (Russell's note.)

28 August

1. *Works*, 6:217. The line correctly reads "I never nurs'd a dear gazelle."

29 August

1. Samuel Seyer, *Memoirs historical and topographical of Bristol and its neighbourhood. . .* , 2 vols. (1821–23).

1–2 September

1. Russell dates this entry as September 17th, and that for the 9th as September 18th.

17 September

1. Johann Christian Wilhelm Augusti, trans., *Die Religions-wanderungen des herrn Thomas Moore, eines irländischen romantikers, beleuchtet von einigen seiner landsleute . . .* (1835).

18 September

1. Published in the *Morning Chronicle*, 8 September 1836. *Works*, 9:215–19.

1 October

1. The first two pages of the MS volume, containing the entries for 1–4 October 1836 (through the letters "ban-" of the word "banteringly") are missing and have been supplied from Russell's edition.
2. Jonathan Swift, "The Dean's Manner of Living," ll. 1–4.

4 October

1. Henry Joseph Monck Mason, *Primitive Christianity in Ireland. A Letter to T. Moore, exhibiting his misstatements in his history respecting the introduction of Christianity into Ireland* . . . (1836). Travers's answer to Mason, which was apparently never published as a single work, has not been identified.

7 October

1. *The Dunciad*, 2.243–44.

8 October

1. *Lalla Rookh; or the Ghebirs of the Desert*, an equestrian spectacle. H. M. Milner, *Mazeppa, or, The Wild Horse of Tartary*, a drama based on Byron's poem, first performed 4 April 1831.

9 October

1. Jozef Krystyan Ostrowski, trans., *Les Amours des Anges. Poème de T. Moore* (1837).
2. See Elizabeth Longford, *Wellington: The Years of the Sword* (New York, 1969), pp. 489–90.

10 October

1. Moore placed the passage in square brackets at the end of the MS page, with asterisks indicating its location in the text.

11 October

1. Moore obviously meant Travis. For the controversy see Richard Porson's *Letters to Mr. Archdeacon Travis, in answer to his defence of the Three Heavenly Witnesses, 1 John v.7*, 1790.
2. Juvenal, "Satire 8," ll. 73–74.

13 October

1. "The Boy Statesman. By a Tory" published in the *Morning Chronicle*, 16 July 1836. *Works*, 9:191–93.

18–20 October

1. Moore noted here: "On turning to Rees's letter I find the words as follows—We heartily congratulate you on Macrone's offer, which you should most certainly accept."

30 October

1. Moore made two entries for 30 October.

1–2 November

1. See Dowden, *Letters*, 2:805.

6–7 November

1. Ibid., 2:806.

24 December

1. George Soane, *The Hebrew* (1820), a drama based on Scott's *Ivanhoe*.

1837

[January] {1, 2, 3, 4 &c. [Sunday–Wednesday]—A note from Lord Lansdowne saying that they had been in hopes, when the snow began to melt
away that I would give some signs of life, and asking me to come over soon,
as his time for departure was near approaching—Offered to send the
carriage for me, but told him in my answer that I could manage very well
without it.

5. [Thursday] Walked to Bowood—Feilding who called just as I was starting, riding beside me as far as the Lodge Gate—Found at Bowood Luttrell,
Mr. Reeve (a relation of Mrs. Austin's) and Mr. Spedding, friend of Von
Artevelde Taylor—also, Eastlake, the painter, whom Rogers had fixed to
bring down, but on the evening before changed his mind and sent a verbal
message by him both for Lord Lansdowne & me. Senior[1] too "that mighty
man of demonstration, that great lord & possessor of first principles" still
one of the company—the only female guests I found remaining were Miss
Fox and one of the Lady Elliots—Sung in the evening, Eastlake having
expressed great anxiety to hear some of the songs I had sung when we met
at Lord Essex's—Lord L's anecdote of the handkerchief Lord Holland
brought home one night by mistake during the time that the negociations
were going on which ended in a duel between Lord Winchelsea and the
Duke of Wellington—The handkerchief being marked with the letter W.,
Lord Holland supposed it to be Lord Winchelsea's, whom he had been
sitting next for a part of the night, and he accordingly returned it to him in
a blank cover. It turned out however to be the Duke of Wellington's and the
surprise of Lord Winchelsea on receiving it was extreme, considering the
matter that was just then at issue between him & the Duke—it seemed as if it
was a new-fashioned sort of *cartel* that the Hero of Waterloo was bringing
into vogue[2]—In talking of the Benthamite school & their exceeding conceit, I remarked that, after all, none of them had done any thing remarkable in public life themselves, though so full of pedantic lecturings and

objectings to others—Lord L. in agreeing to this mentioned Lord ———, as an instance in point, and said it was an exceeding mortification to the school to find how ineffective he has proven in public life—Luttrell, apropos of something, quoted two amusing matter-of-fact lines of Crabbe's

> "Letters were sent when franks could be procured
> And when they could not, silence was endured."[3]

Talking of Monk Lewis, I referred to Luttrell's famous scene with him at Oatlands,[4] when, to the great amusement of the company, Luttrell under the mask of a *general* description of a Bore described Lewis to himself most accurately—Lewis unconsciously drawing him out by question after question as to the properties of the animal he was describing—"But if the Bore is so disagreeable a creature" said Lewis at last "why don't you instantly leave him?" "So I would this very moment," answered Luttrell "but that the etiquette of her R. Highness's society forbids me"—Lord Lansdowne mentioned having been present once when poor Lewis was complaining in his peculiarly tiresome way of having been dreadfully bored somewhere, and Payne Knight who was present, at last impatiently cried out "Damn it, why didn't you bore again?"—Talking of the Duke of Baden Lord Lansdowne mentioned that he & his Duchess used to hold separate events, and that when people came to wait upon him after having been with the Duchess, he used to say to them "Made. la Duchesse vous a dit des choses bien aimables, n'est ce pas?" and when they answered in the affirmative, he always rejoined "n'en croyez pas un seul mot."—I mentioned that Holkham (Cooke's place) was made a post-town by Lord Leicester; and, after the job had been a year or two in existence, there came down one morning from the Post Office an official letter to intimate that the issue of letters from Holkham not being sufficient to justify this distribution, there was some intention of withdrawing it. The House being just then full of company, Cooke in announcing this hint from the Post Office, at breakfast, said "Come, ladies, try what you can do for me, in the way of letter writing, for the honour of Holkham," on which they all turned to and never was such a batch of epistles sent out from any country-house before as issued forth that morning—Luttrell remarked on the exquisite humour in the Recruiting Officer of the girl disguised in men's clothes saying to the other girl she is pretending to court, "My dear, my circumstances are not so good as those of the Colonel."[5] Must see this passage.

7 [Saturday]—Left Bowood for Lacock—whither we had been all (Bessy, myself, & the boys) asked to meet the Valletorts before their departure for Devonshire—The Feildings' carriage came for me—expected to meet Bessy in the way, she having driven (not intending to dine there) to Lacock to take

leave of Lady Valletort—but found I was too late—Tom also dined there. Two charades told me by Luttrell "Why do they call that little dog Negus? Because he goes always *wining* and watering about the house."[1] "When a man has a fine collection of paintings, why have you a right to pick his pocket? Because he has picked yours." Pictures

8 [Sunday]—Saw the Valletorts off and returned to Sloperton in the Feildings' carriage

9, 10, 11 &c. [Monday, 9 January–Monday, 16 January] Too busy at my work (trying to make up for lost time) to be able to journalize with any particularity for the remainder of this month. Have not mentioned, I think, the application I had from my brother-bard of Barrow, Martin Doyle, to beg of me to endeavor to procure some situation for him. Through Lord Morpeth and Stanley (of the Treasury) both of whom were very kind on the subject I succeeded in procuring for him a small office in Dublin (Stamper of Newspapers) salary sixty pounds a year which will make a second Croesus of the poor fellow. Received a very cordial letter of thanks from his patron Boyse, on the occasion.—A letter from Spring Rice, in the course of this month dated from Lord Northampton's, begging me to contribute some scrap from my pen to a miscellaneous Volume they are getting up for the widow and family of poor Smedley, an accomplished clergyman whom I knew something about when living in Derbyshire, and who has left his family in much distress. Promised to do what I could—

17 [Tuesday]—Bessy took Russell to Devizes on his way to town, meaning to give him the treat of a Concert this evening at Devizes—Expected Corry down in consequence of a letter from him a week or two since saying he would take us on his way back to Cheltenham from London.

18 [Wednesday]—Bessy and Corry arrived in *his* Fly from Devizes.—He full of influenza, poor fellow, but still full also as usual of kindness and joviality—

19 [Thursday]—Corry left us for Cheltenham—

20 [Friday]—To Devizes, Tom, Bessy & myself—to dine with the Hughes's and attend a Ball in the evening—A tolerably good assemblage, in spite of

the influenza and it consoled me for the weariness of the thing to myself to see my sweet Bess looking so remarkably well, and dancing a country dance (which she did with Captain Amyot, the Steward) so well and actively. Tom, of course, was in a high state of enjoyment. Slept at the Hughes's.

23 [Monday]—Were to have gone for a few days to the Houltons but received a note from Mrs. Houlton putting us off on account of Houlton's illness with the influenza.

24, 25 &c. [Tuesday, 24 January–Tuesday, 31 January] Attacked myself by the prevailing complaint, and was for two or three days a good deal shaken by it, but not, like most other people, confined to my bed. It has, however, increased somewhat the tendency to swelling & inflammation in my foot— Our maid Davis also attacked—Received a letter in the course of this month from a Doctor Schaefer of Strasbourg, who it appears is the author of a German translation of my Irish History[1]—gives a very flattering account of the reception of the 1st. Volume—talks of the general appreciation throughout Germany of the depth of research and "etudes historiques" displayed in it and above all the "haute impartialité" by which it is characterized. The main object of his letter, however, is to suggest that I would, if in my power, furnish him with the proofs of the Second Volume as it goes through the press, in order that he may be enabled to gratify the impatience of the German public who has long been looking anxiously, he says, for its appearance—

February 1, 2, 3 &c &c [Wednesday, 1 February–Wednesday, 15 February]— Received a kind letter from Lardner, expressing his anxiety to know how soon I shall be ready with my second Volume, but at the same time very good-humoured & patient on the subject. Told him in my answer that I thought he might announce me for the 1st. of May, but not sooner. I forget whether I mentioned a former answer of mine to another communication from him in which I said that when it was considered that Lord Lyttelton took 20 years to write the History of *one* reign, it could not be considered *very* slow of me, even in these rail-road times, to despatch *20* reigns in *one* year, which was about the rate I had hitherto gone at.[1]

16 [Thursday]—All went for a couple of days to the Feildings—Company at dinner Captain & Mrs. Rooke & daughter, new comers into the neighbourhood—the Talbots at Lacock, she on her way to town to be confined— glad at all times of Talbot's society, his mind being always full of a variety of

subjects, though without the power, unluckily, of concentrating it efficiently upon any *one.* Is now all agog for *sun*-worship, as against *hero*-worship—but why not both? Had been reading a good deal upon the subject, but, oddly enough, had not looked into Dupuis. Showed me Champollion's posthumous work which is most neatly got up.[1]—Sung in the evening, the first time since my influenza. Thought I could'nt, but *did,* notwithstanding, though having a most common-place auditor in Mrs. Captain R.—

17, 18, 19 &c. [Friday, 17 February–Tuesday, 28 February]—Working away at my proofs—The following is from an Examiner of this month (the 29th) and occurs in one of a series of letters written by Walter Savage Landor, professing ironically to come from a Conservative and Churchman— "There is no person whom, as a Churchman and Conservative I dread so grievously as Mr. Moore. His jocularity is neither tittering nor tempestuous; but inextinguishable as the Greek Fire and blazing upon ten thousand faces."[1]

March 1, 2, 3, 4 &c [Wednesday, 1 March–Friday, 31 March]—This whole month busy—and with the exception of two days to Bath, for commissions, during which I took up my quarters at the Crawfords, have not budged from home & my writing-table—Feilding now & then called, but even those few times, I could but ill spare the half hour to talk with him.}

April {1 [Saturday]—The Longmans in a fright about my Volume, thinking there will be difficulty in getting it out the 1st. of May, the time they have counted upon—Resolved therefore to come up to town, and expedite the printing by being on the spot—Co. all rejoiced thereat—}[1]

5 [Wednesday]—{Started for town—Two ladies and a little Harrow boy my companions—some talk with the latter about Drury, to whom I sent my remembrances by him—the day most bitterly cold, and acknowledged by every body to be the worst we have ever had even this bitter season}— Arrived in Paternoster Row between 9 & 10—found Rees, some cold meat & hot brandy & water awaiting me—Rees, by the bye is about to quit the Firm, and Tom Longman, the eldest son, who succeeds to his place, has been for some weeks past my chief *business* correspondent—{an active, lively young fellow. In my announcement to him of the day I meant to come up, I said they might begin airing my bed &c. as soon as they chose, in answer to which I received a grave letter from him, in the name of the Firm, concluding (after some reference to the progress of the printing)

thus:—"We shall without fail sleep in your bed to-night, and remain with our best compliments, your most obed. serv.

Longman, Rees, Orme & Co."

6 [Thursday]—Set to work at the proofs, revises &c. & remained at it for some hours—started in an Omnibus for the Far West, and executed some commissions—putting in train a new coat, waistcoat &c. &c. Called at Rogers's but did not find him—} A great dinner at the Row, for which I had been secured before I came up, and not a bad thing to start with, as the company consisted of Sidney Smith, Canon Tate (a regular Princeps Editio old fellow whom I had never met with before) Merivale, Dionysius the Tyrant, MacCulloch, and Mr. Hayward, the translator of Faust, but better known as the author of some late Culinary articles in the Quarterly[1]— Sidney most rampantly facetious; his whole manner & talk forming a most amusing contrast to the Parson Adams-like simplicity and middle-aged lore of his brother Canon, Tait, whom I sat next, and who between the volley of Sidney's jokes, was talking to me of "that charming letter written by Vossius to Casaubon" and "the trick played by that rogue Muretus upon Scaliger."[2] Apropos of this trick (which was the imposing upon Scaliger, as ancient, some Latin verses written by himself, and which, of course, Scaliger never forgave,) I took occasion to mention that I had often thought of writing a History of celebrated Forgeries, or rather had thought what a good subject it would be for any person who had time & learning enough to undertake it.—the great variety of topics it would embrace—first, the historical forgers, Philo of Byblos, Annius of Viterbo, Hector Boece, Geoffry of Monmouth &c.[3] Then the *Ecclesiastical* impostures, such as the numerous False Gospels &c—then the *Literary,* including that of "the rogue Muretus," that of Jortin "Quae te sub tenera" &c. (which took in, not designedly however, the learned Gruter) and so on to Chatterton, Lauder, and lastly, Ireland.[4] {Talked of Cross, the *crystal* maker who produced such a sensation at the Bristol Scientific Meeting, and who lately, it is said, has found animal life to be the result of some of his experiments.[5] "I must say" remarked Sidney Smith "that that's the last sort of fluid (Muriatic acid) that I should expect to find employed in a process of gestation." Story about Judge Bailey, and the waiter at Harrowgate. "I say, Waiter, is there any W. in Harrowgate?" "Plenty on 'em, Sir—but Master doesn't like them to come to the Dragon."—} Conversation turned on Boz, the new comic writer—was sorry to hear Sidney cry him down, and evidently without having given him a fair trial—{McCullough too and the Partners seemed surprized and vexed with the Public for taking so much to the drollery of the Pickwicks—} whereas, to me it appears one of the few proofs of good taste that "the masses" as they are called, have yet given—there being {(mixed up with a good deal of coarseness & bad taste)} some as nice humour and fun in the Pickwick

papers as in any work I have seen in our day.[6]—Hayward, the only one of the party that stood by me in this opinion engaged me for a dinner (at his Chambers!) on Thursday next.

7. [Friday] Got to work a little after nine and remained hard at it till near four—Lardner came in dismay, not knowing of my arrival, and (there being now, it appears, really no other volume to substitute for mine) despairing of carrying on his series this month—much cheered by finding that I had no doubt of being ready in time. In a late letter to Tom Longman, I called Lardner & Co. the *Cab.*-drivers—not a bad name for them, I think.[1]—sallied out for the West End—went to Brooks's, where Rogers came to look for me—offered to dine with him to-day which he most heartily agreed to.—Called at Lansdowne House—saw Lady Lansdowne, who asked me to dinner to-day, and on finding I was engaged, asked me for tomorrow—Rogers very agreeable—Mentioned the Duke of Wellington's saying to some enthusiastic woman who was talking, in raptures about the glories of a Victory—"I should so like to witness a victory! &c. &c. "My dear Madam—a victory is the greatest tragedy in the world, except one,—and that is, a defeat."

8 [Saturday]—Hard at work till dinner-time—Company at the Lansdownes Lord & Lady Holland, the John Russells, the Morleys, Lord Seaforth, the Duke of Argyle, Baring, and one or two more. Sat between Allen & Sir George Grey—In talking of my History to Allen, who made some enquiries about it I remarked that I was lucky in being the first to have the advantage of the facilities which O'Connor's Work furnishes to a historian of Ireland, and which before, were in a great measure sealed up. He said that pretty much the same was Hallam's good luck who, in writing his Constitutional History had the advantage of the Rolls of Parliament, then recently made public. {(Mentioned this, by the bye, to somebody since who said that Hallam but little if at all, availed himself of them.) In talking with Lord John after dinner, he said to me *"You,* I know, will be glad to hear that Shiel is as rapidly rising in the estimation of the House of Commons as OConnell is decidedly sinking and going off." This I hear from every one—at least, as regards the immense success of Shiel——and very sincerely rejoice at it.} Some talk between Lord John, Baring and myself on the subject of Parliamentary oratory—the difficulty of interweaving those parts which every orator, to be effective, must prepare with those called forth by the impulse and demands of the moment. Baring quoted, as one of those things of Canning's which must have been elaborately prepared, though appearing to arise out of the suggestions of the moment, and which ended with some such sentence as "We find the bird of Diogenes in the man of Plato."[1] Must

remember to look to Canning's Speeches for the passage. {Had some new light communicated to me by Lord Morley on the subject of lettuce-pills, of which, oddly enough, I had never heard before, but of which he told me he takes very freely and with very good effect. Lord Seaforth the same. Home to the Row, having promised to dine with the Hollands on Monday.

9 [Sunday]—Meant to have gone to the Warwick Chapel, but too busy to spare the time. Sent for Russell to the Charter-House, and dispatched him with a note to Bryan's, saying that I would come to dinner there—Did so, leaving poor Buss (for want of better sport) to dine with one of the Partners in the Row. Made. Manson (Mary Bryan that was) made one of our party. Bryan in very good humour—Back to the Row pretty early, having come to the resolution of moving bag and baggage to Sackville St. on the morrow— the Feildings not being likely to come up for a week yet.}

10 [Monday]—Moved to the West and took up my quarters in Feilding's secluded & comfortable room, where I felt I should be able to work double tides.—Dinner at the Hollands'—company, Sidney Smith, Lord Milbourne, and Lord Kinnaird—{My lady holding forth in the evening on the merits of Scarron's Roman Comique—improper enough, she owned, but still very clever & amusing[1]—Lord Holland looking over Bayle for something— pointed out to me what Bayle tells of a mistake of the Press mentioned by Erasmus as having occurred in a Dedication of one of his books (to the Queen of Hungary, I think) where having said that this Queen "semper mente illa usam esse quae talem faeminam deceret," the Printer made him say "semper mentulâillâ usam esse quae &c. &c."—[2] I remember having referred to this very mistake in some mock learned notes I wrote when in college to some doggrel of my own, under the name of Trismagistus Rustifustius—On my remarking to Lord H. how very convenient was the form of his Bayle (an octavo edition) he said very good naturedly that he would endeavor to procure a copy of the same format for me if I would do him the favour to accept it. Somebody having remarked how ignorant Rogers was on all subjects, except mere English Belles Lettres, a discussion arose on the point, in which my Lady, Sidney & Allen took part *against* Rogers's condition & Lord H. *for* it. The truth is, he *does* know very little either of Science, Ancient Literature, History or Languages—but taking him altogether (and this I remarked at the time) his poetical talent, his acquaintance with, and refined feeling of, the arts, his powers of conversation, his position in society & his wealth, he presents a most extraordinary combination, and Nature and Chance may shuffle the cards between them, for a long time, before they again turn up another such trump as Rogers.

11 [Tuesday]—At work most of the day—Called upon Mr. Grenville—
found Lady Harrowby there who he told me was to dine with him next day,
and asked me to come & meet her & Lord Harrowby—but I was already
engaged—Showed me Sydney's 3d. Edition of his Anti-Episcopal Pamphlet,[1] and pointed out the new note he has added, directed against Lord
Harrowby, which is not only a failure in point of execution (being a most
pedantic attempt at humour) but, as regards Lord Harrowby, it appears
unfounded—Sydney having written it under the notion that Lord Harrowby was one of the most decided of the Church Commissioners, on the
side of the Bishops, whereas Mr. Grenville said (and he had just heard it no
doubt from Lady H.) that so opposed was Lord H. to the views of the
Bishops that it was with difficulty he could be kept from resigning in
consequence. Dined at Lord Essex's, company, my good old friend, Woolriche, Boldero, Rich, and F. Byng. On my happening to allude to the
operation I went through some thirty years ago under Woolriche's hands,
he treated the company with a most minute description of all he had done
to me—the probing, the caustic &c. the extreme danger I was in, all
depending, as he has often told me, upon whether the tumour broke inside
or out—and it was to determine it outwardly that he so successfully tortured me with the probe & caustic that day. Though remembering so
accurately, however, all he himself did, he had again forgot, though I have
often reminded him of it, the Epicurean verses I wrote in the course of that
day of pain, and repeated to him in the evening after the discharge of the
matter had relieved me. I forget all but a few lines of them now, but they
were in the true spirit of youthful bravado. The following are all I remember.

> Even here, in speechless pain, I draw
>   From every pang within, without,
> Such proofs of Pleasure's holy law,
>   As Saints themselves would blush to doubt.
> And if my spirit rise from this,
>   If neither bile nor Woolriche kills me
> Oh, I shall &c. &c.

I forget how the stanza ended—For the sake of the alliteration, I afterwards
made it "If neither bile nor Bailey kills me," Bailey having also been in
attendance on me at the time—To Brookes's for a while and home.}

12 [Wednesday]—Was obliged to leave my work at three and sally forth to
the Printer (Shoe Lane) about some difficulty that had occurred—most
troublesome people, these midwives of the Muse. If they wouldn't take
upon themselves to *think,* one could get on pretty well—but the moment
they begin to "think they're thinking" all goes wrong. Thus, in quoting the

Four Masters in my notes I have always written "IV Mag."—but the wise Compositor or Reader took it into his head to *think* that it ought to be "Mag. IV," and though I go on continually marking so (IV Mag.) and it comes back generally in the *first* revise *right,* yet, in the *second,* it is always sure to be transposed back again, *wrong.* Dined at Lansdowne House—Company Lord & Lady Mahon, Lord & Lady Fitzharris, Lord Clare, the Lysters, Eastlake, the painter, & Barry, the architect—Sat next Lord Mahon, and had some interesting conversation with him. Talked of the Duke of Wellington, for whom I professed (without remembering at the time Lord Mahon's *devouement* to him) all the admiration which he has at length fairly *extorted* from me, in the very teeth of long cherished prejudice and dislike to him. And, after all, too, it is his *pen-and-ink-work* that has made a convert of me—those Despatches of his,[1] recently published, those most interesting despatches, full of traits of thoughtfulness, modesty, consideration for others, patience under misrepresentation, and all in short, that (combined with the vast things he was then accomplishing and preparing) goes to make the character of a great man as well as of a great and fortunate soldier. Expressed myself much to this purpose to Lord Mahon, who of course agreed with me most zealously, and said that there was one part of the Duke's political career,—his conduct in 1832 (during the attempt made by the Tories to construct an administration) which was little known to the public but was sure, some time or other, to come to light, and redound most memorably to his honour.[2] {A phrase used by Lord Mahon, however, let me into the secret I suspect of a great part of the merit (in Tory eyes) of the Duke's conduct on that occasion—for he spoke of "the disinterested devotedness to his sovereign which he then displayed"—rather a questionable ground of praise—at least, till one knows what it was his sovereign required of him—} Some general conversation after dinner about India in the course of which Lord Clare gave no very agreeable idea either of the country itself or of the society there—a great want of beautiful scenery—all being so flat, and even where elevated, being but an ascending series of flats—the society very much of the same description—people take no interest in any persons or events that are not immediately under their noses—"If I were to talk," said Lord Clare, "of Lord Lansdowne or any other of my friends at home, they would think I was coming Captain Grand over them—I therefore carefully avoided all such subjects"—Speaking of Rogers, and the feeling between him and Byron, Lord Clare mentioned having seen Rogers, at Rome (I think) after his visit to Byron, and R's telling him of Byron's having said that there were but two men in the world he felt any affection for. *"You* were one (added Rogers) and I am sorry to say *I* was not the other."[3] {Lord Clare, after mentioning this, turned round to me and said "You, I think, *were* the other."} Lord Mahon, apropos of some story about *souls,* quoted to me my own lines "Says Malthus one day to a clown"[4] (which I had myself quite forgotten) and went through several stanzas of them. It constantly happens to me thus to find people remembering my own things much better than I do myself: which shows at least that the parturition of them was easy—Forgot to mention that the day before yesterday, I think, when I was sitting with Rogers (or rather standing, for we neither of us trouble chairs much) he pointed to a note lying on the table, said, "there's *Glory,*" and on my replying that he must have many such testimonies to his glory, he said "No, but read it"; on doing which I found it was a printed Circular from my rather too active partisan, M{oran}, of the Globe, proposing a dinner to be given to me by my friends and admirers, during my stay in town—Despatched a note off instantly to M{oran} to deprecate the design, telling him that I would explain to him all my manifold reasons when we met. On the same evening Lord Holland produced to me another of these missives (or rather missiles) which had been discharged at *him.*[5]

{13 [Thursday]—Worked till five, when I was again obliged to hurry off to the Printer to arrange some difficulty—Dined at Hayward's, in the Temple—Company, Mr. & Mrs. Leicester Stanhope, Mrs. Herbert, and my old Paris acquaintance, her daughter, Lady Vincent—Mrs. (I forget the name) a daughter of Lady Charleville, and (the only agreeable thing of the party) my hospitable Bath friend, Elwyn. As I was, by order of the Host, leading in Lady Vincent to dinner, Mrs. L. Stanhope, with a smile meant to be irresistible, leaning back towards me, said *"Pray,* let me sit next you at dinner"—but my fair companion, who overheard her, took care to whisk me off quite to the other side of the table. The object of both was evidently not to talk *with* me but *to* me, and our party being small & huddled together by the smallness of the room, the voices of these Prima Donnas and the host's (none of them the most agreeable in the world) being all at full stretch during the whole time of dinner, made such a *charivari* among them as was really intolerable—Elwyn & myself and Leicester Stanhope (whom I have always rather liked) played mutes on the occasion, with the exception of a little quiet whispered talk which Elwyn and I, who sat next each other, contrived to interchange. After dinner Sergeant Talfourd arrived from the House of Commons and [*MS damaged*] for a while the tongues of the ladies by a pretty considerable volley from his own. I should have gone away, indeed, with not a very much better [*MS damaged*] of Talfourd than of some of the rest of the company, but it rather fortunately happened that we both took our leave together and finding that he was returning to the House of Commons, I accompanied him thither. [*MS damaged*] giving me an opportunity of some further conversation with him, I got to like him much better before we parted. He is evidently a *natural* person, and that in itself goes for a great deal. Sat for a short time with him under the gallery, and then went home, having promised to dine with him some eight or ten days hence.

14 [Friday]—Obliged again to go down to the Printer—Called at the Horse Guards, and left my name both for Lord Fitzroy & for General Macdonald—Called upon Lady Grey and sat with her for some time—Found there Lord Clements—met afterwards, in the Square, Lord Grey and had a few words conversation with him—Being bound by no dinner engagement, resolved to treat myself to some Theatre—Dined early at Brookes's, having, in passing Braham's Theatre, left my card for him, saying that I meant to come that evening—Received from him while at dinner an order for a Private Box "for Mr. Moore and party." Very civil this. On my presenting myself, too, the alacrity of the box-keeper &c. all very agreeable. The first Piece one that I have long wished to see, Maitre Jacques,[1] and it a good deal affected me—being alone, I could cry a little without restraint—There came afterwards, however, a party into the next box whose unceasing efforts to get a peep at me and my own to baffle them made me rather laugh again. Before the commencement of the Second Piece a messenger came with Mrs. Braham's compliments that there was a Pitt Private Box at my service, should I prefer it—sent for answer, with my compliments, that I could not be better pleased, but should have the pleasure of paying my respects to Mrs. B. before I left the house—Did so, and while there Braham joined us, in the Grand dress he had worn in the Opera. Could collect from them as well as what I hear from other people that the value of theatrical property has sunk considerably within a short period—the lust for dramatic representation having, from various causes, very much gone by. Braham's other speculation, however, the Colosseum turned him *clear* (as I understood) last year eight thousand pounds.[2] Did not wait for the last piece & got home pretty early—Mrs. Braham full of Lalla Rookh, and asking me questions about some parts of it which I was exceedingly puzzled to answer.}

15. [Saturday] Edward Moore called—A kind & sensible letter from Dr. Taylor. Received within this day or two, by the bye, from Sloperton, an anonymous letter that had arrived there for me since I left home, rather amusing. Begins thus "Dear Moore—I do not know you—I hate your politics, but I love your songs, and it is from the love I bear those songs that I now write to &c. &c." The writer then proceeds to recommend an edition of my Lyrical productions with the music neatly engraved over each Song—Out at four.—Received this morning copy of some new Illustrations of Lalla Rookh, entitled Pearls of the East professing to be portraits of the principal heroines of that work[1]—Not very like the Ladies, I should *hope*. One of the dinners I have been at at Lansdowne House lately, is thus announced in the Court Circular—On such a day "the Marquis of Lansdowne entertained Mr. Thomas Moore, and a number of other literary & scientific gentlemen, at dinner at L. House"—These literaries & scientifics

having been in reality a party of fine Lords & Ladies. Paid some visits—dined at Lord John's—company, the Lansdownes, Lord Melbourne, Lord Grey and his daughter, Lord Carlisle and his daughter and Baron Bulow. {Both} Lord & Lady Lansdowne remarked to me that I had not looked at all well the other day at L. House and I can well suppose that fag and worry do *tell* upon me, in despite of all my buoyancy of spirit, which thank God, seldom fails. Dinner very agreeable—It was remarked, apropos of something, how much more tenaciously the remembrance of historical personages & events are preserved among the country class of people in Ireland than in England. *"You* say, I perceive (said Lord Melbourne, turning to me, in allusion to my Captain Rock) that Lord Strafford is still remembered in Ireland, under the name of Black Tom."[2] I remarked that the Irish were in every respect a people of traditions, dwelling for ever on the past, and Lord Carlisle said, with but too much truth, perhaps, that this is a characteristic of a people backward in civilization—that, as nations advance, they leave their traditions behind them—or (as I think he expressed it) that "according as a people became instructed, their traditions vanished"—A good deal of talk about Cromwell, and his character. In speaking of Talleyrand, after we went up to coffee, Bulow mentioned Talleyrand's having told him that none of those Speeches he delivered in the Convention were his own—had them all written for him and he read them out from the Tribune[3]—Talleyrand attributed the misfortunes of all the rulers who have reigned over France from Napoleon down to Louis Philippe to their neglect of the counsels which he (Talleyrand) gave them. Bulow said that Talleyrand's lameness was owing to a pig having eaten away part of the foot when he was a child—he had been placed en nourrice, according to the old French mode, and the nurse having left him alone, one day, a hungry pig that was near got at him and *rongeait* one of his feet. Have mentioned this since to Lady Holland, and she said there is no truth whatever as to the pig, though the lameness did rise from an accident at nurse. I believe it, however, to be a case of scrofula.[4] Came away with the Lansdownes, who very kindly insisted upon leaving me at my own door, as the night was so very cold. Did intend to have gone to Babbage's soireé (as did also Lord L.) but had staid too late at Lord John's.

16 [Sunday]—At work till half past five, when I dressed for dinner, (though not having to dine till half past seven) and went to Brookes's to relax over the Sunday newspapers—Overtook Sir Robert Peel near White's, who greeted me most cordially—"Ah Moore, how do you do? I am so glad to see you." Told him that I had called upon him last time when I was in town, which he seemed not to have known, and said that at any time when he was at home, if I sent in my card he would be most happy to see me—Dined at Byng's having fixed the day myself, in order that he might get Fonblanque

to meet me—company, Fonblanque, Shiel, Lord Ebrington, Lord Clanrickard, and a German Count (Walstein, I believe)—Some talk with Fonblanque about his paper and its deserved success—the more to be rejoiced at as it told well for the *readers* as well as for the *writer*—the wit being of that high kind which required the *recipient* also to be of no ordinary description—Quoted to him a passage from one of his own Papers as an instance of the sort of condensed wit which I thought required minds very different from those of the common run of readers to seize and appreciate properly. It was one which I may have already mentioned in this Journal, where, speaking of the martial tendencies of the Irish parsons, he says "It is curious to observe how an Irish parson, in hot water, assumes the military colour." Seemed pleased with my remarks on this, and said "from *you* particularly" &c. &c—{Byng told me of his meeting with Strangford lately at Lady Blessington's (Strangford having been *cut* by him, and it appears deservedly, many years ago) and of S. going up to him suddenly & saying, as he seized his hand—"Is there to be no limit to animosity?", "on which," said Byng "I could not help giving way, and so we are now on terms again."—Told me he saw Peel & me together to-day being himself in White's at the time—mentioned the difficulty he felt sometimes as to the mode in which he should address persons of high station with whom he had been for years in habits of familiarity—Peel for instance—whom he however still calls simply "Peel." Confessed that he hesitated on the subject when about to write a note once, to Lord Melbourne, soon after his elevation to the Premiership, but at last decided upon addressing him "Dear Melbourne" as usual. I should like to hear what the two Premiers themselves think of the matter!} On my return home between eleven and twelve o'clock sat down again to my proofs and worked till half past two—

{17 [Monday]—The Longmans signified to me that the whole of the work must be in the hands of the Printer by Friday next (21st.) which rather alarmed me, there being still a good deal to revise—To make the matter worse, some dust flew into one of my eyes to-day, which gave me for some time a good deal of uneasiness as well as apprehension—Not being engaged to dinner any where (as I thought) turned in for the evening with the melancholy prospect of being obliged to pass it without either dinner or light, besides losing the time for my work—By dint of drenching the eye, however, with very hot water, I subdued the inflammation so much as to enable me to work a little—nor was the starvation, perhaps, without its good effect—a slice of the ham that I got Fanny (the housemaid) to boil for my luncheons being all my repast—Got to bed early.

18 [Tuesday]—My eye much better, and indeed nearly well—Received a note, to my consternation, from Lord Essex, recalling to my recollection

that I had promised to dine with him yesterday. He says very good humouredly "My dear Moore—Wherever you dined yesterday, you got, I am sure, a much better dinner than you would have had here—But I had asked some people to meet you, and &c. &c." Wrote to apologize for my forgetfulness, told of the dust in the eye & the dinnerless evening & mentioned two days on either of which I should be most happy to come and dine with him. Dined at Kent House—large party in the evening. Sung with great success. Lady E. Bulteel & her husband at dinner.

19 [Wednesday]—At work all day—dined with Lady Holland—Lord H. having gone to the House of Commons to hear the debate—Company, besides Allen, Sidney Smith, Rogers, Luttrell, and young Gore (Lord John's Private Secretary)—The day odd and amusing—but, in one respect *not* agreeable. People, by living constantly together, contract a familiarity towards each other, which if not restrained by a watchful sense of good-nature and good-breeding is apt to bring out in unseemly sallies of contradiction, interruption, temper &c. and this was rather painfully exemplified in what I observed to-day. Between my Lady & Allen such outbreaks have been always present, but the shortness of their duration and the perfect good-humour by which they are, in general, immediately succeeded, render them far more amusing than offensive. But to-day was otherwise—My Lady broke loose much oftener than I have ever seen her do before, and the Habitués all gave it to her again in return—Sidney, Rogers, and Luttrell, each in his different temper and manner attacking her, and though nothing could well be more lively and dramatic than the whole exhibition, I could not help feeling all the while that I was in bad company and would infinitely prefer (except for a short spurt now and then) living in society much less clever and witty but having more courtesy and good-breeding towards each other. It is curious enough too that it should be the case (but all the men of the party, in talking over the dinner afterwards, agreed it *was* so) that the absence of Lord Holland acted as a removal of restraint—and it was amusing to observe that while each perceived this, as far as regarded Lady Holland, none of them seemed to be conscious that the same emancipating effect was visible also in themselves—His good nature generally interposes to soften away all such shocks & collisions in conversation—Sidney, however, was very amusing, particularly after my Lady had retired—His jokes upon the two words πευκοφρων and κακοφρων under which two heads, he said, were comprised the different classes of children one meets with in stage-coaches—said that he himself when a child joins the party, always speculates according to its looks, whether it is likely to be of the πευκοφρων or the κακοφρων kind—if the former it will be held up to the window—if the latter [it] must take its chance in the coach.—In talking of Bulow's account of the cause of Talleyrand's lameness (which Lady Holland, as I have already said, contradicts) she mentioned a Mrs. or Lady St. John, a

very pretty woman, who when an infant had been attacked by a pig and had one of her *fesses* eaten off—always rode, she said, sitting on a different side from what other women did. Sidney, as a counterpart to this, mentioned another lady, who not knowing there was a stove behind her, retired back upon it, and as he said, bore ever afterwards branded upon her behind the words "John Feytin Londini fecit."—After dinner got away to join Lady Louisa at the Opera, Lady Lansdowne having given me a ticket in the morning—Found her and Lady (Stratford) Canning whom I had not seen for a good while—The Opera the Cenerentola and a new singer, Albertazzi, very agreeable.[1]—Got a note from Lord Essex during dinner, asking me for Friday.

20 [Thursday]—See next page.

21 [Friday]—At work—Got into a scrape with Rogers, having said I would dine with him on Sunday (taking for granted that Edward Moore had not been able to collect the party he was planning for that day) and was now obliged to send him Edward Moore's card "To remind," showing that I had a previous tie for Sunday. R. a little savage about it, but the fit soon over.— Dined with him to-day—a large party—at least for him—consisting of the Hollands, Sidney, Luttrell, Charles Kemble, Mrs. Butler (the renowned Fanny) and her unmarried sister, the Mildmays & one or two more— altogether a dozen. Took down Miss Kemble to dinner a rather dull & pedantic young lady, who deals over much in words ending with "ality." Disapproved much of the sameness of character there is in English society—no "individuality" to be met with any where. Seemed shocked at my taking the part of the *non-individuality* people, and saying that I rather liked that kind of society where there was nothing that departed very much from the common level, one way or the other—that there was an ease in it which, I was ashamed to own, I liked, &c. &c.—She returned however to the charge and at last silenced me by another "ality," saying that if there was any thing she herself disliked more than another it was conventionality— Talked in the evening with Mrs. Butler, whom I found much improved by time and training—She spoke of the Americans with a great deal of good sense & fairness—

20 [Thursday]—(I have by mistake transposed my records of the 21st. & the 20th) Very hard at work these two days, and, of course, near the end of my task—Feilding and the ladies expected this evening—he very ill, and obliged to have the large coach sent down for him, in order that he may be brought up recumbent.—Dined at Lord Essex's, being taken by Rogers &

his sister. Told Rogers, pretty much as I have stated it above, the sort of impression left upon my mind by our last day with Lady Holland, and he seemed to feel the truth of it, though of course not quite pleased to hear it—I instanced also the manner in which he himself had spoken to her at his own table, when, on her criticising the new National Gallery (in which he has been a good deal concerned) he said violently to her "as for you, you know no more of architecture &c." Left Lord Essex's with Rogers & his sister and accompanied them to an assembly at Hallam's, where I staid but a very short time. Had some talk with Mrs. Lyster, who, in speaking of Lady Lansdowne, said that she always felt herself under restraint in her society, though having the kindest opinion of her—that there was a coldness &c. &c.—I spoke, as I always speak & feel of her, as being a most perfect model of a noble feminine character.

22 [Saturday]—Went down to the Printing-Office with almost my last words, there being the Errata of the First Volume to add tomorrow—sent to the Charter-House for Russell, who came to me to the Printer's, and I made him show him the Printing operations while I was engaged with my proofs—Took him then to Leicester Square, and gave him a nice dinner at the French House, which Tom patronizes, after which I packed him off in a cabriolet to his prison—Dined early with Byng, in order to go to the Opera, having refused a fine dinner at Lansdowne House for the purpose— nobody but the Byngs, myself and Lord Russell—The opera Norma, and Grisi most charming in it—

23 [Sunday]—Have been breakfasting with Horatia Feilding almost every morning since they came—nice girl—full of intelligence and sweetness.— Finished the last remains of my task (θεω δοξα) at ½ past five, and des- patched it to the Printer—Dined with Edward Moore—company, Shiel, Wyse, Lord Fingall, Bryan, Mills (Washington Irving's great friend) a Sir Thomas Webb, I think, and some other person—The day middling—never had seen Mills before, and was not a little surprised that such a coxcomb should ever have been Irving's friend. But, if Poverty brings a man ac- quainted with strange bed-fellows, so also does Wealth, and it could only have been the convenience of Mills's luxurious house in the country (af- fording a retreat now & then to Irving) that could ever have made such an ill-matched pair friends. Sate rather late and home. Forgot to mention that I had some talk yesterday with Macrone upon business—I had lately writ- ten to him to say that in looking over the MS. of my first sketch of the Epicurean (which was originally intended to be in verse) it occurred to me that we might subjoin this poetical fragment to his Edition, so as to increase the size of the Volume. Had brought up the MS. with me & gave it to him

to-day to read. He wished me to name the sum I required for it but this I declined or at least deferred doing.[1] Saw him again to-day and promised to breakfast with him tomorrow morning. Forgot to mention that at Kent House, the other night, Lady Georgiana Grey asked me whether I could name any day to dine with them, and I mentioned Monday as a day on which I was disengaged—Received the next morning a very kind letter from Lady Grey saying they would be most happy to see me on that day, but that she feared they would have only a family party to offer me. Wrote back to say what I most truly felt, that the pleasure of dining with themselves alone would be far more delightful to me than the gayest party that they could collect.}

24 [Monday] {Started this morning a free man, independent of the devils &c.—It was still however but a change of business and anxiety, as my first object now was to try and catch Lord Fitzroy Somerset, on the subject of Tom's commission—Called early at his own house, and was lucky enough to find him at home, at breakfast, and my old musical friend, Sir Andrew Barnard along with him—Nothing could be more frank and good-humoured than his manner, and though he held out no definite hope, the assurances he gave me that my son was not forgotten seemed as sincere & well-intentioned as I could expect. Called also at the Horse-Guards and saw General Macdonald—Promised to breakfast with Macrone tomorrow morning, who insists upon my giving birth to another monster by sitting to MacClise for my portrait—this new "monstrum horrendum informe" (as it is sure to be) being intended to form one of the ornaments of the new splendid edition of the Epicurean—Macrone had wished to be allowed to have a print from Lawrence's portrait of me, and asked Murray's permission, but the great John refused—just as I recollect his refusing Lord Dover, who begged of him to allow Lawrence to make a copy of it for him.} Dined at Lord Grey's—Company, besides their own family, the Hollands, Rogers, Lord Duncannon and {"Bear"} Ellice—the day very agreeable—in the evening came some of the Carlisles, and the Duke of Sutherland, with his engaging Duchess, who combines the thoroughly feminine woman with the air of the "high-born ladye" in a most remarkable and pleasing manner. {Lady Morley also of the party—Lady Georgiana & Lady Elisabeth Bulteel played some very pretty things on the Harp & Piano-forte, and I sung most abundantly, my voice being in pretty good order and my hearers not easily tired—Called this morning at Lansdowne House and sate with Lady Louisa, who was looking not at all well—

25 [Tuesday]—Breakfasted with Macrone—had made up my mind not to name any price for the additional "matter," and it was lucky for myself that

I did, as what he offered (£200) was, to say the truth, about twice as much as I should have had the face to ask for it—Called afterwards upon General Macdonald (in consequence of a note from Lady Macdonald, saying that he would be most happy to accompany me to Lord Hill) and was by him taken to the Commander in Chief, who received me very kindly—asked me how long my son had been on his List, and when I told him something more than a year, said smiling "That is not a very long time Mr. Moore" which, I fear, is the exact truth of the case. His manner, however (as far as that goes in such matters) was kind and promising—Forgot to mention a scene in Pall-Mall yesterday which was rather curious—I met OConnell, and stopped to speak with him—but before we had exchanged any words, Sidney Smith came up to me with great eagerness, and taking me away rather *brusquement* from the great Agitator entered with much earnestness on the subject of a dinner which he wanted me to eat with him next Saturday, leaving OConnell (who had touched his hat to him but whom, in his eagerness, he hardly noticed) to stand for some time behind us and then get away as he could. I hesitated for some time as to my ability to give a decisive answer, but Sidney, being in one of his rigid and imperative moods, I did at last promise to defer my intended departure beyond Saturday & to dine with him on that day—Found on my return home that a Card had been sent to me by the Council of the Royal Academy for their great dinner on Saturday and so was obliged, after all, to write an excuse to Sidney— Dined to day with the Longmans at Hampstead, being taken out by the Spottiswodes. Day as usual in that house comfortable & friendly—with plenty of singing from myself and Miss Longman (or rather Mrs. x x x, as she has become lately) reinforced on the present occasion by two Miss Pocockes, daughters of the late dramatic author of that name, but not very agreeable in the singing line. Brought home by the Spottiswodes.

26 [Wednesday]—Breakfasted with Hume at the Parthenon—forgot, I think, to mention that I went with him one of these days to the Treasury, the first time I have presented myself there, in my quality of Grand Pensionary. Called upon Stanley in his office, who asked me to dine with him the following day, but I was engaged.—Dined at Sergeant Talfourd's,— on my way thither met my old publisher, Carpenter, the first time I have seen the rogue for years, and had some talk with him—Company at Talfourd's, Shiel, Harness, the Rutherfords, and a good many other people that I knew nothing of—Some conversation after dinner about the Drama, in the course of which I was much struck by Shiel's efforts to avoid & turn aside any allusions to his own dramatic efforts. One of these was my mentioning that I had once cried over his Evadne during a journey up to town in the Coach—very much as I added from imagining all the while the touching manner in which Miss O'Neill would act it—The whole day far

from being pleasant—Saw, on returning to the drawing room, that there was a determined design to get me to the Piano-Forte—a vile looking upright affair, at which there were two or three young children, banging away with all their might at the keys, and every new thump followed by a laugh from the mother and a set of aunts (as I take for granted) who sate around—One of these urchins came up to me, by command, to say that the company wished very much to hear me sing one of my charming melodies. "Presently, my dear" said I, having already made up my mind what I should do, and being placed near the door, I took advantage of the first entrance of a servant into the room to bolt down stairs and in a few seconds found myself safe in the middle of the Square—Meant to have gone to old Lady Cork's, who had written me rather a touching note in the morning, but it was late & I was tired, so went home to bed. The following is a part of her note—"You visit every body but me! Nay, I heard of your warbling at Mrs. Lister's. Friendship is a fine thing. I cared for *you* when I met you a stripling at Moira House, but you forget and neglect Mrs. Cork in her old age &c."}

27 [Thursday]—Went to the Longman's, for the no less awful purpose than the looking over my account with them for some years past—Had time but for the Sum Totals on both sides, and found the result more satisfactory than I had expected, the interest of the sums deposited by me in their hands some years since having sufficed pretty nearly to cover all the advances they have made me. Shiel, one of these mornings, at Brookes's, told me some good things said by the Irish Barrister, Keller, my god-father—To some Judge, an old friend of Keller's, a steady solemn fellow, who had succeeded as much in his profession as Keller had failed, he said one day "In opposition to all the laws of natural philosophy, you have *risen* by your *gravity*, while I have *sunk* by my *levity*."—Shiel mentioned to me his intention of quoting some time soon in the House Lord Bacon's praise of Ireland (the passage where an allusion to the Harp occurs) introducing it by first quoting some lines of mine to the same purpose, and then saying "You may object that this comes from a poet and an Irishman; but I will now produce to you one who is &c. &c"—Dined at Murray's {(the great John)}—Company, Doctor & Mrs. Somerville, Croker, and Sir David Wilkie & his sister—The first time of my meeting with Croker for many years—he talked a good deal, laying down the law, as usual, upon every topic and though never what can be called agreeable, yet often very amusing—Mrs. Somerville, whom I had never before seen so much of, gained upon me exceedingly—so much unpretending womanliness of manner joined with such rare talent & knowledge is, indeed, a combination that cannot be too much admired—{In the evening had an addition to the company among whom was a very pretty & clever "little girl"—Russian born, but educated in

France, and speaking English (though but just arrived here) almost like an English woman—have seldom met a young lady more full of enthusiasm concerning "Moore" and all that "Moore" has ever done, said, or written. Was determined evidently to try the whole force both of her eyes & tongue upon me. Sung also, and though with but little voice, (sometimes almost inaudible) showed much feeling & taste—Of course, I was also put in requisition, and it gave me great pleasure to find that Mrs. Somerville showed as thorough a *woman's* enjoyment of my singing as even the pretty little Russian herself—Some allusion having been made in the course of our after dinner conversation to Talleyrand's lameness Croker, who seemed to think that it was decidedly a case of scrofula, remarked how curious it was that there should be at one time living and flourishing three such spirits as Scott, Lord Byron, & Talleyrand all suffering under the same infirmity and, as he believed, from the very same cause—

28 [Friday]—Went after breakfast, attended by Macrone & Hume to sit to MacClise for the intended Portrait—Moore, the sculptor, attending at the same time to study my phiz for his own monstrosity—Called at the Morning Chronicle Office—saw Black, & had some talk with him—Said to him that I supposed they cared no longer to have any of my squibs (no intercourse having taken place between them & me since the completion of my last agreed-for batch) but he said, on the contrary, it was the very thing they wanted and could never have too much of it—In the same manner the Cramers whom I called upon yesterday, so far from being saturated (as I had supposed) with the things I had given them, were on the contrary quite ready for more, and proposed to me eagerly to join Balfe in some musical work.—All this satisfactory, whether I think right to avail myself of it or not.—}

29 [Saturday]—After breakfasting at Rogers, went to Macclise's, and gave him a long sitting—ditto to Moore at his house in Howland St—was obliged to be dressed & ready at ½ past four to accompany Rogers to the Academy, in order to have a view of the Exhibition before dinner—The whole thing, Exhibition, Dinner & Company, a spectacle well worth being present at.— Was sorry to see that the Duke of Wellington entirely forgets me—though, to be sure, so many years have passed since I dined at his table in Dublin, when he was Secretary there, that it is by no means to be wondered at—We have been thrown together once or twice, in society, of late years, and then from the few words that passed between us, I was in hopes that he remembered me—but from the manner in which he received me to day when Rogers, after shaking hands with him himself, made a sort of half presenta-

tion of me to him, I am pretty sure he has no recollection of me whatever—Got seated near Jones, the artist, who in talking of Turner's forth-coming designs for the Epicurean, mentioned his having "attempted" some subjects from it himself, and his being curious to see whether Turner had fixed upon the same. Had some talk too with Turner about his task, and in referring to the subjects I had marked for him, he said "There is one you have done yourself"—meaning, as he added, the incident of the Epicurean hanging by the ring.[1]—From the dinner Rogers & I went together to Babbage's, where we staid but a short time & then home—{Sir John Conroy at the dinner mentioned his having seen me at the Opera last night and said that the young Princess had found me out the moment I came in—which was curious enough as it was in one of the highest boxes

30. [Sunday]—Breakfasted with Macrone & went to Warwick St Chapel, the Duke of Norfolk having given me permission to occupy his place in the Foreign Ambassador's seat—from there to MacClise's—Dined at Lansdowne House—company—the Mintos, the Roseberrys, the Howicks, Lord Palmerston, Sidney Smith, Shiel (his first appearance here) & Lord Clare—Got seated between Lord Roseberry & Lord Palmerston—Pressing invitations to come to Scotland both from the Mintos & the Roseberrys—Went afterwards to the Hollands'—found there Lord John, who had sent me a card for dinner on the 7th. to meet, as he now told me, OConnell—said that somebody had told him I should not like to meet OConnell—but I replied, "Oh dear—I should not have the slightest objection but that I am going out of town"—"Well, I *thought* you wouldn't" replied Lord John. Got home pretty early—}

May {1 [Monday]—A day of jobs & businesses—offered myself to Bryan for dinner, and got away from him early to pack.

2. [Tuesday] Started in the Emerald, Lord James OBrien and an old Bath lady being my companions—Some rather amusing conversation with Lord James which I have not now time to notice—The old lady evidently did not know who were her companions till he & I went in to dinner at Marlborough, she remaining in the coach. She had been in the mean time informed about me, and on my return asked me who *he* was. It was curious enough, too, on my mentioning something about my trip to America, she said that she herself was in Windsor (Nova Scotia) at the time when I visited that town and was one of a number of young girls who, having heard a great deal about me, were all most anxious to get a peep at me as I passed. It is Strange to think at how *early* a period my reputation (such as it is)

began to spread—Found my dearest Bessy still suffering from a fall she had over a Stile during my absence—}

3, 4, 5, 6 &c. [Wednesday, 3 May–Wednesday, 10 May] From this throughout the remainder of the month I had neither time, nor indeed, much material for journalizing—every moment being devoted to the careful correction of my Epicurean, both in its prose form, as published, and in the poetical shape which it was at first intended to wear. Found among my papers a part of the latter—viz. a rough copy of a Letter from the High Priest of Memphis,[1] which I had entirely forgotten, but which I have now furbished up and think it one of the best things, in the heroic metre, that I have ever written.

{11 [Thursday]—Went to Bowood, to dine with young Lord Shelburne, and his *two* tutors—Paishley (who has just published upon Crete) and Von Bohlen, the great German Orientalist, with whom he was domiciliated at Koningsberg[1]—The German full of my writings and familiar with them all, even to my newspaper squibs—Read me translations by himself, into German of some of the latter (one of them "Little Men and Little Soul")[2] which I could only judge of by their sing-song, but which, if done at all tolerably, must be no ordinary tour-de-force. Slept there.—The German said (whether truly or not I don't know) that Byron & myself were the English authors most popular among the Germans—Three translations into German of Lalla Rookh, but none, he said, very good—Henry Fitzmaurice mentioned as excellent a thing said by Sydney Smith the other day of Lord John—"He really has not body enough to cover decently that mind of his." By the bye, Saw not a bad colloquy quoted somewhere lately—"Well, Sir do you entertain my proposition?" "No, Sir, but your proposition entertains me."

12, 13, 14 &c. [Friday, 12 May–Wednesday, 31 May]—Had the German and Henry Fitz. one of these days to dinner to meet Brabant, who was in the seventh heaven, and has invited the German to his house, in order that he (Brabant) may superintend his health and that Bohlen may in turn superintend his German.}

June 1, 2 [Thursday–Friday]—Having long meditated a trip to France with Tom for the purpose of placing him somewhere (not in Paris) where he may lay in a little French before he embarks in his profession, I wrote to Corry about this time, asking him to join in our expedition, which he readily consented to do, {and arrived at Sloperton, with that view, on Saturday the 3rd.

4th [Sunday] Corry accompanied Bessy to Church—busy preparing for my expedition—had to dinner Starkey and his brother-in-law, Windham, as well as Henry Fitzmaurice. Mrs. Starkey came in the evening—Starkey delighted with Corry's fun—

5th. [Monday] Started for town, with Corry and Tom, the latter outside—took up our quarters at the St. James's Hotel—the first time of my being in an Hotel for I know not how many years—Had written to Lady Macdonald to beg of her to have Tom's name written down on Lord Fitzroy's Levee List for tomorrow.

6th. [Tuesday] Went with Tom to the Levee—found that our names had been placed high on the List—Received very courteously by Lord F. whose first question to me was "Well, how soon do you wish your son to be employed?"—"Oh, of course," I answered, "as soon as it is in your power to appoint him—for I take for granted you would allow him some period of leave afterwards"—"Two months" he replied "is the time allowed"—He then talked of the places best for boys to go to on the Continent, and mentioned one which, he said, was 400 miles off, and therefore too far perhaps for my purpose—After a few minutes of such conversation took our leave—Met on the stairs an old General Officer, whose name I could not recollect but who talked of times past when we were acquainted, and introduced to me his son whom he had brought there with the same views as my own.—Note from Lord Lansdowne enclosing me a ticket for the Opera.—Dined (Corry, myself & Tom) at Bryan's—Left early, Tom for some public place (I forget where) and I to the Opera—Grisi in Semi-ramide[1]—came in for her Scene on the Throne and was so much affected by the music, that it was [with] difficulty I could keep from sobbing aloud—No one in the box luckily but Lady Lovera, and a great friend of hers, a lady whose name I forget—Lady Lovera perceived (as she told me after-wards) how much I was affected but took care not to appear to notice—Home, and found Corry & Tom in the Coffee-Room—had supper and were very jovial.

7. [Wednesday]—Walking about with Tom—met several gentlemen to whom I introduced him—among others to Lord Anglesey whom we met

riding to Bond St.—Told him that it was such people as he, military heroes, that had set my son wild for the army adding that I was glad he had had a sight of him. "Aye," said Lord A. with a shrug and a sigh "I am now so well worth seeing"—Looks much better, however than from his long suffering could have been expected—Asked me to come to him tomorrow evening— Met also Lady Grey, who stopped her carriage, & asked me to dine with her on Sunday next—of course, can *not*. Dined Tom & I with Rogers in order to go to Made. Devrient's benefit—Miss Rogers and Mr. Mitford (who has lately published some additional Letters of Gray) our only other guests[1]— an Opera Fidelio followed by Duvernay in the Sylphide[2]—On my saying that I would stay but for a *little* of the Ballet, Rogers echoed with much bitterness "a *little* of it!" adding, "I remember once when Moore & Lord Byron and myself were sitting together consulting very agreeably—Moore said he must leave us to go to Lydia Whyte." Seeing, however, that I had given up the idea of going away, he relaxed into better humour, and told some amusing stories, among others one of an old servant who had lived for a length of time with some antiquated maidens, and who after having worn red plush breeches for many years, was by some change of taste in his mistresses obliged to assume black ones instead. "Here" said the fellow, muttering angrily to himself, "Here has my a —— been on fire now for more than twenty years, and now it is as black as a cinder."—R's *humour* in walking home—his taking suddenly to running, and keeping Tom and me in a trot after him—wonderful strength for his time of life—He & Tom had come to the play in a cab together, and not a word (as Tom told me afterwards) had he spoken to him all the time—

8. [Thursday]—Out early for commissions &c.—breakfasted with Rogers to meet Lady and Miss Macdonald—Paid visits afterwards to Lord Essex, and Lord John, taking Tom with me to both—found Lord E. at home, looking wonderfully well, but alluding to some calamity that had befallen him, and, while he spoke, bursting into tears—On enquiring of the servant, as I went out, learned that his daughter, Mrs. Ford, had lately died.[1]—Found Lady John also at home, and soon after Lord John himself arrived—remarked Tom's likeness to his mother—both he & Lady John full of kindness—sent Tom on some commissions, and went to pay other visits—first to Kensington House, where I sate for some time with Sir John Conroy, who again called me to task for not always announcing myself to him on my arrival in town—"immediately on your coming," he said "you ought to write me a note, saying My dear Conroy—I am just arrived in town and mean to stay for ten days, a fortnight, or a month, whatever the time may be—for I assure you he added that the Duchess & the Princess have never forgotten their agreeable meeting with you at Erle-Stoke."—Went to Holland House,

and found Lord H. very ill with gout—having a chalk stone in one of his feet—Woolriche was with him, and Lady Holland came in soon after—made me promise to come & stay some days at H.H. on my return from France—Lord H. told me [he] had sent my Bayle to be bound, thinking that as a present to me it ought to come in proper form & dress.—Left my name at the Duke of Sussex's in returning—Dined at Feilding's, Tom and I—Poor Feilding, whom I have seen almost every morning since I came continues in a state of health not a little alarming—could perceive the first morning I saw him that Lady E. who was sitting beside him could hardly refrain all the time from tears. Was somewhat better to-day, and had himself carried up stairs to join us after dinner—Our party, in addition to themselves & Mademoiselle, being George Montgomery, and a young Italian they had kept at Nice, who [was] a very good singer (though no musician) and gave us some specimens of his voice after dinner—Had some conversation to-day with Lord Tavistock, at Brookes's, about Lord John, his great success, his late admirable speeches &c. Met Lord Francis Gower, and had some talk with him during which the solemn buckram he used to be cased in seemed to me a good deal worn off. Has given Corry this morning a letter of introduction to Lord Granville

9 [Friday]—In talking of my singing, Corry reminded me of what Manners Sutton had once said to me, in his presence, on that subject—namely, that placed as he (Manners Sutton) was, surrounded by much of what the world considers high & prosperous, he would willingly exchange it all to possess those gifts (meaning the union of poetry and music) with which I was endowed. This, which I had entirely forgot, was of course but a strong mode of expressing the pleasure he felt at the moment from my singing—Had Macrone to breakfast who was full of ecstacy at the Letters of the High Priest, which I had sent him up, but does not intend, unless the aspect of the money market improves very considerably, to proceed any further with his Edition of the Epicurean for some time. Forgot to mention that, on my telling Lord Holland of my intention to leave Tom somewhere for instruction in France, he mentioned Caen as a place which he had heard recommended for that purpose—Having taken our places in the Coach for Dover, Tom & Corry and I started at eleven o'clock, and arrived there at eight o'clock in the evening, when we dined—A very poor house—rumours in town, when we left it, that the King was all but dead—Forgot to mention a letter written by Sidney Smith the other day to his daughter announcing his return from Holland, in which he says, (after having been absent about 3 or 4 weeks) "I am now about to return to my native land and should be glad of a letter from you to meet me at Calais, saying what institutions of my country have been changed, and who is the present reigning monarch"— not bad satire—

10 [Saturday]—Sailed for Boulogne, where we arrived at five o'clock after a passage of 4 hours—uncomfortable all the way, unable to speak or move— Walk in the evening along the pier—

11 [Sunday]—Started at eight in the Diligence—our company in the interior (which was constantly changing, from our party being sometimes *out*side, sometimes *in*, Corry & I alone remaining there stationary) consisted of three young men belonging to some wholesale business in London, all of them lively, intelligent & good-humoured fellows and two Italians, one of them long a dealer in hardware &c. in England, was now going for a short time to his own country—an honest, good sort of man— practised my Italian with him occasionally and altogether got on very smoothly & merrily—the more so from my companions not having yet found me out. One of them in the course of the day quoted "The Last Rose of Summer" and another said "As Tom Moore tells us, in his Life of Byron."—Stopped for the night at Amiens, and being, of course, at the mercy of the Coach for our *gîte*, fared not very comfortably—Had a glimpse of the Cathedral before going to bed.

12 [Monday]—Off again at seven—day most tryingly hot—my companions had in the interim found me out—a man on the top having expressed his suspicions as to the fact, and the brass plate on my portmanteau having confirmed them.—Got on very jovially notwithstanding, Corry's stories and mine keeping them, most of the way, on the broad grin—The evening delicious—arrived at Paris between nine and ten & took up our quarters at Meurice's, Rue Rivoli

13 [Tuesday]—Called at Galignani's—both brothers full of courtesy and offers of service—recommended our immediate application for tickets for the approaching Fêtes, and on my mentioning Vicomte Chabot said that he was the man to apply to—"The King will, of course" said Galignani "the moment he hears of your arrival, send to invite you &c. &c."—Called upon Lord Granville and sat some time with him—asked me what was thought in England, as to the consequences of the King's death—evidently anxious not to be disturbed from his very agreeable post, a post which, I believe, both he & Lady Granville fill, in all respects, most worthily. Spoke to him about his son's successful debut in Parliament. While I was with him, the Duc de Broglie came to pay a visit—did not know him at first, but he shook my hand very cordially, and, on my mentioning, in the course of conversation, my wish to place my son somewhere to learn French, and, if possible, to connect with that object some opportunity of military study, he by a curious

coincidence with Lord Holland's suggestion said that he believed Caen was a place well suited for my purpose, and offered to introduce me to a person who could, he said, give me information on the subject.—Sauntered about with Tom & Corry—dined at the Café de Paris, and set out to visit the shows in the Champs Elysées, but a tremendous storm of lightning and rain coming on, deluged the whole scene and drove us for shelter to the Palais Royal, where we sauntered about, had ices and then home—Called upon Chabot in the course of the day & sat some time with him. Had been ill and looked worried & sickly. On my adverting to the chance of my being presented to the King during my stay said that he was sure the King would be very glad to see me—that he would let him know of my arrival, and that it was possible he might send a card for the Hotel de Ville but just as possible that he might not being so much occupied at this moment &c. &c. [It was not from the King, I believe, that these invitations came—but the above was as far as I could collect what Chabot said. He seemed, however, neither to know nor care much about the matter.][1] To this I replied that it was much better perhaps not to take any steps on the subject—at least as to the point of my being presented, which would entail on me the necessity of full-dress &c.—In all this he seemed most willing to agree with me. Heard afterwards that both Chabot himself & Lady Isabella have been always remarkable for taking as little as possible trouble to oblige people. To this Poco-curantism was added, on this present occasion, evident physical weakness & worry. In talking of the existing state of political affairs, he did not speak as if he thought the present good-humoured temper of the public mind likely to last. While at Galignani's Reading Room to-day I received several marks of respect from the strangers there assembled—many of whom took off their hats as I passed them, and one intelligent looking young man who brought me a newspaper he had heard me ask for (evidently for the sake of the opportunity of speaking to me) begged to be allowed to shake hands with me, and offer his thanks for all the pleasure I had been the means of affording him.}

14 [Wednesday]—{A visit, while at breakfast, from the Revd. Dr. Wright, the English chaplain at Caen—Told me of Rothe, my old Kilkenny friend, who is established there with his family, and also of General Corbet, my fellow collegian at old Trinity, who, having suffered in those times for the cause of Ireland, entered into the French army, and after serving through the whole Peninsular War, in the retreat from Moscow, in the Defence of Paris, and, at a later period, in Greece, has now attained the rank of General, and commands the district at Caen—All this very nearly decided me to select Caen as the place for Tom.—Accompanied Tom to the Tailor's & Shoemaker's, to act as his interpreter with those functionaries—no small operation, considering that Tom is of the Dandy genus. Went through it,

however, very patiently—Took him afterwards to the Champs Elysées, and occupied a chair outside while he visited the different shows.—Called at Flahaut's, but found no one at home. Received tickets from Chabot for the Thuilleries this evening. Called upon Lady Canterbury who was anxious for us to come to dinner—Lord C. away in England.} Took Tom to introduce him to Chabot, and were both a good deal struck by the homeliness of his Royal lodgings (up three pair of stairs in the Thuilleries) the arms emblazoned here and there on the furniture being the only things that reminded us of our being in the dwelling of Royalty. Dined at Meurice's at the Table d'Hote, and went in the evening to the Thuilleries—Had three tickets admitting six persons among us three, but were not aware that they admitted to different places—one of the tickets, which was of a different colour, being for the roof of the Thuilleries, from whence the best view of the fireworks could be obtained—Encountered a good deal of confusion in going in from our ignorance of this difference in the tickets, and not liking to separate myself from Corry, I gave Tom that which admitted to the roof while Corry and I took our places in the garden of the Chateau, just under the balcony at which Louis Philippe and la Famille (as they are called by distinction) were seated. Anxious about Tom I again went out, and had to experience fresh difficulties in coming back again during which I was twice irritated into speaking angrily to those fierce fellows with swords in their hands, who, to do them justice, treated my "brutum fulmen" very good-humouredly & concedingly. But there is something so humiliating in being pushed back, that if there was a whole army of them, I could not refrain from speaking my mind to them as I did then. The fireworks beautiful; and what with the flowers, the moonlight, the gay dresses of the women seated around, and the sweet airs played by the military band, I thought it all very delightful but, like all other delightful things, sad and affecting. (The Marseillaise Hymn was among the airs they played!) Nor was it the least touching part of the whole spectacle to see that poor Louis Philippe, whom when I was last in France, I left living happily and comfortably, with his family, like an English gentleman in the country—the ladies all at their work-table in the evening, and the children brought in to play with their hoops about the room,—to see him now placed in so very different a situation, not knowing, from minute to minute, whether the assassin's arm was not levelled at him, and obliged to rise and make obeisance to a set of gazers whom he must both fear and despise whenever any one of them chooses to greet him with a half ironical cheer. It seemed to me in general, indeed, the voice of a child that began the feeble "Vive le Roi" with which he was greeted. From our position, we could not see any of the fireworks but those which rose into the air (whereat Corry grumbled like a great school-boy) but those were well worth seeing, particularly a small balloon which occasionally detached from itself, as it rose, other bodies or offsets of light, as it were, without losing for a long time its own lustre, and the last grand *bouquet* which exceeded all that I have ever before seen, in the pyrotechnic line. Rejoined by Tom who had seen the whole perfectly, and was in extacies—[He had made acquaintance with a Member of the Chamber of Deputies who sat next him, and who promised to send him tickets of admission to the Chamber.—Sauntered about—had ices & home—Tom too late for the Champ de Mars where the sham fight took place while the fireworks were going on.

15 [Thursday]—Doctor Wright again to breakfast—brought with him to show me a copy of a book he has published, a translation from the German of Hug[1] accompanied by notes of Wright's own, which as far as I looked through them, appeared to me learned & clever—the man himself, however, rather oppressive—a good deal of talk with him about Caen, as a place for Tom, both as to its advantages & disadvantages—the latter of which (being himself out of humour with the town and about to leave it) he did not disguise, and the result was my nearly making up my mind to the trial—the great difficulty according to him, was to find a good place to receive a young man as boarder—the college which he said, I think, cost but £30 a year for every thing was for many reasons (viz. Tom's age, their starving system &c.) wholly out of the question—said, at last, that rather than there should be any difficulty, he would take Tom, as long as he remained in Caen, himself—went with Tom and Corry to make calls, at the Gregory's, Mrs. Forster's (who I found was in England) the Lady Forbes's (whose father, poor old Lord Granard, died a few days since) and the Ambassadors, where I went up for a few moments to ask Lady Granville whether it was necessary to wear any full dress at the Hotel de Ville. While I was waiting in the Hall, the Duc de Caze (whom I had never before seen) was shown up to Lord Granville—Lady G. full of good-nature about the dress, and went to enquire of De Caze for me, who said that it would be "plus galant" towards the King to wear uniform—but as I had no uniform, she seemed to think that a cocked hat would be, perhaps, all that was necessary—offered to take me there in her carriage to the Ball in the evening, but as I could not desert my companions, declined.—Learned soon after I left her that, in consequence of the dreadful loss of life last night in the Champ de Mars the Ball at the Hotel de Ville was put off—How fortunate Tom's not having been able to go to the Champ de Mars![2] Dined (Tom & I and Corry) at Lord Granville's—company, Lambton (whom I had not seen for ages) and a pretty wife, Mr. & Lady ——— Fullerton (Lord Gs. daughter whom I sat next and liked very much) Brooke Greville, Lord Leveson, and two or three Attachés.—In the evening Lady Granville hinted a wish that I should sing, her daughter being most desirous, she said, to hear me, but I pleaded with truth a very relaxed state of throat, from the excessive heat of the weather, and promised to call some morning and sing to them.

Found, on our return the tickets from Tom's friend, for the Chamber of Deputies—My arrival having been announced to-day in Galignani's & the different French Papers (the latter all calling me "Sir Thomas Moore") visitations from Poets, Priests, &c began to pour in upon me, and (what I thought I had escaped from, in leaving England) Poets' *Manuscripts* also. To-day received, among other things, some specimens of a translation into French of the Irish Melodies and parts of Lalla Rookh by a young Poet, who speaks thus in a long letter he has sent me—"J'apprends à l'instant votre arrivée dans notre capitale et ma première, comme ma plus douce pensée fut de m'unir a vos nombreux admirateurs, de vous porter aussi le témoignage de mon respect et de mon amour, de mêler ma faible voix au concert et d'hommages que de tous côtés s'elevent autour de vous. Français j'ose m'addresser au plus illustre ecrivain de l'Angleterre moderne; jeune, et inconnu, je ne crains pas d'importance de mon humble veneration un poete parvenu à l'apogée de sa gloire et à la maturité de son génie—He then gets enthusiastic and exclaims "est il si sombre endroit ou ne pénétrent les rayons de votre gloire? est-il un coeur si glacé qui ne s'emeuve s'échauffe, s'exalte en entendant votre nom comme en lisant vos chefs d'oeuvre? Je n'ai pu resister à cet elan de mon ame qui me pousse sur vos pas— Je n'ai pu imposer silence &c. &c. &c. Dés mon enfance je parcourus d'un oeil avide les tresor de la literature anglaise j'explorai les mines fécondes ou nous avons puisé tant de richesses. Alors m'apparut dans mes recherches poetiques un astre sublime qui rayonnait entre tous les autres, une lyre dont aucune autre lyre n'egalait la celeste harmonie, un nom devant qui palissait les noms les plus fameux—je venais de lire Thomas Moore! ah pardonnez" &c. &c.—and so the poor young fellow goes on through four closely written pages of such raving.—Fine as all this is felt much' more flattered this morning on being told by Scroope Davies and Galignani (neither of whom had seen me for at least fifteen years past) that I was not at all altered in appearance since we last met. This, indeed, is an approach to immortality that one *may* be proud of—mentioned the dreadful catastrophe that took place at the Champ de Mars yesterday, where Tom would have been had he not luckily preferred staying at the Thuilleries}

16 [Friday]—{After breakfast sallied out with Tom to go to the Diorama, which is a truly poetical exhibition—the chapel gradually filled with people & light, and the glories in the Temple of Solomon growing upon the eye, while the peal of the organ is heard swelling at a distance—what a magician the inventor of this spectacle would have been accounted a few hundred years since!—Called upon Made. Money, and had to labour up to a cinquième after her—} Went to the Chamber of Deputies and were lucky enough to come in for the briskest "turn-up" (as the gentlemen of the ring would call it) that has occurred for a long time—The question turned upon

a point of order, M. Mauguin having asked for explanations on the subject of the "Traité d'Afrique," and nothing short of an actual *row,* could exceed the agitation of the scene—The following specimen of it, from an account given in the Constitutionnel of this morning, may afford some little notion of what we witnessed—but the gesticulations and violent *acting* of the President it would be difficult to give any notion of

"*M. Berryer.*—Je ne dis pas non.—mais j'ai la parole.

M. Augustin Giraud—On ne peut pas vous empêcher de parler—c'est une tyrrannie (Vive agitation)

M. le Président.—Je dois proteger la liberté de la tribune, M. Giraud, je vous prie de ne pas interrompre la discussion—vous troublez l'ordre.

M. A. Giraud.—Vous devez maintenir la parole à l'orateur. (L'agitation continue.)

M. le Président—M. Giraud, je vous rappelle nominativement à l'ordre.

M. A. Giraud—Et moi, je rappelle M. le Président au sentiment de convenances. (Tumulte)

M. le President—Je vous rappelle à l'ordre pour la seconde fois (Nouvelle agitation)

M. Berryer—(au milieu du bruit)— Messieurs. . . .

M. Garaube—aux voix! aux voix!

M. Berryer—J'ai le droit. . . .

M. de Vauguyon (frappant sans discontinuer son pupitre avec son couteau de bois) aux voix! aux voix!

M. Pataille—(rivalisant de force et d'agilité avec le couteau de M. Vauguyon) aux voix! aux voix!

M. Roul (dont le couteau lutte glorieusement avec les couteaux de MM. Vauguyon et Pataille) aux voix! &c.

and so it goes on—"Tumulte inoui—les cris, aux voix! et les roulemens des couteaux redoublent avec une nouvelle energie; les dames se bouchent les oreilles, l'infatigable couteau de M. Vauguyon domine sur tous les autres couteaux &c. &c."—It was stated in another paper that personalities had passed between the President & some of the agitators, and it looked to me as if all was personality.—[Tom's friend (whose name I am ashamed to say I have forgot) observing us seated in one of the boxes, came up to us—a modest, intelligent looking man, speaking very good English—must ask Tom his name. On our coming out of the box together, he said "Take care, *Sir* Thomas, there's a step here."—Went to Galignani's and wrote letters— Dined Tom and I with Lady Canterbury where we had a few of the Attachés. Some of the party set off to Franconi's in the evening, but finding it shut in consequence of the rain, returned—

17 [Saturday]—Tom and Corry off to Versailles, whither I was sorry not to be able to accompany them, but visits and commissions required my pres-

ence in Paris—Forgot to mention a visit I received the other day from an Irish priest, attached to the Mission Etrangere here, and speaking himself a dialect *étranger,* Mr. ODonelly by name—Got yesterday the following characteristic note from him.—"The Revd. Mr. ODonelly has the honour of presenting his compliments most respectfully to Sir Thomas Moore, and humbly offering his services in facilitating any of the usual inconveniences presenting themselves to travellers in a foreign country"—Went to visit him to-day—not at home; but when I wrote down my name for his old porteress, her eyes brightened up, and she said "Ah je connais ce nom-là." I was beginning to feel flattered at this recognition; but her explanation of it let me into a little secret. The Revd. Mr. ODonelly, she told me, had staid out rather late the other night, and, on her scolding him for this excess, he told her, by way of excuse, that he had been passing the evening with a great "compatriote" of his, whose name she must have heard of—Monsieur Moore.—and this sly fib of the Revd. ODonelly's was evidently the sole source of her knowledge of me—dined at Madame Graham's—Company, Lord Leveson, the Marquis de Béranger, and Brook Greville—It is curious to see how fond the English are of displaying their French—here I found that Graham and some of the others, though long living in the society of the Marquis de Beranger, had never found out (so prodigal were they of their own gibberish to him) that he could speak very good English—far better, as it appeared to me than any of them could speak French— Mention made by the Marquis of a *Memoire* on Spain written by Louis Philippe (founded, I suppose, on his relations with that country in 1810)[1] in which he gives his opinion of the character of the Spaniards, as a military people, quite agreeing with that expressed by the Duke of Wellington, Napier, and other authorities, and entirely borne out by the spectacle they are exhibiting to Europe at this moment.[2]

18 [Sunday] Went all to the Church of the Rock after breakfast—nothing very striking either in music or sermon—Tom & I to Lady Canterbury's, where we lunched—wanted us to dine but we had determined upon the Opera Comique for the evening—dined at Meurice's—the pieces at the Opera, Fra Diavola[1] and a Petite Piece (I forget its name) very touching— Called one of these mornings on Lady Virginia Murray, at Passy—found with her her niece the Princess de la Tremoille, who appeared to be a very nice person—

19 [Monday]—Called upon Dr. Gunning to whom I was bearer of an introduction from Hume—an intelligent, agreeable man—Told him a great deal about William Spencer whom he appears to have known well during his later years at Paris—Miss Poulter was the lady who, from a sort of

romantic fancy for Spencer paid such friendly attention to him at that time, took lodgings in the same house with him, and defrayed the expense of having him buried according to his own request at Harrow, he having said once during his last illness (on being asked where he would like to be buried) "Oh, Harrow, Harrow"—She also was the posthumous editor of his Poems[1]—Talked of Tom Hume—thinks he must be making a great deal of money by his speculations at Hanwell—it appears that on a Competition being thrown open there for two public undertakings—namely, a Road and a Canal—Hume undertook both, and by constructing his road with the materials furnished by the excavation for his canal, has (so Gunning thinks) made a very good thing of it—The property at Hanwell came to him with his wife. Went to the Bibliotheque du Roi—forget whether I mentioned having received a note from an Irishman connected with that establishment a Mr. Dillon offering his services there in any way I might require—The following is his note—"Sir, may I request the favour of a minute's conversation the first day you are disengaged. I have got a very bad French translation of one or two of your excellent works to submit to you and to thank you as an Irishman for your noble and persevering efforts in favour of our common country. I shall wait on you at any hour you appoint, and should you think of honouring the Bibliotheque de Roi with a visit, my connexion with that establishment will enable me to procure you access to its unexplored curiosities, if indeed there be any such.—I have the honour to remain with respect & admiration &c. &c. P. W. Dillon." Shown by Mr. Dillon through the Library—mentioned to him my wish to enquire into whatever records there may be extant respecting the Irish Brigade, or "Legion Irlandaise"—introduced me to Champollion, (the brother of the hieroglyph man)[2] who, with all the promptness of a man of business, enquired precisely my immediate object, and then set in train the readiest process for accomplishing it for me—On my saying that it was fifteen or sixteen years since I was last in Paris, he remarked—"Mais, depuis ce temslà, vous avez fait de belles choses."—Found that there was not much to be expected on the subject of the Irish Brigade, but Mr. Dillon undertook to have *whatever* there might be sought out & copied for me—Went to the Ambassador's, and wrote in Lord Leveson's room a letter to Bessy to go by the bag—a message from Lady Granville, to say that she would have room in her carriage to take me to the Ball at the Hotel de Ville to-night, but, being pledged to my "cumrogues" Tom and Corry, declined—Dined at the Cafe de Paris, where we were joined by OConnor, an old Irish Catholic (a friend of Corry's) who has been long living at Paris—a pompous old twaddler—memorable (as Corry told us) for some Latin misquotation he made once at a Public meeting in Dublin, and who gave us a taste of the same talent, during dinner—In talking of the "taedium vitae," he called it the "Te-*Deum* vitae." Home to Meurice's to prepare for the Ball—amusing scene with the Marchande de [?Modes], who brought us some ready-made white cravats, Lady Canterbury having written to me to say we must positively not wear black ones—none narrow enough for my neck—efforts of the Marchande to make one of them fit me—anxiety of the waiter that I should *not* go in a black one—Laughter & noise of the whole party—ended at last in my *taking* a white cravat to oblige the marchande & the waiter, but putting on a black one to please myself, Tom & Corry going in white—found, in the end, it did not matter one pin which—Called for by Lady C.—but she having come only for *me*, did not separate—at least in going. Were not however five minutes in the Ball-Room before, in the dazzle and crowd we all lost each other. A most splendid affair certainly, but being alone, and not seeing a single creature whom I knew, soon grew weary of the light & the flowers & the almost total absence, as it appeared to me, of female beauty and made my way out again into the open air. Found it no easy matter, however, to penetrate the cordon of troops there was on every side—"on ne passe pas par ici—on ne passe pas par là." To increase my difficulty, too, Louis Philippe had got tired (or rather frightened as it was rumoured) about the same time I did, and the exit of the King & family at the same moment with myself, set every body on the alert.—At last, a most courteous Subaltern (as I think he was) took charge of me, and putting me in a corner where he left me so long that I began to fear he had entirely forgot me, came back again for me, however, most faithfully after he had disposed of his other charge, Louis Philippe, and walking a good part of the way with me, left me safe near a cabriolet-stand, from whence with a very lame horse (which the driver assured me however, was lame only from habitude) I got back to my Hotel—

20 [Tuesday]—Found that Tom & Corry had staid much later than I did—Tom (who had met there Lady Harriet Galway and her daughters), did not get home till two o'clock.—Dr. Wright to breakfast—had resolved to defer his return to Caen (kind bore!) for the pleasure of travelling thither in our company—Received another enthusiastic letter, accompanied by a splendidly bound volume of poetry from a Monsieur A. de Beauchesne, who describes himself as "Ancien gentilhomme de la Chambre de Roi Charles X et Secretaire des Beaux Arts de la Maison de S. M."[1] The following is his letter "Monsieur—Mon nom ne peut être arrivé jusqu'a vous et je commets san doute une bien grande indiscretion en vous offrant le premier de mes Essais Poetiques. Mais l'admiration rend trop temêraire pour que la gloire ne rende pas indulgent, et je me persuade que vous me pardonnerez ce manquement à toutes les rêgles du savoir vivre. Depuis votre arrivée à Paris, je suis malheureux de ne pouvoir trouver un moyen convenable de vous être présenté. L'ouvrage que je vous envoie pouvait me mériter cette faveur, il m'aurait donné plus que n'ai jamais osé attendre de lui. Tous les hommes de gout et de coeur, Monsieur prononcent avec reconnaissance

votre nom dans le monde entier, mais le Poete Catholique de la malheureuse *Erin* doit éveiller encore plus de sympathies chez tous eux qui pleurent sur l'oppression ou l'abaissement de leur patrie. Nous qui défendons ici l'honneur de la vieille France, son vieux culte et ses vieilles institutions, nous avons, ce me semble, plus que les autres encore, le droit de fêter votre bien-venue. Vous pardonnerez donc à un jeune Legitimiste l'entrainement et l'enthousiasme qui lui font aujourdhui oublier toutes les formes de la bienséance pour arriver jusqu'à celui qui s'est appelé Little et que la posterité surnommera Great. J'ai l'honneur d'être avec respect & devouement" &c. &c.—Strange bedfellows, to be sure—an Irish Radical and a French Carlist! but Catholicism is the great reconciler of all such anomalies, & hence it is, that this "Ancien Gentilhomme" of Charles Dix is so much in love with *me* and that OConnell on the other hand, abuses so violently (or at least did a few years since) the French *Liberals.*—Went to call upon Crowe (author of To Day in Ireland and a History of France) and found only his wife, a handsome, Irish woman with five or six Children, living au cinquiême, and with every appearance of but little means—Her nervousness in seeing me—for she had guessed, as she told me afterwards, who I was and "was very near sinking before me."—Complained of Crowe having nothing to do that interested him, his sole employment now being his correspondence with the Morning Chronicle—wished to undertake a History of Germany[2] if the booksellers would give him encouragement—After looking earnestly at me for a minute or two, in the course of our conversation, she exclaimed, "Well, if at one time of my life any body had told me that I would see Thomas Moore in my own house!—" Evidently a warm-hearted creature—Offered, if I could do any thing for Crowe with Publishers, to use my best exertions to serve him—set off to visit the Galways but went to the Avenue de Neuilly, near the Arc du Triomphe, instead of the Avenue de Neuilly, Champs Elysées (the latter specification of the place being foolishly omitted on my Lady's card) and so threw away both my visit & my time—it gave me an opportunity however of seeing the Humours of French Omnibuses, as I travelled in three successive busses to perform this journey & back, one of my stages costing me but three sous.—Dined, Corry & I and Tom at Lady Canterbury's—Company besides ourselves, Lord Sandwich & Prince Belgoioso, the husband of Lord Mulgrave's flame—He & his Princess still live together in the same house, but seldom see each other—went, for a short time, in the evening to Guizot's, where there was an assembly—received very graciously by Guizot, and introduced by him to his sister, with whom I had some talk about the present state of France—expressed that I thought it presented a most puzzling appearance to the distant observers, but found that she, as well as most other intelligent persons I have met with here (Dillon, for instance, this morning) all seem to agree in the opinion that Louis Philippe's policy, however, in some respects, jarring with *Libéral* notions, is that which is best suited to the present state and temper of France—introduced by her to Lafayette's grand-daughter, with whom I talked a little of America, and found she was no friend to the Jackson policy—Had some further conversation with Guizot, who referred to the offer made by different constituencies to bring me into Parliament, and expressed his wonder & regret at my not complying with the call.— remarked very strikingly on the process of *retribution* there was now going on in the fearful obstacles thrown by Ireland in the way of England—with all her abundant means of prosperity England was now actually brought to stand-still by Ireland. On my remarking that the worst of it was, there appeared to be no way of getting out of the difficulty he said that Peel, on conversing with him on the subject seemed to take the same hopeless view of it, and though with his usual caution, entering but little into detail, expressed that he did not see how the great questions at issue between the two countries were to be settled. Returned to Lady Canterbury's, where I found Belgoioso singing, very agreeably—Sung among other things the Chorus "Rataptan, rataptan" out of the new Opera of the Huguenots.[3] I also sung several songs, which Belgoioso (who understands English) seemed to enjoy, and Lady Canterbury was, as usual, all delight at them, though some (as she herself reminded me) were sung, for the first time, to her, thirty long years since!—How one holds out, is a wonder.

21 [Wednesday]—Went, after breakfast, to call on the Galways, & found them at home—On my mentioning what some people had suggested, respecting the prospects of my making an effort to see the King, they said that, by all means, I ought to do so—that he was known to be particularly sore, on such matters—and with English still more than with French. Advised me to see Madame Montjoye on the subject—Called afterwards on Madame de Dolomieu, meaning to consult with her about it, but did not find her at home—Tom being with me, meant to have put on my card "Avec le *petit Tom*" she having known and called him such, years ago, but I forgot it—On my return to Meurice's found another crazy French poet waiting for me—also Albert Philbert's MS. accompanied by a letter—Account of the King of England's death.[1]—Feeling exhausted and by no means well, did not dine, but went with Tom early to Franconi's (the spectacle there being in the open air) and having been much amused, while I staid, returned home to dress for Made. De Broglie's assembly—found her looking remarkably well and still pretty, though 15 or 16 years, I think, have gone since I last saw her. The time of our first meeting (she herself said) was between 21 and 22 years ago. She used to be I recollect *tant soit peu* laughed at for her *sentiment,* at that time, and she now gave me a little specimen of the same, in talking of it. "I was very unhappy then—youth is generally an unhappy time—if it were not for *hope,* the sadness that is in the heart would be insupportable"—Asked me about Lamartine's Jocelyn,[2] and was surprized

and ashamed (on my account) to find I had not read it—Was still more surprized when I told her (which is the fact, though she no doubt thought it affectation) that, poetry is, and has always been, the least favourite of my studies, and that there are few persons of ordinary education that have read less of it than myself. I also mentioned to her Rogers' once saying to me significantly, when I had made this avowal (which he took to be self-gratulatory) in his presence—"Yes—one *sees* that"—meaning, you would have written a great deal better if you *had* read more poetry. On her offering to present me to some people, I begged her not to do so, saying that it was to her alone I came, and having so little time to stay, did not wish to give any of it to others. There was, however, a M. Le Brun (a poet, as she told me) standing near us to whom she did introduce me—apparently a hearty and agreeable man, who told me, laughingly, that there were, at present "eighty great poets in France," and mentioned some Journal (I forget the title of it) which, "every morning, when you took it up, announced, to your surprise, some new great poet." "England," he said, bowing to me complimentarily "is contented with three great poets, but *we*—." Found that he had been to England, & visited Walter Scott at Abbotsford.[3] After a few words with the Duc de Broglie himself, took my departure—Forget whether I have mentioned that one of these mornings I called upon Lady Virginia Murray in Passy—found her looking well & vigorous though complaining of tic douleureux in her little finger—Her niece, the Princesse de Tremouille (a very nice person) with her during my visit.

22 [Thursday]—Wright, the Hyperborean, as usual, at breakfast. Showed us a letter from his wife, full of raptures about me & the prospects of seeing me. "I think I shall die at the sight of him" was part of the phrases which this Reverend gentleman was not ashamed to read out to us accompanying what was *meant* most innocently with numerous winks and intimations, which (though even in *him* procuring more from want of *taste* than any thing else) were any thing but respectable. Took Tom and Corry to the Bibliotheque—my friend M. Dillon not there but two other young men (French) escorted us through the rooms with a kind and delicate earnestness of attention which was as creditable to themselves, as it could not but be deeply flattering to me—To express so much feeling without putting it into words is the very perfection of such tributes—Forgot to mention, I believe, that Mr. Dillon has spoken frequently to me of M. Thierry, the author of the History of the Norman Conquest, and expressed a strong wish that I should pay him a visit—Poor Thierry has, it seems become quite blind. He is employed now in writing a History of the Communes of France, and the Government with very creditable liberality, has appointed for his aid, five or six young men, who collect authorities & transcribe for

him—I saw them at work on each of the days when I walked through the rooms of the Library.—Had some little scruples (as I told Mr. Dillon) about being introduced to him, having, if I mistake not, found some fault with his work in the notes on my History[1]—But this he most probably never saw— Called upon my poor little poet, Albert Philbert, who, on the strength of some laudatory words I either said or wrote to him about his translations of my verses, requested of me to give him some sort of certificate of my approbation to induce the booksellers to publish them—this I fairly told him was toute autre chose adding that it would be necessary for me to read him over again & with more care, before I could venture upon such a step—not having, I confess, read him at all, or at least, *hardly* at all, the first time. This seemed to disconcert him a little, and so we parted—Returned home and had a visit from Alexandre, the great (and truly great) Ventrilo- quist, whom I hardly recognized again. Brought with him one of the Numbers of the Album he is publishing—consisting of drawings and hand writings of various eminent people—Emperors, Kings, Generals &c—Wal- ter Scott's verses to him, on his power of assuming a variety of faces, excellent good fun—Scott, who was at that time Sheriff comes at last to the conclusion that this plurality of persons was a case for his interference and adds "You're a mob in yourself, I must bid you disperse"[2]—Showed me a note of my own wherein I thanked him for what was really very kind—his going to my father and mother, when he was in Dublin (they being unable at the time to attend public places) and giving them a little exhibition of his talents by their own fire-side. Explained to me his plan (which appears to me a very good one) for an exchange of duplicates between all the great libraries and public Collections throughout Europe—Had some talk by the bye, with my friends at the Bibliothèque about the plan, and they appeared by no means to approve of it—were of opinion, that it never would succeed. On my telling Alexandre that I was to dine to-day with Lord Elgin he said that he would volunteer a visit there in the evening, which I encouraged him to by all means. Went with Sewell, Corry and Tom to call upon Bishop Luscombe, who is charmingly lodged in the Champs Elyseés, upon a part of what *was* the Jardin Beaujon—His beautiful walk along the terrace, with nothing but shade and seclusion, on one side, while on the other he sees the moving Panorama of the Champs Elyseés, too far off to disturb, but quite near enough to amuse and enliven—His pertinacity about our dining with him on Saturday next, which I had set aside for a peep at Versailles—held out against him as long as I could, but at last gave way—In talking of the changes that time makes in people Sewell also said that he knew no one so little changed as I was—tant mieux—though, as poor Stevenson used to say "What the devil's the use of looking young, when one's *not* so?" In con- sequence of a note from Lady Adelaide Forbes, begging that I would let her have "the comfort" of seeing me, before I left Paris, called at the Avenue Marboeuf, but found they were in all the bustle of *deménagement* and did not go in—Found another MS. and Letter on my return home. Dined, all of us, at Lord Elgin's—only their own family and the Gregorys—Alexandre in the evening—gave the scene of the man coming down the chimney—the man waked by another knocking at the door—the dogs outside barking and the little puppy answering from within, the wife gradually waking, and joining in the conversation, then the child; and then the men, dogs, woman & child all seeming to join in full cry together—never was any thing so wonderful. Gave us after his changes of face which were no less extraordinary—Lady Canterbury & daughters in the evening—borrowed her carriage to whisk me off to M. Hermanatoff, a Russian, where I was invited to meet some of the Revd. Gentlemen of the Mission Etrangére. Found them all at cards, which they gave up when I arrived. Much interested by the young Hermanatoff—a youth of about eighteen, who followed all my looks and motions so attentively and intelligently—seeming so happy when I gave him my umbrella to hold—but never never speaking a word. The Priests all in their Canonicals (or whatever they call them)—One knowing-faced old fellow talking of the Bourbons, but before almost every sentence, looking courteously around as if he was afraid some spy had come into the room— Said, among other things, (and was so pleased with it, that he said it twice— looking anxiously round each time) that the elder branch of the Bourbons was rather "pour le royaume des Cieux than for that of this world." Talked, some of them, of my Irish gentleman, the Russian expressing his surprize that I had not seen any French translation of it there being, he said, three— Had some tea & took my departure—was called back, when half my distance, by the host to say that his son would be quite unhappy if he was not presented to me—Shook the young fellow cordially by the hand which seemed to give him great pleasure—whisked back rapidly to the Elgins and was taken home by Lady Canterbury, Corry having gone away long before.

23 [Friday]—Breakfasted at home—overwhelmed with visitors and notes— Had to interpret for Tom in his instructions to Tailor & Shoemaker, no short or easy task. Went to the Louvre with Tom & Corry, having got tickets of admission from Comte Forbin—Had great pleasure in seeing again some of my favourite pictures—Corry quite out of sorts at the change there had been in the Louvre since he last saw it in 1814—Could talk of nothing but what was *not* there, while I was full of delight at what *was*—Called upon Lady Helena Robinson and sat some time with her—She remarked of the De Broglies that "they were shy & uncouth people in receiving strangers," which I can easily believe. Had appointed this evening to accompany Dillon to M. Thierry's, but not able to manage it—Home—a visit from Alexandre bringing with him a Russian—forget his name, but had Chambellan de Empereur on his cards—a hearty, talking fellow who had been passing fifteen days in London, where he had met some one in an omnibus with

whom he became suddenly acquainted and who had introduced him to Warburton and several other young Radicals—Spoke of my works, and said that several of my things had been translated into Russian—"But, Sir," he exclaimed "I expected to find you an old man!"—"Well, I *am*" I answered— "quite old enough." He then without any round-about, asked me my age, and, on my telling him, answered "Il faut dire que vous êtes fort bien conservé." Dined at the Cafe de Paris with Tom and Corry for the purpose of going to the Opera, but when Tom and I arrived there was disheartened by the immense *foule* at the door and leaving him to make his way by himself, returned to Corry, who had been joined over his wine by Marney (an old college acquaintance of mine). Sat for some time with them, and then afterward I returned to the Huguenots—got a pretty good place, but I became before long tired of the music & the heat and betook me home- ward—The music, which is by Meyerbeer, struck me as affected—Great fun going out every day between Tom & Corry, who play together like a pair of school-boys, to my no small laughter—Corry's hoaxes on Tom—having invitations written to him in French from the Officers of the Guard, beg- ging him to attend their parades (Tom having professed to be very anxious to attend said parade, but never having been able to rise early enough for the purpose). "Les Officiers de la Garde Nationale ont l'honneur de pre- venir M. Thomas Moore &c. &c.}

24 [Saturday]—{Breakfasted at home—out with Tom for visits and again his interpreter with the tailor and shoemaker—Returned home for some- thing, and found a young lady waiting "to have a sight of me"—a Miss Power, who told me that so great was the agitation that had been caused in the circle in which she lived by the announcement of my arrival that she could think of nothing else, and that at last, though aware how strange such a step must appear, she was resolved to come in person herself and see me. Requested that I would indulge her by writing my name for her, which I promised to do by penny post. Called upon the Forbeses—Lady Adelaide still handsome, by dint of countenance—a good deal of talk with them— told me that Lord Forbes never rested till he got every thing out of the Father, and then involved the whole property so much that it is now reduced to almost nothing—Seemed to think that the insanity with which Forbes was affected during the last years of his life had been brought on by the consciousness of the wrong and ruin he had caused. Made most friendly enquiries about Mrs. Moore, and remarked with a good deal of feeling that *we* too had had our sorrows.—Called twice in the course of to- day on Madame Durazzo, having heard only yesterday of her being still in Paris—was most sorry not to meet her—Went with Corry to Mrs. Graham— who was very amusing about my anxiety to see Made. Durazzo, and urged strenuously my making some effort to see the King—Called afterwards at

Made. de Dolomieu's, but did not find her at home—} Went {from thence} to Made de Flahaut, whom I found sitting in the garden with her beautiful daughter, (a beauty which struck me to be as pleasing as it was brilliant) and Lord Sandwich and another young man along with them. Have seen no hotel so handsome as theirs in Paris. Sat for some time, and regretted very much not seeing Flahaut, who is among the few men I like as well as *admire*.—{Dined (Tom, Corry & I) at Bishop Luscombe's—Company besides ourselves, Sewel & Sir Sidney Smith, the latter of whom, I must confess, beats all the bores that even *I* have ever suffered under.—Our host full of civility and kindness to us, and presented me with a poem addressed to me by his daughter, requesting that I would write something for her in her Album, which I accordingly did—From thence to Franconi's & home—}

25. [Sunday] A visit during breakfast from M. {Buchon}, whom I did not at first recollect, but found out afterwards that I had known him, when formerly at Paris—though his reputation as a writer, has been I believe chiefly acquired since, several collections of old Chronicles having been, I see, edited by him and his name being frequently joined with that of Guizot, as fellow laborer in that line of ancient lore.[1] On hearing of my intention to proceed to Caen, offered me letters of introduction in that quarter. Talked very cleverly & eloquently of the state of France—of Louis Philippe's avarice, his insincerity in holding forth hopes to the people (both his own, and those of other countries) that he would aid them in acquiring popular institutions, while he was holding an entirely different language to their rulers {—Phil. Dalton also at breakfast with us—Forgot to mention that I saw Made. de Dolomieu yesterday, and sat some time with her, but there being two other persons at the time with her, did not mention what I intended about the King. Wrote her a note this morning, before breakfast, in which, after mentioning my having been turned aside from my original intent of making an audience with the King by what Chabot had said to me, I asked something about my grateful remembrance of the hospitable reception with which I was honoured at the Palais Royal, when last in France, and (to go still further back) of the time which I had the honour of passing with his Majesty at Donington Park, when I could well remember being whole hours in his company, in the Library there,—he being the deputy employed in studying the pages of Lord Clarendon. This, or something pretty near this, I expressed as well as my hurry would admit of, in a note to the Dame d'Honneur. Out for visits and commissions—Dined, Tom & I, at Lady Canterbury's—Company Brooke Greville, Aston (whom I did not much take to) and, I believe, one or two Attachés.—Went all to Tivoli in the evening, where there were Tournaments, and Horse Quadrilles, but no possibility of getting any place to see them—Sauntering through the gardens by myself, listening to the music and fancying prettier things, I dare

say, than I could have seen—though, by the bye, I *did* get a glimpse, in the shade, which was well worth having. On the termination of one of the performances in the circle, I saw the six or eight mounted Knights and Dames, who had been exhibiting, issue forth from the enclosure, and crossing the path in which I was sauntering, gallop up a dark walk of the garden, as if in search of other moonlight adventures, in some distant vallies and glades. At least, so it then seemed to my fancy, though I am afraid it was only their way to the stables—Watched for the end of the next exhibition, which was, I understood, a Quadrille by Knights and Ladies on horseback, and saw them again canter past me, in the dark, their armour, bracelets &c glittering as they went, and again lost them in the depths of that mysterious grove. Went to look for the rest of my party, and found Tom, Lady Canterbury & her little girl riding cock-horse in a merry-go-round, and firing at little plaister images from mock pistols, as they passed—Left the whole party there & got home—Tom returned in much tribulation (which I was not much inclined to relieve him from) he & his two cock horse companions having been mulcted in the sum of thirty franks for their diversion—not having had the nous to make any terms with the showman before they commenced. Gave Tom a little lecture for the same & got to bed.

26 [Monday]—Buchon at breakfast—brought my letters of introduction to M. de Rigny, Lafist, the Prince de la Moskowa &c. &c. This being our day for starting had not much time to spare. Was much struck however with the eloquence of Buchon in English for finding that Tom and Corry could not follow him in French, he made an effort (for the first time, he said, for many years) to explain himself in English, and the very straits to which he was driven in endeavouring to explain himself gave a condensation and *character* to his language which was not a little striking—I had asked his opinion of Guizot and found it to be such as most people entertain of the doctrinaire-school. But, as far as I could understand him, his charge against them was not so much their being theorists as their being pedantic matter-of-fact men. Having collected a certain number of what they call *facts* on a question, they then rigidly insist upon conforming to these facts under whatever change of time and circumstances—or, as he expressed it, whenever a fact has *passed* (as through an aperture, I take for granted) there the man must be free to pass through also—I repeat though I admired the force & character of his English I could not well understand his meaning—made my escape alone to Galignani's and there wrote some letters—Galignani, by the bye, had invited us to come to his country house, which is near Fontainbleau, on Saturday, and to stay for two or three days, to make excursions in the neighbourhood—Stopped at a book-stall with [*unrecovered*] to buy something to read on the way, and seeing a Collection

of Archives of French History in 4 Volumes, which seemed in my way, proceeded to marchander for the purchase of it, and having brought down the fellow (a common stall-man) from 18 francs to sixteen, proceeded to tell him where to send it. I had no sooner said "Monsieur Moore—Monsieur Thomas Moore," than his eye lids opened wide at me, and he exclaimed "Ah! je connais."—he then added "Là-le voila" pointing triumphantly to a copy of Galignani's Edition of my Works lying on his stall.[1] This is more than any English stall-keeper would have been up to, let the foreigner who addressed him have been ever so celebrated. Had ordered a job coach to take us to Maison Lafitte, where we were to embark in the steam-boat next day, and, having settled all our matters at Meurice's, set off at two o'clock. Our drive most delightful—had some difficulty in finding the Hotel Talma to which we had been directed, but very well repaid when we arrived there, the situation being charming. Lafitte by offering a certain number of acres to all who choose to build on that spot is gradually raising round him a beautiful settlement which is already called "La Colonie" & promises to be most prosperous—Dined, very comfortably—the inn being kept by an Irishman, formerly in the army, a Captain O'Reilly—After dinner drove in our open carriage, through the forest, to the common, the evening being delicious, and the Road royally smooth & shady all the way— One of my objects, besides showing Tom the place where Henry 4th was born, was to call upon Montmorency Morres, whose lucubrations I have referred to in my Irish History, and who had written to request I would come and see him[2]—Sauntered about with him a little and returned, by the same charming road, to La Colonie, where we slept.

27 [Tuesday]—Off in the steam-boat at eight—Tom's cloak left behind in Paris, the only real loss or accident that has hitherto happened to us. The whole voyage a series of beautiful scenes, hardly, if at all (Corry said) inferior to the Rhine—the want of the castles being, he thought, the only thing in which the Seine was inferior—a large party on board, Dr. Roberton and Wright included—the latter being the only blemish of the whole voyage—The comparison which Homer makes of one of his heroes to a fly, always returning to the charge and never to be got rid of,[1] is quite as applicable to a *bore* as to a hero, and to none more than to the said Wright— Doctor Roberton a good deal in the same line, but I managed to keep him off by pretending to be sick—a Doctor being bound to have a respect for sickness. The Reverend Doctor, however, had no such compunctions but bore away without ceasing. Among the company on board was an American & his wife who had been travelling (as they all are now, in all directions) through Italy—A very Yankee-spoken fellow this, but sensible and good-tempered, the latter of which qualities he showed *most* creditably, in the course of a conversation about the slave traders in which Dr. Roberton and a younger Doctor named Badham, spoke in very bad taste (to say no more)

on the subject. Talking of the slave-dealers (whom the American was not defending but merely explaining & lamenting the position in which they were placed) Roberton exclaimed "They ought all to be thrown into their own lakes "—"There are no lakes" said the matter of fact American "in the part of America where they are chiefly found"—"Then," rejoined Roberton fiercely "they ought to be sent to hell." I showed (as strongly as it was worth while to do) what I thought of this vulgar out-burst, and the American & I became very good friends—Immense bustle on our landing at Rouen, but got to a very good Hotel, the Hotel de Rouen—

28 [Wednesday]—The American & his wife at breakfast—she rather a nice woman but of that *over*-feminine kind which seems to be common in America—On my praising Washington Irving, the man said "Yes, Mr. Irving is a very smart man"—smart being, among them, synonymous with clever. They would say, I have no doubt, that Milton & Shakespeare were very smart men—Went to see the Churches of Notre-Dame & S. Ouen, the latter beautiful—Set off in the steam-boat for Havre between 12 and 1—the weather delightful—a gay party on board, the deck covered with awning and a band of music playing from time to time—nothing could be more agreeable—even Wright was for some time tolerable—Forgot, I believe, to mention one of the things he said to me when we were on the eve of starting from Paris "I will not quit you now till I place you in the arms of my wife"—A lady on board seized with hysterics as we were starting—found that she was the wife of a gentleman (also on board) who turned out to be an old acquaintance of mine, though I had myself no recollection, a Mr. Davis, who succeeded Lord Napier in China—Told me that he was the author of two articles in the Quarterly Review—one of them on Chinese Poetry[1]—Confusion with the luggage, on our arrival at Havre—Found that Mrs. Corry had already arrived, and joined her at the Hotel de l'Europe

29 [Thursday]—Walked about Havre, and found it a much prettier place than I had expected—Had a Fiacre and all drove to a lodging House on the Hill called the Pavillion Fouache, where the Corrys thought of establishing themselves—none but English received there—the environs on this side very pretty—Brought La Martine's Jocelyn, in order to retrieve myself in the eyes of Made. de Broglie &c. by reading it. Shall find it hard work, I fear—Set off Tom and I, a little after four, in the Steam-boat for Caen, leaving with great regret our Jolly Coriander behind—and, still worse, taking Doctor Wright with us—some very intelligent men, belonging to Caen on board, returning from a meeting of a Scientific society (geological, I believe) held annually at Honfleur—Had a good deal of conversation with them—at least as much as a sort of incipient feeling of sea-sickness would allow me to indulge in—the motion of our course having begun to be a little

brackish, if I may so say—found all here were most marvellously well acquainted with my name & works, and all most courteous. Their attentions to me—Lamartine they called, their "best living poet." Told me how much Bulwer was read and admired in France. Had a new instance of my own excessive folly, in allowing myself to be swayed & corrected by *any* body (no matter who) that puts on an imposing face of knowledge and authority. On my quoting, some time since, before Gore (Lord John's secretary) the ridiculous line addressed to me by the Polish poet, Ostrowski,

> Oh Moore, n'es tu pas un archange exilé!

Gore repeated the line, after me, pronouncing the *ch* soft, instead of giving it the hard sound (like *k*) as I had done. Thinking that this was meant for my correction (as I have no doubt it was) and that he was moreover right, I have ever since followed his authority in quoting the line, and did so now, in citing it to these Savans, whereupon one of them very courteously said to me "Nous la prononçons Ar*k*ange." It however was the means of drawing down a compliment upon my French; for, one of the other Savans, thinking perhaps his friend's criticism of my pronunciation somewhat uncourteous, was proceeding to observe that one could not expect a foreigner to be thoroughly acquainted with all those little niceities &c. &c. when the other interrupted him by saying "Mais M. Moore prononce extrêmement bien." Altogether we got on very agreeably, and some of the party had the appearance, both in look and manner, of as thorough John Bulls as could be found between Ludgate Hill & St. James's. One of them, the best bred & most intelligent of the party, said to me, as we shook hands with each other, in parting "I assure you the pleasure I have had in meeting so distinguished a man is more than I can express to you." Nothing could be gayer and more sparkling than the scene along the bank as we glided into Caen—it was the hour of the evening Promenade, and the shore, for a long extent, was crowded with well dressed people standing to see our boat enter. Found, on landing, my old friends Rothe and General Corbet waiting to receive us— Walked home with Rothe and found Mrs. Rothe and her daughter waiting dinner for us—Our reception by the whole party most cordial and gratifying—Some talk with Rothe about the settlement of Tom somewhere, which gave me no great encouragement on the subject, the society of Caen having, by his account, very much deteriorated of late years, and the difficulty of finding a family fit to entrust one's son with being, according to his account, considerable. Had provided apartments for us at the Hotel d'Angleterre, Rue St. Jean, which we found very neat and comfortable—}

30 [Friday]—Breakfasted at our inn,[1] {to which there was but one, but that a grievous objection—its early noise—a Diligence starting daily from the very yard under our windows, at the inhuman hour of four or half past

four in the morning, and from that hour, of course, all sleep at an end—at least with *me*. Tom did not mind it, so I accordingly changed rooms with him, and put him in front of the battle.} Rothe called and we walked out together, the first great object being the *Pension* for Tom. {At one lodging house (for there appeared but little chance of our finding any that combined *education* with board & lodging) the old lady could not take him in because her present lodgers, (English) did not like gentlemen, "Ces Dames ne veulent point de Messieurs," and this she repeated about ten times during our conversation, to my no small amusement—Called (Tom and I) upon Spencer Smith to whom I had a letter of introduction (from Bp. Luscombe) which he read and was exceedingly civil and courteous offering to show me all the attention in his power—Perceived clearly however that he did not yet know who I was, and being rather in a hurry, did not care just now to enter into the explanations, but I had hardly got to the bottom of the stairs, when he cried out from the top (being but barely able to hobble) "Oh for God's sake, Sir, come back again" which I did immediately, and he exclaimed, staring at me, as I came up, "Why you're Tom Moore!" He then said that he had fancied, as I sat before him, that he had seen me somewhere before and now recollected that it must have been at Walsh Porter's— If so, (and it is not unlikely) that must have been some three or four & thirty years ago—Promised to come again soon to him—Rothe having mentioned a Law Professor, a Monsieur—I forget his name—who had once taken an English pupil, the son of some nobleman (whose name I also forget) we now proceeded with Rothe to call upon him—an intelligent but somewhat hard mannered man (a bitter Carlist, as I afterwards learned) his wife rather a nice woman. Seemed well inclined to take Tom, and his lady showed us the room they meant to give him. Said clearly that it was a "maniére d'être" that would be very trying to a fellow brought up as Tom has been, but made the best of it to him, as there seemed but little chance of finding better—The terms, as I understood, were to be 150 francs a month, which was generally accounted high. Called on Wright and found his wife a rather nicer woman than he deserves—their little girl very pretty—Drove about with General Corbet and his brother (also in the army and to all intents & purposes a Frenchman, having been brought away from Ireland when he was but three years old)—took me to the different promenades— Dined at Rothe's, company the Corbets, Wright and one or two more—A party in the evening, chiefly English viz. Lady ——— Wenys, Maxwell (the husband of Lady Lacy) and a number of others, both young & old, whose names I have forgot—A Madame Lemaire, also, a clever French woman with whom I had some conversation—In speaking of Buchot, she said that the natural turn of his talent was for light literature, but that having unluckily taken it into his head that his forte lay in the laborious and profound, he was now throwing himself away upon subjects he was unfit for. This, whether true or not, as regards Buchot, is taken generally as a very possible and probable case.—The English of to-night gave me no very bright view of that portion of the Caen Society.}

July 1 [Saturday] Breakfasted at home—a visit from Wright, bringing with him to introduce to me a very clever and amiable mannered man, M. Bertrand, a Professor of Greek Literature in the University of Paris, and a great admirer, as I soon discovered, of my poetry—has translated several of the "Irish Melodies" and told me himself that it was my poetry first won him into the study of English—A good deal of conversation, during which he explained to me the nature of the Professorships and Colleges through France—after he had gone, Rothe came and we walked out together—Had not gone very far when Wright came running breathless after us, to say that Monsieur Bertrand would, he believed, take Tom—Went with him to that gentleman's house, and found both him and his wife (who is much older than himself) very kind and amiable on the subject. From what I had heard Rothe and others say of him, was of course very anxious to secure so good a position for Tom, and, to my great joy, now found that there was no difficulty in the matter—he himself appearing to be quite as much pleased with the office as I was at his accepting it—Was going, he told me, to his country seat in a month or so, and would take Tom with him—in the mean time would have a room prepared for him at his house in Caen. Asked about Tom's Greek studies, but I told him that my chief object for him now was French and French Literature—On my coming to speak of terms, he assured me that that was the last consideration with him, and that he was chiefly actuated by the pleasure of being able to do any thing that would show his respect & admiration for me—It would be far more agreeable, he added, to leave the settlement of terms to some third person, and, on my mentioning Rothe said that most willingly would he leave the whole matter to him—Drove out afterwards with the General who expressed delight at my good fortune in this arrangement, only regretting it, he said, for one reason, which was that his brother and himself had made up their minds to offer Tom a reception in their house—Had begged of Rothe to settle the terms with Bertrand, but officious Wright had been before hand with him, and it appeared that from 100 to 120 francs a month was all that he would require—Called upon the chief Libraire of the place—an intelligent man and possessing several very rare & valuable books—but finds no market for them, he said, in Caen—is collecting all the remains of the Abbé de la Rue for an Edition of his Works, with autograph Letters from English antiquarians, Druce &c.—Bought of him the French engravings of the Tapisserie de Bayeux[1]—showed me some fine Missals—no encouragement for such an establishment as his in Caen—but sends books to other markets— had had a visit from Payne not long since—Dined at the General's— company, Rothe, Wright, Brummel & one or two others—The poor Beau's head gone, and his whole looks so changed that I never should have recognized him—got wandering in his conversation more than once during dinner—{Told me of the agreeable surprize he had one night, on returning home, to find Lord Stuart de Rothesay seated comfortably by his fire—Happening to be on his way through Caen, he did not like to pass without seeing his old friend Brummell, and accordingly had seated himself by the Beau's fire till he came home—All this, I was told afterwards, is a mere dream—Lord S. did pass through Caen, and sent his servant to enquire after Brummel while he was changing horses—but never saw him—A gay dance at the General's in the evening, several other officers there and a good many English. Was introduced to almost the whole room, officers and all—among others to M. de Fouchet, a strong Carlist, but a fine gentlemanlike old fellow.—Went for a short time to Made. Jaubert's, an English woman, related to Lamartine's wife, and who has therefore thought herself qualified to translate Lamartine's Poem—rather a dingy tea-drinking concern from which I bolted speedily—and home. Have fixed to go with the General the day after tomorrow to Bayeux.

2. [Sunday] The General with us soon after breakfast—drove us to see some of the churches—dined with Rothe in the evening and drove in an open carriage to the Cours Caffarelli with him & the Ladies—a very gay scene, it being Sunday evening—got out of the carriage all and walked—found myself soon pointed out both by French & English, and when we returned to the carriage, Rothe having (designedly, I suppose) made me get in first, I was immediately surrounded on all sides by good-natured stares, some pressing close to the carriage, and one or two French ladies addressed me—one a Made. Tolmar, as I heard afterwards, a handsome woman, who stood for some time by the carriage expressing eagerly to me her admiration &c. &c. I bowed away of course, taking off my hat in all directions, but felt rather awkward, at being left alone in the carriage, and was not a little relieved when the Rothes got in, and we drove off—Went to pay some evening visits (a most dull ceremony, whose shortness seemed its only pleasure) to Made. de Serrand, a fine old lady, turned eighty—to Made. de Rigny, whose husband (query?) is about to stand his trial—and some others.}

3. [Monday] Breakfasted with the General and off soon after for Bayeux Rothe, Tom & myself—my conversations with this worthy fellow have all been most interesting, but I can only note rapidly a few of the particulars—gave us to-day an account of his escape from Kilmainham, where he had been kept a prisoner for two years and a half.[1] The preparations made in the Ball-Court or Tennis Court where the prisoners were allowed to play

every evening—his place of concealment formed in the heap of sand—the ladder of ropes prepared—its failing to reach the persons waiting on the other side—at another time breaking—the night of escape—he himself getting safely over and waiting in vain for his companion—mounting again & looking over the wall for him—seeing that he had fallen & would not venture to try again—obliged to make his own escape—Major Sirr on board the ship in which he lay concealed during the passage—A long life of prosperity & happiness would hardly repay what he suffered during that year & a half.—Reminded him of what he told me, when we last met, of Napoleon's dislike of the Irish—explained it more fully now by saying that it arose out of the rivalry then subsisting between Napoleon & Hoche[2] and the game of the latter being Ireland, which interfered with the designs of Napoleon, both his jealousy & his impatience combined to make all that was connected with Ireland odious to him. Corbet then passed to his detention, along with three other French officers, at Hamburgh, for the details of which, as well as of the negociations, to which it gave rise, I must some time or other consult the public accounts. Having 'served through all the Peninsular War, being in the retreat at Salamanca &c. Corbet joined the Russian army and was in the Battle of Leipsic, then in the Defense of Paris, and was the bearer of a flag of truce from Marmont to the Emperor Alexander[3]—described his interview with Alexander, his deafness, his anxiety to ask questions of Corbet, but whenever Corbet interposed a remark as to his immediate object, referring him to the official person (I forget who or what) by his side—Marmont held out stoutly on that occasion, refusing to capitulate, and insisting upon an armistice, so as to enable the army to join the Emperor—Corbet's name not mentioned in the public accounts of this negociation with the Emperor, which he seemed to think lucky, on account of the unpopularity (if I recollect right) which afterwards attached itself to the transaction. But I must take an opportunity soon of reading about all these events and correcting the impression (if wrong) which I received from his details. Mentioned, as an instance of Clausel's coolness, in the retreat from Salamanca, his (Corbet's) being sent to him at night to say that the English had got possession of a certain important post. Clausel, whom he had found fast asleep, on being awaked & told the intelligence, just paused for a few moments to consider the bearings of his position, and then saying coolly "it is impossible," turned round and went to sleep again.[4] In talking of Scott's Napoleon, Corbet said that it was "an odious work"—he had read with the greatest admiration and delight all Scott's novels, but when he came to peruse his Napoleon, he was utterly disgusted. To say nothing of the mistakes & ignorance with which it abounded, the intentional falsifications throughout the work were such as drove him, however unwillingly to the conclusion that Scott was a "bad man." This opinion must of course, be taken with all the allowance that Corbet's position & prepossessions would naturally suggest—but it was the opinion of a truly honest man, a man (if I am not mistaken in him) of the true, grave and steady nature of which heroes & martyrs have been most generally made. As an old poet well says

> "Your sad, wise valour is the true complexion
> That leads the van and swallows up the cities."[5]

Apropos of this, I found Corbet to be of exactly the same opinion as that held by most authorities respecting the character of Spaniards—"nothing" he said "would make them fight well." Spoke highly of Flahaut, who, he said, was next to Caulaincourt,[6] the best man about Napoleon. In speaking of the French affairs in Africa, he said that Guizot's government was the cause of all the failure in that quarter, as well as in Spain.[7] When Thiers was turned out by Louis Philippe, he was within 15 days (Corbet said) of vanquishing Don Carlos, and the same interrupted Clausel's operations in Africa—In his view of Irish politics the Corbet of 1837 is, as might be expected, very different from him of 1798. Considering division to be a source of weakness to both countries, he is so far now from wishing to see Ireland severed from England that he considers their union in support of good government and free institutions to be essential not only to their own well-doing but also most important, as an example to all Europe. Ought to have mentioned, with respect to Corbet's escape from Kilmainham, that he mentioned the account of it given in Lady Morgan's OBrians & Flahertys, as reasonably accurate in most of the particulars[8]—On our arrival at Bayeux, found that the Bishop was absent—went to see the fine Church—were kept for a good while from seeing the Tapisserie in consequence of a Concile (some town-meeting) being then sitting in the Chamber where it is preserved—{Passed this time very agreeably in conversation with Madame —— the wife of the Sous-Prefet, a very nice woman and a remarkably intelligent little girl, her daughter—Her talk with Corbet chiefly about her husband's unsuccessful attempts to get himself promoted—had been formerly Prefet.} Admitted at last to the Tapisserie, & found it, like many other things in this world, better to be *imagined* than *seen*. {Forgot to look for the indelicate things that are said to be among the drawings, though the work (as is said) of female hands.—} The French engravings {of the Tapisserie} misrepresent it (on the favourable side) most extravagantly—Napoleon, when contemplating an invasion of England, had this Tapestry brought to Paris & exhibited, in order to revive the recollections of the former successful descent—and it was even said, Corbet told me, that the Empress & her ladies were industriously practising embroidery, in order to be able to complete the parallel—During our journey the thought struck me that I might turn the subject of the Tapestry to account, in the way of Poetry with illustrations, and I told Corbet that, if ever I should carry this thought into execution, it would be to him I should dedicate the work—This seemed to please him greatly.—{Dined all of us at Rothe's.}

4 [Tuesday]—{Called upon Wright, who gave me a fac-simile of a note, in the Irish language which is found in an old manuscript of the Gospels, supposed to have been addressed to the celebrated Irish scholar, John Erigena,[1] and therefore supposed to be his hand-writing—Went with my friend the bookseller to the Public Library, where the Librarian showed me a copy of my Epicurean, the only work of mine they seemed to possess— Promised to give them a collection of all my published works—The bookseller, in the course of my conversation with him, asked me whether I could inform him who was the real author of a small collection of English Poems published under the name of Little. Told him that the real culprit stood before him, and he owned that he had suspected as much.} Went to the Museum, where there is a Perugino, which struck me as good, and which it seems *ought* to have been sent back into Italy with the other restored plunder, but, by some accident, remained here—Was struck too by a picture of MalHerbe—A little *Bossu* poet, about half my own height, accompanied me around the rooms with much brotherly devotion—had published, it appears, some Poesies at Caen.—Dined at Rothe's, and went in the evening to drink tea at M. Bertrand's, where I had to go through a fresh round of introductions—In the course of the evening M. Bertrand was requested to recite some of his translations from the Irish Melodies, and I had accordingly to stand the delivery of two of them—both author & translator being seated, side by side, on the sofa, and whenever any reference to "Le Barde" occurred, M. Bertrand would turn round, with a profound bow, to me, while I, with another profound bow acknowledged the compliment. Not sorry when the séance was over; though seeing more & more reason to congratulate myself on my luck in locating Tom.

{5 [Wednesday]—Up at four to start in the Diligence for Honfleur, and before five, Rothe, Corbet & Mr. Bertrand were in attendance to see me off—Took leave of them and dear Tom at five, and off for Honfleur—road very pretty—first sight of the sea through a long avenue very striking— Took steam-boat to Havre—found that Corry & Mrs. Corry had retired to the Pavillon Fouache—walked there, though much exhausted with my early rising & the heat of the journey—left word I would come to dinner, which I did, and was much delighted when they proposed that I should stay and sleep, Corry most kindly insisting upon my taking his bed while Mrs. C. sent in her maid for my dressing-case &c. Thus, instead of stewing in a wretched room at the Inn, over the kitchen (which was all they could give me at the Hotel de l'Europe) I passed the night coolly & agreeably at the Pavillon Fouache having walked, all of us, to drink tea with Gordon the English Consul, who lives quite near, and there met the Miss Fittons old Irish acquaintances of mine, whom I have not met before since my childhood—Slept most refreshingly

6 [Thursday]—Sauntered about with Corry, & Mrs. Corry, who accompanied me into Havre, and saw me off about two o'clock in the Steam-boat for Southampton—A clever fellow, on board, a lieutenant in the Navy, son of the Jerningham (by a first marriage) who married Edward Moore's sister—a good deal of conversation with him—also an old acquaintance of mine, Wilder—}

7. [Friday] After a smooth passage of 14 hours arrived at Southampton—walked about a little with Wilder, and after breakfasting set off in the Coach for Bath, where I dined most heartily & *Englishly* at the White Hart, and then proceeded in a Fly to Sloperton, where I arrived between 8 & 9 in the evening. {Found Bessy much better, and B. Prowse still with her—

8, 9, 10 &c. [Saturday, 8 July–Sunday, 16 July] nothing worth noticing till the

17 [Monday]—Went into Devizes to dine with the Hughes's—Bessy having gone in the morning to attend the Courts.—Company at dinner Bingham & another barrister—Glad to meet Bingham once more & had a good deal of agreeable conversation with him.—Slept at the Brabants', the Doctor himself absent.

18 [Tuesday]—Went with Bessy to the Trials, and was rather interested in some of them. Returned home to dinner, Henry Fitzmaurice walking some part of the way out of Devizes with me.

20, &c. [Thursday] Letters from McCulloch & Murray intreating me to take the Chair at a dinner which is about to be given to Rees, on his retirement from business—Did not however, consider it a "dignus vindice nodus,"—(at least, to go to town *expressly* for,)—and accordingly made my excuse.}

23. [Sunday] An official letter from the Horse-Guards, acquainting me, that, on my lodging the sum of £450 in the hands of Cox, Greenwood & Co., Lord Hill will submit my son's name to the Queen for the purchase of an Ensigncy in the 22nd. Foot.—{Received a letter also from Lady Lansdowne, begging me to attend Henry's election at Calne tomorrow—"I do not know," she says, "whether you are intending to go to the Election at Calne on Monday; but I should feel much happier about it if Henry had

you there as a supporter."—she adds afterwards—"I do not suppose he would be flattered at my asking you to take care of him & therefore I shall say nothing about my request to him."

24 [Monday]—Set off to Calne, but having taken it into my head that it was the Election *Dinner* I was to attend, arrived there too late and found that not only was the election over, and both electors & elected all dispersed but also that there was to be no dinner—Had dismissed the poney-chaise, too before I entered the town, so that I was left there, in a smoking hot sun, without any means of return—Walked to Merewether's & found him at home—pressed me to dine, but I preferred sauntering on to Hughes's, where (having already dined themselves) they hospitably laid the board again for me, and seemed truly happy at my visit—Had a chaise from Calne (no Fly being disengaged) and rattled away home.

25, 26 [Tuesday–Wednesday]—Wrote a private letter to Lord Fitzroy, telling him of the manner in which I had disposed of Tom at Caen & asking leave of absence for him.

28–29 [Friday–Saturday]—Henry Fitz. to tea}

30 [Sunday]—Received the following from Lord Fitzroy "My dear Sir—I have communicated your letter of the 25th to Lord Hill, who desires me to say that he will give your son six months' leave of absence from the time of his being gazetted, but, if you should think that insufficient, he considers that it would be better to decline the commission in the 22nd. with the understanding that your son is to be provided for as soon as he is ready. Probably however leave of six months is all you require. Very faithfully yours &c."

31 [Monday]—{Started for town—no room in the first coach from Devizes—Took a Fly to Beckhampton & there got a seat in the Regulator—A nice girl in the coach with a sort of subdued resemblance to Lady Lansdowne—told me in the course of conversation, that she had not a single relative in the world, all her relations having died when she was a child, and she now lived under the care of some friends, whom she was going to rejoin after a short visit to some connexions of theirs at Bath—evidently a sensible & admirable, as well as good-looking girl—took up my abode at the Royal Hotel for the night—the Feildings, I found, were at Richmond & poor Feilding still very ill—By the bye in} looking back over the Journal of my

French Tour, I find {one or two things omitted which I had better slide in here, before they entirely escape my memory—I forget whether I mentioned Buchon's saying to me "Scott, Byron and yourself are more familiarly known in France than many of our own most celebrated poets." I do indeed believe that, *next* to Byron & Scott (and also "long o'intervals") my name is of all our modern Parnassus the best known in France. In a French advertisement I was looking at this morning, recommending a new work entitled "the Living Poets of England,"[1] it is said "La Poësie Anglaise Moderne n'est guère connue en France que par les ouvrages de Lord Byron, de Moore et de Walter Scott: mais ces noms ne sont pas les seuls que l'on puisse citer"—Among my other visits, I called upon Lord Trimleston, from whom I had received a note directed "Sir T. Moore Bart." Found him far advanced, poor man,—not in years, for he looked most blooming—but in a French translation of Lalla Rookh, the MS. of which he showed me, but forbore asking me to read it, luckily, till it is fairly finished. A Miss Jervis sent me her Album, with a request that I would write my name in it, and concludes her note thus—"She is just beginning life and has the desire to possess herself of the autographs of good & eminent men who are her contemporaries."—} In Buchon's note accompanying the letter of introduction he sent me, he says—"Votre fils trouvera en France une large d'affection; je vous assure ce n'est qu'une faible marque de la reconnoissance due aux nobles et poétiques inspirations de son père. Le nom de Moore s'est naturalisé Français, par l'admiration que nous avons non seulement pour ce qu'il a écrit mais pour ce qu'il a voulu. Son caractère et son talent ont été adopté par nous, comme une gloire universelle. La langue est la forme, la pensée est le fond qui appartient aux hommes éminens de tous les pays.—Votre admirateur & ami, J.A.C. Buchon"

August {1 [Tuesday]—Called upon Rogers between 9 & 10—found he expected some Americans to breakfast—Hamilton (the son of Washington's friend) and his wife & family—so came in (as I almost always do with him) for something new & agreeable. The man himself & his son (a youth of 16 or 17) the best of the party—the daughters being but pretty*ish* & the wife no great thing—Found they were near neighbours of Washington Irving, who has a young niece living with him to whose education as they told us, he devotes a good deal of his time—Altogether a very agreeable breakfast—Rogers suggested to me a good subject for a squib, the Three Young Queens with Three Cruel Uncles. Told me, after the breakfasters were gone, of some young American girl he had lately met who left a tender letter to be delivered to him after she had embarked, and of his own still tenderer letter to her in return; the tears coming into his eyes, as he stated to me the substance of his Epistle. His sister, he said remarked on his reading it to her "Why that's a love letter"—and so it was to all intents and no—certainly *not* to all purposes. Asked me to dinner, to opera, to every sort of agreeable thing. Called upon Miss Macdonald, who was full of surprise & congratulation on my good luck as to Tom—Thence to Horse-Guards, where I saw Macdonald, and heard all the particulars about the Regiment—Said Tom should have leave of absence for six months, but advised me not to ask for more, as there had been an outcry against long leaves. The Duke of Newcastle's case, who procured a whole year's leave of absence for his sons, they being all the while at the University, had drawn much attention to the abuse.—Dined at Rogers's—no one but his sister & Lady Langdale to go to the Opera.—Grisi in Anna Bolena[1]—excellent.}

2 [Wednesday]—{Had called yesterday to see the Lansdownes & break-fasted with them this morning. Just when they found themselves free to escape from town, he had been attacked by gout, and forced to take to the sofa—Dr. Holland, who came after breakfast gave it as his opinion that Lord L. would be able enough to start tomorrow—Told them all about Tom at which they expressed much pleasure—Promised to breakfast with Holland tomorrow—Out to Holland House in Omnibus—a good Whig trades-man in the Omnibus, who when I desired the lad to stop at H. House, looked most pleased at me & said "A highly respectable address, Sir."—Missed the Hollands by a second or two, for as the clumsy driver drew up *beyond* the gate, they drove in their carriage *out* of it—Left my name at the Duchess of Kent's—called upon the Duke of Sussex, and was admitted—"Ah Tommy!" he exclaimed, as I entered—"How long it is since you & I last met! Now, you shall dine with me to-day." "Why, Sir," I answered, "if you will lay your *commands* upon me to do so, I shall not be sorry, but—" here Lady Cecilia, who was sitting with him, very good-naturedly said "No—his Royal Highness never wishes to interfere with previous engagements"—"No—No," he exclaimed, "you shall dine with me on Friday instead." We then talked for some time about politics, the bad aspect of the Elections &c.—From thence down to the Longmans, for the purpose of making with them some arrangement as to the purchase-money for Tom's commission—Meant to manage it in Bills & renewals through my Devizes Banker, so as to keep the sum afloat till my Third Volume of the History should pay it off—Hume also had kindly suggested that, to save me discount, interest &c. he would manage a long Bill upon the Longmans for me through his Banker—But Longman (more creditably for all parties) proposed that I should draw a cheque at once upon his house, for the amount—} Dined at Rogers's—company Lord & Lady Carlisle & daughter, M. & Madame De-del, Falck, Luttrell and Landseer—Day very agreeable—Dedel & Falck both excellent, straight-forward & sensible men—a good deal of conversation with them on the state of France, the prospects of England &c. &c.—{Saw Greville to-day at Brookes's, who gave me a note to his man at the Council.

3 [Thursday]—On my way to breakfast with Dr. Holland met Hume and fixed to join him after breakfast. In Sidney's letter to Mrs. Holland, bidding her (as I have before mentioned) let him have a letter from her to meet him at Dessen's, on his return from abroad, he added "If it is a Republic, I shall stop here."—Went with Hume to Cox and Greenwood's and gave my cheque on the Longmans for £450—Thence to Foreign Office where Hume introduced me to his friend Scott.—To Brookes's, where I met Rogers & walked home with him—found him full of admiration of some extracts given in the Times from a new work of Carlyle's (a History of the French Revolution, I think)[1] written in a strange, mad style—or rather I should say, morbid than mad, for there is even more of disease than of frenzy in it—but in which both the Times and Rogers found much to admire and to praise. They are, perhaps right—but to me it appears that this Germanized gentleman exhibits far more of the "contorsions of the Sibyl" than of her "inspiration."—Saw Lord Essex at Brookes in the course of the day, who showed me some verses written for his daughter's tomb, and begged me to look over them, at my leisure, and suggest any alterations that might occur to me—Dined with him—company, Lord Glenelg, Col. Boldero, and one or two more—Conversation agreeable, Lord Glenelg being more than usually *awake*—Came away with him, in his carriage, and was left by him at Brookes's, where I found them all full of the Middlesex Election—Forgot to mention that I shifted, after the two first nights, from the Royal Hotel, to 19 Bury St., where I again domiciliated myself under the auspices of a new Landlady, Mrs. Durham—}

4 [Friday]—{Breakfasted at home—note from Macrone—called upon him in consequence, and found him preparing to start for Scotland, whither he has been ordered, for change of air—his state of health evidently perilous, and no less so, I fear, his circumstances.—Has got into some wrangle with Goodall, the engraver, about my Epicurean. It appears that Goodall was to have gone half with him, in the speculation, but, taking fright at it latterly, wanted to be off his agreement—but that Macrone would not hear of.—A proposal was then made by the publisher (Sherwood & Co I think) to take the whole of the concern off Macrone's hands, and this he appeared to me disposed to accept—Said to me however, that it was his intention in making his estimate to give in £750 as the sum he had paid to me for the copyright. This I told him he might do, if he thought right, so that *I* had no share in the transaction. He then explained, that his object was not to let *them* have the advantage of the cheap turns upon which he had become possessed of the copyright of the edition, but to let the additional £250 he might thus get from them go into *my* pocket. To this I, of course, decidedly objected, as far as I myself was concerned, and (if I did not misunderstand him) am certainly by no means disposed to think the better of his trading morality

for this very *naive* proposition.—But, so it is—the ethics of the *shop* are all of the same stamp.—To Brookes's—told Lord Essex that I did not like to venture on any change in the verses, for though too long for an epitaph, it would be difficult to shorten without spoiling them. Told me that they were by Eastlake, the artist.—} Forgot to mention that Greville, two or three days ago, gave me a letter to his right-hand man at the Council Office (he himself being about to leave town) desiring him to put me in possession of his (G's.) rooms for the purpose of looking over the Records, and at the same time gave me a letter also to Lemon of the State Paper Office desiring him to attend me whenever I should require it, and give me his assistance in my researches—This all very kind of Greville & promptly and heartily done—{Called to-day upon Lemon, and fixed Monday next for him to meet me at the Council Office—Lord John Churchill having arranged with the Stevensons to take me to dinner at the Duke of Sussex's, their carriage called for me at ½ past six, and I proceeded with Lady Mary and Stevenson to Kensington—Company, besides ourselves Lord John Churchill, Lady Cecilia, Dr. Holland and one or two others—The *talking* part of the performance sustained chiefly by Stevenson, whose free & easy manner towards the Duke was sometimes rather painful—his poor Royal Highness, who has become very deaf, making constant efforts to catch the conversation, while Stevenson continued to address his harangues in every direction except that of his Royal Master.—"Do you hear me, Sir?" he condescended to say once (moved thereto, I think, more by a gesture of mine than of his own courtesy) "Why, I'm *trying* to hear you"—answered the Duke very good humouredly. Stevenson evidently, though, a keen, clever fellow—Talked of Bickersteath—his marriage with Lady Jane, arriving a good deal from her being his tenant, at the time of her mother's death, they being then living in a cottage belonging to Bickersteath and Lady Jane continuing to inhabit it alone—Bickersteath used frequently to call upon her there & at last proposed for her[1]—great difficulty in getting him to accept of the Mastership of the Rolls and the Peerage—My countrywoman Lady Cecilia very heartily, in the course of dinner, made signal for me to take a glass of wine with her.—The Duke himself, too, full of kindness & hospitality—Reminded of OMeara's dinner in Dublin by the hot whiskey toddy being brought on the table immediately after dinner—every one, too, I think, except myself, partook of it—Brought home by Stevenson & Lady Mary.}

5. [Saturday] Breakfasted with Rogers to meet again the Americans—Conversation turned (curiously enough, before the son of Hamilton, though none of us seemed to have thought of this at the time) upon the prevalence of Duelling in America, and Hamilton told some strange stories on the subject. {Mentioned a Judge from the Southern states whom he

himself met at Washington, and who always carried a poniard stuck by his side—had been a pioneer (I think, he said) in his youth, and always retained this habit—Rogers in repeating the story about "Your cloth protects you, Sir" gave a different reading of it, making the answer to be "But it shall not protect *you*." I told the story about Grattan & Gifford—} Mr. Hamilton said that there was no longer now any doubt of his father having been the writer of almost all Washington's Addresses. Gave me an autograph letter of Washington's to his father which tends a good deal to confirm this fact. Among the autographs he showed us were some of Jefferson's, and I was not displeased to see in them a frequency of my own trick of erasures & corrections—Jefferson always opposed to Washington, being always an advocate for French predominance in their Councils—Went, all of us, with Rogers to see Stafford House, which evidently astonished the Americans (as it well might) by its richness & grandeur. They are just come from visiting all the great Palazzi of the Continent, but it was plain had seen nothing like this. After we parted with them, turned in with Rogers for a few moments to the exhibition in Pall-Mall and took a passing glance at some of the fine things there—{Hurried away then to the Charter-House for dear Buss—Brought him away to the West End, where Macrone joined us—eat ices &c. at Confectioner's, and then back again to dine at the Longman's who had forwarded tickets for us for Astley's—McCulloch & Brown only at dinner, together with some well-iced Sauterne—Off to Astley's, which I found as dull as Bussy found it delightful—a bed for him at my lodgings—By the bye, called at Murray's one of these mornings, and had a letter from him since enquiring whether I could furnish him with any more letters, fragments or notices of Byron for a new Edition of the Life he is preparing[1]—Some talk with him about Lockhart's Scott, which he complained of (echoing no doubt the opinions of others) as having been made too much the channel of Lockhart's own political grudges & antipathies—regretted his retaining such things as Scott's expressions about Lord Holland—"I cut him like an old pen" &c and attributed most of these blemishes in the Life to Lockhart's rigid view of the duty of a biographer.[2]

6 [Sunday]—To Brookes's after breakfast, where I found Stevenson. Told me all the particulars of Lord Munster's supposed resignation of the Constableship of Windsor, the Queen's letter to the Duke of Sussex ("My dear Uncle" &c.) bestowing upon him the Office— Lord M's remonstrance, and the Duke's "most beautiful" letter to the Queen (as Stevenson styled it, though most probably written by himself) denying any wish to interfere with Lord Munster's claims on the office—Set off for Hanwell with Russell to see Hume—found on a visit with him the lady (Mrs. Barnard, I think) whose high-flown letters he sometimes shows me—a fine woman, and far

more natural and agreeable than her letters would betoken—Saw the reliques of the festival he gave some time since, in commemoration of me, and at which the Gossets were, I believe the principal handmaids—My bust (the small marble one) crowned with flowers &c. &c.—His place, though still as odd as need be, considerably improved since I last saw it, and the works of *art* he has, scattered about (chiefly the Rothwells, the paintings) throw a degree of elegance over the works of brick which still form his staple—Nothing to be sure, can equal his kindness to me and mine in his own odd way—Sent for a Fly to take Russell & me to Kew Bridge where we took the omnibus to town.—A gentleman sitting next me (who I saw knew me) said, after some little conversation between us, "I am rejoiced, Mr. Moore, to see you looking just as well as you did twenty six years ago when I last saw you." On my enquiring where it was we had met, found that it was at dinner at my old friend's, Dr. Parkinson's, in Kegworth to whom this gentleman was related, and though not quite 26 years ago (being about the year 1812) it is not far from it—found that he recognized me instantly on my coming into the Omnibus—Had written to Lord Essex in the morning offering myself for dinner to-day, but finding no answer from him, ordered cutlets at Brookes's, and was lucky enough to find (instead of a solitary dinner, as I expected) no less an agreeable companion than Lord Dacre who had been drawn to the same resource. Sat talking with him a long time about politics, and found that, though illness has for some time incapacitated him for public life, his head is as sound on the subject as ever—and one strong proof (in *my* opinion) of his sound-headedness was that he saw the mischief of, and stood aloof from, the rash measures of the Reform Bill—}

7 [Monday]—Breakfasted at home and was at the Council Office by ten, where I was joined soon after by Mr. Lemon—Looked over the Indexes of the Papers with him, and found him, in every respect, the man for my purpose—being most well-versed on the subject, but also most readily disposed to assist me in the way most useful to me—Explained to him how I was situated with respect to my History, being now more than ever aware that in less than two Volumes more I should not be able to do justice to my subject, and yet from the inadequate pay I receive for my labour (compared with what I should make by employing myself otherwise) being unwilling to expend so much of my time so unprofitably.—He remarked that nothing unluckily was more common than to see historical works which had been commenced & continued to a certain extent with most exemplary carefulness then begin to show signs of relaxation & haste, and at last hurry on to the end in the most careless & clumsy manner—gave as an instance Turner's History of Henry Eighth, in which a small part of

Henry's reign occupies the great bulk of the work while the remainder is despatched in a very few pages.[1] Must see how far this is the case—[Called for by Hume according to agreement at 12—Went with him to call on my old friend Emma Foster—now Mrs.—I forget what—she too full of compliment about my looks, not having seen me before for I believe 15 or 16 years—called also upon Martin Shee, and sate (or rather stood) some time with him.—Met the Miss Dillons (daughters of Lord Edward's Hostess) coming out as I entered—They too, in talking on the subject of my looks, said it was impossible to couple the idea of age with me—Parted from Hume & called on Mrs. Shelley, who I was told was at Mrs. Norton's—Went thither & found them both—poor Mrs. Norton much changed, but hardly rendered *interesting* even by adversity.—Glad to see Charles, her uncle, who is I think, a thoroughly *good* fellow, albeit a *Sheridan*.—walked out with me—called at Lansdowne House, on poor Von Bohlen, who has been laid up for weeks there—took Charles S. in with me, and found poor Bohlen, with emaciated looks, copying most neatly a Sanscrit MS. which they have lent him from the India House—Dined at Lord Camperdown's—company only Bailey (of Seymour Place) and two or three uncouth Scotchwomen—a *dies non.* Got off earlyish (Bailey lending me his carriage) to Miss Rogers's, where I found Miss Stephens & her niece, and was lucky enough to hear them sing a most delicious duett—wanted me to sing, but I pleaded hoarseness, & took flight—Forget whether I mentioned that I lost the opportunity of meeting the Duke of Wellington yesterday at Rogers's by perhaps rather a squeamish delicacy on my part—Rogers had asked me to dine with him, saying that I should meet Lord Hertford, and that he had invited also the Duke of W. but was not sure that he would come—As Lord Hertford however is one of those on whom I most seriously laid the lash, in my early squibs,[2] and have never since met him in society, I thought it as well (knowing R's nervousness about his dinners) not to risk any awkwardness by the recontre, and therefore declined the invitation—Had I been sure that the Duke would come, I should have been less delicate perhaps.—The party were (besides the Duke & Lord Hertford) the Tankervilles, Lord Hill, Lord Fitzroy Somerset, and Luttrell, and all were invited by the Duke to dine with him tomorrow. Sheridan's Toast "The Duke of York and his brave followers"}[3]

8 [Tuesday]—Breakfasted with Rogers to meet a Frenchman of the name of William Brown—his grandfather I believe was English, but he himself cannot speak a word of English—Found him alone when I arrived, and in the course of conversation he guessed (from my portraits, as he said) who I was—During breakfast arrived Count Krasinski, an intelligent Polish refugee, and man of letters—Told me how familiarly all my works were known

in Poland particularly the Irish Melodies {which had been translated there [*unrecovered.*]} The great favourite among his countrymen is "Oh blame not the Bard"[1] and he himself was acquainted with a young poet who always made use of the authority of this ode, when reproached with being an idle fellow—Remarked that there was a strong similarity between the Poles & the Irish, and mentioned as an instance of this a countryman of his, who having on some occasion knocked a man down for being, as he thought, insolent to him, was expostulated with for having done so, by some friend, who remarked that, after all, what the man had said to him was not very offensive—"No—it was not" answered the other—"but still it was safer to knock him down."! The Fire-Worshippers, he told me, had been translated in Poland, in a *Polish sense,* and there was also, he said, a Russian translation of that poem—{Went afterwards to the British Museum—Looked over some of the publishers Rolls, and also referred to Doctor OConnor (Annals of the *Four Masters*)[2] in consequence of a letter I had received, before I left home, from Cooper, the Irish Priest of Marlborough St. Chapel, containing the following passage—"What did poor Doctor Lanigan do to you that you inflicted that "unkindest cut of all"? Now you referred to no authority and there is no authority to bear you out in attributing an enactment to Kells Synod repressive of the practice of clerical concubinage."[3] Immediately on reading this, I turned to the passage in my History (Vol. 2 p. 191) and found that I had omitted to note the very trust-worthy authority which (in spite of the little priest's dogmatic taunt) I was, of course, furnished with for my assertion—Extracted now, in order to send them to him, the very words in which the Record of the Four Masters describes the wives & mistresses of the Priests, and which are as follows "Mna cuil—cair deasa"—i.e. "bad naughty women and beloved wives"—} Dined with Rogers to go to the opera—Party at dinner, Wordsworth, and Miss Rogers—A good deal from Wordsworth about his continental tour—In talking of travelling, in England, said that he used always to travel always on the top of the coach, and still prefers it—has got at different times subjects for poems by travelling thus—a story he has told in verse (which I have never seen) of two brothers parting on the top of a hill (to go to different regions of the globe) and walking silently down the opposite sides of the hill, was, he said, communicated to him by a fellow traveller outside on a coach—also another story about a peat-hill which had been preserved with great care by a fond father after the death of his youth who had heaped it up—must look for these stories in his Poems[4]—On my mentioning that I had met with a young man at a café in Paris who had seen him (Wordsth.) in Italy, he asked me who he was, and on my answering that I did not know his name, and that it appeared he had merely *seen* Wordsworth, the sublime Laker replied "Oh—Virgilium tantum vidi"[5]—but immediately conscious of the assumption of the speech, turned it off with a laugh—{There is certainly something sublime in his self-[?exceptancy].

9 [Wednesday]—Called upon Lord Fitzroy at the Horse Guards, and had some talk with him about Tom's regiment—said that there were no dashing young men of rank in it—that the office next above Tom was the son of the Dean of Christ Church & that the rest were all old fellows—this all right.— Called upon Strangways at the Foreign Office—In coming out found Lord Melbourne just getting off his horse and had a few words with him—on telling him that I had just received from the Horse Guards the very great favour of being allowed to lay out my money, he exclaimed, as he slid off his horse—"Yes—to be sure, what a thing it is!" Called upon the Miss Dillons and on Charles Greville, with whom I sat for some time—and then to Hutchins the Dentist, to have my teeth cleaned—Dined with Lord Essex, who, by the bye, rated me yesterday for not coming to him on Sunday— saying that I ought to have remembered "silence gives consent." Had asked me to meet the Duke of Sussex at dinner some day this week, but the Duke having appointed Saturday, when I hope to be at Sloperton, told Lord E. I could not come.}

10 [Thursday]—{After breakfast set off for Richmond to see the Feild- ings—Found them in somewhat better spirits about poor Feilding than they had been, as they told me, for a long time—I had written to Lady Elisabeth, soon after arrival in town, offering to come down to them, but her answer, which was written in a very melancholy tone, made me doubt whether she would like to receive me—*Him* I knew, I could not see. Resolved to-day however to take my chance, and found them all, as I have just said, in tolerable spirits—Lady Valletort and Ma'mselle being with them—Walked with Horatia down to the old walk beside the river—the whole place & scene looking most beautiful—Lunched & returned to town—} Dinner at Rogers's—almost over when I arrived. Company, Wordsworth, Landseer, Taylor & Miss R.—a good deal of talk about Campbell's poetry, which they were all much disposed to carp at & deprecate—more particularly Word- sworth. I remarked that Campbell's lesser Poems, his Sea-Odes &c.[1] bid far more fair I thought for immortality than almost any of the lyrics of the present day, on which they all, Rogers, Wordsworth & Taylor, began to pick holes in some of the most beautiful of these things—"Every sod beneath their feet Shall be a soldier's sepulchre" a *sod* being a sepulchre! (this perhaps *is* open to objection)[2] The "meteor flag braving the battle and *the breeze*" another of the things they objected to.[3] Then his "angel visits, few and far between" was borrowed from Blair, who says

"or, if it did, its visits
Like those of angels, short and far between"[4]

Taylor remarked that "The coming events cast their shadows before" was also borrowed but did not so well make out his case. "Iberian was his boot"[5]—another of the blots they hit—altogether, very perverse industry. To the Opera, all except Wordsworth—The Gazza Ladra, charming—notwithstanding that a stick {(named Ivanhoff)} was substituted for Rubini.[6] In talking of letter-writing this evening, and referring to what Tucker has told of Jefferson's sacrifice of his time to correspondence, Taylor again mentioned the habits of Southey in this respect, and Wordsworth said that for his own part, such was his horror of having his letters *preserved,* that, in order to guard against it he always took pains to make them as bad & dull as possible.—

{11 [Friday]—Breakfasted at Moxon's, Company, Rogers, Wordsworth, Moxon's brother & sister, and somebody else—Went to take my place in the Emerald for tomorrow, but found it was full—took it for Sunday—On mentioning at Brookes's that I was not going till Sunday. Lord Essex said "I'll make room for you then tomorow, if you'll come."—Told him it was the very thing I had counted up on—Dined at Longman's—Doctor Lardner, McCulloch &c. Speaking of Lord Bacon, (in referring to Macaulay's Article in the Edinburgh about him)[1] Lardner talked some sad stuff, while McCulloch spoke, as he always speaks, with clear, downright good sense. In walking away with McCulloch told him of my intention to endeavour to make some better arrangement with the Longmans, on the subject of my history, than at present exists between us—it being hardly possible to do justice to the remainder of my task in one Volume, and yet on the terms upon which I am now working I *cannot* afford to carry it further. Advised me to speak at once to Longman himself, on the subject, and said he had always found him the most liberal of the whole Co. Rees was, he added, the skin-flint of the party, and so I have sometimes myself suspected—[Have seen reason since to think that the skin-flint of the party (whoever he may be) did not die with Rees—1840]}[2]

12 [Saturday]—{Breakfasted with Rogers—Talking of Life & Futurity—the punishments threatened hereafter—so disproportioned to the life and transgressions of poor foolish fleeting Man. "Here come I"—said Bobus Smith once to Rogers "who for all the harm I have ever done deserve about three good hard knocks on the back—and yet they talk to me of hell-fire!"—On my mentioning how sorry I was at having let my squeamish scruples deprive me of his dinner the other day, Rogers said—"That's a sort of feeling, my dear Moore, that has done you more good through life than almost any thing else." He then told me of the failure of a former dinner he gave to the Duke, when Lord Holland was one of the party, and felt so little easy, on the occasion (I suppose from the part taken by him in the affair of Ney, which the Duke resented so much)[1] that he quite "lost countenance."

This reconciled me a good deal to my own disappointment.} Rogers showed me some pretty verses of his own upon Youth—the last, he said, he had ever written or should write. Said he could cry over them all day—and was very near bursting out into tears, while he spoke. Part of the feeling of them consists in sadly anticipating all that youth has before it in life of wrong, as well as of suffering—of wrong that will be regretted in after days[2]—{He then told me that once at Scone (or as he, to dignify the scene, said "in a Palace") Lady Mansfield's having brought down to present to him a pretty young daughter of hers Lady Mary not yet come out, he said, as he looked at the girl (having his own verses then freshly in his mind) "ah! she will do many things in life that she will be sorry for," on which Lady Mansfield, naturally enough, on hearing such a prediction exclaimed "poor Mary!" and the sisters all echoed "poor Mary" in their turn. He afterwards sent the verses to Lady Mansfield, and explained to her (as I understood him) the poetic influence under which he had uttered the reflection.— Forgot to mention that the Longmans said yesterday they were sure Moxon would lose by his speculation on Wordsworth—£1000 being what he gave him, I believe, for the Edition of his works. What will the worshippers say to this?—In talking of Wordsworth the other day to Bulwer, at Brookes's (Bulwer being, by the bye, a far more profane scoffer at the Idol than I am) I referred to the famous line "The child is father to the man,"[3] which is made one of the tests of the true faith by the Wordsworthians. If you do not see the merit of this, then truly they think thou'rt d——d. But, after all, (as I remarked to Bulwer) we have here only the very natural and obvious reflection that as is the child so will be the man, put into a quaint and startling form; or as Bulwer, in agreeing with me, very happily expressed— "Take away the affectation, and you leave a common-place." —An excellent instance of the sort of wordy pomp with which Wordsworth sometimes overlays his matter may be seen in the version he has given of an anecdote which Wilkie related to him as well as to Rogers and which the latter has told very simply & effectively in one of his Notes—"I often think that we and not they are the shadows."[4] This simple and touching sentence Wordsworth has mounted upon stilts most Gargantually—dined with Lord Essex— company, the Duke of Sussex, Lord Albemarle, Creevey, George Keppel &c. &c.—day agreeable enough, the Duke being in very good spirits and taste. Got home as early as I could to pack—

13 [Sunday]—Off at eight in the Emerald—having the Coach to myself almost all the way—*Mem.*—Luttrell at Brookes's about the complacency with which a smug Parson, after reading over some chapter full of blood & horrors, from the Old Testt. shuts the Book, and says "Here endeth the First *Lesson*"—His story of the Parson leaving out by mistake several lines of the Litany and saying after the word "widows" *so that in due time we may enjoy*

them.—Rogers's remark on the flagellation given to Sydney Smith, by the Quarterly, in its Review of his Sermon,[1] that sooner or later, vengeance is sure to overtake the *Scorner*—it was the same way, he said, with Canning— when the opportunity came for wounding him all who had suffered under his powers as "Scorner" pressed forward to take advantage of it—

14, 15, 16 &c. [Monday–Wednesday] Nothing particular except a couple of days passed at Bowood (Lady L. had asked Bessy & Ellen to come also but Bessy not well enough) and my correspondence with the Longmans for which see below.

20. [Sunday] Lord Shelburne to tea—The Spectator, one of these weeks, thus notices Tom's commission—"Moore's eldest son, Tom Lansdowne, has obtained an ensigncy in the 22nd. Foot." Have received, by the bye, from Corry who is still at Caen, a letter about Tom, giving a most satisfactory & gratifying account of the way he is going on, in all respects.

21, 22 &c [Monday, 21 August–Monday, 28 August]—At work at my Third Volume.—My correspondence with the Longmans adverted to above arose out of a conversation I had with Longman himself on the subject of my History the day before I left town, but which I omitted to notice under its right date. The chief point of my communication to him was the conviction I felt that, to do the *work* justice, it should be extended to Four Volumes; but that, to do *myself* any thing like justice, I could not, on the present terms (£500 for the Third Volume) extend it beyond Three; as, at my time of life, to be expending year after year on a task for which I was so *under*paid, while at the same time offers were tendered to me on all sides, of sums twice the amount for labours not a quarter part so troublesome was a sacrifice of myself and of the interests of those belonging to me which I could not in conscience make. I therefore submitted to him and the rest of the Pro- prietors of the Cyclopaedia whether they would prefer only three Volumes on our present terms, or would encourage me to make it four by giving the same sum (£750) for the third & fourth Volume which they did for the two first. The manner in which Longman received my proposition (his son Tom being the only other person present) augured but ill of the spirit in which it would be met. Instead of viewing the plan fairly as an equalizing force for all the Volumes he tried to make it appear that I demanded £1000 for the fourth Volume. This *shop*-shuffle did not look promising—Received from them on the 17th. a letter of which the following is the part relating to the above—the rest being on the subject of the Record-Commission which I had requested them to make enquiries about

"Dear Sir   August 16

"The Proprietors of your History of Ireland, having considered your proposal of extending the work to Four Volumes beg me to say that it is the universally expressed opinion that the scale of the former volumes absolutely require at the least this extension, but which they did not themselves intend. The price for the former Volumes having been settled with the approbation of yourself & your friends who considered the remuneration very liberal at £2000, the Proprietors are willing to pay you £750 (Scott's price) for a fourth and concluding Volume. The proprietors trust that this sum will be agreeable to you for they would greatly regret that the work should be drawn in so as not to be satisfactory nor indeed creditable to any parties." In a short letter which I had written to Tom Longman immediately on my return from town, I had said that, "as far as regarded myself I should by no means be sorry should the proprietors decide on rejecting the terms I proposed." My answer now (which I have not kept a copy of) was in conformity to the declaration, saying that I had foreseen from the manner in which Mr. Longman spoke on the subject that such would be the decision of the proprietors and that I must now only endeavour to do as much justice to the remainder of my task as the already agreed for limits would admit of. The following was their reply.

"Dear Sir   August 24

* * * * *

"The Firm desire me to say that they exceedingly regret you did not accept their proposal made for a fourth volume of your History of Ireland. They really thought that the terms would have been advantageous to you; particularly as the labour of research would not have been increased thereby, and besides you can not be insensible that the dilemma is of your own creating and should not at least be taken advantage of. If the public should complain of the unequal proportion of the matter, the proprietors of the work will suffer for it; and can they then be contented after paying £2000 for a work so unsatisfactory?

"The instant you communicated your own expectations Mr. Longman felt a painful presentiment that all the agreeable literary and friendly intercourse of so many years was coming to a termination.

"They have only to add that they sincerely wish your new friends may prove more satisfactory to you and (to use your own expression) be less *hard* in all their transactions with you than they have been.

Yours ever truly &c. &c."

Seldom have I felt much more surprise than I did at this sentimental effusion. It was plain they had taken it into their heads that I was about to desert them for some other publishers and had attributed to the plotting of some persons behind the curtain the steps I had taken with respect to the terms for my History. I accordingly instantly wrote to them to say how

surprized and puzzled I was by their letter, adding that though in addressing myself, as I had done, to the whole body of the Proprietors of the
Cyclopaedia with some of whom I was not even personally acquainted, I
might have expressed myself somewhat differently than I would in writing
to themselves whom I had known so long & whose friendship & liberality I
had often experienced, yet even under these circumstances I could not
conceive what there was in my letter to justify the allusions to new friends
and the prognostics of the "termination of our literary & friendly intercourse" which their last contained. "The real fact is" I continued, "the
gentlemen of the Firm have completely misunderstood me, and acting
upon their own misconception they have (through you) addressed me in a
tone which is warranted neither by our past, our present, nor, I sincerely
hope, our future relations with each other. I have always done justice to
their liberality to me on more than one occasion, and particularly in the
instance of my Life of Sheridan, when they of their own accord added £300
to the price already agreed upon for this work—and it was upon the
precedent of that very transaction I had founded my hope and request that
they would *reconsider* the terms arranged between us for the History." I then
added that "in order to set all right again between us, I here retract my
refusal of the terms contained in your letter of the ——th and consent to
accept the sum of £500 for the Third Volume and £750 for the fourth,
being the concluding one." This (as nearly as I can collect it from little
pencil memorandums) was the substance & language of the letter which I
addressed to them and which produced (as I anticipated it would) the
following *Peccavi* reply, written as all the other letters were by Tom Longman.

"Dear Sir   August 26th 1837
"We have read with the sincerest pleasure your letter of yesterday, because it assures us of the misconception with which we were so painfully
influenced in writing our last letter. We believe that new Eastern Romance
which was talked of puzzled our minds not a little. [I had mentioned to
them, among other proposals made to me, one for an Eastern Tale—][1] But
all is now quite right again. Let us all forget this little incident in our literary
history, and once more embrace, as the foreigners term it.

"The terms for the Fourth Volume are £750—Pray, believe us as before
and always your sincere friends—

Longman & Co."

I was however, not yet quite done with them, but wrote to Tom Longman
on the 27th. the following letter

"Dear Tom—I had little doubt that when the true state of the case was
laid before them the Firm would perceive how wholly unfounded was the
view they had taken of my conduct and all would again be right between us.
But you must allow me a few last words before I dismiss the subject from

my mind. You may be assured I never *have* received nor ever *will* receive any proposals from other publishers without making your House immediately acquainted with the circumstances. This I repeat has been always hitherto my practice, and I only suppressed the names of the parties in some late instances because I had declined the proposals as soon as made, and the mention of the names would have been therefore as unnecessary as it might have been insidious. There is yet another point suggested by our late correspondence to which I shall here advert, and without feeling, I assure you, the slightest ill-temper on the subject. Though most happy still (and long, I hope) to continue my private correspondence with you and my other friends of the Row in the same hearty & confidential way I hitherto have done, I think it better for all parties that I should henceforth address myself, on all matters of serious business, to the entire Firm, and receive my answers from them accordingly. This will save at least some collisions which, between individual and individual, are seldom agreeable. For instance, you must own, I think, that to be told by you, my dear Tom (as I was in one of your letters) that I was "taking advantage" of the Firm was a charge rather *awkward,* to say no worse of it, in a letter from one gentleman to another.

"Having thus said to yourselves, according to my custom, the utmost that I would say to others of you, I am, dear Tom &c. &c."

Received, in answer to the above a very friendly and gentlemanlike letter from Tom Longman, which being rather long, I shall here extract only the following passages of it.

"August 29, 1837

* * * *

"It is with the deepest regret that I find it was possible any expression in the letter could have been felt as an individual opinion &c. &c.

"The Firm desire me to add, with their kindest regards that you have called their attention to an expression in their letter which they are grieved to find might perhaps strictly bear the meaning which, on review, they do not wonder has wounded your feelings; but they wish you to be assured that no part of your character is more strongly impressed upon them than that it would not be possible you should wish to "take advantage" of any one, and that their observation had reference to *their own* position *alone,* without supposing for a moment that it was capable of a personal interpretation.

"For myself I shall only add &c. &c."

29 [Tuesday]—Went into Devizes, in consequence of a letter I had received from Corry, from Southampton, announcing that he would bring Mrs. Corry to Sloperton on his way home—Called at the Scotts', thinking that Corry would make his first resting-place there, but found they had heard

nothing about him—had an early dinner at the Hughes's and in the evening the Corrys arrived—returned home after having seen them, and fixed for them to come to us tomorrow—

30 [Wednesday]—The Corrys to dinner.

31 [Thursday]—Had a Fly and went with the Corrys and Ellen to show them Bowood—the day delicious and all enjoyed it very much—the Lansdownes themselves away at Windsor, on a visit to the Queen—}

September {1 [Friday]—Walked with Corry & Mrs C. to Spy-Park, which was in high beauty—went afterwards into Devizes with them (Ellen & I) to dine at the Scotts'—company, Luttrell & Miss Tiley—Returned (Ellen & myself) to Sloperton at night parting with the Corrys, who stay at Devizes till the day after tomorrow and then are off home—}

2, 3, 4 &c. [Saturday–Monday] Received a note from Lord Holland announcing that his present of Bayle was on its way down by the waggon. The note was accompanied by an amusing string of rhymes full of fun and pun a la Swift—and the next day's post brought me what he calls "Editio auctior et emendatior" of the same, which I shall here transcribe

> "Dear Moore
> Neither poet nor scholar can fail
> To be pleased with the critic I send you,—'tis Bayle.
> At leisure or working, in sickness, or hale,
> One can ever find something to suit one in Bayle.
> Would you argue with fools who your verses assail?
> Why, here's logic and learning supplied you by Bayle.
> (Indeed as a merchant would speak of a sale,
> Of the *Articles* asked for, I forward a *Bayle)—
> But should you, in your turn, have a fancy to rail,
> Let me tell you, there's store of good Blackguard in Bayle:
> And although they for libel might throw you in jail,
> Pray what would release you so quickly as *Bayle*†?
> Your Muse has a knack at an amorous tale,—
> Do you want one to versify? turn to your Bayle.
> Nay, more—when at sea, in a boisterous gale
> I'll make you acknowledge there's service in Bayle;
> For, if water be filling the boat where you sail,
> I'll be bound you'll cry lustily, "Bail, my lads ‡*Bayle*,"
> A mere correspondent may trust to the mail,

But your true *man of letters* relies on his Bayle.
So much knowledge in wholesale and wit in retail,
(Tho' you've plenty already) greet kindly in Bayle.

Holland House, 3rd Septr"

*Aliter, Bale   †Aliter, Bail   ‡Aliter etiam Bail.

{8 [Friday]—A lively letter from Spring Rice, as follows—
   "It is a sin and a shame that we have not good words for our God save the Queen. We could tolerate doggrel from old habit as long as "great George our King" filled up the verse. But they are now actually yelling out

"God save Vic-to-ri-ā"

and a formidable disunion of syllables is effected by these repeaters of the "voice and verse"
   "Besides, somebody has said that, if the old line is preserved of "Send her Victorious" it will be considered as a cry for a husband, being the masculine of the Queen's name. Do pray think of this and save us from the ignominy of the horrible cacophonia now not only coined but uttered."}

9, 10 [Saturday–Sunday]—Perceive, on looking back, that while I have noted down trivial & ordinary occurrences I have made no memorandum of a loss which will be long felt at Sloperton, the death of poor Feilding, one of our kindest and most amiable friends. His sufferings were so long and so helpless, that his death, at last (Septr. 2) came as a relief both to himself & to all who felt for him.—Received a letter from Talbot informing me that the funeral is to take place next Friday and that Lord Valletort & George Montgomerie are to attend—Wrote to him to ask whether it would be agreeable that I should also come.

11 [Monday]—A letter from Talbot saying that he is sure it would gratify Lady Elisabeth if I also would attend the funeral.

15 [Friday]—Drove in the poney carriage to Lacock—twelve being the hour appointed for the funeral—found there the persons I have already mentioned, and also one of the Audreys—{the attorney—a dry chattering fellow, whose manner jarred most offensively with all the feelings of such an occasion.} The whole ceremony most painful, though the form and

manner of it were (with the above mentioned exception) as simple and as worthy of the man as could be desired—We followed the coffin on foot through the pleasure grounds & the garden (which were then looking in their highest beauty) without any crowd of gazers to disturb or distract us, and the funeral service was read touchingly and impressively by Paley. It was poor Feilding's wish (expressed some years ago, it seems) that his coffin should be made of the oak of an old Man of War; and Talbot, on applying to the Admiralty, got some of the same wood of which Nelson's coffin was made—After luncheon walked home, Talbot & Montgomerie accompanying me a great part of the way—Besides the loss of poor Feilding, I have had some other losses lately, not touching me closely, but which combined with his, comprize all that is meant by events that "come home to the *business* and *bosoms* of men"[1]—for while he came under the latter description, my good old partner of the Row Rees, may be classed among those *business* ties, the breaking of which by death cannot but be felt solemnly, if not deeply. Poor young Macrone, too—whose death however did not take me by surprize, as I saw, when I last parted from him, that he was not long for this world—

16. [Saturday] {Went to Bowood—Lady Lansdowne having written a kind note, asking us all over to pass to-day & tomorrow, but Bessy not well enough to go—Company Sir E. Codrington and two daughters, Joy, Mr. & Mrs. Milman and the Merrewethers—Talking of Lyndhurst's break-down the night I heard him, in the House of Lords, on the Catholic Question, Lord L. said it was owing entirely to Ls. endeavouring to lay a foundation for his then projected change, on the subject, and some particular phrases he had prepared for the purpose not immediately occurring to him, he became embarrassed & was obliged to stop. Lord Lansdowne (who sat next him at the time) felt confirmed in the supposition by Lyndhurst saying to him "It was particularly unlucky as I had just come to a point which I wished to put strongly."—} It was mentioned by Joy that Sir William Scott, to save the Legacy Duty, made over the £20,000 he intended for his son William during his life-time—but William who died before his father made a Will leaving the sum back again, so that Sir Wm. did not escape the Duty after all, and now a question has arisen out of this complex transaction whether Lady Sidmouth (to whom the sum was bequeathed by Sir William) can establish her claim to it—adding one more instance to the many already extant of great Lawyers committing blunders in the management of their own legal affairs—Sir William, who placed this money in the Three per Cents used to congratulate himself "on escaping (as he said) from the perplexities of Land to the pure {simplicity of the} Three per Cents."— {The Miss Codringtons sung in the evening, as did also my own proper self

a great number of songs, being in good voice. Merriwethers the only departures at night.}

17 [Sunday]—Took a long walk with Lord L. the Codringtons, {Joy having gone home after breakfast—} In the course of conversation Milman asked how happened it that the Irish after having produced such pure writers of English as Swift and Goldsmith should have broken out into the peculiar style now known by the designation of "Irish"? Something called my attention away, or I should have asked him why he left out such additional examples as Bishop Berkeley, Burke & Sheridan?—Milman mentioned having heard one of Goethe's tragedies performed with a Chorus, in the ancient manner—said that the effect was good—asked him if it was like a Chaunt—he said "somewhat, but more monotonous"—Attended prayers, Milman doing the duty—{In the evening tried over some of the fine things in Latrobe's collection with the Miss Codringtons—a great desire among the whole company for me to read one of Lover's Irish stories for them but the book was not there—All begged me to stay over to-morrow, and to send to Sloperton for the book & I half consented—

18 [Friday]—On second thoughts, recollecting that my dear Nell leaves us so soon, resolved not to stay to-day, and told them so at breakfast—Lord L. in showing the pictures to Codrington, mentioned the circumstances under which he bought the picture of the little girl's back & shoulders in one of the rooms. Having seen during his visits to the Louvre when last in Paris a young woman busily employed in copying some of the paintings in the Louvre, he asked her, when about to quit Paris, whether she had any work of her own to dispose of, as he should like to become the purchaser of it. She answered that she had nothing much worth his notice "Mais, si vous voulez les épaules des ma soeur, je viens de les peindre"; and this was the picture he bought of her. At breakfast, this morning, in talking of De Montron, and his living constantly with Talleyrand, Lord L. mentioned that on some one remarking to Montron how odd it was that, constantly abusing each other as they did, Talleyrand should yet like to have him so much with him—"Mais, il aime tant le vice," answered De Montron. Found, what I never knew before, that De Montron's first English *début* was his presenting himself on board Codrington's ship, when off ————?, as a deserter, being tired of remaining on shore in such dull quarters. Codrington, for some time, suspected him to be a spy and treated him as such.[1]—Some talk with Milman about Lockhart's Scott having mentioned to him Lockhart's desire that I should give him some account of my visit to Abbotsford. The letter I received from him, Lockhart, on the subject was as far back as June last,

and I doubt whether I mentioned it in this Journal—but the following is an extract from it. "I approach the time of your first acquaintance with him and have to beg of your kindness some brief notice of your visit to Abbotsford and impressions there. It seems to me desirable to have something of this sort from every great & esteemed contemporary of Scott's to whom I can have material access and I should be especially sorry to omit you."[2]—In talking with some people lately about Lockhart's Life, I find the impression it produces of Scott's character is not altogether what one could wish. Among other things the story of the "Button," I see, acts upon most people's minds exactly as I told Rogers it would when I deprecated or rather lamented (for the deed was already done) his communicating of it to Lockhart. It was the worse to do so, as the story was told to R. by Scott himself, and to take advantage of a man's candour against himself is hardly fair. I have heard more than one person say in speaking of particular traits in Scott's life, "you trace the *button* there."[3] In talking on this point now with Milman, I found him owning fairly that such was the impression he perceived to be made upon most people by this story, but at the same time declaring that it had never struck him in that light, and that he did not even now see why it should be so taken. The fact is that a certain *instinct* is necessary for the purpose. Altogether, I can perceive from what I hear (not having yet read the work myself) that the manner in which Scott's violent politics are put forth in the Life, as well as the lengths to which he carried his trading turn (so much so, it appears, as even to go about recommending people to employ his partners while concealing his connexion with them) has done harm to Scott's memory & I should think, *unjust* harm. The solution, too, which some people give of it, is that Lockhart disliked Scott, and never forgave his opposition to the marriage with his daughter. But is it true that he opposed it? Milman seemed to think *not*.[4]

22. [Friday] Set off to Bath with Bessy and Russell, and our dear Ellen, whose too short visit had reached its close, and who had fixed to sail from Bristol on the morrow—Arrived in Bath soon after twelve—left them to shop and called at the Prowses' and the Crawfords—the latter wished me to stay to dinner or to dine tomorrow on my return from Bristol—Called also upon Lord Camperdown, who also pressed me to dine either to-day or tomorrow—Started for Bristol with Nell, in a Fly, at five o'clock, Bessy also departing at the same hour for Sloperton with Russell—Had a very comfortable dinner at the Gloucester, at eight o'clock

23 [Saturday]—A fair breeze and plenty of it for Nell, whom I saw off in the Killarney between 12 and 1—an immense number of passengers none of whom for a long time had any notion who I was—but, as soon as the

word was given by somebody who knew me, there was no lack of kind and *Irish* recognition, most of the party being Green-Isle folks. Had taken my place on arriving last night, in the Devizes Coach, and set off for home at ½ past three—took a Fly from Melksham—Found, on my return home, that Bessy had been surprized by a visit in the morning from Bentley (the great Omnibus of the publishing world) attended by Moran—On finding that I was at Bath, they had proceeded thither, partly for the chance of catching me, and partly to see the place, having never been there—but were to return and breakfast with us on the morrow.}

24 [Sunday]—Bentley and Moran to breakfast—Bentley full of impatience and ardour for something of mine to publish—a light Eastern tale, in 3 Volumes, scene, Circassia, events, founded on the struggle of that people against Russia, and price £1500, with two thirds of the copy-right my own— {his great ambition being to transmit his name to posterity connected with mine. All this I was of course obliged to turn a deaf ear to, at least for the present—he however suggested that perhaps, in the interval between the 3rd & 4th Volumes of my History, I might be able to snatch enough of time, were it only for recreation, to despatch a work such as he required. This I allowed him to think was possible, and so, after much conversation on the subject, *that* part of the business was got rid of. They had been to Bowood before breakfast to get a glimpse of the pleasure-grounds, and} after we had lunched I walked them over to Spye-Park, the day being delicious. Bentley had now started on another scent—the Edition of my poetical works—which, after telling him the difficulties that at present beset the plan, I confessed to him was one I had so much at heart that *whoever* would enable me to accomplish it should have my best wishes & cooperation, even though I myself should not gain a penny by it. I then told him the state of my poetical copy-rights, Lalla Rookh and the Melodies being in the hands respectively of the Longmans & Mrs. Power, and the rest all my own, those of Carpenter having now returned to me—Was amused at the sanguineness with which, on hearing this (not having before known that so much of the property was my own) he seemed to consider the whole thing as settled or at least settle-able without any difficulty. He would see Mrs. Power and the Longmans on the subject, and had little doubt of bringing them round to his terms—Told him (while doubtfully shaking my head at all this con-fidence) how sanguine I had always found men of business in such matters and that, in fact, I had constantly, in my dealings with them, been obliged to take the business line, and to repress as much as I could their "gay soar-ings." On more than one occasion have I endeavoured to keep the Long-mans within bounds as to the number of copies in an Edition, when the count has proved that *I* was right, not they. The imaginations, indeed, of some of your *matter-of-fact* men (as they are called) beat those of us poets

hollow.—{After dinner, and a good bottle of port, crowned by a glass or two of real whiskey toddy, our guests departed by a fly for Devizes to take the first night coach—One of the agreeable results of their visit was the interest Bessy awakened in them for our little friend Mary Hughes's lithograph speculation, which they undertook to manage for her without any expence whatever, but, (on Bessy's objecting to this) with the least possible expence

25, 26 &c. [Monday–Tuesday] Have had no time to journalize—being obliged to occupy every moment that society & correspondence allow me to call my own in doing something (little enough God knows) towards advancing my unfortunate History.}

October {1, 2, 3 [Sunday–Tuesday]—On the third Bessy and I went to dinner at Bowood, the carriage being sent for us between three & four—Company, besides Lady Davy, whom we were both of us glad to meet again) Brabant, the Youngs, the Starkeys & one or two more—Sung in the evening—Young also sung one of my songs—rather a slangish person and will not long keep his ground, I prophesy, at Bowood.

4 [Wednesday]—After breakfast Bessy walked to see Mrs. Hughes, and from thence the Lansdownes' carriage took her to Sloperton—I walked home—asked Brabant yesterday, by the bye, whether I had not once heard him express a slighting opinion of Mackintosh's work On Ethical Philosophy[1]—said that he had no doubt I had, for he considered it a work very unworthy of the subject.

5, 6, 7 &c. [Thursday–Saturday] Bentley has lost no time, I find, in forwarding his views with respect to the edition of my Works—has not only been with Mrs. Power on the subject, but has entered into a negociation with Cuming (who holds the Irish copy-right of the first Seven Numbers of the Melodies) to buy up his share of the property. Having learned from him all this, and finding that his zeal might prove more mischievous than otherwise, wrote to beg that he would, before proceeding any farther on the subject, go at once to the head-quarters, in the Row, and acquaint them with his design—A letter from him to say that he had done so, and that they had treated him very uncourteously, if not insolently—Wrote to try to express my regrets, &c. and had an answer from him saying that though no consideration would induce him to let the Longmans have the advantage of the copy-right he had purchased from Cuming, it should be entirely at my service, whenever I pleased.[1]

8, 9. [Sunday–Monday] Letters from Tom Longman on the subject of Bentley's interference—which I have not now time to notice—but all very kind and good-tempered towards *me*—They have sent down to Mrs. Moore a large paper copy of Heath's Picturesque Annual and also a copy of Goethe's Letters to a Child,[1] being the first reminiscences of the kind that have come from them for many a day. The fact is I had allowed them to become *too* sure of me—Dined on the ninth at Merewether's—Company, Thomas Methuen & his son, Miss MacDonald (that was) and her husband, together with two or three Curates. Singing in the evening by two of the ladies, and of course by myself—was in good voice—Slept there—Bessy had refused coming having taken this opportunity of paying a long-promised visit to Mrs. Scott at Devizes.

10 [Tuesday]—Meant to have returned home immediately after breakfast, but Merewether finding that I had never been up to the White Horse or to Abury, prevailed upon me to accompany him thither—the day delicious— our party consisted, besides Merewether himself, of his daughter, Miss Gabriel & Guthrie—[Merewether mentioned that, in a late account by Sir Pulteney Malcolm of Napoleon's departure from Torbay in the Northumberland it is said that some fears were entertained on board lest an idea which had been entertained of taking advantage of the Habeas Corpus Act, in his favour, should be put in practice and that this apprehension was increased by the appearance of two lawyer-like men who followed the ship closely in a boat as it sailed out of the harbour. This was Merewether & a friend of his who went there from curiosity.][1]—Merewether's carriage took me afterwards to Hughes's, where I found them most opportunely going to dinner and the poney chaise being in waiting for me, got home before dark—In speaking of Abraham Moore and his irregular life Merewether said that it was a frequent saying of Moore's that he was sure he should "die in a ditch"—and so he actually did, somewhere in America.

11 [Wednesday]—Bessy returned from Mrs. Scott's}

12 [Thursday]—A visit from Lord John, who arrived yesterday at Bowood and walked over to see Bessy this morning. Sat with us for some time, and then he & I sauntered on together to Bowood, where I had promised to

dine to meet him and Lord Melbourne—Nobody at dinner but Lord Melbourne, the John Russells and a young Lady Strangeways, very pretty— In talking of Chateaubriand and of his having got deaf lately, Lord Lansdowne quoted Talleyrand's saying of him that "Il se croit sourd parcequ'il n'entend plus parler de lui." {Lady Lansdowne told me that the Queen says she knows of Lord Melbourne's arrival, the moment he comes within the walls, by the sound of his laugh. It is, to be sure, a most preternatural laugh, and also, but too frequently, a "sound signifying nothing."}[1] In talking of Windsor, Lady Lansdowne objected to the numbers of dirty houses that come up quite close to the Castle—this Lord John said he liked—it was feudal; and he preferred it much to the insulation of the great houses of the present day. Was at first inclined to agree with him, but on recollecting the *dependence* implied in this juxtaposition of the great & the small, retracted my concurrence, and was all for the stand-off system of Lady Lansdowne—each rank in its own station. To be sure, it might have been retorted upon me that my own social position is little better than that of a hut placed cheek by jowl with palaces—{but mine is somewhat different from sticks and stones and I may say I think without much vanity, that the parallel does not hold—that merit makes some difference in such a [*one word unrecovered*] as mine—} and not a bad neighbourhood either do I find it.

{13 [Friday]—Lord L. after breakfast expressed a hope that I would stay today, but not if it prevented me from coming again on Monday next, when he wishes particularly to have me—Told him I hoped to be able to manage both—Bessy being at Buckhill I walked to see her after breakfast—Addition to our company at dinner, the new Bishop of Salisbury and his Chaplain, also Guthrie. In the evening, I sung, not a little nervous at first, but got on better afterwards—A good deal of conversation in the evening, about Phrenology &c. &c.—The Bishop a very mild gentlemanlike person—

14 [Saturday]—After breakfast joined Bessy at Buckhill, and went in the poney carriage with her to call upon the Feildings, for the first time since our poor friend's death—A *tete-à tête* between Bessy and Lady Elisabeth, which the latter said, had been a relief & comfort to her—Home to dinner

15 [Sunday]—A visit from Rogers and his sister, on their way to Bowood— he in high good humour, but did not quit us without, as usual, leaving a little sting behind. On his noticing the prints in our dressing room, I said something about their being all "personal friends" and that I wanted his portrait to add to the number. But, without noticing this, and wishing

(more suo) to take the conceit out of me, as to their being "personal *friends,*" he exclaimed, "Why, you've got all your *patrons* here! You ought certainly to put up Sir Robert Peel also."—Worked a little in the evening.}

16 [Monday]—A note from Lady Elisabeth to Bessy, saying how much good she had done her, and begging of her to come again to Lacock, during my absence at Bowood—Poor Bessy rather fearing a repetition of the painful scene of Saturday, but still felt that she could not refuse, and promised to come tomorrow—To Bowood to dinner—the party increased by the addition of Lord Suffolk & his daughter, Lord Glenelg, Sidney Smith and the Rogers's.—Much amusement excited by the article in the Spectator Newspaper about the "Conclave" assembled at Bowood. "At the Bowood meeting of Ministers" says the journalist "it is not credible that any consideration of what is due to the people of England—of what they require and deserve—will clash for an instant with the main object of securing office for as many Whig Lords and gentlemen as possible"—Had this Sour-crout politician been present at our dinner-party to-day he would have seen that one main object of ministers was certainly laughter & good cheer, and that while the Bowood cook took care of this latter branch of policy, Sidney Smith administered amply to the other—Talking of proverbs after dinner, Lord John mentioned his own definition of a Proverb "the wit of one and the wisdom of many," which Mackintosh (I think he said) quoted in one of his works.— {R. told me that there was evidently a growing estrangement between the Queen & the Duchess of Kent, the former having come to the knowledge of (what he says there seems now no longer a doubt of) the too great intimacy that existed between the Duchess & Conroy—the distinction made during the latter part of the late King's life, was "the *Royal* family at Windsor and the *Con*royal family at Kensington"} [1]—Sidney, speaking of Mackintosh & his Memoirs remarked on the proof they afforded of his having been so very honest a politician—the more striking certainly as there was always a sort of tarnish on his name in this respect, which was a good deal perpetuated by Parr's antithetical contrast between him & Quigley, addressed it is said to Mackintosh himself, on his saying some thing in disparagement of Quigley—{"Yes—Tommy—but he *might* have been worse—he *was* a Priest, he might have been a Lawyer—he *was* an Irishman, he might have been a Scotchman—he was a traitor, he might have been an apostate."}

17 [Tuesday]—Bowles came after breakfast—more odd & ridiculous than ever—his delight at having been visited yesterday by the Prime Minister & Secretary of State, Lord L. having taken them both to Bremhill—The foolish fellow had left his trumpet at home, so that we could hardly make him hear, or indeed do any thing with him but laugh. Even when he *has* his

trumpet, he always keeps it to his ear while he is talking himself and then takes it down when any one else begins to talk—To-day he was putting his mouth close to my ear, and bellowing away, as if I was the deaf man, not he—We all pressed him to stay to dinner, but in vain—and one of his excuses was—"No—no—indeed—I cannot. I *must* go back to Mrs. Moore."—Rogers very amusing afterwards about this—"it was plain, he said, where Bowles had been all this time"—"taking advantage of Moore's absence &c. &c." {Rogers arranged to go with his sister to Bremhill on Saturday, to stay there some days—no room for me, which (all circumstances considered) I was not at all sorry for.—Walked a good deal with Rogers through the pleasure-grounds. Put to him the case, respecting Barnes, which I have for a long time, felt anxious about, and which (though already no doubt mentioned in this Journal) I will here briefly re-state. During the time when I furnished squibs to the Times newspaper, there was usually an advance of money made to me, which I worked out as the fancy struck me, and kept myself an account of the articles I had written— At the time when, in consequence of their change of politics, I separated from the Times, there was still of the last sum they had advanced me, some forty or fifty pounds over what I had supplied articles for. I therefore wrote to Barnes, acquainting him with this circumstance and saying that I would, as soon as I could conveniently, pay him the balance—To this he answered very kindly that he would not hear of any such payment—that there was but one person in the concern whom he ever consulted with, on such matters (meaning Walters) and that *neither* would consent to my refunding—It was at the time rather convenient to me to leave the matter so, and I felt the less scrupulous about it, as Barnes had often assured me in his letters that they were all well aware I was underpaid for my services, but that the expences of the paper would not allow them to go any farther. I was however determined as soon as I could afford it to refund the said sum and it was upon this I now consulted Rogers, both as to whether he did not think it right I should do so and as to what he thought the best manner of doing it—His first impulse was very generously to proffer the money for the purpose, but this I told him would soon, I hoped, be conveniently within my own power. He then advised that I should not do it by letter, but call upon Barnes, when I next visited London, and explaining that I had waited till I could without inconvenience, proffer the sum, insist as a favour, that he should accept it from me.}

18 [Wednesday]—Joined Rogers & Sidney in a walk before breakfast— Sidney said to me when Rogers had left us "There are two points in the character of our noble host which, I think, must strike every one who knows him, and none more than yourself—one is the patriotic feeling with

which, neither wanting nor liking office (for whatever he might have done formerly, he certainly does not like it now) he yet takes upon himself its trammels for the public service, and the other is the gentlemanlike spirit and courtesy which unvaryingly pervades his whole manner and conduct never swerving a single instant from the most perfect good-breeding and good-nature." To this tribute I most heartily subscribed, after an acquaintance with the subject of it more than thirty years, and a close intimacy of more than twenty—{talk of Lord Melbourne's *tone* of conversation—his saying last night, with that preternatural laugh of his, that "every thing would go on just as well if we had no law at all"—"Yes" said Sidney—"drunken paradoxes!"—Lord John at breakfast telling, with high glee, of a rumour there is in the Tory papers of a misunderstanding among the Ministry.—Rogers showed me what Miss Martineau says in her last book about the relative reputation held by the present rise of English writers in America—According to her account, Bulwer & Mrs. Jamieson take the lead there[1]—Bulwer one knew already to be their coryphée—but as to Mrs. Jamieson—not having read her, can't say. Of *me* they do not appear by her account to have even *heard*. Mentioned also an American Volume he had seen, containing all the Pleasures—viz. Imagination, Hope, and his own, Pleasures of Memory.[2] In a Preface, prefixed to this last, it was remarked, he said that it was a Poem totally devoid of originality; and he, in some degree, admitted the justice of this charge, saying that it had been always his delight as a young man to cull every little beautiful bit and phrase he could find in the course of his reading. I remember, indeed, his often pointing out to me, years ago, little sparkling things in his poems, which he owned to have borrowed and mentioned freely where he found them—One of these, I recollect, was "caverns full of night" which he found in Thomson, I believe;[3] and another time I remember his saying of four lines in his Columbus "You would hardly believe what a number of books have contributed to the making of these four lines." But this can hardly be called plagiary—it is at least a power of selection and combination which is almost equivalent in its result to originality. Mentioned to him what Sidney had said of Lord L.—but he demurred thereto—The fact is, Lord L. does not attend sufficiently to his conversation—at least, so Sam thinks—"He is never very *courteous* to *me*."} After breakfast set off to return home, and Rogers accompanied me—Nothing could be more agreeable and amiable than he was. In talking of his age (he is now some months turned 75) he said "If I was asked what ailment I have, I really could not say that I have any"; and yet, so delicate was his health up to the age of between 30 and forty that it was difficult to keep him alive. We walked up and down between the Sandy Lane Gate & the Calne Road three or four times, I still turning back with him and he then retreading his steps with me. In the course of our walk, he said "You know Mrs. Moore is my almoner"—I anticipated what was coming, and both for Bessy's sake and the poor people's, rejoiced in my heart. He then took out of his pocket five sovereigns and gave them to me for the Poor of Bromham. One of my embarrassments indeed, during his visit has been the fear lest Bessy should thank him for the five pounds I brought her, in *his name*, for the same purpose two or three years since. But I had taken an opportunity of warning her against doing so, saying that it would look like asking for more. I now told him the circumstance of my having imposed upon her, as just stated, not saying however that it was in his name I had done so. I need not say how great was Bessy's pleasure on my producing this new fund for her old women.

{19, 20 [Thursday–Friday]—On this last day, Bessy, who has been long meditating a visit to her mother in town started in the coach from Buckhill for that purpose—A note from Lord Lansdowne yesterday to say that as he is so soon going to town he hopes I will come to dinner on Saturday, adding that it would be very amiable of me if I could stay over Sunday also—An invitation from the Salmons to Bessy and me to dine with them on Monday next—answered that *I* would come.

21 [Saturday]—To Bowood—Company, Lord Glenelg, the Vernon Smiths, and Lord & Lady Grosvenor—Lady G. always a great favourite of mine—Sung a good deal in the evening for them, and was in excellent voice—}

22 [Sunday]—{After luncheon walked to call upon the Hughes's and the Merewethers—found that the Sergeant & his son were also going to dine with the Salmons tomorrow—offered to take my portmanteau for me to Devizes in the morning which I accepted at first, but afterwards luckily declined}—Read a story of Lover's for the party in the evening—{A good deal of conversation with Lord Glenelg and some one else about Boz, whose merits I as usual stood up for, but found the same fastidiousness in Glenelg, on that head, as I find in most of the people, of this grade, that I meet with—In reference to my general view of the doom that attends our later literature, from the great increase of readers, and the consequent lowering of the standard of literary taste, Lord Glenelg said with some justice that such writings as those of Boz, which mixed up as I seemed to think so much talent with this vulgarity would but hasten that decline which, according to my opinion, was in progress, by extending the taint also to those higher classes where the parting Astraea of Good Taste might be expected the longest to linger—(This latter flourish, my own—but it conveys most briefly the substance of his meaning.)

23 [Monday]—Day lowering & disagreeable, and the prospect of my journey to Devizes (even if I could effect it, which I had never thought of before) not at all inviting—would have first to come home & from thence get, how I could, in the cold open carriage to Devizes—With this view of the matter before my eyes, it was no wonder that when Lord L. came, in his most persuasive manner, to beg of me to stay over to-day, I was not very tardy in complying—I told him however of my engagement to the Salmons & the necessity there would be of sending a man & horse to Devizes with my apologies, all which he was most ready to perform, and I accordingly, nothing loth, consented to stay—The Vernon Smiths off this morning, and the only company now left the Grosvenors & Lady Caroline Strangways— In talking with Vernon Smith, by the bye, about Novel reading, he quoted what Mackintosh, who was himself much given thereto, said in defence of it, that "it is right for a man to be acquainted with that which interests large masses of the community." This as I told him would be quite as good a defence of dram-drinking, for that also interests large masses of the community. But this was very much Mackintosh's *feelosophic* way of putting things. Dinner and evening very snug and agreeable.

24 [Tuesday]—The Grosvenors off before breakfast—I staid till after luncheon, having some historical memoranda to collect in the Library, and then walked home—Found a letter there from Bessy, saying she would be at Buckhill in the evening—Despatched the poney carriage with George for her, but the hour was so late that she deferred coming home till the morning—

25 [Wednesday]—Bessy home again—glad to have paid her visit, but tenfold glad to be back again—

26, 27, 28 &c. [Thursday–Saturday] Resumed my work and continued at it with but few interruptions—A note from Lady Adelaide Forbes, who is now with Lady Hastings in Scotland, in reference to a request she had made of me to procure some situation if possible, for an old servant of their family whom she & her sister are obliged to part with, not being able to afford to keep him—alas, the changes of this world!—I had so long delayed answering her that I was afraid she might consider it unkind, and expressed myself so when I wrote—Her reply begins "As your most kind letter for which I can never be sufficiently grateful (I speak for my sister Caroline as well as myself) may lead to your wishing to write to her &c. &c." At the end she says "I cannot tax myself with ever having had an unkind suspicion of you, one of my oldest & kindest friends"}

November, 1, 2, &c [Wednesday–Thursday]—At work busily, and with but few interruptions—none, indeed, except a visit now & then from young Henry Fitz-Maurice, who is, I rejoice to say improving in his looks.—As I generally read for about 20 minutes or half an hour after I go to bed (always something different from the task I have been employed upon during the day, in order to get that out of my head) I have taken lately, as my night dose, a dry book on Ethics, by I know not who, in answer to Mackintosh,[1] which Brabant lent me; and I here discover the source of Brabant's low opinion of Mackintosh. It does, to be sure, take the shine out of Mac's Ethics prodigiously—and the instances of confusion of thought, and even of ignorance which he cites from Mac's book are, some of them astounding. Cannot help making a memorandum here of one (indeed, the most glaring) of the proofs brought by him of Mackintosh's marvellous ignorance (marvellous in *him*), or what is much more likely to have been the case, excessive carelessness. Leibnitz, in a familiar letter to a friend gives a short account of a book which had just appeared, "de principio Iuris Naturalis," and, after mentioning several other things discussed in the book, he says "Quaeritur deinde, utrum custodia societatis humanae sit principium juris," and adds "Id negat vir egregius (the author) contra Grotium, qui societatem, Hobbesium, qui mutuum metum, Cumberlandium et similes qui mutuam benevolentiam, id est, semper societatem, adhibent." In other words, the author, of whom Leibnitz is giving an account, enquires "what is the origin or 'principium' of Law," and decides that it is *not,* as Grotius, Hobbes & Cumberland have supposed, a regard to the conservation or guardianship of human society—but simply, as he subsequently endeavours to prove, the Will of the Creator, "Iussum Creatoris." In ranging, too, on the same side of the question, Grotius, Hobbes & Cumberland, this author shows that he considers all their several opinions on the subject to be resolvable into one and the same—namely, that a regard to the safety & consideration of *society* is the origin of human law. I have put clearly, I flatter myself, in the foregoing few lines what it has cost the castigator of Mackintosh more than half a dozen pages to explain. This being the state of the case, let us now observe how Sir James, with much pomp & plausibility, disserts upon the subject. Having given it as his opinion that preceding inquirers had not been very clear in their theories of morals, he proceeds as follows. "It is little wonder that Cumberland should not have disembroiled his ancient & established confusion, since Leibnitz himself in a passage where *he reviews the theories of morals* which had gone before him, has done his utmost to perpetuate it. 'It is a question,' says he, 'whether the preservation of human society be the first principle of the law *of nature.*' This *our author*[2] denies, in addition to Grotius, who laid down sociability to be so, to Hobbes, who ascribed that character to mutual fear, and to Cumberland, who held that it was mutual benevolence; which are all three only different names for the safety and welfare of society? Here the great philosopher (continues Mackintosh) considered benevolence or fear, two feelings of the human mind to be the first principles of the *law of nature*,[3] in the same sense in which the tendency of certain actions to the well-being of the community may be so regarded. The confusion, however, was then common to him with many, as it even now is with most. The comprehensive view was his own." The confusion and inaccuracy crowded into this short paragraph of Mackintosh's is really astounding. It requires but the merest school-boy's power of construing to see that the proposition which Mac ascribes to Leibnitz is that of the author on whose book Leibnitz is making remarks; and not content with this blunder, Mackintosh misrepresents also the author of the book, making him say that Grotius and Hobbes considered benevolence and fear to be the first principles of the law of *nature,* whereas this author was not speaking of the law of nature at all, but of the "principium *juris.*" I could not help endeavouring to bring this exposure into a somewhat more concise and intelligible form than has been done by Mac's *Mastix* himself—who is, however, a very clever clear-headed fellow, and, withal, a very disagreeable one. Indeed, so much so that I would almost rather be *wrong* with Mackintosh—cum Platone errare—than be *right* with so harsh & conceited a dogmatist.[4]

November, 1, 2, 3 [Wednesday–Friday][1] &c. &c. Hard at work at the reign of Edwrd 2nd.—Forget whether I have mentioned before that the Record Commission have (as in duty bound) sent me all their published Volumes. Have got down as many as are *immediately* necessary to me, and hardly know how to dispose even of these—my study being already overloaded with learned rubbish, of various kinds, and the floor not being very trust-worthy—Have also got down a number of gigantic books from the Long-mans, so that what with Rymer, Palgrave's Parliamentary Writs &c. &c.[2] poor Sloperton will I fear, hardly hold out. A good number are stowed away in the hall, with Bessy's Club things for her old women, and *very* fit company they are for each other—

{4, 5, 6 &c. [Saturday–Monday] Ditto repeated—with little change or inter-ruption except a visit now & then from Henry Fitzmaurice who with his sister still remains at Bowood—

7 [Tuesday]—Received a note from Henry to come & dine with them on Monday, as they start for some watering-place on Tuesday—

9 [Thursday]—Bessy having offered herself to Lady Elisabeth for to-day, went to dine & sleep at Lacock, while I walked to Bowood—A nice snug & agreeable dinner with only Lord Shelburne, Lady Louisa & Lady Kerry—

In the evening tried over some collections of German Songs which Shelburne had brought with him from abroad—and was much tempted into *words* by some of them

10 [Friday]—Walked home after breakfast—Among my relaxations lately (in the reading way) one has been, looking through Talford's Play of Ion, which (though he kindly sent me a copy) I was not able to read at the time when every body was talking of it—Some of the writing, I must say (with all deference to his eulogists) is in very bad & flashy taste. I will just take at hap-hazard some specimens of what I mean.[1]

> "your glories break
> Through my pavilioned spirit's *sable* folds."

> "As if some unseen visitant from heaven,
> Touched the calm lake and *wreathed* its images
> In *sparkling waves*—"

> *"When pansied turf was air to winged feet."*

See a long passage also p. 80

> "And wreathe a diadem around its brow,
> In which *our sunny fantasies may live,*
> *Empearled,* and gleam in fatal splendor, far
> On distant ages"

> "These are fancies
> Which thy soul, late expanded with great purpose,
> Shapes, as it quivers to its natural circle
> In which its joys should lurk, as in the bud
> The cells of fragrance cluster."

What the d—— does this mean?

> "The gods have prompted me; for they have given
> One *dreadful voice* to all things which should be
> Else *dumb or musical;* and I rejoice,
> To step from the grim round of waking *dreams*
> Into this *fellowship* which makes *all clear.*"

Oh very *clear!*

> "and the brood
> Of dizzy weakness flickering through the gloom
> Of my small curtained prison caught the hues
> Of beauty spangling out in glorious change."

I have heard of *shelling* out *change*—and if the change be in new sovereigns, perhaps *spangling* out is not an unpoetical way of describing it.

> "tell me how it gleams
> "In bloody portent or in saffron hope."

We have been accustomed to "bright hope"—"sunny hope," and even "rosy hope"—but *"saffron* hope" is to be had only at the druggist's, I should think. And the above is more than enough.

11, 12, 13 &c. [Saturday–Monday] On to the end of the month. Hard at work, and since the day I dined with Henry at Bowood, have not been beyond the garden. Bessy not at all well, and obliged, by Dr. Brabant's orders, to go through a course of Blue Pills, which produced a good deal of pain & exhaustion in the process, but has certainly made her much better— Letters from Tom very agreeable, and confirming me more and more in my self-gratulation on the step I took in placing him where he is now, Bertrand having turned out every thing I could most wish and having also inspired a friendship & affection for him in Tom which it will do the boy good to remember. Among other things he tells me in one of his letters, that Bertrand reminds him constantly of *me*.}

14, 15, 16, 17 &c. &c. [Tuesday–Friday]—No change or novelty in my mode of existence—still the same still-life picture. It is some comfort, however, to find that, while so quiet at home one has still the capability of kicking up a row abroad.—Witness the "turn-up" I was the cause of the other night (the 21st.) in the House of Commons—the subject of Debate was the Pension List, and the best mode of recording what took place is to insert here the scrap from the Times' Report of the Debate[1]

{18, 19, 20, 21, 22, &c. &c [Saturday–Wednesday]—Still the same quiet course of life. Forgot to mention a letter I had from Napier who is in London wishing me to recommend him to the Longmans for an immediate object he has in view of raising a small sum of money by the publication of a tale he wrote some time since together with the right of making an engraving (to accompany it) from a picture he has himself painted in illustration of said Tale—His object is to have it bought by the Longmans for their Keepsake—Sent him a letter to the Co. and also one to Bentley, should that fail, but at the same time advising him to enlarge the Tale if possible, and publish it by itself[1]—The newspapers (particularly the Irish ones) all full of allusions to the late assault upon me in the H. of Commons by "that Bateman" (as the Dub. Eve. Post calls him)—But that which gives me the most real pleasure among all these notices, is the following truly generous paragraph in the Standard—this not being the *first* time that Gifford has done himself honour on the same subject.[2]

23, 24, &c. &c. [Thursday, 23 November–Thursday, 30 November]—Forgot, I think to mention a letter which I received some weeks since from Macvey Napier (Edr. of Edinburgh Review) entreating of me to furnish him with an Article on some subject of my own choosing—alluding to the long time that has elapsed since he & I had any intercourse with each other, he says "Often and often have I thought of breaking silence, and yet, so it is, that my frequent want of your powerful hand and earnest wishes to have its assistance have allowed the time to pass unimproved &c. &c. In a word," he adds, "I wish of all things to have (as I must come at last to the sordid phrase) an *Article* from you. Will you gratify me? Will you be prevailed upon once more to put on your armour and come down to the field under the ancient colours of the *Blue* and *yellow*? We have now-a-days sundry rivals in that field; and the more need of the aid of those gallant knights who have heretofore led us to triumph. I have not however lost courage, but if I could see you once more shake your brilliant spear, I would anticipate nothing but victory."} [1]

December 1, 2, 3 &c. [Friday, 1 December–Tuesday, 12 December] Still confined to my study and garden, and, as long as I have health, not desiring any thing better—An agreeable announcement, in a letter from Mrs. Napier to Bessy, of the approaching marriage of one of her daughters to Lord Arran. The whole of the details promise most prosperously & I rejoice at it sincerely.

13. {[Wednesday] To Devizes Bessy & myself to dine with the Salmons & receive Russell in the evening on his return for the holidays—was glad to be asked again so kindly by the Salmons, having feared that my excuse last time from Bowood might have been taken ill. Company at dinner, Archdn. Macdonald, Mr. Mazindre, and another person, whose name I forget, and the Grubbs—Sung in the evening several songs—little Buss arrived, grown a good deal since last time, but not looking very strong.}

14 [Thursday]—{Pressed by the Salmons to stay over to-day, and for Bessy's sake, consented—her health & spirits are already the better for the change, and besides it gives Brabant better opportunity of seeing and talking with her—} Looked again over the curious Diary of Sir Edd. Bayntun which Salmon has in his possession. There are several Volumes of it, and a curious selection might be made from their contents. Took down the following memorandums for the year 1754, just after Pelham's Death, when a new Administration was about to be formed.
      "March 1754.—Went to the Smyrna—thence to Lady Northum-

berland's—her house the resort of distressed lovers; and herself so compassionate as to neglect nothing for their general relief.

"Do.—To Leicester House—great appearance of faction. Boone said, if Mr. Fox was Chancr. of the Exchequer, it would not be borne—what must become of this poor woman and the children—that old friends must stand together. Thence to Lord Winchelsea to dinner—had much of his confidence touching the new schemes—would join the Duke of Newcastle—any thing to obstruct Sandwich and the D. of Bedford which must be the consequence—that Murray had been ruined by malice, and that there was difference in drinking the P's (quy. Pretender?) health with Tosset or at Oxford[1]—Complained of Lord Granville—VIII (o'clock) to White's & Lord Granville—curious to know where I had been.

"March 15—Went to Mr. Fox who told me he had refused to accept being the Secy. of State—that he had accepted it according to the message delivered by Lord Hartington, understanding that he was to manage business in the H. of Commons under the D. of Newcastle—for more certainty how his Grace understood it he had waited upon him and found, upon his proposing some questions of explanation, that he was not to be the channel between his Grace & the divers applications arising in the H. of Commons—that his Grace even refused to permit him to enquire into the plan left by Mr. Pelham, till his Grace & Dufflin had adjusted it—that, he conceived his being employed in a business he did not understand and secluded from one he did, was a plain project to ruin him, and he rather chose to fall in the station he was—(quy. *in*)—that he could be of no sort of use without this countenance. . . . XII—to Lord Granville who was waiting for Mr. Stone—I told him what Mr. Fox had said, by his direction—my Lord seemed surprized, and said he had heard nothing from the D. of Newcastle—he feared they would trifle in this manner &c. &c.

"March 17—the D. of Grafton in opposition to the D. of Newcastle—the D. of Devonshire inflamed by H. Walpole—the scene[2] deeper laid than appears—Thence to Mr. Fox's—did not stay to see him—to Lord Winchelsea who discovers expectation from these difficulties—the D. of Newcastle shows evident marks of fear—this confirmed by General Lake."

{No one at dinner but Mr. Meek, Salmon's man of business—a very comfortable and quiet evening

15 [Friday]—After breakfast started in a Fly for home.}

16, 17, 18 &c. [Saturday–Monday] At work—Sent one of these days a short answer to Rice's Circular on the subject of the Pension List,[1] which I concluded by saying that my Pension had been given to me without any solicitation on my part, and would be surrendered by me without a murmur should the Committee think right to withdraw it.

19, 20, 21 &c [Tuesday–Thursday]—Some correspondence with the Longmans respecting our projected Edition of the Works—Mrs. Power has asked £1000 for the right of publishing the poetry of which she holds the copyright—This the Longmans think excessive and so it probably is; but my dear generous & just-minded Bessy thinks otherwise, and (though she knows so large an outlay in that quarter must necessarily trench upon *my* share of the emoluments) hopes most earnestly that Mrs. Power will, for the sake of her family, refuse to take any less.—A "rare bird"[1] is Bess, in more ways than one.

{24 [Sunday] A letter from Tom Longman in which he says, after alluding to the difficulties in the way of the Edition "The time has at length arrived when we are resolved on making a desperate effort to surmount them all. We apprehend we cannot buy out Mrs. Power under £1000,—we must buy out the Irish at £50, we must buy out ourselves at £———, We have only left to buy *you* out, and we trust we cannot fail to do this at another £1000, of which £500 to be paid on the publication of the 1st. Vol. & £500 on that of the last." He adds afterwards "we depend upon your doing all you can to make the most of the works by editing, notes &c. &c. and remember we buy you all out and out, for all that is and is to come of copyright."—Must take time to consider of this last clause.

27, 28 [Wednesday–Thursday]—The Hughes's came to dine and pass a few days with us

29 [Friday]—Received a note yesterday from Lord Lansdowne, who has within these few days returned from town, asking me to come over to dinner either to-day or tomorrow—Lord Shelburne had already called in the course of the week, but poor Lady Lansdowne still detained in town, by the illness of Lady Louisa—Had intended to walk over to dinner to-day, but the rain came on so violently that I was prevented—The Hughes's still with us—Read out to the party yesterday evening Colman's John Bull,[1] to the no small delight both of Bussy & Bess

30 [Saturday]—A kind note from Lord L. hoping that it was nothing worse than the weather that prevented me from coming yesterday, and saying

that he would expect me to-day or tomorrow—Weather still very bad, but went in Bessy's poney chaise as far as the Lodge and from thence walked the remainder of the way in a sousing shower—Found Lord Ebrington's carriage at the door to take him away to Hobhouse's—had been at Bowood these two days past—was sorry to have missed him and he expressed very cordially the same with regard to myself in the few words we exchanged at the door—Shelburne also gone to Hobhouse's—Company at dinner only Senior and Miss Fox. In the evening Lady L. arrived from town with her poor sick girl, who is, however, thank God, a little better—joined us in the evening (Lady L. herself) with looks and manner as disengaged & cheerful as if there was no sorrow whatever within—A good deal of conversation with Lord L. & Senior, about Canada & other matters—Senior pointed out a passage in Adam Smith, written while the American Revolution was in progress and full of a strong radical feeling, which, Senior said, prevailed in him to a great degree, though not generally noticed in his character.— Mentioned to Lord Lansdowne the passage in Sir Ed. Bayntun's Diary (quoted above) which contained what Fox said about his "being employed in business he did not understand &c." This Lord L. said, he rather thought was given by Walpole or some other writer of that time, as it struck him that he remembered it—Turned to Walpole's Memoirs,[1] but could not find the passage—read out the report of Pitt's famous rhetorical flourish about the Rhône & Saône[2]—the beginning of which is good, but the complimentary conclusion flat. Lord L. thought this might have been meant as irony—but, even so, it is a failure. Probably the fault is with the reporter of the speech, Walpole himself.

31 [Sunday]—Pressed by Lord L. to stay to-day, which I readily assented to, having, in the anticipation of his wish, prepared Bessy for my not return- ing—Employed the morning in looking over Carte's Ormond (the pre- fatory part) and Froissart's Chronicle[1] for the details of Richard 2nd's visit to Ireland—Had the addition of Henry only at dinner.}

Notes to 1837 Entries

5 January

1. Moore identifies this person as "Tillotson" in a note placed at the end of the MS page.
2. Wellington and Winchelsea fought a duel on 21 March 1829; see entry for 16 September 1830. For another account of the handkerchief anecdote see Greville, *A Journal of the Reign of George IV and William IV,* 1:198.
3. Crabbe, "The Frank Courtship," ll. 141–42, *Tale VI of Tales in Verse* (1812).
4. Outlands was the country estate of the Duke and Duchess of York.
5. George Farquhar, *The Recruiting Officer,* 4.i.

7 January

1. "Negus" is a mixture of wine, water, and sugar, named after its inventor, Col. Francis Negus.

24–25 January

1. *Die Geschichte von Ireland,* übersetzt von August Schäfer, 1 vol. (Würzburg, 1835).

1–3 February

1. George Baron Lyttleton, *The History of the Life of King Henry the Second, and of the age in which he lived* . . . , 4 vols. (1767–71).

16 February

1. Jean-François Champollion (1790–1832), a noted Egyptologist; his brother Jacques Joseph Champollion-Figeac (1778–1867) edited and published posthumously several of his works, including *De l'Egypt et de la Nubie* . . . 4 vols. (1835–45), and *Grammaire égyptienne* . . . (1836).

17–19 February

1. In 1836 Landor published *Letters of a Conservative;* he published thirteen more letters on the Church of England in the *Examiner* from 29 January to 19 November 1837. See R. H. Super, *The Publication of Landor's Works* (London, 1954), p. 63.

1 April

1. See Dowden, *Letters,* 2:808.

6 April

1. Abraham Hayward (1801–84) published a prose translation of *Faust* in 1833. His reviews "Gastronomy and Gastronomers," *Quarterly Review* 54 (1835): 117–55, and "Dinners, Clubs, etc.," *Quarterly Review* 55 (1836): 444–87, were published in 1852 as *The Art of Dining; or Gastronomy and Gastronomers.* Dionysius The Tyrant is Dionysius Lardner.

2. Isaac Vossius (1618–89) and Méric Casaubon (1599–1671) were continental classical scholars who settled in England. Marc-Antoine Muret or Muretus (1526–85), classical scholar; Joseph Justus Scaliger (1540–1609), classical scholar and editor.

3. Philo Herennius of Byblos (b. A.D. 42) was chiefly known for his "translation" of the history of the Phoenicians by Sanchuniathon, a legendary and perhaps mythical figure who was said to have lived before the Trojan War. Fragments of Philo's work are extant.

Giovanni Nanni (1432?–1502) published a volume of spurious classical poetry with a commentary by "I. Annius Viterbiensis" or "Annius of Viterbo."

Hector Boece or Boethius (c. 1465–c.1536) published his *History of Scotland* (under the Latin title *Scotorium Historiae . . .*) in 1527. Scholars have detected imaginative inventions and distortions of facts in the work.

Geoffrey of Monmouth (1100?–1154), the creator of King Arthur as a romantic hero, wrote *Historia Regum Britanniae,* citing as his source an ancient book given him by Walter Colenius, Archdeacon of Oxford. Since there is no record of this book's having existed, the assumption must be that Geoffrey wrote from imagination and oral tradition.

4. John Jortin (1698–1770), classical historian, critic, and clergyman. In 1731, Jortin began a publication entitled *Miscellaneous Observations on Authors Ancient and Modern.* Jan Gruter (1560–1627), whose two-volume *Inscriptiones Antiquae totius orbis Romani* appeared in 1603 and whose seven-volume *Lampas, sive fax artium liberalium* in 1602–34, was one of the authors included in Jortin's work. Thomas Chatterton (1752–70), English poet who committed suicide when his *Poems of Thomas Rowley* was proved to be spurious. William Lauder (d. 1771) published fraudulent verse in an effort to prove Milton's debt to various writers of Latin poetry. William Henry Ireland (1777–1835) forged Shakespearean documents and MSS.

5. Andrew Cross (1784–1855) described his experiments with the formation of crystals in an electric current at a meeting of the British Association in Bristol in 1836.

6. Charles Dickens (1812–70); his periodical fiction was collected and published as *Sketches by Boz* (1836); *Posthumous Papers of the Pickwick Club* was published serially (1836–37).

7 April

1. "In allusion to the *Cabi*net Cyclopedia, of which Dr. L. was the editor." (Russell's note.)

8 April

1. "This is a mis-quotation. The passage, though I cannot find it, was to this effect:— 'Gentlemen opposite are always talking of the people as distinguished from the rest of the nation. But strip the nation of its aristocracy, strip it of its magistrates, strip it of its clergy, of its merchants, of its gentry, and I no more recognise a people than I recognise in the bird of Diogenes the man of Plato.'" (Russell's note.)

10 April

1. Paul Scarron, *Roman Comique* (1651–57), a picaresque novel.

2. See entry for 5 September 1818 and its n.2.

11 April

1. Sydney Smith, *A Letter to Archdeacon Singleton, on the Ecclesiastical Commission* (1837). For Smith's correspondence with Grenville and Singleton on the pamphlet see idem, *Letters,* 2:650–52.

12 April

1. *The Dispatches of . . . the Duke of Wellington . . . Compiled by Lieut. Colonel Gurwood*, 13 vols. (1834–39).
2. See Longford, *Wellington*, pp. 274–76.
3. For an account of Byron's attachment to Lord Clare, see Marchand, *Byron: A Biography*, 1:72, 90.
4. "Dog-Day Reflections By a Dandy Kept in Town," *Works*, 8:263–66.
5. See Dowden, *Letters*, 2:808–9.

14 April

1. Morris Barnett, *Monsieur Jacques: a musical piece* . . . (1836), then playing at the St. James Theatre, which Braham built in 1835.
2. The Colosseum in Regent's Park, which Braham bought in 1831.

15 April

1. *Pearls of the East; or Beauties from Lalla Rookh. Designed by F. Corbaux and drawn on stone by L. Corbaux* (1837).
2. Sir Thomas Wentworth, Earl of Strafford (1593–1641), Lord Deputy and later Lord Lieutenant of Ireland.
3. A reference to Talleyrand's activities at the Congress of Vienna. See Jean Orieux, *Talleyrand*, trans. Patricia Wolf (New York, 1974), pp. 450–81.
4. According to Orieux, Talleyrand was crippled by a fall from a chest of drawers when only a few months old (*Talleyrand*, pp. 10–11).

19 April

1. Emma Howson Albertazzi (1813–47) made her London *début* on this date in Rossini's *La Cenerentola* (1817).

23 April

1. See entry for 31 July 1836 passim. Moore's *The Epicurean with Alciphron, a Poem*, illustrated by Turner, was published in 1839.

29 April

1. The illustration faces p. 58 of the 1839 ed.

3–6 May

1. *Alciphron*, Letter IV, *Works*, 10, 342–52.

11 May

1. Robert Pashley (1805–59), *Travels in Crete*, 2 vols. (1837). Peter von Bohlen (1796–1840), author of several books on the Near East.
2. *Works*, 3:205–7.

6 June

1. Rossini, *Semiramide* (1823).

7 June

1. John Mitford (1781–1859), clergyman, poet, and miscellaneous writer, published a two-vol. ed. of Gray's *Works* (including his letters) in 1816. He published a new, five-vol. ed. , 1835–43.
2. Ludwig van Beethoven, *Fidelio* (1805). *La Sylphide* (1832), ballet, music by Jean Schneitzhoeffer, choreography by Filippo Taglioni.

8 June

1. Genealogical accounts list Essex as having died *sine prole*. *The Complete Peerage of England, Scotland, Ireland . . .*, ed. Vicary Gibbs et al. (London, 1910–59), 5:148, note *c:* "In *Hertfordshire Families*, edit. Duncan Warrand (V.C.H.), p. 100, it is stated that 'a monumental inscription in Watford Church records the death 14 May 1837 at the age of 29 years, of Harriet, da. of George, Earl of Essex.'"

13 June

1. Moore placed the passage in square brackets at the end of the MS page, with asterisks indicating its location in the text.

15 June

1. Probably Johann Leonhard v. Hug, the author of many works on theology.
2. On 14 June 1837 more than 300,000 people gathered in the Champs de Mars for a fete depicting the storming of the citadel at Antwerp. When some fireworks were accidentally set off, panic swept through the crowd. In a rush for the gates twenty-four people were killed and 150 wounded.

17 June

1. In 1810 Louis-Philippe, then in exile in Palermo, received an invitation from the Spanish junta at Seville to lead an army against Napoleon's forces in Spain. After a brief and unsuccessful effort he was ordered to leave Spain by the British authorities. See T. E. B. Howarth, *Citizen-King: The Life of Louis Philippe* (London, 1962), pp. 118–19. Louis-Philippe published *Mon Journal* in 1849 and *Correspondance, mémoire et discours inédits de Louis-Philippe d'Orléans* in 1863.
2. Spain was involved in a civil war between the supporters of Maria-Cristina and her daughter Isabella and those of Don Carlos.

18 June

1. Daniel François Esprit Auber and Eugène Scribe, *Fra Diavola, ou L'Hôtellerie de Terracine* (1830).

19 June

1. *Poems of the late Hon. W. R. Spencer . . . To which is prefixed a biographical memoir, by the editor* (1835).
2. See entry for 16 February 1837 and its n. 1.

20 June

1. Alcide Hyacinthe Du Bois de Beauchesne, *Souvenirs poétiques* (1830).
2. Eyre Evans Crowe, *Today in Ireland* (1825) and *The History of France*, 3 vols. (1830). He did not publish a history of Germany.
3. Giacomo Meyerbeer, Eugène Scribe and Émile Deschamps, *Les Huguenots* (1836).

21 June

1. William IV died on 20 June 1837.
2. Alphonse de Lamartine, *Jocelyn. Épisode. Journal trouvé chez un curé de village* . . . (1836).
3. Pierre Antoine Lebrun (1785–1873), poet and playwright; Scott's Journal for 24 November 1825 records a meeting at Abbotsford with a Frenchman named "Le Noir," whom the editor identifies as Lebrun. *The Journal of Sir Walter Scott*, ed. W. E. K. Anderson (Oxford, 1972), p. 11 and note.

22 June

1. Jacques Nicolas Augustin Thierry, *Rapport sur les travaux de la commission des documents inédits de l'histoire du tiers état* (1837). He also published *Recueil des monuments inédits de l'histoire du tiers état*, 2 vols. (1850–56) and *Essai sur l'histoire de la formation et des progrès du tiers etat* (1853). For the criticism of Thierry see Moore's *History of Ireland*, 1 (1835), p. 251 n.
2. "Lines Addressed to Monsieur Alexandre, the Celebrated Ventriloquist," Scott's *Poetical Works*, ed. J. Logie Robertson (Oxford, 1951), p. 752.

25 June

1. Jean Alexandre Buchon (1791–1846), French historian; one of his important works was *Collection des chroniques nationales françaises* . . . , 47 vols. (1826–28).

26 June

1. Galignani published a one-volume ed. of Moore's *Poetical Works* in 1827.
2. Hervey Montmorency Morres (1767–1839), a United Irishman in the Austrian and later the French service.

27 June

1. The reference is to Menelaus; *Iliad*, 17.570.

28 June

1. Sir John Francis Davis (1795–1890), British diplomat and expert on China. The major article on Chinese poetry in the *Quarterly Review* of that period was the review of Davis's own translation, *Hān Koong Tsew, or the Sorrows of Hān* (1829), *Quarterly Review* 41 (1829): 85–120. *The Wellesley Index to Victorian Periodicals*, ed. Walter E. Houghton (Toronto, 1966), 1:709, attributes this article to Davis.

30 June

1. "Breakfasted about nine [at Caen]" in Russell.

1 July

1. Jean Frédéric Galeron (1794–1838), who founded and directed the library in Falaise near Caen. He published *Notice sur les travaux littéraires de l'abbé de La Rue, et principalement sur ses manuscrits* (1837). The English antiquarian whom Moore mentions is Francis Douce (1757–1834). Gervais de La Rue, *Recherches sur la Tapisserie . . . appartenant à l'Église Cathédrale de Bayeux* (1824).

3 July

1. Corbet was among a group of United Irishmen arrested in Hamburg in 1798 and imprisoned without trial. They were later transferred to Kilmainham prison in Dublin, from which Corbet escaped in 1803.

2. Louis Lazare Hoche (1768–97), French general and early rival of Napoleon.

3. In the battle of Salamanca (1812), allied troops led by Wellington defeated the French forces of Marmont and Foy. See Michael Glover, *The Peninsular War* (London, 1974), pp. 188–205. In the two battles of Leipzig (16 and 18 October 1813), a combined army of Austrians, Russians, and Prussians forced Napoleon's troops into a disastrous retreat. See Jacques Bainville, *Napoleon*, trans. Hamish Miles (London, 1970), pp. 381–84.

After a brief but furious defense of Paris in March 1814, Marmont sought favorable surrender terms from Alexander and the Austrian prince Schwarzenberg, withdrew his forces, and later signed a secret agreement with the Austrians that effectively forced Napoleon's abdication. See Maurice Guerrini, *Napoleon and Paris*, trans. and abr. Margery Weiner (London, 1970), pp. 335–41.

4. Baron Bertrand Clausel or Clauzel (1772–1842), General in the Army of Portugal; he took command in the battle of Salamanca after Marmont and Bonet were wounded. See Glover, *Peninsular War*, pp. 203–5.

5. George Herbert, "The Church-Porch," ll. 247–48. Line 247 correctly reads "A sad wise valour is the brave complexion."

6. Armand August Louis de Caulaincourt (1772–1827), Napoleon's ambassador to Russia (1807–11) and Minister of Foreign Affairs (1813–14).

7. I.e., French reverses in Algeria and in the Carlist revolution in Spain.

8. Sydney Owenson, Lady Morgan, *The O'Briens and the O'Flahertys: a National Tale*, 4 vols. (1827).

4 July

1. Johannes Scotus (815?–77?), medieval scholar and theologian who used the literary pseudonym Johannes Ierugena or Eriugena.

31 July

1. *The Living Poets of England . . . with biographical and critical notices* etc., 2 vols. (1827).

1 August

1. Opera by Donizetti, produced in Milan (1830).

3 August

1. Thomas Carlyle, *The French Revolution. A History*, 3 vols. (1837).

4 August

1. Henry Bickersteth, later Baron Langdale (1783–1851), married Jane, daughter of the fifth Earl of Oxford, in 1835.

5 August

1. In 1838 Murray published *Life, Letters, and Journals of Lord Byron* in one vol.
2. For an account of the controversy between Scott and Holland over a pension for Scott's brother Tom, which Holland opposed, see John Gibson Lockhart, *Memoirs of Sir Walter Scott*, 5 vols. (London, 1914), 2:113 and Edgar Johnson, *Sir Walter Scott*, 1:330–31.

7 August

1. Sharon Turner, "History of the Reign of Henry VIII," pt. 1 of *The Modern History of England* (1826–29), 2 pts.
2. See for example "Parody of a Celebrated Letter," "Extracts From the Diary of a Politician," and "The New Costume of the Ministers," *Works*, 3:160–68, 172–74, 192–94.
3. An allusion to the Duke of York's retreat from Ostend in 1793. See Sichel, *Sheridan*, 1:89.

8 August

1. *Works*, 3:264–66. For an account of Moore's reception in Poland see Eóin MacWhite, "Thomas Moore and Poland," *Proceedings of the Royal Irish Academy* 72 (1972): 49–62.
2. Charles O'Conor (1764–1828), Irish antiquary and librarian of Stowe, who published the Latin translation *Quatuor magistrorum annales hibernici . . .* in 1824.
3. John Lanigan (1758–1828), whose *Ecclesiastical History of Ireland . . .* , 4 vols. (1822) Moore cites in his *History of Ireland*. The quotation is from *Julius Caesar*, 3.ii.
4. "A Tradition of Oker Hill . . ." and "Filial Piety."
5. Ovid, *Tristia* 4. 10. 49.

10 August

1. For example, "Ye Mariners of England" and "Battle of the Baltic."
2. "Hohenlinden," ll. 31–32; line 31 correctly reads "every turf beneath their feet."
3. "Ye Mariners of England," ll. 3–4.
4. Robert Blair, *The Grave* (1743), ll. 588–89. The passage from Campbell is *The Pleasures of Hope* (1799), pt. 2, l. 378.
5. "Lochiel's Warning," l. 56, and *Gertrude of Wyoming*, 2.xiii.8. The latter correctly reads "Iberian seemed his boot."
6. The line beginning "to the opera" and ending with "Rubini" was first recorded at the end of the entry for 8 August. In that entry Moore mentioned Rogers, Miss Rogers, and Landseer as attending with him.

11 August

1. Macaulay reviewed Basil Montagu's edition of *The Works of Francis Bacon* 16 vols. (1825–34), in the *Edinburgh Review* 65 (1837): 1–104.
2. The passage in square brackets is an interlineation, written after the word *suspected*.

12 August

1. The reference is to Wellington's refusal to intervene in the execution of Marshal Ney, with which stand Holland did not agree.
2. "Reflections," *Poetical Works of Samuel Rogers* (London, 1892), pp. 177–79.
3. "My heart leaps up," l. 7.
4. "Lines suggested by a Portrait from the Pencil of F. Stone," l. 117. The pertinent lines read as follows:

> Pondering the mischiefs of these restless times,
> And thinking of my Brethren, dead, dispersed,
> Or changed and changing, I not seldom gaze
> Upon this solemn Company unmoved
> By shock of circumstance or lapse of years
> Until I cannot but believe that they—
> Are in truth the Substance, we the Shadows.

13 August

1. Smith's *The New Reign. The Duties of Queen Victoria: a Sermon . . .* (1837) was reviewed by the *Quarterly Review* 59 (1837): 240–73.

21–22 August

1. Moore placed the explanatory note in square brackets at the end of the MS page, with asterisks indicating its place in the text.

15 September

1. Francis Bacon, Dedication of 1625 edition of his *Essays:* "My essays . . . come home, to men's business, and bosoms."

18 September

1. Casimir, comte de Montrond (1768–1843), was arrested and imprisoned on Napoleon's orders in 1811. In the following year he escaped and fled to England.
2. Moore sent Lockhart a copy of the Journal that Moore had kept during his visit to Abbotsford from 29 October to 2 November 1825. See Dowden, *Letters*, 2:541, 814, and 817.
3. According to the story that Scott told Rogers (and Lockhart included in his biography, 1:76–77), Scott surpassed the top student in his class after noticing that the other boy played with a certain button on his waistcoat whenever he recited. Scott secretly cut the button from his coat, and the boy could not answer the schoolmaster's questions.
4. According to Edgar Johnson, Scott was pleased by Lockhart's courtship of and marriage to his daughter. *Sir Walter Scott*, 1:696–97.

4 October

1. Sir James Mackintosh, *Dissertation on the Progress of Ethical Philosophy . . .* (1830).

5–7 October

1. See Dowden, *Letters*, 2:815–17 and notes.

8–9 October

1. *Heath's Picturesque Annual* (1832–42, 1845). Goethe's *Briefwechsel mit einem Kinde* (1835), trans. *Goethe's Correspondence with a Child,* 3 vols. (1837–39).

10 October

1. While the *Northumberland* was being prepared to transport Napoleon to St. Helena, English sympathizers, notably the barrister Capell Lofft (1751–1824) sought to prevent his exile, first through a writ of Habeas Corpus, then through subpoena from the Court of Queen's Bench. Both attempts failed, and Napoleon sailed for St. Helena on 5 August 1815. See Norwood Young, *Napoleon in Exile: St. Helena,* 2 vols. (London, 1915), 1:62–63. Sir Pulteney Malcolm (1768–1838) was commander-in-chief at St. Helena from 1816–17. His conversations with Napoleon are recorded in his wife's *Diary of St. Helena . . .* (1899). Moore placed this passage (in square brackets) at the end of the MS page, with asterisks indicating its location in the text.

12 October

1. Cf. *Macbeth,* 5.iv.

16 October

1. See Cecil Woodham-Smith, *Queen Victoria* (New York, 1972), p. 70.

18 October

1. Harriet Martineau, *Society in America,* 3 vols. (1837). Anna Brownell Jameson (1794–1860), English miscellaneous writer.
2. *The Book of Pleasures* (Philadelphia, 1836), containing Campbell's "The Pleasures of Hope," Mark Akenside's "The Pleasures of Imagination," and Rogers's "The Pleasures of Memory."
3. Rogers, "To . . . 1810," l. 3.

1–2 November

1. James Mill, *A Fragment on Mackintosh . . .* (1835).
2. "Meaning Leibnitz." (Moore's note.)
3. "The italics are mine to mark his mistakes more emphatically." (Moore's note.)
4. A paraphrase of Cicero's dictum found in *Tusculanarum Disputationum,* 1.17.

1–3 November

1. Moore included the dates 1–2 November in two entries.
2. Thomas Rymer (1641–1713), English archaeologist, critic, and court historian, who published *Foedera, Conventiones, Literae et cujuscunque generis Acta Publica* etc., 20 vols. (1704–35). *The Parliamentary Writs and Writs of Military Summons,* ed. Sir Francis Palgrave, 2 vols. in 4 (1827–34).

10 November

1. The first three quotations are from *Ion* 2.i; the following are, respectively, 2.ii, 3.i, 3.ii, 4.ii, and 1.i.

14–17 November

1. Moore inserted the clipping from the *Times*, which has been omitted in this edition. The debate concerned a question put to the Chancellor of the Exchequer (Thomas Spring-Rice) by an Irish M.P. as to whether the pension was granted to Moore for "making luscious ballads to love-sick maidens or for writing lampoons upon George IV, of blessed memory." The reply by the Chancellor (Mr. Rice) was an eloquent defence of parliament (evoking vocal approval from the House) for granting the pension as a "reward for distinguished talent in literature."

18–22 November

1. Sir William Napier's "Griffone: A Tale of the Peninsula" appeared in Bentley's *Miscellany* 3 (1838): 601–11, and 4 (1838): 74–89.
2. Moore included a clipping from the *London Standard* on the debate in the House concerning his pension. The article was as high in Moore's praise as that in the *Times*.

23–24 November

1. For Moore's reply to Napier see Dowden, *Letters*, 2:819–20. Moore declined to write for the *Edinburgh* until work on the *History of Ireland* was completed.

14 December

1. In 1753 William Murray, the Earl of Mansfield (1705–93) was accused of having had dealings with James Stuart, the "Old" Pretender to the throne. Although he was honorably acquitted before the Cabinet Council and the House of Lords, his enemies kept alive the charge of Jacobite leanings. Pitt's most devastating attack on Murray came during a speech in the House of Lords on 27 November 1754. See O. A. Sherrard, *Lord Chatham: A War Minister in the Making* (London, 1952), pp. 278–80.
2. Moore was uncertain of the reading of "scene" and wrote "scheme?" above the line.

16–18 December

1. See entry for 14–17 November 1837 and its n.1.

19–21 December

1. Cf. Juvenal, *Satires*, 6.165.

29 December

1. George Colman the Younger, *John Bull; or, The Englishman's Fireside* (1803).

30 December

1. Walpole's *Memoirs of the Last Ten Years of the Reign of George the Second* appeared in 2 vols. in 1822, ed. Lord Holland.

2. Pitt compared the alliance of Fox and the Duke of Newcastle to the junction of the Rhône and the Saône. See Sherrard, *Lord Chatham*, p. 306.

31 December

1. Jean Froissart, *Chronique de France, d'Angleterre, d'Écosse et d'Espagne*, covering ca. 1325–1400.

1838

January {1st. [Monday] 1838—Started on the jaunting car for Sloperton, at 12 o'clock, being the bearer of a very comfortable apron from Lady Lansdowne, for Bessy to wear in her little open carriage, with pockets &c.— Expected to have found her departed for Devizes, but found she had waited for me, and at two, she, Russell and I started for that bright place, in order to attend at a Concert in the evening—Dined at Hughes's—no one, besides ourselves, but Brabant & his daughter—Having mentioned to me the other day a notice of my Irish History (which I had not myself seen) in Hallam's last work, Brabant now brought me a copy of the passage which is as follows and comes of course very welcome from such a source—It occurs in a note on the words "Faint glimmer of light in the sixth Century."—"See also the first Vol. of Moore's History of Ireland where the claims of his country are stated favourably and with much learning and industry, but not with extravagant partiality."[1]

4 [Thursday]—Had a large party of the Hughes's, with Tom Brabant &c to dinner—Mr. & Mrs. Hughes and Mary remaining to sleep

2, 3, 4, &c [Tuesday–Thursday][1]—A visit from Lord Lansdowne one of these days—After sitting for some time with me, he sent away his horses and I accompanied him in his walk home as far as the Keeper's lodge—}

9 [Tuesday]—To Bowood to dinner—Company the Phipps's, Joys and Youngs, Mìss Fox & the Duke and Duchess of Sutherland—In the evening the Duchess having expressed a strong wish that I should sing, I sat down & began unluckily with "There's a song of the olden time" which I had not sung before for a long time, and the state of my spirits not being very good, the melancholy both of the song and of my own voice affected me so much

that before I had sung the two first lines I broke out into one of those hysterical fits of sobbing which must be as painful to others as they are to myself, and was obliged to hurry away into the next room whither I was immediately followed both by Lord & Lady Lansdowne and Henry Fitz-Maurice—The exceeding effort I made to suppress the sobbing only made it break out more audibly, and altogether nothing could be more disagreeable, the company that witnessed the scene being unluckily larger and more miscellaneous than is usual at Bowood—Having drunk off a tumbler of Sal Volatile & water which Lady Lansdowne brought me, I returned to the drawing room and after laughing a little at my own exhibition, sat down again to the Piano-forte, and sung through all the gayest of my songs that I could call to remembrance.

{10 [Wednesday]—Accompanied Lord Shelburne & Phipps to Malmesbury to attend a Reform Association Dinner of which Shelburne was to be Chairman—In expectation of a demand for speechifying I had thrown together some materials for an Oration, in which I intended to introduce (qualifying it of course with a large mixture of radicalism) an attack upon the Ballot—On arriving, however, at Malmesbury we found a most beggarly amount of empty chairs, not more than twenty being the number of Patriots forthcoming for the feast, and of these the only Star, God wot, being Lord Andover! It was wisely resolved therefore that we should pretend to no more than a mere Committee Dinner, and should eschew speeching and every thing else calculated to bring the Reporters upon us. Got away about eight o'clock and our four horses whisked us back to Bowood through the frozen snow most gallantly—Dressed and joined the company in the Drawing Room, now reduced to the Sutherlands, Miss Fox & Ponsonby.

11 [Thursday]—After luncheon (which I intended to make a dinner, not expecting to get any at home where a Child's party was to be the order of the day) I set out, accompanied part of the way by Lord L. & the D. of Sutherland for Sloperton—Found Bessy busily preparing for the Juvenile Feast, of which the large cake from Bowood was to be the substratum—Our Company the Schonbergs, Pugetts, Hughes's, Emma Money &c—the amusement Forfeits &c. &c—stole away half starved from the group, and got something to eat—all very gay & merry and Bessy quite in her element, making children happy—The poor & the young being her favourite objects in this life.

12 [Friday] Returned, according to promise to Bowood, where I found only the Sutherlands and Miss Fox—a good deal of agreeable conversation in

the evening, which I have not time now to notice. Before we separated for the night the Duchess, who was to start before breakfast in the morning, asked me to sing a little for her which I did of course most willingly—

13 [Saturday]—After breakfast started for home, and found our dear Tom returned from France, having been this week past expecting him—had been obliged to come to London—

14 [Sunday]—Lord Lansdowne, who was to have started for town to-day, made his appearance to my no small surprize about one o'clock at our gate—Had received a respite from his brethren of the Cabinet till tomorrow and walked over to call upon me—Sate some time with us, and I then accompanied him back as far as the Lodge.

15, 16, 17 [Monday–Wednesday]—At work

18 [Thursday]—Had a dinner-party consisting of Captains Agar and Puget, the Starkeys and Schonbergh—Can't say much of the male part of my company, with the exception of John Starkey. Gave them, however, plenty of wine, and got rid of them about 11 o'clock.

19, 20, 21 &c. &c. [Friday–Sunday]—Nothing particular—Hume sent me a letter to look at written by his *rather* fantastic friend Mrs. ——— to a German admirer of hers, at Berlin, who is about to visit England. It appears from her letter that he had written to her lately about me and his anxiety to become acquainted with me and had said "But I must go through Stultz's hands before I can venture to present myself before Moore" to which she replies that he is mistaken on this point, for "though Moore dresses very elegantly &c. &c."—I don't know how it is that I have got this reputation—except it could have been from a book of Lockhart's some years ago, in which speaking of Jeffrey he says "the greatest Dandy, of a literary man, that I have ever seen,—always excepting Tom Moore."[1] I find, too, in a work lately sent me, called "Literary leaves" written & printed in Calcutta,[2] the following—"Thomas Moore is as neat and particular in the cut of his clothes as in the turn of his verses." Must not forget, by the bye, to answer the civil letter from the author that accompanied this Calcutta book.

22, 23 &c. [Monday–Tuesday]—The following kind note, one of these days from Lady Lansdowne to Bessy "My dear Mrs. Moore—Will you be persuaded to come over either tomorrow or Monday to luncheon and see my sister. She is very anxious to see you, and if you are not able she will go to you—but we all hope that you will come here that we may show you Mary and all her pretty ways. You shall be sent for in a close carriage & safely sent home before dark." Bessy, of course, went, and found Lady E. much better than when she last saw her—Fixed for a date to go to Lacock on Saturday—

26 [Friday]—Hughes and his son to pass a few days at Sloperton.}

27 [Saturday]—My poor Bess, whose state of weakness for some time past gives me many a painful boding (though I trust in God without any real grounds) not finding herself well enough to go to Lacock, Tom & I set off thither in the poney carriage at 3—leaving the Hughes's to keep Bessy company.—None but the Talbots, Lady E. & Horatia at dinner.—Lady E. much better than I could have expected to find her.—Found it very agreeable, though inwardly sad the whole time—poor Feilding seldom absent from my thoughts—In the evening Horatia played over several beautiful things from Bellini, Strauz &c. while I sat in a corner and listened in silent sadness.

28 [Sunday]—After luncheon Tom & I started in the poney carriage for home, and when at the top of Bowden Hill I got out & walked through the fields home—Brought a note from Lady Elisabeth to Bessy which I shall here copy
    "My dear Mrs. Moore—I cannot tell you how very much disappointed I was at your not coming yesterday nor how grieved I am for the cause. You are always most soothing to me, and I am sorry the weather & the winter put a sort of gulph between us. You particularly know how to "minister to a mind diseased."[1] I am glad to have seen Mr. Moore whom I consider (that rare thing) a sincere friend both for the present & the past. His voice reminded me but too much of the gay days of the Abbey—happy days, they can never return.—How often have I thought formerly that it was a mistake calling this world a vale of tears, a thorny path &c. &c.—I always found it such an agreeable world and so pleasant to live—I suppose nobody believes those truths till they feel them in their own person—God bless you—E.F.— Let me hear soon by the Post how you are—We are all anxious about you."

{31 [Wednesday]—Started for town with Tom to provide his outfit for joining his regiment—One of my companions inside old Davies Giddy, and the other as I found towards the close of our journey a Mr. Bachelor, who lives between Bath & Bristol and is well acquainted with most of my neighbors. Found our rooms in Sackville St. ready for us (Lady Elisabeth having kindly allowed me to go there) and was not sorry to find that I was put in Lady E's room instead of poor Feilding's, while Tom had Horatia's—}

February {1st [Thursday]—Found out Captain Agar who undertook to assist Tom in his purchase—went to Tailor &c. &c. Went with Hume to lunch at the Gossets. Dined (Tom and I) at Bryan's. Bryan himself confined to his room with gout, and Madame (who was very kind) our only companion at dinner—Tom off to the Theatre while I remained with Bryan— Promised Lord Tankerville to-day to dine with him, to meet the Sutherlands, tomorrow—Had called in the course of the day at Lord Essex's, and found him in rather low spirits—cried, in talking of his daughter, and said how desolate he found himself without her. Went with Hume to-day (Tom and I) to lunch at his friends' the Gossets

2 [Friday]—Called upon Rogers—Showed me a gratifying letter he had received from a poor *litterateur* who has written some successful things under the name of "the Basket-Maker," his original occupation[1]—With much simplicity he informs Rogers of the comfortable station he has attained by his writings and attributes all his success to the timely donation of two guineas which he had received from Rogers, and which coming as it did, when he was on the very brink of destitution gave a prosperous turn to him in his destiny which has ever since continued. Went to the Charter House & saw dear Russell. Dined at Lord Tankerville's—Company, Duchess of Sutherland, Lord Ossulston, Ponsonby, the Dawson Damers & Sir Robert Gordon, (Lord Aberdeen's brother)—several of the intended guests, the Duke of Sutherland, Lord Lansdowne and others, detained by the Debate in the House of Lords. The Duchess of S. said to me very graciously on our meeting, "I had expected that I should be one of the first that would see you." Called me also to sit beside her at dinner, and was not only agreeable (which so handsome a person could hardly fail to be) but also clever.—The D. of Sutherland, Pozzo di Borgo and some others in the evening.

3 [Saturday]—To the Charter House with Tom, to try and get Russell out for the day, but did not succeed, this not being his turn. Saunders consented, however, as a favour, to let him come to me tomorrow morning— Abundance of tickets for the Theatres provided for Tom by my friend of the Globe, Mr. Moran—Has also invited Tom & his friend Clifford (son of Sir Augustus) to dine with him to-day previous to the Play. Promised that I

would join the party, as a non-eater, being engaged to dine with Lord Essex—Did so—such an affair as it was! Mrs. M. above all—got away in a Cab at ½ past six and was with Lord Essex in time—Only two or three of his regular diners, but as usual, quiet & comfortable—Called by the bye this morning on Lord John Russell, and saw him & Lady John—asked me to dine with him tomorrow, to meet "a family party," which I promised to do.

4 [Sunday]—Found a letter at Brookes's from Lord Churchill, saying as follows—"Having mentioned your name to his R. Highness (D. of Sussex) he now commands me to invite you to dinner this evening at 7 o'clock should you not be previously engaged. Stephenson will bring you out & carry you home." Wrote to say that I had already engaged myself to Lord John Russell, and prayed to be excused &c. &c. After breakfast took my little Russell who was with us at nine o'clock to hear the Military Band at St. James's—after which I took him to see Rogers who was very kind to him and then consigned him to Moran, Tom & Clifford for a trip to Richmond or Greenwich while I set about paying visits—Went out to Little Holland House to call upon Miss Fox, who has been by no means well—sate some time with her—from thence to leave my name at the Duchess of Kent's and to call upon the Duke of Sussex, by whom I was admitted—A most good-humoured man, but certainly the most prosy even of Princes. One whole hour by the Palace Clock did he keep me listening to him, while with little more than an interjection, now & then, on my part, he disserted on all imaginable subjects, beginning with Genesis and ending with the Reform Bill—His religious notions not altogether outworn but quite as unintelligible as if they were—with the exception only of his first leading principle—namely—"that a *finite* can be no judge of an *infinite* being."—He had some peculiar notion about the meaning of God's breathing into man's nostrils the breath of life, but what it was, I could not well make out, not being able to fix my attention on any of his points (or *pints,* as he calls them)—In speaking of Ireland went into long details of what he would do, if sent there as Lord Lieutenant which he seemed most earnestly to desire—would call the great Lords to account—would say to them "Here are large estates granted to you upon certain conditions, not one of which you have fulfilled &c.—" and would take measures to *compel* them to perform their part of the conditions—Among minor things we talked of Bessie Napier's marriage with Lord Arran, the only objection to which he said was the want of money between the parties—Had made several attempts to take my leave, but he still said good-naturedly that it was so seldom we met that he could not part with me so easily, and so, on I staid through the whole hour—Forgot to mention, under yesterday's date that I took Tom to General Macdonald, at the Horse Guards, who seemed much pleased with him and said he was a very promising "recruit." On my enquiring about Lord Hill's Levee he said

very kindly "It will be a better thing for him to be introduced to Lord Hill first privately, & if he will be here to-day at 3 o'clock, I will do it for him." We accordingly were there at that hour, and nothing could be more markedly kind, in his quiet way, than Lord Hill. Shook hands with Tom, and wished him every success, and when I thanked him for his kindness, said that it gave him great satisfaction to have been able to do any thing pleasing to *me*.—Dined to-day at Lord John's—company as he had already told me, an entirely *family* party consisting of Lord & Lady Tavistock, and the Listers—Delighted to see Lady Tavistock again. Talked of old times in Dublin when Lord Harrington was [*unrecovered*] there & Lord Tavistock was making love to her—Reminded her of the dinner and Dance at the Royal Hospital when Lancaster, the Quaker called for a Bible and Candles, and retired to a room by himself, during the dancing—His emergence from thence prematurely, on a false alarm of supper, and his entering the room just as Lady Anna Maria was dancing down the middle—Her looking gaily at him and saying "How did you like that last step of mine, Mr. Lancaster?" and his answering sulkily, being disappointed at the supper—"Young woman, it was a step of vanity." We then talked of the Private Plays, given also at the same time, at the Harringtons', when I could remember as well as if it was but yesterday, Lord Tavistock, who played Frederick, in "Of Age Tomorrow,"[1] frizzing away at Lady Anna Maria's hair—and likewise Lord John, speaking the Prologue (which had been written by himself) with his flat cocked hat under his arm. Gay times those, we all seemed to feel—and (as usual, in such remembrances) with a sigh.—I had asked Lady John to allow Tom (who dined at Sir Augustus Clifford's) to join us in the evening, which he did—Left pretty early and home—On my telling Lady John I had been asked for three different days to the Hollands', she said "Come the day *I* dine there"

5 [Monday]—My usual London cold come on, and no chance, I fear, in this most harsh weather, of getting rid of it.—Tom put on his regimentals for the first time, this morning, to let me see him in them, and looked, I must say, remarkably smart and soldier-like—Visits & Commissions—Dined at the Hollands'—Company, Lady John, Lord Russell, Luttrel, young Howard, & Baron Bulow—Lord H. not well enough to dine with us—called by my Lady to sit next her—A good deal of conversation about Canada, which brought out my own recollections of my journeyings & adventures there, and Lady H. (to whom it seemed quite *news* that I had ever been to America) catechized me not a little amusingly as to my route & doings while in that part of the world—mentioned my having been laid up for a few days at Buffalo, with a sprained ancle which I had got in walking through the woods, and that, at that time, this place (which is now, it appears, a beautiful city) was little more than an assemblage of wig-wams and huts—Sat talking,

for some time in the evening, with Lord Holland & Luttrell—our topic chiefly the poets that immediately preceded our own time—Lord Holland *rather* prosy and *law-giving* on the subject—poetry not being his forte either in theory or practice—Home & glad to get there, my cold being much worse.

6 [Tuesday]—Were to have breakfasted, Tom & I, with the Lansdownes (she having arrived yesterday) but put it off till tomorrow, and breakfasted in bed, instead, which I found myself all the better for—The moment, however, I emerged into the streets, the harshness of the air was really almost intolerable, and I found I must only cut & run as soon as I can.—Lady Lansdowne having kindly asked me to name something that Tom wants, (Lord L. being anxious to make him some useful present) I found on enquiry that strange to say, he has no wants whatever, every thing having been already provided for him; and how I have managed it all God only knows. Discovered, however, that he had just ordered a writing-case, and thinking it possible that I might be in time to countermand it went to the shop & represented the circumstances to the tradesman, who very civilly consented to annul the bargain—Acquainted Lady Lansdowne with this so that a writing-case is to be my Lord's gift to his god-son—In talking, by the bye, the other day to Lady Holland of my not having seen much of Rogers since I came, from my not liking to pester him with my son whom I had now constantly with me, she said, very comically, and but too truly, "You know *nobody* likes other people's children." On my mentioning this to Rogers to-day when I was sitting with him, he followed it up very characteristically, in his own way—"Yes—there have been several cases of *sons*, within my memory—*Hallam* had a son—poor Luttrell also has a son, and &c. &c." looking as only *he* can look, all the time. Was to have dined with the Hollands to-day, but on Rogers mentioning that Fonblanque (the Examiner) was coming to dine tete-a-tete with him, proposed sending an excuse to my Lady, if he would let me make a third at his dinner—Said "most willingly" & I accordingly pleaded illness (with but too much truth) in a note to my Lady. The following her answer—"I rely upon you on *Friday* next, as *you promised*. I cannot let you off. You were so very pleasant yesterday that 'L'appetit vient en mangeant.'[1] You miss a *very* pleasant party to-day."—Our trio at dinner very agreeable, but left little worth remembering—am rather inclined to agree with Luttrell, who said the other day, in speaking of Fonblanque in his *private* capacity (for his brilliancy as a writer no one can gainsay) "It is the fashion to call him agreeable—but I own to me he appears rather dry and unattractive" (or some such word.)—On my saying to Luttrell the other day that I rather believed the Duke of Sussex knew something of Hebrew, having arrived at it *per saltum*, without knowing any thing I rather thought either of Greek or of Latin—he said "I am sure it is, at all events, not Hebrew without *points* he deals in."}

7. [Wednesday]—{Breakfasted, Tom and I, with the Lansdownes—received some notes that had been sent for me to Bury St—one from the Duchess of Sutherland, fixing a morning (now passed) for me to bring Tom to see their gallery—Called there & found her & the Duke—explained the reason of my not attending to her kind note. Asked me to come to dinner on Saturday but unluckily already engaged—Proposed then Monday, but, if I stay so long, must dine with the Lansdownes on that day—The Duke showed me his new pictures, the Murillo from Soult, the French Portraits &c. &c. and on my taking leave of him said very kindly—"I trust you will be able to dine with us on Monday instead of at the Lansdownes'—they have so many opportunities of seeing you." From thence went to call on Lady Francis Egerton, whom I found at home reading Scott's last Volume— Asked me who was the Lady———, of whom Scott told in the anecdote, but I contrived to evade telling her—She too very kindly anxious for me to dine with them some day, and proposed Saturday—but in vain—Called upon Easthope to whom I had sent up from Sloperton, before I left home, a Squib on the subject of the Ballot, with which (as I think I have omitted to mention) he expressed himself highly delighted, but thought it better to defer its insertion till after he should have given his own vote for the Ballot[1]—found him most eager to enter into a new arrangement for occasional contributions from me, and ready to agree to any sum I should propose.—} Dined at Lord Essex's—Boldero and Co. as usual, with the agreeable addition, on this occasion, of Sir Robert Adair, from whom one gets, now and then, an agreeable *whiff* of the days of Fox, Tickell and Sheridan—told one or two things of that date, which I had known before, but which came from him with the stamp of the time upon them and were in so far, more interesting than even better *new* things. {—Got home as early as I could, my cold being most heavy and disabling—Have nearly made up my mind to leave Tom behind for the levee, and start myself for home on Saturday or Sunday—I shall be decided by Bessy's answer to my last letter—Forgot to mention that I called upon Lord Durham this morning and sate some time with Lady Durham before I was admitted to him— found her as nice & feminine as ever—a dreary prospect for *her* (however grand for *him*) to be whisked across the Atlantic with her five young children to Canada.[2]——Her account of Russia most comfortless—the cold being there always a *damp* cold (far different from what she will find in the bracing snows of Canada) and the society almost nothing—Talked a good deal with Durham himself about his office, the arduous responsibility of it &c. &c. Told me of the efforts he had made to avoid undertaking it—had told the Ministers that he would go down on his knees to them if they would assure him that "there was no other person to undertake it, in case he should refuse," and they assured him that such was the fact—that it must be either himself or nobody and upon this, he said, I gave in, but insisting on the fullest powers.—Met him afterwards in the street & introduced Tom to him, as not unlikely to see him in Canada.

8 [Thursday]—Breakfasted alone at Brookes's—Took Tom to see the Gallery at Stafford House and left a little note for the Duchess saying I should be unable to come to dinner on Monday.—Went with him to see his Cot, Arm Chair &c. &c. all very nice and reasonable—Took him to the Ordnance Office where I introduced him to Charles Fox, and asked Charles who I should get to present him. He suggested Sir Hussey, and sent in to his office for him but he was engaged with Lord Anglesey so Charles wrote to him on a scrap of paper that Moore wished either him or Lord Anglesey to present his son on Monday. In a few minutes Vivian came in, all in a hurry, but most kind & hearty, saying that he would have great pleasure in presenting my son—So *that* was agreeably settled.—Dined, Tom and I, at Milman's, a rather inaccessible, but very pretty house in the Cloisters, Westminster—Company, Babbage, Murchison, Hayward & Otway. Talking of Bowring Milman said "I like Bowring's books because I know they are not his own." The day agreeable—Liked Murchison *better* than I had done before and Hayward much *worse*. Home early—

9 [Friday]—Breakfasted at home, and Lord Clifford, Tom's friend to join us—Hume, too, in consequence of a note I had written to him, came early—Called upon Stanley at the Treasury (having first paid a visit to Mrs. Stanley at their house & sat some time with her) Waited a good while for him, being anxious to get him to remove Edward Hughes from his present situation (a land-writer) at Liverpool to a similar post in London—this being the great wish of Edward himself & his father & mother—Had spoken to Stanley already about it, when he spoke as if the thing was feasible—On my mentioning it now, he made instant inquiries of the Clerk to whom he had given my memorandum of the request, and after a little consideration, said promptly & kindly "it shall be done"—Went and took the double good news of my having achieved the job for the Hughes's and my being booked for home on Sunday. Called this morning at Lord Shrewsbury's to answer a card of invitation I had received from them to dine on Sunday—they having sent yesterday to ask for my answer—Forget whether I have mentioned that at the beginning of the week I called upon Lord Shrewsbury, found him at home and sate for a little while—Told me of poor Dr. Lingard having been quite reduced lately in his circumstances by some pecuniary misfortune—found my Lord & his sister now, who expressed regret that I could not come on Sunday—Am leaving my dinners all at sixes and sevens—Got this morning the following note from Lord Lansdowne, accompanying Tom's present which is quite perfection for neatness and fitting up—and among the articles in it what I could swear to be Lady L's peculiar doing—some Account Books.—Lord L's note is as follows—"My dear Moore—I can hardly believe, as Lady L. tells me, that you mean to be off before morning—Will you not relent & dine here and bring Tom with you? I am glad for his sake, he has so few wants, *alias*

encumbrances, tho I wish I could have provided a smarter present for a young officer."—Dined at Lord Holland's—Company, Wood & Lady Mary, C. Buller, Ellice, and one or two more. My Lady again very graciously called me to sit beside her—Saw that she was doing the *aimable* most markedly to Buller, and on my noticing this, she confessed that she was trying to bring him over (i.e. from the Rads) and had little doubt, as she said, of succeeding—Talking of Lord Russell I expressed my regret and wonder at the sort of non-entity he was, to all practical intents & purposes, whatever those who know him intimately may see or *fancy* they see in him. She confessed it was very much to be lamented—said that he really *had* a good deal in him but intimated that the distinction of his life (as it appears to be) [*several words unrecovered*] his habits with women—that from morning till night it is his constant and sole pursuit. This was probably a creation (or at least exaggeration) from the mint of my Lady's own inventive brain.[1]— Came away early—Have had an invitation from the Dawson Damers for next week, which is one of those I should have liked to accept, George being an old "cumrogue" of mine. Got a note, too, this evening from Mrs. Holland (Sydney's daughter) which as a summons to their family party, was *particularly* tempting. "Should you," she says "by any account be disengaged tomorrow evening, will you come and meet my father (who is just arrived) at dinner here."}

10 [Saturday]—{Breakfasted, Tom and I, at Rogers's—Luttrell having the other day complained to me that Rogers seemed entirely out of humour with him; though he could not conceive from what cause, begged me to propose our breakfasting together at Sam's some morning—which I did, and he was now of the party. R. cross a little, but more to me, I think, than to L.—In talking of Lady Holland's worship of worldly success, Luttrell said "You may always judge how you stand in the world by her reception of you"—"Then," I said, "judging by that index, I suppose I ought to be pretty well satisfied with myself for she called me up to sit by her both these last days I dined there." Perhaps it was this speech of mine that vexed R.— there's no knowing. He was, however, full of kindness afterwards.} Talked of Irishmen's unwillingness to pay ready money (their notions of the *ready* being always a Bill at sixty one days' date—Somebody saying that one would think every Irishman was born sixty-one days too late, from there being always that space of time behind the rest of the world ! And Luttrell described the process of purchasing a horse between one Irish gentleman & another—"Price sixty pounds, for which you have no occasion to pay down cash—only commit *your thoughts to paper*." {Finished up some of Tom's business and got ready for flight tomorrow—Dined, Tom and I, at Murray's—Company James Smith, Captain Bach, and one or two others— Meant to have remembered some of Smith's *remembered* jokes (for his are seldom impromptus) but was too much stupefied with cold to be a good

recipient of bon-mots—Got home as early as I could. Forgot to mention Luttrell's story of an old General (or Count) Rambouillet saying to his young wife "On pourroit recommencer, ma chère, mais ça seroit toujours la même chose"

11 [Sunday]—Started in the Emerald at eight—the coach contrary to my expectation (of a Tuesday) quite full inside—My companions, after some time made out to be Linley, the great violincelloist (whom I had often in former times heard play, but had no recollection of his appearance) and a Miss Birch (a new Concert singer) and her brother all going down to Bath for a Concert of Loder's to be given tomorrow evening—Much amused with old Linley—his accounts of different noble pupils of his, Lord Barrymore & his brother, the Duke of Leicester &c. &c. Mentioned the generosity of the Duke (a quality I believe now generally allowed to him) his always giving Linley fifty pounds for the few lessons he takes of him when in London—Linley's fondness for good cheer, his going alone to eat whitebait &c. &c. This coupled with his advice to Miss Birch and her brother "not to dine on the road, but to save their money" all very amusing—Having passed Newbury (the place where usually my *incognito* is dispelled, as the waiters there generally tell my companions who I am) and seeing that I was still undiscovered I said as we passed over the Downs to Devizes, "Well, as I have come to the knowledge of who *you* are, it is but fair you should know also who *I* am & I shall tell you before we separate." It was plain that this speech did not make any great impression upon them & that if I had left them still in the dark they would not have much cared about it, but when having begun my revelation, I said "You have heard I dare say of Moore—usually called Tom Moore"—and then added "I am that person," I certainly have seldom seen people thrown into a state of more smiling wonder—We were luckily then near Devizes and little else than ejaculations passed in the interval—"Well, to be sure! &c. &c." and the young lady exclaiming "Never can I forget this journey &c."—Took a Fly from Devizes—found my darling Bessy looking—as she has looked for too long a time—wretchedly ill.

12, 13, 14, &c. [Monday–Wednesday]—From various causes (some of them most trying and painful) I have not entered any records for more than a month in these pages. But being now, thank God, in a great measure relieved from my anxieties I shall endeavour to note down some of the circumstances that have occurred in that interval.

15 [Thursday]—Tom arrived from town, having attended the Levee the day before—

16, 17, &c [Friday–Saturday]—Had intended to defer Tom's sailing from Bristol (his regiment being at Cork) till Saturday 24th, which we thought would give him time enough to reach Cork by the 28th. the day on which his leave expires—But taking into consideration the uncertainty of the days of sailing and of the weather, resolved to let him go by the first packet next week—Bessy accordingly set about all the preparations with her utmost speed, and worked more than her strength could bear to have all things ready—

19 [Monday]—Though confined to the house by my town cold ever since I returned set off with Tom in a Fly for Bristol—On arriving at Bath, drove to Crawford's—promised if possible to join Crawford at dinner with Lord Camperdown on the following day—Went on to Bristol to our very kind friends the Saunders's with whom we had been in communication on the subject of the Packets, and who asked us to their house—None but themselves and Mrs. Saunders's sister at dinner—Evening very quiet and comfortable—

20 [Tuesday]—Found even more uncertainty as to the sailing of the packets than I had expected—the weather now most unfavourable, and owing to the delay of the packets from the other side, that which was to sail to-day from Bristol would not start till tomorrow—Resolved accordingly as Tom was in such good hands, to leave him and return to Bath—Dined at Lord Camperdown's—Company, Captain Duff (a great friend of the Villamils) Henry Hobhouse, and four or five more—among others, a pretty girl who sung to the Piano-forte in the evening, and, among other things, sung my words "They tell me thou'rt the favoured guest."[1] My cold too bad to admit of my singing a note. Slept at Crawford's.

21 [Wednesday]—Started for home between 11 & 12.—Read on the way a small volume of verse, by Savage Landor, chiefly on Satire and Satirists, in which he speaks very laudatorily of my humble attempts in that line—Talks of the "easy" power with which I hit my mark[1]—Intended to have copied out the line here, but cannot find the book.

22, 23 [Thursday–Friday]—On the latter day a most kind letter from Mrs. Saunders telling all the particulars of Tom's departure, and speaking in most cordial terms of himself—"What a good fellow he is!" is one of her phrases. The weather had moderated a good deal, and all looked most promising she said, for his passage.

24, 25, 26 &c [Saturday–Monday]—The weather had again become very stormy, and some accounts in the Spectator of a frightful snow-storm along the Southern Coast of Ireland on Thursday night (*last* Thursday, as I fancied—just when Tom would be approaching it) threw me into a most distressing state of alarm which continued through the

26, 27 [Monday–Tuesday][1]—during all which time there was still no account from him—My sweet Bess, though evidently full of alarm herself, saying & doing every thing in her power to calm my apprehensions—wrote to Mrs. Saunders, & sent to make enquiries in Devizes &c. while the accounts of storm & wrecks every day were quite frightful. The only consideration that gave me any comfort was the state of the roads in Ireland, which, as I saw by a statement of Lord Morpeth's in the House of Commons, prevented even his official letters from reaching him—

28 [Wednesday]—A letter, to our great relief, from Tom, written on the evening of his arrival at Cork (the day after he sailed) but delayed on its way, as we conjectured, by the state of the roads. So far from any misfortune, his passage had been so quiet and prosperous that he had not even felt sickness till near shore, and the gale that has done so much harm since did not come on till after his arrival—another kind letter from Mrs. Saunders—}

March {1st [Thursday]

4 [Sunday]—Just as we were preparing to go down to dinner my darling Bessy, who had walked to Church and back again was seized suddenly with a fit of vomiting which, at once, filled nearly a large basin, and she had but time to say to me "blood, blood," and then "Russell," when she fell apparently almost lifeless and it was with difficulty that, with the help of the maids, I could get off her clothes and place her in bed—I then instantly ran to Webbe and sent him off on horseback for Brabant, while I dispatched George (lest Brabant should be absent) to Melksham for Mr. Kenrick—Never shall I forget what I felt, for I really thought she was dying, and so as I found afterwards she thought herself from seeing that it was blood and her effort to say "Russell" was from the wish to have him sent for—In a remarkably short time Brabant arrived, and by his advice we dispatched Webb off to Bowood for ice which he ordered us to give her continually and cheered me by the hope that if there was no return of the vomiting, the

attack would not prove serious—one great point appearing certain that the blood was from the stomach, not from the lungs. Kenrick had arrived before Brabant but did not see her. Webb returned quickly with the ice, which the gardener had gone in a boat for to some part of the lake, and it was given to my darling Bess throughout the night.}

5 [Monday]—Brabant with us early (and Kenrick also whom he had thought it right to ask to meet him but who did not see her) and though he gave his opinion with a degree of reserve & caution which in itself was like a dagger to me I was but too happy to collect from him that if there was no return of the haemorrhage no danger need be apprehended—My dearest Bessy herself has preserved, throughout all our alarm, the same collected-ness & sweetness of feeling which she has shown on every trying occasion since I first knew her—thinking of every body *but* herself.

6, 7, 8, &c. &c. [Tuesday–Thursday]—Thank God, all has been going on well & will, I trust in God, continue so. On the morning after her attack Bessy mentioned a pretty story translated by Miss Fisher from the German of an old Man who received Three Calls or Warnings before his death. "I look upon this" she added calmly "as my *first*." But thank God, again and again, the danger now seems past.

9, 10, 11, &c. &c. [Friday–Sunday]—Between my continual and anxious watching of my dear Bessy's progress (for such I flatter myself it is) and my efforts to work, for which I have now more than usual need, from my late expenditure both in time and money, I have not had a moment to give to these pages. {There has, however, but little worthy of record occurred.} In default of other matter I shall here transcribe from a late publication (or rather re-re-publication of Bowles's) a note respecting myself, which in his usual good-natured sensitiveness he has thought it necessary to insert. What the passage about "the Sorcerer Poet" was to which he refers I have not the slightest notion.

"*Sorcerer Poet.*—I trust it will not be thought necessary by one human being for me to disclaim any, the most distant allusion to one consummate master of song, who if in the unthinking gaiety of premature Genius, he joined the Syrens, has made ample amends by a life of the strictest virtuous propriety, equally exemplary as the husband, the father and the man; and, as far as the Muse is concerned, more than ample amends by melodies as sweet as scriptural and sacred, and by weaving a tale indeed of the richest oriental colours, which faithful affection & pity's tear have consecrated to all ages."

12, 13, 14 &c. [Monday, 12 March–Saturday, 31 March]—Nothing much different to add on the subject that now occupies all my cares & thoughts— my dearest Bessy's health. The prospect of losing the advantage of Brabant's attendance by his approaching departure for the Continent gives me a great deal of uneasiness, though *he* looks upon her as past all danger now, and means to leave written instruction for her how to act in case any change should occur. Went to dine one of these days with the Hughes's at Devizes, who were anxious to have me meet their Member, Dundas,—returned home at night. Nothing could be more gratifying than the anxiety manifested in all quarters, both high and low, about poor Bessy's health—every two or three days a messenger comes from Bowood, with a supply of ice, vegetables & such other things as it is known Bessy has been ordered to take.

April 1, 2, 3 &c [Sunday–Tuesday]—Still the same course of life, watching over my dear Bessy's progress, slow, but I trust sure—and working, in the intervals at my History. Sent a squib one of these days to the Chronicle "Sketch of the First Act of a New Romantic Drama,"[1] which Easthope in a note I had from him, told me was very much admired. In the same note he added (what I had suspected myself & mentioned to him) that my former Squib on the Ballot "The Song of the Box," had not produced much effect—{I mean, if I can, to complete about half a dozen of these things for the Chronicle, in order to get a little money, which I sadly want, my late *Military* exertion having made me like these heroes Ossian must mean, when he says "Some of my heroes are *low*"—i.e. in *cash*.} Found, one of these mornings some memorandums of my own in penciling so very nearly effaced I think I had better copy out whatever is worth preserving of them here. They relate, I see, chiefly to Petrarch and must have been collected, I think, for a comparison between him and Catullus which I took as one of my subjects while writing for the Metropolitan, but made little use of, I believe, in the hasty sketch I gave to that Periodical.[2]—{"Propertius's mistress, who was a married woman, ran off with a soldier—elle va suivre les camps"—returns to him, for which "il remercie Apollon et les Muses." The husband of Ovid's Corinna ceases to be jealous of her "cela déplait à l'amant, qui le menace de quibus sa femme s'il ne reprend pas sa jalousie."—Tibullus *shows up* his mistress Delia to her husband & tells him of her tricks and "si ce mari ne suit pas la garder il la lui confie." All these ladies appear to have been topers.—} The Cynthia of Propertius was accomplished, & a poetess[3]—Petrarch's triflings about the *Laurel*—For Laura's coquetry, see Sonet. 31, 39, 40, 41—Canzon. 15 & particularly Sonet. 43, where he describes himself as baffled when just within reach of his object—"Tra la speza a la man quel muro è messo"—See Sonet. 50, where she complains that he was tired of loving her, at the end of ten years—the pretty scene in Sonett. 207, the old man giving the two roses— the beautiful picture in Sonett. 189 Dodici donne—Her pretty action in Sonett. 219, in putting her hand before his eyes when she sees him in a reverie gazing at her—The three celebrated Canzoni which he himself called the Three Sisters 18, 19 & 20—The Canzoni *after* her death allowed to have more truth & nature in them than those *before.* Levommi il mio pensiero Sonet. 261—See this for her veil which she says she had left on earth—See for his trifling decomposition of the name of Laura, or Laureta into three parts—Sonett. 5—In his Dialogues de Contemptu Mundi he says "Scio autem quid hîc mihi solatii est quod illa mecum senescit."—The Eveque de Lombez wrote to Petrarch rallyingly that all his love for Laura was a mere fiction—"De hâc autem spirante Laurea cujus forma captus videor, manufacta est, et omnia ficta carmina, ficta suspiria"—see Academie des Inscrip. Tom 15[4]—{An Italian author of the 15th Centy. (Sonarzafichi) accused Benedict 12th of having been in love with Petrarch's sister, and having tried to persuade the brother "à favoriser sa passion." Petrarch's father threw all his son's Belles-Lettres books into the fire to force him to study the law—but on seeing him so unhappy, snatched out of the flames again Virgil and the Rhetoric of Cicero.}[5]

4, 5, 6, &c. &c. [Wednesday–Friday]—Agreeable accounts from Tom from Ireland—his regiment ordered to Dublin, which will be very delightful to Ellen & make a great difference, in point of society, to himself—Received one of these days the following note from Spring Rice, relative to the Pension List Committee

"My dear Moore—Though you could not have anticipated any other result, still as Committees are strange and unaccountable bodies, I think it may be agreeable to you to know that your case came on yesterday, and was by acclamation confirmed. I think the Committee would have increased the grant had it been in their power to do so—Always my dear Moore, very sincerely & faithfully yrs. T. S. Rice."[1]

{7, 8, 9 &c. [Saturday–Monday]—Have found the Poem of Savage Landor which Crawford lent me, entitled "A Satire on Satirists," and shall here extract what he says of myself, in that capacity.

> No, rather see, while Satyrs dance around,
> Yon little man with vine and ivy crowned,
> Raising his easy arm, secure to hit
> The scope of pleasure with the shafts of wit.

He adds, in a note "Nothing can be lighter or pleasanter or more brilliant."[1] Crawford has promised to introduce me to Landor, whom I have never yet even seen.

11, 12, 13 &c. &c. [Wednesday, 11 April–Monday, 30 April]—Tom all life and gaiety in Dublin—laughing away with his merry little Aunt, dining with the Commander in Chief (a rare honour, I find, for a younker) going with Drummond and his lady to the opera and then supping with the Lord Lieutenant afterwards. The regiment is to be moved, however, to Belfast, which I am not sorry for (nor, he himself, I am glad to find) as all this racketting must interfere sadly with his probationary discipline.—Received, one of these days, an extraordinary letter, inclosing a still more extraordinary poem, from some man at Bristol, signing himself Henry Johnson & asking me to give him five pounds to pay his next quarter's bill for board & lodging. In the course of his letter he says—"You are, so I am credibly informed, Sir, appointed by the Mrssrs. Longman of London to judge upon the demerits of a literary production. I am, with humility do I say it, prevailed upon to appear in lowly garment of thought, as well becomes me, before those gifted publishers &c. &c. &c."}

May 1, 2, 3 &c. {[Tuesday–Thursday]—Still at home and at work, as much as the every day distractions—more especially the answering of eternal letters—will allow me—Sent another squib lately to the Chronicle "Epistle from Henry of Exeter to John of Tuam"[1] which the Examiner and the Dublin Evening Post copied—} Received a letter from Haydon the Painter, written, it appears, a year since, but mislaid, and only just now as he tells me, found again, containing an account of three letters relating to Sheridan which had been brought for his inspection—{The following is his account of them. "One from Sheridan's father to Charles, the eldest son, then at Stockholm, and two from R. Brinsley when he & Mr. Fox were out the first time—The father's letter dated Bath 1772 is authentic, as they are all, and contain some very curious particulars which certainly ought not to be lost though as the letters came to this gentlemen, with some books, without the knowledge of the parties, at present he is unwilling, till authorised, to let them be known. I mentioned to him his duty, when he is so, to communicate them to *you*. Old Sheridan's letter is an admirable one, and complains bitterly of Dick—as he calls him—his "sad son, without an atom of principle, utterly reckless of truth, and playing all sorts of abominable deceptions"—He describes to Charles the whole duel with Mathews,[2] which he says he had from the Postilion & the Second—that the ground was uneven, and Dick tripped & fell, and it was evident to all the party present, *the Duel was not fought in a room*—if old Sheridan be correct—(this is what I urged particularly should be sent to you.)—He then goes on complaining of Dick's marrying a strumpet—"for I leave you" he says "to judge if Dick could be content for three months alone with a woman only ogling & sighing." These are the very words. He alludes to some transaction about a gun which Charles had given him to keep for his sake—but Dick had borrowed money on it, and then told the landlady when the gun was sent for, to say "Charles had taken it with him."—This is all of Haydon's letter that is worth transcribing—} Wrote to thank him, saying that any communication from his hand was better late than never—that I had written so much and of such various subjects since Sheridan was my topic that I had now almost forgotten all about him—adding that what one poet has said of the waves of the sea

> And one no sooner kiss'd the shore, and died
> Than a new follower rose,—

was but too applicable to the multifarious succession of my works,—the "dying," I feared, included.—Apropos of Sheridan, I see by an extract from the Diary of Wilberforce just published that he says I over-rate Sheridan's powers as a wit.[3] This may be so—but I think it rather more likely that Wilberforce *under*-rated them. My opinion was derived not so much from my own knowledge of Sheridan, for he was gone off when I knew him, but from the indestructible proofs of his wit in the School for Scandal and the Critic, and the unanimous tribute paid to it by all his own personal friends.—{Received a letter from a gentleman in Ireland, who signs himself Joseph Huband Smith, and lives at Aughnacloy, sending me a Legend he has founded upon Irish History, and speaking thus kindly of the share I have had in his inspirations

"Sir—As many hints for the inclosed attempt at versifying an ancient legend of our country have been taken from your admirable Dissertation on the pagan state of Ireland,[4] it seems to be best a tribute of justice to lay this trifle at your feet. I hoped to have found an ancestor in the monarch whose fate it records, as he appears to have had his chief residence in the district known as the territory of the Kinel—Farray (as it is commonly pronounced) the posterity of Fiacha Araidhe, from which I, as an OGowan, claim descent. There can be little doubt, however, that he is the same with Laoguire, whom I find to be of the family of Heremon; while the OGowans, as perhaps you are aware, in common with most of the Ulster families, derive their origin from his younger brother, Jr.—I have a gratification also in seizing an opportunity of offering to the great poet and historian of my native country this testimony, however inconsiderable, of the warmest & sincerest admiration of his most obedient &c. &c."}

Sent another Squib, one of these days, to the Morning Chronicle, in reference to the Copy-right Question, entitled "Great Dinner of Type &

Co.—a Poor poet's dream." which has been copied I see into the Athenaeum and placed side by side with the letter of Wordsworth & the famous one of Southey's to Brougham, as our joint protests against the present state of Copyright.[5] To my squib they merely annex asterisks, saying that it requires no signature—Have fixed my projected visit to town for the 17th.—Wrote to Lady Elisabeth (who was so kind when we last met as to offer me lodging at Sackville St.) asking whether she is still in the same mind, and received the following answer—"Only a moment to say I shall be *so* pleased to have you in *casa* mia—I am not such a capricieuse as to have changed my mind since I saw you at Sloperton, and Mrs. Moore looking so well and handsome in her reclining attitude in the fauteuil. Who is Mr. Calvert who talks in such raptures about you? It was agreeable to read his enthusiastic opinions in these prosaic and utilitarian days—Love to Bessie."—{Mr. Calvert is quite new to me, never having heard of him or his praises before—must enquire about it.}

5, 6, 7, 8, &c. [Saturday, 5 May–Sunday, 13 May]—On my explaining to Bessy, at breakfast one of these mornings the nature of the retrospective clause in the intended Copy-right Bill (which I had but just come to understand, myself, not having troubled my head much with the question) she exclaimed, with the directness of aim at the true and the just which, in her, is innate, "Why, that's not honest." Having to write to the Longmans, the same day, I mentioned this circumstance just as I have here stated it, adding "as for me, I, of course, shook my head and said nothing, being an author."

{14, 15 [Monday–Tuesday]—Wrote to Bath, as usual, to bespeak a place in the White Hart for Thursday morning—took for granted, not receiving any answer, that my place was secured.

17 [Thursday]—Left home in a Fly at eight—but found, on the arrival of the White Hart that all inside was full—waited for the Emerald—all full likewise—so took the Star Coach to Reading, hoping the Emerald might drop some of its company on the way—A nice old couple, man & wife, residents of Bath, my companions in the Star—never saw a heartier or happier pair, and we got on most sociably together. The old Lady paid me the compliment of saying she "was sure I was a very good sort of man"; and then, appealing to her husband, asked him "*isn't* he the very picture of good health and good temper?"—Told her I should report this compliment at home—both were wholly ignorant who I was. On our arrival at Reading, found that the Emerald still continued full, and was obliged to remain

there for the night—Had a bad dinner, and worse bed-room, a squalling child being my neighbour, and but a thin partition between us—

18 [Friday]—Started in a Reading Coach for town—and went by a road, new to me, through Windsor Forest—the day very bright and the glimpses we caught of the Castle magnificent—took up a pretty, smart girl before we entered the Forest, who did the honours of the scenery very agreeably— Had written to Lady Elisabeth from Reading to account for my delay— arrived in London at two—found Talbot in Sackville St. where I dined with him, Lady Elisabeth & Horatia, and accompanied Talbot in the evening to the Royal Institution to hear a most interesting lecture of Faraday's— Learned to my mortification that there had been a grand Dress Party at Lansdowne House last night—just the very thing a gentleman from the country would wish to have ready for him on his arrival, and which I lost by the stupid mistake about my place. Had I had the least notion of it I should have put on an additional pound (for it cost me nearly that sum staying at Reading) and posted to town—poor Lady Lansdowne herself had been too much exhausted by the fatigue of the drawing-room in the morning to be able to receive her company, and was forced to retire early.}

19 [Saturday]—Breakfasted with Rogers to meet Ratcliffe and Young the actor—Story of the lady who wrote to Tallyrand informing him, in high-flown terms of grief of the death of her husband, & expecting an eloquent letter of condolence in return—his answer only "Hélas, Madame! votre affectioné &c. Talleyrand"—In less than a year after another from the same lady informed him of her having married again, to which he returned an answer in the same laconic style "Oh ho, Madame!—votre affectioné &c. Talleyrand." {Young's tragic mode of murdering some "very comical" stories which he told us—the grinding emphasis he gave to the joke, quite painful. In one or two instances, Rogers very adroitly told the story over again, giving it as a "new reading" of the anecdote, and putting the point and emphasis where they ought to be. One of the murdered stories was that of a foolish fellow (I forget now who it was) describing to Frere his difficulties in travelling through Spain. "On arriving" said he, "at Manganares, I with great difficulty got a mule." "Was the mare pretty?" asked Frere quietly.} In talking of Office, and its routine business a great deal of which does itself, Rogers mentioned Lord North's illustration of this fact by a sign at Charing Cross of a black man turning a wheel—"People stare at this" said Lord North "thinking that the black man turns the wheel, whereas it is the wheel that turns the black man." {Was asked to dine at Lord Camperdown's to-day, to meet the Duchesse de Cogni, but being anxious to hear Persiani sing, told him that if he would take me conditionally, I would come in case I

could not get a Stall ticket—to this he good-naturedly assented, and not having succeeded in getting the ticket, I told him at Brookes's to-day that I would dine with him—Company only the Duchesse, Lord Duncan & Elwyn, and the day very hospitable & agreeable—saw some of the presents for Duncan's intended bride Miss Philips—Home early. The Duchesse de Cogni rather a nice person.}

20 [Sunday]—{A note from Lord Lansdowne asking me to dine with him on Wednesday.} Went to breakfast with Lord John—found him alone. Longman had called upon him, he told me, on the subject of the Copyright Bill, and had shown him my letter, the whole of which Lord John had read—so much for private correspondence with one's *publisher.* {Told me of his disappointment the day before—having refused a dinner at the Duke of Devonshire's in order to meet the Duke of Sussex at Lord Shrewsbury's, and finding on his arrival at the latter's door, that the dinner had been put off, so had to retire and & betake himself to his solitary cutlet at home. The nation, however, I suppose, profited by it, as he added that he was not sorry, after the first shock, to have the evening for business.—} In the course of our conversation he referred to my praise of the aristocracy at the Bristol dinner, and said he had often since thought of my courage in venturing it—spoke of the tendency of the world now to *Americanize* in every thing—in the forms of government, in literature, in the tone of society &c.— {a "base declension" that; but} the remark I fear but too just. Talked of Bulwer's Athens,[1] and said he found it interesting—Apropos of Americanizing, I remarked what an instance Athens was of the fact that it is *the few* who have hitherto taught and given the tone to the world—what a light surrounds that small spot still! It is the οι πολλοι that will again reduce the world to barbarism. Asked me to come to dinner next Sunday & said he would be glad to have me also on Saturday {but supposed I would not much care to meet a large party of Members of Parliament.} Had in the children for me to see, and showed off all their little ways as nicely as any mother could do. It is indeed charming to see so much gentleness of nature combined with a spirit so manly & determined as is certainly "Johnny's." Talking of Sydney's last letter, which is making such a noise, I said that I had as yet read only the memorable note, but had heard that after having, in that note, glorified him (Lord John) at the expence of all his colleagues, Sydney had, at the end, thrown him overboard as well as the rest—"{God,} he *has,*" answered Lord John, in his quiet way, rubbing the back of his head. He was however animated & earnest in condemning the manner in which Sydney had treated Lord Melbourne, "*affecting*" as he said "to under-rate Melbourne."[2]—{After leaving him made several calls—found the Shrewsburys at luncheon, and joined them at it—Told Lady Mary of her having been denounced by the Age newspaper that morning as one of the for-

midable Papists that were gathering round the throne—had a good deal of laughing about this, Lady Mary being one of the Queen's train-bearers—Called upon Lady Charlemont,—the first time I have seen her for a long while—and sate some time with her—still looking very handsome—found her full of admiration of the Queen and, *next* to the Queen, of Lady Lansdowne, whose adroitness and presence of mind in all the little difficulties that occur to the Ladies in Waiting—the management of the train, the settling of the folds of the robe &c. &c.—she lauded in a way that opened to me a new & unexpected feature of Lady Lansdowne's merits. Her loss, she said, if she were to resign, would be irretrievable. Have since learned that this great admiration of Lady L's expertness as a waiting-woman is to be set down rather to Lady Cs. own utter incapacity in that way than to any surpassing adroitness of Lady L.—Called on Mrs. Shelley, who told me, in speaking of Bessy's illness, that vomiting of blood had been a very common complaint (and without any serious consequences) during this late harsh weather. Returned home & drove out with Lady Elizabeth & Horatia—called at Lansdowne House, and saw Lord Lansdowne—not looking at all well—from thence to Lord Valletort who has been for a long time confined with illness—found him lying in a water-bed, and looking very ill—sate some time with him—Dined at Miss Rogers's—company, Lord & Lady Holland & Allen—Lord Lansdowne, Stevenson, the American minister, and his lady, Milnes, Rogers's nephew, Sydney Smith, and somebody else.—In the course of conversation after dinner, the Copy-right Bill being one of our topics, I mentioned the circumstances of my letter to the Longmans, as above stated, and instantly the whole table was divided on the point, the great majority (particularly Allen, Milnes & Lord Holland, who I found were great sticklers for the new Bill) being all against my view of the case, but, Lord Lansdowne and Sydney Smith, I was glad to see, entirely with me, and thinking the determination I had formed to be the just and honest one. On being introduced, before dinner to the American Minister, he said that he had seen me once before, so long back as when I was in America (no less than 34 years since) and, mirabile dictu, that he would have recognized me again any where. Came away with Sydney Smith, whose carriage left me at Brookes's—The American said to-day that the appearance of a new novel of Bulwer's "makes always an Era" in America.

21 [Monday]—Breakfast at Brookes's and went afterwards to the British Museum—Found the books that remained to be consulted by me, (at least in the present stage of my task) far less numerous than I had supposed, which was no small relief—The pamphlets relating to the reigns of the Charles's seem the most abundant part of the materials here.—Called at Shee's—Sir Martin out—saw my Lady & the two Misses—Paid some other visits—Dined at Bryan's, by my own invitation—the George Bryans &

children there—Mrs. Bryan's delight at the splendour of Lansdowne House, the other night, where she went, through the mediation, I take for granted, of Lady Shrewsbury. Bryan *"wouldn't go—certainly* not, to people he didn't visit." Has not been at Brookes's yet, though a Member for several months past—the waiters, he fears, would not know who he was—offered my humble escort some morning, to get him over the difficulty, which he was pleased to accept—A good fellow, but odd, and fractious, like one or two others of my dear friends.}

22 [Tuesday]—Breakfasted at Milnes's (son of the man called Single-Speech Milnes) and met rather a remarkable party consisting of Savage Landor & Carlyle (neither of whom I had ever seen before) Crabb Robinson, Rogers, and Rio. A good deal of conversation between Robinson & Carlisle about German authors of whom I knew nothing nor (from what they paraded of them) felt that I had lost much by my ignorance—Robinson had witnessed the performance of Schiller's Bride of Messina[1] with the ancient Chorus, but I forget now what he said as to its effects. Savage Landor a very different sort of person from what I had expected to find him—{the few things I have read of his having prepared me to expect somewhat of a stilted coxcomb, instead of which} I find in him all the air and laugh of a hearty country-gentleman, a *gros rejoui,* and whereas his writings had given me rather a disrelish to the man, I shall take now more readily to his writings from having seen the man. {Told a good story of the present Lord Londonderry having once at Vienna indulged himself in the unmanly liberty of pinching the derriere of a young lady who stood before him in a crowded assembly. Indignant at this insult she mentioned it immediately to the old Prince de Ligne, who, going up to Londonderry, said to him in a sort of confidential tone, "Une autre fois, milord, quand l'envie vous prend de pincer une derriere, *voici la mienne,*" turning the part round to him at the same time contemptuously. Talking of Sir W. Scott's prose style, Rogers pronounced it, as usual, to be very bad, an opinion which Landor followed up by saying "I always thought Scott's the worst possible prose style till I read Bulwer."—A volume of Blake's (the lunatic poet & designer) produced, full of most marvellous things—the fancies in the poems being often as striking & beautiful as the designs are many of them graceful & Stodhart-like.—Had reserved myself to to-night's Opera, and having got a Stall-ticket, and a dinner with Moore expressly for the purpose, managed it all very agreeably—Dined solus cum solo, about a quarter to seven, and got to the Opera before the Overture—Moore proceeding to his box, and I to my stall—The Opera (Parasina), not very agreeable, but Persiani charming. An Act of Norma however, afterwards, in which Grisi soon convinced me of her immense superiority in every respect, as woman, as singer and as actress. Had an old acquaintance, Lord Arthur Hill, seated before me—

Went afterwards to the Ball at Devonshire House, which I found insufferably hot—encountered, during the twenty minutes I staid there, a multitude of old acquaintances by whom my dinner-list was almost filled up for the time I remain in town. Among others, Lady Georgiana Grey said she should not be forgiven at home if she did not fix me some day for dinner, and I mentioned Thursday the 31st. as the only one I had open—had before fixed Wednesday 30th. for a dinner at Mrs. Cunliffe's—Forgot I believe to mention that before I left home, I received a letter from Messrs. Smith and Elder of Corn Hill proposing to me to furnish twelve short poems for a new *Annual* (of all things, at this time of day) which they are about to publish—Took the opportunity, one of these days, when down at Longmans, to go on to Cornhill, and deliver my answer (negatively, of course) in person—Had to stand a pretty considerable stare from some half dozen persons collected in the shop as I issued from the bibliopole's Sanctum Sanctorum. By the bye, received an odd note since I came to town, directed originally to "Sir Thomas Moore, Pickwick Hotel, Cheapside", but the Postman having written on it "no such Hotel in Cheapside, try &c. &c.", the note reached me in Sackville St.—The following are its mysterious contents, which have, at least, none of the *fun* of a hoax in them—the handwriting evidently a woman's.

"My dear Sir Thomas—I called in hopes of seeing you upon the subject Mrs. M. last mentioned to you which *must* be attended to on Tuesday morning next. Therefore knowing she understands very little of business perhaps you will immediately go to Dungamor [This name not legibly written][2] Cottage and advise her how to act for the best. I am sure you will excuse my thus troubling you and in hopes of your being convalescent, believe me, my dear Sir Thomas,   yours

"Excusé (thus spelled)   truly, *Mary*}

23 [Wednesday]—Breakfasted at Brookes's—went and sate some time with Valletort, whom I found much better—Called at Bulteel's and saw his nice wife, Lady Elisabeth—Bulteel full of the North-London Hospital performances, having left a case behind him in Devonshire more extraordinary than any of them—read me a letter from the gentleman in whose house this phenomenon of a young lady is residing giving an account in the most serious and *bona fide* manner of such downright miracles as throw all we have hitherto heard of in that line, into the shade. Among other things, she can, *in the dark*, by passing her two forefingers down the page of a book, take off the impress, as he expresses it, of the whole contents of the page, in about two seconds & repeat it all correctly! Proposed to me to accompany him to the North London Hospital one day to see Dr. Elliotson's manipulatory experiments.[1]—[Met Hume by appointment at the Parthenon to luncheon—accompanied him afterwards to call on the Gossets, Mrs. Foster

&c. &c.—} Dined at Lansdowne House, a grand dinner to the Duke of Sussex, and a very splendid thing it was, in every respect—Company, besides the Duke of Sussex and Lady Cecilia, the Duke & Duchess of Cleveland, Duke & Duchess of Somerset, Lord & Lady Minto, Lord & Lady Breadalbane, Lord Camperdown, Lord John Russell, and plain *Mister* Moore.—Sat next Lord John. The D. of Sussex on my coming in exclaimed, as usual "Ah Tommy!" and called me to account for not having been to see him, but I told him I *had*—In the course of dinner, taking wine with different people, and lumping three or four together, at a time, in order to *diffuse* the compliment, he cried out on proposing wine to some at *our* part of the table, "Lord Minto—Lord John—and last not least—Tommy!"—on which Lord John said gravely in an under voice "Last *and* least"—thus, putting in his claim, as I told him, for the small modicum of superiority he has over me in that respect,—whereat he gave one of his very agreeable & playful laughs. {Home early.}

24 [Thursday]—{Breakfasted at Rogers's to meet Sydney Smith, Mrs. Norton, Charles Sheridan and *Statesman* Taylor.[1] Sydney very amusing about Allen—said that there was a dark place with bars to it at Holland House which people did not know the use of, but it appears that Allen keeps a clergyman there whom he torments occasionally—he then imitated Allen's face while torturing his victim—Went off afterwards very comically on the fancy of Allen himself being shown, in a cage, at Exeter Change—the Keeper, to show him off, giving him a poke occasionally, crying to him "blaspheme, blaspheme" Allen's growl &c. &c.—In the course of conversation, Lord Lansdowne became the topic, and Sydney was (as he always is) very fair to him—Rogers, as usual (in this instance) *denigrant*—a comparison between Lord Holland & Lord Lansdowne—Lady Holland's Character—and one or two other topics passed in review.—} Went down to the Longmans—bad prospect for the Edition of my Works, and consequently of the supplies I expected from it. The uncertainty of the effects of the Copy-right Bill, and, as yet, of the very nature of its enactments must naturally suspend all undertakings dependent upon it. {But, in the mean time, the Partners are about to take a step, for their own peculiar advantage, which will completely I fear anticipate the harvest of the projected Edition. Already they have a new illustrated Edition of Lalla Rookh to bring into the market, and now they think of availing themselves of Mrs. Power's copyright which was purchased for the purpose of the Collected Edition, to print also an edition, on their own account, of the Irish Melodies and my other Lyrical works; this entirely preoccupying, to my exclusion, a great part of the advantage to be expected from a collective Edition. There is, of course, nothing to be objected to all this, in the way of trade—but still it is sheer tradesmanship, and, as such, not very agreeable to a poor devil of an

author.[2]—Called upon Easthope—Forgot to mention that Charles Philips whom I met yesterday (walking with OConnell) spoke of something in that day's Chronicle significantly, as if supposing it to be mine—had barely seen it myself, without reading it, but now had some talk on the subject with Easthope who was highly amused at the recollection of some things I had told him, respecting my annoyance at the sort of stuff that was sometimes attributed to me—particularly my account of Lord Essex's having once produced from his pocket-book some trashy doggrel (as I found on reading it) which he had been treasuring as mine—"ah—I have you here—there's no mistaking you." Easthope now showed me these verses of yesterday, which were in their way (the serious & bitter style) not bad, and, as I suspected, written by my chief *Singe*, Paul of Corsham. It was, however, by no means agreeable to me to be thought to have written so violently against Burdett, whom I like too much for *himself* and have also estimated always too justly the extent of his capacity, to allow his late conduct either to surprize or to make any very great change in my feelings towards him. He is in fact just as good and gentlemanlike a fellow—and as far from a *sensible* one—as ever he was.[3] In remarking how few people there were that knew good from bad, in matters of taste, Easthope said "Be assured it is only your having obtained the stamp of the few good judges that makes the many who cannot judge for themselves admire you." This, whether true or not, as regards myself, was not ill said—Met Lord Headfort and walked with him some time—proposed to take me to his house to see Gustavus & Adelaide—found the latter at home and looking *so like* her mother!—but Gustavus out.} Have not mentioned, I believe, that on my first visit to the Longmans after my arrival, when I found them in high delight at Mrs. Moore's "opinion on Copyright", I took care to impress upon them that it was solely from what I thought due to myself and my own feeling of what was right that I had come to the determination of not availing myself of any such law to change or unsettle my agreement with them. "There has already," I said "been too much *sentiment* mixed up with this Bill—sentiment for *authors*—and I wish you to understand that it is not from any sentiment towards *publishers* that my present views have been adopted"—{Dined at Lord Francis Egerton's—Company, Lord & Lady Grosvenor, Lord Morpeth, Lord Fitz-Alan, Lady Keith & Flahaut (just arrived) with their nice daughter, Lady Charlotte Greville, and Charles himself—Sat next Lord Francis & found him very agreeable—The party broke up early, being all bound for the Duke of Sussex's Ball—Went to Lord St. Vincent's, where I found a few people (still fewer of whom I knew)—but shortly, however, the plot began to thicken, and there came in the Jerseys, the Duke of Wellington and others. It is curious to see how little fastidious your fine folks are as to *where* they meet so they but meet *each other*. The scene of this reunion was at Ellis's Hotel in St. James's, in two small drawing-rooms, where the ladies' *bustles* could hardly find room to move about—but then they had the

Duke of Wellington and Miss Jervas's singing, to say nothing of the now sadly faded Lady Jersey. To my great delight, the Duke was pleased to recognize me and gave me a very courteous shake of the hand. After some charming Tyroliennes by Miss Jervase, I was pressed much to sing something, and Lady Jersey "hoped that I would consider how *very* long it was since she heard me"—but I fought *shy* and came away. An admirable picture, the Duke & Lady Jersey sitting in confab—bending towards each other across a flower-stand that was between them, she talking eagerly and he with his hand behind his deaf ear advancing it to catch her accents. "I wonder" said some one "*which* clause of the Irish Municipal Bill it is they are now dooming to destruction."[4] Home.

25 [Friday]—Breakfasted at Brookes's—find no memorandum of what I did in the course of the day—Asked by the Duke of Norfolk, whether I wanted a Fast-dinner to-day? Dined at Byng's, a dinner made by him for me—company Bulwer, Fonblanque, Shiel, Charles Greville &c.—Fonblanque rowing and bantering Shiel, upon the appropriation Clause, in that Public-School style which we Irishmen can so little understand or bear—At least, I speak for myself. Shiel bore it with much good humour—Home early where I found Kit Talbot and Lady Charlotte—sat some time talking with the Feildings—Received to-day, to my great surprise, a most laudatory Poem from Miss Landon, on my singing accompanied by a very kind note. I say, to my surprize, because the only time I ever sang in her company she gave me the idea of sneering at it all through—so much so as to disconcert and annoy me exceedingly. I must have done her, I suppose, injustice. The Poem, she tells me, is to appear in Fisher's Drawing Room Scrap Book[1]— the following is her note.

"Dear Sir—As the expression of my earnest and respectful admiration can scarcely be held a liberty I venture to send you the accompanying lines. They will appear together with your portrait in the Drawing Room Scrap Book for next year. Messrs. Fisher will of course do themselves the pleasure of sending you the Volume when published, in the Autumn, but I shall then have left England. I could not deny myself the gratification of sending you the MS. copy.

Pray accept my best wishes and allow me to remain yours Dear Sir, most admiringly and sincerely L. E. Landon"}

26 [Saturday]—{Breakfasted at Brookes's, and conned over my Speech for the day—accompanied Lady Elisabeth and Horatia to Straus's music at the Hanover Square Rooms (where, by the by, I went a day or two before with Rogers) and enjoyed very much the sweet snatches of melody that, every now & then came, though far too short, and succeeded by clangor quite

deafening. Having seen Lady E. & Horatia out before the end of the Concert, returned and sate by} Lady {Charlotte Greville, who} having just received a letter from Paris {(from her son Henry)} giving an account of Talleyrand's death, gave me the note-paper sheets of his letter to read, according as she read them herself. The account curious and very well given—the management of the Archbishop, in leaving the whole conduct of the death-bed scene to an Abbé, who intermediated, and the evident anxiety of {Madame de Dino} to give as orthodox an air to the whole transaction as was possible, all very amusing. Talleyrand more than once said during his dying moments "la machine s'en va," and these words were his last. {Joined Miss Jervase afterwards who was there with Miss Burdett, and Rogers acting as their chaperon—walked a little way with them and then to Lansdowne House, where I found that Lord L. was to call upon me, to go to the Literary Fund Dinner, at six o'clock—} Had received notice in the course of the day that I must be early in attendance at the Freemason's Tavern, as one of the Stewards, to receive the President[1]—but found it far more agreeable of course to go *with* him, Henry Fitz. being also of the party.—Immense bustle on our arrival—was invested with my wand, as Steward, and all made our way to the head-table, the room being already crowded—got seated between Bulwer and Wise, within two or three of Lord L.—and opposite me sat Sir Harris Nicholas, with his flaming star (being a Guelph) whose book of the Privy Council I had lately been studying—The whole proceedings of the day interesting and to me, in an almost overwhelming degree, flattering and gratifying. Lord Lansdowne by general admission, a most admirable Chairman—more particularly for such a purpose—his feeling and taste being, I think (whatever his ambition might once have been) far more towards literature than politics—{Shall give on the following page a scrap from the Morning Post, containing a pretty good report of what he said on proposing my health, and also an account of the manner in which the toast was received.[2] Flourishing and overdone as is all the Petrarch-and-Virgil part of this description it scarcely does justice to the burst of cordial & *personal* feeling towards me displayed on this occasion. It really, as I with truth told them, "overwhelmed" me.— Came away with Lord Lansdowne & Shelbourne at about 11 o'clock.

27 [Sunday]—Having made out a pretty accurate Report of my speech, took it to the Morning Chronicle Office & left it there for Black.[1] Called, in the course of the day on Barnes, and found him at home—Received me very kindly and asked what day I could dine with him—told him my Dinner List was now overflowing, but that when I next came to town I should announce myself, in time, to him—"Be sure you do" he said "that I may get some one to meet you—should you have any objection to meet Lyndhurst?" I answered "No—certainly—if he would have none to me"—"Oh—he's not the

sort of fellow to mind those things" Barnes answered with a laugh. Told him I had just been taking the precaution of giving a Report of my Harangue yesterday to the Chronicle, and was now sorry I had not made a copy of it for the Times—on which he said, that if they would send a slip of their Report to the Office he would take care to have it inserted—I accordingly rattled off in my Cab to Black's and left a note for him to that effect. Had an instance in one of today's papers of the downright necessity there is of taking these precautions, against misrepresentation—one of the Sunday Reporters making me say, "That I had now amassed a considerable fortune by my literary labours," and the newspaper from which I have extracted the above scrap, though so evidently inclined to do me justice, puts the saddest trash into my mouth, in their Report—Went to sit with Lord Valletort, and found my old acquaintance, his father, with him, whom I have not met for many years. The Mount-Edgecumbes were among the first fine folks I got acquainted with in London, and I remember how proud I used to be of the privilege of visiting Lady Mount E. in her Opera box and occasionally supping with her, too, afterwards. At one of these suppers I found myself seated next Mrs. Siddons, the first time I had ever seen her off the stage, and I remember the ludicrous effect it had to hear her say, in her most solemn & tragic tones "I do love ale dearly." Found the old Lord as fresh and full of facetiousness as ever.—Dined at Lord John Russell's—Company, Bulwer, Shiel, E. Stanley, Lords Boringdon, Torington (good rhymes, by the by) Radnor &c. &c.—sat next Lord John. No ladies of the party but joined them in the evening, Lady Morley, Mrs. Lister, Mrs. Stanley &c.— They *would* make me sing, though neither myself nor the piano-forte were in tune for it—made out a few songs for them, however, which pleased at least Mrs. Villars, for she very good-naturedly exclaimed "*That,* I always say, is the music for *me.*}

28th [Monday]—

> {"I, my dear, was born to-day—
> Shall I salute the rising ray?"

to which I answer? that I do not at all see why I should *not*—for old as this day makes me, time has done but little, thank God, either to cool my heart, weaken my head or impair my strength. Forget what I did in the morning— found every body pleased with my speech, and Lady Elisabeth said "she felt it to be what speeches are not very often, quite touching"—meaning, I take for granted, the allusions to myself as working for the means of daily subsistence. Met Lord Mulgrave at Brookes's, just arrived from the Vice-Royalty—thanked him for his kindness to Tom, whose regiment, he told me, was expected back in Dublin, in July. Called upon Miss Jervase whom I found at home and alone—Sung some charming things for me, particularly a Tyrolienne of her own composition, full of spirit and dramatic effect. Made me sing also for her & seemed really to *like* it—"What a beautiful voice!" she exclaimed once, and I *did* happen to be in pretty good vocal order. The rain which has kept off so well since I came arrived to day at last—Bought myself a pair of India rubber galoches—} A note from Mrs. Smith to say that Sydney would take me to the Longmans to-day if I liked—had already half promised to go with Lardner, but sent a note to put him off—on our way to Hampstead Sydney talked of his Letter,[1] rather nervously, I thought—forget whether I have mentioned Luttrell's saying to me the other day—"Well, my dear Moore, could you have conceived any man taking such pains to upset a brilliant position in society as Sydney has been doing lately?" In the course of our talk Smith mentioned his having received a letter lately from Lord Carlisle, in acknowledgement of a copy of the pamphlet S. had sent him—repeated the substance and I suppose nearly the words of the letter which appeared to me a very polished but pointed condemnation of the pamphlet—Lord Carlisle, it is clear, in writing it, felt himself bound to express as politely as possible, what he knew to be the opinion of the persons he lived with on the subject; and being himself unscathed by the pamphlet, he could of course do it with a better grace. This, however Sydney did not seem to me to feel. While we were on the subject, I thought it *my* duty also to tell him what I thought of his attack on Lord John[2]—his representing him to be so totally wanting in feeling as to bear with unconcern the loss of the Channel Fleet, the dying of a man under an operation for the stone &c. &c. through his means. This he denied to be the purport or effect of the passage in question which meant merely, he contended, that you would not *perceive* by Lord John's manner that he felt it. In the course of our conversation afterwards, he happened, in speaking with great bitterness of Lord Castlereagh to say something of his indifference to the mischief & ruin he might cause by his measures, which amounted in purport exactly to the same which he has said of Lord John. I, therefore, instantly interrupted him, saying—"There—that's precisely the impression you produce in your character of Lord John." "You *don't* say so?" he exclaimed—"I assure you," I answered "that such is the way in which it is viewed by all whom I have heard speak on the subject"—"Then I must certainly" he said "set myself right on that point, and as there is a new Edition just coming out, I shall not lose a moment in doing it." On our arrival at Hampstead, he absented himself from the drawing room for a short time, and I found afterwards it was for the purpose of making this correction. [It is merely a short note denying that he meant to impute any want of feeling to Lord John—but the arrow had already sped and no one now minds the note.][3] {Company besides ourselves, Lardner, MacCulloch, a clergyman (of Hampstead, I believe) whose name I now forget, Mr. & Mrs. Hart Davies (whose ward, a remarkably nice girl, Tom Longman has just married), Mrs. Marcet, and one or two more—The day very hearty and agreeable with "lots" of singing as usual in the evening, for which my voice mustered in tolerable strength, and in which Mrs. H. Davies, and Mrs. Tom Longman also took their part. A pretty song sung with great feeling by Mrs. H. Davies "Oh the merry days that are gone" touched me exceedingly. As they would not let me go away with Sydney, I remained & was taken home by the Spottiswodes. My speech praised very much, and I found from T. Longman that I was very well heard.

29 [Tuesday]—Breakfasted at home with Horatia—Received one of these days, through the hands of L. Col. Sir Charles O'Donnel, a portfolio sent me by a foreign lady of Irish descent, and with no less charming a signature to Irish eyes than the following—"La Contesse Eveline ODonnel."—The Portfolio is ornamented with a drawing by the Contess herself—the subject of it my song of "Love Valour and Wit" in the Irish Melodies, and the following her eloquent letter, which she dates "Vienna."

"Si les poetes n'etoient en quel que sorte une proprieté intellectuelle dont chacun prend sa part à raison de la puissance qu'ils exercent, je ne saurois en verité comment faire pour justifier mon courage—car il en falloit beaucoup pour avoir osé consacrer mon pauvre talent d'amateur à vos délicieuses poésies, et plus encore pour en renvoyer le pâle reflex à son veritable auteur. J'espére toutefois que ma sympathie pour l'Irelande vous fera juger ma foible production avec cette heureuse partialité qui impose silence à la critique: car si je n'appartiens pas a l'Isle Verte par ma naissance ni mes rélations, je puis dire que je m'y intéresse avec un coeur Irlandais et que j'ai conservé plus que le nom de mes peres. Cela seul me fait espèrer que mes petits voyageurs ne subiront pas le triste noviciat des étrangers. Puissent-ils remplir leur mission sur le sol natal, en agissant conjointement et toujours pour la cause Irlandais et amener enfin une ère nouvelle pour cette héroique et malheureuse nation.—Vous dirai je, Monsieur, les doux moments que je dois a vos ouvrages? ce seroit repéter une fois de plus ce que vous entendez tous les jours et de tous les coins de la terre. Aussi j'ai garde de vous ravir un tems trop précieux par l'écho de ces vieilles vérités. Si jamais mon étoile me conduit en Irlande je ne m'y croirai pas étrangère. Je sais que le passé y laisse de longs souvenirs, et que la conformité des désirs et des espèrances rapproche en dépit de l'espace et du tems. Jusque là recevez, je vois prie l'assurance &c. &c."

Went to a variety of places—Lady Elizabeth decidedly of opinion that I ought to wait for the Levee, and says Lady Lansdowne thinks the same—wrote this to Bessy, adding that I did not myself think it of consequence, but that if she could get on without me for a day or two after Russell leaves her, I *would* go to the Levee which is to be tomorrow week—Dined at Lord Shrewsbury's—(forget whether I mentioned that he asked me to dinner last

Saturday to meet the Duke of Sussex, saying in his note that Lord John had just sent him an excuse and hoping that I should be able to take his place— which I of course could not—that being my Literary Fund Day.) Company, the George Bryans, Lord & Lady John Somerset, and some English Catholics, whose names I forget—also Hertz, the great German Piano-forte player, the sight of whom completely put to flight whatever intentions I had of *singing* for my Lady in the evening. To sing before great foreign musicians, who perceive all that is *wrong* in my singing & accompanying, and cannot understand what there may be of *good* is an operation which I have always, when I could, avoided—Dinner very grand, none of the dishes on the table (just as it was at Alton) and an awful interval between the guests— sat between my Lady herself and the kind good-tempered Lady Mary—In the evening Hertz played, and I dare say very finely, but as I was all the time meditating flight, could not much attend to him—Saw it was quite a settled point that I was to sing—but being resolved (ungracious as it might appear) *not* to sing, watched my opportunity, and was down stairs and out of the house in less than a jiffey

30 [Wednesday]—Breakfasted at Rogers's—Company, the three very handsome (and all, in their ways, clever) sisters, Mrs. Norton, Lady Seymour, and Mrs. Blackwood.—had once thought Lady Seymour rather goose-ish— but find there is a quiet humour about her very amusing—the other guests, Mrs. Shelley and her friend Miss Robinson, Lord Mulgrave, and the very pompous and uncouth gentleman, Mr. Von-Arteveldt Taylor—The whole party, however, amusing, in their several ways. Lord Mulgrave saying how surprised he felt at the ladies not curtseying to him.—Received both together a letter from Corry, announcing his departure from Cheltenham, and a card betokening his arrival in London—called at his lodgings, but he was out—Wrote to Easthope on the subject of my squib-money.—Dined at Mrs. Cunliffe's—company, Lord & Lady Brabazon (she very handsome), Lady Monson (I believe) a very pretty little woman, Wilmot Horton and one or two more—Conversation amusing—Wilmot Horton full of old stories & giggle—Sung a good deal in the evening having very pretty as well as *encouraging* auditors—By the bye, wrote a civil note to Lady Shrewsbury this morning to excuse the apparent churlishness of my flight last night.

31 [Thursday]—Breakfasted with Jolly old Corry, whom I found better a good deal than I expected—drove out with him and Latham to make calls— went to Lady Listowel's, and found her & her sister and niece at home— Left Corry & Latham there while I went on to Holland House—saw my Lady for a few minutes and offered myself for dinner there on Saturday— This I did, because Luttrell told me a day or two since that they were not

pleased at my never having dined there since I came to town—Wrote to Phipps, by Lady Lansdowne's desire to beg he would look to Henry Fitz-Maurice who is going down to a Yeomanry dinner and to get him off the dinner if he can—at all events to see that he does nothing to make himself ill, his health being now, poor fellow, but too delicate—added that it would be as well not to let him know of this interference as young fellows don't like to be superintended. Received a note from Lady Grey this morning putting me off my dinner engagement to them for to-day, in consequence of the dangerous illness of their grand-child—Called at Lord Essex's while I was out, with Corry to offer myself for dinner there, but his table was full—asked me to come either Saturday or Monday and I fixed Monday—So here I was dinnerless for the day—but luckily "me servavit Apollo" for while I was mentioning to some one at Brookes's, that I had been put off from Lord Grey's, Lord Grosvenor who was writing at a table near me, took me aside & said "Do you mean to say you are disengaged for dinner to-day?—then pray come and eat a family dinner with us—we ourselves, as you see, are in mourning, and were obliged to put off a party we had asked—but if you'll come we shall be delighted."—I, of course, consented—a desperate deluge of rain came on just as I was about to start, and there appeared no chance of a hackney coach—but again Apollo, (or rather Venus herself) came to my aid, for there was Lady Valletort and her carriage at the hall door, having brought her mother home, and most kindly and opportunely she conveyed me to dinner—The party entirely a family one, consisting only of the old Duchess Countess, the Duke of Sutherland, Lord Robert Grosvenor, Lord & Lady Francis Egerton and Mr. Grenville. The conversation particularly agreeable, and the whole thing, in its way, a God-send.—Left at home by the Egertons.

June 1 [Friday]—Breakfasted at Brookes's—received a very civil note from Easthope, enclosing a still more civil note for £100, part for work *done* and part for work to *come*—Met Hume by appointment at the Parthenon to lunch—had previously made several visits, among others one to Milman, & found him and Mrs. M. at home—Went with Hume to the Gossets and to Mrs. Forster, the latter of whom I had not seen for a great number of years and she told me "the flattering tale" that I was not a bit altered since we last met.—Paid a visit also (without Hume) to old Lady Cork, who had written me a note, beginning "Oh Tommy, Tommy, come, come, any time you can &c. &c."—A most wonderful specimen of antiquity she is, to be sure—found her as full of dinner engagements &c as ever. "Where do I dine tomorrow?" she asked sharply of a little Lady in Waiting that attends her—Made various efforts to fix upon a day for me to dine with her, but as our several engagements made it impossible, she said in her little old-witch-like way—"Well, well, good bye—I'll make no appointment with you till I am a hundred"—95 is I believe the age she now marks herself at.—Called upon Mr. Reade, the poet—that *would* be. Poor man, if intensity of desire could make him one, he would be among the first—Six or seven years, I think, he told me, have been devoted by him to the Poem on Italy he has just published,[1] besides I don't know how much of his income which it has cost him to lay it before the world. And there it lies and *will* lie, I fear, unread. His case is, indeed, *not* one to be laughed at, for his whole soul is bent upon making a fame, and a fame at this time of day (as a poet at least) he has not the slighest chance of making. *Read* may *write* but no one will read *what* he writes.—Dined at Tom Longman's—company much the same as at Hampstead the other day—sat next his pretty wife at dinner, and sung abundantly in the evening—By the by, I think I have not mentioned a curious MS. put into my hands the other morning, at the Longmans', being nothing less than the copy of a Speech *intended* to be spoken by Longman Senior, in giving my health the other day after dinner, at Hampstead, but which in consequence of a fit of shyness coming over him was left *un*-spoken. It is, however, capital in its way—After beginning in the usual manner, "Ladies & Gentlemen—proposing a toast—which I am sure you will drink with pleasure—I should say with enthusiasm"—he proceeds, or rather *meant* to proceed, thus—"a gentleman who has so often been the delight of these rooms—and, I may say, of Pater-Noster Row also—not to mention all England—and all Ireland—and I should not speak the whole truth if I did not add of all Europe—and America—and Asia—and of every country where the use of letters is known." Then comes the following exquisite touch of *shop* gallantry—"But I cannot feel satisfied, Mr. Moore, without including Mrs. Moore's name in the toast, for I shall never forget Mrs. Moore's noble exclamation, "Why, that's not honest," on your mention of a certain clause in the new Copy-right Bill.—Are you all charged, ladies & gentlemen?"

2 [Saturday]—Breakfasted at Rogers's—company Mrs. Norton, Mrs. Shelley, Miss Robinson, Taylor, Rio and young Kean—after breakfast came Lady Seymour. Kean's account of Murray (the publisher) whom he sat next at the Literary Fund Dinner—Murray quite drunk and grumbling most audibly all the time Bulwer was making his Speech—"I wouldn't give that fellow a hundred pounds for the best novel he ever wrote"—at last, he burst out with "that's a damned lie," and then ducked down his head, while every eye was directed towards him (Kean), and he felt quite disconcerted lest people should think it was from him these words proceeded. He was, however, relieved by Murray's rising from his chair, and staggering away, as well as he could down the room, showing clearly who it was had so ejacu-lated. Was rather in a scrape about my dinners for to-day & tomorrow, owing to my uncertainty as to whether I should remain so long in town, and

the half promises I in consequence gave to different people—To-day's case a most lamentable one, as after having *volunteered* to dine with the Hollands, I found, in calling yesterday at Bryan's, that I was expected to dinner *there*. What was to be done? *Temper* was to be encountered in *either* quarter, while *agreeableness* was only to be had from *one* of them. However the worst temper of the two carried it, (as I am afraid will generally be the case) and I resolved to dine with Bryan—Wrote as apologetic a letter as possible to my Lady—and, at seven o'clock, instead of finding myself among the *elite* of Holland House, sate down with a table full of Bryans—the only small addition thereto being a young attaché of the French Embassy. Bryan himself however was very good-humoured, and being always to me a most hearty friend, I felt I did the right thing, though thinking now & then, of a line of my own in an Epilogue I wrote once for Corry at Kilkenny, where speaking of the sacrifice we (the actors) were ready to make for our manager,[1] made him say

"For him—oh friendship!—I act *tragedy*."

The following is the whole of the passage.}

"Tis said our worthy Manager intends
To help my *night*—and he you know has *friends*.[2]
Friends, did I say? for fixing *friends* or *parts*,
Engaging *actors*, or engaging *hearts*,
There's nothing like him! wits, at his request,
Are chang'd to fools, and dull dogs learn to jest;
Soldiers, for him, good "trembling cowards" make,
And beaux, turn'd clowns, look ugly for *his* sake;
For him even lawyers *talk*, without a *fee*,
And I—oh friendship!—I act tragedy!

{Another scrape about dinner for tomorrow, having in like manner half promised Mrs. Norton & Edward Moore—Mrs. Norton, however being the prior one, determined for that—Moore called upon me at Brookes's, on the subject, and went off in a huff on finding I wasn't to dine with him—"You *don't* go to the country then?"—No, I do not" " and it is not with *me* you dine?"—"No, I—" "Very well—that's enough" and off he strutted, like a much injured gentleman in a tragedy, without waiting for a word of my explanation. Forgot to mention some little particulars about the breakfast this morning—one of our chief subjects of conversation was a brother "statesman" of Taylor's named Stebbing,[3] whom it pleases Taylor and a few others to cry up as a most wonderful person, though God knows for what he is wonderful except the having such a piece of work made about him. We had him at Bowood, I recollect, some days, without being a bit the wiser or brighter for him. It appears, however, that "there is no such man as

Stebbing."—Rio told me that my Loves of the Angels have been brought a good deal into discussion lately by the appearance of LaMartine's new Work "L'Ange Déchu,"[4] in which Rio says La Martine has at last completely *unchristianized* himself having been in the process thereto for some time.— In speaking of my foreign reputation, said that my Irish Gentleman[5] had rendered me "still more popular than ever abroad."

3 [Sunday]—Breakfasted at home with Horatia—went afterwards to the Catholic Chapel at Warwick St. and was unluckily too late for the opening of the Mass by Persiani, but the rest charmingly sung by Mrs. Bishop, Phillips &c.—Got placed in Flop's pew (the Howards') rather too conspic-uous a station to enjoy the music in—Had to stand, as usual, a general stare, in leaving the Chapel—Paid a number of visits, at Mrs. Shelley's &c. &c.— Dined at Mrs. Norton's, which was a very *manqué* proceeding—Charles Sheridan having been obliged to dine out, and the only guests at dinner being the Seccatura Taylor, Mrs. Blackwood, and some young fellow, whose name I did not enquire. Joined the ladies almost immediately after dinner and found additional company, among whom were Alvanley and a Mrs. Barton (daughter, they told me of Kit Hutchinson & by the way of a beauty). Found I was doomed to sing, and commenced by a Duett "Dost thou remember?" with Mrs. Norton—Mrs. Blackwood also sung—but there was a running accompaniment of *chatter* throughout all our performances which was by no means encouraging (Mrs. Barton being the Prima Donna of the talk) and accordingly, as soon as I could well manage, I made my escape, and finding that I *had* a voice determined to carry it, well wrapped up, to Edward Moore's, (where I knew there were to be ladies in the evening) and thus re-instate myself in his favour—Found there a very nice & hearty party of Irish—Lady Morgan & her niece having just departed— and, after some talk with Shiel's daughters-in-law, two very nice and smiling girls, *volunteered* (a rare thing with me) to sing. Found my audience rather a different one from that which I had left, and sung right-ahead more than half a dozen songs—One of the most pleased of my auditors being *Rio,* who was all animation & eloquence at the "era" which he said it made in his life to have heard me sing the songs of Ireland among my own countrymen & countrywomen & witnessed the delight which it gave them—Edward Moore himself all *couleur de rose* again—Left at home by the Shiels.— Among the evening company at Mrs. Norton's were two *once* beautiful persons, Mrs. Tom Sheridan and Lady Graham—the latter still handsome but changed.—the other—alas, how unlike her I saw at the Boyle Farm fête some ages ago!

4 [Monday]—Having made up my mind to go to the Levee and so told Lord Lansdowne, (who said if I went with him, he would save me much fuss by

taking me in by the private entrée) I went this morning to leave my name at the Chamberlain's Office, and found the Levee was not to be till Friday— Resolved therefore, as I had announced myself to Bessy for Thursday, not to disappoint her (particularly as Russell leaves her on that day) and was just in time to stop Huffell in cutting up the cloth for my dress-coat, as well as Mrs. Gibbon, in making my stock and shirt-front—Met Lord Cawdor (now turned Tory) and had some talk with him about the refusal of the other two great Clubs (Boodle's & White's) to join us of Brookes's in giving a Fête to the Queen—[Very lucky for me that this grand design went off, as I had put my name to the requisition, at Ponsonby's request, and I dare say it would have cost me no less than 25 pounds or so. At least Lord Hatherton, in talking to me of the backwardness there was about it said "The fact is, men are not so ready now as they used to be to sport their £25. on such an occasion."] Mentioned the rumour we had heard that the reason of White's people not joining us was their not liking to coalesce with a Club that contained OConnell, and he said that was really the cause—Met Lady Lilford in Grosvenor Place who asked me to come to her in the evening which I promised to do—Went with Corry to the Exhibition, and met there Codrington and his daughter, who asked me to dine with them the day after tomorrow, but couldn't—[Forgot to mention Corry's story of Bushe saying when somebody remarked of Lady C. Lamb's threatening to stab some man how ready she was with her *knife* "Aye, and with her *fork* too" said Bushe.][1] Dined at Lord Essex's—Company, besides my Lady, Sir Robt. Adair, Boldero, and somebody else—forget who—On leaving Lord Es. walked to Lady Lilford's, but it being then early found from the servant that there were but two persons yet come, Captain Stopford and his lady, and not liking to encounter this paucity (the Stopfords being strangers to me) turned on my heel & went to Brookes's.

5 [Tuesday]—Took my chance of finding Rogers at Breakfast, and found him as usual, surrounded by company—a lady and gentleman, whose name I forget & four or five daughters—all very smiling and agreeable—R. offered me his Stall-ticket for the Opera in the evening, and an early dinner, which were just the very things I wanted, not having made any engagement—Walked out with R. and met Macaulay just returned (the evening before) from India looking most hale & prosperous, having brought home his health & talents unimpaired and about forty thousand pounds, I suppose, in his pocket—said in the course of our short conversation some words tantamount to his being "bound to no party" which struck me as significant—A characteristic touch of Rogers putting the lancet thus soon into Macaulay after their long separation by reproaching him for not calling upon him before he went away—which had evidently rankled in R's memory ever since. Macaulay, who had forgot Rogers

enough to be surprised a little at this reminiscence, pleaded his having been so hurried on his departure as not to be able to call upon any body—but this wouldn't do—Sam wouldn't let him off so easily—"Oh yes"—he said— "you called upon Sharpe"—Walked out with Rogers—called at Miss Jarvis's, but she was not at home—then to Brookes's—had told him a day or two since of the Longmans' meaning to publish an Edition of the Melodies & Lyrics immediately, to the adjournment, if not total abandonment of our joint Edition of the Works, and he advised me not to stir any more in the matter—they couldn't he said do without me, and therefore the best way was for me to rest on my oars. This I thought very good advice, and shall certainly act upon it. On my mentioning to-day, however, that I had been down to the Longmans, he, without waiting to hear what had taken me there, instantly flew out with "There, now—that's just like you—you'll never follow my advice—that was just the way with the Byron Manuscript—you took Luttrell with you on that occasion, instead of taking *me.*"—and so he went on, calling up as (I couldn't help telling him) he had just done with Macaulay, "the ghosts of old grievance."—So much for the *Pleasures* of *Memory!*[1] Dined with Rogers, no one but ourselves & Doctor Henderson, the writer on Wines, whom he had asked to join us—The Opera Parasina,[2] not very good—but a dancing Interlude, with Taglioni, which was beautiful in its way.

6 [Wednesday]—Breakfasted with Corry—and afterwards took a giro pretty extensive in paying Bills—went down with Lardner, Mrs. Shelley & Miss Robinson to the London Hospital, in the hope of seeing some private experiments on Okey[1] &c.—but, being a holiday, all the Somnambulists were gone out walking & I could not wait.—Dined at Sir Charles Lemon's, being taken by Horatia—Company, the Wilbrahams, Bailey, Lady Davy &c.—In the evening Lady Lansdowne's Music, a select though large party, and very well done, in every respect—Left after the first Act, having to be off early in the morning.

7 [Thursday]—Started at eight in the Emerald—a very pretty & agreeable woman one of my companions, who was going to visit her father & mother at Bristol, and who having married a Catholic (Mr. Lescher, I think) had herself become Catholic—I managed to preserve my incognito, till I was near the end of my journey when I saw the lady opposite me (who was also an agreeable intelligent woman looking with all her eyes at my cloak which was lying across my knees and which had a card stitched on the inside with Thomas Moore, Sloperton Cottage, written on it. She then looked over at the other lady whose eyes followed hers to the card, and so I found myself in a very few minutes discovered—It did not however make the remainder

of the journey less agreeable—I found the pretty Catholic was as well versed in my Irish Gentleman as in my Songs, and we struck up a warm friendship before we reached Devizes—Found my sweet Bess pretty well & most glad to have me back.

8, 9, 10 &c. &c. [Friday–Sunday]—Forgot to mention that Rogers, while I was in town repeated to me some verses he had written (to be introduced into his Italy,[1] I suppose, being in blank verse) very good & spirited, as they struck me, and delivered by himself from memory, with a vigour both of action & voice that was quite remarkable in a man of his age and look. It had all the effect of an eloquent & powerfully delivered speech. [Forgot also to mention Greville's taking out of his pocket (at Lord F. Egerton's) my verses "They tell me thou'rt the favoured guest,"[2] and asking me whether I was the author of them—some woman having given him a copy of them—praised them as the most beautiful verses he had seen for a long time.][3]

11, 12, 13 &c. [Monday, 11 June–Thursday, 21 June]—Nothing worth recording—have returned to my task, and am trying to make the best of my time.

22 [Friday]—A Squib of mine against that sublime *raff,* Brougham, in the Chronicle, entitled Animal Magnetism[1]—forget whether I mentioned that Lardner, while I was in town, expressed a very anxious wish for some contributions of this kind from me to the Monthly Chronicle, and proposed my being paid by an *annuity* from them. But this regular task-work will not do for me—I found, while writing for the Metropolitan, how completely the periodical return of the task unfitted me for the performance of it. Received a letter from Lardner about this time, coupling Bulwer's urgent request with his own that I would do something for them this month.—Would have sent them the thing about Brougham, (having asked Black while I was in town whether there would be any objection to my thus *sharing* my labours with the other concern & he said none whatever) but that I thought it likely, from the tone the Monthly takes about Brougham, that they would not like to insert any squib against him—

23 [Saturday]—A new farce brought out at Covent Garden, under the name of "The Irish Lion"[1] of which I have the honour to be the hero, and which (thanks to Power's acting) appears to have had prodigious success. A common Irish fellow, whose name is T. Moore, being mistaken for me, is introduced to an assembly of ridiculous Blues (the scene being laid at

Devizes) by whom every thing he says is received as oracular, and pronounced by a Dandy of the party to be "dem'd foine." John Starkey, who
saw it, says that nothing could be more comical—}

July, {1, 2 [Sunday–Monday]—On this latter day Bowles and Hughes came
to dine with us—Bowles very desponding about his health, though looking
as well as he has done for years, and when poked up a little, as full of fun &
oddity as ever—Had a few evenings since a visit from the Talbots—Forget
whether I mentioned that, while in town I took Talbot to introduce him to
the Longmans, in consequence of his wish to publish with them (instead of
Rodwell, whom he employs at present) a small work he is engaged upon
relating to Classical Antiquities[1]—(as I think the title is.)—Find he has
nearly printed it. In talking of the incident of poor old Lord Rolle losing his
footing the other day at the Coronation, when he was approaching the
Queen, and her advancing so nicely to give him her hand, I mentioned the
joke of Jekyl (as I thought) about Lord Rolle's large feet—namely that,
when he is caught in a heavy shower he merely lies down on his back and
raising his feet about his head makes them serve him as an unbrella—But,
nil sub sole novum—I find from Talbot that this was said, in old times, of the
Egyptians

3–4, 5, 6 &c [Tuesday–Friday]—At work & little else—Received a letter by
post, which cost me half a crown, directed to Thomas Moore Esqr. the
delight of all circles & the idol of his own, London. There were the usual
finger-post marks on it "Try Bury St—Try Brookes's" &c. &c. sending the
Postman in various directions after the said "Idol" and "delight"}

7, 8, 9, 10 [Saturday–Tuesday]—Nothing remarkable—working away at the
reign of Henry VII. Received a letter from my countryman Dillon of the
Bibliotheque du Roi, introducing some friends of his, and sending me two
or three brochures published lately by Guizot, of which he says—"You will
find them not unworthy of your attention, independently of the value
which you will naturally attach to a souvenir from such a writer.[1] Mr.
Guizot has mentioned your name to me more than once. He, in common
with the distinguished portion of his countrymen appreciated fully those
talents & that sterling patriotism which have earned for you the esteem &
admiration of every dispassionate mind in England."—{Dillon also sent
letters introducing to me two friends of his, Mr. Burke & Monsr. Philaréte
Chasles, which these gentlemen not finding me in town forwarded to me
here—Monsr. Chasles (whom I see one of the London papers represents as
connected with the Journal des Débats)[2] writes, in his letter, as follows "Je

serais très honorè, Monsieur, et très heureux, si vous pourriez [m'indiquer] par lettre une heure et un jour aux quels je puisse avoir le plaisir de vous rendre mes devoirs et de lier personellement, connaissance avec l'un des esprits les plus variés et les plus brillans de l'Europe Moderne, dont j'ai étudié et souvent relu tous les ouvrages et dont personne plus que moi n'apprécie la portée et l'influence—Agréez, Monsr., je vous prie l'expression de mon respect et de mon admiration."

11, 12, 13, 14 &c. &c. [Wednesday–Saturday]—The Globe newspaper, one of these days, in noticing the Report of the Pension List Committee, has extracted the accounts given by Southey and myself of our respective claims in the answers returned by us to the Circular of the Committee, and remarks on the "modesty" of mine compared with the pompous list of his, honorary titles &c. furnished by Southey.[1] But one very good reason (*besides* my Irish modesty) for *my* not giving in any such list of titles, is that I really have *none*—even the precious Royal Academy of my own country not having deigned to make me an honorary member of their body, though this is (if I recollect right) one of the multifarious feathers and very deservedly paraded in Southey's cap. I recollect, in my private answer to Rice on the subject of the aforesaid Circular I told him that I had felt half inclined to give myself in as a Member of the Polu*fill*tatic Society, that being the only learned body I had ever belonged to—and a right merry body it was, William Spenser being our Grand Toper and wearing, on great occasions, a crown formed of a circlet of wine-glasses on his head while in his hand he bore a gold sceptre, in the shape of a cork-screw. Our minor Toper, the facetious Will Madocks, wore, for *his* costume, a gold goblet inverted on his head, with "Hoc Age" inscribed upon it. We had all learned names—I forget what William Maddocks's was, but Spenser was Grynaeus, Lord Limerick from his family name & his being an Irishman was Περιταυρος (a coinage of Spenser's), Pigou was Πριηπος, and so on. Our ritual song, every verse ending with "the Polufilltatics, Toll de Roll loll &c" used to be sung by old Joe Madocks and chorussed by the whole party. We all wore dresses hung round with grapes, and I remember that Lady Castlereagh, on one great occasion, provided us with grapes for the purpose. We used to give in compositions now & then, which were all inserted in the *Purple Book* of Grynæus, and I myself contributed to it an *Eleventh Book* of Diogenes Laertius giving an account of an ancient Sect, omitted by that author (transmitted to us) called the Polufilltatics, and founded by a namesake of *our* founder, Grynæus. What has become of this thing, I know not, but have been told, that our Purple Book fell into the hands of John Madocks, the nephew of our Member Joe. The name of the Club (and I believe also its formation) originated in some Greek verses addressed by Spenser to a party of friends with whom he had been passing a few agreeable months in

the country, and one of the lines of which was as follows
Ἐμοῦ φιλέοντες, ἐμοὶ πολυφίλτατοι αἰεν

15, 16, 17 &c [Sunday, 15 July–Tuesday, 24 July]—Niente.

25 [Wednesday]—In consequence of oft-received invitations from our kind friends at Farley, we agreed at last to come to them, on this day, to meet a party consisting of their own family. Setting off in our own poney chaise for Belksham, Bessy & I were there met, as usual by the Houlton's carriage & got very snugly to Farleigh—The party we found there (besides their own home materials, including John) were Isabella & her husband (Vivian) and Catherine with hers (Ward)—another young Ward, the Fiancé of Flora was also of the party and altogether it was as pretty a Tableau de Famille as could be desired. My dear Bess not strong enough to join us at dinner, but appeared, with the music in the evening and enjoyed the whole exceedingly—Crawford came to dinner—talked of Savage Landor, who told Crawford of his having met me in London, and expressed himself highly pleased &c. &c.

26 [Thursday]—The weather not at all good—our party at dinner lessened by some of the family going to dine with Henry Hobhouse, who sent *me* also an invitation by Crawford yesterday, but I declined.

27 [Friday]—Sauntering about & looking over the Houltons' old Books— selected a Stow[1] to bring away with me—Company to dinner, consisting of a Colonel or two (quartered at Trowbridge) the young wife of *one* of them, and her sister—Sung a good deal with Catherine in the evening, as well as a great number of my own songs—

28 [Saturday]—After breakfast set off for Melksham in Houlton's carriage, and from thence took a Fly home.}

August, {1, 2, 3 &c. &c. [Wednesday, 1 August–Sunday, 12 August]

13 [Monday]—Called at Bowood, Lady Lansdowne, Louisa & Henry having been down some days—found Lady L. looking not at all well,—asked me to stay to an early dinner, the annual fete of her school-girls & boys

being to take place in the evening—did so, and had a very agreeable dinner with them, the old Lady Ilchester (Lady L's mother-in law) being of the party, and also Horatia Feilding—Lady Elisabeth who is also staying at Bowood, having gone for the day to Lacock to meet Talbot—After the sports of the children were over, I set off to walk home not expecting that Lady Elisabeth would return to Bowood, but, on my arrival at home, found she had been there with Bessy on her way from Lacock back to Bowood, so that I missed her at both places—I have not mentioned, I believe that I wrote lately to Lord Lansdowne, hearing that he & Lady L. meant to visit Ireland this autumn, to ask of him how soon he thought they would start, as I should like to time *my* trip to Dublin so as not to miss them there. His answer expressed uncertainty as to when he himself should be able to get away from London and likewise as to Lady L's health being restored enough to admit of their going to Ireland this year at all. One of my objects in writing to him was to give myself a chance of being asked to accompany them, if it should happen to be convenient to them to take me—But, as he said nothing in his answer, to this effect, I soon after closed with a suggestion of Hume's that he & I should go to Ireland together, on the same very *easy* terms (to *me*) upon which we both travelled thither some two or three years ago. On mentioning now to Lady Lansdowne my letter to Lord L. on the subject I found he had told her of it, and that from what he then said, she quite *concluded* that I was to be of the party, if they went.

14 [Tuesday]—Bessy & Emma Prowse (who has been staying with us for some time) went into Devizes to the Sessions & I had to dine and pass the evening alone}

15, 16, 17 [Wednesday–Friday]—A letter this latter day from Lord Morpeth, to whom I had written in consequence of one I had received from Drummond, his Under-Secretary—Shall here copy his note, on account of the good fun it contains in allusion to Durham's late Ordinance, which makes it a capital offence to bid "farewell" to Bermuda.[1]

"My dear Moore—Many thanks for your good news of your intended sojourn at Dublin next month. It will be my compensation for getting no holidays at which sometimes I am half disposed to repine—You are sometimes accused of treasonable tendencies in your poetry; but there is one passage containing in its outset such a direct incitement to capital crime that I wonder it has never been branded as it deserves.

> "*Farewell to Bermuda*—& long may the bloom
> Of the citron and myrtle its vallies perfume;

May Spring to eternity hallow the shade
Where Ariel has warbled & Waller has stray'd.[2]

Most sincerely yrs. &."

{18, 19 &c. [Saturday–Sunday]—Received a letter from Lord Lansdowne
(Lady L. having told him of his omission to make any offer to take me with
them to Ireland) very kindly explaining & regretting the omission, which
was owing very much, he said, to his uncertainty as to whether Lady L.
herself would be well enough to undertake the journey at all—Bessy, one of
these mornings, showed me a passage in Pellico's Duties of Man (translated
by Roscoe) which I was not before aware of—After mentioning that Bryon
was desirous of having his daughter educated in the Catholic faith, he says
"The friend of Bryon & the greatest poet, since his departure, of whom
England can boast, Thomas Moore,—after having spent years of doubt in
regard to the choice of a religion, would seem to have directed the whole
force of his active mind to the investigation of Christianity &c. &c." He then
adds that I "wrote an account of the researches I had made & the irresistible conclusions to which I had come."[1] A note from Lord Lansdowne, who
has at last escaped from his harassing parliamentary toils, asking Bessy &
myself & Buss (who has also escaped from *his* toils) to dine at Bowood on
Friday next to meet Lady Elisabeth & Horatia—

24 [Friday]—To Bowood to dinner—but could not persuade Bessy to accompany me—the operation of sitting through a long dinner being too
much for her—Company only the Fieldings, Mademoiselle, George
Montgomery & Guthrie—Day agreeable—Horatia playing pretty Waltzes
in the evening—Some talk with Lord L. about Brougham's vagaries—
Forgot to mention, by the bye, two squibs which I have let off, since the
"Animal Magnetism"—viz. "Announcement of a new grand Acceleration
Company for the promotion of the Speed of Literature" which appeared in
the last Monthly Chronicle and a "Song of Old Puck"[1] (meaning that
sublime Scamp, Brougham) which seems to have made some little sensa-
tion, having appeared a few days since in the Morning Chronicle—Slept at
Bowood.

25 [Saturday]—Bessy had promised to drive over to breakfast, but the rain
prevented her from coming till about twelve—Poor Lady Lansdowne not at
all well to-day—Lord L. walked part of the way home with me.
    On Monday the 27th. I mean to start from London & from thence via
Liverpool to Dublin.

27 [Monday]—Went to Buckhill in a Fly & took the Coach to town—day hot, and the coach crowded, there being two children besides the four adults—a *row* had occurred before I joined, in consequence of one of the passengers of the room having usurped the place of the other, and the ejected gentleman (who was a powerful fellow) having collared & shaken the other, without waiting, as the latter alleged, to hear his explanation or give him time to resign the place—The collared gentleman, who was a little fellow, continued to be wroth during the whole journey, and at every stage renewed his demand of the other's address who, however refused to give it. Of the two, I felt rather in favour of the small gentleman, as the other, after showing himself a bully at first was evidently anxious to shirk the ulterior consequences. On our arrival in town, the collarer (who was accompanied by a rather suspicious looking elderly lady) having called a hackney-coach to convey away himself & his luggage, the little fellow having again reiterated in vain his demand of the other's address, called aloud to his servant and ordered him to follow that hackney coach in a cab & not to quit it till he had ascertained where the pretended gentleman was set down—The servant accordingly placed himself in a cab behind the hack, and off they set together, leaving me very much disconcerted at not being able to follow & learn the result of the adventure—Drove to the Royal Hotel St. James's, and planted myself there for the few days of my stay.

28 [Tuesday]—Went to Longman's and had some talk with Tom L. on the subject of our projected Edition of the Works—called upon Lemon at the State Paper Office and had a good deal of conversation with him—got into a little scrape while remarking on the tendency of those employed by the Record Commission to puff up their own wares—gave, as one of the instances, Sir Harris Nicolas, who, in the Preface to the Proceedings of the Privy Council, Vol. 1, speaks of the correspondence of Richard 2nd. given in that volume as "of much interest" and "affording much information on the state of Ireland"—mentioned how my own expectations were raised by this announcement & my disappointment on finding that these bepuffed letters contained nothing of which the substance was not already familiarly known. This was all very well, but I then unluckily began to extend my observations to the State Papers of the reign of Henry Eighth, in the first vol. of which (for Ireland) a document is given (the paper by Pandarus) of which the substance had already been laid before the public by Leland[1] and yet of this previous promulgation of the document no notice whatever is taken by the Editor;—when I came to touch on this ground I suddenly recollected that Lemon himself was implicated in the "State Paper" case, and therefore shuffled out of the remark as well as I could. Indeed, these Volumes are of true & real importance, and will be of incalculable advantage to me in the part of my task I have just now entered upon. Was rejoiced

to find too from him that, though no money will be granted by government towards the arrangement of the Privy Council Papers, Charles Greville has managed to do a good deal towards that object and is employing Lemon in arranging & indexing them[2]—the expence being defrayed quietly by small accounts, sent in now and then, of 20 & 30 pounds, so as not to alarm the oeconomical wakefulness of the Treasury. By this means (as I understood him) I shall have all the Council Papers of Elisabeth's reign accessible and consultable, which will be a most important object for me—Dined at Greville's, having volunteered to do so by the Poodle's advice—a large & good party, consisting of Shiel, the two Villars's (Sir George & his brother) Stephens, Amyot, and—I forget what others—

29 [Wednesday]—Called at Mrs. Macrone's, and had a good deal of conversation with her man of business who told me of the Creditor having permitted the concern to be still carried on in her name. It being the great wish of the Longmans as well as my own, to include the Epicurean[1] in the collected Edition, one of the objects of my visit to Macrone's was to see what chance there was of the Edition meditated by poor Macrone coming out, as I am bound not to produce any other untill 12 or 14 months after the appearance of his.—Found that this Edition was in a state not only of contemplation but of progress.—at least so said the man of the shop. Called upon Rogers & found him at home—is staying at Holland House, and advised me to volunteer myself as a dinner-guest there to-day—did so and was very cordially welcomed both by my Lady & my Lord—found there Kenny and March domiciliated, and Sneyd & Sir Stephen Hamick guests.— very agreeable conversation, which I had not time to take note of—brought in at night by Sir S. Hamick—Promised Lady H. I would come to dinner again on Friday.

30 [Thursday]—In consequence of a promise to Hume that I would give him a few hours at Hanwell, went out there in omnibus immediately after breakfast—found domesticated with him the same lady I have before mentioned as his guest but in what relation, besides that of patient, she stands towards him I do not permit myself to conjecture—*innocent* it is, no doubt, *perforce*, but still odd and suspicious. She did however the hospitalities of the mansion most kindly—played on the harp after luncheon and led me through Hume's grounds with all the air of a person *at home*. Returned to town with the incumbrance of a premature dinner, and not knowing what to do with it or myself for the remainder of the day—not having formed any other engagement. Performed some commissions, and had an early supper, alone, at nine o'clock at Brookes's—listening to the high treble laugh of the Chancellor of the Exchequer who was at dinner

with a party in the adjoining room—Was asked by Lord Sudely to dine with him tomorrow, but engaged to the Hollands.}

31 [Friday]—{Bustled about a good deal—went to the Longmans, and held a long conference on the subject of the Edition with Tom Longman & Turner, the solicitor—their notion was that Power of Dublin had, in his disposal of the Dublin Copyright of my things to Cuming, withheld a great many, and that it was necessary to ascertain this point before we could proceed with our arrangements[1]—The manner of Tom Longman was by no means what it ought to be—and, in saying this I by no means intend to imply that he was wanting in civility or cordiality—but [*one line heavily deleted and unrecovered*] making me regret, more & more, the loss of [*unrecovered*] Rees's [*unrecovered*] and mellowed [*unrecovered*]—In referring to the offer made me (made me by themselves) of £1000 for my share of the Edition young Longman seemed to hesitate—as to that sum, [*half a line heavily deleted and unrecovered*] but I am resolved to take no less. Undertook to make enquiries as soon as I got to Dublin, with respect to William Power and his further claims—Called upon Black and sate some time with him— His amusement on my telling him that Brougham was the author of the famous recommendation to the people of England to use "bludgeons and brick-bats" for which the Times was so much abused—Thinks that Brougham will be at *me* for my squibs against him—having alluded to them evidently in the Preface to his Collected Speeches, and also in an article lately in the Sun (which is Brougham's paper) where he speaks of the ministers setting on their "petty pensioned poets" to abuse him. This article Black said he could swear to as being Brougham's own. Having had to send Tom £10 for the payment of some of his Bills, found myself hard run for cash & told Black that I should be obliged to draw upon Easthope for a little more squib-money. This, he said, would be most cheerfully supplied—} Went to H{utchins} the dentist, to have my teeth cleaned—told me of his nephew who is practising as a dentist in India being employed to make a set of teeth for the King of Delhi—the difficulty at starting was that the dentist required to be allowed to take a model of the King's mouth, and the idea of a Christian putting his hand into the royal mouth was an abomination not to be heard of—It was at last, however, agreed that by washing his hands, before the operation commenced, in the water of the Ganges, the dentist might qualify himself for the contact. The teeth succeeded wonderfully & one of the courtiers, who from jealousy of the Englishman, had declared they would be good for nothing was desired by the King to put his finger in & try, and, on the courtier doing so, his Majesty nearly bit the finger in two—The affair turned out, however, unluckily, as the King, whose appetite was enormous, being enabled by these new grinders to gratify it ad libitum brought on a plethora which nearly killed him, & the teeth were

thrown into the Ganges—{Called upon C. Greville, who offered me his Cab to take me to H. House and was half inclined to send out there to say he would join the party at dinner—Party at Holland House, March, Allen, Rogers, Kenny, Lord Kildare & his brother Lord Gerald, and (for the first time of my meeting him) Dickens, the author of Pickwick—Found him a good humoured, common-place mannered young man, with no indications of the vein of humour that abounds in his writings—Forgot to mention, by the bye, that when I dined here the other day, I found my Lady, to my no small amusement, full of Boz and his merits, though when I was last in town, she would not suffer one even to mention his name—"For God's sake, don't talk to me of that Boz" was then her language. I ventured to predict, however, at that time, that Boz would before long take even Holland House by storm, and so, to my great amusement, I now found was the case. My lady even boasted to me, with great pride, the other day that he had entrusted to her the denouement of one of the stories he has in process, and that she had suggested to him an alteration which he most readily adopted. On her alluding now, however, to the circumstance, he told her, bluntly enough, that on further consideration, he had found that the dénouement she had suggested would not do at all, and he must follow his own course.—Lady H. showed us some presents which they are about to send out to be given to the Negresses on their West-India Estate—necklaces aigrettes and ornaments of every kind, all looking like real jewels & gold but the whole batch not costing more, I think, than three or four pounds.— Left with Boz, who set me down at Brookes's, and went to join his wife at Astley's—The young Fitzgeralds very fine youths—one like the Duke & the other the very image of the mother.—} Called one of these days at the Admiralty & saw Sir John Barrow, whom I found to be an old acquaintance of mine—my object was to make some enquiry as to the person at present holding the Deputyship of my unlucky office at Bermuda. During peace there is little to be got or lost by it—but if, in the present combustible state of Western politics, a naval war should break out some fine morning, I might possibly be brought into the same scrape by my Deputy (though of the Governor's appointment) as that which fell upon me like a thunder-clap, {formerly.}[2] Barrow agreed with me that I ought to look to the matter, and likewise that it would be the most prudent step, all circum-stances considered, to resign the office.

September 1st [Saturday]—Started in company with Hume for Bir-mingham & Liverpool by the rail-road. From this point my journalizing was not very accurately attended to—the whirl of society in which I was kept not allowing me to "take note of time"—I will not add "save by its loss" for it was any thing but lost time to gather such a harvest of kindness and welcome as awaited me in Ireland, at every step.—the interruptions of our journey by the change from rail-road to coach & from coach back again to rail-road by no means agreeable—On our arrival at Vauxhall, too (near Birmingham) where the train stopped, the whole scene but too strongly bore out the notion of those who see a tendency to *Americanize* in the whole course of the world at present—the way in which we were trundled out of the carriage, like goods, and all huddled together in the same room—the rush up stairs to secure beds—the common supper-room for the whole party, and the small double-bedded room in which Hume & I were (to my no small uncomfort) forced to pig together—all struck me as approaching very fast the Sublime of Yankeeism.

2 [Sunday]—Took the rail-road to Liverpool, and was quite enchanted with the swiftness and ease of our course—there I sate all the way, lolling in a most comfortable arm chair, and writing memorandums, in my pocket-book, as easily and legibly as I should at my own study-table, while flying through the air at the rate of 30 miles an hour. Did the journey in about four hours & twenty minutes, and had but little time to look about us, when we found ourselves on board the Liverpool packet—{The Captain, my former friend Townley, who very kindly gave up to me his own cabbin all to myself, without any *fume* of *Hume*, as in my former trip, to annoy me.

3 [Monday]—Landed early & got on by the rail-road to Dublin, accompanied by the very good-natured fellow OReilly (the brother of an old fellow-templar of mine) whom we had picked up by the way, and found most *serviable* through our journey—All breakfasted together at Arthur Hume's, after which I proceeded to my dear little Nell's lodgings, and sat comfortably installed in the same rooms, and with the same attendants, that made me so snug when I was here with her three years ago. After an excellent lunch of cold fowl & sherry, I shaved, dressed & sallied forth— Went to the Castle—saw Macdonald, Lord Morpeth's secretary, and had much talk with him.—By a letter from Tom to Nell I had been led to fear that he would not be able to come up to Dublin, during my stay, but Macdonald now said that he was quite sure I should find no difficulty in getting leave of absence for him—saw Mrs. Meara & other kind friends, all radiant with smiles in their reception of me—The Lansdownes (Lord L. & Shelburne) arrived to-day from Holyhead—saw them for a short time, and asked Shelburne to go with me to a breakfast in College tomorrow morning—the breakfast-*giver* being no other than the Reverend ——— Todd, author of the Pope's Letter, whom I so profanely handled in a certain *squiblet* of mine.[1] Being Librarian of the College, his assistance was of the utmost importance to me; but having perpetrated the said squib I naturally despaired of all favour in his eyes. He has himself however volunteered, in

the kindest manner, through Hume, to afford me all the aid in his power. Possibly he may know nothing of the lampoon—and I know hardly whether to hope or not that he *doesn't*. Asked his leave to bring Shelburne with me, which he granted with alacrity—Dined with Arthur Hume, to meet his nephew and Kemmes, & some others.

4 [Tuesday]—Called upon Shelburne and took him to Todd's, where we found a rich display of Irish Antiquarianism, Petrie & Betham being added to our host himself. The conversation was accordingly "germane" to the occasion and Petrie & Betham having got on the subject of the different colonies that settled in Ireland (as indicated by the remains of stone & bronze weapons &c. &c) a breeze was very near springing up between them which was however got rid of laughingly by my saying that if there *was* to be a duel between them, the formula must be "Choose your weapon, bronze or stone."—Was little aware, till Petrie enlightened me afterwards on the matter, of the heart-burnings there have been on the subject of Irish antiquities lately—Sir W. Betham more especially, having drawn down much ridicule on himself by endeavouring to show that a certain Etruscan inscription, well known to scholars, is, every word of it, Irish.[1] To make this out, he has, it appears, disjoined & connected syllables without scruple, and what is still worse as Petrie intimated, has shown nothing so clearly, either Irish or Etruscan as his own entire ignorance of both. A good parody on this paper of Sir William's has been produced by a Mr. ODonovan (the translator of the Four Masters)[2] in which an attempt is made, in the same manner, to prove some lines of Virgil's Aeneid to be Irish, not Latin; and the object is in the same way attained by dividing & connecting the syllables ad libitum—There is also a translation given of this Virgilian Irish into good English doggrell, and the whole squib is happily imagined & executed—We afterwards went to the Library where Shelburne left me and I remained at work for some hours.—Went from there to a Concert at the Rotunda, where no less than Rubini & Persiani were among the performers—My arrival having been announced in the newspapers, the course of staring I have now to stand began in full force—Dined at Lord Morpeth's in the Phoenix Park, Lord Lansdowne having called to take me—A tolerably large party at dinner, and in the evening an assembly and Concert in two acts, with Rubini Persiani, Negri &c. &c.—Among the diners were my dear old friends, the Powers of Kilfane, with a very handsome daughter sprung up since the "olden time" whom I sat next to at dinner

6 [Thursday]—Have, I perceive, let a day slip through—but this must naturally be expected in the sort of rail-way course I am now rattling along—Had written to summon Tom Boyse to town, and accordingly he

was with us to breakfast this morning—a fine fellow, and as happy to see me, I flatter myself, as *I* am to see *him*—Sauntered about with him most of the day—Dined, Lord Lansdowne, Shelburne & myself with Lord Morpeth, to go to the play—None but ourselves—went to Calcraft's Box—Lord L. left us early, and soon after, the audience having found me out, I was most vociferously cheered and applauded—rose and bowed once or twice, which at last procured silence for the actors—"I foresaw this would be the case" said Morpeth, and I had myself indeed observed, that in arranging the chairs for us, on our entering the box he had placed mine so as that I should be *en evidence* before the House. Wrote to Tom this morning to inform him that the Commander in Chief had told me he should have leave of absence, and to bid him start as soon as he could—Had no money to send him, but trusted there would be enough remaining from the remittance I forwarded to him the other day from London to enable him to come up.

7 [Friday]—Lord L. and Shelburne off this morning—are very anxious I should stay here till their return—A very kind note from the Lord Lieutenant who is at the Curragh regretting that he should lose any of my time here, and inviting me and my son, if with me, to dinner at the Park on Monday—Dined at Arthur Hume's, Boyse being of the party, and the day very agreeable—

8th [Saturday]—A letter from poor Tom, informing that he has been very ill, and still confined to his room, though much better.—Talks of being well enough in about ten days to join me here, but by that time I shall be ready to start—Dined at Lord Morpeth's, who invited Boyse also, to accompany me—a large party as usual, and as agreeable as such "upright slating" *can* be—Morpeth, himself always full of courtesy and kindness—Forgot to mention that I found here Alexander Mac Donnel, (the former protége of Abercrombie & Lord Lansdowne) in the capacity of Irish Clerk, as I believe it is called with a salary of about seven or eight hundred a year—seems out of sorts with all around him—says that Dublin is still a mere military garrison—an entrenchment of Toryism. Poor fellow—the way in which he has been let drop by his patrons is rather lamentable. *Over*rated at first, he is now left perhaps, *below* his due level.

9 [Sunday]—Went after breakfast accompanied by Boyse to the Marlborough St. Chapel where I was invited to collect for the Mendicity Society—the affair, however ill managed—and Boyse & I had but little on our plates beyond what we ourselves put there—viz. a donation from me of three pounds and of five from Boyse. Mine was in reality only *two* pounds,

but owing to his having none but thirty-shilling notes, Boyse could not manage a less sum than six pounds, so he set down the sixth pound to my account.—Dined all, Boyse, myself & Nell, at Cumings's in the country— sung a good deal in the evening—some *very* bad singing also by others.

10 [Monday]—A letter from Tom saying that the Doctor is *now* of opinion he may join me in Dublin, and that he will be here on Thursday next. Dined at the Lord Lieutenant's—a small party and only one lady, Mrs. ———— I forget her name, but who, as I have learned since is supposed to be the present *regnante* with his Excellency—Lady Normanby, who arrived from England on Saturday, not well enough to appear—Sung a good deal in the evening, being in excellent voice—Have not said any thing yet about my studies, but not a day passes without some hours of it being devoted to work, and I shall give, at the end, a brief review of what I have done—}

12 [Wednesday]—Having appointed to go out to the Park to the Ordnance Survey went there with Petrie—Shown the whole by Mr. Larcum, and was as much struck with the man himself as by any thing he showed me—the whole full of interest—called in my way back on the Lord Lieutenant, and was told by Liddell, before I saw himself that his Exy. had bid him say to me that he hoped whenever I was not engaged elsewhere I would come and dine with *him*—{The same repeated to me by Normanby when I saw him. "I know," he said "you must have numbers of friends in Dublin who will be anxious to have you but mind, whenever you are not engaged else where I shall be most happy to see you here"—This all very kind and hospitable— In the course of conversation, asked me "what are you going to do with yourself to-day?" to which I answered that not having any particular en- gagement I should be most delighted to dine with him—which was imme- diately fixed—Wrote my letters as usual at Lord Morpeth's office, where I find, in Macdonald's room, free entrée, every day, and besides writing materials, get franks into the bargain.—A small party at dinner, and in the evening Lady Normanby joined us—Sung a good deal to her, and was more than rewarded by seeing her enjoy it so much—dashed off from there, in my Shanderadan to assist at dear Nell's party—had seen all the preparations in the morning, and nothing could look more promising for gaiety—found them all in high dance, and some very nice girls among the group, particularly Georgiana OKelly, a Miss Byrne and (though a little gone off, from ill health) Mulvany's sister—Sung a great number of songs for them, my voice being luckily in full force, and was paid with plenty of smiles & applauses from all around. I have sometimes complained of my country women that they were not half such encouraging auditors to sing to as the English-women—but this accusation I now retract—at least to a

greater degree—supper charmingly managed, and then came dancing again—so that we did not get to bed till three o'clock.

I had here (from some confusion in my memorandums) mixed together two days, the 11th. and the 12th—and even now cannot recollect what became of me on the 11th.—it can't however be helped. Received either to-day or yesterday a remittance of £30 from Easthope}

13 [Thursday]—Roused up about seven from my short sleep, by the arrival of Tom, who tramped up at once to my bed-room, looking very pale & ill—I had not told him of the night appointed for Nell's party, lest he should have made an effort to be there by starting sooner than his Doctor might think prudent—Took him, after breakfast to Crampton, who gave me every hope of his being soon brought round again—Went all of us, Nell, Tom & myself to dine with the Finlays to-day—In speaking of Irish History, it was not ill said by Finlay—"the lies are bad,—and the truth worse."—{Was asked one day, this week, to dine at the Commander in Chief's,—but couldn't, being engaged. Tomorrow night is to be my *benefit* at the Theatre, Calcraft having written to beg of me to order a play. The following is the announcement in the newspapers. Oddly enough there is but *one* Irish Melody among the Songs here [mentio]ned—Have found another newspaper scrap, giving an account of my reception the night I went with Morpeth to the theatre, which I may as well, also wafer in[1]—

14. [Friday]—Tom, who is better, but too weak to walk much, drove about most of the day with Nell—I at my work—Dined, Tom & I, at Lord Morpeth's—forget who were the company.}

15 [Saturday]—{Hume growing rather impatient to be off—should not be sorry if he did bolt as Lord Lansdowne is expected back here next Wednesday, and what with the Holyhead passages, the Menai Bridge, and his agreeable society, it would be rather a better sort of thing. Hume, however, is a right good fellow, in his way, and so—have with him! Rather nervous about my exhibition to night—people were afraid the Howth Races would thin the audience, but it promises marvellously well, I hear, for this time of the year—} Agreed to dine with Crampton *en famille*—nobody but his own family, and a little after eight He and I and Tom proceeded to the Theatre—found I was rather late—took my place in the front of Nell's box between two very pretty Sultanas she had provided for me, Georgiana OKelly and Miss Burne—The explosion on my appearance was tremendous and when—but it will save trouble to insert the Morning Register's account of the whole affair.[1]

"Unusual as it is to speak from the boxes of a theatre, I really cannot sit any longer silent under these repeated demonstrations of cordiality and affection, and therefore have nothing for it but to say, with *Mr. Muddlework*, in the farce which we have just witnessed, "and now for my oration" (laughter). It would require a voice, I fear, of far more compass than I command to make myself heard by the numerous kind friends who have here assembled to greet me; though, had I the voice of Stentor himself, combined with the eloquence of a Demosthenes, or of your own O'Connell (loud cheers), I should fail to convey to you a hundredth part of what I feel at this great, this overpowering kindness: not that I pretend to consider myself as wholly unworthy of such a reception—for that would be to do injustice to *you*, my kind friends, as well as to myself. No; you have had in other times, and you have still, far more able and eloquent champions of your cause (no, no, and loud cheers). But, as the humble interpreter of those deep and passionate feelings—those proud, though melancholy, aspirations—which breathe throughout our own undying songs—as the humble medium through which that voice of Song and Sorrow has been heard on other shores, awakening the sympathy of every people by whom the same wrongs, the same yearnings for freedom are felt—in this respect I cannot but flatter myself that I am not wholly unworthy of your favour (enthusiastic cheering). It may be in the recollection of most of my hearers, that, in one of the earliest of those songs, I myself foresaw and foretold the sort of echo they would awaken in other lands:—

"The stranger shall hear our lament on his plains,
The song of our harp shall be sent o're the deep."[2]

(loud cheers) This prediction I have lived to see accomplished—the stranger *has* heard our lament on his plains—the song of our harp *has* been sent o'er the deep—and wherever oppression is struggled against, or liberty cherished, there the strains of Ireland are welcomed as the language native to such feelings. It is a striking fact, that on the banks of the Vistula the Irish Melodies have been translated in a Polish sense, and are adopted by that wronged and gallant people as expressive of their own disastrous fate (loud cheers). Not to trespass any longer on your attention (hear and cheers), I shall only add, that there exists no title of honour or distinction to which I could attach half so much value, or feel half so anxious to retain unforfeited through life, as that of being called *your* poet—the poet of the people of Ireland (enthusiastic cheering)." {Supper at Nell's afterwards, very gay.

16 [Sunday]—Received the following note from the Freemans Journal Office—"A reporter from this office does himself the honour of waiting on

Mr. [Moore] to request the favour of an outlining of the speech which he delivered last night at the Theatre. He was unfortunately unprepared with the means of taking notes on the occasion; and, as the subject is of the highest interest to the public, Mr. Moore's compliance with this request will confer an important favour on his humble servant and enthusiastic admirer—Mr. Havertry." After breakfast wrote out the Speech as accurately as I could, and then took it to the Freeman's Journal, and begged of them to send slips of it to the Morning Register & Saunders'—the Register having also sent to me to ask an outline of the oration—Dined (Tom, Nell & I) at Meara's, at Kingstown—a long way off & a very large party of ODwyers, Cassidys, OMaras, Fitzsimons's &c.—all most kind and hearty—Carleton, the author of Irish Tales,[1] likewise of the party—Sung a good deal for them}

17 [Monday]—{Attended a show of Flowers at the Robinsons having received a ticket from the Committee thereof—a very gay show of ladies also—was rather too modest in not making full use of my ticket which I found afterwards entitled me to join the Lord Lieutenant's party, and enjoy as they did the privilege of *eating* the fruit as well as of *looking* at it—} Went with a party consisting of Mrs. Fitzsimon (OConnell's daughter) and some others to see the National School in Marlborough St. and was much pleased—particularly with the *infant* part of it which we found in the playground and certainly never before saw so many happy, pretty & picturesque urchins assembled together—Went to dine, Tom and myself with Lord Morpeth & had rather a whimsical adventure—In going out to the Park I have generally used one of those cabs, (or *shanderadans,* as they call them) which my sister recommended me, driven by an odd fellow, called Ennis, and thinking it was he who had driven me the last time I went to Lord Morpeth's, I merely said now at starting "go to the same place you took me to the other evening"—The length of the avenue to the house rather struck me, and when we arrived and were told they had gone to dinner, some mention of "the Groom of the Chamber &c." made a sort of passing impression upon me, which instead of startling, produced insensibly, I suppose, that change in all my associations which prepared me (so otherwise unaccountably) for what followed. After a little delay we were ushered in to—the Lord Lieutenant's dining-room, where only himself, Lady Normanby & the aid-de-camps were seated at their family dinner, and it was only by taking close order they were able to make room among them for Tom & myself. To Lord Normanby there was just sufficient, in the general invitation he had given me for *any day,* to prevent his being greatly surprized at my present intrusion—but my bringing my son also must have appeared to him a somewhat strong measure. Nothing, however, could be more kind than our reception by the whole party, and I was helped to soup and had finished it before the actual fact of what I had done and where I

was, flashed upon my mind. "Good God!" I exclaimed "what a mistake I have committed!" "What!" said Lord Normanby, laughing, and at once seeing the whole fact of the case "were you to have dined with Morpeth? that's excellent—Now we have you, we'll keep you." Upon which he instantly ordered the aid-de-camp to send a messenger to Morpeth's to say "we have stopped Mr. Moore on the way." The dinner very agreeable, but soon after we had retired to the drawing-room, I said "Well all this is very delightful *so far;* but I really must now go to the *right* place," upon which Lord N. very kindly ordered one of his carriages to take me to Morpeth's, but it turned out that my own Shanderadan had waited for me—so off Tom & I set in it for the Secretary's where we found a very large party, and I sung away for them at the rate of a dozen songs per hour to make up for my default—

{18 [Tuesday]—Attended a show of flowers &c. &c.—John Scully, who I feared was not coming in time to see me has at last arrived, and Nell to-day gave us a snug dinner at home—our party being only John, Meara, Tom & myself—Lord John expected every day in Dublin, but will not be here, I fear, before I start—Having now concluded nearly all my business, shall be able to be off, I hope, on Saturday—An attack upon Tom has appeared in the United Service Gazette, within these few days, accusing him of being "rude to some respectable females" of Belfast. It also brings severe charges against the Colonel of the Regiment; and as the officers expressed a wish that he should notice the part of the attack relating to himself, he has sent a short letter to the Editor of the Gazette denying the charge *in toto;* there being, it appears, not the slightest ground for it.[1]—Dined, Tom & I at Arthur Hume's—rather a heavy concern—

19 [Wednesday]—A *dies non*—at least can find no trace of it, either in my own pencil memorandums or in my letters to Bessy.

20. [Thursday]—Have arranged with Hume, who has long been anxious for our departure, to set sail on Saturday, the day after tomorrow—A letter from young Shelburne to tell me the route of Lord L. and himself, and mentioning the time at which he thinks they are likely to be in Dublin. It *was* my intention to let Hume set off by himself & wait for them, but, all things considered, my present arrangement is the best—and at all events, my sweet *Bess* will think so, as I shall be with her so many days the sooner.— Have read the article in the Gazette against Tom and his Regiment and rather doubt whether if I had seen it at the time, I should have allowed him to take any notice of it—the whole *animus* and style of the thing is so

essentially blackguard. Has shown me letters that some of his brother officers have written to him on the subject, and all are creditable both to themselves & to him—so that the ill luck of having his name blazoned about thus prematurely is, I should hope, the only thing bad in the circumstance. Dined, Tom & myself, with Lord Morpeth, and met (I *think* it was on this day) Pigot, the law-adviser of the Irish government, who struck me as one of the most sensible, well-mannered (to say nothing of good-looking) Irishmen I have met for many a day—Brought Tom and me home in his Fly—not one of the least of his merits, by the bye, was a very warm & apparently sincere relish for my singing which he had never heard before—

21 [Friday]—Annoyed & surprized to see an announcement in all the papers of another night at the Theatre under my patronage for the Benefit of the Mendicity Society—Went, as soon as I could get out to the Theatre to learn what this meant, and found that it was all a hoax, by some stupid, if not malicious person who had gone to the trouble and expence of sending & paying for this advertisement at all the newspaper offices—Poor Nell a little downcast at my approaching departure—Nothing, to be sure (not even *herself*) could be sweeter, kinder, or more cheerful than she has been during my visit—Dined, Tom and I, at the Lord Lieutenant's—had expected that Lord Lansdowne & Lord John would have been there, but neither yet arrived, so that I shall be off without seeing them—A large dinner party, and some of them new arrivals—viz Lady Stuart de Rothesay and her fine daughter—Sir Charles Lemon & his sister Lady de Dunstanville—Gore (Lord John's secretary)—young Lord Mulgrave, John Ponsonby—&c. &c.—Forgot to mention that I walked about yesterday a little with Lemon—went with him to look at the Castle—Chapel &c.—Sat next Lord Cloncurry at dinner, and was invited by him & my Lady to come to Lyons & bring Tom—promised for *him,* though I couldn't for myself which I regret—Sung in the evening, but my voice a little the worse for my racketting, and the Piano-Forte (a new one) unluckily tuned a quarter of a note above concert-pitch—managed, however, to get through a few songs, before the evening company came crowding in for the dance that was prepared for them—Saw a number of people whom I had much wished to see among the rest, Mrs. White (Routhe's daughter) a very handsome person—Lady Howth, &c. &c. and then set off home, leaving Tom behind to quadrille it with the young ladies.—}

22nd. [Saturday]—The day not very favourable for our passage—but I cannot expect to be lucky in every thing—Tom danced till two in the morning at the Lord Lieutenant's—Went the first thing after breakfast to the Royal Irish Academy to look over a MS. Life of Red Hugh[1] which Petrie yesterday told me of—Had luncheon at Nell's at three o'clock, and then set off—Hume and I, accompanied by Tom—to Kingstown. Encountered an odd scene on going on board—the packet was full of people coming to see friends off, and among others was a party of ladies who, I should think, had dined on board, and who on my being made known to them, almost devoured me with kindness, and at length proceeded so far as to insist on each of them *kissing* me. All this time I was beginning to feel the first rudiments of coming sickness, and the effort to respond to all this enthusiasm, in such a state of stomach, was not a little awkward & trying—However I kissed the whole party (about five, I think) in succession, two or three of them being, for my comfort, young & good-looking, and was most glad to get away from them to my berth, which, through the kindness of the Captain (Emerson) was in his own cabin. But I had hardly shut the door, feeling very qualmish & most glad to have got over this osculatory operation, when there came a gentle tap at the door, and an elderly lady made her appearance, who said that, having heard of all that had been going on she could not rest easy without being *also* kissed as well as the rest. So, in the most respectful manner possible I complied with the lady's request, and then betook myself with a heaving stomach to my berth—{The first half of our passage very stormy and rough, but by keeping myself in the same horizontal position I escaped actual sickness, and even slept a little.

23 [Sunday]—Arrived in Liverpool, after a passage I believe, of something more than 12 hours.—It being Sunday, no train was to set off till between one and two, which gave me an opportunity of going to call upon Bessy's god-daughter, Eliza S. who lives at Wavertree a few miles from Liverpool—After breakfast took a Fly, and proceeded thither, Hume & myself—sat for about half an hour with Eliza & her husband, who appears to be a sensible good sort of young man—Arrived at Vauxhall in time to partake of the general scrambling dinner, and then leaving Hume there, to start for London in the morning, I proceeded to the Castle at Birmingham, where I slept.}

24 [Monday]—{Started in the Coach, at ½ past eight for Bath—and at Cheltenham picked up Admiral Bayntun & his daughter Miss Avenall, who made the time pass very agreeably till we got to Bath—Much puzzled there (it being then late) as to whether I should proceed home till morning or not—Home however carried it—a Fly was ordered for Sloperton and though I had to rouse the cottage from its slumbers, and rather frightened my poor Bess, I was not sorry, when all was over, to find myself in my own bed once more.}

I shall now note down briefly, as well as I can recollect them, some particulars respecting my studies during the time I staid in Dublin— scarcely a day having passed without my devoting some hours to the chief object I had in my visit. In the College Library I found the Abstract of the Book of Pandarus which I wished to see—I also found some curious things (but *only* curious) in the Catalogue Todd is making of the Manuscripts of the Library[1]—Went through the Manuscripts likewise & took memoran- dums of the few things I saw much worthy of my notice—among others the contents of four of the Books given by Archbishop Laud to the Bodleian,[2] which I shall take a trip some time or other to see—Went through the Annals of Clonmacnoise, and the annals of Inisfallen[3]—One of which Books of Annals was, if I recollect right, at the Royal Irish Academy, and the other at the College. But the book to which I devoted most time was O'Donovan's Translation of the Four Masters,—beginning at the period where OConnor's translation of the Four Masters ends[4]—This work I found in the possession of Smith & Hodges, the booksellers, and passed some hours of almost every day, for the last ten or twelve of my stay, in looking over & making extracts from it—found nothing however, of much importance—their *omissions* of some remarkable events being far more remarkable than any thing they contain—For instance, the second visit of Richd. 2nd. to Ireland is entirely unnoticed by them.—The day before my departure, Petrie reminded me that I had not looked through the MS. life of Red Hugh at the Royal I. Academy—accordingly immediately after breakfast the next morning I went to the Academy, and taking with me the second Vol. of Sir W. Betham's Antiquarian Researches[5] which professes to give an Abstract of the said MS. found that the Abstract would be quite sufficient for my purpose. Forget whether I have mentioned among my memorandums a visit or two which I made to Betham during my stay— Found many curious things in his Library (some of which, they say, have no *right* to be there) but almost all relating to periods later than that on which I am at present employed—Among some *accessible* books I found was the Index to the Rolls of the English Parliament which contains many refer- ences of importance, respecting Ireland & of which I must procure a copy—Have also I think omitted to mention my going to see the Black Book of Christ-Church, under the auspices of the Bishop of Kildare (a fine old man), who was remarkably kind to me, and wanted me to dine with him to meet Lady Stuart and her handsome daughters, but I was unluckily en- gaged—went with him to Kirk's to see his bust—my Shanderadan being our conveyance—Only think—Tom Moore & a Bishop cheek by jowl in a cab! {Received almost every day letters, addresses, Poems &c. from unknown, but [*MS damaged*] kind & enthusiastic correspondents. One Poem begins thus

> "Thy country hails thee, Moore, thou truly art great,—
> If greatness consists in that being or state

> Wherein man has done good for his country & kind,
> And showed all that power & greatness of mind,
> Which humbles the tyrant, gives praise to the good,
> And, as a river bursting its bounds by a flood,—"

at which line the writer himself bursts all bounds of metre & sense, and goes splashing on through two sheets of letter-paper till at last he subsides into the following very matter-of-fact prose. "My pen is so bad that I fear you will find it difficult to interpret what I have written. There are two things that I find it difficult to obtain—a good pen and a good razor." Another unknown correspondent incloses me some Irish airs not included in my published collection, thus headed "An Address on behalf of sundry natives of the dear Poet's 'Emerald gem of the Western World,' being airs of a very respectable character who, with great deference, consider they are entitled to form (in conjunction with the illustrious Bard's immortal verse) the 11th. and 12th. Numbers of his far-famed Irish Melodies—

> He comes again—of Love and Wine
> The sparkling melodist divine!
> Doth it not glad green Erin's shore
> To hail her patriot bard once more?"

and so on through two or three pink pages, in the same couleur de rose strain. Another of these kind tributes reminds me in the following lines of a story of Corry's—

> Dear Moore where'er I hear your lays
> My soul bursts forth in willing praise;
> The melody of thy sweet songs
> Makes us more deeply feel our wrongs.}

It was Billy Murphy, I believe, who, fresh from reading my "Captain Rock" said to Corry, with the tears running down his cheeks—"oh, it's a beautiful book—I never before knew how ill we are used." {The following are a few more specimens of this poem.—

> Your country's foes have felt your ire
> When, swelled with patriotic fire,
> Your genius comes, with magic wand,
> To save our much oppressed land,
> From cruel tyrants' stern decrees,
> And haughty churchmen's grinding fees.

Received a printed paper from Wales, respecting the approaching festival of the Cymrecgyddion, which I take for granted came from Rio, both because I *half* promised him to attend there, and because the address, in a woman's hand (his wife's I take for granted) was as follows. "The Thomas Moore Esq. par excellence, Dublin."

Here are some other stanzas, not bad, from an "Address to Thomas Moore on his arrival in Dublin."—

> Loud be thy welcome, oh minstrel of Erin!
>   With shamrocks and myrtles thy bright path be drest!
> O'er Liffey's blue water her blue banners rearing,
>   Ellana breathes love to the Bard of the West.
>
> What bliss, in a moment of hope to behold thee
>   Revisit the land of thy tears and thy songs,
> As loving, as loved, as when first she enrolled thee,
>   The saddest, the sweetest that wept for her wrongs
>
> When faded the wreath that, for centuries blooming,
>   Thy "own Island harp," in its brighter day, wore
> Like the rainbow on rose-wood, enriching, perfuming,
>   Thou gav'st it a sweetness it knew not before.
>
> And, snatching it forth from the Hall of its slumber,
>   Thro the desert of Slavery with Erin to stray,
> Like the tree in the waters of Mara, thy numbers
>   Could sweeten the bitterest fount on her way
>
> * * * * * * * * * * * * * * *
>
> But thus while in Fame's brightest halo thou shinest,
>   Tho the first of her bards, and historians thou art,
> As the leaves of the rose in its center are finest
>   The best of thy beauties are found in thy heart.
>
> Then, loud be thy welcome, oh minstrel &c.

But of all the honours that, in this way attended me the following simple and striking letter from a young man in rather humble life, gave the greatest pleasure. I shall here wafer in the original, as it is worth preserving, in its own honest form.

Honoured Sir/

I came from a distant part of Ireland to see you, as the man of old came to see Livy from some remote section of the Roman dominions—Unwilling to trespass on your valuable time, I have waited for several days at the College gate but have not succeeded in my object—May [*MS damaged*] trouble in one line to inform me where or when I may see one whose writings have filled me, in common with thousands, with admiration.

                    I remain one of the humblest of your admirers,
                              James Raleigh Baxter

City of Dublin Hospital
Upper Baggot Street

Not liking to disappoint so unpretending an admirer, I wrote him a note to the Dublin Hospital, saying that I should make it a point to be at the College gates, a little after three the following day, and should feel much gratified by his presenting himself to me. In answer to this I received the following note from his brother

"City of Dublin Hospital
½ past 11 oC.

Sir—My duties here prevent me from waiting personally on you and accounting for my brother's not seeing you. He is a very young lad and having just gone to Kingstown, I am unable to make him aware of your kindness. A young man named Downes, who was on a visit at my house told my brother you were very busy just now, which prevented the young enthusiast waiting on you at your residence. We shall both see you (if we can get room) in the Theatre this evening. With many apologies I remain for my brother, and in my own behalf, your most humble servant, W. Raleigh Baxter."}

This is all, I think, of the communications received during my trip that deserve any particular notice—I forget whether I have mentioned the recollections that gradually came over me, at Lord Morpeth's table the day Lord Lansdowne & myself dined quietly with him to go to the Theatre. I had remarked in the course of conversation, that it was a significant proof of the politics that had prevailed in the Castle during my life-time, that I was but once before a guest in that house—When I came to recollect, however, it turned out, that in the *one* instance which I had then called to my mind, Sir Henry Harding had been my host; and that I had dined (whether at the Castle or park I now forget) both with Elliot and—(never to be forgotten day)—with Sir Arthur Wellesley. I say never to be forgotten, because on that day, the conversation happening to turn upon my poor friend Emmett, I was afforded an opportunity, within those ministerial walls of speaking of him as he deserved, and with Sir Arthur Wellesley for my most attentive and apparently most interested listener. Such a flight of daring at an Irish Secretary's table was, at that time, little less than a portent. But the merit was far less in the speaker than in the great listener—for even the most ordinary of Irish Secretaries could, from his very position have consigned me to silence with a look. But I was encouraged by the attention of my auditor, and, that very night, undressing for bed, I remember saying to myself, "Well, thank God, I have lived to pronounce an eulogium upon Robert Emmett at the Irish Chief Secretary's table."

October {1, 2 &c [Monday–Tuesday]—I must now dispatch rapidly my few memoranda of this month & the following—

4 [Thursday]—Dined at Bowood—Party, the Starkeys, Heneages, Lady E. Cole and daughter—slept there—

5, 6, 7, 8 [Friday–Monday]—

9 [Tuesday]—Went with Lord Shelburne to dine at Guthrie's, in Calne—party Phipps, Atherton, the Vivashes & two ladies, Guthrie's nieces—brought home by Phipps. Much talk with Henry about Madlle. Flahaut, he being about to make another experiment in that quarter—wish him success most heartily—

10 or 11 [Wednesday–Thursday]—Went in, Bessy & I, to dine with the Hughes's, and meet the Boyses in the evening—also the Cletheroes, Brabants &c.—Sung a great deal and was in high voice—Found that Mrs. Boyse & I had met ages ago—so far back as "bonae sub regno Cynarae,"[1] when I was making love to that *very* pretty Cynara, Mrs. Barbat, somewhere about the year 1806, I think.—Received one of these days an addition to my Irish glorifications in the shape of an Address from the inhabitants of Fermoy who it appears supposed that I was visiting at Lord Listowel's, in their neighbourhood (at the time Lord Lansdowne was there) and fired this most flaming eulogy at me. Have not time now to transcribe it, but it is laid by among my κειμήλια —[2]

16 [Tuesday]—Bessy and I went to dine at Bowood—no company but ourselves & all very snug & agreeable—in the evening Lord Lansdowne read aloud to us some of the characters from Brougham's late article in the Edinburgh—slept there

17 [Wednesday]—After breakfast, Bessy walked to see Mrs. Hughes, and the Lansdownes' carriage then brought her home—I myself walked home.}

20 [Saturday]—Went to dine at Bowood—Company staying there my old friends the Miss Berrys, Mr. Twopenny & Henry's quondam tutor, Mr. Paishley—Sung in the evening—Miss Berry, as I now found from her, was present on that very evening (to *me* long memorable) when I made my first appearance as a singer, in London. When I call it "*first* appearance," I mean before any very large or miscellaneous company—Miss Berry's description of the effect I produced tallied very much with my own recollection, & she also described (what I did not of course myself observe) the sort of contemptuous titter with which the fine gentlemen & amateurs round the Piano-forte saw a little Irish lad led forth to exhibit after all the fine singing that had been going on—the change in their countenances, when they saw the effect I produced &c. &c.—I don't know whether I may not already

have mentioned somewhere, that, on that night, as I was leaving the Pianoforte, I heard a lady say as I passed her "and he's going to the Bar—what a pity!" Old Hammersley himself, who, it appeared, had also heard her, begged me when I was taking my departure to call upon him in the morning; and, I found, on going to him at the time appointed, that his object was to express the regret he had felt at the foolish speech uttered in my hearing by this lady, and to advise me not to allow the admiration thus bestowed on my musical & poetical talent to divert my mind from the steady pursuit of the profession chosen for me. This I always thought most kind & fatherly in old Hammersley—A good deal of talk also with Miss Berry, about the agreeable times we passed together at Tunbridge, in 1805–6—Would I had begun journalizing then! our ever memorable party consisting of the Dunmores, Lady Donegal & sisters, the Duchess of St. Albans, Lady Heathcote, that Dragoness, Lady Anna Hamilton, with the beautiful Susan Beckford (now Duchess of Hamilton) under her care, Thomas Hope (making assiduous love to Miss Beckford), William Spenser, Rogers, Sir Harry Englefield &c. &c.—Miss Berry reminded me of several odd incidents of that period—{among others, the poor Duchess of Albans taking unconsciously a play-book to Church, and holding it upside down before her eyes, as if reading, while a saintly lady in the next pew was cognizant of the whole abomination—Her story about Flop—[I had been telling her about Flop (young Howard) when I asked him what o'clock it was, turning to his servant, and saying "che ora?" and then looking at me with that foolish face of his and drawling out, "He's a German" as if to account for his speaking bad Italian to him—She then mentioned her friend Flop having written a learned Essay about a Phoenician colony in some part of England (Cornwall, I suppose) stuffed full of learned authorities, and sending it to Sydney Smith, of all people, who wrote him immediately a letter back, saying he was surprized at his omitting any reference to a number of other learned authors, on the subject, and then subjoining a list of forged names ending in *us* which threw poor Flop into despair & set him ransacking all possible libraries—][1]

21 [Sunday]—Being anxious to work a little, started before breakfast for home—and had a note from Lady L. hot-foot after me, saying how surprized they were at my non appearance, and asking me to come at least tomorrow, if I would not return to dinner to-day. Promised for tomorrow.

22. [Monday]—To Dinner to Bowood—same party—In talking, after the ladies left us of Bishop Berkley's theory, Lord L. referred to the opinion that, if pursued to its utmost, it would prove the non-existence of any body at all—but I do not see this—As long as what is called *mind* exists, impressions producing the notion of external existence may according to

Berkeley's system continue to be made upon it—Speaking of English or rather German French some one told of a lady saying "Mes Suisses ouvrent a tout le monde"—substituting the letter C for S, rather awkwardly—Brougham's saying "Je passai la nuit fort agreablement avec (or *entre*, I forget which) Made. de Brogli et Made. un telle" *to* which I cited, as apropos, the lady who said "Je couche toujours entre deux *matelots*"—meaning mate*las*—

23 [Tuesday]—Returned home after breakfast

25 [Thursday]—To Bowood again, to stay till Saturday—Company, Lord & Lady Barington, Lady Williamson (Lady Bs. sister) Lord Boringdon, and Lord Bathurst—In talking of thermometers, Lord Bathurst mentioned one of his own construction (I believe) which he generally consulted, and when we asked him how it succeeded, he answered with some fun, that he would "trust a new hat to it." Singing in the evening by Ladies Barrington & Williamson, as well as by myself—Lady Ws. voice one of great power and truth, but seems already beginning to feel the "touch of time."

26 [Friday]—Walked home after breakfast to work a little at transcribing—In talking of Pozza di Borgo, one of these days & remarking how extraordinary it was that Corsica should have sent forth at the same time two such men as he and Napoleon, Lord L. mentioned Pozzo's having said, when Napoleon was sent to Elba, "L'empire du Diable est fini—reste à voir celui de l'Homme"—returned to Bowood to dinner—great doings for these some days at Devizes, with the Yeomanry &c. at which all the gentry of the county are assembled—Lord Lansdowne and Lord Barrington gone to the great dinner there to-day and some of the Ladies going to the Ball in the evening—had not the least thought of going to the latter myself, till at dinner Lady Barrington & her sister insisted that I should be of the party and when I alleged their want of room for me in the carriage, said I should sit Bodkin—so off we set with our four horses, Lady Louisa and Lord Boringdon, completing the five inside—Some handsome persons were the Lady Bruces, Lady Aylesbury &c. at the Ball—old Lord Aylesbury himself most lordly drunk (the first time I believe any one ever saw him so) and in talking to Lady Barrington (she sitting and he impending over her) was very near tipping over, to her no small alarm—Came away pretty early and in our two carriages & four got home about half past one.}

27 [Saturday]—Had some beautiful singing in the Chapel from Lady Barrington & Lady Williamson—Combe, the organist, having been brought

over from Chippenham to accompany—{In one or two of the things Lord Barrington (who is no musician, but has a good Bass voice) took a part.} Lady Williamson sung "Let the bright Seraphim" with great spirit and power— They sung also Haydn's beautiful "tu di Grazie," in which I *could* have joined (as I told them afterwards) but did not volunteer.—Walked late in the day to Sergeant Merewethers to dinner—nobody but Sergeant Cross and his lady and daughter to dinner—Sung a good deal for them in the evening, and had a Fly home—at least *thought* it was a Fly (though much surprized at its smartness) till on coming to *pay* I found it was Sergeant Cross's carriage—

{28, 29 [Sunday–Monday]—At home, for a wonder—

30 [Tuesday]—To Bowood—Company there Lord & Lady Grosvenor, Luttrell, the Vernon Smiths, the Bishop of Salisbury, and his Chaplain Bouverie—The Grosvernors very good-natured & agreeable—she, the latter, most particularly—the Bishop also very mild & gentlemanlike—

31 [Wednesday]—Worked a little—walked with Luttrell to Buck-Hill, where Bessy was staying with Mrs. Hughes and sate talking some time. In looking over Burnes's Travels[1] (in the East) which lay on Hughes's table, found the following—"The well-known inscription which has been immortalized by Moore [Light of the Haram][2] still remains on the walls, emblazoned in letters of gold. The correct translation of it runs thus:—'If there be an Elysium on earth, it is this.'[3]—The Elysium has indeed vanished, the peacock thrones as well as the precious roof have disappeared." Same company at dinner as yesterday, with the exception of the Bishop who, after breakfast this morning consecrated the Mausoleum, and then took his departure.}

November {1 [Thursday]—All the guests gone before breakfast, the Grosvenors, the Vernon Smiths, and Luttrell—breakfasted with the Lansdownes, and then walked home, Lord Lansdowne accompanying me the greater part of the way and, after having stopped then, for some time, to continue our conversation, I saw him back again the greater part of *his* way.

Novr. 2, 3, 4 &c [Friday, 2 November–Tuesday, 13 November]—Quiet and at work

November 14 [Wednesday]—Having fixed with the Longmans to come up to town, on the subject of the projected Edition of my works, went to

Devizes, accompanied by Bess, to dine with the Hugheses—company, Brabant, Edmonston, Miss Cooper, Major Oliver, &c.—rather agreeable but too much wine—the occasion of the dinner was old Hughes's birth-day (I believe) and he made us a very apposite & vigorous speech on the occasion—Knowing too that my dear Bess's birth-day was to be on the morrow, he proposed her health also cordially & cleverly—In talking of him afterwards with Brabant entirely agreed with his remark that if old Hughes's training, in early life had been of a better & higher kind he would have been no ordinary man. The clearness of his mind [*MS damaged*] how strong it must have been originally—slept at Hughes's}

15 [Thursday]—{Off at nine by the White Hart—an intelligent man in the coach (accompanied by his wife,) with whom I had a good deal of conversation on a variety of subjects—Knew all about the literature of the day, as well as about literary men. Talking of Scott's physical strength, told of his having lifted, with one arm, a fellow out of his seat in the front of a box in the Edinburgh Theatre, and deposited him body & bones in the pit—the fellow having rudely refused to make way for some ladies by whom Scott was accompanied. In speaking of the difficulty of providing for one's boys in these times, he mentioned the Duke of Sussex having given him, for one of his sons, an appointment to the [*MS damaged*] and added that it was not from any intimacy of his own with the Duke, but from his [father's] having been the tutor of the Princes at Kew—This affords a clue to my companion—His [wife] a much more ordinary sort of person was part of the time employed in reading and at one time burst out suddenly into a loud laugh at something she found in her book. I remarked how gratified the author would be at this unrestrained tribute to his fun, and found it was the Heir of Law[1] she was reading. At Newbury they left the coach & I suspect him to be a clergyman residing in that neighbourhood—on my arrival in town went to the St. James's Hotel, that being Corry's head-quarters, and found him at dinner, the letter I wrote to him last night from Devizes to announce my coming not having been I suppose put in the post. Joined him at his repast, and ordered a bed in the Hotel.

16 [Friday]—Breakfasted with Corry at Hotel—went together to Longman's—asked by Tom to dinner to meet Sydney Smith and Boz—but I did not like to leave Corry—Tom said he would at all events send the carriage for me at six—Talk about our edition—the first great object to ascertain whether Carpenter has (as it seems he pretends, and they believe) any copyright of my works out & out—strong persuasion being that he has not—Suggested that I should take the opportunity of calling upon him now with Corry—did so, though not much liking the operation, it being now so

many years since I was inside his doors. Luckily, however, we met by accident in the street, about a year ago, and then all was friendliness between us. So it was also now. Corry's being with me took off all appearance of formality or prepense design in the visit. A very few words on the subject of the Edition convinced me that he had no right or assignment from me of those works he published. "Those *you* have," I said carelessly "are out aren't they?"—"Yes, in *time*," he answered. This was quite enough for my object. He then added something of my having said once to him that he might do whatever he pleased with them; but this of course was nothing at all to the purpose, and I immediately passed to something else. What I found to be uppermost, indeed, in his mind was a projected work, or fragment of a work, upon "Pious and Learned Ladies,"[1] which I had once an idea of publishing, and even proceeded so far (it seems, though I had entirely forgotten the circumstances) as to have had part of the work printed which he has now sealed in his hands.—For this he gave me, he says (and I have no doubt of the fact, though entirely forgotten it) eighty pounds; and I of course assured him that this should be settled as soon as he pleased & the work redeemed from his hands. Some of the verses in it, I have since used, I think, for my Sacred Songs, but the rest cannot be worth much; though the odd reading with which it abounds cost me a good deal of trouble & time. In parting with him promised to name some day to dine with him, (having been first taken to Mrs. Carpenter, who was equally glad to see me), and the whole visit and business was dispatched in little more, I think, than a quarter of an hour. Called upon Lady Elisabeth Feilding (who has been staying with Lady Valletort for her confinement) and her first words were, most hospitably, "You are at Sackville St. I hope?"—"No," I answered—"I could not think of going there without first asking your leave, and there was not time for that"— on which she said, "Well, mind henceforth, you must always, when you mean to come to town, write to the housemaid at Sackville St. and desire her to prepare a bed for you."—This, I will say for it, is *real* hospitality—Talked of Durham's case, and the shabbiness of the Ministers in deserting him[2]—"Lord Melbourne doing so (Lady E. said) particularly surprized her, as she had always considered him so manly & off-hand a person,"—but, I could not join in her surprise, nor in her view of his character; there being, as I told her, but little necessary connexion between the real manliness of character and that bluff & jolly swagger for which alone the Premier is I think remarkable—Poor Valletort rolled in his chair, during my visit, still weak and suffering—Invited me most kindly to come & dine with them, whenever I was not engaged elsewhere—Called upon Lord Essex, whom I found quite *rajeunè* by his marriage—never indeed was there a Benedict above one [&] twenty more *rayonnant* for the torch of Hymen than he is at this marriage, being as he himself told me, in his eighty second year.—it was quite enlivening to see him—} Found a good many droppers-in at Brookes's, notwithstanding the dead season. Rich mentioned his having met Alava at dinner the other day, and his telling of Pitt's prophecy of the Spanish war a short time before his death—his saying that nothing was now to be done by the Sovereigns; it must be a war of the people and it was in Spain it would begin—{Dined with Corry at the Hotel (Tom Longman's carriage having come for me in vain) and in the evening, having heard from Byng that the Hollands were in town dressed and went to South St. but they were gone to the play to the Duke of Bedford's box—set off to join them there, but felt tired and got home to bed.}

16 [Friday]³—{Breakfasted at Hotel, by myself—Corry having started in the morning meaning to pass tomorrow with Bessy, at Sloperton, and then proceed, on Monday, to dine with Lord Francis Egerton at Bath—Forgot to mention his telling me, among other amusing things, of the nature of the place which poor Harry Bushe held, in Dublin, and which, according to Harry's own account was "Resident Surveyor, with perpetual leave of absence"—Went down to Longman's to report my proceedings of yesterday, with which they were well satisfied, and there is now every prospect of our arranging something about the Edition—In talking of my Bermuda scrape old Longman mentioned (what I had myself forgot) that the original amount of the claim was grossly exaggerated by a man (of the name of Moore, I believe) who had some remote concern in the business, and kept us for a long time deceived as to the real amount of the defalcation—} Called upon Moxon, the publisher, to enquire about Rogers, whom the Hollands left behind them at Paris, and who has chosen an apartment for himself to which there are 120 steps of stairs to go up to—this being Rogers's system to keep the *physique* for ever in play—if you once give it up, he thinks all's over.—Talking of my edition, Moxon said there could be no doubt of its success—Wordsworth's (published by him, & for the Edition of which he gives Wordsworth £1000 the same the Longmans give me) sells, he said, very well—has already sold near 2000 copies—the Longmans printed, according to him, only 1000 of Southey⁴—they mean, however, I believe to print eight or ten thousand of mine—{Dined at Lord Essex's—had met Lady Essex & her niece at Cramer's in the morning, giving orders about a new small Piano-forte they are making for her, the old Lord's passion for her singing having kindled afresh, like all his other feelings—Company, Rennie, Boldero, and Hayter, the Painter—A good deal of pleasant conversation and, in the evening, singing—Lady Essex and Miss Johnson sung charmingly together some Italian Duetts, and then made me sit down and sing song after song for them—till Lord Essex, evidently impatient to have his dear Kitty at the piano-forte again, said from time to time, "Now *do* relieve him a little"—which they did at last. By the bye, I made an allusion in the course of the evening about which I was a little

doubtful as to the way it might be taken, to an Essay inserted some years ago in one of the periodicals, giving the preference to simple singing above all the higher flights of the art, and summing up by declaring in favour of "Nature, Kitty Stephens and Tom Moore." I reminded her of having mentioned this to her before and added that few eulogies had ever pleased or flattered me so much. It just struck for me a moment whether, being now an actual Countess, the familiarity of the old name "Kitty" might not a little jar on hers, or my Lord's, ear—but they both looked very much pleased, and I am sure my momentary suspicion did them injustice.—Had a very wet walk home—promised to call upon Hayter tomorrow to see his new picture of the Queen—} When at Cramer's this morning, had some conversation with Addison and was glad to learn from him that the old things of mine he has had from Mrs. Power (the Irish, the National Melodies, the Sacred Songs) are still doing wonderfully well—hardly a post arrives that does not bring orders for some of them—expressed himself quite surprized at the popularity and vitality there is still in them—All this very agreeable to hear—Was curious to know from him which of the settings of my words "They tell me thou'rt the favoured guest"[5] was the most asked for and popular—Balfe's or the pretty air I originally wrote them to, and was sorry, though not surprized to find that, though both sold very well, Balfe's was the most in request. In the same way, I found that a Song of mine which I myself had entirely forgot "The Dream of Home"[6] (so little had either the words or music interested me) was one of those that sold the best. I wrote it, if I recollect right, to an air not of my own choosing, and the same ordinary *sing-song* style which caused it to make so little impression on my own mind was what recommended it to the great mass of song-buyers. I *may* be, all this time, calumniating both the song & its singers, for I took but a glimpse at it, when Addison produced it—but, if I had *felt* it very much I certainly should not have so entirely forgot it, particularly as little more than a year could have elapsed since its production—{Was glad to find them still so eager to have something from me—they indeed named no less than three composers with whom they wanted me to engage in some works—viz. Barnett, Balfe, and somebody else—Barnett's plan being a series of songs founded on Schiller's *Bell*.[7]

17 [Saturday]—Breakfasted at Hotel—to Brookes's—a good deal of talk with George Keppel—in speaking of the unmanly allusions to Lord Melbourne and the Queen in some of the newspapers (more especially the Spectator) I added my own opinion that a man of Melbourne's age and experience ought to have foreseen that such would be the consequences of his lounging abuse of the sort of relation which must naturally subsist between a Prime Minister and his Royal Mistress but which a delicate & high-minded man would have fenced round with all the formalities—

relations which in the case of so young a woman ought to have been fenced round with even more than the usual formalities and observance of distance—instead of which Melbourne has made himself the boon companion of the Queen rather than her Minister. I don't know whether I exactly said all this to Keppel, but such is my feeling on the subject, & I have expressed it whenever the subject has been mentioned—In speaking of Melbourne's voice and laugh, Keppel said it was rather odd that the Queen could bear it so well, as she was rather particular & sensitive about voices, and he mentioned, as an instance one of the Queen's [?bed] attendants (Lady ——) of whose voice the Queen was constantly complaining—Spoke of the strength & self-possession with which she went through all on the day of the Coronation, (which had completely exhausted every one that had anything to do with it) she was in high spirits and talking at dinner—Two or three days after, (owing to the absence of some of the higher attendants) Keppel happened as he now told me to sit next the Queen at dinner, and either asked her, or she volunteered to tell him, how she felt the night before the Coronation—She had not slept very well, she said, and getting up some time before her attendants came to call her, to look out of the window when she beheld the immense mass of people already collected in the parks waiting for [her]—"I saw it [rain]ing" she said "and was sorry for them." (The day afterwards was [MS damaged] one) There is something touching in all this, whether on [MS damaged] the people who are to be ruled over by such a mere girl as the poor girl herself who is to rule them—The Queen given very much, Keppel said, to little quiet quizzing—often bantering his father (Lord Albemarle) on his want of taste for wine—Called upon Lady Elisabeth—talked of Conroy—told her of his letters to me about his pedigree, which I fear I have forgot to notice in its place, though well worthy of commemoration—His object is to make out (in contemplation of his expected peerage) an ancient pedigree for his family by tracing it up to the Maol-Conrys, a great Irish sect, and having come to a slight hitch in the descending steps, the object of his letter is to ask my assistance (both through my own knowledge of Irish antiquities, and my acquaintance with the chief antiquaries of Dublin) to help him over this stumbling block. Poor man—I fear from something Lady Lansdowne said the other day, when I mentioned the subject, that he has not the slightest chance (from the present ministers, at least) of being Lord Mael-Conry or Lord any thing else—Called upon Sir Martin Shee—found him and family at home & sat some time with him—Found that one of his daughters is a great collector of every thing of mine (at least that she *thinks* to be mine) among the squibs of the day—Called upon Miss Rogers—Rogers still in Paris, detained she thinks by the bad weather—Thinks Lady Holland has been quite spoilt by her trip to Paris and the fuss that was made about her there—Went to Brookes's—found there Lord Howick, Hood, Guest &c.—Dined at Lord

Holland's—mislaid my memorandum book, and therefore cannot say (with the exception of Luttrell and Sydney Smith) who was the company—

18 [Sunday]—My memorandum book had not turned up again, and what became of this day, I cannot recollect; but rather think I passed some hours of it at the British Museum. Remember now that I dined at Stevenson's—the company Bob Adair, Lord William Russell, Lord Say and Seal, George Keppel, and one or two more.}

19 [Monday]—{Called in the course of the day at Hayter's, not having been able to go on Sunday, as I promised—found him at home—His picture of the Queen appears to me very good indeed—not at all like what I remember her, but the most like, they say, altogether of any that has been done—On my mentioning the surprize I had felt at hearing people call her beautiful, he said "down to that (pointing where the nose terminated) she *is* beautiful"—The effect of the ray of sunshine across the picture very remarkable—it actually made me look to the window (though none but a poet could have looked to *such* a sky for sunshine) to see whence it came, and he told me many people were deceived in the same manner.—From thence to the Museum (not yesterday)—Found all transformed & transplanted—the new regulations for the tickets rather troublesome. Found Panizzi at his post, who, on learning it was my first visit to the new site, took me over all the rooms &c.—Went from thence to Bentley's, who had written to me to fix a day for dining with him, & to name my own company—Suggesting, from himself, Campbell, Dickens, Hume [*MS damaged*] more. Asked me whether Sydney Smith could be prevailed upon to come—[*MS damaged*] to ask him.—From thence to Brookes's where I found Lord Albemarle & Lord Sligo. Some talk with Lord A. about Adair—told him how sorry I had been, from my conversation with Adair yesterday, to find that he was still only *thinking* of committing to paper his recollections of Fox and the other men of that day he lived with—In my conversation with him yesterday evening, I found that his mind (if I may so say) had *stopped* at the year 1806—at least that his interests and sympathy had not come down much lower. That was about the time I think, when he was employed diplomatically under Mr. Fox, and a being from another planet who heard him talking of the affairs he himself was then engaged in would think it something that last week's newspapers were full of—in such fresh preservation were the *mummies* of that period in his mind—Poor fellow—he is haunted by the *past* in more ways than one, for Lord Albemarle told me that all the time he was at his (Lord A's) country seat lately he was suffering torture from the tooth-ache, though not having a single tooth, false or true, in his head.—} Had fixed

with Sydney to call to take me to dinner, and in fixing the hour, he said, "Remember, I'm a *prose* writer—so, be ready when I come." *Was* ready—Tom Longman's our dining-place—Company, besides the Longmans from Hampstead, Sergeant Talfourd, the Hart Davies's, Merivale Junr. and one or two more—{Had told Sydney on the way that he must prepare himself to be dosed with my singing, as they never cried "ohe, jam satis," at Longman's—Told him at the same time the agreeable thing Rogers once mentioned to me as having been said by Luttrell one night, at some party, when (being hard pressed to it I dare say) I sat down again to the Piano-Forte—"Good God, are we going to have more of this." Sydney indignant at the idea of any one's reporting such a speech, even if it had been said, which he did not believe, never having met any one, he added, that was not pleased with my singing—After all, it was a very harmless speech for Luttrell to make, and I dare say I should have come out with the same against St. Cecilia herself, if I had had enough of her, for the time. In the evening Sydney *did* get a dose of it, to be sure, and so, I [*MS damaged*] did Sergeant Talfourd, superabundantly—not being, I suspect, much given to music. He, however, *seemed* to be very much pleased and with my *gay* songs particularly—Tom Longman's very pretty wife sung one or two Italian duetts with me, and Mrs. Hart Davies gave her very touching song "oh the merry days that are gone," which I could have cried at like a child, if I had been in a corner by myself—Sydney brought me home—both agreed that we had never found Talfourd so agreeable as he was to-day.}

20 [Tuesday]—{Breakfasted at Hotel—called Carpenter's—found him rather changed and more on his guard—In talking of the sealed work in his hands, I said (what was quite true) that I had entirely forgot the circumstance, and begged he would just let me *see* a copy [of] it to refresh my recollection; but he did not seem very willing—said, if he could [*MS damaged*] a copy, he would. Was more confident, too, in his tone as to copyright—[*MS damaged*] the works he has in his hands having been made over to him for [*MS damaged*] on which I immediately said—"Oh if that be the case, you ought to take steps immediately to enforce your claim—there is no reason why the Longmans should have any unfair advantage on you." He did not wish, he replied, to interfere with my interests but I repeated that he ought, in the first place, to look after his own, and put in his claim to the Longmans—but he let the subject drop, and, on the whole, strengthened my impression that he has no hold over the copyrights.—To Longman's—had my accounts—was startled at the immense balance against me, but found that they had omitted putting to my credit the sum of money of mine they have in their hands—when this was done, found all right—no greater balance being against me than the sum they advanced me on the Third Vol. of my History, for the purchase of Tom's commission—They

then spoke of the high interest (5 per cent) they had been so long paying me on one of the sums in their hands (that for Russell) and expressed a wish to invest it elsewhere, to which I said "of course, as soon as they pleased," and expressed my thankfulness for their having allowed it to "fructify" so long in their hands. The young Longman rather fussy & self-important, of which I found it necessary to give him a little hint, saying to the Father laughingly—"One sees he is a *young* man of business, who likes to *talk* about things." This, quiet as it was, he felt, and I only hope it will do him good, as he is, in some respects, a very nice young fellow. Altogether, the result of this day's business was to make me resolve to have done with the whole Co. as soon as I can conveniently manage it—Called upon Moran—showed me some of the materials he has been many years collecting for the illustration of my works, and which, he said, should be entirely at *my* service whenever I wanted them—*not* the Longmans'. They consist, as far as I could see, of all possible scraps from newspapers, magazines &c. about me as well as all possible monstrosities in the way of portraits of me.—In talking with Luttrel, at Brookes's, about Bentley's dinner, found he would like to be of the party and notified the same to Bentley—Forgot to mention that I called upon Black at his lodgings yesterday, and found him [*MS damaged*] delight at my two last squibs—that against Phillpots (the new [*MS damaged*]) and the Church Pastoral about Mrs. Wolfrey "Leave us alone"[1]—pronounced them inimitable. Must own I was myself not a little amused by the four following lines—(in speaking of the newspaper writers on the subject)

> "The dev'ls have been at it for weeks,
>   And there's no saying when they'll have done,—
> Oh dear, how I wish Mr. Breeks
>   Had let Mrs. Wolfrey alone!"[2]

Was a little puzzled about my dinner engagement for to-day—had promised *somebody*, most certainly, but who it was, I could not for the soul of me recollect—Had begged of Rich yesterday to ask Lord Essex whether it was to [him I had] engaged myself, and Lord Essex who supposed it seems that I [*MS damaged*] by my message to offer myself for to-day, wrote back expressing most kindly his regret that he could not have me, as his table was full—The fact was, I wanted this day to myself most particularly, in order to go see the Lions at Drury Lane, and now finding I was free sent off to Bunn, the Manager (which Murray most good-naturedly managed for me) begging he would put me in some good place for the sight—In talking with Murray about Sidney I remarked how deadlily bitter was the opposition taken in the Quarterly of those words to Falstaff "get to your prayers old man &c." and Murray said "Yes—Croker had warned him that if ever [*MS damaged*] (Croker) he should have it in return"—}[3] Dined at Brookes's alone

and having received a message from the Theatre to say that if I would come
to the Stage Door there would be a person waiting to receive me, set off
there accordingly & had my choice of private boxes given me—In the
course of the piece was joined by Bunn and went behind the scenes with
him where the mixture of material, both human & bestial, was to be sure
most astounding—In one place was a troop of horse from Astley's, with the
riders all mounted, and about and *among* them were little children with
wings, practising their steps, while some maturer nymphs were pirouetting
and all looking as grave, both riders, urchins and nymphs, as if the destiny
of the world depended upon their several operations—A few steps farther
you came upon the lions, which I did rather too closely, and was warned off
by Bunn. While I stood looking at them there was also another gentleman,
a grave & respectable looking young man, standing with his arms folded
and contemplating them in silence, while the animals were pacing about
their cage without minding any of us—This, to my surprise (I found from
Bunn was Mr. Van Abrogh, their tamer, and having heard since that he is
under the impression he will one day or other be the victim of one of these
animals (the lesser Lion, I think) I must say that the grave earnestness with
which he stood silently looking at them that night was such as one might
expect from a person propossessed with such a notion—Dreadfully wet
night—Got home in a Cab.

21 [Wednesday]—{Breakfasted at Brookes's—went from thence to the Library of the Institution in Albemarle St., to see if they had any books for my
purpose—Looked over some of the Reports of the Irish Record Commission and found a few things worth taking note of—} Called on Lady E.
Feilding, who is staying at the Valletorts—sat some time with Valletort—
talked of the Duke of Wellington, who is (deservedly) an idol of Vs.—
{referring to Gurwood's book[1] mentioned a note of the Duke's to Blucher
at Paris, after Waterloo, appointing to dine with him at some restau-
rateur's—"Mein Liebe Furst &c—et nous aurons, j'espere un joli agréable."—Must look for this.} The Duke's grief at Fitzroy Somerset's wound—
Saying to some one who was congratulating him on the victory—"Don't
congratulate me—I never was so torn up by any thing in my life." {Went to
Brookes's—talking of the change there has been in the composition of the
Club of late years, Kensington said—"But think what a change it must be
since *I* first entered it, who remember Fox and Sheridan here." He then
mentioned some particular occasion when Pitt dined with Michael Angelo
Taylor, and, as Pitt and his party were on their way from thence to White's,
in the evening, Sheridan gave a hint to the [*MS damaged*] at Brookes's, to
attack them as they were passing, and in the midst of the scuffle Sheridan
himself ran out, apparently shocked at the outrage, and giving his arm to
Pitt who was very drunk, begged to be allowed to see him in safety to

White's which he did & got great credit thereby—Found, on coming home the following note from Lady Holland, showing that it was to her I had engaged myself for yesterday—"What prevented you from coming to dine and take me afterwards to the play? I waited some time for you, and was much disappointed. If you wish to be forgiven you must dine with me at Holland House on Sunday, and stay the night, if you please." Shocked at my forgetfulness, took a Cab immediately & went to South St. to make my apology—told her the whole case, as mentioned above, my sending to Lord Essex &c. &c.—It was however to the Olympic she went which was not my object—} Dined at Bentley's, Luttrell & I going together—The company all the very *haut ton* of the literature of the day. First (to begin *low* on the scale) myself, then Mr. Jerdan of the Literary Gazette, then Mr. Ainsworth, then Mr. Lover, then Luttrell and lastly Boz and Campbell—Poor Campbell, I was sorry to see, broken and nervous. Our host very courteous & modest and the conversation rather agreeable. Lover sung and I was much pressed to do the same, but refused, saying, rather unluckily that I should feel as doing something unnatural to sing to a party of men. Forget, by the bye, one of the cleverest fellows of the party, Barham, the Minor Canon, my friend Hume's friend [Hume inclosed to me some time after, a letter he had received from Barham, giving an account of the dinner, and in which (aware no doubt of Hume's habit of circulating his letters from friend to friend) he thus speaks of myself—"After praising Luttrell's conversation, he adds—'Still he did not extinguish his neighbour, who sat between him and Campbell and who beyond all question bears away the palm from any man that I, and I believe any one else ever met in society.'"][2] and also Moran of the Globe. {Forgot to mention that I went to the Charter House this morning to see dear Russell—walked for some time with him in the play-ground. He was all over smiles, the dear dog, on seeing me.}

22. [Thursday]—Breakfasted at Brookes's, and from thence to the Longmans—calling at Beaufort Buildings in my way, to say I should come later in the day. Turner (the Solicitor) not yet arrived—the signing and sealing of our agreements, as to the Edition having been fixed to take place to-day—Had an advance of £100 from them—The sum they are to give me for the Edition, £1,000—The reading over and signing all the different papers took a good deal of time—Went up to their old Book-loft to look over the volumes of the Record commission (belonging to me) which I have not yet had down to Sloperton—Found nothing more among them that could be of any use to me. A man employed there in tracing the autographs of Melancthon, from an old MS. Common-place book which is now proved to be all in his hand-writing and which Butler, the Bishop of ——— bought some time since from the R. Longmans for eighty pounds. Had it been known then that the manuscript was all Melancthon's own, the book would have

brought, the Longmans think, two or three thousand pounds—[Of the two, in my present mood towards them, I [*MS damaged*] of the bishop's gaining by it than I should of the bibliophiles—] It is curious that Melancthon appears to have had three or four entirely different sorts of handwriting—and that not for the purpose of concealment or mystification as he seems to have sometimes employed them *all* in writing the same letter or article—a curious whim! The pages, also full of odd & grotesque drawings by the same hand.—Dined at Murray's, company—Lockhart, James Smith, Murchison, Penn and some others—Murray mentioned to me his having two MS. Volumes of Captain Morris's songs sent to him by the Widow, with a view to publication—all *proper,* for a wonder. I had not the least notion that he had written so many produceable lyrics—said that the widow indulged in most extravagant notions of what she was to make by them—talked of 10,000 pounds! Asked me should I like to look over them, and I said yes, very much.[1]—[In the evening a young lady, a friend of the Miss Murrays, sung some songs very prettily, and I also sang a great deal, though having the rudiments of a cold very perceptibly—at least to myself—James Smith sung one of his Fol-de-Rols, and I accompanied him on the Pianoforte, joining in the Chorus.

23 [Friday]—Having now dispatched my business, resolved instead of waiting until tomorrow's coach, when I should have to start in the midst of darkness [*MS damaged*] to go a part of the way to-day by the Reading Coach—and accordingly started from Piccadilly at half past 3, in a coach which ought to have started at three, having one gentleman for my sole fellow passenger—The Coachman who had appeared to me to look tipsy, in order to make up for lost time, set off at a furious rate, and as he drove with only a single leader, that measured both sides of the way, we swayed & swagged most uncomfortably, to the alarm much more of my companion than myself, who thought it might be but the friskiness of the first start—At last, when we had nearly reached Hyde Park Corner, we came bang against something, and on looking out, I saw, in front, our unicorn all abroad, and behind, the horse of a gentleman's cabriolet (which we had overset) *accroché* on one of our wheels—We were soon surrounded by a crowd of gazers, and I, knowing the delay that must ensue before we were ready for another start, as well as the disagreeableness of starting at all with such an equipage ordered my luggage to be taken down, and put into a hackney coach—great efforts were made as well by the coachman himself, as by some Reading gentlemen (*habitués* evidently, of his coach) to persuade me to go on with him, and among the latter was my inside companion, who (as I reminded him) had expressed much more alarm and displeasure at the rate of driving than I had myself. Their solicitations, however, were in vain, and after having with difficulty disentangled myself & luggage from the crowd that

had collected, and spoken a few words to the gentleman who had been overturned, but luckily not hurt, took my luggage back to the White Horse Cellar, and having received a promise from the book-keeper that he would make some arrangement to prevent my losing my fare, I took my place for tomorrow morning, and ordered a bed in the Gloucester Coffee-House. Was now thrown upon the town dinnerless having refused a dinner at the Hollands, and besides, it was too late now to unpack and dress—resolving *not,* however, (if I could help it) to dine alone, I called first at Lord Valletort's—no one at home, the servant said, but Lady Elisabeth & Miss Horatia, and they were then dining (he added, as if guessing my purpose) on *a* chicken. Feeling that I should certainly be *de trop* at such a repast, I left my compliments, and went to Rogers's as his sister had told me he was expected about to-day. "Mr. Rogers not yet returned." Being so near Byng's, thought I had best *pay a visit* there. Found him and her, and sate some time before any thing came of it. At last Byng said "What are you going to do with yourself to-day? (it was now near half past seven) [—you are] engaged, of course?"—(I had already told them my adventure)—"No" I answered—"except to a solitary dinner at Brookes's." "If you can condescend" he said "to partake of an Irish stew—" "My dear fellow," I exclaimed, "say no more, I'm your man." He then told me he expected Lord Russell and Lord Torrington to dinner, and in a few minutes they came. A good deal of talk about the Court &c. (Torrington being one of the Royal train as well as Byng himself) and, after dinner, even Lord Russell found his tongue a little—Got to my disagreeable hotel (though better than I expected) pretty early.}

24 [Saturday]—Started at seven alone, and continued so, with but a short interruption all the way, having Swift's Tale of a Tub, which I bought at a stall for my companion—at Calne took a Fly and got home to Bess, rather early.

Mems. Received some time this month from my Paris friend, Dillon, of the bibliothéque, a copy of M. Thierry's Etudes Historiques,[1] sent me through his hands, by that gentleman (the author of the History of the Descent of the Normans).[2] I had seen this work, at Millikin's, some years since and read the Article in it, on my Melodies, which is very flattering & gratifying. The following is part of Dillon's note. "M. Thierry handed me a few evenings ago the accompanying book, in order that I might forward it to you as a faint expression of admiration for your great talents and character. You will find these feelings expressed in one or two eloquent fragments of the work itself—a proof that they are not of recent growth in Mr. Thierry's bosom. Should you think proper to acknowledge this little souvenir by a letter or line to Mr. Thierry, he will feel very proud of it, I am sure, and doubly so were you to send him a copy of your Melodies, which he often speaks of as the source from which he derived the purest & best of his literary inspirations—I was delighted to see the other day the reception given you in Dublin. The Irish people deserve all that zeal & eloquence which you have displayed in their behalf. They are a grateful people and a grateful people ought never to be despaired of. &c. &c."

I of course sent a copy of the Irish Melodies to Mr. Thierry—received also, through Dillon, some time ago, two or three new brochures of Mr. Guizot, sent me from himself as "hommages."

{25, 26, 27 &c. [Sunday–Tuesday]}

December {1st. [Saturday]—Resumed my daily work, and was left for some time quiet, but continued to suffer for nearly a fortnight after my return from a severe attack of influenza, which I brought, I think, from town with me. Had Kenrick to attend me, and by dint of good nursing and (after a little time) good feeding, got tolerably well again.

10, 11, 12 &c [Monday–Wednesday]—The Hollands at Bowood—a note from Lady Lansdowne asking me to come over—that they would send a warm carriage for me, and it would do me all the good in the world—but Bessy thought I had better not—Received a letter from Fisher the Publisher, saying that he had a proposal to make to me and begging to be allowed to wait upon me at Sloperton for the purpose—Told him [*MS damaged*] that I was too much occupied with other tasks to think of any new [*MS damaged*] but, at the same time, should he consider it worth his while [*MS damaged*] journey, on such an uncertainty, I should be happy to receive him—

13 [Thursday]—Another note from Bowood—made up my mind to go the day after tomorrow—wrote to Mr. Fisher to spare him the trouble of the journey

14 [Friday]—Young Shelburne came in the carriage to take me away and would have [*MS damaged*] without me, but I thought it better to wait till tomorrow—lunched with us—

15 [Saturday]—Russell returned yesterday from school, and will take my place as Mamma's companion—Carriage from Bowood at the appointed

hour—Had hardly arrived there, when a visitor was announced to me who turned out to be the poor Newgate St publisher—Having set off from town last night he did not of course receive my note, and getting to Sloperton in [MS *damaged*] chaise came on after me here. Had him shown up to the bed-room [MS *damaged*] that his object was to get me to be Editor of the Drawing-Room Scrap Book which L. E. L. has been hitherto the doer[1]— Expressed my regrets at his [MS *damaged*] such fruitless trouble and as-sured him that such was the pressure of my [MS *damaged*] that I could not, in justice to myself, or others, undertake any thing in [MS *damaged*] still urged his point—it would give me so little trouble—the subjects [MS *damaged*] my hand, as I had but to write something *apropos* to each of the [MS *damaged*] provided—[when] he came to speak of terms, however, I found that the payment to poor L. E. L. for *her* 60 pages of verse (for such was the quantum required) amounted at first, only to £100, though after-wards to £120 or 30—On hearing this, I could not help telling him laugh-ingly that even if I *could* have agreed to write for him it was plain he knew nothing of the sort of *scale* by which my prices (however undeservedly) had hitherto been measured. Lalla Rookh for instance—3000 guineas. He an-swered that price should make no difference between us and requested earnestly that I would give the matter further consideration which I con-sented to do, for *his* satisfaction—though quite sure, as I told him, that the result would be no otherwise than at present—And so the poor publisher took his leave, evidently a good deal disappointed—In the course of the day received the following letter from him

"Devizes, Decr. 15, 1838
Sir—Though pleading the cause of my own and a favourite child at the interview with which you honoured me this morning, I fear I proved a very deficient advocate, for I have since thought of many reasons I might have urged in favour of your taking the Drawing Room Scrap Book under your auspices. As however you are the judge upon whose decision the issue of my bantling's cause must rest, you will not, I am sure allow it to fail &c. &.c—We will, if you desire it, reduce the number of poems to thirty two to occupy from 50 to 60 pages and for this [MS *damaged*] you a cheque for Five hundred pounds—which taking into [MS *damaged*] quantity of matter, and this being we trust an arrangement to [MS *damaged*] many years, will not eventually be much less than the sum you [MS *damaged*] for Lalla Rookh. Several of the plates &c. &c. &c."

[MS *damaged*] company at Bowood, Lord & Lady Holland, Allen, Lord Suffolk and his daughter

[16 Sunday] Day too bad to get out—a good deal of conversation with Lord H. with Allen and my Lady—In talking of Prior, Lord Holland repeated me an Epigram of his own in imitation of Prior—so good that I asked him for a copy of it—and here it is.

> Mentor to Jack, on leaving college,
> Cries "Well, you've laid in store of knowledge.
> [MS damaged] a living & a wife,
> [MS damaged] and you are snug for life."
> [MS damaged] past, he meets the lad,—
> [MS damaged] Jack, and why so sad?"

> "I gave you good advice"—"tis true;
> "That good advice I follow'd, too—
> "With one small diff'rence, worthy friend,
> "That I began at t'other end;
> "First got the child, then married Bet—
> "But for the living,—that's to get."

[MS damaged] story of the old monk, on his death-bed, saying to his brother monks, who were [MS damaged] preaching to him &c. "Taisez vous—taisez vous—Ne croyez pas [MS damaged] le métier tant d'années sans en avoir appris les secrets—"}

[*The entries for the rest of 16 December and for 17 December 1838 (beginning with "In talking of Hume's charming style") are taken from Russell's edition; the MS page including these entries is missing.*]

In talking of Hume's charming style, Allen said it was curious to trace the gradual formation of it (for it was the work of time and elaboration) from his earliest essays till it reached the point at which we see it in his History. Somebody ought to publish an edition of the History, correcting the mistakes.

17th. [Monday]—Bowles sent me, this morning, a Latin epitaph (ancient, I believe) and his own translation of it, with both of which he seems mightily pleased. The original (as well as I can remember) is as follows: "*Hic jacet Lollius juxta viam, ut dicant præterientes, Lolli vale!*"

Translation.

> "Here Lollius lies, beside the road,
> That they who journey by
> May look upon his last abode,
> And 'Farewell, Lollius,' sigh."

This last line as bad as need be, and so Lord Holland seemed to think, as well as myself. I suggested, as at least a more natural translation of it,

"And say, 'Friend Loll, good bye!' "

Which Lord H. improved infinitely by making it,

"And say, 'Toll Loll, good bye!' "

Some talk with Lord Holland about Morris's songs,[1] the MS. volumes of which Murray sent after me from town. Repeated to him the pretty lines:—

> "My muse, too, when her wings are dry,
>   No frolic flights will take,
> But round the bowl she'll dip and fly,
>   Like swallows round a lake;"—

which he was, of course, pleased with, but did not seem to think much of Morris's talent, in general. Certainly in the immense heap which the two MS. volumes contain, I found none but the few already known to me that were at all worth saving from oblivion, and this I told Murray in returning them. There was one, a political song, which I had forgot, but which for its rhythmical adaptation of the words to the air is wonderful. It begins:—

> *"We be*
> Emperors *three*
> Sandy, and Franky, and little *Boney;"*

and preserves this structure most lyrically throughout. The following scraps I have thought worth transcribing for old recollection's sake:—

> "Old Horace, when he dipp'd his pen,
>   'Twas wine he had resort to;
> He chose for use Falernian juice,
>   As I choose old Oporto.
>
> "At every bout an ode came out,
>   Yet Bacchus kept him twinkling,
> As well aware more fire was there,
>   Which wanted but the sprinkling.
>   * * * *
> "Then what those think, who water drink,
>   Of those old rules of Horace,
> I won't now show, but this I know,
>   His rules do well for Morris."

And the following, from his excellent mock praises of a country life:—

> "Where nothing is seen
> But an ass on a common or goose on a green.

And it's odds if you're hurt, or in fits tumble down,
You reach *death* ere the doctor can reach *you* from town.

In the country how sprightly our visits we make
Through ten miles of mud for formality's sake,
With the coachman in drink, and the moon in a fog,
And no thought in your head but a ditch or a bog.

To look at fine prospects with tears in one's eyes.

But a house is much more to my taste than a tree,
And for groves—oh, a fine grove of chimneys for me!

But in London, thank heaven! our peace is secure,
Where for one eye to kill there's a thousand to cure.

In town let me live, then, in town let me die,
For in truth I can't relish the country, not I!
If one *must* have a villa in summer to dwell,
Oh give me the sweet shady side of Pall Mall."

Notes to 1838 Entries

1 January

1. See Henry Hallam, *Introduction to the Literature of Europe* . . ., 4 vols. (rev. ed. 1876), 1:5.

2–4 January

1. Moore included the date 4 January in two entries.

19–21 January

1. John Gibson Lockhart, *Peter's Letters to His Kinsfolk. By Peter Morris the Odontist*, 3 vols. (1819). Cf. Letter 24 (1:298): "In short, he [Jeffrey] was more of a Dandy than any great author I ever saw—always excepting Tom Moore and David Williams."
2. David Lester Richardson, *Literary Leaves* . . . (1836).

28 January

1. *Macbeth*, 5. iii.

2 February

1. Thomas Miller (1807–74), English poet and novelist.

4 February

1. Thomas John Dibdin, *Of Age To-morrow* (1800).

6 February

1. Cf. Montaigne, *Essays*, "Of Vanity," 3.9.

7 February

1. "The Song of the Box," published in the *Morning Chronicle*, 19 February 1838, *Works*, 9:181–84.
2. John George Lambton, Earl of Durham (1792–1840), was appointed high commissioner and governor-general of British North America in 1838.

9 February

1. This passage is badly garbled in the MS, with a number of words struck through at least twice. The lines recovered seem accurately to reflect Moore's meaning.

20 February

1. *Works,* 5:218–19.

21 February

1. Walter Savage Landor, *A Satire on Satirists, and Admonition to Detractors* (1836); Landor mentions Moore in ll. 248–49.

26–27 February

1. Moore made two entries for 26 February.

1–3 April

1. Published in the *Morning Chronicle,* 22 March 1838, *Works,* 9:173–76.
2. Moore's article "Catullus and Petrarch" was published in the *Metropolitan* 5 (1832): 378–83, and 6 (1833): 126–32.
3. Albius Tibullus (ca. 60–19 B.C.), Roman elegiac poet, author of *Delia* and *Nemesis.* Sextus Propertius (ca. 50–16 B.C.), Roman elegiac poet, the principal subject of whose poems was Cynthia.
4. Giacomo Colonna (Bishop of Lombez, appointed ca. 1329). Moore's source is evidently the *Journal des Savants* (founded 1816), a publication of the Académie des Inscriptions et Belles Lettres.
5. For an account of this incident see Ernest Hatch Wilkins, *Life of Petrarch* (Chicago, 1961), p. 5.

4–6 April

1. In August 1835 the Melbourne ministry had granted Moore a pension of £300.

7–9 April

1. "A Satire on Satirists, and Admonition to Detractors" (1836), ll. 145–48.

1–3 May

1. *Works,* 9:223; published in the *Morning Chronicle* on 19 April 1838.
2. See entry for 24 September 1818 and its n. 1.
3. *The Life of William Wilberforce, by his Sons . . .* (1838), 5:260.
4. Probably Moore's *History of Ireland,* 4 vols. (1835), 1:1–18.
5. Moore, Southey, and Wordsworth supported Serjeant Talfourd's copyright bill. See entry for 17 March 1842 and its n. 1. For Wordsworth's and Southey's correspondence on the issue see *The Letters of William and Dorothy Wordsworth: The Latter Years,* arr. and ed. Ernest De Selincourt, 3 vols. (Oxford, 1939), 2:923 ff; and *New Letters of Robert Southey,* ed. Kenneth Curry, 2 vols. (New York, 1965), 2:473. Moore's squib appeared in the *Morning Chronicle* on 3 May, and copied from the *Chronicle,* in the *Athenaeum* on 5 May 1838, no. 549, pp. 323–24. See also *Works,* 9:261.

20 May

1. Edward Bulwer-Lytton, *Athens, Its Rise and Fall* (1837).
2. Sydney Smith, "Second Letter to Archdeacon Singleton" (1838); see *Works of the Rev.*

Sydney Smith, 3 vols., (3d ed. London, 1845), 3:160–83. Smith accuses Melbourne of failing to take the issue of clerical reform seriously enough (*Works* 3:166–67). He concludes the letter with an indictment of Russell, Melbourne's adviser, for his zeal in support of church reform (*Works,* 3:182–83).

22 May

1. *Die Braut von Messina* (1803).
2. Moore's note at the end of the MS page.

23 May

1. John Elliotson (1791–1868), English physician and physiologist; founded a mesmeric hospital (1849); founder of the Phrenological Society.

24 May

1. Probably Sir Henry Taylor (1800–1886), poet, contributor to *Quarterly Review;* held appointments in Colonial Office (1824–72). See entry for 28 February 1835.
2. Moore deeded the publication rights to the *Melodies, Songs,* and *Airs* to the Power brothers in 1812. The copyright remained with Mrs. Power after her husband's death in 1836. Moore's collected *Works,* edited by himself, appeared in 1841. The following note is scribbled across the face of the MS at this point: "A very mistaken view. T. Longman."
3. The verses entitled "And It Is Come to This" appeared in the *Morning Chronicle* for 23 May 1838. The subject is a public meeting at which Burdett was to act as chairman, to consider the propriety of petitioning for a postponement of the Coronation. Burdett, who was unpopular, having turned on his former friends, was prevented by the rowdiness of the crowd from holding the meeting.
4. The Irish Municipal Corporation Bill, before Parliament for five sessions, was passed in 1840. The Tories agreed to the necessity for reform of Protestant corporations in a Catholic country, but they resisted the replacement of the suppressed municipal corporations by democratically elected councils. See the *Annual Register* 80 (1838): 126 ff.

25 May

1. *Fisher's Drawing Room Scrap Book . . . with Poetical Illustrations by L. E. L. . . .,* 20 vols. (1832–51). "L. E. L." was Letitia Elizabeth Landon (1802–38).

26 May

1. "Of the Literary Fund." (Russell's note.)
2. The excerpt is an account of the flattering toast to Moore offered by Lord Lansdowne.

27 May

1. Moore's speech appeared in the *Morning Chronicle* on 28 May 1838.

28 May

1. See 20 May 1838, n. 2.
2. See Sydney Smith's *Works,* 3:182.
3. Moore placed the passage in square brackets at the end of the MS page, with asterisks indicating its location in the text.

1 June

1. John Edmund Reade, *Italy: A Poem in six parts* (1838). His *Poetical Works* appeared in 1852.

2 June

1. "Poor Richard Power. The Epilogue was spoken in the character of Vapid, in the Dramatist." (Moore's note.)
2. "This simple line, from its truth, brought peals of applause." (Moore's note.)
3. Henry Stebbing (1799–1883), preacher, historian, editor, and minor poet.
4. *Works*, 8:3–106. La Martine, *La Chute d'un Ange* (1838).
5. *Travels of an Irish Gentleman in Search of a Religion*, 2 vols. (1833).

4 June

1. Moore placed this and the passage above in square brackets at the end of the MS page, with asterisks indicating their location in the text.

5 June

1. A pun on Roger's poem of that title.
2. Gaetano Donizetti, *Parisina* (1833).

6 June

1. "The name of the heroine of the performances at the North London Hospital." (Moore's note to his squib "Animal Magnetism," *Works*, 9:177–80). See entry for 23 May 1838 and its n. 1 and 22 June 1838. n. 1.

8–10 June

1. Samuel Rogers, *Italy* (1834).
2. *Rhymes on the Road*, Extract 10, *Works*, 7:313–15.
3. Moore added the passage in square brackets at the end of the MS page.

22 June

1. The squib appeared in the *Morning Chronicle* for 20 June 1838. See *Works*, 9:177–80.

23 June

1. J. B. Buckstone, *The Irish Lion* (1838).

27 June

1. John Stow (1525–1605). Two of his chief works were *The Woorkes of Geoffrey Chaucer* (1561) and *Summarie of Englyshe Chronicles* (1565).

1–2 July

1. William Henry Fox Talbot, *Hermes, or Classical and Antiquarian Researches* (1838–39), nos. 1 and 2.

7–10 July

1. "Sent to me from Guizot himself." (Moore's note.)
2. *Journal des débats politiques et littéraires* (1789).

11–14 July

1. See entry for 4–6 April 1838 and its n. 1.

15–17 August

1. John George Lambton, Earl of Durham (1792–1840). As governor general of Canada, he transported political prisoners to Bermuda and issued an ordinance declaring it to be high treason for them to return to the provinces.
2. "A Dream of Antiquity," one of the "Odes to Nea," *Works,* 2:259. In a note to the passage, Moore acknowledges Dr. Johnson's doubt that Waller was ever in Bermuda.

18–19 August

1. See *Opere Compiute di Silvio Pellico,* 2 vols. (1834), 1, "Discorse dei Doveri degli Uomini," capo 4.3. Pellico cites Moore's *Travels of an Irish Gentleman.*

24 August

1. "The Grand Acceleration Company," *Monthly Chronicle* 2 (1838): 190–91; "The Song of Old Puck" appeared in the *Morning Chronicle* for 13 August 1838. See *Works,* 9:240 and 226 respectively.

28 August

1. The *Book of Pandarus,* the abstract of which Moore searched out at Trinity College, Dublin (see 24 September 1838, n.1). The work, dated in the reign of Henry VIII, discusses the Irish government, and includes proposals for reforming and making the country more profitable for the King. Two copies are extant: Trinity MSS 581 and 842. Moore probably refers to John Leland (1506–52) and Leland's *Itinerary,* 9 vols. (Oxford, 1710). Leland, library-keeper and antiquary to Henry VIII, kept records on his antiquarian tours.
2. A reference to Sir Charles Greville's difficulties with the officials of the British Museum in acquiring the volumes of the Council Registers necessary in the preparation of his indexes to the State Papers. See C. C. Greville, *A Journal of the Reign of Queen Victoria from 1837 to 1852,* 3 vols. (1885), 2:162 ff.

29 August

1. *The Epicurean* and *Alciphron, Works,* 10:1 and 293.

31 August

1. In 1837 Cuming sold Moore's Irish publication rights to Richard Bentley, on behalf of Moore. See Dowden, *Letters,* 2:821.
2. See entry for 29 August 1818 and its n. 2.

3 September

1. James Henthorn Todd, "Sanctissimi Domini Nostri Gregorii Papae XVI Epistola ad Archiepiscopos et Episcopos Hiberniae . . . translated from the Latin" (1836). The work was a mock endorsement of Archbishop Whately's pro-Catholic system of Irish national education. Thinking Todd had tried to pass the letter off as genuine, Moore attacked him in his "Letter, from Larry O'Branigan to the Rev. Murtagh O'Mulligan" (*Works*, 9:194–96), to which he added a note of apology in later editions.

4 September

1. A reference to "The Affinity of the Phœnician and Celtic languages . . ." *Transactions of the Royal Irish Academy* 17 (1837): 21–36.
2. John O'Donovan, "Four Masters," in *Annala Rioghachta Eireann*, 7 vols. (1848–51). Moore had access to O'Donovan's MS; see entry for 24 September 1838.

13 September

1. Moore tipped in two clippings at this point. The first was an announcement that the Theatre Royal, "under the immediate patronage of Thomas Moore, Esq.," was to produce on 15 September *The Man about Town* by W. B. Bernard (1836) and *Charles the Twelfth* by J. R. Planché (1828). Three Irish Melodies, "The Last Rose of Summer," "Oft in the Stilly Night," and "All That's Bright Must Fade," were to be performed as well. The second excerpt announced a concert on the 6th at the Theatre Royal, where Moore attended and received the accolade of the audience.

15 September

1. The excerpt from the *Morning Register* gave an account of another enthusiastic reception by the audience when Moore attended the Theatre Royal on 15 September. Moore's reply to the repeated applause of the audience, quoted in full in the article, has been retained in this text of the *Journal*.
2. "Oh! Blame not the Bard," *Works*, 3:266.

16 September

1. William Carleton, *Tales of Ireland* (1834).

18 September

1. Moore's son Tom was accused of insulting a girl on the street in Belfast. He publicly denied the charge in a letter to the *United Gazette* for 19 September 1838. See Dowden, *Letters*, 2:839 and note.

22 September

1. Hugh O'Donnell (1571–1602), Irish patriot who joined Hugh O'Neill, Earl of Tyrone, against the English. See Moore's *History of Ireland*, 4:101, 136–42.

24 September

1. *Catalogus Librorum, quibus aucta est Bibliotheca Collegii SS. trinitatis*, etc. (1854); *Catalogus librorum impressorum qui in Bibliotheca Collegii . . . trinitatis . . . juxta Dublin, adservantur* (1864).

2. As Chancellor of Oxford (1629–41), William Laud (1573–1645) endowed the Bodleian.

3. Chronicles of pagan Ireland. See Moore's *History of Ireland,* 1:153 ff., and George Petrie's *Remarks on the History and Authenticity of the Autograph Original of the Annals of the Four Masters . . .* (1831).

4. See 4 September 1838, n. 2. Dr. Charles O'Conor, *Rerum Hibernicarum Scriptores Veteres,* vol. 3 (1826), translated the annals to the year 1171. O'Donovan reedited and extended the translation through 1616.

5. *Irish Antiquarian Researches* (1826, 1827).

10–11 October

1. Horace, *Odes* 4. 1, 1. 3.
2. Treasures, heirlooms.

20 October

1. Moore placed the passage in square brackets at the end of the MS page, with asterisks indicating its location in the text.

31 October

1. Sir Alexander Burnes, *Travels into Bokhara,* etc., 3 vols. (1834).
2. Moore's note at the end of the entry.
3. From *Lalla Rookh.* See l. 655 of "The Light of the Haram," *Works,* 7:51.

15 November

1. George Colman, the Younger, *The Heir-at-Law* (1797).

16 November

1. The *Pious Women* was an early (1813) satirical work written by Moore but never published. See Dowden, *Letters,* 1:242.

2. John George Lambton, Earl of Durham, was appointed High Commissioner for Canada after Parliament passed an act in February 1838 that suspended the legislative assembly of Lower Canada for two years and provided for a special council to govern. Durham's conduct in office was felt by his former supporters to be high-handed. He consequently sent in his resignation.

3. Moore made two entries for 16 November.

4. *The Sonnets of William Wordsworth* (1838). *The Poetical Works of Robert Southey,* 10 vols. (1837–38).

5. *Works,* 5:218, and 7:313.

6. *Works,* 5:217.

7. Schiller's poem "Lied von der Glocke" (1797).

20 November

1. "Some Account of a New Genus of Churchmen Called Phill-Pot" appeared in the *Morning Chronicle* for 26 October 1838. "Leave Us Alone" was in the *Morning Chronicle* for 14 November 1838. For the latter see "Songs of the Church," *Works,* 9:220. The squib on Bishop Phillpots was not included in the *Works.*

2. The last stanza of "Leave Us Alone."

3. "The New Reign. The Duties of Queen Victoria: A Sermon Preached at the Cathedral Church of St. Paul's by the Reverend Smith" appeared in the *Quarterly Review,* vol. 59 (1837),

pp. 240–73. John Wilson Croker criticized the sermon severely in the same issue, particularly Smith's attributing the *Nunc dimittis* to "the Psalmist" (it is found in Luke 2:29). Croker (p. 269) quotes Prince Hal, "I know thee not, old man. Fall to thy prayers" (*2 Henry IV*, 5.v), and continues, "What can we think of the fitness of a man to address his Queen and his country . . . who does not know the New Testament from the Old; the Psalms from the Gospel, David from Simeon."

21 November

1. John Gurwood, *The Dispatches of . . . the Duke of Wellington . . . compiled . . . by Lieut.-Colonel G.* (1837).
2. Moore placed the passage in square brackets at the end of the MS page, with asterisks indicating its location in the text.

22 November

1. See below 17 December and its n.1 for the publication of Morris's songs.

24 November

1. Jacques Nicolas Augustin Thierry, *Dix Ans d'études historiques* (1834).
2. *History of the Conquest of England by the Normans* . . . trans. from the French by C. C. Hamilton, 3 vols. (1825).

15 December

1. See 25 May 1838, n. 1.

17 December

1. Morris's works appeared in 1786 as "A Collection of Songs by the inimitable Captain Morris," and, posthumously, as *Lyra Urbanica, or the Social Effusions of Captain Morris; of the late Life Guards* (1840).

1839

Jany. 1—Tuesday—At Bowood, Bessy, Russell and myself, having come here on Saturday last—Company in the house, Charles Fox, Lady Mary, Lady Kerry and Paishley with the addition yesterday of Lady Elisabeth and Horatia—Fine fun for Russell, as two of the nights we had acted Charades, in which Charles Fox, Shelburne and Russell were the performers, and yesterday a large party went out riding of which Russell made one—Charles gave us his imitations of the national singing of different countries, the conversations of Hottentots &c. and the whole time has been very cheerful and amusing—yesterday took place the usual dinner to the children of Lady Ls. school in the conservatory which was very pretty and interesting, all the ladies attending upon them, and Bessy, of course, quite in her element—{The day we arrived My Lady Bess *took* me *in,* rather amusingly—As I had got out, at the Green Drive to walk part of the way, she & Russell, after seeing their rooms, came out to meet me—"such a hole as they have put us in!" she exclaimed. "I could not have supposed that there was any thing so shabby in Bowood"—This, I remarked was rather odd, there not being just now much company in the house. When she took me to the rooms, however, I found it to be an apartment fit for a Prince, which I do not believe either she or I ever saw before—three most splendidly furnished rooms, our two bed-chambers & her dressing-room. My dearest Bess full of her usual arch fun about it, and I told her she would be like Nell in the Farce—}[1] our whole visit very agreeable. Forget whether I mentioned that I wrote to the Scrap-Book man declining definitively his proposal. It is too provoking to think that while I have been now nearly two years at work at the 3rd. Volume of my History (not even yet finished) for which I am to receive but £500, [2] I should be thus obliged to refuse the same sum for a light task, which I could accomplish with ease in three months!—

{2,3,4,5 &c. [Wednesday-Saturday] Understanding from my sister Ellen that Tom had left her to return to his regiment by no means in good health, and that she had wished him to come for a change of air to Sloperton, I wrote to Philip Crampton, whose account of him not being very favourable, I applied to Macdonald (of the Horse Guards) to obtain leave for him to come to Sloperton, which he most promptly and kindly granted—

6, 7. &c. [Sunday, 6 January-Monday, 14 January] Better accounts from Tom, who though very thankful for the leave, thinks it on the whole better that he should not now accept of it.—The Major commanding the Regiment on Tom's declining the leave (not thinking, I suppose, that he would much persist in declining it) begged him to consider before he refused that there it was, perfectly at his command. But, Tom told him that having been already indulged with such long leave, he could not think of interfering with the right of those other officers whose turn of leave ought now to come on which the Major said—"Well since you have made up your mind on the subject, I must say that I approve very much of your conduct and shall report accordingly to the Horse Guards"

15 [Tuesday]—Received the following letter from Sir John Macdonald
Horse Guards
14 Jany. 1839
My dear Moore—I'm sending you for your information the accompanying letter, which I have just received from the officer commanding the 22d Regt. I must not fail to offer you my compliments and congratulations upon the very creditable feeling which your son has shown on this occasion.
Yrs. very faithfully
J. Macdonald

16, 17 &c. [Wednesday-Thursday] Monsr. Thierry, to whom I sent at Dillon's suggestion, a copy of my Irish Melodies, has just acknowledged them in the following letter.—}
"Monsieur—Rien ne pouvait m'être plus agréable que votre lettre et le présent que vous avez eu la bonté d'y joindre. Je suis heureux de tenir de vous ce livre que j'admire et dont, je me suis inspiré. Votre poësie patriotique me parut, il y a bien des années, non seulement le cri de douleur d'Irlande, mais encore le chant de tristesse de tous les peuples opprimés. C'est de la vive impression qu'elle fit sur moi après nos désastres de 1815, qu'est venu, en grande partie, le sentiment qui domine dans l'histoire de la conquête de l'angleterre. Le livre, auquel vous avez la bonté d'accorder un suffrage qui m'est bien précieux vous doit beaucoup, et je suis heureux de vous le dire. On en fait en ce moment une édition plus ornée and plus correcte qui les précédentes—permettez moi de vous l'offrir; dès qu'elle sera imprimée, vous en recevrez un exemplaire. Agréez-le, Monsieur,

comme un témoignage de gratitude, et croyez aux sentimens de haute estime et d'admiration avec les lesquels j'ai honneur d'être &c. &c.

18, 19 &c. [Friday-Saturday]—Received a letter one of these days from Mrs. Shelley, who is about to publish an Edition of Shelley's works, asking me whether I had a copy of his Queen Mab as originally printed for private circulation;[1] as she could not procure one & took for granted that I must have been one of those persons to whom he presented copies. In answering that I was unluckily *not* one of them, I added in a laughing way that I had never been much in repute with certain great guns of Parnassus, such as Wordsworth, Southey, her own Shelley &c.—Received from her, in consequence, a very kind & flattering reply, in which she says, "I cannot help writing one word to say how mistaken you are. Shelley was too true a poet not to feel your unrivalled merits—especially in the department of poetry peculiarly your own, songs and short poems instinct with the intense principle of life and love. Such, your unspeakably beautiful poems to Nea—such, how many others! One of the first things I remember with Shelley was his repeating to me one of your *gems* with enthusiasm—In short be assured that, as genius is the best judge of genius, those poems of yours which you yourself would value most were admired by *none* so much as Shelley. You know me far too well not to know I speak the exact truth."

20, 21 &c. [Sunday-Monday]—I am not sure whether I have mentioned that, when last in town, I spoke to Hobhouse about our little Russell, and his wish to become an Indian soldier—Hobhouse then said that his cadetships for that year had been all given away, but that *if* (emphatic, as it well might be) his official life lasted long enough, my son should not be forgotten. I have lately reminded him on the subject, & he most promptly & kindly has appointed Russell to a Cadetship. We have accordingly taken him from the Charter-House, and in order to prepare him for Addiscombe have sent him to a Preparatory school at Edmonton, Dr. Firminger's.

{21, 22, 23 &c. [Monday, 21 January-Thursday, 31 January] Hard at work—having generally three different tasks in hand—During the day and in the evening my History—Then, for an hour after I go to my bed-room, I employ myself in revising for the Edition of my Works, and in the morning from the time of waking & during my toilet-hour, work at some squib for the Chronicle or mould a sentence or two into shape.}

February 1, 2, 3 &c. [Friday-Sunday] The same monotonous course of life, which leaves but little for Journalizing—Have again played the same trick upon Bessy, with respect to her supplies for the Poor, as I have done more than once before—having confidentially got Boyse to send her a five-pound note, as if from himself, for the poor of Bromham—it makes her happy, without the drawback of knowing it comes from my small means, and in the way she manages it, does a world of good.

4, 5, 6, 7, &c. [Monday-Thursday]—Received a letter from my Calcutta friend, whose first letter I took a whole year to answer, though he sent me a Volume of Poems with it that showed a good deal of talent[1]—he is however in very good humour with me and bears testimony to my accuracy, as an Orientalist, which from such a quarter is not a little satisfactory—After saying some flattering things such as that "a man who has the admiration of nations need concern himself very little about the opinion of a small poetaster in Calcutta," he adds—"and yet, after all perhaps my local knowledge of Orientalism may render me in some respects by no means a contemptible judge of the fidelity of some of your Eastern descriptions. It appears to me that the character of most oriental scenes and nations exhibits that general resemblance which enables a person familiar with a part of them to judge pretty fairly of all oriental poetry. If this be true I may venture to speak with some confidence of the exquisite fidelity of your oriental descriptions. I have been for some few years a Professor of English literature at the Hindu College (a noble institution for the instruction of the natives in the literature & science of the West) and I have always found your poetry greedily devoured by the students."

{4, 5, 6 &c. [Monday-Wednesday][1]—In consequence of the present Anti-Corn Law agitation, they have brought forward I see my old squib "Says Cotton to Corn t'other day" and it is now taking the round of the newspapers—but oh the havoc those devilish printers make with one's moods and tenses! the mending of Mrs. Malaprop's "cakelology" was nothing to it. The line "What claim canst *thou* have upon lords?" was printed in the Chronicle "What claim canst *those* have upon Lords?" This didn't matter much, being so obvious a mistake, that it couldn't possibly, one would think, fail to be corrected in its progress—but so far was this from being the case that, on the following Sunday, the Spectator, (copying no doubt from the Chronicle) not only preserved the above misprint, in this doomed line, but added another error of their own free gift, making it "What claim canst *those* have upon *the* Lords?"[2]—the devil! the devil!—In the gossiping book published by our old Leicestershire friend Gardiner[3] there is a good deal about ourselves & the visits he paid us at Mayfield and Hornsey. But among other things, queerly told, but having a spice of truth in them, he breaks out into the following outrageous bouncer—Byron's Ms. Memoirs "for the suppression of which Moore received £3000"! In sending me his volumes he had begged that I would let him know if there were any incorrectness in his statements respecting myself in order that he might remove them— "incorrectness" this with a vengeance! Wrote to tell him that, instead of receiving £3000 for suppressing the Ms. *myself,* I had paid down 2000 guineas on the nail for the suppression of it, by *others,*—some slight difference, this.—Added, however, that I did not wish him to take the trouble of correcting his statement, as the fact was well known to those whose opinion I cared much about, and besides both the truth & the lie were now perhaps forgotten by all—

8, 9, 10, 11 &c. [Friday-Monday] A visit from Lady Lansdowne the day before she went to town—sate some time with us, and left some money with Bessy for a poor woman of Bromham.

12, 13, 14 &c. [Tuesday, 12 February-Monday, 25 February] Sent to Bentley for his miscellany a squib which I had written at Lardner's urgent request for the Monthly Chronicle of January last. Soon after this request for a contribution from me, Lardner had changed the plan of that publication from a Magazine to a sort of *Monthly-Quarterly* (as *Dinnis* himself would perhaps call it) thus raising it above the lower region of squibs, and rendering my contribution of no avail—This, however, he had not the politeness to apprize me of, so that my trouble would have gone for nothing, had I not thought of offering the thing to Bentley, who gave me the same sum for it that Lardner would have given, i.e. twenty guineas, and most seasonably, it came—though I suspect Bentley at first imagined that I meant it as a free & gratuitous offering at his shrine, which would have been *indeed* contrary to the natural order of things. The squib I sent (entitled "Thoughts on Patrons, Puffs and other matters, in an Epistle from T. M. to S. R")[1] was begun the last time Rogers was down here, on his saying to me as he looked round our drawing-room "Why, you've got all your patrons here!" The first dozen lines or so were written after he left me, and the remainder lately.—}

26 [Tuesday]—Bessy & I started for Napier's on our long promised visit— {had a Fly from Fry's—found them all well, the girls growing into young women and very *pretty* young women to boot.—Napier very much in his usual state of vigour & intenseness—Exclaimed to me, on my first entrance "Why, you're grey?" "Yes"—I answered "but not yet *white*" this being his own case.} Found Roebuck[1] with him whom I was very glad to meet and even more surprized than glad, as nothing could be less like a firebrand than he

is—his manner & look being particularly gentle. But this is frequently the case—my poor friend, Robert Emmett was as mild & gentle, in his manner as any girl. Roebuck stayed but a short time, having to return to Bath by the boat, which I was sorry for. {His father-in-law Dr. Falkner has within these few days died.—In the evening Napier read to us a journal he kept of his trip to Manchester, Liverpool, & the Menai Bridge with Soult—very characteristic and amusing—Soult seems to have growled, like an old tiger in training, all the way, and Napier's attempts to commune with him in French must have been excellent—glad to see Mrs. Napier in such good health & spirits—the marriage of her daughter Bessie seems to have made quite a new woman of her.}

27 [Wednesday]—Young Falkner, the brother-in-law of Roebuck, came and soon after Roebuck himself joined us.—Conversations on various subjects, America, Mesmerism, &c. &c. all very agreeable—Some allusion being made to my squibs, Roebuck said that I had described *him* (which I had myself forgot) dancing a fandango with Recorder Shaw[1]—On the subject of Mesmerism, I found Roebuck to be much of the same opinion as myself that the next folly to that of swallowing all its marvels is that of rejecting them all—The very circumstance, as I remarked, of its rising again and again into notice, at no very distant intervals, after having been crushed as it was thought, by the ridicule of the world, and the quackery of its own professors, shows that there is some real germ of truth and life in it. {Roebuck described Elliotson[2] (who is a great friend of his) as a most sincere truth-intending man.—} Was sorry when Roebuck & his brother-in-law left us as they would have been a most welcome ingredient in our evening party.—but they were obliged to go.—{Napier ill in the evening and obliged to go early to bed—Miss Bowie & the Napiers played some pretty waltzes, and wanted me to sing—but as I have hardly once tried my voice since my influenza, I declined.—}

28 [Thursday]—{Napier better and at breakfast with us.—It had been proposed that we should all go to the Bath Theatre, in the evening, but as it would be too much I thought, for Bessy, we gave it up. Set out, Bess and myself, after breakfast for Bath—} Went shopping and made a purchase which I have long dreamed of, but could never muster up courage enough for the out-lay—namely, a fire-proof Box for valuable papers—it cost me, after all, but five pounds, and the ease of mind it will give me on that score is well worth the money—{Went to see Bessie (Lady Arran) and her lord—or rather two lords—for we were introduced to the young Baron Sudley, now just seven weeks old—Nothing could be happier than Bessie or more *evidently* glad to see her old friends—Arran himself too seems a very good-

tempered and amiable fellow. Went from thence to the Crawfords, and had luncheon, and started in a Fly for home at 3 o'clock.}

March {1, 2, 3 &c. &c. [Friday–Sunday] Again relapsed into study and snuggery—and most snug it is, I must say—My dearest Bess, however, has been again ailing, and her weak and worn looks often sadden me.}

4, 5, 6, 7 &c. [Monday–Thursday]—Bessy better, thank, God.—From an account of a Duel between Roebuck and Lord Powerscourt which has appeared in the papers, I find it must have taken place the very morning after the day when we last saw him at Freshford.—

8, 9, &c. [Friday–Saturday] A letter from Mrs. Napier to Bessy from which it appears that Roebuck was on his way to town that Wednesday for the purpose of the duel with Lord P. having left Mrs. Roebuck under the impression that he was to pass the night at Napier's—I must say, with such an affair on his mind, the composure and cheerfulness of his conversation and manner was not a little remarkable—

{10, 11, 12 &c. [Sunday–Tuesday] Received from Mrs. Shelley the first Volume of her new Edition of Shelley's works,[1] with a note in which she says "I send you my Volume, a tribute due—I hope it will please you. A letter came into my hands not long ago of Shelley's which when I see you I will show you, and you will see the admiration he expressed & I *know* felt for your genius."

13, 14 &c. &c. [Wednesday–Thursday]—Having written to Talbot to congratulate him on the success of his sensitive paper &c. received the following note from him, in answer "We do not mean to be satisfied until we make "every man his own portrait painter"—Instead of sitting to Sir T. Lawrence he is to sit to his own Camera. One sitting will be sufficient; indeed a second would be prejudicial unless he were to sit exactly in the same place—But, adieu to *flattery* in portrait-painting. The French philosophers are making experiments with great zeal on this & the kindred subject of phosphorescence caused by the solar light. The materials which they are making trials upon do not at first sound very dignified (oyster-shells & marrowbones) "mais la Science ennoblit tout." I could not help smiling at the commencement of M. Daguerre's last communication to the French Academy, which begins "Take a large marrow-bone." &c. &c. &c.[1]

15, 16, 17 &c [Friday, 15 March–Wednesday, 27 March]—Nothing to record about myself, excepting that I am busy recording about others. History (somebody says) means simply *His*-story, but it is also now *my* story, and a very dull story too.—Sent a squib to the Chronicle about the 17th. or 18th. of this month, entitled "New Grand Exhibition of Models of the two Houses of Parliament."[1]—Got letters from both Easthope & Black two or three days after, full of consternation at the loss or mislaying of my MS. which Black had left in one of his *Black*-letter folios, and the servant had shut the book and put it by, nor could he, by a general hunt through his Library again find it. Sent him another copy.}

28 [Thursday]—An amusing letter from Byng, telling me one or two ludicrous things which have lately happened, evidently, I think (though he does not say as much) for the purpose of tempting me into squibs thereon. The following are extracts from his note—"Are you aware that Grosvenor Square is at length completely lighted with gas? are these new lights preparatory to taking office? If you have not already been told, you may be glad to hear that the High Church at Oxford having, as you know, acquired an enormous subscription to build a temple or monument to Cranmer sought out and at length as they thought found the very spot where he was buried—and, still more fortunately discovered his bones. The bones were sent to Professor Buckland who having examined them pronounced them to be the bones of a *Cow*."

April {1, 2, 3 &c [Monday–Wednesday]—A letter from a brother-officer of Tom's, Captain Kidd, informing us that Tom is very ill, and that he thinks change of air quite necessary for him—A letter which we had received from Tom himself two or three days before, though saying nothing about his illness, was written with such a trembling hand that we could hardly make it out—Wrote immediately to the Horse Guards to ask leave of absence for him—a day or two after received a letter from Crampton (to whom Tom's brother officer had also very kindly written) telling me that he had, immediately on hearing of Tom's illness gone to D'Aguilar, who without any delay or form had given the leave of absence & he expected Tom in Dublin in a day or two—This all most prompt and kind.}

4, 5, 6, 7, &c. [Thursday–Sunday] {From Crampton's letters it appeared that Tom's illness, had he been left in the hands of such physicians as it was his ill-luck to have about him in Belfast might have proved very serious, being no less than a nervous attack "closely allied to epilepsy" as Crampton describes it—Said he would keep him under his own examination for ten-days or a fortnight and then send him to us to Sloperton—} Received a letter one of these days at which on the first glance we were rather alarmed, thinking it was our own J. Russell that had met with some accident while at play. It was as follows—dated from Ipswich—"Sir—Mr. J. Russell, while amusing us with his entertainment here, a short time since, stated, when speaking of phrenology, that Mr. Deville was visited by yourself and Dr. Lardner, that you were pronounced a mathematician and the learned Doctor a poet. Mr. Deville assures me the assertion is incorrect. May I beg the favour of a reply?—Apologizing for troubling you on so trifling an occasion, I have the honour &c. A. B. Cook." Wrote in answer to him that the story, though a very good one, had not the slightest foundation in truth. Something analogous to it, however, *did* happen which I had half a mind to tell him. When Deville first examined my head, without the least idea who I was, he found in it a great love of *fact*, which Rogers I recollect laughed at, saying "He has discovered Moore to be a matter-of-fact man."—Deville, however, was quite right in his guess. I never was a reader of works of fiction, and my own chief work of fiction (Lalla Rookh) is founded on a long & laborious collection of facts. All the customs, the scenery, every flower from which I have drawn an illustration were enquired into by me with the utmost accuracy, and I left no book that I could find on the subject unransacked. Hence arises that matter-of-fact adherence to orientalism for which Sir Gore Ouseley, Colonel Wilks, Carne and others have given me credit.

{8, 9, 10, 11 &c [Monday, 8 April–Saturday, 20 April]—Good accounts about Tom

21 [Sunday]—Tom arrived from Dublin, much better than we expected to find him.

22, 23, &c [Monday–Tuesday]—Received letters from some *very* mad people—madder even than the common run of my unknown correspondents. One of them sent his long packet under cover to Lord Lansdowne, thinking he had the power of franking weights, a mistake which has happened more than once, and which gives both Lord L. & myself a good deal of unnecessary trouble—In alluding to the small majority on the Irish question which narrowly saved the life of the Ministry the other night, Lord L. says, in his letter to me—"Some friends of ours are very happy at the result of last week's tedious debate. I cannot say that I am myself. Shiel however has added greatly to his reputation as a brilliant debater"[1]

24, &c. [Wednesday]—The following *entoosy moosy* note from a young lady of Kidderminster, begging me to subscribe to her Poems—"If the immortal author of Lalla Rookh would generously permit his illustrious name to appear in the subscription list herewith enclosed, Miss L. M. Holl, a young, but eager adventurer, in the tangled paths of literature would be impressed with the kindness & honour to the latest period of her existence."[1]— Assented of course—so much "immortality" & "illustriousness" being assuredly cheap at five shillings.—A letter from Dolman, the publisher, sending me the 1st Vol of his edition of Dodd's Church History to which I am a subscriber, and asking me to contribute to the Dublin Review, which OConnel has made over to him[2]—The following in a late Examiner—

"How we should rejoice to be endowed with the power of administering an oath of prohibition to these delinquents!—(Parris, Corboulds &c, &c.)— the Form of it should be thus. 'I, M. or N., as the case may be, a penitent member of the vicious school of art, do hereby undertake and swear to abstain for the term of five lawful years from the delineation of *All* the heroes and heroines of Lord Byron; ditto, of Lalla Rookh; item of such personages as Rebecca, Jeannie Deans, Lady Ashton and Amy Robsart'"[3]

25, 26 &c. [Thursday–Friday]—Forget whether I mentioned a long poem I received lately from Bristol, without either name or address,—or, I might add sense or metre. It is in a lady's hand, and the fair writer describes, at very great length, her own feelings on first reading Lalla Rookh, which took place, as well as I can understand her, in India—

> "Twas in a beauteous realm of sun, of flowers bright;
> That first I oped the page, and wildered drank its light,
> The flowing sun was setting as I sate by that lone shore,
> And turned & turned & turned the breathing pages oe'r."

She then asks, "Say, wilt thou smile on these young efforts of the heart," and so proceeds through more than a hundred lines.—Received one of these days by post, directed to me—"Sloperton, England" an American newspaper, published at New-York, and giving an account of two or three different festivals, held on St. Patrick's Day last, in all of which the name of "Tom Moore" shines out most uproariously. First there's the "Shamrock Benevolent Society"—then the "Democratic Sons of St. Patrick"—then celebrations of the Day, at Providence,—Boston, Philadelphia &c.—At all these dinners my songs were sung, and my name commemorated in the speeches & toasts.—Thus, after "the memories of Fitzgerald, Emmett, Shears &c." the song of "Oft in the Stilly night" follows, and the suceeding toast is— "Thomas Moore the patriot poet and minstrel—'To whom the laurel & the lyre were given, and all the glories &c. &c.'"—In a speech by the President of this dinner, the lines "Unblest were her sons &c." are cited—At the Providence Festival, I am thus introduced—"Tom Moore—the illustrious Bard of Erin; at the sound of whose melodious notes the drooping spirit of the exile is raised to the pinnacle of hope, and the icy heart of the despot is melled." (Song, the Bard's Legacy)[1] At this dinner, I appear to have had a rival Irish bard, by the name of White, with whom I am thus gloriously coupled in rhyme.—Speaking of Ireland,—

> "All she wants to set her right
> Are men with souls like *Moore* and *White*."

To this brother bard of mine I owe also the following discriminating eulogium, in proposing my health—"Erin's immortal Child of Song, the heaven-born bard of Liberty. May he soon sing the death-song of Saxon oppression. In my public lectures I have *occasionally* united Moore, Emmett and Washington, as the purest models of patriotic virtue." He then, as an after-thought, to "render the galaxy even more splendid" adds "Dan OConnell"—and why not also Frederick White himself,—almost as fit a man surely to stand by the side of Washington as any of us.

30 [Tuesday]—Dined at Spye-Park to meet the officers of the troop of lancers now at Devizes—Company, besides, the Moneys &c. &c. On being asked to sing in the evening, refused, at first, not having uttered scarcely a note, since my attack of influenza, and being really fearful that my singing was at an end. But on sitting down to the Piano-forte, I found my voice as good as ever, and accordingly sung away as much as they liked—}

[May]{1[Wednesday]—Corry, who had previously announced himself by letter, arrived from Bath to see his friend Bessy, and made us both most happy as well by his visit as by his good looks—being quite himself again. Having been asked to the Schonbergs in the evening, he consented to accompany me thither and there I again sang, to his no small pleasure, and I confess my own, being rejoiced to find that my voice had not taken flight.

2[Thursday]—Accompanied Corry into Bath—called at the Crawfords', who invited me to take up my quarters with them, but were engaged out to dinner—Dined with the two Miss Crawfords, intending to go to the Theatre in the evening, but there was none. Had in the course of the day met Savage Landor and walked with him for some time—talked much of Lady Bulwer's novel, that heroine being now herself in Bath and the reigning subject of all conversation[1]—A Poem, too, has just appeared, in answer to her novel, which is swallowed down here as Bulwer's, and, if it *were* his, (which it evidently is not) would quite complete the matrimonial and literary mess between the parties—Lady Bulwer had proposed to dedicate her novel to Landor as a special hater of her husband, and the Savage had accepted the honour—But his sister, who is in a dying condition, as I understood him, sent her husband to him to entreat that he would not accept of the Dedication, as the disturbed state of his own matrimonial relations (his wife & he having been long separated) would render such an extension of his patronage both awkward & remarkable and would give infinite pain to his said sister. He had therefore declined the dedication, and had thereby offended Lady Bulwer so much that she now would not speak to him[2]—"You observed" he said "that in passing us just now, she avoided looking at me"—I *had,* indeed, seen a very handsome woman pass us, in a Bath chair, who arrested my attention, I confess, a good deal more than did Landor's long story, but whom I did not recognize to be Lady Bulwer.—Went in the evening to Le Maetres, where Corry had dined & proceeded from thence with him & a Miss Corry (rather a fine girl) to Lady Belmore's, where I found a large assemblage of Bath tabbies collected at cards—Instantly, on our appearance, the cards were abandoned, and a whole Babel of tongues opened upon us, my old friend Miss Colville's among the number. I soon saw symptoms of my being asked to sing, but by appointing to call again tomorrow, & half promising to do whatever they wished *then,* I contrived to escape.—Slept at Crawford's—}

3[Friday]—{Corry & I, accompanied (at his own request) by Savage Landor proceeded to pay our respects at Prior Park—Found the Bishop at home and were received with much courtesy by him—The whole place has risen with improved beauty from the flames—The Bishop taking me aside, showed me a Hymn Book, full of beautiful subjects, he said, for Sacred Songs, which he had long wished to place in my hands knowing to what account I could turn them—Sealed the book & gave it to me when I was coming away—} On my saying something, by the bye to Landor of my consciousness of the little value that any thing *I* had done in the way of poetry must bear in *his* eyes (meaning the eyes of his school altogether) he answered "on the contrary—I think you have written a greater number of beautiful lyric poems than any one man that ever existed."—{Well done, Savage.—But I see that he is a man of extremes, and does not mince the matter either in praise or blame. "Scoundrel" is one of his most favourite terms for great men—"That scoundrel, Burke!" "That scoundrel, Johnson!" &c. &c.—} Corry reminded me of a good criticism on our Kilkenny theatricals, by some one who said that of all our Stage company he infinitely preferred the Prompter—and why? "Because he is least seen and best heard"—{mentioned} also a very Irish description given by Harry Bushe of the place which he held under government—namely "Resident Surveyor, with perpetual leave of absence.".—{After lunching at Crawford's,} I took the Devizes Coach home, having bought at Bath to amuse myself with on the way—Select Funeral Orations of Thucydides, Plato, Lysias &c. in the *original!*[1]—I had the help of notes, however.

{4, 5, 6 [Saturday–Monday]—

7th. [Tuesday] Bessy and I & Tom went over to Lacock for a couple of days—none but ourselves and their selves—not forgetting their pretty little children—Talbot took off several photogenic drawings for Bessy, during our stay—

8th. [Wednesday]—A splendid day—walked over to Corsham to show Tom (who went on horseback) the pictures—sun very hot; found the walk a little too much, but was all the better for it afterwards—Tremendous storm at night—the old Abbey towers seemed to rock. Received the news of the Ministry being out, and rejoiced thereat for their own sakes, as well as that of the country.[1]

8th. [Wednesday][2] Returned home—Bessy in her poney chaise & I walking}

9, 10, 11, 12 &c. &c. [Thursday–Sunday] A visit from Bowles one of these days—showed me some new progeny of his Muse, which really breeds rabbitt-fashion—This was prose, however, and theological, tracing the Catholic adoration of the host to the circular image of the sun worshipped at Heliopolis—But why not take the Cross itself which formed a part of the religious worship of the Egyptians? [The Egyptians were acquainted also with the Trinity—as would seem by the inscription on the obelisk in the Circus Maximus, at Rome— ΜΕΓΑΣ ΘΕΟΣ, ΘΕΟΓΕΝΗΤΟΣ, ΠΑΜΦΕΓΓΗΣ —.][1] This however would involve somewhat more than the mere Catholic case, and is therefore let alone. The Catholics, however, instead of shrinking from this sort of paralellism between their religion and that of the heathen are, on the contrary, proud of it; and Bishop Baines the other day in showing me some magnificent engravings executed at Rome, representing the grand ceremonies of the Church, remarked how closely the fans borne by the attendants resembled the flabella carried in the holy rites of the Egyptians. This shows good sense, I must say, as well as fearlessness, and affords, in itself, a pregnant distinction between the ancient and the mere upstart.

13,14 &c.[Monday–Tuesday]—The following are a few of the things that struck me in my Greek studies the other day in the Bath Coach. γνωμη μη αξυνετος—a mode of expression resembling the English one "He is no fool"—meaning that he is a man of very good sense. Plato, too, in one of these orations uses the same form of speech— ου πανυ φαυλη i.e. αγαθη — Thucydides thus tersely & sensibly describes the difficulty there is in hitting the true medium in oratory χαλεπον γαρ το μετριως ειπειν. The following sentence, quoted from Sallust. de B. Iug. might aptly be applied to our great Duke—"Ac sane, *quod difficillimum imprimis*, et prœlio strenuus erat et bonus consilio."[1]

{15–16. &c. &c. [Wednesday–Thursday]—I mentioned above some mad letters which I lately received—one of them is from a half-pay sea-officer, who has become an entire mad poet, taking it into his head that the spirit of Byron has become impersonated in *him*—"In plain language (he says) though to others appearing to be quite myself, I am consciously to myself, become quite another person—Byron. I have his predilections and his prejudices—his imperturbable coolness, and his unbending pride. Much do I question whether, at such times, I could not hit a four-penny piece nine times in ten at fourteen paces &c. &c."—He at last arrives at the main object of his Epistle, which is to request that I would read over the voluminous effusions which he has penned under this self-delusion, and give my candid opinion of them—"Only turn your still-once-young-and but Little-though-now-greatly-*Moore*-than-nine-days-marvellously observant eyes upon the *tournure* of a once-young-and still-but little-though greatly-more-than-nine days old-marvellingly observant kitten, who, during that three quarters of a circumgyration conventional, the immemorial and possibly prescriptive preliminary to a graceful feline recumbency, can wishfully contemplate the retiring extremity of her own Tail, yet who marking, if not *re*-marking, upon the tremulous temptation can even—but let that pass. Tis but poor similitude to express my present tantalizing richness of rotative imagination, and the Stoic sternness of my self-denial." This is but a specimen of the odd, mad, but still cleverish rigmarole with which this strange fellow covers more than five closely-written pages of foolscap paper. The other odd letter I have alluded to, written in a very gentlemanlike hand, begins with two verses of Doggrel, corrected and re-corrected, so much as to be almost illegible, to the following elegant strain

Now, prithee be aisy
Tis not long I'll taize ye
About Thomas Little
Now call'd Thomas Moore.
When he thought himself little,
He little did think of
His namesake, the great Thomas Moore.

After a few more such verses, the writer passes suddenly into the following prose.—"Will Mr. Moore favour Mr. Hassal, of Hambly House, Streatham, with a call at his Chambers, in '*the Building*,' in the Garden, whence came the above effusion (the first he ever thought of putting on paper) and so talk upon subjects, grave and gay. Mr. H. will remain at home on Thursday—or he will be in town on Tuesday next, by eleven, at his Tailor's, Reeve, 5 South arcade."—Who this worthy dealer in fact and facetiousness is I have not the slightest notion—

17 &c.[Friday, 17 May–Sunday, 26 May] Since I last noticed politics a most unlucky turn has been given to the state of affairs, by the Whigs returning again to office, and under circumstances by no means creditable to them,—though how they could well have avoided the step, in the awkward position they had got both themselves and the Queen into, it would be difficult to point out. Heart-sickened as I felt at the nature of the cry they have set up of "the sovereign! the sovereign!" (this from Whigs!) I was so much interested about the men themselves, that I felt rather glad the public in general did not see the matter in the same light I did. But the echo to their cry through the country has been but faint and partial, and the embarrassment they have brought upon themselves, will not I fear *end* with themselves, but extend far and deep into the future.[1] In quoting above (under the date of April 22, 23) what Lord Lansdowne had said, of the result of the previous debate I forgot to mention what I myself had written to him on the same subject, which was, to the best of my recollection, as follows—"There are but two persons concerned about whom I feel any very warm interest, yourself and Lord John, and I own I shall welcome the day when I see you both well out of the scrape." Alas, they have now got but deeper *into* it.

May 27 [Monday]—To town—had intended to have started yesterday, but by a mistake in the time of sending the Fly, was too late for my chance of the coaches at Buckhill & had to walk home again—Found myself among friends, as usual, in the coach, though I had never laid eyes on any of them before—one of my companions proved to be a Revd. Mr. Cooke a great friend of Tom Boyse's, and the lady Mrs. Willis (whose husband an active preacher at Bath was one of the outsiders) proved to be intimately acquainted with all I had done, sung, or written, and not only did she & I become dear friends, on the way, but I happened to touch a spring which brought her & Mr. Cooke also into relations of acquaintanceship with each other, so that we were all friends for life before we arrived at the end of our journey. Mr. Cooke mentioned some punning complimentary verses, addressed to a lady named *Green,* by our friend Boyse, which he (Mr. Cooke) was repeating once in a stage-coach, when a young gentleman one of the passengers who had not till then uttered a word, asked eagerly if Mr. Cooke would oblige him with a copy of those verses, as he himself was then paying his addresses to a young lady named "Green," and these might be of the greatest service to him—Got to Sackville St very early—had written to Lady Elisabeth yesterday to account for my non-appearance in the evening— Dressed & went to Brookes's—ordered cutlets and returned in about half an hour (after having seen Lady Elisabeth & Horatia) to my intended solitary dinner, when I found Rutherford (the Lord Advocate) young Abercromby, Hastie and one or two others about to sit down to *their* dinner, and it was in vain I endeavoured to evade their importunities that I should join them—so join them I did—and accordingly instead of my dinner costing me but eight or nine shillings, my share of the general bill was no less than a guinea, and all this surplus for champaigne & claret of which I did not taste a single drop. One of the diners, Mr. Hastie, is the possessor of Burns's punch-bowl, and fixed a day for us all to dine with him (near three weeks hence) in order to bumper out of this bowl.

28 [Tuesday]—Breakfasted at Brookes's,—went to Huffel's, to order trowsers &c. and from thence down to Paternoster Row on my way to the Flower-pot (whither Tom Longman accompanied me) to take the omnibus to Edmonton—A good deal of conversation with Firminger about Russell— also about the old Lady Crew, whom I found he had known very well and likewise Harry Greville—"old Delirium," as William Maddocks used to call him, in consequence of a Love-Poem he wrote called the Delirium. This expedition to Edmonton took the greater part of my day—Met the Lansdownes in their carriage & had some talk with them, she having already sent me a ticket for the opera in the evening.—Dined at home with Lady E. and Horatia, and then to the Opera—to Lady Lansdowne's box—Grisi charming. Went between 11 & 12 down to the Morning Chronicle office to correct the proof of a squib I had sent up from Sloperton, and which was to appear on the following morning—][1]

29 [Wednesday]—Went to breakfast with Lord John, having written yesterday to say I could—No one but his sister Lady Georgiana (who now lives

with him) at breakfast—had the children in for me to see them.—Talked of poor Lord Essex, whom he had seen and sate with two or three days before his death—his spirit & his interest in politics unflagging to the last—Urging Lord John to do something bold and decisive, and when Lord John said, in replying "yes—We must take some steps—" "some steps!" said the gallant old fellow, interrupting him—"Why, {damme} the carriage is at the door, and you've nothing to do but to *step* into it and drive on." Speaking, at the same time, of the change of feeling that had taken place in all ranks, Lord Essex said "I remember when we used to wear our stars of a morning.— now, even in the evening we are inclined to hide them under our waist-coats."[1] He then told Lord John an anecdote of his walking in the street one morning with the late Duke of Queensbury, when both were young men (returning, I believe, from some night party) and the Duke had on a large star. As they passed some labouring men, one of them looked at the star, and then turning to his companions, gave a significant laugh or smile— "What!" said the Duke, after they had gone by, slapping his star, as he spoke—"Have they found out this humbug at last?" All this lively talk took place but *two* days, I believe, before Lord Essex died, and he in his eighty second year!—His death leaves a great gap in the social circle—{Talked of Gladstone & Puseyism—} praised Macaulay's late article in the Edinburgh[2] and agreed with me in lamenting that his great powers should not be concentrated upon some *one* great work, instead of being scattered thus in {detached} Sibyls' leaves—inspired, indeed, but still only leaves. I did not express the thought quite in this way, but such was my meaning. Went from Lord John's to Rogers's—met Savage Landor on the way, who walked with me through the Park.—I previously called at Lord Carlisle's & found Lord Morpeth with whom I sate for a little while, and then, being so near, paid a visit to Lady Lilford, and saw both her beautiful self & her beautiful boy— Told me that Lord Holland was very far from well—{To return to the Savage,—found him as gentle and tractable as could be—on asking after his idolater, Fonblanque told me to my surprise that he had not seen him since he came to town, nor expected to see him.[3]—left me at Rogers's door. After staying some time with R., his carriage being at the door, he offered to take me part of my way to Paternoster Row, my object being to go with Tom Longman to the East India House, to be introduced to some city people who were likely to give me some information as to Russell's appointment— Having given up, by Firminger's advice, the sending him to Addiscombe, my wish now is to get a *direct* appointment for him to India—Saw Shee's son, who appears to have a good situation there & to deserve it—was introduced to several persons, among others, Smith an Ex-Director, with whom, it turned out (as usual) I had already some acquaintance—every body full of kindness, but no very great advance made in my object, while on the questions I wished for information about (namely, Addiscombe or direct appointment? and in the latter case, cavalry or infantry?) I found each new adviser differing in opinion from the last. Forgot to mention Rogers having shown me before we started some beautiful letters written lately by a poor woman previous to committing suicide—nothing could be more touching, and Rogers's remarks upon the subject were full of true feeling and charity. In reference to the poor frail ones of the sex, of whom this was one, he said that no more genuine mark of divine inspiration could be found in all Scripture than the singling out, as in the case of Mary Magdalen, one of the most fallen of her sex to invest with qualities of the most amiable and touching kind, and make her the attendant & favourite of the Redeemer,—Asked by Trevanion to dine, to meet Benett & some others, but had engaged myself to Easthope before I came up. Company at Easthope's Warburton, Mc.Gillivray, Tom Duncombe, and about a dozen more—It happened that Warburton was the hero of the squib of mine that had appeared in the morning,[4] which I felt to be a little awkward, but Easthope told me they had all been joking him about it, & that he took it in perfect humour—"Did he know it to be mine?" I asked—"Know it!" answered Easthope—"who could doubt it?"—In the course of the dinner Warburton asked me very good-naturedly to drink wine with him.—Went from Easthope to Lady Valletort's where there was music by Doctor Weber, Henry Greville & others—The Greys there, who asked me to dine with them on the 7th.—poor Lord Valletort himself confined to his bed with the gout.—Lord John had asked me to join his family party in the evening, but this music of Lady Valletort's prevented me, which I was sorry for—particularly as she did not want my help, having foreign and professional singers *de la haute volée.*

30 [Thursday]—Breakfasted at home & corrected a sheet of the Epicurean—to Brooke's—had some talk with Luttrel about the present state of affairs—agreed with him that "Lord Melbourne *ought* to have saved the Whigs from coming back."—called upon Mr. Grenville and sate some time with him—Gave an amusing account of the late Duke of Norfolk making a set speech (as was a habit of his) on meeting the lawyers who were to prepare the settlements &c. when his son Lord Surry was about to be married—no one present but the two lawyers & Lord Surrey—said "he rose to address the company assembled," spoke of his past life and vindicated himself from the charges made against him on the score of his illegitimate children—still addressing from time to time, his few auditors as "the company here assembled"—When the Duke was on his death-bed, some clergyman (Mr. Grenville said) took all possible pains to get admittance to him and at last succeeded—but old Jockey would have nothing to do with him—Took a cab & went out to Holland House—was told by the *porter* that my Lady & Mr. Rogers were walking in the grounds, and went accordingly to look for them; but on second thoughts, turned back, as, once

in Rogers's hands, I should be *confisqué,* I knew, for the day.—Left word with the Porter that I would come to dinner either to-day or tomorrow should my Lady have a place for me, and hastened away again in my cab.— Called at Kent House on my way back, having met Boringdon in the morning—Found Lady Morley at home & sate a short time with her.—Went then to Lady Morgan's, where all were at home also, and Milady begun immediately about the rumour of Rogers's marriage to Josephine—Forgot I think to mention that the day before yesterday, on calling at Rogers's soon after breakfast, I heard sounds of music from the upper regions of his house, and on going up stairs, found Josephine Clarke & her sister, and a Miss Courtenay and her brother all singing away most deliciously some of the prettiest things of Bellini—accompanied by an old piano-forte of Rogers's, which I recollect being sent up there in a huff by him some ages ago, on account of some delinquency of mine, in the way of refusing to sing, or some such transgression—It was a most charming suprise to me and with difficulty could I keep myself from bursting out into tears at some [of] the things they sung—But to return to to-day—was hardly at home before I received a note from Lady Holland saying "We shall be extremely happy to see you at dinner to-day—Lord H. will enjoy your society much and you will find a *small* party. Tomorrow oh! if you would come, you would so greatly oblige me—I have Lady Lansdowne & Louisa to dinner & no one to make the party endurable—come, for once be amiable & comply—you will meet Luttrel to-day. Yours &c."—Met Lady Lansdowne, who was uneasy about Lord L's being obliged to attend the House of Lords, though still suffering from gout. Wrote to Lady Holland saying I could not come to day, but would tomorrow—my intention was to go to the Haymarket in the evening, to see Power in King ONeil[1], and I left a note for him at the Theatre, begging him to put me in some private nook for the purpose.— dined at Brookes's and remained there talking & reading newspapers till bed-time, Power's note (arranging most civilly my *whereabouts*) having come too late for me to avail myself of it.

31 [Friday]—Breakfasted at home, for the purpose of working a little— Had brought up the volumes that are to compose the *first* Volume of my General Edition, hoping I should be able to complete its revision & correction in town, but find this a vain hope. Got out about one—called upon Rogers, who took me in his carriage to the Board of Control & left me there—Hobhouse whom I wanted to see not yet come—Rogers talking of the late scandal about Lady Flora Hastings, said he feared there was something in it, that all was not right.—Mentioned what the Duke said to the Duchess of Kent that the whole thing must be put a stop to—that they must keep together (she & the Queen) and put a stop to all further agitation of the matter—"By G——d, Madam it must be put a stop to—

otherwise the question will be Madam not who is with child at court, but who is there *not* with child—the court will be looked upon as a sort of rabbit warren."[1] Saw Hobhouse (who was very kind)—told him that, distracted as I was by the conflicting advice I received on the subject of India, my ultimate decision was *for* the Infantry and the appointment to be as soon as he could manage it.—Called upon Lady Minto, who asked me to come to her tomorrow evening after the Opera.—left cards at Sir Robert Peel's and Sir Henry Harding's—then home to drive out with Lady Elisabeth—called at Lansdowne House with her—her account of the shock that Henry's late affair with the swindler gave Lord Lansdowne, who received the first intelligence of it from the newspaper in which the account appeared.— Lady L. (who was herself equally ignorant of it till then) saw him let the paper nearly fall out of his hand, as he read it, and he then threw him self down upon the sofa, and Lady Elisabeth has little doubt that the shock contributed very much to his present illness.[2] Lady Lansdowne not able to go to Holland House—would have taken me had she gone—Called at the Horse Guards upon Macdonald, who was all kindness about Tom & said he should have a renewal of his leave should it be required—Out to Holland House to dinner—Nobody but Sir Stephen Hameck, Luttrell and myself— Lord Holland wheeled in after dinner, looking more ill & broken than I had ever seen him; and even his temper, which I had never before seen even ruffled, evidently in rather an irritable state—In the evening, how- ever, on allusion being made to his famous Diary of a week at Holland House, and my saying that, strangely enough, I had never heard it, the Diary was produced, and though propped up on the sofa, and obviously suffering he read it out with a spirit & power of mimickry which was quite wonderful. Grattan is the great personage of the scene, and what with the pointedness of the things said by him, and Lord H's. exact mimickry of his manner & voice it brings the very man himself, living & speaking, before one.—Brought home by Hamick}

June 1st. [Saturday]—{Breakfasted at home—Lord Lansdowne obliged to put off his dinner to-day—not being well enough for it. I had been asked by him to this dinner but had previously engaged myself to the Spot- tiswode's—Sent to Mrs. Spottiswode whose dinner party I had declined (promising however for the evening) to say I was now free, if she had room for me at her table—was accepted. Called upon Bryan, and sate some time with him—Showed me letters that had passed between him & Melbourne, in consequence of his applying to M. for a peerage—Bryan having referred to his unsuccessful pursuit of the Slane Peerage, on which he had expended so much money, Lord Melbourne slily hints in his answer, that the having *failed* to establish his claim to a peerage seemed rather an extraordinary ground upon which to *ask* for one.[1] He does not of course hit it directly thus, but very nearly so—Melbourne's letters to him, on the whole, are very slovenly—Before I went to Bryan had called upon Rogers, and found as usual a party with him at breakfast, consisting of Taylor, Luttrel, and some ladies, (strangers to me) with their brothers or husbands—Fixed a day for me to dine at his sisters—In speaking of Brougham, & his present state, all agreed that he was "still perfection in *society*"—}[2] Saw by the Bills that my counterpart "Tim Moore" was to be acted once more "by desire" this evening & resolved not to miss it[3]—went to Haymarket & left word that I would come—Dinner at Spottiswode, Mrs. Robt. Arkwright, Longmans &c. &c. a very large party—told Mrs. S. that I must leave her for a short time (not saying where I was going) at ½ past nine but would positively return— she, though a little distrusting me, very good humoured about it—her guests, however, on seeing me rise to depart, warned her not to let me slip out of her hands, as I was sure not to return—Got a swift cab & rattled off to the Haymarket (from Bedford Square no trifling distance) but found they had told me too early an hour; as the piece preceding Tim Moore was still not nearly finished—This rather *contrariant*.—but I was well rewarded for the effort, having been seldom more amused. The instructions of the Blue Lady to her sister Blues (the scene laid too at Devizes) as to the manner in which they were to receive the supposed Poet—their getting him to write in their Albums—&c—the old Dandy who is to cry "Dem'd foine," at every thing the poet utters—all very comical. The Medley too which the Blue lady sings, made out of the first lines of the different Irish melodies as well as of the first few bars of each air, is exceedingly well contrived & was most tumultously encored. When she came again, it was with an entirely new selection from the melodies, equally well strung together—Altogether, between the fun of the thing, and the flattering proofs it gave of the intimate acquaintance of the public with me and my country's songs, I was kept in a state between laughing and crying the whole time. The best of it all, too, was that I enjoyed it all completely incog. being in a little nook of a box where nobody could get a glimpse of me—dashed off again, before it was quite over, to Bedford Square, and found that already *more* than suspicions had begun to be entertained of my fidelity—lost no time in making up for the delay, by sitting down immediately after Mrs. Arkwright, and singing as well as the breathless bustle I had been in would let me.—{In talking of the Queen, either this morning or yesterday, Rogers mentioned some circumstances which show that her little Majesty has a temper of her own—has on more than one occasion, it seems, (while at Kensington) days have passed it seems without her exchanging a word with her mother— since she came to be Queen refused to let the mother go in the same carriage with her—the Duke of W. saying to the Duchess of Kent "This must not be—go with her—insist upon it." Rogers mentioned too a little Royal adventure of his own, which seemed to have rather mortified him and I hardly wonder it did—He was induced (I forget why) to send a splendidly bound copy of his Poems[4] to Queen Adelaide, then *regnante,* and received, through some official channel a civil message in return. Shortly after, R. procured permission to see the Library at Buckingham House (or some such other Royal establishment) for the purpose of showing it, I think, to some foreigner, and Adelaide, knowing that he was to be there, posted herself in one of the recesses with Lady Howe—One would conclude (as I did when he was relating the circumstance) that this was for the purpose of availing herself of the opportunity to say something courteous to him in return for his homage—but no—it was merely to indulge the curiosity of seeing him, as he passed; for she vouchsafed no further mark of recognition towards him than merely a silent acknowledgement of the bow which he and his companion made in passing her. This, I must say, was most stupidly royal or rather royally stupid on her part—but, at the same time, he somewhat deserved what he got—Why go out of his way to make presents to Royalty? In the same manner Campbell sent his works[5] to Victoria on her accession, and wondered that I did not follow his example. But the fact is I neither think so highly of my works or so lowly of myself as to volunteer any such offering.

2 [Sunday]—Breakfasted at home—went to the Warwick St. Chapel, but found it too full and hot for me to remain long inside—Called for by Rogers in his carriage at Brookes,—took me to see his sister—Went from thence together to the Zoological gardens, where we walked about a little— As we stood looking at the rhinoceros, he said, "Now, if you had sate up all night to make that thing, you wouldn't think you had been well employed, would you?—or even *that* (the camelopard)—you would have given it a little more *behind,* I think."—R. himself a most marvellous production of nature—his activity of body, as well as of mind, quite astonishes me— Evidently proud of it himself, for he takes now to *running* occasionally, and to-day, on my complaining a little of loss of time and "wanting to be somewhere else" (as he puts it) he set off, between run and walk, at a pace that was quite marvellous. Volunteered to dine at Bryan's—had been asked to Edward Moore's but promised to come in the evening—No one at Bryan's, but Mrs. George (I *believe*) & themselves—From thence to Edward Moore's—large party and Rogers (!!) among the number—nothing but the fair Josephine could have brought such antipodes together.—My old fellow-traveller Camac[1] one of the party, and alarmed me by the intimation that he *kept a diary* at the time he & I travelled together—so that, for my comfort, I am "written down an ass" in company with himself. This comes of "strange bed-fellows." —Some nice singing by Josephine, and some tremendous squabbling by a pretty looking foreign girl recently arrived— forget her name—Lady Morgan furious about Lover, whom she has found

out, she says, to have been the author of some very *un*loverlike attacks (in one sense) upon her, in a low Irish paper called the Comet—wished evidently to enlist *my* "amour propre" also against the said Lover, by telling me that he had set him self up as a rival Thomas Moore and was getting numbers of people (as I understood her) to take him at his own valuation— with all my heart—he's welcome to the people and the people are heartily welcome to him.[2]

3 [Monday]—Breakfasted at home—went to the Exhibition—met Cuming the Irish artist there, and walked about with him for some time to view the pictures—said that he has not for a long time seen me looking so healthy, and so, indeed, every body tells me—Apropos of this, met little General Thornton the other day, and was glad to have an opportunity of telling him how much pleased Mrs. Moore was with the Volume of Sermons by Doctor Vincent which he (Thornton) had published and of which he had pre- sented me with a copy.[1] While I was speaking to him, he suddenly inter- rupted me with the exclamation, "How young you look!"—Alas, alas, this, fairly translated, means "how old you *ought* to look!" —Dined at Holland House, taken by Rogers—Lord Holland much better—nobody but them- selves and Allen—Lord H. evidently, I think in hopes that Henry Grattan may do something to Brougham—make him fight or thrash him or some such righteous Judgment, and I confess I should not much grieve thereat myself, for Brougham is an "abomination—before the *Lords*".[2] Rogers brought me in to town, his carriage dropping him first at an Assembly at the Archbishop's and then taking me home.—Received the following letter from my Music publishers sent up to me from Sloperton, which is gratify- ing; for I had begun to think this branch of my Castalia[3] had run dry, and that people wanted no more of my songs: "Dear Sir—From the length of time that has elapsed since our last, we fear you have entirely abandoned Mr. Barnett's suggestion respecting Schiller's Songs of the Bell. We hope to be more fortunate in our present application, as we are anxious to produce something new by you & convince our friends that you have not quite deserted us. We venture to submit to your notice three melodies by Mr. Balfe in the expectation that you may be induced to give them an imper- ishable fame by an alliance with your poetry—" &c—}

4 [Tuesday]—{Forgot to mention that I had gone to a party at Burdets' one of these evenings having received a very kind note from Lady Burdett, asking me—met a lady there who started on seeing me & whom I found to be Miss Meredith (the companion of Miss Burdett Coutts) who had not seen me for many years—Miss Coutts also there, who asked me to call upon

her, which I did one of these mornings—remarkably nice and graceful girl, and as unpresuming with all her great wealth as if she was no better off than any of her neighbours—Received a note from her this morning asking me to dine with her tomorrow and accompany her to see Kean. Was sorry I could not—} Breakfasted this morning with Rogers—the party Sir Robert Inglis (my first time of ever meeting him) Babbage and Milnes the M.P. and poet[1]— Sir Robert Inglis very agreeable, and like most men who are *strong* in their *opinions,* mild and gentle in manner—Received me with marked kindness, notwithstanding our Antipodism.—{From thence to Brookes's, having made an appointment with Macdonald (the Captain, our quondam neighbour at Bromham) to talk over Indian matters with him in reference to Russell—A son of his in the infantry has written home requesting that he would get him changed to the cavalry, and Macdonald has been accordingly making enquiries, on the subject among his East India friends, the result of which has been to determine him *not* to put his son in the Cavalry—. "If you want," said some one to him, "to make your son a spendthrift and fine gentleman, put him in the cavalry," and Sir R. Campbell, the Director, (an old friend of his) told him, on the same grounds, that if he had his pocket full of appointments to the cavalry, he doubted whether he would give him one. This all tells very strongly on one side, but there is an almost equal amount of authority on the other.—Macdonald, of the Horse Guards, for instance, the other day, when I put the case to him, exclaimed instantly "Oh the cavalry by all means."—Dined with Rogers, for the Opera, only ourselves—talked of the Duke of Wellington—showed me a note from him accepting a dinner-invitation of R's for two successive Sundays—R. having got together for both those days some people he liked—Miss Jervis, I take for granted, among the number. The Duke has been obliged lately (R. mentioned) to give up being so much with this little girl, as people said he was going to marry her[2]—In talking of our respective starts in society, I mentioned it as remarkable, that I should so immediately on my coming to London have got into that upper region where I have remained ever since—a circumstance which I had myself forgot, till the other day, in referring to the dates of some letters of mine to my mother I found so early as the year 1800, mention made in them not only of the Moiras and the Prince, but also of the Mount-Edgecumbes, the Harringtons and others of that volée whom I was then acquainted with and occasionally visiting[3]— Rogers on the contrary mentioned that he himself had reached the age of 35 before he was introduced into any of this sort of society. But what a station he occupies in it now!—Went to the Opera (he & I) to the Lansdowne's box—where we found Lady Louisa and ——— a relative of the family, I forget her name, with a little daughter. The Opera, the Puritani.[4]—Rogers, among his other marvels, has lately taken (as I believe I have already mentioned) to fits of running, and performed a feat of this kind, as we walked home to-night, to escape a beggar-woman, with a child that was teazing him—off set Rogers at full speed and off set the woman after him, and this feat was executed by both more than once.

5 [Wednesday]—Breakfasted at Brookes's, having appointed with Hume to come to me there—went together to Moore's the sculptor who had asked me to give him some sittings for the completion of my bust. "—monstrum horrendum informe". Called afterwards on Miss Coutts—fixed to go with her to the Dulwich Picture Gallery on Monday next—had been there herself yesterday, and when she mentioned that she had been on a Dulwich party, I thought she said a *dullish* party, which is not quite so picturesque an affair.—Called upon Lemon at the State Paper Office, to learn what Irish materials there were for the reigns of Edward VI & Mary—Said there was very little—the chief notices being about the Almaine miners—has no doubt that the implements mentioned by Crofton Croker as found in the South of Ireland were tools belonging to these people[1]—mentioned a fact which told badly against the interest taken by my countrymen in their own history, that scarcely a set of the State Paper Volumes about Ireland had been sold in that country—the dearness of the original price of these Volumes is, of course, one of the reasons.—talked of Tytler[2]—seemed to disapprove of his *modernizing* plan, and mentioned a mistake which it appeared to him he had made—one of the writers says to his correspondent you will pay me a visit in the course of your journey "*guest*-like," as Tytler makes it; but Lemon (if I understood him right) said it was evidently *joust*-like, or journey-like—that is you will take in *passing*.—To Brookes's, where I found a rumour that the Duke of W. was with the Queen—Sent a note to Lady Holland to excuse myself from dining there to-day, Lady Elisabeth having wished me to dine at home & go with her and Horatia in the evening to Mrs. Cunliffe's—Met numbers of old acquaintances there— saw among the "*new* lights" two Miss Gwynnes, very pretty girls—Went from thence to Lady Grosvenor's, a large assembly—talked with Lady Tavistock and her sister, with Lady Stuart de Rothesay & her daughter &c. &c. and had a hearty shake of the hand from Peel—found from Lady Stuart that the Bp. of Kildare has been in England, and that he has talked more than once of his jaunt with me in a Cab.—Some conversation also with Lady Stratford Canning about poor Mary Godfrey who is very ill—Barbara &c.—got away soon and home—The following answer from Lady H. to my note of excuse—"Her serene Highness is in a passion" as Lingo says—"I am *really* disappointed and half angry—I reckoned upon you. Lord John would have brought or at least taken you back. Oh fie—these are cruel tricks upon those who enjoy your company."—Sorry to have missed Lord John.—Received an odd note to-day from a Yankee gentleman, beginning "Most talented Sir" and proceeding as follows "About 5 years ago I was in this country, a veritable Yankee, and from my early love of the poet who has

for ever and aye charmed me, even as far back as when you were in Philadelphia, and the intimate friend of *my* friend Dennie," &c—&c.—must call on him.

6 [Thursday]—Breakfasted at home—went to Brookes's—on returning home found Sydney Smith with Lady Elisabeth—full of fun as usual—walked out with me—said gravely "It's very odd—I find the women of fashion confound you very much with Sir Thomas Moore—only they can't well understand how you could have lived in the reign of Henry 8th."—There's no nonsense he can't give a spirit of fun to, by look & manner, if not by words.—Set off when I parted with him to call upon Barnes—found he was living out of town—& left a note for him to say I hoped we should meet.—Called upon that immortal old witch, Lady Cork & found her, with only the pretty little girl who attends her & whom she calls her "Memory"—Proposed to me to dine with her either to-day or tomorrow a party of 18 being to dine with her each day.—Said to-day I could if she had room for me—made the little girl read out the list, and it appeared there was still one vacancy—Lady Cork's doubts about it, and the girl's eagerness to assure her there was room—"The truth is" she said "this child's in love with you—she has every line you ever wrote by heart." It was at last settled I should dine with her to-day—In talking of Lady Morgan, she said comically "I liked her very well, as an Irish blackguard, but as a fine lady I can't bear her." Took me to look at her conservatory &c. which seemed to me to be (like *herself*) exactly in the same state of preservation as I remember it thirty five years ago—Reminded her of our *spectacle* here about that time—the reading of Comus, when Lady Charleville, being too lame to stand, sate in a chair as one of the Bacchantes, with her crutch bound round with vine-leaves & flowers. The rest of the Dramatis Personae were myself (the originally intended) Comus, Lydia White, the Lady, and George Lamb & William (the present Lord Melbourne) the two brothers. There was also a select group of Bacchanals. As for myself, foreseeing that the affair would turn out rather ridiculous, I pretended a bad cold, and on coming to rehearsal one day, declared to Lady Cork that it would be impossible for me to undertake the Comus. This seemed to disconcert her very much, and having left me for a short time she returned with something wrapped up in paper in her hand, and to my no small surprise began to fiddle with my waistcoat as if to unbutton it, saying—"Oh this will quite cure your cold—it's a pitch plaister, the best thing in the world for &c. &c."—Whether she was really going to apply it then and there, I know not. Neither did I wait to see, but, disengaging myself from her, ran off to the other end of the room, and took refuge among the Bacchanals. This story, I see (by extracts in the newspapers) has been told, and ill told in some Memoirs of Lewis lately published, where they say in true "taffeta phrase" that "Moore, then the

darling of the day, was chosen as the fascinating medium through which Comus &c. &c."[1]—Met Taylor & walked some time with him—told me I had been expected at Rogers's yesterday morning, where the Clarkes &c. were breakfasting & singing.—Dined at Lady Corks, where we had the Lonsdales, Tavistocks, Kinnairds, Lord Segrave, Lady — Bentinck, Hallam, Sir. G. Warrender &c.—but no Lord John. Sate next Lord Tavistock—In the evening a large party of all sorts—Mrs. Fonblanque among the number, who was very anxious that I should sing *with* her, but I fought shy and ran away home.—In talking of Brougham with Lord Tavistock he gave me an account of the memorable night of the council after the King had dismissed Melbourne—Brougham's fidgettiness to be off, so much that Melbourne suspected him of meditating some mischief and when he went away sent some one to watch him—It was then that Brougham proceeded direct to the two morning papers, and fixed both trains in a way to damage all parties—*himself*, luckily, most of all.[2]

7 [Friday] Breakfasted with Rogers—the party, Sir Robert Inglis (my first time of seeing him) Babbage & Milnes—Sir R's reception of me most markedly kind, and I must say (Tory & Anticatholic as he is) I took to him in return. His conversation & manner very agreeable—Went out with Rogers in his carriage to pay visits—to Lady Hastings, whom we found at home, and a young fellow with her of the name of King—then to the American Ambassador's where we sate some time with Mrs. Stevenson—then to Miss Jervis who sung for us beautifully a new wild thing of her own—Asked me to dine on the 13th. but already engaged—we then mentioned the 22nd. to meet the Duke of Wellington which I promised to do, if I should stay in town so long. From thence we proceeded to Lansdowne House, where we were admitted & sate some time with Lady L.—R's. remarking afterwards what a place London is, and illustrating it by the course of visits we had paid that morning—he himself, certainly not the least wonderful thing it contains. Talking of Wordsworth—evidently impatient & angry at the idolatry of him & his works that has sprung up of late—Taylor, it appears among the foremost of the worshippers—his praising to Rogers some lines where Wordsworth talks of the waves flowing "innocuously" upon the shore—such a devil of a word to use! but Wordsworth, it appears, had already employed the word "innocently" a few lines before, which left him no resource next time but this "devil of a word, innocuously"—I would sooner have cut my hand off, said Rogers, than use that word.[1]—Dined at Lord Grey's—company, Lord & Lady Canning, Lord & Lady Morley, Sydney Smith and one or two more. In the evening, Alava & others—Sang a good deal, and apparently to every body's contentment—Lady Georgiana's particularly. Alava much pleased with my Song "Where shall we bury our shame" which I was made to sing three times over.[2] Went from thence to Lady Valletort's,

where I had been asked to dine—found Lady Lincoln and Lord & Lady Elliot—sung again a good deal, and so did Lady Lincoln, one or two songs most charmingly. Reminded her of some things I had heard her sing with the Duchess at Bowood some years since—a very pretty person.

8 [Saturday]—In dismay on recollecting that I had been for the last few days promising *both* Sydney Smith and Rogers to come to breakfast this morning. What was to be done? Luckily their hours were different, Sydney's being ten, and Rogers's any time before eleven—So accordingly at ten, au coup de l'horloge I was with Sydney—Found there among others Mrs. Austin, the savante, and Webster,[1] the newly arrived American; a man whose *head,* at least, implies great rapacity, and the little I saw of him at this sitting kept the promise of his head—I was, however, on tenter-hooks lest I should be too late for Rogers, and accordingly bolting without any preparation, got a cab and was in good time at breakfast the second. Found there also a Transatlantic party, consisting of the Stevensons, and young Van Buren and his wife[2]—There was also Milnes, and (a lion quite new to me) Thirlwall the historian[3]—His manner constrained and collegiate, and,—in short I did not *much* take to him—A good deal of conversation about Savage Landor & other matters in which Milnes was as usual more prominent than agreeable; or rather I should say more agreeable to himself than to others.—a clever good-humoured fellow, notwithstanding and repeated some very pretty things of Savage Landor's—Went from thence to the Longmans—Find that they now talk of marking time [*unrecovered*] of the Edition, though while [*unrecovered*] on the subject there was no mention of more than *eight.* They never seem to have the least notion either that this sort of [*several words unrecovered*].—By the bye, I forgot, among the company at Rogers's this morning there was a sort of Anglo-Abyssian gentleman (whose name I did not arrive at) who has been passing a great part of his life among the Abyssians & Arabs, and has left the greater part of his English behind him. Told me that whenever he wanted to recommend himself particularly to the Arabs, he always repeated to them some verses from my Melodies, translated into Arabic. The verses they liked best were "How dear to me the hour when day-light sets."[4]—Dined at home with Lady Elisabeth and Horatia & to the opera with them in the evening—the Box Lady Elisabeth's—Forget the name of the Opera, but the young fellow who was such a friend of theirs at Nice (the son of the then Governor) was one of the performers, and promises to be very successful. Home early}

9 [Sunday]—{Breakfasted at home—went to Warwick St. Chapel—stood with young Shee looking at the Catholic gentry, as they went off in their carriages, and learned from him their names—"Peter, the Creeter" among

the number.—Called upon the Cannings (Sir Stratford) and found them at home—sate a little while—then to the Normanbys then to Miss Coutts's, whom I found at home and Kean[1] with her—a good deal of talk with him about his father, whom I found I knew more of than he did himself—told him several anecdotes of him which I have not time to repeat here. Said to me with a look & manner which made me a little ashamed of myself—"I wish, Mr. Moore, you were as enthusiastic about me as your son is"— Explained as well as I could the little taste I have for fiction, whether on the stage or in books—if it touches me, it touches too much—if not, it *bores*. I had happened to mention to Miss Coutts my having heard so much of Marjoribanks and all he could do (in the course of my East India enquiries) and I suppose she had reported this, as I received to-day or yesterday a note from Marjoribanks (who was long years ago an acquaintance of mine) reminding me very kindly of old times, and inviting me to dinner some day to meet Miss C.}—Dined at Miss Rogers's, {being taken by R.—Company, the Rutherfords, Miss Coutts (whom I sate next) and a good many more. A large addition to the party in the evening, which prevented me from singing, as was wished, and as I should have done, had there been fewer people}—Some talk with Webster, the American, who said in a very marked manner that it gave him great pleasure to make my acquaintance— It is always agreeable to me to be kindly received by Americans. Told him of my having received a letter within these few days from a countryman of his, dated from the Coho Falls—an odd letter too it is. Here are some specimens of it—"Many are the nights that have seen my head pillowed on a Volume of your Poems and I am now reading your Life of Byron for the thirtieth or fiftieth time with increased zest." He afterwards breaks off into the following sally:—"But I must tell you that, at this very moment as I am writing, a beautiful young lady in the next room is singing a certain lyric which I presume you have seen, commencing "Oft in the stilly night"[2]—I must stop and hear it. . . . Beautiful, by Jove!—You have visited our Country—May we not hope to see you again. Do you remember writing some years ago some stanzas at the Coho Falls?[3] Do you remember the cataract and the scenery adjacent? Do you remember the humble cottage in which you became domesticated? That cottage is still standing—the cataract and adjacent scenery are still the same, unless it be that the forest is shorn of its scenery. I spent a few days in the same cottage, during the past summer, and used probably to walk in the same paths which your footsteps had so often trod. I endeavoured to discover your favourite haunt, and through the assistance of the family now occupying the cottage was enabled to do so. The accompanying lines were written at the spot and under the influence of the association & scenery. They were pencilled in a blank leaf of a volume of your Poems {&c. &c. &c"—Left Miss Rogers with R to go to the Duchess Canizzaro's Concert—very full—got in a small room opening on the Concert room, with Lord Grey, Burghersh & others where we heard better &

more comfortably than we could any where else—I had received no invitation for this Concert, but felt that I might safely volunteer my presence, and found that I did not "reckon without my *hostess*," as the Duchess received me very cordially saying "You know *you* have a general invitation." Every body was there, so that I could not have had a better *Panorama*.}

10 [Monday]—Breakfasted at home, and corrected a sheet of the Epicurean.—Have not had time to continue my corrections of the 1st. Vol. of the Edition—Went to the Row, for the purpose of arranging the order of the Works with Tom Longman—Learned from him the astounding fact that my scribblings in verse amount to between 80 and 90 thousand lines!— "Lord Fanny spins a thousand such a day"[1]—and why shouldn't I?—Did not get away from the Row till ½ past four, making more than four hours of work.—{Dined with the Arkwrights—he himself too ill to appear. Company Lord & Lady Hastings, King, Charles Greville &c.—very dull—with the exception of an apparition of Brougham that presented itself at the door, while we were at dinner—supposed, (if not his *fetch*)[2] to have been a mistake, and that he was coming to dine with some other party in the house—the Arkwrights being lodged at the Clarendon—Brougham's phyz, however, was an *incident*, and the only one of the day. Charles Greville wanted me to go with him to the Fonblanques in the evening. But a long Journey, in an unprofessional cab, was not very tempting—I however got away, as soon as I had heard a foreigner (Schatz, I believe) thump some most unintelligible sounds out of the piano-forte, and, with some little remorse (for I knew Mrs. A. expected I would sing) escaped to the Hay-Market Theatre, where Miss Coutts had asked me to join her—Found the Box empty, but staid and enjoyed (Solus) two very excellent farces—Had some conversation, by the bye, with Lord Hastings after dinner which rather interested me—Told him how sincerely I regretted my never having been able to come to Donington, and how much pleasure I should have in doing so, whenever I could—Enquired if the old clock, which I saw still extant, when I was last there some years ago still stood in its place, and he told me (with evident pleasure at my enquiry) that it did & that his delight was to preserve every thing as much as possible in the state in which his father had left it.

11 [Tuesday] Breakfasted at Brookes's, and went from thence to the British Museum; to look over Vallancey (about the OBriens) and Dr. OConnor's Historical Address.[1]—From thence at four to the Council Office, to meet Lemon—Very little about Edward VI & Mary in the Council Papers.— Dined with Byng—Company, Sir Arthur Paget, Lytton Bulwer, Aston, Byng (Lady Agnes's husband) and—some one else—found Sir A. Paget,

whom I had never met before, very hearty & kind—Went from thence with Bulwer to the Opera—he himself looking far more like an *opera* Apollo than a regular Parnassian—so bedizened was he with rings, ringlets and thinglets in all directions. Am sorry for this, for as far as I have seen, there is much to be liked in him. Went to the Lansdownes' box, where I found Lord L & Lady Louisa, and from thence afterwards to Miss Coutts's box where I was re-introduced to my old acquaintance Marjoribanks.

12 [Wednesday]—Bd. at home & then to Brookes's where I had appointed Hume to meet me—some conversation about his ———— which was very painful from the excitement it produced in him—Also about his being made a magistrate—said he meant to tell Lord John *quietly* that "the Home Office is a liar"!! Went from thence to Rogers's, where I found, as usual, a gay breakfast party, Miss Courtenay & her brother, Taylor, Louis Buonaparte, the American Hughes & some one else—Miss Courtenay anxious that I should sing, but told her I was then rather in a hurry going to the British Museum, upon which she said that their house was exactly opposite the Museum, and begged I would call upon her when my studies were over which I promised to do—Off to the Museum, and afterwards to Miss Cs. where I found that Taylor had come with them from Rogers's in the hope that I should sing—*Did* sing for them several songs, which they seemed to like, and afterwards Miss C. & her brother sung for me (and very charmingly) in return—Called upon Miss Coutts, where I again sung for her & Miss Meredith—Dined at Longman's at Hampstead—Company, the Hart Davis's, the Merivales, Colonel Johnson &c. &c.—Sung most abundantly in the evening, and was brought into town by some ladies in a Cab, having a drunken driver, and meeting with various adventures on the way—found some difficulty in getting the gate-keeper of the Regents' Park (who was also drunk) to let us in. "You know we're all private here," said the fellow, with a most confidential air to one of my companions, enquiring at the same time the number of her residence &c.—Got in very late, though with a good deal of laughter to console me for our delays.}

13 [Thursday]—What I wrote to my dear Bess yesterday was but too true, that the manner in which I am pulled about here, in all directions, by callers, diners, authors, printers' devils, is quite too much for one little gentleman to stand. {Breakfasted at Milne's—company, Montalembert, Sir Wm. & Lady Chatterton, Lord Lyttleton, O'Brien, & one or two more.— The New School, to which Montalembert belongs, all against English improvements, machinery &c. and holding that wherever they are adopted, poverty and immorality follow in their train—have drawn up Maps of the different countries of Europe, all *shaded* according to the different degrees

of misery & poverty prevalent in each, and showing, according to their notion, that the blackest are those where English manufactures and improvements most flourish. There may be more truth in this startling notion than appears at first sight. Montalembert, a clever, agreeable man. After breakfast, had music—duetts between Lady Chatterton and her husband, and singing—*such* singing! ye Gods!—from our host; song after song, volunteered, with as free and easy an air as if nobody could *help* admiring it. I also sung, and people seemed to like it, though not a millionth part so much as Milnes liked his own.—Went to State Paper Office, but could do nothing, Lemon not being able to attend to me—Dined at Lansdowne House—Company, Lady Morley, Luttrell, Lord James Stuart, Bulwer and Lady Corke—sate next Lady C.—Went in the evening to Lady Grey's, where there was every body, Lady Holland, Lady Cowper (still looking so handsome) &c. &c—While I was sauntering about among them, thinking I had nothing else to do for the night, Lady (something) Paulett said to me "I am just come from where you *ought* to be"—This, (as I then recollected) was Miss Jervis's, to whom I had most emphatically promised to come—Set off thither immediately, and found my old friend, the Duchess of Hamilton and a small party—Sung for them a good deal, and had also some pretty Songs from Miss Jervis—Lady Holland told me this evening of Rogers's "crossness" the other night at Holland House—his not waiting for his carriage but setting off to walk home.—Home—Called this morning upon Bryan's daughter, and found there had been the devil to pay about his intention of taking her to Ireland with him, and that it was this prevented their going last year—a compromise, however, has now been made, and she is to be lodged in a small house *outside* the Jenkinstown gate![1]

14 [Friday]—Breakfasted at home—Hume with me, during it, and our conversation respecting his ——— very painful—Called on Rogers—speaking of Miss Jervis & the Duke—the women very much against her & reported that the Duke was going to marry her, which has obliged him to give up being so much with her—Went with R. to call on his neighbour, Lady Sondes, who was very gracious and said how much she had long wished to know me.—Received a note from Lord John, asking me to breakfast with him to-morrow, which I dare say was in consequence of my having said to Lord Tavistock the other day, that I refrained from troubling him with any calls knowing how occupied he must be—Went to State Paper Office, where I found Tytler at work, who very kindly offered me all the assistance in his power, towards my enquiries &c. Worked, for some time, at our respective tasks, side by side, till I felt almost emboldened to exlaim "ed io anche sono istorico!"—Dined with Ellis (the Bear)—Company, Lord & Lady Kinnaird, Lord & Lady Roseberry, Alava, Count Zimoisky, the Seymours and some others—Sung for them in the evening and Ellis's

daughters also sung some Canadian things—gave me an account of their frightful adventure in Canada, where, poor girls, they were for some time in the hands of the rebels[1]—Went from thence to Lady Valletort's music—found they had been disappointed of Doctor Weber, a new & very good singer of this season—Miss Gent sung & so did I a good deal.}

15 [Saturday]—{Breakfasted with Lord John—no one but his sister—gave me a description of the variety of small businesses he has to attend to, being obliged, in many instances, to do the duty of his colleagues as well as his own. Told him of Bryan's comical indignation at the way in which he had been treated by him, one day when he had accompanied the Irish Attorney General (by appointment) to call upon him—On Lord John's asking the Atty. General to go into the next room with him, Bryan thinking that the invitation extended also to him, got up to accompany them, when Lord John laying his hand on his shoulder, said in his quiet way, "No—*you* stay there."—"By God" exclaimed Bryan (in his fiery way, while telling me the circumstance) "I never saw any thing so insolent." It was in vain I tried (laughing all the time at his good-humoured rage—for such it was) to set him right as to his entire mistake on the subject—assuring him that it was all but manner, on Lord John's part—he still sputtered & God-d-n-d, and I found all my eloquence, as well as my laughter thrown away.—Lord John very much amused at all this—} Went {afterwards} to the British Museum, and having been told it was a holiday, asked for Panizzi, who was full of kindness, and told me the Library should be at all times accessible to me, and that I should also have a room entirely to myself, if I preferred it at any time to the public room. He then told me of a poor Irish labourer, now at work about the Museum, who, on hearing the other day that *I* was also sometimes at work there, said he would give a pot of ale to any one who would show me to him the next time I came. Accordingly, when I was last there, he was brought where he could have a sight of me as I sat reading, and the poor fellow was so pleased that he *doubled* the pot of ale to the man who performed the part of showman. Panizzi himself seemed to enjoy the story quite as much as I did.—Received a note from Montalembert, full of kind and well-turned praise, which I fear I have lost,—should have been glad to transcribe it here, along with those many other tributes which I feel the more gratified by from an inward consciousness that I but little deserve them. Yet this is what to the world appears vanity—a most egregious, though natural mistake, it is the really self-satisfied man that least minds or cares what others think of him—{Called upon Miss Jervis, who talked much & flatteringly about my singing—promised her two days, I think, for dinner, one of them to meet the Duke of Wellington, and on *both*, sure to meet nothing but Tories—poor Lord Dover used to say "I like to show Moore to the Tories."—Dined at Murray's—had been asked to the Listers to

meet Lord John, and was sorry to miss him, but promised to come in the evening—company at Murray's, Lockhart, Sir —— MacNeil (late away to Persia) and his lady, the Milmans & one or two others—Lady MacNeil told me she had read Lalla Rookh in the Palace of Akbar—went to the Listers, where I found Macauley, Lord John and Lord Clarendon—some very agreeable conversation—Macauley always rather too much a holder-forth, and not improved in that respect by India.—George Villars not at all spoiled by his title.—Forgot to say I *lunched* to-day with Horatia—*her* breakfast! she having been at a ball till half past five in the morning. How women can stand the life they lead here is marvellous—but they actually *thrive* on it.}

16 [Sunday]—Breakfasted at home and went afterwards to Rogers, who was most kind and agreeable—as he has been, indeed, through my whole time here—made me stay with him—said that whenever he is asked where Mr. Moore is? he always answers, "he is at this moment in three different places"—{Forget whether I mentioned our having called together at Lord Sondes's—showed me a note now he had received from him, all full of "regret at being obliged to leave Mr. Moore"—} Walked with me on my way to Moore's, the sculptor's, where I sate for some time.—Went ¼ before three to Westminster Abbey to meet Lady Lansdowne & Louisa, for the purpose of hearing service—I sate with Milman in his prebendal seat & they somewhere else—A beautiful anthem—{but spoiled by poor Knyvett's cracked voice—} Dined at Holland House—had been asked to Lady Morgan's—called there, on my way out, to say I should be with them in the evening—Company at Holland House, Lady Keith & her charming daughter—Lady Cowper (looking as young & handsome as *any* daughter), Lord Clarence Paget, Byng & Lady Agnes—sate at dinner between Lady Cowper and Mademoiselle Flahaut—To my astonishment, on our joining the ladies in the evening, saw a fine piano-forte prepared for the occasion—a most new & portentous appearance at Holland House, and why there now I could not understand, though I saw my own fate clearly in the apparition—Madlle. Flahaut played a little, and then I sung three or four songs—{all to the accompaniment of Lord Duncannon's creaking shoes which were in full play during the whole time of my singing—Lord Clarence Paget also sate down to the Piano-forte and accompanied himself in an Italian boat-song very agreeably.—Came away with Byng & Lady Agnes, Lady Holland having of course tried to make some *different* arrangement—three in a chariot being, she said, not right in Lady Agnes's present situation,—but the Byngs only smiled at her fuss, and with them I went—Set me down at Lady Morgan's, where I found a sort of resurrectionary groupe of old fashionables and dowagers whom I had thought long dead and buried—among the rest Lady Clare.—There were also the Burghersh's and Shelleys—Shelley reminded me of our first meeting, some seven or eight and thirty years ago, when (as I now told him) he must have thought me in a fair

way for becoming a scamp of the first water, as our meeting took place at Mrs. Hodges's, and I was introduced there under the auspices of Augustus Barry, the hopeful brother of Lord Barrymore—I well remember his coming to me that evening, as I sate alone in my little two-pair-stair lodging in George St. Portman Square, and telling me that I must make my toilette instantly and go with him to a party where I should meet some of the first people, and among the rest my friend Lord Moira—(who had at this time taken me up very kindly) I accordingly went with him, and sung, I recollect, a good deal—being puffed off I dare say by Barry, as a young Irish fellow whom *he* had taken under his protection—the persons I met there that night were Lord Petersham (then living with Mrs. Hodges, as the deputy of Charles Windham) Lord Lorne (now Duke of Argyle) and Sir John Shelley. In talking over it now with Shelley, he said "Except for your hair, which I see taking its departure like that of all us, elderly gentlemen, you are looking exactly the same as you did then"—not saying much, as I told him, for my *then* looks. Among Lady Morgan's other guests was Rosetti, the old Italian improvisatore, who gave us a specimen of his art in a long rigmarole, coupling Lady Morgan & myself together in a way of course highly flattering to me. There was also some singing by the Clarkes, none by me, for I stoutly refused—Brought home by Lord Normanby.

17 [Monday]—Hume with me at breakfast-time—went with him to call upon Bushe (the chief Justice) whom I had not seen for many a long day—found him much the same both in mind & looks—a fine fellow in his way. Went to Longman's, and from thence in a Cab to Edmonton to fetch Russell—employed myself, on the way, in correcting a sheet of the Epicurean—Did not get back with Russell till pretty late—Dined at Sir F. Burdett's—Company, Rogers, Bear Ellis, Miss Jervis, Miss Coutts and somebody else—Had a good deal of singing in the evening—Lady Burdett not able to bear my songs and obliged to go away for some time! Few people are so much affected by music, and by *my* voice, she says, particularly. This I do not wonder at, for there is a melancholy in it, even to my own ear, which often brings tears from me when I am singing alone. This the first time I have seen any thing of Burdett (except passingly in the streets) since he joined openly with the Tories; and whether it be from old age or Toryism, I know not, but he struck me as a good deal altered—his spirits particularly not at all what they used to be. I enjoyed my day, however, a good deal—the *woman* part of the establishment being great favourites of mine, and Burdett himself hardly less so—

18 [Tuesday]—To day the whole world of fashion summoned to a fête given by my hostess in the Regent's Park, Lord Dundonald's house, which is now on sale having been hired by her for the occasion & Sackville St stript bare

of almost all its furniture for this gay frisk.—It was literally throwing the house out of the windows all this morning.—Went after breakfast to the Museum, to study a little before my gaieties commenced—rather a trying mixture of duties, particularly in such hot weather—Returned home to dress about three & set off in a Cab for the Regent's Park—a sudden torrent of rain then most unluckily coming on and all the open carriages flying through the streets to escape it—Returned home for my galoshes, and was half doubtful whether I should encounter the fête—but recollecting that possibly my services, in the musical way might be wanted, if the people were all driven in-doors, I set off again & found the gardens and the ladies all shining out as if nothing had happened, but the gazon also glittering & the walks unwalkable—Nothing could be prettier however than the whole spectacle—the women looking their best to make up for the fault of the weather, and to do them but justice all the world might be defied to bring together so many beautiful women as London can thus, at a call, supply.— Amidst the gay groups, too, *who* should have got together (not with *his* will, I am sure) but Rogers and old Lady Corke, arm in arm!—she seemed to have a hag-like pleasure in making him *beau* her. Feeling that I myself too was rather misplaced amidst so much gaily-drest youth & beauty, and finding that I should not be wanted for music, as dancing was to be the order of the evening, I accepted the offer of a seat in his carriage—from some dear old friend of mine whose name I have not the slightest notion of, and what became of me for the rest of the evening I quite forget except that I had a late dinner by myself at Brookes's.}

19 [Wednesday]—{Breakfasted at Rogers's—to meet Leicester Stanhope and his wife, Mrs. Shelley and Miss Robinson—Stanhope himself I always liked, but the wife!! never did pretty and, I suppose, clever woman contrive to make herself so disagreeable, nor exhibit contorsions of mind and face so disfiguring—The talk chiefly about Bulwer & his wife, and their odious feuds—Stanhope affecting to defend Bulwer, but leaving him deeper in the mire at every step—God defend me from your literary people—They are really the very worst society going, as well for morals as for temper and character. I must, as far as manners go, exempt Mrs. Shelley from this denunciation, for she is at least feminine—but your Mrs. Bulwers, Mrs. Stanhopes, and such blue Diablesses are my aversion—I have allowed part of the above denunciation to stand, but it was too general,—as well as also too *particular*—Missed Hume whom I had appointed to meet—Went to Macrone's about the Epicurean—saw one or two of the engravings from Turner's drawings, which promise beautifully—Sorry to find however that the swinging of Alciphron from the ring is one of the subjects he has chosen[1]—I recollect his mentioning this scene to me as one of the instances, in which I had made out the whole subject myself, and I supposed from

this that *he* did not mean to touch it, on the principle that what had been left vague and *unparticularized* (if I may so say) by the writer was that which afforded *best* scope for the fitting up by the artist—and vice-versa. But I find I mistook him & that his conclusion on the contrary was that as *I* had so much *brought out* and elaborated this extravagant scene it left *him* an easier task in extravagating also—a lame conclusion. Appointed to go with Mrs. Macrone's factotum (her brother, I believe) to see the drawings at Goodall's tomorrow.—Dined at Marjoribanks's—Company, Miss Coutts, Lord Boringdon, Lord Sondes, my old friend Lord Strangford, Warrender, and a very pretty little woman whom I sate next, Mrs. White.—} Some pleasant talk with Strangford about old times,—the times when he and I were gay young gentleman (and both almost equally penniless) about town, and that rogue Carpenter was tricking us both out of the profits of our first poetical vagaries. The price of a horse (£30) which Carpenter advanced—the horse falling lame at the same time,—was all that Strangford, I believe, got from him for his Camoens and my *Little* account was despatched in pretty much the same manner—I remember, as vividly almost as if it took place but yesterday Carpenter's coming into my bed-room, about noon one day (some ball having kept me up late the night before) and telling me that on looking over my account with him he found the balance against me to be about sixty pounds—such a sum was to me, at that time almost beyond counting. I instantly started up from my pillow, exclaiming "what *is* to be done?", when he said very kindly that if I would make over to him the copyright of Little's Poems (then in their first flush of success) he would cancel the whole account—"My dear fellow," I exclaimed, "most certainly—and thanks for the relief you have given me."—I cannot take upon myself now to say how much this made the whole amount I received for the work, but it was something very trifling—and Carpenter himself told a friend of mine some years after that he was in the receipt of nearly 200 a year from the sale of that volume.—{Called for by Lady Elisabeth, to take me to the Dutchess Canizzaro's, and came away immediately, leaving, I am afraid, some disappointment behind at my not staying to sing.—Warrender, by the bye, very anxious that I should stop at Clifden for a day on my way into Wiltshire, and I promised, if I possibly could, I would—it is a visit I have long intended & wished to pay, the place looks so beautiful from the road— Found the Poniatowskis[2] in full song at the Duchess's—very good and fine, I suppose, but much too noisy—Saw a number of old acquaintances there— went from thence to Lady Mansfield's, where I was received very cordially by his Tory Lordship, and saw a few more friendly faces of other days—} The following is the note which I mentioned having received some days since from M. de Montalembert—

"Sir—as I dare not hope to have the good luck of finding you at home when I call on you, I cannot refrain from writing these few lines in order to express the deep gratification I have felt in meeting you & hearing you at

Mr. Milnes. Your poems have been the earliest and one of the highest objects of my admiration. They were particularly my guide and delight during my journey in Ireland, when I used to hear the "Melodies" sung & really felt in every priest's house and every peasant's cabin where I halted. To hear them from the lips of their own inspired author and to enjoy his company even for so short a time has been a pleasure greater than I could have anticipated and will for ever remain stamped in my remembrance. Allow me to offer you the inclosed pages (which were the first production of my humble pen) not as any thing in the least worthy of you, but as a slight token of my ardent sympathy for your country & yourself.—I remain &c. &c."

{20 [Thursday]—After breakfast went with Hume and Mrs. Macrone's brother to Goodall's the engraver to see Turner's drawings for the Epicurean & the engraving as far as it had gone—Some of the drawings beautiful, but the gentleman with the ring on his finger as bad as it might be expected to be—our companion insisting on paying the Cab, saying that it was to be "put down to the account of the Epicurean"—Goodall showed us a most beautiful landscape of Turner's (one of his early ones) on which he (Goodall) is now employed.—Went to Paternoster Row, calling upon Hume's friend Barham, on our way—Staid at the Longman's some hours arranging the volumes of our projected Edition with Tom L.—Called upon Majoribanks on my way back, having been alarmed by a note of his, wherein he mentioned the death of his friend Admiral Douglas—feared that it was my own dear old Admiral, but found it was not. What had confirmed me in my apprehension was my having learned at Douglas's house some weeks since that he had gone out of town rather unwell.—Dined at Lord St. Vincent's—was disappointed to find that the Duke of Wellington could not come, as I should have been glad and proud to have once more sate at the same dinner-table with him—Company, Lord Hertford, Lady ——— Paulet, Lord Maidstone, and a good many more, most of them strangers to me—Was saved from a little scrape in the evening by Lord Maidstone's saying that he was going home to prepare for Lady Westminster's—On my enquiring what was the preparation (as I was going there myself) found it was to exchange his black neck-cloth for a white one, as the Queen was to be at Lady Westminster's—on my enquiring a little more about it, he said—"The only difference it makes is (but *that* is indispensable) that you have a *white* neck-cloth and something tight below—" meaning either breeches or tight pantaloons—As this was the case, and I was black & loose in both these required tests of loyalty, I thought it better not to go—so went to Brookes's, read the evening papers and then home to bed—Had Lady Westminster put on her card "to meet the Queen," I think

I should have gone to the trouble of enquiring & making myself orthodox for the occasion. But it would never have done to have a gold-laced lackey looking suspiciously at my neck-cloth, and exclaiming to his fellows—"Hic *niger* est—hunc tu . . . caveto."—This was the first time of my meeting with Lord Hertford since the days when I got into such disgrace with him & his Royal Master by writing

Come, Yarmouth, my boy, never trouble your brains &c.[1]

and other such uncourtly productions. He has become wretchedly decrepid: I happened to be standing near the drawing-room door when he was going away to-night, and seeing that he had some difficulty in opening the door, I stepped forward and opened it for him, upon which he made me a very generous bow. I do not think I was *ever* personally acquainted with him—if at all, it was very slightly. A kind note from Lady Burdett one of these days sending me an old MS. collection of music to select from.

21 [Friday]—Breakfasted rather early at Brookes's, and went from thence to breakfast at Rogers's, where we had Lord & Lady Grey, and Sydney Smith—of course all very agreeable—Was obliged to come away soon, this being my last day. Rogers coming out into the hall with me and bidding me good bye most friendlily & cordially—"God bless you, my dear Moore"—Went off to the Longmans to despatch my remaining business—performed several little commissions in the course of the day.—Lady Elisabeth all in amazement at my not waiting for Lord Morpeth's grand Dejeuner tomorrow—Dined at General Macdonald's—Company, Tierney, Lord Morpeth & Shiel—very agreeable—home early to pack.

22 [Saturday]—Started in the Emerald for home—Nothing worth remembering on the way.—

July 1, 2, &c [Monday, 1 July–Wednesday, 10 July]—Three or four days after my return our dear little Nell arrived from Ireland, so that with her & Russell we have a snug family party—decided upon sending Russell to a school at Calne—notes followed me down from town—among others an invitation to dine with the Powerscourts, whom I didn't know I knew.

11 [Thursday]—Dined at Money's, a family party—sung a good deal—and had a most enthusiastic audience—walked there and also back at night

12, 13, 14 &c [Friday–Sunday]—On the 13th. a visit from Mrs. Long, our County Member's wife, a very agreeable person—sate some time—The Boyses on the same day.

15, 16, 17 &c [Monday–Wednesday]—See by the newspapers that Rogers & I have been made Arcadians (Arcades ambo) by the old Dowager Society of that denomination, in Italy, and that Signor Somebody is on his way to England with our diplomas

18, 19, 20 &c [Thursday, 18 July–Saturday, 27 July]

28th. [Sunday]—Bessy, Bussy, Nell & myself went to see the laying of the first stone of a new Church about to be built at Studley—a grand ceremony attended by all the neighbourhood—and Guthrie preached & Lord Lansdowne made a speech thereon—heavy rain on our return and all got ducked in the sacred cause.}

August {1st [Thursday]—A visit from Shelbourne & Lady Louisa who sate some time with us.

2, 3 [Friday–Saturday]—Nell on a visit for nearly a week with the Hughes's, who took her [on] different trips in the neighbourhood—to Salisbury, Stonehenge &c.

4 [Sunday]—Note from Lady Lansdowne to Bessy, asking us to dine with her and Louisa next Tuesday at three o'clock—but we were engaged for that day to the Hughes's—I wrote, however, to offer myself for tomorrow, having to go to Calne to look after a schoolmaster for Russell—Accepted.

5 [Monday]—Started after breakfast for Bowood, and from thence went on their jaunting car to Calne, where I called upon Guthrie & was by him accompanied to Mr. Jacob's, the schoolmaster—found him a very quiet sensible-mannered person & agreed to send Russell to him—From thence returned to Hughes's, walked through the pleasure-grounds to Bowood, and at three o'clock was seated at dinner with Lady L., Lady Louisa, Guthrie, and Shelbourne. "We have no servants" said Lady Lansdowne

"and are *so* happy!"—and so she seemed.—A most snug dinner, after which we amused ourselves in trying over at the Piano forte some new Waltzes &c. which Shelbourne has brought from abroad—One, a pretty Valse by Libitski, called L'Aurore, tickled my fancy exceedingly, & I resolved to write words to it—Walked home in the cool of the evening, after a very agreeable day.

7th. [Wednesday]—To Devizes to dine with the Hughes's, and go to a Concert in the evening—(Bessy, Nell, Russell & myself)—I walked in—very small audience, but some of the music very good.—slept at the Hughes's

8th. [Thursday]—Walked home after breakfast.

9th. [Friday]—Had almost all the Hughes's to dinner—Old William, Old Robert, Mrs. Brabant, Johnny Hughes, & little Mary—all went off very snugly & gaily, and the Buckhill part of the company remained to sleep.

10, 11 &c. &c. [Saturday–Sunday]—Received one of these days some verses from an Anglo-Dutch lady, who signs herself Mary Merrit dated from the Hague. She incloses some song stanzas of her own—"Air, the Silver Horn," which are *very* Dutch indeed. But her verses to myself begin rather prettily

> "But who is she
> Whose minstrelsy
> Across the sea
> Is sent to thee?"

and again

> Then if worth aught
> My song be thought,
> Be pleased to smile
> Reward the while.

She adds, at the end,

> "And show my song to thy ane ladie,
> And win too a smile from her for me."

On the outside of her letter is written "In Hands"— meaning, I suppose, "by hand"

10, 11? &c. [Saturday–Sunday][1]—Wrote one of these days a letter to Tom's Professor, Mr. Bertrand, in which there was some little treason against my friends the Ministers which I would not have ventured to any one nearer home—"It must appear to you" I said among other things "that our statesmen here smell a little of the *nursery* as well as our sovereign."

12–13 &c. [Monday–Tuesday]—Have mentioned before, I believe, that while in town I agreed to write some more songs for Messrs. Addison & Beale—This makes the *fourth* task I am working at—"driving four in hand" as I described it in a letter to Rogers. viz.—the History, the Edition of the Epicurean, these songs and the General Edition of my works.—Received from Miss Burdett a book of MS. music which she had borrowed from Lady Sandon for me.

17 [Saturday]—Walked over to Bowood, and was surprized to find Lady Kerry & her little child staying there—was delighted, too, to see her looking so much better & happier (though still partly in her widow's dress) and in higher beauty than ever. After looking out my references in old Rymer, lunched with her, and she then walked with me through the grounds, on my way to Buckhill—Walked home from thence in the evening, and met Lady Kerry again returning from a visit to some sick cottager. In a note from Addison & Beale they say—"We are delighted with what you have done for us. 'The dawn is breaking'[1] is beautiful—your fire seems to glow" &c.

18 [Sunday][1]—Have already before mentioned, I believe, my having undertaken at their own most urgent request to write new songs for the Cramers' establishment. Have been occasionally occupied at this task as well as at my History, the new Edition of the Epicurean, and the general Edition of my Works. The Cramers delighted with what I am doing for them, and also liberal enough to tell *me* of their delight, using no less romantic terms than "charming"—"enchanting" &c. &c.—rather rare, I suspect, from tradesmen to their *employés*. The following is a specimen of one of their notes, speaking of an air I had myself composed for one of the songs.— "Your melody to 'Oh do not look so bright and Blest'[2] is quite captivating and must prove a successful effort"—Received some time since the following curious letter from a man (originally, I believe, a basket-maker) to whom Rogers was very kind.—I do not quite know what to make of it— whether it is all really true and honest, or merely—his old trade of "basket-making."

"Mr. Moore—Some years since I ventured to prefix your name to a little

volume of mine entitled "Songs of the Sea Nymphs"; and you was pleased
to acknowledge it—and even gave me encouragement to proceed further. I
have proceeded and with greater success than I believe I deserve, so far as
fame goes—and I have adventured my more matured authorcraft once
more under your far-famed name. I have my reasons for doing this—Some
three years ago I applied to you for a favour which I am now convinced you
could not grant, and the refusal of which caused me to think unkindly of
you; when I ought rather to have thanked you for the denial. Nay, further,
I fear that I may at that time have named it to others. I allude to my asking
you to apply to the Literary Fund for me &c.—It was not until my acquaintance with Mr. Rogers (to whom I am indebted for many favours) that I
became aware of the annoyances to which such men as yourself are subjected, and I then became convinced that I had wronged you both in
thought and word. I am aware that all this can be of no consequence to you;
as whatever I might have said could never harm you. To me however it is;
and I have dedicated my "Fair Rosamund" to you as the only means by
which I could appease my own conscience; and that all may see (to whom in
my bitterness I named the circumstance) that I did wrong—Yours respectfully—Thomas Miller."

Wrote civilly to the poor man, accepting his "Fair Rosamond," and assuring him—I forget what, but to the effect that I had never before heard of
what he now so conscientiously communicated to me.

15 [Thursday]—Our dearest Ellen left us for Bristol on her way back to
Ireland—Bessy accompanying her as far as Bath—the packet to sail on the
17th

17, 18 [Saturday–Sunday]—Very stormy weather came on which made me
most anxious about poor Nell—had advised strongly her going by Liverpool instead—Wrote to Mrs. Sanders of Bristol begging her, if Ellen should
not have sailed, to insist upon her taking the Liverpool way, & inclosing a
cheque for £5, in case her stock of money should not be sufficient.}

19, {20 &c [Monday–Tuesday]—Kind letters from Mrs. Saunders—Nell
had sailed on the Saturday—A letter from her the latter end of the week—
her passage a most stormy one, but safe & quick.

In the above memorandums I have omitted no less an event than a visit
of a whole week from} our old friend Kenny {Jeremy Diddler}[1] who came
to us about the 5th. or 6th, and being joined here by his daughter, who is
living as governess with our neighbours, the Oliviers, remained with us a
whole week. The letter, in which he announced his intention of coming to

us written last June is, for its cleverness & *tournure* well worth copying here. The application of Erasmus's words tickled my fancy (and *vanity* of course) exceedingly

"My dear Moore—I am very glad of a pretence for writing to you, for ever since the time we were roosting like a nest of owls in the Ruins of Bellevue, when you were wont to clamber up the crazy stair-case to cheer me with your sunshiny visits, I have ever and anon regretted the very brief as well as the "few and far between" renewals of our intercourse; for, how true what Erasmus has said of you—"Thomas Mori [Query! so written by him][2] quid unquam finxit natura vel mollius, vel dulcius, vel felicius?" and, recollecting those days, who more sensible of its truth than I am? and, again, "Thomae Mori domus nihil aliud quam Musarum est domicilium." But this all the world knows. Yet even Erasmus says nothing of the peerless lady (in addition to the Muses) of which this domus is also the domicilium— and this brings me to the "pretence" of recalling myself to your mutual recollection." He then tells us of his daughter being in our neighbourhood, and asks of Bessy to "give her once in a way a half holiday at Sloperton"—"I know," (he adds) I am making this request to one who has resisted ever the lures of the great world to follow the quiet ways of her own heart; and she may reckon this among the charities that are wont to occupy her." A subsequent letter from Kenny announced his coming and we had his daughter to meet him—

{23 [Friday]—Went all to Bowles's to dinner, Bessy having given Bowles some venison for the occasion that had been sent to us—she herself not well enough to join the party. Two or three parsons (Mr. Salt one of them) and a *she* parson, Mrs. Archdeacon Knares, our company—the *she* by far the best of the group. The astonishment of the clerical gentlemen at our not knowing who "Charlotte Elisabeth" was—a writer to whose authority they had frequently referred in the course of the dinner—"Charlotte Elisabeth, in her last &c." and "you know what Charlotte Elisabeth says on that subject." They had evidently a very low notion of our knowledge when they found us so totally unread in the works of Charlotte Elisabeth[1]—Bowles in high fun and folly—his fears of death mixing so ludicrously with his thorough enjoyment of all the nonsense of life—"how do you think I look?" being his constant and anxious question—Has put up a cast of a head of Christ in his Church, and chuckles at the notion of being taken for an idolater. Miss Kenny charmed them all by playing (beautifully, as she does) some Valses on Mrs. Bowles's atrocious old Piano-forte—they wanted me to sing—but no—with such an instrument, and such *parsons*—it would never do. Got home very agreeably, the evening being delightful—had stopped in the morning at Bowood to give the Kennys a glimpse of it. Kenny in a very "nil admirari" mood the whole of the time he has been with us.

27. [Tuesday]—Kenny and his daughter left us.—I must have misdated exceedingly some of the memorandums of this month, as Bessy has just reminded me that Ellen did not leave us till some days *after* the departure of the Kennys.—Received an application, either this month or last, from Mr. Schloss, asking me to take poor L.E.L.'s place, as contributor to his Bijou Almanack[1]—Declined, of course—though it would have been almost worth doing for the sake of the motto I might prefix—"Parvum parva decent"— Mr. Schloss says, in his letter, "Should you condescend to accede to my request, it shall be my most strenuous endeavour by the mode of its 'getting up' and decoration, to render it worthy of its admirers and of the patronage of the 'King of Song' . . . By your kind compliance with my request you will relieve me of great anxiety & secure for the 'Fairy Chronicle' its desired success."

September 1, 2, 3 &c [Sunday–Tuesday]—The strange fellow who wrote to me some time since about "the extremity of his retiring tail" has again been at me, and, between his madness and his cleverness, is rather a difficult subject to deal with[1]—Sent me lately some verses about poor Lady Flora Hastings which had a good deal of feeling in them, and which I believe I acknowledged the receipt of, with some expressions of praise. Then came a tremendous and mad attack, (in prose) upon Lord Melbourne, which I but opened, glanced through, and packed off without a word of comment to its author; which (to him) mysterious proceeding brought me in return a letter of which I must here (before I tear it up) record a few *morceaux*.—The parcel containing his MS. was I recollect rather carelessly put up, as my "neat-handed" Bess was otherwise occupied and I did it myself. This circumstance will explain what follows—"The outer envelope (says this odd fellow) which had originally been sealed with a common wafer impression was broken into, as also the seal connecting the twine with the paper; and the twine itself without altering the knot was loose and seemed evidently to have been slipped off—The date also had been altered by a careful erasure and the alteration apparently was in a different hand. I repeat that to me all this is of little moment, even though the time which has elapsed since the date of your last letter in which was stated the MS. having been already despatched is sufficient to allow of its having reached London for examination and even its having been copied. I have no present thought of its publication, but when I consider your political as well as literary position in society (consideration, perhaps that ought to have struck me before) the facts are rather startling. An MS., to concede the least, somewhat violent, and in part inimical to one, ostensibly Head of an Administration you are understood to support, is *(supposititiously)* ascertained to come from you, addressed to a person comparatively unknown, without comment, and in a single and evidently tasteful instance corrected, while the portions most

violent are unnoticed and may therefore be deemed tacitly approved of—
your own letter so explanatory, if accompanying the MS. is of course
unknown to them. [A short letter, acknowledging the receipt of the parcel,
which I had some time before written to him][2] In the event of your having
a watchful *surveillant* of the *mouche* order in your vicinity, is there not
possibility that distance and mistrust might arise between yourself and
parties of whom you are the reputed private and open political friend? So,
I confess, has it appeared to me; and I therefore hasten to identify myself
strongly as possible with that manuscript—to say, for the purpose of showing (if I found necessary) even to Premiership itself that I and no other am
responsible, as author of its every word, and that, until in its complete state,
you never saw it or heard of its existence, unless by letter from myself a day
or two previous to its arrival. That the seals—which being of easy imitation
might have been renewed without trouble—were left broken almost
seemed as an intended hint from *power* that my sentiments were known and
appreciated,—to be noticed of course in due season. These things are
notoriously common of occurrence in continental politics, to which I fear
we are assimilating only too rapidly; and such may be more common here
than I am aware of—" &c. &c.

4–5–6 &c &c [Wednesday–Friday]—Paid a visit to Lacock for a couple of
days—no company but Vivian—

9, 10, 11 &c &c [Monday, 9 September –Tuesday, 24 September]—Hard at
work at my four tasks, the History, the Songs for the Cramers, the Edition
of the Epicurean (which I have for the twentieth time re-corrected) and the
general Edition of my Poems. Have had no time therefore for journalizing.
Even in the *squib* line I have done but one thing for many months "Retrospect of a well-spent Life" (I think it is called) versus Brougham.[1] One of
my few out-of-door frisks was to the Heneage's (after many askings) on the

25th [Wednesday]—Company, the Merewethers, Joys, Col. Murray (Lord
Mansfield's brother) and his sister—Sung at a great rate for them in the
evening, being in tip-top voice

26, 27 &c. &c [Thursday–Friday]

October—1, 2, 3 &c. [Tuesday–Thursday]

7. [Monday]—Again to the Heneages, being called for & taken by Lady Elisabeth & Horatia—One of the guests, John Moore, son of the archbishop & brother to my old acquaintance, Charles Moore—Sung a good deal in the evening—Forgot, by the bye, a story told by Joy, the last time I was at Heneages—Talking of little men having tall sons he mentioned, as an instance, Sir James Graham's father, who it seems was a man of small stature; and some one having said to him, in allusion to this "why your son could put you in his pocket," old Graham answered "you quite mistake— *he's never out of mine.*"—Received one of these days the following note, inclosing a Spanish air.—"Sir—The inclosed is an original Spanish air that has fallen into my hands. It appears to me not to be without merit, and as you have been making a collection of national Airs, I have taken the liberty to send it, leaving it to your own truly lyric genius to adapt words to the air. I am with great respect & profound admiration of your splendid & singular talents your obedient servant—Euphemia."

8, 9, 10th &c [Tuesday–Thursday]—Great good luck for Tom, though somewhat trying to my small or rather *no* means.—By a concurrence of circumstances, (deaths, among the rest) he stands first for purchase of a Lieutenancy, and I am obliged to raise the money, how I can, for the purpose.

11, 12, 13 &c [Friday–Sunday]—Have contrived, by again mortgaging my brains, to raise the £250 for Tom's lieutenancy[1]—

14, 15, 16 &c [Monday–Wednesday]—Nothing particular, except being particularly hard at work.

17–18, 19 [Thursday–Saturday]—The new edition of the Epicurean announced for publication next November—six copies sent down to us by the publishers, with an intimation that there was a copy binding in Morocco for Mrs. Moore.

20 [Sunday]—An onslaught in the Spectator on Mr. Moore's "New Poem"— as the new Edition of the Epicurean with the few Poems at the end has been styled in the advertisements—very foolishly, and quackishly. I had, in my anxiety that poor Mrs. Macrone should gain something by it, allowed that the verse part should be called "Alciphron, a Poem"—but the manner in

which it has been advertised, making these few fragments the work, and sinking the work itself into a mere appendix is nothing less than an imposture. A fine opportunity, however, for my old friends of the Spectator, who having the start of the reading public by about ten days (the work not being to appear till the 1st. of November) have made the best use of their time—not scrupling about the means—to damage the work to their hearts' content. Sinking altogether the Preliminary Notice, in which I have stated that the subjoined poems were merely the fragments of a first attempt to write the story of the Epicurean in verse, (and therefore written nearly 20 years since) they cleverly—for their purpose—review the work as a newly written Poem, and going off upon this lucky assumption, play what is elegantly styled "hell's delights" with the whole thing—"an utter failure"—the mere "manes" of a poem—an "old rake endeavouring to write like Mr. Little &c. &c."[1]—precious fellows!

21 [Monday]—Thought it as well to counteract the impression of this article and sent off a note to the Chronicle as follows

"Sir. The writer of an article in yesterdays Spectator on the forthcoming edition of the Epicurean, has fallen into a mistake respecting the Poems subjoined in that volume, which I think it due to myself to correct. Not having read, I presume, the Preliminary Notice which accompanies the present edition, he represents these poems as being a "versification of part of the prose narrative" and also as recently written. The very contrary, however, of this statement happens to be the fact; the poems, now published having been written nearly twenty years since and then laid aside on my adopting the plan of writing the story of the Epicurean in prose. As some of the conclusions built by the critic on his own error are, to say the least of them, not very charitable, he will himself, I doubt not, rejoice to be thus set right. Your obedient &c."[1]

22, 23 &c [Tuesday–Wednesday]—Have had a pending engagement for some time to go to Bristol to attend a Bazaar in which our kind friend Mrs. Sanders is much interested, and to which, at our request, (though not much liking it, as Bristol is out of her circuit) Lady Lansdowne gave her name as one of the patronesses—My poor Bess being too ill to go, I had also intended to slip out of the engagement & wrote a letter to that effect—but receiving one from Mrs. Saunders the very next day which showed that she confidently counted on my coming, wrote immediately to say that I *would* come.

25 [Friday]—Started for Bristol in the Devizes Coach—found Sanders at home & accompanied him to the Bazaar—The rooms crowded with very

gay company, who were not long (with Mrs. Sanders's assistance) in finding me out—and I soon became the object of a general stare—groups forming round me for the purpose without shame or scruple so as to abash a little even so old a lion as myself—Mrs. Sanders, however, continued most eagerly to assure me that it was all for the good of the charity, so I stood it gallantly for more than three quarters of an hour—there being some very pretty faces among the starers which I tried to *out*stare in my turn, but they quite dazzled me down. Went afterwards to Strong's, the bookseller's, to look over some of his old books—haunted out some things in Leland's Collectanea.[1]—Sanders invited Grantley Berkeley to join us at dinner, which I was very glad of, my prospect at first being a dinner with my host & hostess only, who though excellent people would make rather a long evening of it.—Berkeley's dress at dinner was in itself worth going to Bristol to see—a rich salmon coloured waistcoat, the lapells of the coat lined with red and thrown back to let their "light so shine," and the wrist-bands of the shirt turned over neatly so as to come nearly half-way up the coat-sleeve.—A clever fellow notwithstanding, and made the evening pass away very agreeably.

26 [Saturday]—A little clergyman at breakfast—forget his name—but a lively and sensible man—Went into Bristol to perform some commissions—then to Bazaar "for the second time of appearance" but far less oppressive than yesterday, as the room was comparatively thin—introduced to several Bristolians by the Sanders's, and very glad to hear from S. that I am a great favourite with the people of Bristol. I had already flattered myself that I was so with their young quakers, whose pretty faces and coquettish bonnets are always unfailing attendants of my progresses here. Heighho!—"oh the days that I was young!"—but if I *was* young, they wouldn't be half so forthcoming. Started in the Devizes Coach for home about three o'clock—

27 [Sunday]—A long notice in the Spectator of my letter to the Chronicle which they are pleased to designate as "a well-tempered and gentlemanly letter."[1] Am sorry I can't return the compliment. They admit they *had* read the Preliminary Notice, and then barefacedly repeat all their former misrepresentations. This was of course their best plan, for their own purpose and *métier,* and I have therefore no right to be either surprised or angry at it. But that such fellows should set up as judges of what is "gentlemanly" is rather *too* comical.

28 [Monday]—Have just stumbled upon a letter which I received some three months since from an old fellow-lodger of mine, Mathew O'Reilly,

who used to occupy the first floor at No 45 I think George St, Portman Square (my first London lodging) while I soared above him *au second.* Whether it was then the spirit descended upon him from the second floor I know not, but that he has himself since become a poet, the following extracts from his letter will show.—"When I met you last autumn in Dublin, after exclaiming as Dante did on some similar occasion "Onorate l'altissimo Poeta" I casually mentioned that I passed my life reading & riding, to which you replied with quickness and kindness habitual to you and "I hope in writing"—I answered &c. &c." He, Reilly, then proceeds to say that living as he does in one of the wretchedest parts of Ireland "can seldom feel any of that inspiration, that fire I sometimes imagine I caught from you—wild and imperfect as it is—when we were youths together, laughing & drinking well-iced blackstrap [We used, I recollect, to send for a bottle of port to Lloyd's Wine Vaults in Manchester and having first iced the very life and soul out of it finish the contents between us.][1]—those days as you called them (for I never forget anything good) of "bad port wine and good spirits." Nevertheless as natural propensities will break out &c. &c."

29 [Tuesday]—Pretty much about the same time with the foregoing letter I received one from the Revd. Mr. Husenbeth (the famous Catholic controversialist) addressing me not as a poet, but as theologian—for as Mrs. Malaprop says, I am, "like Cerberus, a gentleman with three heads"—Mr. Husenbeth writes as follows "Dear Sir—As you so kindly accepted some former publications of mine on controversial subjects, I venture to beg you to extend the like favour to another which has recently appeared. He then proceeds to say that Mr. Poole, the writer whose book he answers "belongs to the growing party of Puseyites, or Oxford Tract Writers, who are causing serious alarm among the *mere* Protestants, as their rivals amusingly term them." The Revd. gentleman concludes his letter to me thus—"As you have deeply investigated St. Cyprian, among other Fathers, this little work may somewhat interest you."[1]

November 1, 2, 3, &c. &c. [Friday, 1 November–Thursday, 14 November]—At work with but few interruptions

15 [Friday]—Bessy & I went for a couple of days to Lacock—only themselves—

16 [Saturday]—Shelburne came, in his four-in-hand, with a young German Baron, whom he made a friendship with abroad—Lady Elisabeth asked them to stay dinner, which they did—My poor Bessy suffering from the

pain in her face, but still enjoying (as far as it will let her) the hospitality and comfort of this agreeable house—Discovered among the veterans of the Library a book I had much wanted—the Monasticon Anglican[1]—transcribed from the account of the Priory of Wygmore some particulars respecting the Earl of March.

17 [Sunday]—Home after breakfast

18, 19 &c. [Monday–Tuesday]—Drew on the Cramers for £100—Receive almost every day some curious letter or poem which it would be amusing to preserve—but have not the time to transcribe them—Here is one, however, which arrived about a week since and of which the substance, writing, locality, names are all peculiar & characteristic

London 6th Novr. 1839
Revd. D. Meldola
10 Beve's Marks
City

"To the author of Lalla Rookh (the sweet companion of their leisure hours) [This is worded as if the *author* was the "sweet companion of their hours."][1] the Misses Moss beg most respectfully to offer the accompanying volume of Poems. Should he deem it worthy of acceptance he will deeply gratify those who have no other means of thanking him for the delight afforded them in committing to memory that beautiful & far-famed Romance. If at any time he should waste a moment in perusing it, his candid opinion would be greatly prized by his sincere admirers

Celia Moss, Marion Moss
aged 18 & 16 years."

20, 21 &c. &c. [Wednesday–Thursday]—Forgot to mention that the Spectator has been again at me on the score of my new set of songs, and goes so far as to assure the world gravely that I have not a single musical notion or feeling. I thank thee, Jew, for that oracular dictum[1]—the fact is, I have little else than musical feeling—it was that alone that made me any thing of a poet, and accordingly the verses I have written connected with music are the only ones of mine that have a preserving salt in them for after time—if, indeed, even *they* have it. The answer of the Cramers respecting my draft shows that they are by no means ill-pleased with their bargain.

21 [Thursday]—Dined with the Hughes's at Devizes—a large party consisting of the Ludlow Bruges?, Methuen, the clergyman, Mr. & Mrs. Grubb, Brabants, Phipps's, and one or two more—A good deal of talk after dinner

about Coleridge—(Methuen & Brabant having seen a good deal of him) none of it very creditable to that master of profound Humbug—Brabant mentioned one instance, in which he heard Coleridge take up very strenuously (on some theological question) the very reverse of the line of argument which he had taken, quite as strenuously the day before. He had entirely forgot that Brabant had been among his audience at the former display. Found the ladies, when we joined them, exceedingly impatient at our long *sèance*—the carriages having been some time ordered and one or two of the ladies (Mrs. Bruges, a very handsome person) & a Mrs. Savage being on the tenter-hooks of impatience to hear a song from me before they went—Did not like to refuse, and, happening to be in voice sung half a dozen songs running for them. Slept there

22. [Friday]—Brought home by the Hughes's after breakfast.

23, 24 &c. [Saturday–Sunday]—A kind note from Lady Lansdowne asking Bessy & myself to come for a few days on the 27th. to meet the Mount-Edgecombs & the Feildings.

27 [Wednesday]—My sweet Bess not well enough to go to Bowood, though, thank God, suffering much less from her horrid pain. Went myself, leaving Bessy Prowse (who has been on a visit with us some time) to keep her company—The party in the house, Mrs. Burke (Lady Kerry's sister) and her husband, the Feildings, and young Ellis.—Lady Mount-Edgecumbe having gone to join her Lord at Bath.

28 [Thursday]—Worked & walked to see the Hughes's—same party at dinner—Sung a good deal in the evening

29 [Friday]—Very much pressed to stay over to-day, and Lady Lansdowne proposed to write and ask Bessy to join the party, saying she would send a nice warm carriage for her—But I stole quietly away, and had a very dirty walk of it home.

30 [Saturday]—Bessy Prowse left us, after a visit (I was surprized to find) of three months—a very nice girl, and rather improved than spoiled (for a wonder) by taking to saintliness. Hers, however, a mild form of the disease. Have cut the above out of news papers in the course of this week[1]—must keep a look out after Lalla to see whether she wins or not—}

December {1, 2, 3, 4 &c [Sunday–Wednesday]—Too busy at home and abroad to think of journalizing my movements *en détail,* so must dispatch them *en gros.*—

5, 6, 7 &c [Thursday–Saturday]—Lord John expected at Bowood—Have been taking steps towards Russell's outfit for India, the time being now near when I expect the cadetship for him from Hobhouse—The sum that Lord John deposited with the Longmans for him many years ago now amounts to between four and five hundred pounds, and I am about to apply it, with Lord John's concurrence, to the expences of the outfit— Another enormous outlay has come upon me lately for Tom's Lieutenancy (a series of lucky accidents having made him first for purchase) and this I was only able to accomplish by the old expedient of mortgaging my unfortunate brains—the Longmans having advanced me the sum (nearly £270) in part payment of what I am to receive for the Edition of my Works.

Received last month (Novr. 14) from Lord Holland, the following additional string of rhymes to Bayle, which I thought he had already quite exhausted, and to my shame, as a rhymer, made that my excuse for not "following suit."

"Dear Moore—I have impudently taken your name, and supposed an answer from you to my own nonsense

Yrs. Vassal Holland

"Answer to the Verses to Thomas Moore"

Let me ask what the devil your Lordship could ail . . .?
To string all these pitiful puns upon *Bayle?*
Did you fancy your pains were of any avail
In exhausting the rhymes that will answer to *Bayle?*
Ah, believe me such hopes are exceedingly frail,
There's no end to the English that jingles to *Bayle.*
Consume all your cabbage, you come to Sea Cale,
So you'll never root up verses ending in *Bayle.*
No cross so abundant on mountain or vale
As of words in our tongue corresponding with *Bayle.*
They're at hand, and they ask neither thrashing nor flail,
It should seem the whole language was rhyming with *Bayle.*
Some are scarce, some are common, some fresh & some stale,
But they all go down swimmingly, seasoned with *Bayle.*
Any poet who's fluent would pelt you like hail
With words everlasting that answer to *Bayle.*
He would say, on the head you had hit the right nail,
When for rhyme you selected the syllable *Bayle.*
He would pour forth effusions, would fill a large pail,
So copious the flow when he's spouting to *Bayle.*

> For none but a bungler, as slow as a snail,
> Long could falter or boggle when rhyming to *Bayle*.
> A mere novice in Crambo would spout like a whale,
> If the skill all consisted in rhyming to *Bayle*.
> Nay, a fellow who'd drink a whole gallon of ale,
> Yet would stammer out sounds that would rattle to *Bayle*.
> But as tedious I grow as the call of a Quail,
> With one wearisome note ever harping on *Bayle*.
> So as songs, like most animals, should have a tail,
> Good bye—though of rhymes I have plenty to *Bayle*.

—Forgot to mention last month my receiving a letter from a Piedmontese poet, Giovanni Flechia, accompanied by a copy of the "Profeta Velato"[1] (his own translation) and telling me that, having come to London, for the purpose of teaching Italian, and not finding any pupils, he is about to return to his own country,—but having unluckily spent all the little money he brought with him, he is left totally without the means of getting back again—Begs me to apply for him to the Royal Society of Literature, and refers to Panizzi as knowing him—He adds "lorsque je serai retourné en Italie "si animus vacuus sit curis," je finirai de traduire Lalla Rook—Le succès qu'eût le Prophète Voilé separé me fait espèrer que le Poème entier sera acceuillé avec un grand plaisir par les Italiens."

8–9 &c. [Sunday–Monday] An unexpected visit from Tom about this time—He had written to tell us of an opportunity that had occurred for his exchange into a regiment going abroad—first to some West India island, and soon afterwards (as represented by the Exchange Agent) to Canada. Tom, all agog for this, himself cites all the authority of Captain Kidd (an officer of his regiment whom he knows I have a good opinion of) as thinking the step an advantageous one. Not the least of the temptations to Tom is the leave of absence he is to have previous to going and the sum of money he is to get for the exchange—Proposes to devote £50 of it to travelling and offers to take me to Rome!—Wrote to him to say that if the exchange was so prosperous a one as he & his friends represented it, I gave of course my full assent to his effecting it. Alluding jokingly to his romance about our getting to Rome & back again for £50, I told him that even if we went there, as Caesar did on the top of the Diligence (according to the school-boy's translation of "Caesar ibat Romam summa diligentia") we could not well manage to effect it for that sum—Inclosed him a note to deliver to Macdonald—On receiving my letter, Tom got leave of absence from his Colonel, and set off for London, where having staid a day or two, and seen Macdonald, he came down to Sloperton; and a most lucky fellow he has been to be so seasonably stopped in the imprudent step he was about to take. It appears that the accounts given of the destination of the regiment he was about to exchange into were all deceptive & unfounded—the regiment being about to proceed to some West India island, there to remain for many years, and without any chance of going to Canada. Macdonald desired him to come instantly down to me & tell me to write without delay to Lord Fitzroy Somerset, begging him to stop the papers for the exchange which there is but just time to effect. Nothing could be kinder or more fortunate than this interference of Macdonald. Wrote immediately to Lord Fitzroy, as well as to Macdonald, thanking the latter for his most seasonable kindness—Received an answer from Lord Fitzroy saying that Lord Hill would not oppose the stopping of the papers—What good luck to have had so kind & thoughtful a friend as Macdonald at head-quarters! Wrote to thank him & said that if I had not good grounds for believing in my own paternity, I should have suspected him to be "a father in disguise." After staying a few days, Tom left us to return to Ireland.

13. [Friday] Received a note two or three days since from Lady Lansdowne asking me to dinner to-day to meet Lord John—but something (I forget what) made me put it off till Monday—}

15 [Sunday]—{To Bowood—Sorry that I had not taken advantage of Saturday's invitation, as to-day's dinner turned out to be a "gathering of the clans"—Phipps's, Joys, Southrons, & Heneages &c. Was lucky enough however, to get seated next to Lord John, whom I rejoiced to find looking well—notwithstanding his labours—Joy's powers of boring much increased during his long absence from the neighbourhood—his cut-and-dry stories even more dry and of a worse cut than ever—not that he does not remember and tell a number of very good anecdotes, but they come any *thing* but "mended from his tongue," and the art of *letting well alone* in story-telling is wholly unknown to him—} A thing Lord John said to me to-day struck me as peculiarly melancholy (coming from *him,* so highly placed as he is in every respect)[1] though it is a sort of feeling that often comes over my own mind. On his speaking of the speed with which time seems to fly, I said to him, "if you find it so now, what will you say of it when you are as old as I am."—"I don't know" he replied, in his quiet manner,—"for my part, I feel rather glad it's gone."

{16 [Monday] Brought down with me to breakfast a most ridiculous prospectus sent me lately, of a great poetical Work, or Works, about to be communicated to the astonished world by a Mr. Macklin of Dublin—As my reading of it produced roars of laughter, I shall give a few specimens of its merits here.—He begins by announcing to the world his intention to "become as soon as possible a publisher (i.e. of his own works) upon an extensive scale."—A translation of Homer's Iliad is the first thing threatened, Cowper's being all "feeble and insipid," and as to Pope's, "it is my intention (he says) to point out *seriatim,* the gross & scandalous errors into which Mr. Pope has fallen."

On second thoughts, I shall not give myself the trouble of copying this thing out, but, as it is really worth preserving (for its exquisite absurdity) shall wafer it in here, body and bones. What amused them most at Bowood was his estimating the merit of all preceding poets by the number of lines contained in their several poems. He is certainly a rare fellow, and beats even his namesake, an old college friend of mine Hugh George Macklin, whom we used to call Hugo Grotius Braggadocio. In reading this Manifesto[1] over the breakfast table I had refrained from tiring my auditors with any of the verse specimens; but the moment I threw it down, Joy seized upon the paper and most characteristically proceeded to bore them with all that *I* had purposely omitted.

17 [Tuesday] After breakfast Lord Lansdowne proposed a walk, and he & Lord John and I went to see the new Church, which is advancing very fast—Nobody at dinner but Lord Camperdown (who arrived this morning) Lord John, & the family party—Sung a good deal for them in the evening.

18. [Wednesday] Obliged to go into Devizes to raise money (how I could) for a purpose I shall here be silent on—trusting for the sake of all parties that such painful trials will not again occur—Drew upon the Longmans for £200, and (the occasion having been too pressing for me to give them previous notice) made the Bill payable at three months date. Lady L. offered me the carriage, but I had already ordered a Fly from Calne—got home to dinner. Was obliged to tell Bessy the circumstances.}

19, 20 [Thursday–Friday]—{Received a letter from my Italian translator, M. Flechia, from which it appears that my application for him to the Literary Fund has succeeded—They have given him fifteen pounds, & he expresses himself as highly grateful both to them and me for "ce genereux secours."—My last songs, from every thing I hear of them appear to be very successful—Miss Burdett writes to me that *her* favourite is "The Language of Flowers"[1]—Mrs. Crawford some time since wrote as follows about them—"I immediately proceeded to try them over, and most beautiful, indeed, I pronounce them to be. No. 1, 2 and 4 particularly so." In turning over my letters found one which I received the latter end of last month, signed E.P. the hand-writing of which seemed familiar to me, but I was a long time puzzled to think whose it could be—At last, it suddenly flashed upon me that {the writer must be} Miss Pigot of Southwell, {who was so kindly serviceable to me in furnishing materials for the early part of my Life of Byron.} Inclosed in the present letter was a Poem written by some young lady, a relative of the writer and addressed to me. {As it has just now turned up before me, I may as well give some specimens of it—}

Lines addressed to the Author of Lalla Rookh.

"And what is writ is writ,
    Would it were worthier."[2]

Enchanter, wake! thy harp that sleeps,
The Muse that now neglected weeps,
    Silent have lain too long;
Oh let one lingering heaven-born note,
Like an expiring echo float,—
    Arouse thee, Child of Song!

Shall envious spirits smiling tell
How passed the mighty wizard's spell?
    No—wake each slumbering strain,
Prove thy bright genius ever young,
And let thy hand in fervour flung
    Strike thy own harp again.
            * * *
Then, by thy loved, thy Emerald Isle,
By Beauty's once so worshipp'd smile,
    By rock and tree and flower,
By the green sea & the blue skies,
By woman's love, by woman's eyes,
    Recal thy former power.

By thy young spirit's golden dream,
By all that once did joyous seem,
    By what thou wert of yore;
By earth beneath, by heaven above,
By all that you have loved, or love,
    Awake thee, Thomas Moore!

{And so the young lady goes on through three or four more stanzas—The writer of the letter (Miss Pigot as it proved to be) in which these verses were inclosed, speaks thus of the young authoress—"A pretty little bright-eyed girl of 18, who went poetically mad at ten years of age, from reading Lalla Rookh &c. &c."}

21 [Saturday]—Lord John came over to Sloperton to see Bessy and brought his little children with him; but unfortunately Bessy had gone upon some business to Devizes, and so missed him—Nothing can be more touching

than to see him with these children, and he has them almost always with him, {nor does one see the least difference between his manner & feeling to his own little girl and that which he manifests towards the boy & girl by Lady John's first marriage. He is indeed (as the ladies at Bowood all agree) a pattern for a mother.} Took them up to my study which he wished the children to see, and I there sung the Crystal Hunters[1] for them—the eldest girl (who is clever & has shown a taste for drawing) having made a sketch from that song—In going away, he promised to bring the children again some day when he is sure of finding Mrs. Moore at home. The youngest little girl (his own child) who is a very odd, original little thing, sings a song about "long live *keen* Vittoria" in a very amusing style.

{22, 23. [Sunday–Monday]—Have forgot I believe to mention any thing about Lord John's money for his god-son, our Russell—viz. the sum which (then between two and three hundred pounds, I believe) he deposited in the hands of the Longmans many years since, to be employed for Russell when he should want it, to start him in life. This sum, now increased to more than four hundred, I was about to draw (with Lord John's entire concurrence) out of the hands of the Longmans for the purpose of fitting out Russell for his Indian expedition as soon as the cadetship we are now expecting from Hobhouse shall arrive. But a difficulty has arisen with the Longmans who think that notwithstanding Lord John's letter to them (directing the transfer of the money to me) they may still be liable to Russell's coming upon them for it, when he is of age—This unexpected hitch will, I fear, leave me wholly without the means of providing for his outfit, as I have not only exhausted, but largely anticipated all my own resources for a long time to come—so that what I am to do I know not.

26 [Thursday]—To Bowood—Lord John still there, Lord & Lady Dumferline, John Ponsonby, and Senior—Lord Duncannon went away yesterday—we had also my favourite (and every one's favourite) Miss Fox.

27 [Friday]—The Russell money obliged to be given up, the Longmans having sent me a letter addressed to them by their solicitor, Turner, saying that they could not with safety deliver it over, that they would be liable &c. &c. In one of my letters to them on the subject, I told them, laughingly, that their custody of money reminded one of the old simile of the rat-trap, easy to get into but the devil to get out again—Told this to Lord John, whom it amused.—Lady Elisabeth and Horatia came to dinner—Sung a good deal in the evening, Miss Fox staying to the last to listen to me, though Lady Lansdowne wanted to get her to bed.}

28 [Saturday]—Miss Fox showed me after breakfast a letter she had just received from Lord Holland respecting the case of Frost,[1] she having written to him, it appeared, in favour of leniency—was struck with the clearness & precision of style with which he stated his own opinion on the subject, though the letter was evidently a hasty one written just as he was about to hurry away to the Cabinet. {Found that Lord John had fixed to go with me to day, when I was returning home, & to take the children to Mrs. Moore—After luncheon set off with them in the Coach—They staid a good while at Sloperton, the little thing singing her "Teen Vittoria" over & over again for Bessy who was delighted with her & thought the other girl & young Ribblesdale very pretty. Gave the little thing the last Miniature Almanack, in which there is a portrait of me and a magnifying glass to look at it through—Lord John was to have left Bowood to-day, but stays till Monday morning

29 [Sunday]—Received a letter from Moran some days since in which he says "I heard to-day that three of our notorieties have gone mad, Southey, Miss Martineau, and Faraday, the chemist"

31 [Tuesday] Lady L. before I left them on Saturday asked me to come over again to day, and I at first hesitated—but on hearing that Hobhouse was coming, I most readily assented, being anxious to see him on the subject of the cadetship. Found at Bowood (besides Hobhouse) the Dumferlines still and one or two more.}

Notes to 1839 Entries

1 January

1. Moore probably is referring to Douglas Jerrold's *Nell Gwynne; or The Prologue* (1833). Interest is evoked by the witty dialogue between Nell and King Charles, who comes to her in disguise.
2. Vol. 3 of Moore's *History of Ireland* was published in 1840.

18–19 January

1. *The Works of Percy Bysshe Shelley*, ed. Mary Shelley, 4 vols. (1839). Percy Bysshe Shelley, *Queen Mab; a philosophical poem* . . . (1813). See Dowden, *Letters*, 2:838–39.

4–7 February

1. David Lester Richardson, *Miscellaneous Poems* (Calcutta, 1822), and *Literary Leaves, or Prose and Verse* (Calcutta, 1836). He later published *Notices of British Poets Biographical and Critical from Geoffrey Chaucer to Thomas Moore* (Calcutta, 1878). See Dowden, 2: 835 (letter no. 1146, dated "Sloperton, July 8th 1838"), where Moore requests John Richardson (solicitor, writer, and friend of Scott) to transmit a letter to "Captain Richardson of Calcutta."

4–6 February

1. Moore made two entries for 4–6 February.
2. Controversy over the Corn Laws continued in 1839. On 28 January 1839 the *Times* denounced "the oppressive system of the Corn Laws" and, during the following fortnight, became the official organ of the free trade movement. See Halévy, *History*, 3:309–11. Moore's squib "Corn and Cotton" (*Works*, 8:201–2) first appeared in the *Times* on 6 October 1826. It was reprinted in the *Morning Chronicle* on 1 February 1839. It appeared in the *Spectator*, no. 553, 2 February 1839, with the line as Moore quotes it. *Cakelology* is a slang term meaning "foolishness."
3. William Gardiner, *Music and Friends; or, pleasant recollections of a dilettante*, 3 vols. (1838–53).

12–14 February

1. *Bentley's Miscellany* 5 (1839): 326–28. The *Monthly Chronicle. A national journal of politics, literature, science, and art*, ed. Dionysius Lardner and Bulwer Lytton. For "Patrons, Puffs . . ." see *Works*, 9:275–79. For Moore's letters to Bentley, see Dowden, *Letters*, 2:842–44.

26 February

1. John Arthur Roebuck (1801–79), radical member of Parliament.

27 February

1. See *Works*, 9:212–14, "Thoughts on the Late Destructive Propositions of the Tories. By a Common-Councilman." Moore's note: "These verses were written in reference to the Bill brought in at this time, for the reform of Corporations, and the sweeping amendments proposed by Lord Lyndhurst and other Tory peers, in order to obstruct the measure." Lines 51–52:

> *There* ripe for riot, Recorder Shaw
> Was learning from Roebuck, "Ça-ira."

2. John Elliotson (1791–1868), physician; in 1849 he established a mesmerist hospital; founder of the *Zoist*, a magazine dealing with mesmerism.

10–12 March

1. Mary W. Shelley, ed., *The Poetical Works of Percy Bysshe Shelley*, 1839, 4 vols.

13–14 March

1. In 1838 William Henry Fox Talbot (1800–1877), using the *camera obscura*, developed a process for producing photographic prints that he patented in 1841 as the "talbotype" or "calotype" technique. The advantage of Talbot's technique over that of Daguerre, which was announced on 9 January 1839, was that the negative image could be reproduced on paper as a positive any number of times.

Moore's placement of quotation marks in this passage creates an ambiguity. It is not clear whether everything after "his own portrait painter" is part of Talbot's note or Moore's own comment.

15–17 March

1. Published in the *Morning Chronicle*, 23 March 1839. *Works*, 9:236–39.

22–23 April

1. During the week of 15 April the House of Commons debated a resolution of Lord John Russell's "that the Executive Government of Ireland deserves the support of the House of Commons." On 19 April Richard Lalor Shiel spoke and voted for Lord John's motion, one of a majority of twenty-two that passed the resolution. See *Parlia. Debates*, ser. 3, 47 (1839): 4–447.

24 April

1. Louisa Margaret Holl, *The Indian Captive and Other Poems*, etc. (1839).
2. Charles Dodd, pseud. (i.e., Hugh Tootell), *Dodd's Church History of England . . .*, 5 vols. (1839–43). With vol. 6 (February and May 1839) of the *Dublin Review*, O'Connell changed publishers, from William Spooner to C. Dolman.
3. The quotation occurs in the *Examiner*, no. 1630, 28 April 1839, p. 263, in an article on the "Exhibition of the society of British Artists. . . ." The heroines are characters from Scott's works: Rebecca, *Ivanhoe*; Jeannie Deans, *The Heart of Midlothian*; Lady Ashton, *Bride of Lammermoor*; Amy Robsart, *Kenilworth*.

25–26 April

1. "Unpriz'd are her sons": see "Oh! Blame Not the Bard," *Works*, 3:265; "The Bard's Legacy," *Works*, 3:244, 245.

2 May

1. Rosina Doyle Bulwer-Lytton (Baroness Lytton), *Cheveley, or the Man of Honour,* 3 vols. (1839).
2. The *British Museum Catalogue* lists a poem entitled *Lady Cheveley; or, the woman of honour. A new version of Cheveley, the man of honour. A satire, in verse.* By Rosina D. Bulwer Lytton, Baroness Lytton (1839). See Malcolm Elwin, *Landor, a Replevin* (London, 1958). According to Elwin, Lady Blessington intervened in the matter of the dedication of *Cheveley.* She wrote to Landor to warn him that the story was primarily an attack on Bulwer and that "Lady Bulwer obviously intended that the dedication should excite gossip by the analogy of her separation from her husband to Landor's from his wife" (p. 331). Landor and his wife separated in 1835. According to the *DNB,* Elizabeth Savage Landor (1776–1854), Landor's sister, died unmarried.

3 May

1. *Thucydidis, Platonis, Lysiae, orationes funebres* (1790?).

8 May

1. After a very narrow victory in a vote on the question of suspending the constitution of Jamaica, taken on 6 May, the Ministry resigned on 7 May.
2. Moore made two entries for 8 May.

9–12 May

1. The passage in square brackets was placed at the end of the MS page, with asterisks indicating its proper location in the text.

13–14 May

1. Gaius Sallustius Crispus, *Bellum Iugurthinum,* 7.5.

17 May

1. When Peel, the obvious Tory choice for Prime Minister, and the Queen reached an impasse over the Queen's refusal to ask her Ladies of the Household to resign (the "bedchamber question"), the Queen recalled Melbourne, and the Cabinet remained in office. Though the Whigs capitalized upon public sympathy for the Queen, attacking Peel's insensitive attitude toward her, public opinion soon swung to the side of Peel, who emerged from the episode with his influence in the House unimpaired. See Halévy, *History,* 3:243–45.

28 May

1. "New Hospital for Sick Literati" appeared in the *Morning Chronicle* on 29 May 1839. *Works,* 9:247–50.

29 May

1. When Victoria succeeded to the throne, the temper of the government became more democratic. See Halévy, *History,* 3:242, n. 1.
2. Edward Bouverie Pusey (1800–1882), Regius professor of Hebrew at Oxford, in 1835 joined the Oxford Movement, which objected to the rationalism of the Church of England

and emphasized the Church's divine institution. William Gladstone (1809–98) defended the principle of a single state religion in *The State in its Relations with the Church* (1838). Thomas Babington Macaulay's review of Gladstone's work appeared in the *Edinburgh Review* 69 (1839): 231–80. Macauley dissented from Gladstone's opinions but admired his talents.

3. Moore added, between the lines, "Have heard since that it is not Fonblanque but a Mr. Forster [John Forster, 1812–76] who writes the eulogies on Landor." See, for example, "*Dramatic Scenes*. By Walter Savage Landor, Esq.," the *Examiner*, no. 1575, 8 April 1838, pp. 211–12. Albany Fonblanque (1793–1872) was editor of the *Examiner* from 1830–47.

4. "Hospital for Sick Literati." See 28 May 1839, n. 1.

30 May

1. *King O'Neil, or The Irish Brigade* (1839).

31 May

1. Lady Flora Hastings, one of Queen Victoria's maids of honour and a lady in waiting in the Duchess of Kent's household, was accused of being pregnant. On 17 February 1839, upon the Queen's insistence that she clear her character, Lady Flora underwent a medical examination that established her virginity. The Duchess of Kent opposed the examination. Despite the examination, rumors of Lady Flora's pregnancy persisted. On 5 July 1839 she died of cancer. See Halévy, *History*, 3:245–46; Cecil Woodham-Smith, *Queen Victoria* (New York, 1972), pp. 164–80.

2. The episode involved Lord Lansdowne's son Henry, Earl of Shelburne and later fourth Lord Lansdowne. Shelburne, desiring a loan, gave Henry Stafford a bill of exchange for £5,000 at 8% interest. Stafford absconded without giving Shelburne the money, thus leaving Shelburne liable for £5,000. Henry Richardson offered to secure the return of Shelburne's bill, asking as payment from Shelburne two bills of exchange for £500 each. Shelburne agreed and, upon receiving his original note for £5,000, destroyed it. Richardson was apprehended with Shelburne's two £500 bills on his person and charged with negotiating the recovery of stolen property. Though the magistrate bound Richardson over to the next court sessions, he declared the case weak since Shelburne had destroyed the evidence. Furthermore, Richardson's lawyer applied for one of Shelburne's two £500 bills of exchange as his fee. The account appears in the *Spectator*, no. 566, 4 May 1839, pp. 410–11.

1 June

1. From 1830 to 1835 George Bryan unsuccessfully argued his claim to the Irish barony of Slane, asserting himself to be the heir general of the twelfth and fourteenth Lords Slane and the coheir of the tenth Lord. The Slane barony had been dormant since 1771. See *The Complete Peerage*, 12:pt. 1, 23 and appendix, 6 and 7.

2. Brougham's political reputation, which had dimmed since 1835, was at this time very low because of his radical and frequent attacks on Melbourne's ministry. Frances Hawes, *Henry Brougham*, p. 272.

3. John Baldwin Buckstone, *The Irish Lion* (1838).

4. *Poems*, 2 vols. (1834).

5. *The Poetical Works of Thomas Campbell*, 2 vols. (Albany, 1810). Moxon brought out an edition of Campbell's works in 1837, apparently the one sent to Queen Victoria.

2 June

1. Moore and Camac were occasional companions in Florence in October 1819, when they also traveled from Florence to Rome together.

2. Samuel Lover collected materials on Ireland, including *Legends and Stories of Ireland* (1831–34) and *Songs and Ballads* (1839).

3 June

1. William Vincent, *Faith, Doctrines, and Public Duties*, 2 vols. (1817–36).
2. Brougham led the opposition in the Lords to the Melbourne ministry.
3. A spring on Mount Parnassus, sacred to Apollo and the Muses.

4 June

1. Sir Robert Inglis (1786–1855), Tory politician. Richard Monckton Milnes (in 1863, first Baron Houghton), M.P. for Pontefract, published *Memorials of a Tour in Some Parts of Greece: Chiefly Poetical* in 1834 and *Poems of Many Years* in 1838.
2. The name of Mary Ann Jervis, daughter of Edward Jervis, Lord St. Vincent, was connected with the Duke of Wellington's from about 1833 until 1840, when she married David Ochterlony Dyce Sombre, Esq.
3. See letters to his mother, Dowden, *Letters*, 1 : 18–28.
4. Vincenzo Bellini, *Puritani di Scozia* (1835).

5 June

1. The Almaines were employed in mining for silver and lead at Clonmyne, county of Waterford. *Literary Remains of King Edward VI*, ed. John Gough Nichols (1858), notes the State Paper Office documents *Irish Correspondence*, 9, 10, and 11, no. 1 for references to these miners. Ibid., 2 : 417.
2. Patrick Fraser Tytler, *England Under the reigns of Edward VI and Mary*, 2 vols. (1839).

6 June

1. *The Life and Correspondence of M. G. Lewis*, ed. Margaret Baron-Wilson, 2 vols. (1839). See 1 : 363–64 for the anecdote.
2. At a confidential meeting on the night of 14 November, Melbourne, the Prime Minister, informed Brougham, his Chancellor, of the dismissal of the Ministry and received the latter's promise of silence until after the Cabinet had met the following morning. The next morning's *Times*, however, announced the Ministry's dismissal. Brougham was widely blamed for informing the press, but his guilt was never proved. Halévy, *History*, 3 : 175–77, Frances Hawes, *Henry Brougham*, pp. 257–59.

7 June

1. "Where the salt sea innocuously breaks, / And the sea breeze as innocently breathes," *The Excursion*," ll. 516–17.
2. *Works*, 4 : 217.

8 June

1. Daniel Webster (1782–1852) visited England in the summer of 1839, following his reelection as the United States Senator from Massachusetts.
2. Abraham and Angelica Van Buren, son and daughter-in-law of Martin Van Buren, then President of the United States. Angelica was hostess at the White House.
3. Connop Thirlwall (1797–1875), wrote a number of books on history including *A History of Greece*, 8 vols. (1835–44); 8 vols. (1845–52) as part of Lardner's *Cabinet Cyclopaedia*.
4. *Works*, 3 : 241.

9 June

1. Charles John Kean (1811–68), son of the famous actor Edmund Kean (1787–1833), was an actor himself.
2. *Works,* 4 : 167–68.
3. Moore saw the falls in 1804. "Lines Written at the Cohos, or Falls of the Mohawk River," *Works,* 2 : 306–8.

10 June

1. Alexander Pope, "The First Satire of the Second Book of Horace," l. 6.
2. That is, apparition.

11 June

1. Charles Vallancey, ed., *Collectanea de Rebus Hibernicis,* 6 vols. (1770–1804). On 4 May 1795 Arthur O'Connor gave an eloquent speech in the Irish parliament in support of the Catholics.

13 June

1. Bryan's daughter was Lady Doyle, who in 1820 deserted her husband for a Mr. Brown. Such conduct would have made her *persona non grata* in Ireland. See entry for 18 August 1820.

14 June

1. Moore refers to the Canadian rebellions of 1837, which arose from the Canadian Reformers' dissatisfaction with the unresponsive British government.

19 June

1. See entry and note for 29 April 1837.
2. Prince Józef Michal Poniatowski (1816–73), composer of masses and operas.

20 June

1. "Horace, Ode XI. Lib. II," *Works,* 3 : 183–87.

10–11 August

1. Moore made two entries for 10–11 August.

17 August

1. *Works,* 5 : 266–67.

18 August

1. Moore follows this entry for 18 August with one for 15 August and a second entry for 17–18 August.
2. *Works,* 5 : 259–60.

19–20 August

1. The chief character in James Kenney's *Raising the Wind* (1803).
2. Moore placed the phrase in square brackets at the bottom of the page, with asterisks indicating its proper location in the text.

23 August

1. Mrs. Charlotte Elizabeth (Browne Phelan) Tonna, author of various devotional works and editor of vols. 1–25 of *The Christian Lady's Magazine* (1834–49).

27 August

1. *The English Bijou Almanac* (1836–41, 1843). L. E. L. is Letitia Elizabeth Landon.

1–3 September

1. See entry for 15–16 May 1839.
2. Moore placed the passage in square brackets at the end of the MS page, with an asterisk indicating its proper location in the text.

9–11 September

1. "Dreams of a Well-Spent Life" appeared in the *Morning Chronicle* on 7 September 1839.

11–13 October

1. See Dowden, *Letters*, 2:848. Moore drew £250 from an account at Longman's intended for his son Russell.

20, 21 October

1. The *Spectator*, no. 590, 19 October 1839, pp. 998–99.

21 October

1. See also Dowden, *Letters*, 2:849 and notes.

25 October

1. John Leland, *Collectanea*, ed. Thomas Hearne, 6 vols. (1715).

27 October

1. The *Spectator*, no. 591, 26 October 1839, p. 1021.

28 October

1. Moore placed the passage in square brackets at the end of the MS page, with asterisks indicating its proper location in the text.

29 October

1. See entries for 19–21 January 1834, and 29 May 1839 and its n. 2. For the quotation from Mrs. Malaprop, see Sheridan, *The Rivals*, 4.ii.

16 November

1. Sir William Dugdale, *Monasticon Anglicarum* (1693).

18–19 November

1. Moore placed the passage in square brackets at the end of the MS page, with asterisks marking its proper location in the text.

20–21 November

1. *Merchant of Venice*, 4.i.341. The *Spectator*, no. 592, 2 November 1839.

30 November

1. At the top of this MS page there is space for a clipping, now missing.

5–7 December

1. Giovanni Flechia, trans., *Il Profeta Velato* (1838). See Dowden, *Letters*, 2:850–51.

15 December

1. Lord John Russell was Colonial Secretary at this time.

16 December

1. The incomplete clipping is a description, by Thomas Thornton Macklin, of his own poetical works and an appeal for subscribers to the publication of his *Poem on Poetry*, a work that he contended was superior to all other works of criticism, from Aristotle's *Poetics* to Pope's *Essay on Criticism*.

19–20 December

1. *Works*, 1:264–65.
2. Byron, *Childe Harold*, IV, clxxxv, ll. 5–6.

21 December

1. *Works*, 4:193–94.

28 December

1. John Frost (d. 1862) led an abortive Chartist rebellion in Newport, Monmouthshire, 4 November 1839, was transported, and later pardoned (1854).

1840

[January 1st 1840 [Wednesday]—After breakfast took an opportunity of speaking to Hobhouse about the expected Cadetship, when he exclaimed "What! have you not taken it up?—it is there lying for you." On further explanation I found he was under the erroneous notion that it had been a direct appointment he had given me last year and that with this impression, he had dismissed the whole matter entirely from his thoughts, leaving me thus at the end of my year's waiting, nothing but the old & to *me* utterly useless order for Addiscombe![1]—This was too provoking. Though startled by my certainty on the subject, he still retained his own impression that it was a direct appointment that was forthcoming for me—but said he would write up directly about it, and let me know.—Returned home—Had the Hughes's to dinner.

2, 3, [Thursday–Friday] The Hughes's remained with us these three days— In talking of India, it struck me that I might as well write to Lord Auckland about Russell, as it was just possible he might in some way or other be able to serve him—Did so.

6 [Monday]—Went (Bessy & I & Russell) to Lacock—none but themselves & Lady Mt. Edgecumb who had come over from Bath, where she & Mt. Edgecomb have been staying some time for his gout. In the evening, a gay ball given by Talbot to his tenants & the servants of Lacock & Bowood— The great Hall of the Abbey being lighted up and tastefully decorated for the occasion—the effect very striking. The Ball was opened by Lady Mount-Edgecumb & myself, followed by Horatia & Russell, and Bessy & Montgomery—We danced down three country-dances (very long sets) and it delighted me to see my dearest Bessy dancing away so actively and enjoying herself so much. Neither had I myself quite lost my old elasticity of toe; and had it not been for dignity's sake which made it proper for us to

withdraw after these three dances, we should, all of us, I think, have liked a little more of the fun.—Some hours later we were apprized that glee-singing was about to commence, and returning to the Hall, were treated with three or four good old glees (the Red-Cross Knight, Peace to the Souls of the heroes &c.) exceedingly well sung by some young men of Lacock, and accompanied by one of themselves on the Piano-forte—Altogether the evening most creditable both to the Host & Hostess & their guests

7 [Tuesday]—A beautiful day, which I employed the greater part of in walking about the gardens, and working at the proof-sheets of my history—Same party at dinner, and in the evening, Lady Mt. Edgecumb & little Valletort left us to return to Bath.

8 [Wednesday]—Home—I walked, and the ground being very slippery with an incipient thaw, I came suddenly down upon my back, in descending the hill into the Spye-Park fields—Called upon John Starkey in my way home, and staid some time with him.—

9 &c [Thursday] A good deal jarred by my fall, and not well able to move my left wrist for a day or two

10, 11, &c. &c [Friday–Saturday]—I had begged of Lady Lansdowne & Lady Louisa to look for subjects for me in Lalla Rookh fit for Jones's pencil to illustrate,[1] and the following note from Lady Lansdowne contains the result of their search. "We have been trying to make a selection of subjects from Lalla Rookh; but it is difficult; as those we prefer are not sufficiently *tangible* for an illustration. It is impossible to represent the Peri; so we have left her out entirely. The girl playing to Azim on the lute and the others looking in at the windows—Hinda, where she is under the rude awning in the Robber's boat—or when in the tower Hafed appears; and Lalla Rookh when she discovers who Aliris is. These are what we prefer—but Jones is a man of such taste, I think you might leave it all to him.

12, 13, &c [Sunday–Monday]—After all the pretended difficulty about Russell's money, the Longmans have, of themselves, come forward to offer it to me—without any further light being thrown upon the matter either by them, or their adviser Mr. Turner. I strongly suspect, however, that some little hints I have in one of my letters of the grievance it would be to *themselves* to continue so long paying such high interest on the sum (five per cent) had led them to find practicable for their *own* sakes what they considered so wholly impossible for mine. This is, to be sure, after listening to them a most marvellous stroke both of selfishness & stupidity—but taking them as a Co. it is hardly more than they deserve.

14, 15, 16 &c [Tuesday–Thursday]—Received a letter towards the latter end of this month from Hobhouse (in consequence of one I had written to him) saying that I had been right in my impression, and that it was the Addiscombe appointment alone that was forthcoming for me. He added, however, that if he could get any one to give him an equivalent in military appointments, for a writership which he had to dispose of, he might still be able to oblige me.

17, 18, 19 &c [Friday–Sunday]—Thought I had better, while waiting my chance of something from Hobhouse, endeavour to exchange my Addiscombe appointment for a cadetship—With this hope, wrote towards the latter end of the present month to Miss Burdett Coutts, asking her to use whatever interest she might possess, through Marjoribanks or others, to effect for me such an exchange.—

20, 21 &c. [Monday–Tuesday] Received a most kind answer from Miss Coutts saying she would use all the exertions in her power for me.}

February 1, 2 [Saturday–Sunday]—The following note from Miss Coutts— "My dear Mr. Moore, I have this moment received with the greatest pleasure the enclosed note from Mr. Lock through Mr. Marjoribanks. I lose no time in forwarding it to you, as I feel how anxious you must be on the subject, and I must again beg you to accept the assurance of the very great gratification it has given me to be of any service to you." She adds in a postscript—"Should your son be in town any time, I hope he will do me the favour of calling."—This news gave us all great pleasure; though my poor Bessy saw in it the sad certainty of her soon losing, or at least being separated and perhaps, for ever, from the one whom (*next* to myself) she most clings to and loves.

{3, 4, 5 &c [Monday–Wednesday]—Received one of these days a poem printed for private circulation upon a half sheet of letter paper, comparing the dinner lately given to Macready with that which commemorated some years since the departure of Kemble from the stage and bitterly (though rather weakly) contrasting the public characters by which these two dinners were severally attended. In the following lines, referring to the Kemble banquet, he mixes me up (under a title which Charles Phillips I believe first gave me) with Erskine, Campbell & Canning

> So bright a galaxy was rarely seen
> As that day offered—Party forbore its spleen,
> Science with music, poetry with lore
> Culled from the tomes of deep Philosophy,
> There mixed—for what? to show a people's sense
> Of Genius!—Hope's Bard with Erskine joined;
> "The Muse's Nightingale" was likewise there,
> And filled the social glass with Canning.

The writer, whoever he may be (and the initials W.R. are subscribed to his verses) is evidently not among the worshippers of Boz, as the following passage denotes. Proceeding to contrast the Macready dinner with that given to Kemble, he says,

> "There was a Feast—and round the generous board
> Great talent sparkled; but methought the beams
> Were like Archangels fallen, when compared
> With that foregone. Campbell and Moore were *there;*
> But *here* was Dickens, whose low mind has shed
> Its baneful influence oe'r his country's taste,
> And sent the Boudoir's denizens to seek
> Wisdom and pleasure in the squalid haunts
> Of vice and murder! and that witling bard, [Bulwer, I suppose][1]
> Whose melo-dramas are now deem'd fit mates
> For Shakspear's Tragedies! &c. &c. &c."

6, 7, 8 &c [Thursday–Saturday]—Have just found, in turning over some letters, an American Newspaper which was sent to me some time since [*incomplete*]

6, 7, 8 &c. [Thursday–Saturday][1]—In looking over the Anthologia Hibernica for September 1793[2] found the following lines, very happily descriptive of Curran, quoted from a Poem in a paper called "the Gleaner," written, I think, by Sir William Smith—

> "With staring, senseless, vulgar broad flat face
> Got Flummery up to ope the Plaintiff's case.
> *Him zeal-fraught Simio followed, ripe for sport,*
> *(An uglier Christian does not come to court)*
> *He smack'd his lips, and turned his saucy head,*
> *Then cock'd his little keen, pert eyes and said,—"*

9, 10, 11 &c [Sunday–Tuesday]—Sent up lately to the Cramers a new song I have written, "Come, play me that simple air again,"[1] the music taken from a pretty Waltz of Lobelske's. Received last week a proof of the Song, as arranged by Goss. The publishers say in their note—"We are happy to say that the last six songs are becoming very popular, and we shall not lose an opportunity of again tempting your Muse with some fresh melodies."— Shall soon be obliged to run up to town, to make enquiries respecting poor Bussy's expatriation, which in this most harsh weather will be by no means agreeable.}

12, 13 &c. [Wednesday–Thursday] Received a letter lately from Crampton, in answer to a note I wrote him under the apprehension that he was seriously ill. Happy to find that the attack (gout) has passed off & that he is himself (he *could not* be any thing better) once more. The following which he tells me about Tom is at once frightful & ridiculous. "I forget if I told you that I strongly suspect that I have discovered the exciting cause of Tom's convulsive attack. The infernal folly of our military service (I mean of course that part of it which regulates the dress of soldiers) has deter- mined that to *look* like a fighting man an unfortunate soldier must *be* a choaking man; and poor Tom, who is the pink of soldiers, wore his stock & his collar so strictly according to order that the jugular veins were so compressed that the blood could not return from his head. I observed that his face had a violet tint and that the veins on the temple were full to bursting. On examination I found the collar so tight that I could not pass the tip of my finger between it and his throat. He confessed to me that he was "half choaked," and that he could not stoop or turn his head to the right or left. I need not tell you that I soon made him violate the Queen's order; and he has lost all the uneasy sensations, which he used to experi- ence in his head, from that hour."

{12, 13, 14 &c. [Wednesday–Friday]—A late number of the Spectator designates me as—"the poet who, as Dr. OToole would say has the run of the kitchen of Lansdowne House."[1] I have gone on taking this gen- tlemanlike paper, instead of the Examiner, lest they should think I was angered by their abuse, and because the Hughes's of Devizes have hitherto let me have the reading of *their* Examiner. But as they have now left off taking that paper, I really *must* treat myself to it, and throw my friend the Spectator over board

15 [Saturday]—Have had some correspondence lately with Tom Longman, arising out of a letter addressed to me by the Firm, in somewhat of the

Slave-Driver tone, urging me to get on with the Fourth Volume of my History (the Third being but just published,) and requiring of me to say, as nearly as I could, how soon I thought I should be ready with it. I am not sure whether I have noticed in this Journal a letter which I received some short time since from him (Tom Longman) taking me to task civilly, but still in a tone I did not quite like for the expence I had put them to, by my numerous corrections & alterations in the course of the printing of the Third Volume of my History. It appears to me that I equally indulged this habit of revising & correcting in both of the former Volumes (as, indeed, in every thing else I have ever printed) and yet never before was it thus made a matter of complaint against me. Was resolved not to let this new tone of the Row pass without animadversion—it being so different (as I told Tom Longman) from what I had experienced during the administration of the good old Rees—"bonae sub regno Cynarae." After a few letters on both sides the whole *embrouillement* worked itself clear again. The fussy letter from the Co. about my Fourth Volume was said to have been meant entirely in joke, and, as happens with most of such seasonable thunder-storms, the air has been left all the clearer for this little passing out-break.}

16, 17 [Sunday–Monday]—It had now become absolutely necessary for me to go to town on Russell's business, and accordingly I prepared, or rather my sweet active Bess, with her usual diligence, prepared every thing for my departure.

{18 [Tuesday]—Had a Fly to Buckhill, to take my chance by the First Coach—Long conversation with Hughes before starting, about India and all that was Indian. Found him quite unhappy at Russell's appointment being for Madras—besought me earnestly to move Heaven & Earth—and the India House—to have him sent to Bengal instead—Told him that I had heard such contrarieties of opinion upon every thing connected with India, that although possibly *he* might be quite right, yet I should not be surprised if the next person I talked with on the subject would say that Madras was as good, if not better, than either of the other Presidencies—Got a place in the first Coach—the York House—a young lady from Bath with her maid inside—Were joined soon after by a good-looking & courteous young man, who from his general information and good manners I thought at first must be a person of some station—though the word "Gent," which he almost invariably used instead of gentleman told rather against this supposition—Found he had read and was well acquainted with the writings of late French travellers. In talking of the Clubs in London, he said that there was one he should like much to belong to—the Athenaeum—if his station in life was such as entitled him to do so, and it then turned out that he was a young attorney, whose mother being left a widow, he & she lived together, and most of his evenings were passed at home with her & his books. I should have liked much to learn his name, but at Newbury he left us, and was there I dare say told who *I* was, as while we stopped before the inn door, he brought a lady past the Coach for the purpose of showing me to her. Being now left with the young lady only, we commenced a conversation which continued with but little interruption, all the rest of the way. Falling on the topic of India, it was not long before what I had predicted to Hughes in parting with him actually took place, as this lady told me that a brother of hers had been lately ordered with his regiment to Madras, and that her father, having heard a bad account of that Presidency, was about to move heaven & earth (as Hughes had bid *me* do) to get him changed into some other regiment—But on referring to more trust-worthy authorities, he found Madras to be, on the whole as good as any other place, and the young man was accordingly about to proceed with his regiment. She added that her father, she was sure, would be happy to give me all the information he had himself acquired on the subject. Told me her name,— Miss Bruce—her father a gentleman of Glamorganshire, who had lately taken the name of Pryce for an accession of fortune and the female part of the family at present residing at Bath. After having taken down her father's address, I told her that as she had done me the honour to be so kindly communicative, it was but right she should know who I was. I then told her my name, adding laughingly, that it was "a name pretty well known"—but some minutes elapsed before she *understood* and a few more, evidently, before she *believed* me—her face being in the meanwhile lighted up both with blushes & smiles. When we alighted in Piccadilly, she introduced me to her brother-in-law, who had come to meet her and both very courteously expressed their wish to see me at his house in Grafton St. Drove to Sackville St. and found Lady Elisabeth & Horatia just about to sit down to dinner— had a most comfortable evening, and found my bed-room and all as snug as could be—Told them all about my coach-companion, who, by the way, was well acquainted with all that concerned the Talbots, her family being neighbours of Kit Talbot, and not liking Kit himself, I found, any better than I do. In the evening, Lord Ilchester & William Strangways came, and were both of them very amiable and agreeable.}

19 [Wednesday]—{Breakfasted at home—Tom Longman called with a Petition on the Copy Right Bill for me to sign, if I should approve the object of it—the question being about to be brought forward this evening—Had not much time to consider the matter—but seeing Rogers's name to it, thought I might safely sign—Tom L's. feeling that Rogers disliked him—} My first visit to Rogers, whom I found remarkably well & full of kindness—{In a letter which I had written to tell him of my coming, I had said that I was

sure to find, as usual, at Hyde Corner, "a cold waiting to catch me, or rather for *me* to catch it"—and so it has turned out—for I started this morning with a confirmed London cold—Talked of various things—Macaulay's failure the other night—the advantage taken of his saying he was "the first Cabinet Minister" who had risen to address them—His dating from Windsor, an unlucky mistake[1]—inconceivable that any man with the least knowledge of the world could fail to foresee the sort of advantage that would be taken of such a Cockneyism—this my own opinion & I believe R. agreed with me. Told me a number of ribald jokes about the Queen's marriage[2]— one innocent enough—that Albert's allowance was "half a crown a day and a Sovereign at night." Then there was the list of the newspapers sent down to Windsor—"Two Globes, a Standard and eight Times, two Observers &c. &c."—} Agreed with me that the three men now most looked to by the people of England were the Duke, Lord John & Peel—mentioned, apropos of this, what he had told me of the Duke saying to him last year, in speaking of the Ministry—"Lord John is a host in himself." When he found I had not yet engaged myself to dinner, proposed that I should call with him at Lord Ashburton's where he was to dine, and where he was sure they would be glad to have me—but I did not much fancy it—Walked out with him & went to Lansdowne House where he left me—Found Lady L. Lady Louisa & Lady Kerry—Taken by Lady K. in her carriage to Sackville St. and thence to Brookes's—where she dropped me. A most charming person, and gains more upon me every time I see her. Something, quite touching in her present position—*in* the world but not *of* it—The very cheerfulness which she has now, I am glad to see, regained, has a calm and deep sentiment mixed with it which (even without the weeds) sufficiently tells her story.[3] {Dinner-hour very near approaching, without any dinner offering itself when, at last—Byng having informed Standish that I was disengaged, that distinguished Amphytrion came smiling to me, and after enumerating the names of his guests, Mrs. Fox Lane, Lord Carrington, Maxie (Called "Go it, Maxie") and his wife Lady Louisa (I think) proposed that I should join the party at ½ past seven—As he had often asked me before—but in vain—was glad on every account of the occasion, and readily accepted.—Found, besides those he had mentioned, Fitzroy Stanhope, whom I had not met by his own account, for these 30 years past—Our dinner of the most recherché kind; and I sate marvelling both at dishes & guests; the never-ending succession of the former and the never-exhausted appetite of the latter. Mrs. Fox Lane gave, very cleverly & amusingly, an account of the habits of Yorkshire some nineteen years ago—the drinking, gambling &c. of the great squires—more like old Irish doings, than any thing I could have supposed in England at so recent a date. The fair raconteuse herself is not a little extraordinary in her way—for notwithstanding her known career, there are, I am told, two mature noble lords (Duncannon one of them) who, if her husband were to die tomorrow would be ready, either of them, to occupy his place.—The house where Standish lives (Lower Grosvenor St) is, it seems, divided into two sets of Chambers, and some guests (Lord Burghersh, one of them) who were going to dine with the other occupant, to meet the Duke of Cambridge, came to us first by mistake—Had a good deal of small talk about the Queen—a subject that now predominates usque ad nauseam.—and will soon reduce conversation to the mere tittle-tattle of waiting-maids.—An assembly to night at Lady Normanby's to which I thought of volunteering but did not—Called on Mr. Cabell at Hobhouse's office who gave me a good deal of information about India.—Among the quantities of small events I have had to notice lately, forgot I believe to mention my having written to Bertrand, my friend the Professor at Caen. Thinking that Russell's departure would not take place till about June it struck me that the intervening time could not be better disposed of than by sending him to Caen (if Bertrand would take him) and letting him have a little of the advantage which Tom enjoyed in picking up a smattering of French—Wrote to Bertrand about it and received a very kind & friendly answer, agreeing most readily to my proposal.} By the bye, was taken to task to-day by R{atcliffe (the Colonel)} who is just come from Ireland, for not making a larger allowance to Tom—such as would enable him "to live like a gentleman"—B{yng}, too, who was by, joined in the same cry. I told them (in the very few words I could trust myself with saying to them on the subject) that they little knew how hard I was pressed to make out even the allowance I at present gave him, and that there were some men, as good as he or any of us who lived on their pay, without any additional allowance at all. "Aye, they said—these are rare instances."—then why, I asked, should not my son be *one* of them?—But there was no use in any such appeal—He ought to be enabled to "live like a *gentleman*"—as if the living like a *man* was not something far higher & better. But such is the standard of station at present in England, where (as has been lately remarked) poverty is ignominious—Nor can we wonder at young, giddy school boys and ensigns having such notions, when their superiors and guides, the Colonels, Tutors, Fellows of Colleges &c all set them the example and make money, money alone the test of the man and the gentleman. I think I must have mentioned in this journal a somewhat parallel case to R{atcliffe}'s view of the matter, in what {Saunders} of the Charter-House said to me when it was intended that Tom should go from thence to the University. After informing me that the exhibition coming to him from the Charter-House would be, on an average, about £100 a year he coolly added "so that you would have to give him from yourself only £150 a year."—that is the *half* of the *only* income (my Pension) that ever I possessed in my Life without working hard for it—aye, and sharing my earnings, all the time, with almost every body related to me. If *I* had thought but of "living like a *gentleman*" (as these Colonels & Tutors style it) what would have become of my dear Father & Mother, of my sweet sister Nell, of my admirable Bessy's mother?

{20 [Thursday]—Breakfasted at home—had appointed to come to Tom Longman early—called at Rogers's, who *would* come out with me, though I told him of my hurry, and *would* make me go into the National Gallery, on my way, to look at some pictures—At *last* put me into an Omnibus & left me. Forgot to mention that Tom Longman invited me yesterday to meet at dinner with him on Tuesday next no less considerable a personage (to *me* at present) than Sir Samford Whittingham, the newly appointed Commander in Chief at Madras—this most lucky—Remained some hours in the Row arranging the Volumes of the Edition with Tom Longman—A good deal of explanation [*unrecovered*] by him as to the proceeding of the Co.—talked of the difficulty there was in bringing so many partners to agree and dwelt particularly on the jealousy which he said Orme had always felt towards his father (T. Longman) and which had a good deal disturbed the Counsels of the Firm. All this (though he did not expressly say so) was of course meant to explain to me the reasons of whatever conduct on the part of the Co. I might, at any time, have disliked—On my way back called upon Mr. Cabell, at the Board of Control, who had written to me so civilly about Russell's appointment. In talking comparatively of the Presidencies, said that Bengal was at present most in favour as being most the scene of service, but that Madras was not without its advantages, and might also before long be brought into activity by the Burmese. Showed me the Military Map of India and explained on it what he meant—Dined at Rogers's—to meet Mrs. Shelley, the two Miss Robinsons and Ratcliffe—All went in the evening to Musard's, where Rogers had taken a box for the party, to listen to an astounding *tintamarre* of violins for two or three hours. R. & I went afterwards to an assembly at Miss Burdett Coutts's, where I met a number of people I had not seen for a long time—and among the rest Chantrey & Sir Henry Hardinge—poor Chantrey's looks a good deal alarmed me—It seems that some months since, he had a paralytic seizure but himself & Lady Chauntry told me that he was now much recovered—He looks, I must say, perilously—another very old friend I met with there was Admiral Beresford—talked to him about Douglas—Saw also Lady Listowel & the Bushes

21. [Friday]—Breakfasted at home—went to call upon Mr. Cabell, at the Board of Controul—(this I put by mistake among my doings of yesterday)—Called at Merewether's, and was asked by them to dine to-day—Byng had asked me to dine with him and go to the play—but as I *owed* the Merewethers a dinner, agreed to come to them—Was lucky enough to meet Hobhouse in the Park, on his way to his office—made me turn about with him, and was very kind about Russell. His burst of school-boy laughter at my confounding the Caubul Elphinstone (whose work was of such use to me in Lalla Rookh)[1] with the Lord Elphinstone who is at present Governor

of Madras. The fact is, I had never even *heard* of the *Lord* Elphinstone till now—Said he would give Russell a letter of introduction to him—Went to call on the Hollands, having received the following note from my Lady—"I wish you could dine with us to-day? Why have you not called or asked for a dinner?—Come early, you will see the Lansdownes—dine here on Sunday or Monday—We are engaged out till then."—Found her & Lord Holland—Rogers with them—Lord H. in a very uneasy state and she very worrying to him—*wouldn't* let him sit as he wished—*would* put a screen between him & the fire, whether he liked or not &c—Told her I could come to dinner on Monday. Rogers came away with me—Called on Lady William Russell whom I had not seen for many years—Found her very agreeable & in some points much improved—sate some time—Brookes's—told Byng I would join him after my dinner—Dined at Merewether's—a large party, chiefly of their own family—there was also Mr. Long the magistrate—wanted me to sing in the evening, but I got away to the Theatre—Found Byng & Mrs. in Duke of Bedford's Box—were joined there by Lord William Russell—staid but a short time & home.

22. [Saturday]—Having promised to breakfast with Rogers to meet Miss Coutts, was at his door about ten, but found to my great relief that she was not coming & he was still in bed—so hurried off to Brookes's, and break-fasted there—from thence to Lord John whom I found at home—took me up stairs to see the children, and then said if I would wait a little, he would walk across the Park with me—Said he had had six hours' good sleep last night which was a great thing for him.—Started at a quick pace across the Park & had not gone far before we were joined by Lord Clarendon—"I hope," I said laughing, "I shan't be taken for a Cabinet Minister"—"What! you think we're so down in the world?" said Lord Clarendon. Told them of Hobhouse's horse-laugh at me for taking the Elphinstone now at Madras for the Caubul Elphinstone—Lord John said that he too would give Russell a letter to Lord Elphinstone.—Lord Clarendon asked me to come & meet Lord John this day week at dinner—told him my stay was uncertain—but asked how long he would keep the place open for me? "Oh, to the last"—he said. Left Lord John to call on the Mintos—found Lady Minto at home & sate a little time with her and then returned to Lord John, whom I found just going into Council, and having heard me express a wish to see Lemon, said he would send him out to me for "two minutes," which he did—All I had to tell Lemon was that he might expect shortly to be again troubled by me, on the subject of Records &c. & he expressed himself as usual most ready & willing to attend to me.—Returned home, found Lady Elisabeth in the drawing-room and was talking with her, when the servant announced to me Admiral Douglas. "You shall receive him here," she said and flitted away as actively as a young girl.—Walked out with my dear good old friend,

who was very anxious for me to fix a day to dine with him "I am eighty-three, Tommy" he said, laughing, while he said it, and I bid him keep the secret to himself, as no one would find it out—Left him at the United Service Club & got into an Omnibus to go to the Row—Worked again with Tom L. at the arrangement of the Edition—He then accompanied me to Jones, who showed us some beautiful things of his own, and while we were looking over them, Maclise arrived—a fresh instance, as I said, of the marvellous good luck that almost always attends me of happening upon the very persons and events I most wish for at the time—Endeavoured to fix a day for our all meeting together at Longman's, but could not well manage it.—From thence went, (Longman and) I to the East India Agency Office in St. Martin's Place—was introduced to Captain Grindlay, one of the partners, who told me that he had been intimately acquainted with an old friend of mine, Macklin, in India—"What!" I exclaimed, "Hugo Grotius Braggadocio!" I then told him of Macklin having this nick-name in College, (his Christian names being Hugh George) and he had evidently known him well enough to see and enjoy its appropriateness—I also told him of Macklin's saying when asked was he well prepared in his Conic Sections?—"I could whistle them" and his being put down in the disorderly list of a Society to which we both belonged, as "fined sixpence, for whistling Conic Sections"—Captain Grindlay told me, in return, what I was gratified to hear that Macklin always spoke of me in the kindest & most affectionate terms—that he had a Portrait of me hung up in his room & used frequently to apostrophise it & hold forth on my merits—Grindlay in the kindest manner offered his services to me in every way I might require for my young Cadet, and begged me to consider myself free of that Office or Club-room and all such sources of East India intelligence &c. as it contained—From thence to Brookes's—found myself too late with my letter to Bessy, the Post time having been made earlier by an hour since the new change—The waiters told me, however, they could send a messenger into the city with my Letter—did so, to my great pleasure, as it would have grieved me to disappoint my sweet Bess of her daily letter.—Went to Rogers's—found he was about to dine alone, & offered myself as his guest.—Showed me in the evening an early publication of Poems by Wordworth—1794, I think,[1]—sad trash in them, but pompously expressed. Showed me also his own recollections of the conversations of Horne Took, Grattan, the Duke of Wellington &c.—has made use of much of these in his own notes on his Poems—Told me that of his first publication, the Ode to Superstition,[2] there were only 15 or 16 copies (or even less, I believe) sold in the course of two years. Consulted me now upon some minute points in his Poems which I can recollect him to have been working at for nearly 30 years past—Home.

—As every body seems to be of opinion that the sooner Russell sails the better, the plan of Normandy must, I feel, be given up. Went this morning to Mrs. Durham's (my old quarters in Bury St) and finding that her first floor was disengaged, begged her to keep it so for me a few days, as it was possible I might want it for Mrs. Moore & my son.}

23 [Sunday]—Met Hume by appointment at Brooks's—went with me to Paternoster Row, where I had fixed to meet T. Longman—Returned in an Omnibus, Hume to proceed home and I to pay a visit to the D. of Sussex at Kensington—Buckland was with the Duke, and I had to wait a little time. Found that Buckland had been showing and explaining to him a new invention for the taking off or copying, any printing or engraving by means of electricity—Bank notes for instance, can be thus copied instantly and accurately—Could hardly refrain from throwing in the pun of "*flash* notes" while he was describing this to me—Complained strongly of the encroachment there was now going on of the spiritual on the temporal and the confusion it was producing—{Asked me could I dine with him on Wednesday next—but told him that Byng had collected some people whom he knew I wished to meet for that day. "Well," he said, "write and tell me when you will come, and give me, if you can, two or three days to choose from." He had already said that there was an old acquaintance of mine (meaning Lady Cecilia) "who would be very happy to see me."—Dined at Lansdowne House—a small party and odd enough, with the exception of John OConnell (whom I sate next & liked) all strangers to me. Home.}

24 [Monday]—{Breakfasted with Rogers to meet Lord Normanby—there were to have been some women—I forget who—but they didn't come—Buchon, my old Paris friend, broke in before we sate down to breakfast and set off at full score, as usual, in talk, but Rogers gave him no encouragement to stay—Talked of Guizot, to whom he is evidently no friend. "But he's liked in Paris?" one of us said—"Oh yes" said Buchon "we shall like him very well when he is with you."—meaning, of course, that they'd be glad to get rid of him. Normanby, very agreeable—is always best I think, when there are no women by; and I know several other men to whom the presence of women is, in this sense, a disturbing ingredient. I suppose it is that their vanity is then most awake. Mentioned what I had never heard before, the last King's dislike to Lord John—used to say "I do not like that young man." In talking of George 3rd.'s madness, I mentioned a circumstance told me by Manners Sutton, as being in his father's Diary, of the King knowing by the perfume that the Prince had been in the room; and Normanby reminded me that it was by the smell Charles Windham found out the Prince, when Mrs. Armitage, on Wyndham arriving unexpectedly, shut up her royal paramour in a closet. It was then C. Windham turned her off.—The King one

day, it seems, being very violent, the Keeper knocked him down—and so awake was Royalty in the old fellow, that in getting up again, he said "my foot slipped"—thus saving his dignity—N. told of a young fellow, a patient in some mad-house who was supposed to be recovered enough to be allowed to walk about the rooms with his father who had come to see him— but in passing a shower-bath the young fellow who had often suffered under it himself, popped the father in & shutting the door let down the whole inundation upon him.—Went to the East India Office—had a good deal of talk with Christian, one of the partners, whom I found very intelligent & civil—long conversation with him as to the choice between cavalry and infantry, and with a young fellow I met there, who is in the cavalry, and just returned from India on leave of absence. I have little doubt (from what they & others have told me) that the advantages, on the whole, are on the side of cavalry—But there is no use now in thinking of it, as I see no chance of my being able to get such an appointment.—Found Byng at Brookes's, and found I had made a sad jumble about the day of the dinner he had promised to get up for me, which was not Wednesday, as I had thought but Tuesday—and I had now engaged myself somewhere else for Tuesday and refused the Duke of Sussex for Wednesday. Bulwer who was one of those asked to meet me at Byng's was now with him when all this murder came out—Byng very good-humoured about it and said he must only put off the others he had asked.—Wrote to Lady Cecilia Underwood to say I was now free for Wednesday, if the Duke would be graciously pleased to have me—Received from her a note saying "The Duke is not at home, but I know I may say yes—that he will be most happy to see you at 7 o'clock on Wednesday"—signed Cecilia—} Dined at Holland House—{Bear Ellis & his lady, and my old friend Woolriche. Thanked Allen for having, as I found, given directions at the State Paper Office about the Calendar &c—} A good deal of talk about Erskine, and the particulars of his first brief— much of which, as now told by Rogers, was quite different from the account given me of it by Jekyll—but Rogers, it seems, took it all down from Erskine's own lips—{some bad traits mentioned of him—a good deal of talk with Woolriche about old times—My lady very graciously pressing me to prolong my stay in town, in order to dine with her next Sunday—and also to go with her some night to the play—} Came away with Rogers, and went to Lady Minto's, a large assembly—saw there many a familiar face to which I could annex no name, and while, some persons I dare say were passed by formally whom I once knew well and intimately, there was one lady whose hand I seized cordially (on her making some movement which I took for recognition) and it turned out that she was an utter stranger to me. Luckily, however, I was not such to her, for on my apologizing, she said, with much sweetness & good-breeding—"Mr. Moore must be well aware that to be addressed by him, whether known or unknown, cannot be otherwise than a compliment." {Home.}

25 [Tuesday]—{Breakfasted at Brookes's—had been asked to Rogers's to meet Buchon & some lady, I forget who—but had too much business on my hands to trust myself with Rogers—} Performed some commissions & went down to Pater Noster Row—having first made my excuse to the Milmans for Friday—Worked at the Edition and transposed a good deal of the matter—they think of publishing the 1st. Vol. in April, which is alarming.—Found from Tom Longman that there is some chance of their being able to bring out the History some time or other in a better shape than that vile Lardnerian *format*. Showed me the items of the expence of our forthcoming Edition (the Poems) amounting to more than £7000.—{Dined at Tom Longman's, company, Sir Sanford Whittingham, the new Madras Commander in Chief, and two young men, his relatives, I believe, and aid-de camp, Hayward, the old Longmans & one or two more.—The dinner heavy enough—Much pressed to sing, indeed *unconscionably,* when I joined the ladies, but actually *could* not—Miss Rogers among the company in the evening—Having heard Mrs. Tom sing a song or two, came away with Hayward, who improves on one a little—My cold getting worse every day.}

26 [Wednesday]—{Breakfasted with Rogers—Company Miss Burdett Coutts, Miss Meredith, Charles Murray & one or two more—somebody mentioned a show there is at Paris: The Infernal Regions, admittance one shilling—Talked of the late correspondence between Lady Seymour & Lady Shuckborough which appeared in the Argus of last Sunday, but took place some months since—R. sent for the Argus, and some one read out the letters, which are unexampled for vulgarity, on both sides, though a *little* redeemed, on Lady Seymour's part, by fun & cleverness.—Murray mentioned that all sorts of mischievous & blackguard letters, parcels &c are addressed almost daily to the Queen—In one lately there was some combustible or detonating matter, which had there not been suspicions entertained of it, and precautions accordingly taken would have seriously injured those who opened it—They are obliged to watch lest any of these beastly or dangerous things should reach her [*MS damaged*] devilish spirits there are now at work in all directions!}—Went to call upon Marjoribanks, and on my mentioning the desire I had, to get Russell's appointment changed, if possible, from Madras to Bengal, he advised me to go at once to Lock the Director, myself, and ask him to do it for me—Wrote a letter for me to take to Lock, very strongly & kindly expressed, and I instantly set off with it to the India House—saw Mr. Lock, who received me most cordially (though we never, that I know, set eyes on each other before) and in a very few minutes my object was accomplished. On my mentioning what my wish was he said "I rather think I have got *one* Bengal appointment left"—then ringing the bell, he ordered the person who answered it to bring him some paper which he described, and having run his eye down this paper, said, to

my very great pleasure, "I find I *have* one Bengal appointment left, Mr. Moore, and it is very much at your service." After a few words more of conversation, I took my leave, and thus was despatched in a few minutes a favour which (from knowing no channel through which to apply) I had given up all thoughts of seeking for—Called at Marjoribanks on my way back to say how much obliged I was to him, as well as to his friend.—{A note from Miss Coutts, asking me to join her this evening at the Theatre to see the Queen & Prince Albert come in state—but my dinner at Kensington puts it out of the question—Went in a Cab to Kensington—company, besides Lady Cecilia, Lord & Lady Mark Kerr, Lady ——— I forget her name—a sister of Lord Arran's (whom I took into dinner) Fonblanque, and one or two more men.—A good deal of talk with my fair neighbour about the Arrans—The day altogether very quiet and home-like. In the evening, cards—of which I find Fonblanque is a very devoted worshipper, and at which I left them all very seriously occupied between 10 & 11 o'clock.— Found neither Cab nor Coach on my way, and had to walk into town—Went for a short time to Brookes's & home.}

27. [Thursday]—{Breakfasted at home—Called on Lord John, and sate a little time with him—Told him I should stay over Saturday to meet him at Lord Clarendon's—asked me to dine with him on Sunday—but then recollected his having promised to dine with the Hollands (where, by the bye, if I could have staid so long, I was to have met him).—Left word at Lord Clarendon's that I would come to dinner on Saturday.—Went to the Milmans whom I had promised in the same conditional way for Friday— saw her & told her I should come on that day.—Called upon Rogers who, I found, was to dine to-day at Lansdowne House—fixed for him to take me. In talking of my boy Russell found that Hobhouse had been less civil to him (R.) than he had been to me, in circumstances nearly similar. He had given an Addiscombe appointment, as I understood, to one of Rogers's nephews, who was, however, not able to pass the examination; and in the course of a correspondence that ensued, on the subject, (the boy's friends wishing to get him a direct appointment) Hobhouse said, in one of his letters, "If Mr. Rogers's nephew is a dunce, that is no fault of mine." This doesn't *sound* civil,—but without knowing the details of the transaction one cannot judge of it; and certainly Hobhouse has behaved very differently to *me*.} Dined at Lansdowne House, taken by Rogers—Company Bobus Smith, Lord Ilchester, and one or two more—Bobus exceedingly agreeable, and said several very lively things—short, apt, and pregnant. Took me away in his carriage, and left me at Miss Berry's, where I found his brother Sidney, in full plume and play. Two very remarkable men—both wits of the highest order, but of entirely different *genres*. {Lord Haddington also of the party—Home.

28 [Friday]—Breakfasted at home—Met Hume by appointment at Brookes's—Accompanied me to Ratcliffe's, who had begged me to call upon him and give him some notion of the way to sing my new songs—Had received a letter from Mrs. Shelley, (to whom he had been singing them) full of raptures at their beauty—Found now that Ratcliffe, though very eager to show off in them, did not know much about them—Played over one or two of them for him, and as far as my cold would allow me gave him an idea how they were to be sung. He then sung for me a song of Mrs. Arkwright's I had never heard before and gave it with much feeling—his voice being a very melancholy one. Went to Marjoribanks, in consequence of a note he had sent to me—then to Longmans, where Hume and I lunched & he left me. Went on to Lubbocks' to draw upon my Devizes' bankers for £10, but had hardly mentioned my intention to the clerk, when I recollected that I had no right to draw on any money from them (Lubbocks) having no credit with them—As soon, however, as my name was mentioned, a general smile mantled over the cheeks of clerks, partners &c. and the ten pounds was forth-coming in a twinkling. I am afraid, however, that a larger sum would have tried the magic of my name rather *unromantically*—Got back to the West end, and called at the Hollands—was shown in to my lady whom I found at dinner though it was early and none but herself and Miss Rogers. Entering, as I was, with my great coat and umbrella, (the latter of which I had laid down upon a chair) I said, "You will excuse my coming in upon you this way"—"Yes"—she answered "but there was no occasion for you to bring in your umbrella"—On a little further explanation I found she had thought I was coming to dine & to go to the play with her—as she had asked me to do (this being the second night of the Queen & Prince Albert going in State) and I had entirely forgot it. She had also sent me a present of Two Volumes of Criminal Trial, which she said she thought would interest me, and these I had failed to acknowledge, though I found afterwards written in them to Thos. Moore Esqr. from his friend E. V. Holland—A sad amount of offences, and made me rather ashamed of myself—the more so as she was so very good-humoured about it—Company at Milman's, where I dined, Rogers (who took me) Lord Northampton & his daughter (whom I led into dinner) Mrs. Austin &c. &c.—A large party in the evening, for whom it was expected I should sing—but my cold gave me a more than sufficient excuse for refusing—Rogers went away early, but as I knew that Lord Lansdowne (who was among the evening guests) would take me home, waited for him—}

29 [Saturday]—{Buchon, in sending me his "Panthéon Litteraire"[1] had sent with it an immense sheet of blank paper which a good deal puzzled me to make out what it could mean—Found by a note from him, this morning, that I am to fill it with an autograph!—it would take a whole chapter full of

hand-writing like mine.—The following (as far as I can decypher it) are the contents of *his* scrawl—"Mr. Thomas Moore me feroit un bien grand plaisir s'il vouloit bien prendre la peine de copier sur la feuille de papier que j'ai remise chez lui, en même temps que mon volume, un de ses délieceiux chants, veritables Odes, que j'ai lu autrefors avec tant d'enthousiasme." Among others, he says, "gravés dans son coeur is "Oh blame not the Bard"²—quelle belle poésie! et quelle situation dramatique d'une nation et d'un homme!"—He concludes by begging me to copy out this Melody for him, "en y mettant ce nom qui reveille à lui seul tant de nobles souvenirs." Thought the last verse would be quite enough to copy out for him, and having done so, left it at his Hotel.—There came, yesterday evening, by the bye, a mysterious present for Bessy,—the Beauties, or Heroines, of Lalla Rookh—handsomely bound, and accompanied by the following note, in a particularly neat female hand—"Mr. Moore need fear no "rival" in a bosom so early trained in admiration of him, as was the present Incognita; and since he has furtively glanced into her "book," the Sybils predictions must be concluded; and she gives him sure promise that his fame through nations, the love of his friends, and the praises of all elegant minds will increase each of the days that Fate has in store for him—Heaven granting they may be many! This invitation into *present* & future must not be communicated to any one, however dear. But he may acknowledge that it has not miscarried by adopting some word out of this leaf, en parenthèse, when he writes again, he must guess where."—Found an album from Wordsworth's niece, I believe, Miss D. Wordsworth, with a request I would write a few lines in it—did so.—} Set off to Cornhill, and secured a cabin for Russell—near midships—I suppose, a good position—In my way back called upon Jones, who is employed upon a sketch from my Fudges in England—am sorry that he chose a subject from that work—He mentioned his surprise, that Maclise should have found any difficulty in meeting with good subjects in the Irish Melodies—To him (Jones) all my poetry "appeared to abound with picture." Might have told him, in return, that his painting abounded with poesy—{Went to make my parting call at the Hollands—found my Lady, who was most kind and smiling—said that Lady Palmerston had just been with her, and had bid her collect some agreeable men for her Ball to-night—asked me would I go? and on my saying, I would if possible, wrote off a note to Lady Palmerston, speaking it aloud as she wrote, saying she had just found an agreeable man &c. &c.—Dined at Lord Clarendon's—company, Lord & Lady Howick, Lord John, Lord Normanby, Charles Greville &c. &c.—Got placed between Mrs. Villars & Lady Howick—From thence to Lord Northampton's Assembly of Savans, where I staid but about five minutes, and then got home—being far too tired to go to Lady Palmerston's Ball, and besides having to be up early in the morning.

February 1st. [Saturday]¹—Off for Sloperton, with as bad a cold as need be—nothing remarkable on the way—Russell at Calne to meet me.—

February 2nd. 3, 4, &c. &c. [Sunday–Tuesday]—As I have to return to town so soon, on the sad mission of our dear boy's departure for India, all the interval between must be devoted to business, and I can have but little time for journalizing.—

5, 6, 7 &c [Wednesday–Friday]—Forgot whether I have before mentioned an allusion I met with lately, in some periodical publication, to a work (recent, I suppose) of the great German scholar, Gesenius, in which alluding, I suppose to what I have said of the pretended "Irish," found in Plautus, he says "etiam Thomæ Moro placuisse"—Must see *where* he says this, as well as *what* it was that pleased "Thomæ Moro."—A civil letter from a gentleman named Verity, asking for my "eminent autograph"—concludes his letter thus "In the hope that the effusions of your pen may be lasting to add (if possible) greater luster to your well-merited fame, I have the honour &c. &c."—This reminds me, by the bye, of what I ought *not* to have forgotten, a very agreeable tribute which met me on my arrival in town, the other day, being a translation into German, by a lady who signs herself Minna Witte, of "Paradise & the Peri" & the "Fire Worshippers,"¹ accompanied by a very flattering letter, in the following good English.—"Sir—I take the liberty of sending you hereby a poetical German translation of mine of your Fire Worshippers &c the reading of which inspired me so much as to make me try to play with the bold finger of an apprentice the *Master's* lyre, in repeating in our language your lovely songs, which have enchanted and will enchant still so many. The kind approbation my countrymen have given to my little work—which I certainly owe to the beauty of your composition and the sweetness of your images gave me courage to accept most thankfully of Major de Plat's offer, who promised me to deliver &c. & &c." She concludes thus—"I am very happy of having had this opportunity to express to you a part of that admiration which your charming works have excited in me and in all those of my countrymen who are able to value the beauties of your language."

2, 3, 4, 5 &c. [Sunday–Wednesday]—My chief employment turning over the former volumes of this Journal in order to gather there any remarks or anecdotes that may be useful to me in the Prefaces I mean to introduce in our new Edition.}

6, 7, 8 &c. [Thursday–Saturday]—At work, and looking over my journal—many parts of which brought tears from me—particularly the details of my dear child Anastasia's death. Much struck too by the falling off there has been, from various causes, of many of my former friendships and intimacies—people with whom I once lived familiarly & daily, being now seldom seen by me & that but passingly and coldly. This partly owing to the estrangement produced by politics and to the greater rarity of my own visits to town, of late years—but, altogether, it is saddening.

{9, 10, 11 &c. [Sunday–Tuesday]—Received a poem without any signature, "the Emerald Wreath," dedicated to "the Bard of Erin"—nothing in it worth mentioning—Wrote to Wildman to express my regret at having missed him in town & received a very kind answer from him, in which he says "I was really gratified by the sight of your hand-writing; and still more by the assurance it conveyed that the inhabitants of old Newstead still held a place in your recollection." He adds afterwards "It would give us very sincere pleasure to see you once again at Newstead, which would be greatly enhanced if you could prevail on Mrs. Moore to accompany you."—Wrote to thank Talfourd for a copy of his Speeches on the Copy-Right Bill which he sent me and said incidentally that I had once intended to beg of him to take some opportunity of publicly mentioning in the House the resolution I had formed from the first not to avail myself of the retrospective clause originally intended to be introduced into the contemplated Bill giving a reverting interest to the author.[1]

12, 13 &c. [Wednesday–Thursday]—Received from Talfourd a copy of his collected Speeches on the Copy-Right question.}

14 [Friday]—In thanking Talfourd, mentioned that I had once intended to request of him to take some opportunity of stating to the House the resolution I had from the first formed not to avail myself of the clause, once contemplated, giving a reverting interest to the author. In replying to my letter, he says,—"I think Lord John Russell, in the few remarks he made the session before last on the Copy-Right Bill, alluded to your generous determination not to avail yourself of the reverting interest which it then contemplated; but I shall be too proud of gracing my cause by the mention of your name not to avail myself of any that may arise more distinctly to express your feeling—which cannot be irrelevant, as it will show the disinterested spirit in which the general cause of literature is advocated by a poet who has no personal interest to bias him."

{15, 16 &c. [Saturday–Sunday]—In a speech lately made at some Religious Liberty meeting, by Sir George Strictland, I think, the following passage occurs—"If the voluntary principle began in Oxford,[1] where were they not to expect it to extend? *Oxford,* which was supposed to extinguish all the daring outbreaks of liberty of conscience! It reminded him of the words of Moore, who said "how can you expect to put out the conflagration, when the extinguishers themselves take fire? *(Cheers)*"—

17, 18 &c [Monday, 17 February–Saturday, 29 February]—Employed principally in looking over the past years of this Journal—Have likewise made some progress in the Preface for the First Volume of our great Edition—

March 1, 2, 3, 4, &c. &c. [Sunday–Wednesday] Among my odd correspondents there are few that transcend the joint writers of the following letter. Taking into account the place it is dated from, there could hardly be a more striking instance of the literary mania that is now seizing the whole community—custom-house officers not excepted.—I should be sorry not to have time to transcribe it—but here goes, for at least a beginning:—

"Office No. 27 Custom House, Liverpool
March 4, 1840
"Sir—Grateful for the enjoyment derived from a perusal of your beautiful collection of Poems, under the title of Lalla Rookh, my friend Mr. Evan MacColl, the author of the Mountain Minstrel[1] &c. and myself desire to thank you for the gratification we have received from that charming Work, and perhaps we should by quoting passages endeavour to show you what portions please us most,—but where *all* are Beauties, selections would be invidious—for surely when it is considered that every reader, according to his own peculiar taste and pursuit may here find himself entranced amidst his own ideas and associations, we shall not be considered egotistical if we say that the enumeration would be great, indeed:—since the soldier for instance needs only to glance at that portion which refers to the stealthy invasion of the Arabs into the fortified Mount of the Fire-Worshippers, when, with the warmth and energy of his profession, will he not rush from the Temple where the Gheber lights his funeral pile, from which abstraction he will only be roused by the death-shriek of the Arab's daughter piercing &c. &c. &c. So, with the Lover, who, when his eye drinks in, as it were, those mellifluous & soul-stirring lines &c. &c. &c. does he not with Azim hear from her lips the &c. &c. is he not "awoke into horrors as the echo of her oath bursts" &c. &c.—In short, as the eager eye of each individual falls upon every succeeding line, new charms will burst upon his

&c. &c. &c.—For me, who am not worthy of being called a poet, but am, indeed, the least of all rhymers, it would be presumption even to offer an opinion; but with my friend Mr. McColl the case is widely different, since he has written many pieces which will cause him to be long remembered. . . . Allow me, Sir, to wish you every happiness you can possibly wish yourself, in which wish my friend cordially joins me; and allow me to say that we look forward with pleasurable anticipation to the expected appearance of a new work from your pen, and that in the event of such a desideratum, we shall use our utmost endeavours to bring it speedily to a Second Edition. Believe us to be, Sir, your admiring humble servants,

B. McRill on the parts of Self and
Evan McColl."

I find I undertook too much in attempting to transcribe the whole of this Epistle.

5, 6, 7, 8 &c [Thursday–Sunday]

10 [Tuesday]—A letter this morning from a Winchester boy, asking me for a scrap of Byron's writing, and thus bursting out about Lalla Rookh, "I have just seen your Lalla Rookh for the first time, and words cannot describe the delight & admiration &c. &c."—he then proceeds to say, "I had written thus much without giving you the slightest clue to conjecture who I am or what situation I bear in life. You will start when you hear that I am only a youthful student at Winchester College, but I entrust myself quite to your clemency" &c. &c. &c.

11, 12, 13 &c [Wednesday–Friday]Niente

14, 15, [Saturday–Sunday]—The following note sent me by Hume, addressed to himself by the Secretary of the St. Patrick's Day Anniversary. It really lies heavily on my conscience having now, for so many years, absented myself from that meeting.—

"Sir—I am directed by my Masters to mention to you, as the constant & liberal benefactor to this charity, their earnest wishes to win Mr. Thomas Moore to their festival on Tuesday next, could such an advantage to its interests be accomplished. We have heard that the great poet is in the neighbourhood of London.—I am, Sir &c. &c.}

16, 17, 18, &c. &c. [Monday–Wednesday]—Received, about the latter end of this month some letters from Ireland, respecting this strange movement in the Temperance direction which is now in progress there.—Had but a few days before sent a squib to the Chronicle, on this very subject,[1] but not in a tone I fear that my worthy correspondents would approve of—One of them, a Quaker, rather a sensible sort of fellow—at least sensible enough to feel some little doubts respecting the stability of this Anti-Whiskey enthusiasm—Presses me much to lend my aid to the cause. The other, a Priest, also invokes my pen—"And oh!" he exclaims, "if it were not too much that, in addition to this rather pious effusion (a card he had sent me to add some lines to) you would write us a Ballad of a few verses for our Irish peasants, boys & girls, who are to walk with their medals on the 15th. of August."— The Quaker, pretty strongly hints that I *owe* some reparation of this sort for the many effusions in the opposite direction which I have been guilty of.

{19, 20, &c. &c. [Thursday, 19 March–Tuesday, 31 March] Nothing more to the end of this month, excepting the anxious and (to my poor Bessy) most painful preparations for the departure of our dear boy, Russell, for India. Her heart seems but the more wrapped up in him, the nearer the time comes for losing him. The day of the ship's sailing is now fixed—the 13 or 14th of next month.

April 1, 2, 3 [Wednesday–Friday]—Had written to Lady Elisabeth to know if *I* might come to Sackville St.—the lodgings for Bessy & Russell having been already provided in Bury St. at No. 19

4 [Saturday]—Bessy & Russell started for London.

5 [Sunday]—Note from Lady Elisabeth saying "I am very sorry you are thinking of coming to town just now, as I am leaving it, and very sorry too that *this* time you cannot be *niché* in your old nest, because I am going to paint *part* of the house in hopes the smell may be gone off by the time I return, after Easter." She then adds that the Mt Edgecombs having sold their house in Dover St. all her vacant rooms were now stuffed up with their furniture "I feel much," she says "for Mrs. Moore and fear I shall just miss her, though I know one could offer no consolation that her own good sense has not already suggested." In alluding to the Ball just given to the Queen at Lansdowne House, she says "I wish you had been there—it was such a comfortable way of seeing her in detail & examining her at leisure. As a sight the whole thing was magnificent—*très roigné* and perfectly *well done*. The Statue Gallery was all wreathed in roses—the antiques must, I think, have been quite surprised at being enveloped in the honey-moon

flowers! There were so many beautiful things, it was impossible the Queen could have time to notice one half."—Passed a very lonely Sunday—Schomberg called in the morning and asked me to dinner—Promised for tomorrow.

6 [Monday]—At work—dined at Schomberg's—company, the Starkeys, Tugwell and Captain Wallace—amusing enough.

7 [Tuesday]—Another lonely day.—Such solitude doesn't at all agree with me

8 [Wednesday]—Started for town—two old acquaintances my fellow passengers inside Clutterbuck and Lord Camperdown—plenty of talk on the way, and some of it amusing—Found my dear Bess & her boy lodged as comfortably as could be expected, and a back bed-room (one I have often occupied) prepared for myself—Bessy had said indeed in one of her letters "We are as comfortable as *dirt* and a good natured landlady can make us."— No time had been lost about Russell's outfit, Bessy having passed all her days between Hemphill (the tailor) and Grindlay, Christian & Co. St. Martin's Place—with the exception of Sunday which she devoted to a visit to Hornsey to see the grave of our dear child Barbara and look to its being all decent and right. Had dinner and some sherry from Sloperton which my provident Bess had brought with her.}

9 [Thursday][1]—Sallied forth after breakfast Bessy Russell and myself to visit the ship in which our poor boy is to be taken away from us—Called at Lubbock's in whose hands I had placed the £339 remaining of the sum destined for the out-fit &c. Went from thence to the East India Docks where the ship was lying—the operation of getting Bessy up the steep ladder that led us on board added not a little to my exceeding nervousness on the occasion—Had never myself been on board so immense a vessel—the accommodations for passengers almost as roomy as those in a good-sized house—Forget whether I have mentioned that Sir Lionel Smith the new governor of Mauritius goes out in this same ship, together with his family, a wife and daughters—The cabins prepared for them quite a suite of rooms, and very handsomely furnished—but our dear Russell's berth was, of course, the chief object of our attention, and I was most agreeably surprized by its roominess. We had determined from the first, that though increasing so much the expence he should have a cabin to himself and we now had all his things brought & stowed away, under the mother's eye

comfortably. The Lieutenant, a hearty good-natured Irishman, and, even before he knew who I was, full of most cheering kindness—But when he re-appeared, his increased cordiality showed most *comfortably* what he had heard, in the interval, and with the Captain, it was exactly the same case. Indeed, every step I take in this to me most painfully interesting task (though painful chiefly, on the dear mother's account) makes me feel with gratitude the value of a friendly fame like mine—I call it friendly, because from the manner in which it manifests itself, I cannot help feeling that the tribute is as much—nay, I should hope, much *more* to the man than to the author—{On our return called again at the East India Agency Office and paid the sum for Russell's passage (£110) by a cheque on Lubbock—Stopped at Farance's, the confectioner's, and had ices &c. &c.—} Had written to Lady Holland to tell her of my arrival, but expressing doubts of my being able to see her during my stay—Got in return a note from her, in which, after naming some days for me to dine with her, if I can, she adds—"I hope Mrs. Moore is in good health and heart for I fear it is a pang to separate from her son which will require both." {Seeing that Macready & Power were to act to night resolved to make an effort to get Bussy and Bessy good places for the performance; and having learned Macready's address at the stage-door of the Haymarket Theatre set off in a Cab to his residence in Regent's Park—was lucky enough to find him at home, and he most readily & good-naturedly said that I had but to ask for "Mr. Moore's private box" and I should be comfortably placed—Had dinner early, and off to the Theatre—Bulwer's Play, Richelieu[2]—clever, certainly, but not of a high order of dramatic talent—Power, in one of the farces that followed, very amusing—but I always miss the *real* Irishman in him—

10 [Friday]—After breakfast set off with Russell to get his papers from Mr. Cabell. It just struck me, as we were on our way, that if there were many forms to go through, we should have enough to do to despatch them in the limited time left us—Having finished all that was required at the Board of Controul, we found that there was still the most important business remaining—namely, the passing at the India House. Cabell said something, too, of a possible difficulty we might have to encounter, but gave me no very clear idea either of its nature or extent—When we got to the India House were shown into the office of Mr ———, the person with whom this part of our business lay (as complete a personification of what is called a Jack in office as could well be conceived) and were by him told smirkingly that we had come too late, that the Council for the passing of the Cadets &c. had sate yesterday, I think, or the day before, and that no other could be got together till Wednesday next. What was then to be done? I had been told the ship was positively to sail on Tuesday, so that all we had been doing—the payment of the passage money, the fitting up of the cabin & sending things

aboard was now all to go for nothing! I have seldom felt more alarmed or annoyed. This jaunty gentleman (Mr. Clarke I think his name is) then advised that I should enquire immediately of the Captain whether he really sailed on Tuesday, or whether it was not possible he might be detained till Wednesday. Set off to Grindlay's, where I found that the ship was *certainly* to sail on Tuesday, and that though she *might* linger a little in the Downs so as to give my son a chance of getting on board on Wednesday, yet if a fair wind was to spring up she would be off. A gentleman whom I had found on entering Mr. Clarke's office (a Doctor Kembell, as I understood afterwards) took a good deal of interest in my difficulty, and showing me a List of Directors said that as three or four, (I think) were all that were necessary to form a Council, I might possibly know some who would most readily attend to oblige me. But they were all unknown to me. At length (not to dwell further upon this most disagreeable *hitch* in my operations) the official gentleman, Mr. Clarke whose whole object had been evidently to enhance his own services began to find out that it might be *possible* to get a sufficient number of Directors together tomorrow to despatch my son's business. I therefore came away without any very serious fears as to the result [see below[1]—On arriving at home found Rogers with Bessy, all kindness,—as he is invariably, indeed, wherever she is concerned. Begged that she would make use of his carriage, which was at the door & left us, having fixed for us to dine with him on Sunday—Wanted me to dine with him also tomorrow, but I had promised Corry—Drove to see the Douglas's—found only her & the girls—from thence to the Drive in the Park, which was quite full, and made several turns up & down, to Bessy's great amusement, the day being very fine & the whole world abroad—Russell, of course, with us—every minute of him now being precious—painfully precious—to the poor mother.]—dined late at home—Bessy went to see her mother.—Went to Brookes's and had a mutton-chop, and was joined by Otway Cave, who came for the same hasty sort of dinner having to start by the Mail—finished a pint of port, to my own share, and thought I felt the better for it—home early.

11 [Saturday]—Hume to breakfast—and set off with us for the India House, but recollecting on the way some payment he had to make at a particular hour, left us & returned—Found on my arrival at Mr. Clarke's that the immense difficulty had been got over, and that Russell was to be passed. In talking of his own exertions in the cause this official gentleman mentioned his having applied to Sir Robert Campbell, "who, I am sorry to say, (he added, with much solemnity) refused to attend." As I found that not only he, but some of his brother clerks were anxious that I should buy at that office a copy of the great Hindoostanee Dictionary (on the sale of which they have I believe some profit) thought I had better do so, as Russell

must have the book, and it is as well, too, to give him the chance of occasionally studying it on the voyage—so ordered a copy (price six guineas or pounds) to be sent on board for him.—Returned home, with my heart somewhat lighter (as to *one* difficulty, at least) than it was yesterday. (Find that it was to-day, *not* yesterday, that all about Rogers's carriage, and our drive to the Park &c. as mentioned above took place.)—dined, Hume and I with honest Corry, at his Hotel—a very snug & good dinner and both these kind friends most cordially interested in all my proceedings—went early to Rogers, who had wanted me to dine with him, having a large party—Found the gentlemen yet at the wine! joined them. Have forgot in my bustle who were the party, but Gladstone and his wife, and Von Artevelde Taylor were among the number—A good deal of conversation with Mrs. G., Lady ? and one or two other pretty women that were of the party and then home early—there having been strong importunities that I should sing, but, between *couldn't* and *wouldn't*, I *didn't*.

12 [Sunday]—Having left word when we called at Lord John's yesterday that I would breakfast with him this morning, did so—very kind about Bessy and Russell & regretted his not having seen them.—Bessy & Russell went to St. Paul's this being Sunday and I forget what I did myself during the day.—All three dined at Rogers's, a large dinner of relatives, the only exceptions to the family tie, out of a party of 15 or 16, being ourselves, the Leslies the painter & his wife, and old Maltby—Bessy had Rogers's carriage again to day, and took me to Macaulay who has promised me several letters for Russell.

13 [Monday]—Edward Hughes with us early & very useful in helping to pack; this being the day of our dear boy's departure for Gravesend—I forgot to mention that Corry, yesterday or the day before, suggested, in the kindest & most delicate manner, that if his joining us at Gravesend would be at all agreeable to us he would be most happy to come—accepted eagerly his offer—Left town in the Coach, Bessy, Russell & I about one—had been recommended by Luttrell to go to the Waites's, I think, which we did.—A most excellent house in every respect—the dinner (ordered by Corry) good & comfortable, and our beds the same. But the ship that was to carry our dear boy from us was there lying before our eyes and, as long as any daylight remained, the poor mother continued to gaze upon it.}

14 [Tuesday]—{The whole of this morning passed in watching the preparations of the Reliance for sailing—my darling Bess bearing up wonderfully through it all, and Corry and I, as well as dear Russell himself doing our

best to cheer away the time. As it approached two o'clock the arrival of Sir Lionel Smith (who, together with his family was to sail in the Reliance) seemed to be all that was waited for—I do not recollect whether I have before mentioned that on finding Sir Lionel Smith was to be on board (going to take the government of Mauritius) I wrote to Lord John begging he would give me a letter of introduction to him for Russell; and the following note from him will show how promptly & efficiently he complied with my request.

"My dear Moore—I have written to Sir Lionel Smith and sent the letter directly to him. Shall I write to Lord Auckland by the Indian Mail?

Yrs. ever, J. Russell[1]

The steamer from London with Sir Lionel [*incomplete*]}

It being now time for our dear boy to leave us, a few parting words were said, and he then set off in a boat to the ship, which was to be towed by steamers to the Downs. As long as the vessel continued in sight my poor Bessy remained at the window with a telescope, watching for a glimpse of her dear boy, and telling me all she saw,—or *thought* she saw him doing.— Corry having set off in the Coach we hired a little open Fly in the town, and got comfortably to town in the evening—{Went & had dinner, I think, at Brookes's}

15 [Wednesday]—Forgot what I did this day, except walking about a little with Bessy and (after I had left her at home) calling upon Rogers. In speaking of Bessy, he said "We are told marriages are made in heaven, and certainly none but God Almighty could have brought you two together— she has beauty, sense,—" and so he went on most kindly about her.

{16 [Thursday]—Started, Bessy and I, in the York House for Sloperton, Johnny Hughes being one of our outside fellow-passengers—Inside we had that great man, Nield, and accordingly we had not proceeded far on our way to the rail-way station, when the coach broke down, and we were obliged to get on, as we could, in another. Nield very good-humoured about his share in producing the downfall—Found him agreeable and courteous throughout the journey. Got home from Calne in a Fly.

17, 18, 19 &c. &c. [Friday–Sunday]—*Ex nihilo nihil* fit—no events & therefore no journalizing. A rash or eruption which came out on my leg before I went to town, and which both then, and while in town, I entirely neglected, has been thus let go too far to be easily removed—am obliged therefore to nurse it.

20, 21 &c. &c. [Monday, 20 April–Thursday, 30 April] At work writing a Preface to the First Vol. of our forthcoming Edition.—Had Kenrick to my leg, who ordered lotion and rest.

May 1, 2, 3 &c. &c. [Friday–Sunday]—Have found the following extract in some newspaper (from a work lately published) professing to give an account of my reception in the Edinburgh Theatre, the night I went there with Scott & Jeffrey—Like all such clumsy reports, it is both *over* done and *under* done. But I am glad to see any public record of the circumstance, for it is one I remember with much pleasure, and I have myself made a memorandum of it, I think, in this Journal.[1]

4, 5, 6 &c. [Monday–Wednesday]

14 [Thursday]—Went to Devizes, Bessy and I to dine with the Hughes's—chiefly a family party—slept there.

15 [Friday]—Brabant examined my leg—found the eruption more extensive than he had supposed—ordered me to discontinue the lotion, and put on a plaister of simple lard—returned home.

16, 17, 18 &c. [Saturday, 16 May–Sunday, 31 May]—At work—as much as the want of my loco-motive powers (always essential, or at least habitual to the play of my mind) would let me—

June 1, 2, 3 &c. [Monday–Wednesday]—The same sort of life—with only a most disagreeable addition to my bodily grievances in the appearance of spots, or eruptions in other places besides the leg.

4, 5, 6 &c [Thursday–Saturday]—In looking over some old papers, found the following neat verses in a female hand—by whom written, I know not, or at least have forgot.

"Impromptu, on their repealing the Act against
Witchcraft in Ireland

"So you think, then, the days of witchcraft are past,
    That, in Ireland, you're safe from the magical art;
Those who hold this belief may rue it at last,
    When the force of a spell is found in their heart.
That the maidens of Erin in witchery deal,
    By those who have seen them can ne'er be denied;
While the spell of their bards o'er the senses will steal,
    As by some hath been felt, and by Moore hath been tried.
Then think not to scape on such dangerous ground,
    Nor fancy that magic and *witch*-craft are o'er;
For in Ireland those powers will ever abound,
    While her *witches* are fair and her *Wizard* is Moore!"[1]

4, 5, 6 &c [Thursday–Saturday][2]—Having a good deal ill-used the copy of
the State Papers (Henry VIII 2 Vols)[3] lent me by Lord Lansdowne, thought
I had best procure for him a new copy, instead, and applied to my State-
Paper-Office friend, Mr. Lemon, to help me in procuring one, which he
did. Apprized Lord Lansdowne of this, asking at the same time, whether
the Vols. were to be sent to London or left at Bowood. In the letter he wrote
in answer, he says, among other things, what follows—"The Protestant
carnival is now in full action, and society overflowing as it is with currents
from all parts of the world becomes a drudgery—However it will always
have a place for you, so I hope you will appear soon with spirits fresher
than ours." He adds "Our Irish friends are so irritated by the success of
Stanley's Bill[4] that it is difficult to keep them in order sufficient to prevent
their marring their own cause." With respect to the S. Paper Volumes, he
merely says they may be left at Bowood to come to town by the first
opportunity. Two or three days after, received another letter from him,
saying "My dear Moore—It was very stupid in me not to say when I wrote
to you a few days ago that, if you had not actually got another Volume to
substitute for mine of the State Papers, I should value my own much the
more for any notes, marks and scratches of yours (the more the better)
bestowed upon its margins."

7, 8, 9 &c [Sunday–Tuesday]—In the course of my search through old
papers, I have lighted upon the Letter I received from Stockholm in the
year 1807, acquainting me with my having been elected a Knight of the
Order of St. Joachim. I remember my first impression on receiving the
letter, was that it must be a hoax, and that the Patron-Saint of the Order
was, in reality, not St. Joachim but St. *Joke-him*. The letter is a very long one,
but I shall transcribe some parts of it, premising that the direction it bears is

as follows "Sir Thomas More K. J. Elect, at his Chambers in the Middle Temple, this Letter is transmitted to Messrs. Hammersley's & Co.—to be by those gentlemen consigned to Mr. D. Symonds No. 20 Paternoster Row, who is requested to deliver it into the hands of the Author of Epistles, Odes and other poems whose name is Moore." The following are extracts from the Letter—"Sir—The ingenious works wherewith you have enriched the literature of your country and the brilliant reputation you have thereby acquired in the Republic of Letters are circumstances well known to the learned on the Continent. The Literate in Germany and throughout the North are well acquainted with your name and your merit; and it is precisely on those accounts, that the Princes, Nobles and Gentlemen who compose the general Chapter of the most Illustrious, Equestrian, Secular and Chapteral order of St. Joachim have deemed it expedient, Sir, unanimously to elect you as a Knight of the Third Class of this order. Your nomination & election took place on the ninth of December; that day being the anniversary festival of the Patron; and you may rest assured, Sir, that I experience a peculiar pleasure in having been selected as a proper person to notify these matters to you—which being the present state of the case, the Serene Grand Master, the Knights Capitulars and the whole Equestrian Confraternity now await your ultimate decision respecting the points of acceptance or refusal of the proffered honour."

The extent of the letter may be judged when I say that the above forms about an eighth part of it. The writer proceeds to enumerate all the distinguished persons in different parts of Europe who have borne the honour of Knighthood, and at last goes back to my namesake Sir Thomas More, whom he disserts on in the following grandiloquent style—"Sir— even the very names you bear recall to our remembrance those of one of the brightest luminaries which shone on the dawn of English literature—of a man who in his day was one of the greatest ornaments to the Bar and to the Supreme Court of Iudicature wherein he presided—May Providence, who seems to have destined you to be the successor to his transcendent genius & extraordinary talents, to his elegant wit and profound learning, may that Providence, Sir, equally enable you to attain the highest dignity of the law wherewith he was invested, and preserve you from an end like his, at once tragical and unmerited."

The writer then comes to something more germane to the matter, and tells me what I found to be true, that Lord Nelson had been elected a Knight of St. Joachim, and that not only had the title been acknowledged by the English Court, but on his death was made hereditary in his family. I took the trouble, I recollect, of writing to Sir George Nayler for some information respecting this order, and learned from him that the Duc de Bouillon, I think, was the last Knight of St Joachim acknowledged by the British Court and that it was no longer so sanctioned. I had never much idea of accepting the honour, (*certainly* none of ever assuming the title) but this information, which the writer of the letter withheld from me, determined me at once to decline the distinction, which I did in a respectful answer. The person who wrote to me gave as his address "Monsr. Monsr. Le Commandeur Hansson, Vice-Chancelier de l'ordre de St. Joachim."[1]— Received a letter from Napier about the beginning of this month, in answer to one I had written him, asking whether he could give me any information respecting the particulars of poor Brock's death,—the gallant fellow whom I knew at Niagara, and who was killed at Queenston 8 or 9 years after.[2] In accounting to Napier for my not yet having had time to read the last volume of his Peninsular War,[3] I said that I was I was so hard at work, endeavoring to carry on the war myself (in a different sense of the word) that I could not find time for any thing else. In reply to this he says—"I am sorry to hear you are obliged to carry on the war so busily—I am rather in hostilities of that kind myself, as my bookseller has contrived to have 7000 *copies,* not *sets,* of different volumes still on hand unsold, and yet forces me to print 1000 more of the 3rd. Vol.—He says they will all *go off!*—but I fear it will not be on golden wings—their going will be with sugar and spice and all that is nice, like young girls."

10, 11, 12 &c. [Wednesday–Friday]—The following letter, dated January 1816 has just turned up among the old scraps of things I have found among my papers, and (as it amused me, I recollect, at the time) I shall give it in extenso—or at least a part of it—here.

"18. Duke St.Bloomsbury Square
Jany. 27 1816

(Confidential)

"Sir.—Having some concern in an Institution for Free Debate held in Bond St, in this metropolis, and the question for Friday last being a contrasted investigation of the poetical merits of Lord Byron, W. Scott, Thomas Campbell & yourself, which question is adjourned to the 2nd. of F'bruary (as you will see by the File of the Morning Chronicle in your city [I take for granted I was in Dublin at the time]) I beg to make you a proposal. If you wish to have an account of the different speeches & proceedings on the 26th. instant & the ensuing nights, I can send you an ample report by the Post. I exerted all the little eloquence I possessed to prove your superiority, and being a countryman of yours, and, besides, unsuccessful in my speculations in England during the last 25 years, I take the liberty to suggest to you that for the sum of five pounds, British, I will convey to you the intellignece to which I alluded. You may send the amount, £5, an English note, cut in two, and on the receipt of the first half, I shall immediately transmit to you the report.—I am, Sir, your humble servt.

S. Fleming

"P.S. Being engaged in literary pursuits in this city I can execute any commissions of that kind with punctuality & despatch."

13, 14, 15 &c [Saturday–Monday]—Received a letter from a Mr. Joseph B. Boyd, dated Cincinnati, State of Ohio, April 9, 1840, asking for my autograph, as he "felt very desirous to enrich his collection with a specimen of the chirography of one so preeminently distinguished as the author of Lalla Rookh."—Sent it to him accordingly.}

16 [Tuesday]—Found the following verses, addressed to me, in 1823, on reading the Loves of the Angels by Miss Lefanu:[1]—

> "Beloved of heaven, how passing bright
>   The wreath thy three-fold lay has won!
> So varying shines with hallow'd light,
>   The rising, ris'n, and setting sun.
>
> To Lea, first, the spell-word given,
>   Teaches to range yon starry sphere;—
> Virtue a mortal lights to heaven,
>   While Vice detains an angel here.
>
> A bolder chord now shakes the lyre,—
>   See Rubi in his radiance move,
> Where Lilis kneels, with soul on fire,
>   That lov'd to learn and learn'd to love.
>
> But, hark!—what notes, at day's decline,
>   With sweetest, holiest influence, steal,
> And all a *Seraph's* flame divine,
>   And all a *mortal's* love reveal?
>
> The closing strains, like parting day
>   A flood of soften'd radiance pour;
> For Virtue points the moral lay
>   And Genius twines the wreath for Moore."

{17, 18 &c. [Wednesday–Thursday]—Still laid up with my tiresome leg.— Took advantage of the visits of Norman (the great Bath surgeon) to our poor neighbour Phipps, who has been in a very dangerous state from stricture in the urethra, to get his opinion respecting my small malady— Had him three or four times—on the first visit took the 2 sovereigns I presented to him, but declined all fee afterwards.

19, 20, 21 &c. [Friday, 19 June–Tuesday, 30 June] The change of lotion and ointment ordered by Norman produced good effects at first, but they were not lasting—so that I am still on a reduced allowance of walking, which with *me* is as bad for mind as for body.

July 1, 2, 3, 4 &c [Wednesday–Saturday]—Found another laudatory copy of verses among my papers,—when written, I know not—but here they are. The hand-writing a woman's—

> "Three poets in an age of rhymers born,
> Britannia's and Hibernia's isles adorn.
> Each to the laurel crown prefers his claim,
> And proudly represents his country's fame.
> Byron, in bold, sublime, impassioned lays,
> Thy lofty spirit, Albion, well displays.
> Famed Scotia sees, in Scott's romantic strain,
> Her feuds and fiery chieftains live again;
> And Erin's sons her ancient lyre behold,
> In Moore's rapt hands, triumphant, as of old.
> While rival states sustain their bards' renown,
> And, for her favourite, each demands the crown;
> Too wise to suffer a disputed throne,
> The realms of wit their joint pretensions own;
> The sway of Byron, Scott and Moore proclaim,
> And hail the Great Triumvirate of Fame."

5, 6, 7, 8 &c [Sunday–Wednesday]—In looking over Murray's Omnium Gatherum edition of Byron's Works (I mean Omnium Gatherum, as regards the annotations) I find p. 549, the following note. "Mr. Moore considers "Thyrza," as if she were a mere creature of the poet's brain." He then quotes what I say about Thyrza, and adds—"It is a pity to disturb a sentiment thus beautifully expressed; but Lord Byron in a letter &c. &c." My critic then sets off upon a track which shows that neither he nor Dallas (whom he quotes) knew any thing more about Thyrza than they *suppose me* to have known.[1]

9, 10, 11, &c. [Thursday–Saturday]—Here is another scrap that has turned up (relative to my Travels of an Irish Gentleman in search of a Religion) which I found in a French Ecclesiastical Magazine:—"Le 9, Juillet, il y a eu une rèunion de l'académie de la Religion Catholique, où le Pere Olivieri a donné une analyse de l'ouvrage de Thomas Moore, intitulé Voyage d'un gentilhomme Irlandais à la recherce d'une religion. En rendant hommage au talent, au savoir et aux bonnes intentions de M. Moore, le docte académicién relève néanmoins quelques expressions peu exactes de l'auteur Irlandais." I take for granted this must refer to what I have said about St. Augustine which though, in my opinion, perfectly true, has touched upon rather a sore point of Catholic ecclesiastical History.[1]

12, 13, 14 &c [Sunday–Tuesday] Received letters both from Hume & himself, announcing the arrival of my excellent friend, Philip Crampton, in London—he had written to us from Dublin, announcing his intention of coming, and likewise of running down to Sloperton to see Bessy and give his advice about her health. Unluckily, Bessy's god-daughter, Mrs. Swindon, is at present on a visit to us with a little child & a nurse, which so overlays our small establishment, that we shall not be able to receive Crampton—wrote to him to say so.}

15, 16, 17, &c. [Wednesday–Friday] Received from the Cramers a copy of Bunting's newly published Collection of Irish Airs,[1] which they have often written to me about, as likely (they hoped) to furnish materials for a continuation of the Melodies. Tried them over with some anxiety; as had they contained a sufficient number of beautiful airs to make another volume, I should have felt myself bound to do the best I could with them, though still tremblingly apprehensive lest a failure should be the result. Was rather relieved, I confess, on finding that, with the exception of a few airs, which I have already made use of, the whole volume is a mere mass of trash. Considering the thorn I have been in poor Bunting's side, by supplanting him in the one great object of his life—(the connexion of his name with the fame of Irish music) the temper in which he *now* speaks of my success (for, some years since he was rather termagant on the subject) is not a little creditable to his good nature and good sense. Speaking of the use which I made of the *first* Volume of Airs published by him, he says "they were soon adopted as vehicles for the most beautiful popular songs that have perhaps ever been composed by any lyric poet."[2] He complains strongly however of the alterations made in the original airs, and laments that "the work of the poet was accounted of so paramount an interest that the proper order of song-writing was, in many instances, inverted, and instead of the words being adapted to the tune, the tune was too often adapted to the words,—a solecism which could never have happened had the reputation of the writer not been so great as at once to carry the tunes he deigned to make use of altogether out of their old sphere, among the simple & tradition-loving people of the country; with whom, in truth, many of the new melodies, to this day, are hardly suspected to be themselves."— He lays the blame of all these alterations upon Stevenson—but poor Sir John was entirely innocent of them—as the whole task of selecting the airs, and in some instances, shaping them thus, in particular passages, to the general sentiment which the melody appeared to me to express, was undertaken solely by myself. Had I not ventured on these very allowable liberties, many of the airs now most known & popular would have been still sleeping, with all their authentic dross about them, in Mr. Bunting's First Volume. {It would have been just as rational to blame me for not adopting the character imposed on each air by the sort of words I found it originally with—in which case, many of these melodies that are now wedded with words that breathing their own melancholy spirit would have still continued to be thrown away upon mere [*incomplete*]} The same charge is brought by him respecting those Airs which I took from the Second Volume of his Collection. "The beauty of Mr. Moore's words," he says, "in a great degree atones for the violence done by the musical arranger to any of the airs which he has adopted."

18, 19, 20, 21, 22, &c. [Saturday–Wednesday]—A thought having crossed my mind that Lord Lansdowne, in accepting the dedication of my Collected Works, might have forgotten the numerous squibs & satires with which some of the Volumes must swarm, I thought it as well to bring this circumstance to his recollection & therefore wrote to him to say that though I myself saw no reason why a Dedicatee should be considered responsible for all the freaks of his dedicator, yet as it *might* be a matter of question, I thought it right to submit the point for his consideration—Received in answer from him the following letter, which I shall give entire, as containing the first account we received (though a note soon followed from Lady Lansdowne giving Bessy the same intelligence) of the acceptance of Shelburne's proposal by Lady Georgiana Herbert.

Richmond, July 23

"My dear Moore—{I was sorry that I got home too late for the post yesterday afternoon, and was thus prevented from answering you by return of post, as I ought & intended; but} you will allow I had some excuse for hurry and delay, when I tell you (what I am sure you will be glad to hear) that, in addition to my expected avocations during the day, arose others unexpectedly, from the circumstance of Shelburne's having proposed to & been accepted by Lady Georgiana Herbert in the course of the morning—an event which, as she is, I believe, a very amiable person, gives Lady Le. and myself great pleasure.

"But I have wandered from the Dedication, which I should be very sorry to decline, on the ground you mention. By receiving it, I am not responsible for all that the volumes contain; and, if I was, as I could only be made a party to any thing that might be thought exceptionable by being also a party to that far greater portion which all will join in admiring, I should be a gainer by it, independently of the value I attach to the expression of your friendship and kindness.

{"I am sorry to hear mention again made of the leg—I trust you have taken the best advice you can for it—

Yrs. very truly
Lansdowne

24, 25 &c. &c. [Friday–Saturday]—Having made up my mind to try a *change* of *some* kind, and London being, on many accounts, the most desirable, wrote up to Lady Elisabeth to know if she could receive me, but got for answer that Talbot being now in town, I could not have the room till he was gone. Resolved therefore to try Bury St.—

26 [Saturday]—Started for town—A gentleman & his sister my companions, very agreeable. She handsome. Became as usual most intimately acquainted with them before we parted—the young lady full of Lalla Rookh, &c. Drove on my arrival to Bury St., and found that the room Russell occupied when we were last there was vacant—agreed to take it by the night. Went to the Fieldings, found them at dinner & joined them—Talbot & Montgomery of the party—Left them early & home.

27 [Monday] My bed most uncomfortable last night, and my feelings altogether sore & uneasy—the spot on my hip having become heated & irritated with the journey—Called on the Feildings—from thence to the Lansdownes, where I found all bustle & smiles—Lady L. herself looking radiant with happiness, and Shelburne full of business—The Calne people want Lady Lansdowne to put off the intended Bazaar, on account of a meeting of Clergy,—but she declares she will not unless the "Queen of Beauty" (Lady Seymour so nick-named)[1] can also put off her coming, as she is resolved not to lose the advantage of her presence at the Bazaar—Had called in the morning at Rogers's, but found he was at the Archbishop of York's, and, so went to breakfast at Brookes's—Went afterwards with Hume down to Longman's &c. &c.—Dined at Rogers's, having had a letter from him, before I came to town, to secure me—Company, Lord & Lady Grey, Lady Georgiana, & Colonel Gray—Lord & Lady Redesdale, Sydney Smith, Count Zamoiski, and Pahlin—great personal likeness between Pahlen & Zamoiski, though diametrically opposite to each other in every other respect. About nine o'clock heard a loud firing in the direction of the Park, which we were puzzled to account for, when Sydney exclaimed "Oh it is the destruction of all the Canons!" the Ecclesiastical Bill being passed that very night.[2] This of course produced a great effect. (Found afterwards the firing was for the Duchess of Cambridge's birth-day.) Had a good deal of conversation with Lord Grey—The Greys were to set off for Howick in the morning, leaving Lord Durham in a state, hopeless, but not (as they then thought) immediately threatening—Forgot to mention that I went this morning with Lady Elisabeth & Horatia to the Dutchess Canizzaro's Music—not having been invited but venturing on the general invitation she has always given me—Mostly warmly received, and almost *hugged* by her, which was more than I bargained for.—A very pretty girl there, Miss Gurwood,

the daughter of the Duke's Gurwood[3] by a French mother. Some very good singing by Rubini, Da Nuovo, Lord Ossulston &c. &c. Lord Ossulston's style of singing very agreeable.

28 [Tuesday]—Bd. at Brookes's—went with Hume down to Longmans &c.—made visits—to Lady Mt. Edgecomb, to Holland House where I found both Lord & Lady H.—a good deal of conversation—asked me to name a day to dine there—fixed Thursday—talking of Rogers, she complained of his having got into an entirely new set & deserted *them.* Speaking of dentists, I happened to say I must go to Hutchins, when she exclaimed "What can you possibly want with a dentist?" from which I conclude that my old grinders still look speciously. Went from thence to the Duke of Sussex's—found him at home & alone—kind & loquacious, as usual—Read me a long passage from Mandeville, about the Clergy,[1] which to a man in a hurry was any thing but seasonable. Bid me a fix my own day for dining with him & I mentioned Friday. Was sorry to find him so out of sorts with the present state of things, and still more sorry when he got on the very ticklish subject of his foolish speech, the other night respecting the Regency.[2] A good-natured man, however, all through, and most laudably unaffected and good-natured. Being anxious to hear the Opera to-night, had fixed to dine alone with Byng & his wife—He read me some curious letters from Lord Clanrickarde, who is a very old friend of his, written while he was at Petersburgh, and giving most amusing private details of the doings & the adventures of the Russian Court—an account of a masquerade, at which both the Emperor & the Empress were, fancying they were disguised both from each other & the company, and presuming on this supposed incognito, though every one knew them perfectly, and both the husband's intrigues and the wife's hovering around him & watching him were the diversion of the whole company. [A good deal more later *incomplete*] A woman who had once lived in Clanrickarde was then the great object of the Czar's pursuit. Much more lively talent in these letters than I have ever given the writer credit for. Went to the Opera—to Miss Burdett's box—the Lucrezia[3] and the new dancer Cerito, who is very pretty. Went afterwards to Miss Coutts's box,—home early, not feeling easy about my leg. Have forgot, I believe, to mention that I called upon and sate a little while with Lady Burdett in the morning—Made up my mind to go to Brodie, & wrote him a note saying that though it was like putting Hercules to the distaff to ask him to attend to such a trifling case, yet I would so far presume on his good nature.

29 [Wednesday]—Another visit from Hume, who had come in expressly to urge me to go to Brodie, and to let him accompany me, as Brodie, he said,

would like to have a consultation about it!—Poor Hume! how exactly the same man as he was in the year 1806–7, when he *would* have a finger in the pie (much to my annoyance) at a real and serious consultation held by Bailey & Woolriche on my then case.[1] Told him now that it would be quite ridiculous. He is intimate I believe, with Brodie, but the idea of his going with me to make a fuss about "consultation" &c. on such a trifle, quite angered me, and I begged him not to think of it. So he returned home re infectâ.—Went to Brodie, who received me very kindly, and made me much more comfortable respecting my leg, which I had found all broken out afresh in several places this morning—Put on a plaister which he said he had often found very beneficial. When I offered him his fee, he exclaimed "Oh no," most cordially, quite hugging me at the same time, and adding how happy he was to do any thing for "a man who is such an honour to our country"—Nothing indeed could be kinder—To Brookes's—Lord Villiers Stuart mentioned to me a young Pole who has translated parts of Lalla Rookh & who is very anxious to see me[2]—Said, if he would come some morning to Brooke's about eleven o'clock I should be glad to see him—Had called upon Bryan in the morning and told him I would dine with him—did so—none but himself & Madame

30 [Thursday]—Breakfasted at home—Went to the State Paper Office to see Lemon—sat some time with him—The Calendar for James's reign complete—showed it to me—but they have got no farther—Called at the Mintos—Saw only the young ladies & sate with them a little time—thence to Lady Elisabeth & after with her to Lady Mt. Edgecumb's, from whence we all proceeded to the Duchesse Canizzaro's Concert. (Have misplaced my memorandum of this Concert which took place two or three days before—see the preceding page under date 27)—Met there several old acquaintances—Lady Beauchamp—Mrs. Bradshaw, Lady William Russell, Lady Essex (looking quite an old woman) &c. &c.—A remarkably pretty person there Miss Gurwood—but all this I believe I have mentioned before.—Dined at Holland House, being taken by Lady E. & Horatia—Lord H. at the House—Company, Mr. Austin, Bulow, Luttrell & I forget who else—Lady H. anxious for me to sing in the evening—but I pleaded cold—Horatia played—Brought home by the Feildings.

31 [Friday]—My leg having discharged a good deal of matter, since Brodie drest it, I thought it as well he should see it again, and, calling at his house, luckily found him disengaged—Said it was going on, he thought, very well. Had breakfasted with Rogers, having taken my chance of finding him at home which I did, with a table-full of Moxons around him, and in all his matutinal good-humour.—forget what I did through the day, except drive

about with Lady Mount-Edgecombe, who is in high beauty and spirits & has just been made one of the Queen's attendant ladies—Dined at the Duke of Sussex's company, Lord & Lady Marcus Hill, two or three of the Duchess's sisters, Charles Gore & one or two other men—Sate next the Duke who was full of good humour & hospitality—Had agreed with my cabman to come for me about ten—went to Miss Coutts's Concert which consisted of purely English music—and chiefly (as far as I heard it) of English *glees.*—Among others, "By Celia's arbour all the night," my words & I beleive Horsley's music—Also my "Jubilate,"[1] which was very much applauded & encored. Saw Strangford there and his son, to the latter of whom (quite a youth) Lady Ossulston is making fierce love—their flirtation very amusing, and, as I sat behind them, her back & shoulders looked quite young enough for any thing—but when she turned round her face—alas! it wasn't even "Ancient Phillis with new graces," for the "graces" were to me full as old as herself.—Came away after the first act of the Concert.

August 1st. [Saturday] Breakfasted at Brookes's—drove about with the Feildings—Lady Mt. Edgecombe insisted upon my singing for the young Macdonalds (daughters of the late Macdonald of Clanronald who live with her) and I was very glad she did; as I had feared, from six months' disuse, it was entirely gone—but I found it come again most wonderfully, and was quite grateful to her for charming it back—the more so, as I was to dine with Lord John, where I knew I should be *made* to sing.—Company at Lord John's, the Clarendons, the Lady Mintos, Mrs. Villiers, and two or three M.P.s—. Sung most abundantly in the evening, and to all appearances with great success—Came away with the Lady Mintos who left me at Brookes's. —In talking, this morning, of the bills that are sent in, right or wrong, when one's tailor dies, Ferguson (Sir Ronald) said it was an old remark that "nothing was so dangerous as a dead tailor."}

2nd. [Sunday] {Went on the chance of finding Rogers at breakfast, but found he was at Holland House—Bd. at Brookes's. Went to Wardour St. towards the end of the Mass, and was lucky to come in for Mozart's beautiful "Benedictus"[1]—Curiously enough, too, the whole concluded with my own Jubilate,—whether impromptu, from having seen me come in, I know not.—My having been present, when it was sung at Miss Coutts's the other night (and, I find, encored) has been mentioned, I am told, in some of the newspapers.—Drove about with Lady Elisabeth & Horatia, they paying visits, and I lounging the while in the barouche enjoying the air & sunshine.—}[2] In passing through Brompton showed them the house which Bessy and I occupied on our marriage, and where at a breakfast we gave a few months after I introduced her to Lady Donegal, Miss Godfrey, Rogers,

Corry, and one or two other very old friends. "How handsome she must have been then!" said Lady Elisabeth—and she *was* certainly, in *my* eyes, *very* handsome—Dined at Lansdowne House—a dinner of men only, Lady L. being at Bowood—Company, Macauley, Lord Clarendon, Lord Clanrickarde, Rogers, young Fortescue, & Fonblanque. Sate between Macauley & Rogers, {and marvelled not a little at the confidence with which they both disserted upon Goethe, Schiller, the Greek Dramatists, &c. comparing the merits of these different poets and laying down the law respecting them with as much self-complacency as if the language and works of both Greek & German play-rights were perfectly familiar to them. How it may be with Macauley I know not—but Rogers certainly knows not a word of either Greek or German. For me, who am equally devoid of German, I should quite blush for myself if, in giving any opinion of writings in that language, I did not interpose such confessions as "judging by the translation"—or, "as far as one ignorant of the language may judge."} Of Macaulay's range of knowledge any thing may be believed—so wonderful is his memory. His view of Goethe as being totally devoid of the moral sense as well as of real feeling—his characters, therefore abstractions, having nothing of the *man* in them, and in this respect so unlike Schiller's—Such, at least, as far I could collect it was his view of Goethe—Some conversation with Fonblanque, who in speaking to me of my own writings, remarked how full of idiom they are—"There was in no writer (he said) so much idiom"—This odd enough as I told him, considering that I am an Irishman. Take for granted, however, that in saying this, he had chiefly my lighter, playful style of writing in his mind.

{3 [Monday]—Day very hot—Had promised Webster to dine with him at his villa near Richmond to meet Rogers but Lady Holland has assured me that Rogers did not mean to go & that therefore I had better dine with her—. This all to get me away from Webster, who was in great alarm lest she could succeed. Wrote her a note, and set off with Rogers, in his carriage, to Webster's—none but themselves, Boddington, Eastlake, the Painter, and another man whose name I did not learn. Their Cottage (called Little Marble Hill, I think) situated close to the river, and opposite the Duke of Buccleugh's, which I had before my eyes all the time of dinner, forming, with the boats, full of gay people, gliding past & the children playing upon the banks, a most gay & sunny picture—Liked this part of my day very well—but not the rest. Returned at night with Rogers.

4 [Tuesday]—Called upon Miss Coutts to fix about to-day's dinner—four o'clock the hour—beautiful weather only too hot—Called upon Lady Mt. Edgecombe, who told me that the Queen had given her her picture last

night, on the conclusion of her first term of attendance—Went to Miss Coutts at four, and set off with her, & Miss Meredith & Miss (I forget her name) for the Star and Garter, Richmond—found there William Banks, and Lord Templeton, and were soon after joined by Lord Templeton [*sic*]— drove in the Park, for a short time before dinner—the day most lovely, and the prospect in its highest beauty—The Marjoribanks also at dinner— walked about in the evening, and got back to town (brought by Miss Coutts) between 10 & 11.

5 [Wednesday]—Breakfasted at Brookes's—had called yesterday at the lodgings of the young Pole (Lord Dudley Stuart's protegé) and fixed for him to come to Brookes's to-day.—accordingly he came at the appointed time—a gentlemanlike & intelligent young fellow & speaking English remarkably well. Was one of those students who began the revolution, and has translated a number of my things[1]—His health drunk, he said, at one of their great meetings in Paris, as "the translator of Moore."—mentioned that several translations had been made into Polish of detailed parts of my works. Hume came afterwards—went with him to Moore's, the sculptor, who has been again tormenting me to sit to him—Lord Charlemont having ordered a bust of me from him—sat now for a little while.—rather melancholy to see him plucking off the clay curls by handfuls; so much have my poor locks fallen away since I last sat to him.—Went from thence, Hume & I to the Longmans—some talk about the Edition—Dined at Easthope's, (from whom I received before dinner £60 *squib*-money, and very seasonably it came)—Company, Villars, Joseph Parkes, Easthope's son, and three or four others—Went home & refreshed a little and then to Lady Palmerston's Ball—the last of the season, and beautiful in every respect, the house, the company, Lady Fanny & all. Saw numbers of old acquaintances, among others the Leicesters, Lady Gwyder (what is she now?) and several more

6 [Thursday]—Breakfasted either at Rogers's or Brookes's, I forget which— called upon Bryan who looked a little ruffled on finding that I had no day to give him for dinnering before I left town—Went to Miss Coutt's, by appointment, having promised to sing, if I could, for some friends of hers.—Found there the Majoribanks, Lord Templeton and a few others— Her rooms very noisy which afforded me some excuse for endeavouring to be off my promise—but they took me into a variety of other rooms, all having piano-fortes in them, till at last I fixed upon one which was quiet itself & had a quiet instrument in it. There I sate down to sing, and though it was with the greatest difficulty I could keep from bursting into tears, (so nervous had the whole operation made me), I soon recovered myself sufficiently to make *them* cry, instead. I was made to sing every song twice &

some three times. [Dined on this day (6th) at Rogers's—company the Ruthvens, the new Bishop, Thirwall (whom I liked much better than on my last meeting with him) Milnes & one or two more.][1]—

7th. [Friday] Dined at Holland House, having received a note from Lady Holland two or three days since, saying "As you stay till Sunday you may bestow another day upon us."—Taken by Rogers—Forget who were the company, except that there were three Esculapiuses, Brodie, my good old friend Woolriche and Sir Stephen Hamick—Got a little tired of the efforts at conversation in the evening, and seeing Brodie preparing to depart, resolved to take my flight along with him; though shaking in my shoes at the prospect of Rogers's ire tomorrow—Said nothing of my intention, to a creature, (except Brodie) and got snugly off.

8 [Saturday]—Must copy here the very pretty note I received from Miss Coutts, the other day, reminding me of my promise to come and sing for her. "Dear Mr. Moore—I write these few words to recall to your mind your kind promise of coming to take luncheon about two o'clock tomorrow (Thursday) *pray* do not forget it, but add another golden day to this August so that we may at any rate have *two* days in our lives we would live over again—Yours most truly &c." Forgot to mention that I called, either yesterday or the day before on Mrs. Smith (my old Dublin friend, who wrote to tell me of her arrival) and was taken there by Miss Coutts, who, having dropped me at the door, drove about a little & then called for me again—Wrote to Rogers to offer myself for dinner to-day (the last of my stay) and received the following answer, which I shall wafer in, as a specimen of his clear & beautiful writing, at such an advanced age 78, (I believe)—Not so old?

> I *do* dine at home to-day & at any time you like. You may come & go when you like. If you like, you shall find a stall at the Opera at your service or will you go for an hour to the Concerto d'Eté? Could you call here for an instant this morning—I am not going out—& you would find breakfast for two. Yours ever [*signature missing*]

I have mentioned that, on the day I dined with East-hope (the 5th.) he paid me sixty pounds—it was in a fifty pound and a ten pound note, and on my return home I put the fifty pound note in the under part of my dressing-case, and have often looked at it since—This morning, before I went out, I saw it all safe in its place, but on returning home to dress, I found to my no small horror that it was gone!—From a habit of confidence in those about me, it is only wonderful that I should have hitherto escaped so well in this & other lodging-houses. The only precaution I had taken this time was to *lock* the dressing-case—but I had been so foolish as to leave the key lying beside it!—Immediately, on discovering the loss I rang for my landlady Mrs. Durham, who apparently shocked at the circumstance, began rummaging among the few papers that remained in the dressing-case—but of course with as little success as myself—Unfortunately my having to dine with Rogers and to set off for Sloperton early in the morning prevented my taking any immediate steps—for I could not get off my engagement with him without telling him the circumstances; and of that I should never hear the end. Went to dinner, accordingly, "with what appetite I might"—Rogers had got Eastlake to meet me, and after dinner all went to the concert d'Eté,—my mind, of course, running all the time on my poor £50-note—Being *obliged* to be off in the morning, thought I had best acquaint Eastlake with the circumstance, and beg him to take such steps as might give some chance of my recovering the note—Did so—and nothing could be more kind than the interest with which he entered into my unlucky loss. Having gone through the ceremony of sitting through a part of the Concert, I got away pretty early (not without some grumpy looks from Rogers), and hastened home to pack for the morning. Mrs. Durham "quite sure I could not have left the note in my room &c. &c." but I have not the slightest doubt that I *did,*—who*ever* may have been the abstractor of it—

9 [Sunday]—Off in the New York Coach—no companion inside for a good part of the way—The Arch-*Kiddy* Craven in the same Coach with me on the Rail-road and he & I had a good deal of talk together—a cleverish fellow, in spite of his odd costume—Was joined by a young man about half-way, who, I found, had passed a good many years in Italy—turned out to be the eldest son of Reynolds, the successful play-wright—told me that his father had made nearly five and twenty thousand pounds by his plays—Found my poor Bess looking not well with *any* thing but a *visage de fête* for the gay doings we are about to have at Bowood.

10 [Monday]

11 [Tuesday]—To Bowood, Bessy and I, Lady Lansdowne having sent the carriage for us—Lord L. not yet come down, nobody at dinner but ourselves and Miss Fox—in the evening arrived Lord & Lady Barrington

12 [Wednesday] Lord L. arrived. Bessy busily employed with Lady L., Lady Louisa, Lady Barrington, & the Feildings (who arrived to day) in arranging the stalls in the Conservatory for tomorrow—Lord Barrington & I occa-

sionally employed as porters. Lady Seymour arrived to dinner—Singing in the evening from Lady Barrington & myself.—

13 [Thursday]—The grand day of the Bazaar—weather beautifully fine, and the whole thing very lively and prosperous, the receipts having amounted to more than £400—Bessy held a stall with Lady Louisa, & their joint receipts were very good—The other holders of stalls were Lady Barrington, Lady Bruce (a very nice person) Lady Elisabeth, Horatia, Mrs. Heneage & one or two others—Lady Aylesbury, and Lady E. Bruce also helped in the sale, but went away before dinner—Company at dinner, besides ourselves, the Barringtons, the Bruces, the Feildings, the Talbots & Lady Seymour—Singing in the evening from Lady Barrington, with an accompaniment of talk, all through, from Lord Bruce & "the Queen of Beauty"

14 [Friday]—The company all departed, except ourselves, and the Feildings; & Lady Lansdowne having expressed a wish that we should stay over the day, did so, and found it very comfortable, and quiet after the bustle of the preceding days—

15 [Saturday]—Came home, soon after breakfast, in the Lansdownes' carriage.

16, 17, 18 &c. [Sunday–Tuesday] A long spell of rest—no tidings of the lost note, though Eastlake and Tom Longman, to whom I wrote on the subject, have done all that *could* be done towards its recovery—I had written to Easthope for the number of the Note before I left town, and notice was given of it to the Bank. Tom Longman also took the Police to Mrs. Durham's to examine the people there, but nothing came of it—A sad loss to me, at *any* time, but particularly just now—My poor Bess having expected some money, on my return, for our little bills, and I am neither able to give her any nor can venture to tell her why, as the loss would haunt her mind incessantly—On the 21—a letter from Tom from Bristol—Set out on the 22nd to see him. [Met him coming to Bath, and turned back with him—both dined with Dr. Crawford—23 Returned home & Tom returned to Bristol][1]

19, 20, 21 &c [Wednesday, 19 August–Wednesday, 26 August]—A very civil letter, one of these days, from a Clerk in Grindlay's office enclosing me the following extract from a Calcutta paper and saying that he will have great pleasure in looking out and communicating to me any intelligence that he thinks may be interesting to me in the East India Journals—The extract is as follows:—"We hear that a son of Thomas Moore, the poet, is coming to India as a cadet. A writership for his son would, we should have thought, have been within the reach of one who has so steadily adhered to his political party, independently of his separate claims, as a man of uncommon genius. But we believe the young man has a military penchant, and preferred the charms of the Cantonment to the luxury of the Cutchery. On the arrival of Tom Moore's son, India will be able to boast that she has provided for the progeny of four of the first poets of Great Britain—Burns, Walter Scott, Allan Cunningham (?) and the author of Lalla Rookh."

27 [Thursday]—A note from Lady Aylesbury reminding me of a promise I made her at Bowood to come to Tottenham Park. She says our meeting at the Bazaar had afforded her very great pleasure, "as," she adds, "I had the satisfaction of renewing an acquaintance begun long since. So, for "auld lang syne" you must come & pay me and Lord Aylesbury a visit (which you know, you promised you would)—and as the Caernarvons are coming to us next Thursday the 3rd. Septr. pray, say you will come and meet them."— Should have liked very much to meet Lord Caernarvon, whom I think an agreeable and excellent man, but on the whole—preferred staying at home.}

28 [Friday]—Received soon after I returned from town a letter from Lord Holland sending me a translation by himself of some Italian verses (Metastasio's, I believe) which I recollect his mentioning to me when we last met. The following is his letter:—

> "Dear Moore
>   Chi ciecamente crede,
>   Impegna a serbar fede;
>   Chi sempre aspetta inganni
>   Alletta ad ingannar.

"I said I could not translate them—nor have I to my fancy. But, tant bien que mal, I have thus compassed the job.

> "Who trusts in those with whom he deals,
>   Inspires the same good faith he feels;
>   But he who still suspects deceit,
>   Tempts others in their turn to cheat.

"I have another version which perhaps renders the thought more correctly, but which seems to me, I know not why, more prosaick and more like a flat epigram than a pathetick stanza, and yet less natural and easy. Here it is, shorter than the other by two words.

> "Who trusts in all with whom he deals,
> Invites the very faith he feels;
> Who constantly suspects deceit,
> Lures those, he so suspects, to cheat.

> Tis thus I turn th'Italian's song,
> And deem the meaning is not wrong.
> But, with rough English to combine
> The sweetness that's in every line,
> Ask for your Muse and not for mine.
> *Sense only* will not quit the score,
> We must have that and a *Little More*.
>   Yrs. Vassal Holland."

29 [Saturday] {Sent a few days since a squib to Easthope "Mrs. Nethercoat"[1] I believe and at the same time begged him to remit me £30, which he did most readily and kindly—

29 [Saturday][2] In looking over a Collection of Songs at Crawford's the other day, (the day I went to meet Tom, the 22nd of this month) found the following passage in the Preface. "It was the desire of Sir Joshua Reynolds that the last words he should pronounce in the Royal Academy should be the name of Michael Angelo. The Editor will conclude this imperfect introduction by naming the men whom he reckons to be the great song-writers of our nation,—Ben Johnson, Burns and Moore." (*The Songs of England and Scotland,* published by Cochrane) He had applied to Power, as he states in the Preface, to be allowed to insert some songs of mine in his Volume, but was refused.—} Another letter from Lord Holland (about the 16th. I think, of this month) as follows

"Dear Moore—A little helped by Rogers, and a little by my own reflection, I now read my translation thus.

> Who trusts in all with whom he deals,
> Inspires the confidence he feels;
> But he who still suspects deceit,
> Tempts others in their turn to cheat.

>   Yrs. Vassal Holland

"I send you too a melancholy Epigram of which I have alas! seen many witness the truth—

"A minister's answer is always so kind!
I starve, and he tells me, he'll keep me in mind.
Half his promise, God knows, would my spirits restore;
Let him *keep* me,—and faith, I will ask for no more."

This epigram very good.—Wrote to tell him I thought so.

September, {1, 2, 3 &c. [Tuesday–Thursday]—Received a little work giving an account of Caernarvon and its neighbourhood from the Revd. Hews Bransby,[1] with a very civil note of which the following is a part. "It can be no affectation in me to say that I wish the book were more free from faults; but, in common with hundreds and thousands, I owe much to your delightful pen, and I am anxious to seize an opportunity of expressing my gratitude, and of assuring you of my sincere & affectionate respect."

4, 5, 6 &c [Friday–Sunday]—A letter from a gentleman near Leeds, who signs himself Samuel Lord, asking for my autograph—"In addressing," he says "so distinguished a person as yourself, I feel a considerable degree of diffidence; but still, from what I can gather from your admirable works, I judge I am addressing one of whose character I have formed the right opinion. I trust you will pardon me when I make bold to solicit the favour of your autograph, with a line or two of your writing to my address which will rank among the highest honours conferred upon me by men of genius &c. &c."—This gentleman mentions, in the course of his letter that "the poet Shenstone once asked to see Mrs. Jago's hand-writing that he might judge of her temper."[1]

7, 8, &c. [Monday–Tuesday] Another note from Lady Ailesbury, saying "I hope the Fates will be more propitious this time & that you *will* come to us &c. &c." Was obliged again to refuse

7, 8, 9, &c. &c. [Monday–Wednesday] Received a letter from Boston, Massachusetts, dated 14 August signed Benjamin F. Emery, Counsellor at Law, and making enquiries respecting the character of Mr. Frederick P. White, the Irish musician & poet, who, it seems has been trading on his pretended intimacy with me, in several parts of the United States, and (as I conclude from this gentleman's letter) has taken in several persons by this false pretence. "He came here," says the writer, "professing to have been your intimate friend and associate in England and Ireland, and, by strength of your name, succeeded *at first* in commanding some notice." Wrote to Mr. Emery to say that one interview with this young man at Wexford (where he seemed to be very much liked) and a letter or two exchanged between us afterwards formed the whole of my acquaintance with him.

10, 11, 12 &c [Thursday–Saturday]—Found another poem, in a female hand, among my old papers—but who was the writer—(if I *ever* knew)—I have quite forgot. Here it is:—

To Mr. Moore

Thy strain shall wake full oft again, but not,
   oh not for me,—
The billow's roll, the sea-bird's wail, my melody
   will be:
Thy strain will echo here, where now, my silent
   footsteps glide,
When desolate the place of her, who stems the foamy tide.

Thou of the deeply thrilling tone, whose touch hath power
   to shake
The slumbering chords of memory's lyre, and bid their
   music wake,
Thou that hast skill to touch the strings, broken erewhile
   and mute,
As summer-winds draw forth a dirge from some neglected lute.

Thou, at whose wand the shadows rise, from many a
   mouldering tomb,
And visions float, as visions came, ere life had lost
   its bloom;
Thou, at whose spell the broken heart, the bleeding soul,
   once more,
Arabia's balm—a gush of tears—yet once again may pour.

Thou! thou henceforth, must be to me, a dream,—a very dream,—
A thing whose very being is—alone in memory's stream;
A shade of parted splendour, like the visions fancy threw
Round youth's fair moon—so be it then!—one long, one
   last adieu.

It is rather odd that I should have forgotten who was the writer of these verses.

13, 14, &c [Sunday–Monday]—On the 17th. young Villamil, the son of our Spanish friends arrived on a visit to us.

18 [Friday]—Villamil, who had brought his guitar with him, sung for us in the evening [*MS damaged*] many of his mother's pretty Spanish Songs

19 [Saturday]—In talking of the modern French poets, Villamil quoted with admiration some lines from Dumas' Caligula, where in speaking of Christ, he says

> "Ils croyaient clouer ses mains à une croix immonde,—
> "Ma mere, ils etendaient ses deux bras sur le monde."

This couplet (which is evidently not given correctly)[1] was he said considered very fine—I dare say it is. Another "fine thing" which he quoted from Lamartine, was as follows:—

> La douce et blanche tourterelle
> N'a qu'une note dans la voix,   quy. sa?
> Mais cette note est eternelle,
> Et ne dort jamais sous le bois.
>
> C'est un souffle qu'amour agite
> Un *soupir qui pleure en sortant,*
> C'est un coeur émer qui palpite
> Une ame sans voix qu'on entende

These verses of Lamartine's by the bye bring to my mind the passage in his Méditations Poetiques, which I once parodied in the Edinburgh Review.[2]—

> "Lorsque du Créateur la parole féconde
> Dans une heure fatale, eût enfanté le monde
>   Des germes du Chaos,
> De son ouvre imparfaite il détourna sa face,
> Et d'un pied dédaigneux le lançant dans l'espace,
>   Rentra dans son repos.
> Va, dit-il, &c. &c.

———

> When the Deity saw what a world he had framed
> From the darkness of Chaos, surprised and ashamed,
>   He turned from his work with disdain;
> Then gave it a kick, to complete its disgrace,
> Which sent it off spinning through infinite space,
>   And returned to his slumbers again,
> Saying, "Go, and be &c. &c. &c."

—Two or three days since received a letter from the Music Publishers (Addison & Beale) which shows that *they* at least are not yet tired of my Songs—Inclosing to me a MS. air, they say "The enclosed melody is one which we have at last found, and think would be likely to meet with your approbation—If you are of the same opinion we shall be happy to hear from you; as we trust that many years will elapse before you publish your "last ballad."

20. [Sunday]—Received an unexpected visit from Hayward (the Quarterly Reviewer & Translator of Goethe)[1] who is on his circuit, as a Revising Barrister, through this neighbourhood—Having already planned an excursion for the following day to Bowood & Laycock in order to show those places to Villamil, invited Hayward to join our party & to dine at Sloperton afterwards.

21 [Monday]—Had a Fly, and proceeded to Laycock, having previously asked leave of the Talbots—met there by Hayward—received most kindly by the Master and Mistress & Mademoiselle Emmeline, and after partaking of a nice luncheon & being conducted over the Abbey, set off to Bowood—From thence returned all to Sloperton, to dinner, and in the evening, Villamil sung his guitar songs, and I sung a great many of my own, much evidently, to Hayward's delight.

22 [Tuesday]—Villamil left us—}

23, 24 &c. &c. [Wednesday–Thursday] Another poem has just turned up among my old papers (which I am now rummaging for to find materials for my auto-bio-graphical prefaces) equally a mystery to me [*incomplete*] Another poem has just turned up (in the general rummage I am now making among my old papers) of the source of which I am as entirely ignorant as in the instance mentioned a page or two back:[1]

"Impromptu, on their Repealing the Act against
Witchcraft, in Ireland

"So you think, then, the days of witch-craft are past,
    That, in Ireland, you're safe from the magical art;—
Those who hold this belief may rue it at last,
    When the force of a spell is found in the heart.

That the maidens of Erin in *witchery* deal,
    By those who have seen them can ne'er be denied;
While the *spell* of their bards o'er the senses will steal,
    As by some hath been felt,—and by *Moore* hath been tried.

Then think not to scape, on such dangerous ground,
    Nor fancy that magic and witchcraft are o'er,
For, in Ireland, those powers will ever abound,
    While her *Witches* are *fair*, and her Wizard is *Moore!*

{25, 26, &c. &c. [Friday–Saturday] A letter from Hayward to Bessy, speaking with great delight of his day here, & referring to what has been said of my singing in the last Quarterly—which is as follows—"The same might be said of many of our finest pieces of lyric poetry, as set to music [That poetry tells with most effect when united with music.][1] and originally sung by Mrs. Arkwright—Campbell's 'Hohenlinden,' or Battle of the Baltic,[2] for example, which certainly never fall with such a fulness of expression upon the ear or mind as when they are presented with the accompaniment. But then the music is made to play an unostentatious part, and (like Mr. Moore's songs in his own exquisite singing) it is as pieces of impassioned recitation that they please." Quarterly Review, No 132, p. 512.[3]—

Hayward bids us observe that, though expressing what he himself felt, this eulogy on my singing must have been written and printed *before* his evening at Sloperton.}

October {1 [Thursday]—A letter from town saying that Bessy's mother was dangerously ill—in consequence of which my poor Bess started for Buckhill, hoping to catch the twelve o'clock coach for town—Received a note from Mrs. Hughes saying that Bessy had been too late for the 1st. Coach, but that there was still another in which she hoped to get a seat—

2 [Friday]—Drove in to Devizes, to get Dr. Brabant or Rufa, to revise the Proof of Von Bohlen's translation of "Little Man & Little Soul."[1]—Returned to my lonely dinner

3 [Saturday]—Heard from Bessy that her mother was better & that she herself would be home in the evening—Drove to Buckhill—Found from Hughes, that Bessy had been obliged to post on (a great part of the way by herself) to the station at Faringdon—

4 [Sunday]—Bessy arrived at home, having slept last night at Buckhill.}

5 [Monday]—Still searching among old papers,—found the following verses.

"Lines suggested by the perusal of Mr. Moore's
Poem in the "Metropolitan," on receiving the gift of the
Inkstand of the late Revd. George Crabbe[1]

"And canst thou, Moore, thou gifted one,—
Each Muse presiding o'er thy birth,

Deem, mid the coursers of the sun,
　Thyself alone a Child of Earth?

Perish the thought! tho Albion mourns
　Full many a star's departed light,
To thee, with hope renew'd she turns
　To shed a splendour o'er the night.

Though hush'd in holiest, last repose,
　The "Village" bard, the rural sage,
Who sang the peasant's joys and woes,
　From blameless youth to reverend age;

Though on the northern blast is borne
　A fitful wail, on viewless wings,
And spirit-voices, plaintive, mourn
　A Master-lyre's all-broken strings;

Though He, of flight like eagle strong,
　And with delirious anguish brave,
Hath pour'd his tortured soul in song,
　And found in distant Greece—a grave;

While Poesy her choicest rays
　Concenters round thy favoured head,
We hail the living Minstrel's lays
　Nor miss the living or the dead;

Then deem not, thou all-gifted one,—
　Each Muse presiding at thy birth,—
Among the coursers of the Sun,
　Thyself alone a child of earth.

{9th. [Friday] A letter from the Doctor, saying that Bessy's mother was again in a dangerous state, in consequence of which my poor Bess had again to start for town

10 [Saturday]—To Devizes, to dine with the Hughes's, Company, the Magendies, Mr. Savage, Mrs. Seagrim, Brabant, and one or two more— Slept there—

11 [Sunday] Home after breakfast.—Called one of these days at Bowood, & lunched with Lady L. & Louisa

12 [Monday]—Drove to Bowood—found Bessy returned, worn out with fatigue—her mother had died about 3 hours before her arrival in London—Luckily she had the assistance of Moran in the arrangements for the Funeral &c.

13, 14, 15 &c [Tuesday–Thursday] The air which the Cramers sent me some weeks since not having much pleased me, I told them so, but at the time time added that if they could find me some pretty airs I should be very glad to employ myself upon them—At the beginning of this month received from them three or four tunes which rather take my fancy and which, as I told them, I shall try to turn to account.

15 [Thursday]—A letter from Hume one of these days, in which he quotes the following passage from a late work of Leigh Hunt's, speaking of my Life of Sheridan—"Life and Memoirs &c. written by a distinguished living Poet, with an information no less abundant than his wit."

15, 16 &c. [Thursday–Friday] Had intended to run up to town, as well for the purpose of seeing Brodie, as for other little businesses and commissions, and had gone so far as to arrange about my bed in Sackville St. and to take my place in the York House Coach. But some kindly urgent notes from Lady Lansdowne pressing me to stay for the party expected at Bowood, induced me to put off my journey—Received, on the 16th, the following note from her:—"Dear Mr.Moore—Cannot you put off your journey for a week? as our party will be otherwise gone before you return, and will be succeeded by one not so much to your taste,—the Bishop of Salisbury & his Clergy who come to consecrate the church—Lady Cunliffe, Lady Morley and Mr. Rogers come next week—do, revise your plans."}

21 [Wednesday]—Went to Bowood to dinner—Found, besides those Lady L. had mentioned,[1] Lord John and his children, Lady Macdonald and Macauley—The dinner and evening very agreeable—Macauley wonderful!—never, perhaps, was there combined so much talent with so marvellous a memory. To attempt to record his conversation {(or rather his monologues)—} one must be as wonderfully gifted with memory as himself—

{22. [Thursday]—Passed the greater part of the day with Rogers—Same party at dinner as yesterday—Sung a good deal in the evening, and all seemed much pleased—Macauley held out his hand to me after I had finished, and said very cordially "Thank you—this is the first time I ever heard you sing." Told him it was well I had not known this before I began, or it would have increased my nervousness—a good deal of conversation—}

23 [Friday] While I was dressing this morning, the Maître d'Hotel came to my room with the distressing & startling intelligence that Lord Holland was dead!—He had been sent by Lady Lansdowne to tell me, with a request also that I would inform Mr. Rogers of the sad news. Went immediately to Rogers's room who was equally shocked with myself at the sad intelligence—Met all at breakfast—Lord Lansdowne showed me a letter which he had received on the subject from Dr Holland, giving an account of all the particulars of the death, which took place after a short illness. My own opinion was that our party ought to separate, but I found to my surprise that both Lord & Lady Lansdowne's wish was that we should stay—Having expressed my opinion to Rogers, he thought it right to mention it to Lady Lansdowne, but her earnest wish was that we should stay, and Rogers returned to me from her crying like a child {from something kind she had said to him.} It is right to say, however, that both he & all felt (as who would not feel?) that a great light had gone out, and that not only the friends of such a man but the whole community in general had suffered an irreparable loss. {One of the grounds, indeed, on which I advised our separating, was the unfeeling appearance I feared it would present to the Public if a party met for the purpose of pleasure should remain together after such an event. Forgot to mention that Bowles called at Bowood yesterday, and was altogether much better than I expected to see him—Rogers unluckily out of the way & Bowles would not wait—The only signs of wandering I saw in him more than usual was his saying to me "How beautiful you look! you ought to get your picture drawn immediately"—He said much the same to Rogers—Poor Bowles! Same party at dinner, and both then and in the evening, one of those natural consequences took place which might have been foreseen from so large a party remaining together—We all forgot too much (at least outwardly) the sad event that had just happened, and it often occurred to me, in the course of the evening, how little a stranger ignorant of the circumstances, coming among us, would suspect how great a void had just been made in the lives of those present.

24 [Saturday]—A note from Bessy rendering it necessary that I should return home—Mrs. Hughes not being able to stay over to-night with her—Made my excuses to Lady Lansdowne—Rogers not at all pleased about it, and, with all his love for Bessy, couldn't see why she shouldn't be left to pass the night alone at Sloperton—Walked with me home, full of talk & vigour. Sate some time with us, and then walked back to Bowood—went with him part of the way. Much as Rogers has always shown an anxiety to have me with him, it has been even more urgent & restless this time than ever. The fact is, a listener who he thinks can appreciate him is quite as necessary to him as a mirror to a beauty—he wants something on which to make an

impression of himself, and receive back from thence the reflection of his own thoughts & tastes.

25 [Sunday]—Lord John came soon after breakfast to see Bessy with his two nice little children—Rogers also came with them—sate some time with us—Rogers walked back and I went a good part of the way in the carriage with Lord John—met the Shelburnes in the avenue, the first time I have ever seen Lady S.—A note from Lady Lansdowne asking Bessy to come to the consecration of the new Church tomorrow

26 [Monday] The Lansdownes carriage sent for Bessy at nine o'clock—went with her—found them at breakfast—no ticket for me, Lady L. not having expected that I would come—Sate talking with Rogers & Lady Morley—After luncheon Lord John & Lord Lansdowne walked a great part of the way to Sloperton with me.—the conversation very agreeable.—

27, 28, 29 [Tuesday–Thursday]—Sent on the 29th. a squib to the Chronicle—viz "Latest accounts from Olympus"[1]—}

31 [Saturday]—{Received from Easthope an advance of £45—} Rogers mentioned, among other agreeable things, a curious parallel found in the Odyssey to the well-known story of the Indian Chief, at Niagara who was lying asleep in his boat, just above the current of the Falls, when some wicked person cut the rope by which his boat was fastened to the shore, and he was carried down the cataract. The poor Indian, on waking up had made every effort by means of his paddle to stop the career of the canoe, but finding it to be all hopeless, and that he was hurrying to the edge, he took a draught out of his brandy-flask wrapped his mantle about him, and seating himself composedly, thus went down the Falls. The parallel to this in Homer is when the companions of Ulysses, in spite of all his precautions let loose the Bag of the Winds, and when with the same dignified composure Ulysses submits to his fate. The natural action of wrapping round the mantle is the same in both. Cowper thus translates the passage

> I then awaking, in my noble mind
> Stood doubtful, whether from my vessel's side
> Immersed to perish in the flood, or calm
> To endure my sorrows and consent to live.
> I calm endured them; but around my head
> Winding my mantle, laid me down below[1]

[Rogers mentioned his having said lately (to one of the Fitz-Clarences of some one who was sitting between Lady Wilton & Lady Mary Fox, "Why he is seated between Miss Farren & Mrs. Jordan—"He is, indeed, answered Fitz-Clarence[2]—R. remarked, in reference to his own conversation "People don't care for stories now as they used to do—there are so many Memoirs published. They don't listen to me—seem to think I am come to my *anec*dotage &c. &c."

31 [Saturday]—Young Drury, our new Curate—dined with us, Hughes being at the time staying at Sloperton

November 1, 2, &c. [Sunday–Monday]—Among the letters I received during these last few weeks was one from Byng (the husband of Lady Agnes) which rather amused me—"Dear Mr. Moore—Will you pardon my presumption in asking you to become sponsor to a Quadruped—as I am at a loss for an appropriate name for a sister to Garryone (so called from being the son of St. Patrick & Excitement) and venture to take the great liberty of appealing to the source preeminently qualified to remove my difficulty." In my answer to him I suggested either Shelah or Nora-Creina, but it seems these names have been preoccupied—"I beg" he says in his reply "to offer my thanks for your kind reception of an application which might have appeared impertinent and to express my regret that the names which you suggest are already recorded in the stud-book. Shelah has long since been put in requisition for some of the numerous offspring of St. Patrick and nobody *except* the Author of the Irish Melodies could expect that Nora Creina would have remained to this day without namesakes." &c. &c. Among the applications for autographs last month, I find the following, from a Mr. Löhr—"Can you grant the favour of your autograph to one who, whether in the quietude of a peaceful house or amidst the severe pursuits of Alma Mater, owes to the varied productions of your pen the grateful remembrance of many hours of unalloyed intellectual enjoyment? &c." Received from Moxon about the same time a copy of his Edition (in one Volume) of Wycherley, Vanbrugh, Congreve & Farquhar, which he has been so kind as to dedicate to me.[1]

Received through Ellen some time since the following verses written by a friend of *her* friend Miss OFerrall

"Lines addressed to the swan's quill
with which Mr. Moore wrote his name in Miss
OFerrall's Scrap-Book

"How little didst thou think
   Oh fair & lovely plume,
While resting by the water's brink
   That thou should'st e'er presume
To give thy gentle form
   To that high hand of fame,
And thus, with feelings warm,
   Inscribe so bright a name!
Were I a plume like thee,
   I'd with my sires have vied,
And, uttering such sweet melody,
   Have closed my wing, and died.

3, 4, 5, &c [Tuesday, 3 November–Tuesday, 10 November]

11 [Wednesday]—Went to Laycock to dinner, to meet the Shelburnes—Vivian also of the party—Sung in the evening—The Shelburnes returned at night to Bowood

12 [Thursday]—Staid at Laycock—no company but Vivian—Horatia & Mademoiselle playing beautifully in the evening—a charming Notturno of Field's which I asked them to copy out for me that I might try words to it.

13 [Friday]—A tremendously stormy day—difficulties about my getting home—at first Vivian's post horses were to take me part of the way, but on his consenting to remain over to-day, they were most anxious I should do the same; and at last Mrs. Talbot proposed going with me to Sloperton, in order that if Bessy has not yet come from Buckhill, I might return with her to Lacock—The wind so tremendous that, on Bowden Hill, I had great fears that the carriage would be blown over—Found Bessy at Sloperton, she not having gone to Buckhill—Mrs. Talbot therefore returned without me.

14, 15, 16 [Saturday–Monday]—Had sent to the Music-people (Cramers, alias, Addison & Co.) two or three of the Songs I had done for them—one of them a translation from Dante's Dream of the Two Sisters[1]—Received from them, on the 17th. the following *entoosy moosy*[2] note. "We have received the songs you were so kind as to send, and are extremely pleased with them; your translation from Dante is one of the prettiest and most successful things we have ever seen—nothing can be more chaste." A remarkable effusion this from a London Co.! and the most *poetical* part of it is their pronouncing the thing to be *already* "most successful." If the Muses thus get behind the Counter, there is no saying what will happen next.

17, &c. [Tuesday] Among the people lately asking me for autographs, one vulgar fellow begins his letter thus. "I write you, because you are a poet"

18 [Wednesday]—Bessy and I went to dinner to Bowood, Lady L. having sent the carriage for us—Lord Ebrington expected next day—forget who were at dinner, but Lord Ebrington arrived in the evening, accompanied by young Fortescue and young Romilly—

19 [Thursday]—After breakfast Bessy & I sate in the library and had a long conversation with Lord Ebrington—Told us all about Father Mathew of whose sincerity and honesty he has a high opinion[1]—the value of property in Ireland much improving—judges this as well from his own property as that of others—gave us both a most pressing invitation to accompany him to Dublin in his yatcht the 7th. of next month, and stay some time with him at the Phoenix Park. His sister also goes with him—It was not improbable, Mrs. Moore told him, that *I* should join the party and she hoped I would, but to her it must remain only a pleasant dream.—Nothing could be more hearty & cordial than the manner of his invitation—In the evening I sung a good deal.—While Bessy & I were dressing for dinner, I asked her anxiously whether she had provided herself with a nice evening cap, and she said, "Yes—I laid out eight pence halfpenny on it yesterday." This extra expence for the Lord Lieutenant was I found quite true, and though I felt a little alarmed about the result, she looked as nicely for that sort of quiet dinner (even among grandees) as need be.—There is nothing like *nature's* dignity, after all.—even an eight-penny cap can't sink it.

20 [Friday]—After luncheon, Lord L. asked me if I was inclined for a walk, and he and I and Lord Ebrington took the round of the pleasure grounds &c. and had a good deal of talk on the way—Bessy returned home after breakfast—Company at dinner the same—

21. [Saturday]—Lord Ebrington and his party off before breakfast and Lady Lansdowne brought me (*after* it) to Sloperton on the jaunting-car—a most inclement day.

22, 23, 24 &c. &c. [Sunday–Tuesday]—The following little note written I know not when by that nice girl, Clara Burdett, has just turned up from among my papers.—"I have sent the Album as I promised. A few lines of your *own* will please Mama more than a poem from any other pen.—If giving pleasure to others is pleasure to oneself you ought to be very happy, as you gave us all so much last night, and not least of any to your sincere *ammiratrice*, Clara Maria."

25 &c. &c. [Wednesday] I think I have never yet transcribed the following verses in this Journal, though sent to me some time since

> "Address to Thomas Moore, on
> his arrival in Dublin
>
> Loud be thy welcome, oh minstrel of Erin,
>   With shamrocks and myrtles thy bright path be drest!
> O'er Liffey's blue waters her joy-banners rearing,
>   Eblana breathes love to the Bard of the West."
> What bliss in a moment of hope to behold thee
>   Revisit the land of thy tears & thy songs;
> As loving, as lov'd as when first she enrolled thee
>   The saddest, the sweetest that wept for her wrongs!
> When faded the wreath that, for centuries blooming,
>   Thy own "Island Harp" in its brighter day wore,
> Like the rain-bow on rose-wood, enriching, perfuming
>   Thou gav'st it a sweetness it knew not before;
> And, snatching it forth from the Hall of its Slumbers,
>   Through the desert of slav'ry with Erin to stray,
> Like the tree in the waters of Mara, thy numbers
>   Could sweeten the bitterest fount on her way.
> Oh, bright shall thy name, through all ages descending,
>   Be blazon'd in beauty & light on her shores,
> Her poet, her lover, her annalist, blending
>   The proud fame of Erin for ever with Moore's.
> But thus, while in glory's bright halo thou shinest,
>   Though the first of her bards and historians thou art,—
> As the leaves of the rose in the centre are finest,
>   The best of thy beauties are found in thy heart.
> Then, loud be thy welcome, oh minstrel of Erin,
>   With shamrocks & myrtles thy bright path be drest,
> O'er Liffey's blue waters her joy-banners rearing,
>   Eblana breathes love to the Bard of the West."}

December 1, 2, 3 &c. &c. [Tuesday, 1 December–Tuesday, 29 December] The whole of this month has been passed in such a state of agitation, from the pressure of business, the calls of society, and last and worst, the news we received of our dear Russell's illness, that I have not had the time or the heart to record any thing in these pages, and I must now only give a hurried retrospect of the whole interval with such extracts from letters, as I can get into the few remaining leaves of this Volume. We had received most kind letters from Lord Auckland & Miss Eden announcing to us our boy's arrival at Calcutta, and their having taken him to lodge with themselves at the Government House:—The following is a part of Lord Auckland's letter dated Septr. 17, 1840.—"My dear Moore—Your letter, announcing the departure of your boy from England reached me about three weeks after his arrival in Calcutta, and I and my sisters had already been glad, in the recollection of you and of the many happy hours we have passed together, to welcome him to India. I can, as you are aware, be of no substantial advantage to so young an officer, but I have had pleasure in giving him a room in Government House for so long as he may remain in this city: and I have endeavoured to impress him with the precepts which I look upon as most important, namely, that he should study the native languages, that he should expose himself as little as possible to the sun, and that he should apply to the doctor upon the smallest ailment till he shall have learned to deal with himself & the climate. He shall have letters from me when he goes up the country & I will endeavour even at a distance to have some cognizance of his progress. He has been in all things most amiable and every one here has liked him."—Lord Auckland then proceeds to tell me of an illness Russell had had, in consequence of going out fishing, but from which he had then recovered, and adds "I have not pressed his immediate appointment to do duty with a regiment near to the Presidencies. It is well that he should remain here two or three weeks more, and perfectly recover strength; and in the mean time, the severities of our season will be passing away." In addition to this most friendly letter, there came also one from Miss Eden to Bessy containing equally comfortable & gratifying details.— By the next mail there came another letter from Lord Auckland dated October 19th. which was as follows:—"My dear Moore—your boy has given us a fright, but he is now doing exceedingly well. He was recommended change of air, soon after I last wrote to you and we sent him up the river Naper at Moonshedabad where he was hospitably and kindly received, and was for a short time without fever. But he again became ill and rather seriously so, and, at his own request, he returned to us—and ever since his return he has been daily improving, and we may be confident that, in another week he will be as well as he was when he landed here. We will keep him with us till he is quite strong, and I will do my best to get him appointed to a regiment stationed in the dry climate of the Upper Provinces. His attack here may have been accidental, but I think it desirable that he should not pass a bad season in the damp atmosphere of Bengal. For the next few months however the weather is not likely to be oppressive or unhealthy—I write these few lines at the last moment before our overland Mail goes out. Most truly &c. &c."—This I look upon to be *thorough friendship,* and such, as if I lived to the age of Methusalem, I could never forget.—In this state between hope and fear, has the poor mother and myself been left ever since the receipt of the foregoing letter, which, I must add, was accompanied by one from Russell himself, of an equally encouraging character. Still, the fears predominate with us both, and I know not that I ever have passed so painful an interval. (Written January 10th. [Sunday] 1841)

I forget what more I did in December, with the exception of the occupation which my monthly Volumes and their Prefaces pretty abundantly give me—{A remark, in the Times, respecting the first Preface that it "was more egotistical than might be expected from the good sense of the author" rather alarmed me, as giving forth from the "High Place" of the Press the very cry, respecting vanity, egotism &c. which I had both foreseen & feared from my rash launch into auto-biography—What annoyed me more, too, was Tom Longman's going (without, of course, any authority from me) to inform Barnes how much I had been disturbed by this remark. The truth is I had expressed my determination to cancel the Prefaces (already printed) to the Second & Third Volumes and give up my autobiographical scheme entirely—This of course alarmed the Co. exceedingly, but their behaviour, I must say, through the whole of the crisis thus created was both courteous & considerate—Barnes too, behaved with the utmost good-humour & cordiality, and by his most flattering article on the succeeding Volume made up (if any making up was really needed) for the annoyance his remark on the First had given me. It was done, indeed, (as I told him in a note, on the subject) both generously & skilfully.

December—30th. [Wednesday]—Went to Bowood—having received a note from Lord L, saying that he wished me to come and meet Lord Clarendon & Macauley—found that Lord Clarendon had been summoned by the Queen to Windsor and could not come—Company, the Belgian Minister, Vander-veer & his lady, the Feildings, Senior, and Mr. Dundas. Sung a good deal in the evening—

31 [Thursday]—Paid a visit to Hughes—Company at dinner the same, with the addition of Macauley, & the Milmans—Sung again in the evening.

I shall now fill the remaining space of this volume with such scraps, letters &c. as it will afford room for.—The following very liberal tribute appeared in the Times lately in the course of an Article respecting Dr. Chalmers:—"And, in like manner, while neither the Liberalism of Lord Byron & Thomas Moore, nor the Toryism of the Duke of Wellington and Sir Walter Scott has materially modified the common admiration which the country awards to those eminent men, according to their distinctive merits, we are not surprized to find that the genius & service of Doctor Chalmers &c. &c. &c."

Received the following kind offer in the course of this month—"Mr. G. T. Vigne (an Oriental traveller) presents his compts. to Mr. Moore, and having observed, for the first time, in the papers of to-day that his works edited by himself are in a course of publication, and being in possession of a complete series of drawings taken in Kashimir, has the honour of making him an offer of the free use of all or any of them, for the illustration of Lalla Rookh, provided that he (Mr. Moore) has an interest in the sale of the work."—Answered this, thanking the gentleman & informing him I had no interest in the sale of the work.

A letter from a Monsr d Foudre of Paris, accompanied by two large-sized volumes of his poetical works, and threatening a further visitation in the following words: "Veuillez les lire avec indulgence, et me permettre de prendre avec vous l'engagement de vous offrir à l'avenir toutes mes publications."}

The following *timely* suggestion is I think worth preserving:—"Sir, Previously to the publication of Lalla Rookh in the collection of your Poems now issuing from the Press, allow me to suggest what many of your readers, as well as myself would consider a great improvement—that is to versify the short introductory notice to each part. To emerge from the splendour of poetry into the vapidness of prose is a terrible damper. So pray, be propitious to this humble petition of your obedt. servt. Ignotus."

Received a letter from Mr. Dudley Costello, in consequence of my mention of him in my second Preface in which he says "By this act you have done for me what no exertion of mine could ever have accomplished—you have given me the assurance that my name must descend to posterity, and that in the most enviable manner by linking it with the associations which you have rendered immortal"[1]

{An Application from a Miss Pontigny, which her own words will best explain.—"The matter is this—One of a set of 9 Songs, composed by Berlioz, and dedicated to yourself have been given me to translate into English verse. From several expressions in the song, such as L'Isle Verte, which I take to be no other than your own Emerald Isle, which you have so often & so beautifully celebrated, together with the circumstance of the dedication, I have been led to imagine that it is probably itself a translation from some original verses of yours" She then, after some more introductory words copies the French verses which are (as she might easily have found out, without applying to me) a translation of the melody "Rich and rare"[2]—The following is the first verse

> "La belle Voyageuse
>
> "Elle s'en va seulette
> L'or brille à son bandeau;

> Au bout de sa baguette
> Etincelle un joyau.
> Mais sa beautè surpasse
> L'éclat des rubis
> Et sa blancheur efface
> La perle au blanc de lis." &c. &c

Application from a lady, the author of "the Eglantine"[3] (which she sends me) asking permission to name me as one of the patrons of her Second Volume—Consented, of course.

Received a translation into Italian of "the Last Rose of Summer"[4] done by L'Abate Giuliani at Pisa—not good

Wrote to Lord Dudley Stuart to ask the name of the young Pole he introduced to me in London, wishing to mention him as one of my translators[5]—and received the following answer—"Dear Mr. Moore—I am delighted at receiving a note from you and assure you no apology is necessary for addressing any enquiries to me on a Polish subject from *any one* or from you on *any* subject—&c. &c."

Received an odd application from an Edinburgh lawyer, dated Chambers 24 Queen St.—"Sir—At page 156 of the second Vol. of your Life of Sheridan, 2nd. Edition 1835, there is a letter quoted from Mrs. Sheridan to Mrs. Lefanu &c. &c." He then proceeds to enquire of me where this letter can be found, as it would be of much importance in establishing the claim of one of their clients &c. &c. &c—Have had some correspondence with my poor "Graeculus esuriens" of Peckham, who had requested me to join my influence with that of Lord Monteagle in endeavouring to procure for him some relief—wrote to Lord Melbourne, in his behalf, and was glad to find that our joint exertions had been of some use.[6]—"You will be highly gratified (he says) to learn that, through your endeavours, and those of other influential friends, the Royal Bounty which was forwarded to me at first in the goodly shape of £100, was shortly afterwards *doubled*."

Received lately the following curious Epistle, in a hand-writing, as odd & plebeian as its contents—"Honored Sir—I am about to publish a small treatise upon the rudiments of arithmetic, and what I want from you is a small acrostic poem, as being from the same place that had the honor of giving you birth. Honored Sir, if you condescend to do it, please direct your answer to be left at the P. Office. I give the real name as it would be useless to do any thing. I have the honor to be, Honored Sir, your &c. &c. Thomas Beham

"P.S. I enclose a postage, so that Honored Sir you will be put to no trouble, except to write it, which if you do, Honored Sir, I shall ever pray in duty bound."

A Letter from the Bristol Mechanic Institution, informing me that they were endeavouring to collect a Library, and mentioning the number of books they had already got—amounting, I think, to only thirteen, though

Grantley Berkely & four or five other such dashing politicians are among the contributors—Sent them with a civil note three or four books, among which was a nicely bound copy of Boyce's Usurpation of Buonaparte,[7] and received the following acknowledgment. "Sir—We have the honour to return you the thanks of the Committee for your valuable present volumes entitled Boyce's Usurpations of Buonaparte, which have been received & deposited in the Institution. The handsome manner in which they were presented enhances the value of the gift, which is considered a most interesting addition to our Library, and most deservedly appreciated as containing your Irish Ode in praise of the Conqueror of the Conquerors of Europe."—This ingredient of the work I was not myself aware of.

Forget whether I have mentioned that Basil Hall wrote to me to procure for him from Mrs. Arkwright a copy of the air which she wrote to some words from my Anacreon—In her letter enclosing the song she says—"It needs no letter to recall you to my recollection—What with music, poetry and never to be forgotten conversation, you are, as Mrs. Malaprop says, "like Cerberus, three gentlemen at once," laying hold of one, at [*MS damaged*] times & in all places."—} The following scrap was sent me lately by Moran, extracted from Miss Lloyd's "Sketches of Bermuda" published by Cochrane London. "I had the pleasure of being introduced to the family of Nea, celebrated in Moore's Odes. Nea is no more (dated August 16th, 1819) but she still lives in song, and in the fond recollection of her friends. From a likeness which I saw I should judge her to have been a fine woman; but it is sad that she was indebted in her fame less to her beauty than to the fascinating & easy gracefulness of her manner."—I should like to know whether they have hit the *right* Nea—though it would be rather hard for them to do so, as the *ideal* Nea of my odes was made out of *two real* ones.[8]— {Have found lately some verses written to me so far back as the year 1808, entitled lines upon Mr. Moore's declaring that he disliked singing to men." The following are the opening couplets:—

> "By Beauty's caresses, like Cupid, half spoil'd,
> Thus Music and Poesy's favourite child,
> Exclaim'd 'tis by Heaven a most terrible thing
> Thus before a *he* party to sit and to sing"

Received some time since a Volume of Sonnets with a polite note from the author, a Revd. Mr. Pulling, and left it for some time unacknowledged—till, finding it contained a very kind sonnet to myself, I hastened to atone for my apparent ingratitude by a civil letter, which has thrown the poor man into ecstacies—"To have been tolerated" he says in his answer, "by the author of such numerous works, fraught with all the beauties of composition, as well as the finest thoughts, would be no mean praise, but to have elicited from so celebrated a man &c. &c."

In a note from Moran, received about the last days of this year or the very beginning of the following, he mentions a curious circumstance (if true) respecting Mahony—alias Father Prout—a clever *Vaurien* who writes for Frazer's Magazine—"The Revd. Mr Mahony has called on me to day, in his way from Syria to Ireland, and, in the course of our talk, alluding to the Collected Edition [told] me, among other things, how sincerely he has long since recanted his errors and heresies relative to the squibs he let off at the Melodies in Fraser and other quarters"[9]

Verses by Sydney Smith
in his own hand-writing
On Robert Baldwin Printing Verses

Great was the Stink
& foul the Ink
of Baldwin printing Vapidly

Late was the hour
The Beer was Sour
The Candle burning rapidly

Runes would not come
Bob was Humdrum—
he went on writing Mulishly

But all unsold shall be the Book
& Dumb and Dumpish to the Look
of Printer printing foolishly.}

Notes to 1840 Entries

1 January

1. Hobhouse had offered Russell a cadetship in Addiscombe College, an institution owned by the East India Company to train young men for its service. See Jordan, *Bolt Upright*, 2:590, and entries for 14 January–20 February 1840, *passim*.

10–11 January

1. George Jones (1786–1869) illustrated the 1840–41 edition of Moore's works and drew some of the vignettes for the 1853 edition.

3–5 February

1. The phrase in square brackets was added as a marginal comment, with an asterisk indicating its reference to "witling bard."

6–8 February

1. Moore made two entries for the dates 6–8 February.
2. *Anthologia Hibernica; or, Monthly Collections of Science, Belles Lettres, and History*, 4 vols. (1793, 1794).

9–11 February

1. *Works*, 9:415–16.

12–14 February

1. *Spectator*, no. 606, 8 February 1840, p. 132.

19 February

1. On 1 October 1839 Macaulay dated a letter to his Edinburgh constituents from Windsor Castle, where he was staying. This pretension and his use of the phrase "first Cabinet Minister" in his speech in the House of Commons on 29 January 1840 provoked ridicule by the Tories. See Richmond Croom Beatty, *Lord Macaulay* (Norman, Okla., 1938), pp. 217–22.
2. Queen Victoria was married to Prince Albert of Saxe-Coburg Gotha on 10 February 1840.
3. Lord Kerry died on 21 August 1836.

21 February

1. See entry for 6 June 1829 and its n. 1. Mountstuart Elphinstone (1779–1859) was the fourth son of the eleventh Baron Elphinstone. The Governor of Madras, John Elphinstone

(1807–60), was the thirteenth Baron Elphinstone. Mountstuart Elphinstone wrote *An Account of the Kingdom of Caubul* . . . (1815).

22 February

1. *Descriptive Sketches. In Verse. Taken during a Pedestrian Tour in the Italian, Grison, Swiss, and Savoyard Alps* (1793).
2. *An Ode to Superstition, with Some Other Poems* (1786).

29 February

1. Jean Alexandre Buchon, *Chroniques étrangères relatives aux expéditions françaises pendant le XIIIe siècle* . . . (1840), a volume in the *Panthéon Littéraire*, 135 vols. (1835–45).
2. *Works*, 3:264–66.

1 February

1. Moore made two sets of entries for February 1840. The notes that follow are those pertaining to the second set of entries.

5–7 February

1. Minna Witte (von Mädler) published sections from Moore's *Lalla Rookh* in 1837.

9–11 February

1. Sir Thomas Noon Talfourd, *Three Speeches delivered (18th May, 1837, 25th April, 1838, and 28th February, 1839) in the House of Commons in favour of a measure for an extension of Copyright* (1840). See 1–3 May 1838, n. 5, and Dowden, *Letters*, 2:853.

15–16 February

1. A reference to the Oxford Movement (ca. 1833), which was toward High-Church principles in the Church of England.

1–4 March

1. Evan MacColl, *The Mountain Minstrel* . . . *poems and songs in English and Gaelic* (1836).

16–18 March

1. "Come, Send Round the Tay-Pot" appeared in the *Morning Chronicle* on 9 March 1840; it is a parody of "Come, send round the wine," *Works*, 3:256.

9 April

1. Russell begins this entry with the words "In town," which are not in the MS.
2. *Richelieu; or, the Conspiracy* (1839).

10 April

1. The note "see below," written between the lines, and the square brackets enclosing the passage are Moore's.

14 April

1. The passage beginning "I do not recollect" and ending "Yrs. ever, J. Russell" is encircled in the MS. An asterisk after "Mail" indicates a footnote, in Moore's hand but struck through, reading "This to be a note."

1–3 May

1. See entry for 12 November 1825. The clipping that Moore wafered in is from Benson Earle Hill, *Playing About: or, Theatrical anecdotes and Adventures, with scenes of general nature, from Life*, 2 vols. (1840). It recounts the enthusiastic welcome given Moore and Scott at the Edinburgh Theatre.

4–6 June

1. See entry for 23–24 September 1840.
2. Moore made two entries for 4–6 June.
3. See entry for 28 August 1838 and its nn. 1 and 2.
4. Lord Stanley's Irish Registration Bill limiting the Irish franchise. By Parliamentary management the government prevented this Tory measure from becoming law. See Halévy, *History*, 3:328.

7–9 June

1. See *Works*, 2:xxv–xxvi, and Dowden, *Letters*, 1:141 and note.
2. Sir Isaac Brock (1769–1812) in 1804, when Moore knew him, commander at Ft. George; killed in the War of 1812.
3. Vol. 6 of Napier's *History of the War in the Peninsula* (1840).

16 June

1. See entries for 7–9 and 10 February 1823.

5–8 July

1. Byron's *Works*, ed. John Murray (1837–40). Murray also included this note in Moore's 1832 edition of Byron (9:15–16). For Byron's letter to Dallas, see Marchand, *LJ*, 2:110.

9–11 July

1. A reference to Moore's allusion to Augustine as a Manichaean. See *Travels* (Paris, 1835), p. 103.

15–17 July

1. Edward Bunting, *The Ancient Music of Ireland* . . . (1840).
2. For an example of Bunting's jealousy of Moore, see James Corry's letter to Moore, from Dublin, 9 July 1813, in *Memoirs, Journal, and Correspondence of Thomas Moore*, ed. Lord John Russell, 8 vols. (London, 1853–56), 8:149.

27 July

1. Lady Jane Georgiana Seymour (1809–84), a granddaughter of Sheridan, was designated "Queen of Beauty" at a tournament at Eglinton Castle, Scotland, in 1839.
2. Lord John Russell's "Ecclesiastical Duties and Revenues Bill," by which large cathedral endowments would be reduced and redistributed to support a greater number of smaller livings.
3. John Gurwood (1790–1845), private secretary to the Duke of Wellington.

28 July

1. Probably Bernard Mandeville, *Free Thoughts on Religion, the Church, and National Happiness* (1720).
2. The Duke of Sussex's speech on the bill appointing Prince Albert regent in the event of the Queen's death. The bill passed on 16 July 1840. See *Parlia. Debates*, ser. 3, 55 (1840): 850–58.
3. Gaetano Donizetti, *Lucrezia Borgia* (1833).

29 July

1. See entry for 27 April 1836 and its n. 1.
2. Stanislaus Kosmian, Polish revolutionary. See the entry for 19–21 February 1844. See Eóin MacWhite, "Thomas Moore and Poland," *Proceedings of the Royal Irish Academy* 72 (1972): 53–55, for other translations.

31 July

1. Mendelssohn set the song to music. "Jubilate" refers to the refrain of "Hark! The Vesper Hymn is Stealing," *Works*, 4:169.

2 August

1. "Benedictus, qui venit in nomine Domini," from the unfinished *Requiem* (1791), or "Benedictus sit Deus," from the *Offertorium pro omni tempore* (1769).
2. Russell begins the entry at this point with the words "In London," which are not in the MS.

5 August

1. Stanislaus Kosmian. See 29 July 1840, n. 2 and 19–21 February 1844.

6 August

1. The passage in square brackets was placed at the end of the MS page, with asterisks indicating its location in the text.

16–18 August

1. The passage in square brackets was placed at the end of the MS page, with asterisks indicating its location in the text.

29 August

1. "Musings Suggested by the Late Promotion of Mrs. Nethercoat," *Works,* 9:254.
2. Moore made two entries for 29 August 1840.

1–3 September

1. James Hews Bransby, *Description and Historical Sketch of Beddgelert* (1840).

4–6 September

1. Margaret Underwood, second wife of Richard Jago (1715–81), a minor poet and friend of William Shenstone (1714–63).

19 September

1. Alexandre Dumas, *Caligula* (1838). The couplet reads as follows:

> Croyaient clouer ses bras contre une croix immonde
> Ma mère! ils étendaient ses deux mains sur le monde.
> (1. ii)

2. Alphonse Marie Louis de Lamartine, *Méditations Poétiques* (1820). The passage opens the meditation titled "Le Désespoir." For Moore's version, see his article "The French Novels," *Edinburgh Review* 34 (1820): 372. See also entry for 24 February 1821 and its n. 4.

20 September

1. Abraham Hayward (1801–84), essayist and translator of Goethe's *Faust* (1833).

23–24 September

1. See entry for 4–6 June 1840.

25–26 September

1. The passage in square brackets was placed at the end of the MS page, with asterisks indicating its location in the text.
2. *The Poetical Works of Thomas Campbell* (1832), 1:183 ("Battle of the Baltic") and 191 ("Hohenlinden").
3. The quotation appears in a review of Prince George of Hanover's *Ideen und Betrachtungen über die Eigenschaften der Musik* (1839).

2 October

1. *Works,* 3:205. Peter von Bohlen (1796–1840), German Orientalist and translator. See entry for 11 May 1837.

5 October

1. See 18–19 July 1832, n. 1.

21 October

1. Russell adds parenthetically, "Lady Cunliffe, Lady Morley, and Rogers."

27–29 October

1. *Works*, 9:268.

31 October

1. *Odyssey* 10. 59–64. See Cowper's *Homer* (1791), 2:220.
2. Rogers's joke resides in the fact that Lady Wilton was the daughter of Miss Elizabeth Farren (1759?–1829), well-known actress, and the Earl of Derby, whom she married in 1797; and Lady Mary Fitzclarence Fox was the daughter of Mrs. Dorothea Jordan (1762–1816), prominent actress, and the Duke of Clarence, later William IV, whose mistress she became in 1790. The children of the Duke of Clarence and Mrs. Jordan were given the name Fitzclarence; Lady Mary Fitzclarence Fox was a relative of the Fitzclarence to whom Rogers was speaking.

1–2 November

1. *The Dramatic Works of Wycherley, Congreve, Vanbrugh, and Farquhar,* with biographical and critical notices by Leigh Hunt (1840).

14–16 November

1. *Works*, 9:411; from *Purgatorio*, canto 27.
2. Byron wrote that John Braham, the tenor and cantor, pronounced "enthusiasm" in this way. See Marchand, *LJ*, 3:209.

19 November

1. Hugh Fortescue, 2d Earl Ebrington (1783–1861), was Lord Lieutenant of Ireland, 1839–41. Father Theobold Mathew (1790–1856) was an Irish temperance priest.

31 December

1. Mr. Costello sent Moore a goblet from Bermuda. See *Works*, 2:x, and entry for 20 March 1834.
2. *Works*, 3:236.
3. *The Eglantine; or, Annual Memorialist for 1839* (1838, 1839).
4. *Works*, 3:314–15.
5. Stanislaus Kosmian. See 29 July 1840, n. 2 and entry for 5 August 1840.
6. Spring Rice (Monteagle) and Melbourne were both active on the Pension Committee.
7. Edmund Boyce, *The Second Usurpation of Buonaparte* (1816).
8. Susette Harriet Lloyd, *Sketches of Bermuda* (1835). For the "Odes to Nea," see *Works*, 2:245–74. The models for Nea were Miss Hinson and Hester Louisa Tucker (1786–1817), the latter of whom was married when Moore met her.
9. "Vaurien": a good-for-nothing scamp (OED). Francis Sylvester Mahony (1804–66), Irish humorist and Jesuit (until 1830). In *Fraser's Magazine* and elsewhere Mahony published his own own Greek, Latin, and French translations of Moore's songs and poems as the "originals" that Moore had merely translated. See *The Reliques of Father Prout*, comp. F. Mahony (1860), pp. 131–62.

1841

[The first two pages of the MS for 1841, covering the period 1 January through 11 April, are so badly damaged that only a few scattered words can be recovered. The entries for that period are taken from Russell's edition.]

January 4th, 1841. [Monday] The Lansdownes anxious that Bessy and I should have gone there to-day; but she is in such a state of suspense about intelligence from Russell, that I could not prevail on her to leave home.

7th. [Thursday] Brabant left us after breakfast. In the evening took place the usual annual ball on this day, to the servants and tenants, which Bessy enjoyed so much last year, and would now, had not her anxiety for news from Russell prevented her from coming. I danced with Mademoiselle, and went down an Engish country-dance of fifty couple on the stone floor, no trifling achievement for a sexagenary.

From the last date till the day on which I am now writing (July 6th), a long interruption has occurred in this Journal; the first of any such length that has yet broken the chain of these records. The chief cause of this has been the monthly pressure upon me of the successive volumes of the new edition of my Works, which, slight as may appear what I have done for it, has kept me the whole time in a state of busy worry, and quite convinced me (if I wanted any such additional proof) of my utter unfitness for *periodical* labours. In addition to the responsible task of revising and correcting all my past writings, the series of prefaces which I rather rashly volunteered to write, imposed upon me a duty which, both from its difficulty and its periodical recurrence, has left me no peace nor pause; and I rejoice most heartily that I am now so near the end of it.

Among the worrying mishaps I have had lately, was the miscarriage of the MS. of one of my prefaces, after my having destroyed all the rough copy of it. Most marvellously, however, I was able to recall the whole to my memory; and on the MS. being afterwards found, I found I had departed hardly by a syllable from my original copy.

Being anxious to introduce in one of my prefaces some anecdotes about my old friend William Spencer, and our *Poluphitetic* revels together, I meant to take as a peg to hang them upon, his translation into Italian of one of my songs, "The wreath you wove;" but on consulting Frederick Montgomery, and getting Rossetti to look over the verses, I found they broke Priscian's head even more grievously than I had supposed, and were not fit to be published. It may be worth while here, as a curiosity, to preserve both Spencer's translation, and Rossetti's remarks on it; placing first the original song, of my juvenile productions.

ORIGINAL SONG[1]

"The wreath you wove, the wreath you wove,
  Is fair—but oh, how fair,
If Pity's hand had stolen from Love
  One leaf to mingle there!

"If every rose with gold were tied,
  Did gems for dewdrops fall,
One faded leaf where Love had sigh'd
  Were sweetly worth them all.

"The wreath you wove, the wreath you wove,
  Our emblem well may be;
Its bloom is yours, but hopeless Love
  Must keep its tears from me."

SPENCER'S TRANSLATION, WITH ROSSETTI'S REMARKS ON IT

"Son soavi quei fioretti[1]

[1]"Questo verso è ottonario, mentre debb' essere settenario: '*soave*' in Italiano è di tre sillabe e non mai di due.

Ch'annodasti per me,[2]

[2]"Questo verso non ha convenevole accento: l'avrebbe se potesse legarsi 'annodasti,' ma sarebbe strana parola.

L'imago degli affetti
  Però tra lor non è.[3]

[3]"Questi due ultimi versi son buoni. '*Immago*' è più usato che *imago*, che ha intanto qualche esempio. '*Non v'è*' suona più italiano.

"Perciò ch'i nostri amori[4]
  La sorte fa languir,

[4]" '*Perciò che*' non è voce poetica, nè è quella che il senso chiederebbe: '*poichè*' dovrebbe dirsi, ma il ritmo non l ammette.

Che veggia almen i fiori[5]
  Con essi impallidir!

[5]" '*Chi'io veggia*' determina meglio la prima persona ad allontana l'oscurità.

"Se l'oro i lacci fece
  La ghirlanda a legar,
Se di rugiada in vece,
  Vidi gemme cascar,

"Questa strofa non presenta netto e limpido il senso, e il secondo e il quarto verso non son ben collocati. Sarebbe stato bene che mi fosse stato mandato l'originale Inglese, poichè non son sicuro di essere entrato nell' idea vera dell' autore. Io intendo che il nastro che annodava il mazzolino fosse di seta e d'oro, e che tra i fiori sieno stati mescolate della gemme, se pure questa parola non è qui metaforica.

"Un *foglio* inaridito[1]

[1]"Se dice '*foglio* di carta' e '*foglia* d'albero,' di pianta, di fiore e parmi che l'idea esiga la seconda e non il primo.

Ch'amore pianse in su[2]

[2]"Sintassé non Italiana; sarebbe tale se dicesse, '*Su cui pianse amore.*'

Da me saria gradito[3]
  Oh quanto e quanto più!"

[3]"Se gli ultimi versi s'invertissero ne guadagnerebbe la dizione, ma perderebbe il ritmo che richiede la rima tronca al termine della storfa."

April [Monday, 12 April]—On the 12th of this month set off for London, taking up with me a part of the Preface for our next Volume, meaning to finish it in town—Arrived in London between 3 & four—As I made no memorandums during all the time I remained in town I shall here give extracts from my letters to Bessy to supply their place—

Brookes's, 20 minutes past four April 12th.—I have had a most amusing Journey of it, my companions being my old eloquent friend H{arris} of Calne (who made me laugh almost as much as you sometimes do) and our new neighbour V{ivash} who I am glad to tell you is a very nice fellow and one likely to make a very good neighbour. {He and I & his brother (the *waistcoat* fellow) have all put up at Hatchett's, and I have got a tolerable room on the ground floor. [Talbot being at Sackville St. I could not go there.]}[1]

13 [Tuesday] {Began to feel myself a little more in my element to-day, notwithstanding a most wretchedly noisy and, of course, sleepless night at Hatchett's—have within this hour moved myself and chattels to [*MS damaged*] Hotel in [*MS damaged*] where I hope to be better off—*worse* I could not be. You will be surprised to learn that poor Mrs. Bryan died

nearly a week since. The first I heard of it (for it was not, I think, in any of the papers) was from Edward Moore this morning, & I called instantly at Bryan's—but he will not yet see any body—being it seems deeply affected by his loss. I was to have dined with Lady Holland to day, but she has put me off, and I shall therefore have another lonely dinner which I don't at all like—} This morning I breakfasted at Miss Rogers's (having walked there with Rogers) to meet Barbara and her husband—Barbara herself but little altered and he seems a very excellent fellow. They pressed our visiting them in Worcestershire most urgently & kindly—{N.B. I don't know whether I told you yesterday that Lady Lansdowne mentioned some thing of a bad fall which Lady Elisabeth has had. I hope this is not the case, but you had better go or write to Lacock to enquire.}

14 [Wednesday]—You will rejoice to hear that all my fears & scruples about my Prefaces have been removed. I find they are liked exceedingly & the only fault found is my not telling enough. This is a most agreeable relief to me. My poor old friend Douglas (the Admiral) is I fear near his last breath but this last attack must have come on, I think, quite suddenly, as Mrs. Douglas and his daughters left him at his sister's yesterday, and went to the country. I saw the sisters about half an hour since and he was then insensible—but they said if he revived at all they were sure he would be glad to see me & would send for me. {After I wrote to you yesterday I had a God-send of an invitation [MS damaged] Brookes's that I had been put off by Lady Holland [MS damaged] to join his family party. This I did, and [MS damaged] him, Lady [MS damaged] their nice children to a show (the North American Indians) in the evening—All very agreeable, and the more so from being sudden and unexpected—[MS damaged] last, but *not* a *home* one.

15. [Thursday]—Sat down to catch [MS damaged] before I set off to pay a visit to the D. of Sussex, at Kensington—fearing that his long-winded Highness might out-talk the Post hour, and leave *your* Royal Highness without your letter.—Lord Auckland's letter is delightful, and must have given my own darling great pleasure—Lady Lansdowne has asked me to dine at Richmond on Sunday, but I think they would as lief be without me, being alone, and so shall not go, I think. [This turned out to be a mistake, as they had a large party of Mintos, Lord John &c.][1]

16 [Friday]—Dined yesterday at Lady Listowel's—a wedding party, her nephew having married in the morning—I am driven very hard for the corrections of my proof and must breakfast with Rogers tomorrow morning, which I fear will be the ruin of the few hours I shall have left for it.

Barbara's husband called upon me this morning, to entreat I would come see Aunt Mary when I leave London—so I suppose I must—

17 [Saturday]—Have been at work three or four hours to-day at my Preface, and have not [*MS damaged*] done with it—But on Monday it *must* go into the hands of the printer. [*MS damaged*] agreeable dinner yesterday at Burdett's—*you* were enquired after most kindly by the girls. This morning my day was broken into by a breakfast at Rogers's to meet young Jekyll and his wife. Bryan left his card with me yesterday, the funeral having taken place the day before.—To-day I dine with Rogers to go to the Opera—[Had two Operas, Grisi in one and Persiani in the other—both charming but far too much of it all for one sitting, and Rogers would not suffer me to stir till the last coup d'*anchet*, at one o'clock! Saw in coming out poor foolish Edward Moore escorting a large woman (handsome, but enormous) to whom he is acting the part of "Limberham," or the kind keeper[1] What a mistake for a plusquam sexagenarian!]

20 [Tuesday]—I was myself nearly as much shocked and surprized as you were at this large demand on my unfortunate purse [A bill drawn upon me by Tom for £112, to enable him to prosecute his overland journey to Cairo—this added to £40 I sent him to Paris! I have mislaid, I find, the sweet, thoughtful letter which my poor Bess wrote in sending me up the bill.] —but hard as it is—*dreadfully* hard with me, I have been a good deal consoled by learning that it is not sixpence more than was absolutely necessary. Immediately on reading your letter, I posted off to Grindlay's and he gave me the enclosed items to send to you, from which you will see that the expences of the journey were quite enough to consume all the money that Tom has had from me. I shall, however, be sure to impress on him strongly the heavy infliction this has been upon me. In the mean time "let not *your* noble spirit be cast down," as the song says, for I shall be able, please God, to get through all valiantly—since I wrote the above, have been out to Holland House, and to various other places—Have just been asked by Edward Moore to meet the person of all others I most wished to meet—Easthope, of the Chronicle. [Easthope could not come and had only Mills and the aforesaid lady][1] In the evening I go to the Opera or a Child's Ball at Dr. Holland's—I don't know which I shall choose—A very agreeable dinner yesterday at Lord Grey's—our company Allen, Charles Fox, Lady Mary &c. In the evening sung a great deal—

21 [Wednesday]—Hume, whom I saw to-day was very [*MS damaged*] offers have been busy corresponding all the morning and did not get out till [*MS*

damaged] three—since which I have been to Shore's Lane to the Printer's—Dined yesterday at Edward Moore's—afterwards to the Opera and from thence to a dance at Mrs. Holl[and's]

22 [Thursday]—Have just returned from Hume's Demimonde Dame, where I went to lunch and to sing—the day bitterly cold—and I began to feel a little the worse for my runnings about, day & night. It was but this morning, however, that I have given my last proofs of the present Preface to the printer—Easthope (my only hope in the *money* way) I have not yet seen. A most dreadful dinner yesterday with Bryan and Mary, Edward Moore and George being the only other guests

23 [Friday]—Dined yesterday at Tom Longman's and sung in the evening to rather a large party with great success—You will be glad to hear that I have arranged the means of settling that frightful bite. [Through Easthope who advanced me £150, for which my poor wits are now deeply pledged. Alas poor wits! To write under such circumstances is indeed (as somebody said of a situation somewhat similar) "like putting a tooth-drawing instrument into a man's mouth & bidding him sing"!]¹

24 [Saturday]—I have been for some hours looking through large volumes of the Times Newspapers, to ascertain the dates of some of my squibs and am most heartily tired and head-achy—I am getting daily into scrapes about my dinner-engagements, and, owing to one of them, shall have lost dining with the Lansdownes at *all*, during my stay, though they have asked me three times.—This morning I breakfasted with Lord John & the nice little children. He is very well and, as usual, *charming*. Today I dine with Barnes.

25 [Sunday]—Sunday—no letter—dined with Lady Holland. (Had promised to meet Lord Denman this morning, at breakfast, with the Jeffreys, but unluckily forgot it)

26 [Monday]—Thanks, my dear lassie, for your nice note of to-day. I have begun to cough a good deal and shall not be sorry when the time comes for my return to my nest. Shelbourne's is a very nice & feeling letter. [A letter he wrote to me from Avignon]¹ I dined yesterday at Lady Holland's, to meet Macaulay &c.—*all* men. To-day I dine with Lady Elisabeth—poor Mount-Edgecombe is in a wretched state, propped up in bed and scarcely

able to move hand or foot. She, in great beauty. Lady Macdonald whom I saw today, in speaking of Russell, said that to have the fever soon after arriving she thought rather a good thing as it seasons people.

27. [Tuesday]—I think I can now tell you something of my plans—Barbara & her husband were so very anxious I should come for a day or two to see Aunt Mary, that I promised them most decidedly I would, & that I should go to them from London. From my stay here however having been longer than I expected I cannot manage the visit in this way being obliged to go directly home for the purpose of getting through the Preface to my [*MS damaged*] volume. I shall therefore write to them to say that they may not expect me [*MS damaged*] weeks—and if *you* could make up your mind to join me in the visit, it would be very *nice*. My present intention is to set off for home on Sunday next [*MS damaged*] the Lansdownes can [*MS damaged*] dine with them on that day I shall put off my departure till Monday. The sudden opening of summer upon us has set every body perspiring, and has made me throw off my great coat. I have just now, to-day been driving about in an open carriage with Lady Elisabeth which (added to the throwing off the great coat) was rather hazardous. I called to-day in Buckingham St.—but found only Anne—the rest of the family having gone to see at some milliner's the bridal [*MS damaged*] of Lady Fanny Cowper, whom by the bye, I surprised on Sunday last, at Lady Palmerston's in the midst of her marriage bustle and had a most cordial shake of the hand from her. The marriage is the great town topic now. To-day I dine with Murray to meet a party of Quarterly Reviewers. [A note from Empson, in the course of that day, after mentioning Denman's disappointment at our not meeting, adds "His feelings towards yourself are quite in accord with those which you expressed respecting him the other evening. He is exposed to so much unjust censure that the good opinion of those on whose opinion he sets value is a great gratification to him"]] [1]

29th. [Thursday] {Soon after I received your nice note this morning, I called at the Lansdownes, and saw Lady L. and Louisa—the latter professing to be very well, but looking wretchedly, and Lady L. herself suffering very much from rheumatic pains—I offered [myself] for dinner on Tuesday next, but Lord L. is engaged from home on that day so [*MS damaged*] I shall go away without dining there— . . . To-day I dine with Charles Fox, having been asked to a variety of other places. Yesterday's dinner was at Murray's, where we had the Milmans, Lockhart, Coleridge,[1] and a curious Parsee (from Russell's country) who would have amused & interested you.} Went {from thence} with the Milmans to {keep} Miss Berry's last soiree for the season. [On my saying something to Miss Berry of the liberty I had taken, [as] an old friend, of coming there unasked, she reverted, in her odd way, to the early days of our acquaintance, and said "I didn't so much like you, in those days. You were too—too—what shall I say?" "Too brisk and airy, perhaps," said I.—"Yes" she replied, taking hold of one of my grizzly locks, "I like you better since you have got these." I could then overhear her, after I left her, say to the person with whom I had found her speaking "That's as good a creature as ever lived."][2]

[30 [Friday]—I had been led by the hope of meeting Croker to promise to dine with Lord Oranmore to-day, but finding Croker could not come have succeeded in freeing myself from this out-of-town dinner, and shall dine with Lady Holland instead. (Went in the evening to Lady Vincent's, & found there the Caernarvons, Seftons &c. &c.)

May 1. [Saturday] A very agreeable day yesterday at South St.—Lord Glenelg, Jeffrey, the Charles Fox's, my old friend Woolriche, Rogers &c. &c.—To day I am to dine with Lord Ducie, [The company at Ducie's, Lord & Lady Caernarvon, Lady Clinton, Lord & Lady [*MS damaged*] Lord Dalmeny, Lord & Lady Sherburne—also the handsome daughter of my old friend Lord Decies.—Memorandum—"Ghosts?—oh, there are quantities of them in Suabia"—"Doing his master's business by his mistress's orders"][1] and tomorrow take my parting dinner with Rogers. (Met at Rs. Lady Wm. Russell, Lady de Dunstanville &c.)

May 3rd. [Monday]—Returned home to Sloperton—so that here my extracts from the Letters cease.

A month or two before the visit to town of which I have here given some memorandums, a sad event in the family of the poor Lansdownes (the death of Lady Shelburne) had taken place. It would have been difficult to select a young person more formed in every respect, to make Shelbourne himself and all belonging to him happy; and to Lady Lansdowne particularly the loss has been most sad and trying. A few weeks before I went up to town she came to call upon us (her first visit to any one since the funeral and while she sate with Bessy in the drawing-room Shelbourne walked about in the garden with *me*. I could see he was labouring with something he wanted to say or ask of me, and at last out it came that he was anxious I should sing for him at the Piano-forte that most melancholy of all my songs "There is a song of the olden time."[1] The request startled me and, though, seeing how much he had set his heart on it, I quite grieved to be obliged to refuse him, I yet felt, as I told him, that neither of us would be just then able to bear that song. With a good deal of [*MS damaged*] and sweetness he told me how much he had set his heart upon hearing it, and the only way in which I was able to get off from what I knew would lead to a painful scene with us both, was by assuring him that I would, before long, comply with his request.

4, 5, 6 &c. &c [Tuesday, 4 May–Monday, 31 May]—Occupied with my Preface for the June Volume of the Work.}

June {1, 2, 3, 4 &c. &c. [Tuesday, 1 June–Sunday, 20 June]}

21st [Monday]—Set off on my long-promised visit to the Godfreys in Staffordshire, taking Cheltenham and Corry in my way—started by a coach, thinking I was soon to have rail-way, but found I had got into "the wrong box," and after an accident with our horses which delayed us at Chippenham more than an hour, had nothing but coaching all day and did not arrive at Gloucester till between six and seven in the evening—Was most lucky, however, in the weather and would not have lost the succession of beautiful scenes I passed through for twice the speed of the rail-way— Took the Mail at Gloucester and got to Cheltenham between eight & nine— not having had any thing for twelve hours except a biscuit & glass of sherry during our stay at Chippenham—{Despatched a note to Corry & had some mutton-chops & ½ pint of sherry at the Plough which were like nectar and ambrosia to me—Went to Corry's, who, I found had no bed for me, so passed a miserable night at the Plough, all my kit having been locked up & made unapproachable till morning.}

22 [Tuesday]—Going about all day with Corry, his sister Connelan, and her very gentlemanlike & agreeable son, seeing all the pretty places of this most beautiful town and neighbourhood—{Among other things went to see Lord Northwick's pictures, of which it may be said, as of most collections, "Sunt bona—sunt quaedam mediocria, sunt mala plura"—the latter class, however, as usual, predominating—}Dined with Corry & Connelan at Mr. Ramsay's (whom I had never before seen) brother to Lord Panmure—a small party and the daughter of our host, pretty—which was at least something to look at—Sung a good deal in the evening for them—

23 [Wednesday]—Started by rail-road for Hughes's—a good story, by the bye, of Williams's (the Circulating Library man) of a stranger passing through Cheltenham, who wishing to devote the few hours he had to stay there in visiting the scene of the Great Battle of Worcester,[1] walked out there alone and having enquired of some man he met as to the spot on

which the battle had been fought was accompanied thither by this person who at once entered, with much communicativeness, into the subject of his enquiry—showed him exactly where the battle had taken place—mentioned how soon the first blood was drawn & quite delighted the antiquarian with the minuteness of his historical knowledge—"It was certainly a great battle" exclaimed the latter—"Oh wonderful, Sir," answered his informant—"nothing but Spring's wind could have carried him through it." {With my usual luck encountered in the rail-carriage, an old fellow-collegian, Peacock, who had forgotten me (being so blind, however, as to be obliged to use an opera-glass) till I mentioned my name to him—Was a furious Orangeman, I recollect, in old times—Invited me most cordially before we parted, to come and pass some time with him at his living when I next visited Ireland—} Had received a note from Barbara to say that I should find Hughes, her husband, with the carriage for me to Wolverhampton—and there he was.—Poor Mary Godfrey much affected at our first meeting—she has lost the use of her limbs, but in all other respects is as much herself as could possibly be expected, after such a lapse of time—{Philippa, though so much younger, looked much more altered—The Hughes's children charming little things, both girls.

24 [Thursday]—Walked with Hughes toward Ward's—found Mrs. & Miss Ward, and also the tutor who is about to marry the young lady—The present noble proprietor is, it seems a "most heavy declension," (in all ways except wealth) from the last one.—Had a pelting thunder-storm, coming back. Another comfortable & cordial dinner with my dear old friends—sung for them in the evening most of their favourite old songs. I forgot to mention that at the Wolverhampton Station yesterday I saw Cavendish & Lord Levison, just arrived from town, and the latter asked me to come to his house (not far from this) for a few days—promised him I would, but the weather looking threatening, and the operation of getting to [*MS damaged*] rather troublesome (my host having to drive me to Bridgeworth, where Levison's carriage was to meet me), I gave up the expedition, and wrote him an excuse, though rather sorry to do so as I like himself much, and hear his wife is a nice person.

June 25 [Friday]—Driven by Hughes to Wolverhampton & from thence railed it to Cheltenham—Found Corry to whom I had written to announce myself—dined and slept at his house—

26 [Saturday]—Set off, Corry & I, by rail-road—he to proceed to London, I, home—Met Lord Lansdowne, just arrived from town, at Chippenham—

wanted me to go on with him to Bowood, but, having ordered my fly, did not—Sorry to see him looking far from well—found Bessy and her companion Bessy Power (who has been on a visit with us for some time) not expecting my return—the letter I wrote from Cheltenham not having yet arrived.

26, 27 &c. &c. [Saturday–Sunday]—Received lately from a Frenchman (of Falaise) rejoicing in the name of Cephas Rossignol, the following note accompanying a Volume of Poems.—"Je vous addresse, avec prière de vouloir bien l'accepter, un livre de poësies que j'ai publié sous le titre de *Dieu et Famille.* Puissé—je apprendre que ce livre a été lu par vous avec une partie du plaisir que j'ai eu lisant vos belles poésies—Je le désire, mais j'ose peu l'espérer—&c. &c—"

28, 29 &c. [Monday–Tuesday] A very flattering article in the last number of the Dublin Review on my Poetical Writings—find by a scrap of paper which accompanied the copy sent me that the author is a priest.[1]—The following odd note from a lady who signs herself Comtesse de Verpucis reached me lately written under the impression that I was, at the time in town. C'est a l'hasard que je dois le plaisir d'avoir faite votre connaissance—cet [*MS damaged*] me favorisait'il une autre fois? Hélas! d'y conter serait folie. Il aime donc mieux de courir au moyen le plus [?sur], celui de vous prier directemen[t *MS damaged*] Etrangere je desire connaitre tout ce qu'il y a de supéri[eur *MS damaged*] & du [*MS damaged*] cette vaste et c'est donc tout naturel que [*MS damaged*] demande la faveur de renouveller votre connaissance. Si vous êtes matinal, voulez [vous] avoir la bon[té de ve]nir partager mon dejeuner dimanche matin vers les 10 heures—Je vous fais [*MS damaged*] sans cérémonie et dans le seul espoir d'avoir le plaisir de prolonger votre visite—Comtesse de Verpucis}

July 1, 2, 3 &c [Thursday–Saturday]—Have just found the note my poor Bess wrote to me in sending up to town Tom's bill upon me for £112—"I can hardly bring myself to send you the enclosed—it has caused me tears and sad thoughts—but to *you* it will bring these and hard *hard* work. Why do people sigh for children—they know not what sorrow will come with them. How *can* you arrange for the payment, and what could have caused him to require such a sum? Take care of yourself, and if you write to him, for God's sake let him know that it is the very last sum you will or *can* pay for him. My heart is sick when I think of you and the fatigue of mind and body you are always kept in. Let me know how you think you can arrange this." I have already mentioned the difficulties to which the Bill of Tom's reduced me, and I had not been more than a week or two at home, when another Bill of his drawn upon me at three months, for £100 was sent to me for acceptance. This blow coming so quick after the other was, indeed, most overwhelming. It seems, on his arrival at Bombay he found that his regiment had been ordered on active service, and he was accordingly obliged to provide such an outfit as would enable him to join them. I could not do otherwise of course than accept the Bill, but how I am to pay it, when due, Heaven only knows—The following note from the Priest who wrote the Article in the Dublin Review on my Writings,[1] reached me about the beginning of this month—

"Respected Sir—It gives me the sincerest pleasure to find that you are pleased with the short article in the Dublin Review on your writings, for I feared very much that, from my slender acquaintance with English literature—especially the poetical part thereof, I could hardly produce any thing that would not be unworthy the subject. What you are pleased to term the "overplus of praise" was certainly not meant or believed by me to be such. The little I said of your Irish Melodies & Humourous Poems falls short of what I conscientiously think of their merits—especially as regards the Melodies—Allow me to add that I feel highly honoured by your kind note, and by the too flattering wish you express of knowing me personally. It is many, many years since I first longed to catch a glimpse of Thomas Moore. Circumstances which have occurred within the last month oblige me to delay the article which I promised on your Histy. of Ireland, and which I would not have thought of undertaking but for the earnest request of that most pious and most learned of prelates, Dr. Wiseman. The same circumstances compel me (sorely against my inclination) to wear my mask till next autumn. I shall then eagerly seize the first opportunity thus so unexpectedly offered of gratifying one of the warmest wishes of my earliest years. In the mean time, I have the honour to be most respectfully, your faithful servt. Author of the Art. on Thomas Moore."

{Have been looking over some of the notes I received while in town last, and found several from poor Lady Holland showing rather painfully the sort of monomania that haunts her on the subject of dinner-giving —it [*MS damaged*] whole object & thought, and the sending notes in all directions to attract guests for the succeeding day is her sole occupation and solace. I have found four at a time from her awaiting me. Sometimes they say she cries through the whole of dinner. What a singular state of mind!—reminding one a little of some doggrel lines (I know not whose they are)

> Sometimes a sob of grief and then "some mustard"
> And now a sentiment and now—a custard

One of her first notes to me after my having [*MS damaged*] her was as follows "My dear Mr. Moore—I was so charmed at having the earliest opportunity of seeing you that I proposed your dinner here tomorrow, tho you have agreed to Wednesday—Alas! in my eagerness I quite forgot that my table was too full. I omitted Charles and Mary in my list and they come to meet the bishop, his former tutor. So, my dear friend—let me beg you to come as originally settled, Wednesday—Thursday, Friday, Saturday, are all free days. Forgive me and join in regretting my annoyance"

In another note she says, on my volunteering to dine with her—"With the greatest pleasure I shall receive you tomorrow, Sunday—fix also some other day & evening with me—it is the only solace, the seeing friends."

The following note from Rogers, which I received the day before [*MS damaged*] for town, is so characteristic of him in every way—of his neatness, his alertness, his hospitality, that I shall preserve it here in statu quo—

My dear [*MS damaged*]

I need not say what pleasure your letter has given me—All enquire when will he come—& come you must—why not to me? But come you will no doubt to Sackville St. You do not say when. To-morrow I go to the Deepdens for 2 days. Barbara Hughes is in town for a few days—Lady Holland talks of going to Holland House on the 17th for a few days—Pray come & stay—My love to Psyche—Tell her to come too—I hope she is well as you don't say No. Sidney is in great force & [*MS damaged*] & Jeffrey—

Yours as ever,
S. Rogers

April, 1841

Had a letter about a month or two since from Shelbourne, in allusion to that song of mine which still seems to haunt him. He dates from Avignon— "I was very much disappointed at leaving England without seeing you again, and claiming your promise about that song—It is foolish, I dare say, to care so much about it—but I had quite set my heart upon hearing it. There is something to me so soothing both in words and air that I cannot express to you how much I feel it—particularly when sung by you to whom I have been attached from childhood by bonds of the greatest kindness on your part, and gratitude [*MS damaged*] as well as admiration on mine. You will be surprized, I dare say, at this effusion from me, but I could not help writing a few words to say I should still claim your promise when we meet again, and recall myself to your recollection and dear Mrs. Moore's."

Such tributes as the following gave me the more pleasure from being rarely bestowed upon that barren and outlawed section of my literary labours, the poor History of poor Ireland

Beaumont, Cork
April, 1841

Dear Sir—Allow me to offer for your acceptance the accompanying [*MS damaged*] little work which, from its connexion with the National Labours which have been lately [*MS damaged*] unworthy of your perusal—and I gladly avail myself of the opportunity thus presented me to express the high respect & utmost [*MS damaged*] I entertain for [*MS damaged*] and historian—I have the honour [*MS damaged*]

The work of this gentleman, which, as [*MS damaged*] as I have had [*MS damaged*] appears to be learned & interesting, [*MS damaged*] my History.

Have just received the following jeu d'esprit from Dr. Holland, which he copied out for me when last at Bowood—Why he says "after Prior," I know not—unless he means after the manner of Prior

"After Prior"

Mentor to Jack, on [*MS damaged*]
Cries "[*MS damaged*] of knowledge;
"Now get a living and a wife,
A child and you are snug for [life."]
Some winter past he meets the [*MS damaged*]
"Why, how now, Jack? and why [*MS damaged*]
I gave you good advice"—"tis true,
That good advice I followed, too.
"With one small difference, worthy friend,
"That I begun at t'other end;
First, got the child—then married Bet,
"But, for the living,—that's to get."

About a month since received the following communication from Brabant (who is at Hamburg) through his daughter Rufa

"My dear Mr. Moore—In a letter I have just received from Papa, from Hamburg, he says 'At a very large dinner-party of professors, Doctors, Parsons &c. I met a very intelligent physician from Transylvania. He spoke of Mr. Moore, and has given me what I enclose—pray translate it and send it to Mr. Moore' "—Here follows Rufa's translation—"Johann Schüller, Rector of the Gymnasium in Hermannstad, has very beautifully translated a considerable number of the Poems of Thomas Moore into the German language. These translations are to be found scattered in the Siebenbürgen Wochenblatte published at Koonstadt in Siebenburghen—also in two distinct volumes published at Hermanstadt in 1830 (second Edition) and lately in 1840.[2] These poems so admirably rendered by Schüller excite universal admiration and delight—June 16, 1841."

Among the tricks of people to get a letter from me, the following worth selecting for the bare-facedness of its pretence

"5 Porland Place, Southwark.

"Sir—Being altogether unacquainted with you personally, I have to apologize for the liberty I am taking in troubling you with the accompanying request. I have just become connected in the publication of the life and papers of an individual, lately deceased, of considerable celebrity. Such a pursuit is quite foreign to what have been my usual avocations and aware of the valuable experience of the biographer of Lord Byron in such matters, I am bold to ask the following favour of him—Would you give me, when your leisure will permit a brief sketch of the plan best to be adopted in commencing such an undertaking—[*MS damaged*] This modest gentleman subscribes himself my "sincere admirer, [*MS damaged*] More." I have already mentioned [*MS damaged*] of the [*MS damaged*] write to her—I did so, of course, and [with] as much brevity as was consistent with good breeding, saying that I had heard of [*MS damaged*] possessing all those qualities which ought to adorn that woman [*MS damaged*] Princess [*MS damaged*] the Woman her proper precedence over mere Royalty, which, [*MS damaged*] writing [*MS damaged*] of the Revolution was, I think, all right. So long an interval, however, elapsed before any notice was taken of my letter that I had nearly forgot both the woman and Princess when the following gracious note arrived—"Je mets un [*MS damaged*] Monsieur, à la lettre flatteuse que vous m'avez [*MS damaged*] et que je dois [*MS damaged*] doute á ce que Mr. Cowell, vous aura dit de Mons. [*MS damaged*] pour vos ouvrages. Je la conserverai comme un témoignage flatteur pour moi, et elle enrichera d'un nom bien célèbre une collection déja précieuse, ou le souvenir du Barde d'Erin sera placé à cote d'illustrations [*MS damaged*] par lui.—Je désire qu'une circonstance m'offre l'oc[casion *MS damaged*] vous remercier moi même; on dit que l'homme amiable n'a rien [*MS damaged*] au poète, que sa societé est de celle qu'on recherche avec empressement et si j'allois en Angleterre je me ferois un droit de la lettre qu'il m'a ecrite pour réclamer le plaisir de vous connoître—Recevez je vous prie, Monsieur, l'expression de ma considération la plus distinguée, Stephanie."

7th. July [Wednesday]—Was surprised by a visit from Sir Francis Burdett, accompanied by Starkey—He is come down about his election, and stays at Southron's—A good deal of conversation—was rejoiced to see him looking so fresh and well—

8, 9, 10, &c. &c. [Thursday–Saturday] Occupied a good deal, about this time, with the general Index to my volumes, which the Longmans have got their regular practitioner in this line to construct, and a rare fellow he must be in other lines as well as his own. "These charming Poems" he says (meaning *mine*)—and under another head alluding to the pun on St. Joachim, in the Second Preface, he describes it as "a pun by the author's susceptible imagination"[1]—The introductory part about the Duke of Wellington begins thus "The Duke of Wellington, pugnacious"—No book could have survived such a tail to it—of course, I lopped away most abundantly—

11, 12, 13 &c. [Sunday–Tuesday]—A letter from Mr. Gilmore dated "Fairy-Mount-Ballynacarrig," containing specimens of his poetry, and requesting my opinion—Answered civilly, but dissuaded him from losing his time in rhyme—

14, 15, 16 &c. [Wednesday, 14 July –Thursday, 22 July]—An invitation from Mrs. Walter Long to come to Rood-Ashton, and offering to send the carriage for me—which left me without any excuse. Met her at a Ball at the Coulsons.

23 [Friday]—To Rood-Ashton—A good merry party at dinner—among others Mr. & Mrs. Ray—sung in the evening as did also Mrs. Ray

24 [Saturday]—Brought home after breakfast by Mrs. Long, driving her [*MS damaged*] little poneys up hill &c. &c. [*MS damaged*] fearlessly—the day very [*MS damaged*] Bessy not at home, but they remained some time looking [*MS damaged*]. Forgot to mention a grand Ball we had at the Coulsons a rich and odd family not long come into the neighbourhood—Bessy and I and Bessy Power (who has been some time on a visit with us) joined the gay crowd there, to the great amusement of both Bessys—my sweet wife looking almost as handsome as in her younger days, and mixing in the country dances with great glee—Met there a very old acquaintance whom I had not seen for ages, Lord William Somerset (Uncle to the Duke of Beaufort) who with wife & children has been for some time on a visit at the Coulsons—A great deal of talk with him about the London life of other times when (be it said with all respect for his *present* [*unrecovered*] he was as thorough a pickle and scamp as need be—Spoke with great interest about John, the old money-lending waiter at Limmer's, who, he tells me was still alive & flourishing and to whom he always pays an affectionate visit when he is at London}

{[Sunday, 1 August–Monday, 9 August]}

10th [Tuesday]—A visit from our friend Philip Crampton who kindly made an effort to give us one of the few days he had to spare during his short English trip. His first intention was to come down by rail-road, eat an early dinner with us, and then return by another train so as to accomplish his other dinner-engagement in town. This feat, as being one worthy of his dash and activity, I was rather anxious he should perform. But, as it was, we had longer enjoyment of his society, and in addition to the pleasure of having him for a night under our roof, he gave most cheering assurances as to the state of Bessy's health. After a long conversation with her on the subject of the attack she had {(a discharge of blood from the stomach)} two or three years since, he assured me that her health was, he thought, improved and certainly much better than when he last saw her, about ten years ago. This all very delightful to me to hear. Sate talking together till a late hour.

{11 [Wednesday]—Crampton left us soon after breakfast.}

18 [Wednesday]—Having arranged with Hume to take a short trip with him to Ireland started for Lacock Abbey this morning on my way to town— The day beautiful—and I found grouped in full sunshine upon the grass before the house, Kit Talbot, Lady E. Feilding, Lady Charlotte & Mrs. Talbot, for the purpose of being photographed by Henry Talbot who was busily preparing his apparatus—Walked alone for a while, about the gardens, and then rejoined the party to see the result of the operation—But the portraits had not turned out satisfactorily nor (oddly enough) were they at all like; whereas a dead likeness is, in general, the sure though frightful result—{at least,} of the daguerre process.—The evening agreeable— {even Kit Talbot *won* upon me exceedingly}

19 [Thursday]—Breakfasted comfortably (thanks to the rail-road) at ten o'clock, with Mrs. Talbot only—the rest of the party being in their bedrooms—and then set off in their covered cart to Chippenham, from whence I started in the 12 o'clock train Was lucky enough to have Paulet Scrope for my companion, who was very agreeable—took up my quarters in Sackville St—Called on Rogers, who had nearly finished a solitary dinner—wanted to have more dressed for me but I made my escape & called at Burdett's who asked me to join him & his daughter Johanna at dinner—But this did not look very promising, and I declined. Thought then of Bryan, who it was probable I should find returned from Ireland, and an evening with him would be at least doing my duty; but I found (though expected today) he was not yet arrived. It was now past seven o'clock and my chances of getting any thing better than a solitary cutlet at Brookes's had become desperate. Resolved however to go and leave a card at Lord John's before I turned in for my cutlet—Lord John not at home—but I had hardly given in my card and resumed my seat in the cab, when the servant looking out, said "Here's his Lordship coming, Sir." "How long have you been in town?" asked Lord John—"About an hour or two"—"Then you can dine with *me?*"—"Why, I've not dressed, and it now past seven o'clock"—"Oh we shan't dine till near eight, and you've got a cab"—So I instantly took the

hint, jumped into my vehicle, and in the course of about an hour found myself seated at table with a large party of Mintos, Russells, Villerses, amounting to about fourteen or fifteen in number—Sung abundantly for them in the evening, and was made to repeat several of the songs—{one of the party was a young brother of Lord John's, a sailor who came to me in the hall when I was taking my departure, said how glad he was to make acquaintance with me, that he was going immediately to be married and was sure that I would approve of his choice.}

20 [Friday]—{Breakfasted with Rogers—Hume has put off our departure which gives me a much longer time in London, and enables me to accept an invitation to dine with Maido-[*MS damaged*]—Had a note from Lord Lansdowne asking me to dine with him to-day, "Will you also do so frisky a thing as to go with me afterwards to take [*MS damaged*] party to Vauxhall?"— Performed some commissions, but did *not* go to the Longmans, not being in very good humour with them—I had before I left home written a sort of appeal to them on the subject of the Prefaces which I had volunteered for our new Edition asking whether it was not their intention, (in consideration of this help to the work) to make some addition to the sum originally agreed for it, and citing, as a precedent for such an after-thought, their own example in the instance of my Life of Sheridan, when in consequence of the success of the work, they of themselves added £300 to the sum already agreed for. Their letter, in reply, though I dare say all right in their own view of the matter, is both disappointing to me and not very creditable to *them*—In short as Rogers said on the subject, "They are a shabby set of fellows." I may however be doing them injustice—[*several words unrecovered*] Rogers walked out with me, and as usual, [*several words unrecovered*]—} Went to the State Paper Office and sate for some time turning over the Calendar for Elizabeth's reign to see what sort of task I had before me—Dined at Lansdowne House, company, Lord Minto, Lord Ebrington, Lord Seymour & one or two more. From thence to Vauxhall with Lord L.—as I told Bessy, in my letter, "we went to Vauxhall like a couple of young rakes as we are and found it very bright and pretty though I so far forgot my character of rake as to wish for *you* there"—

{21 [Saturday]—Breakfasted with Rogers—who *would* afterwards take me on a course of Panoramas with him, though knowing it was my last day for the various Commissions I had to despatch—I was to meet Hume too, at a little after one to arrange for our departure on Monday—but in vain did I tell him all this—he *would* take me first to Damascus then to Jerusalem, and so on, asking particulars of the showman about every mosque and gateway—not that he cared one pin about the things himself, but for the mere pleasure of exerting power and preventing *me* from leaving him—At last my time for meeting Hume was within a few minutes, and I fairly balked, running all the way to Brookes's—but I was too late—for he had been already there to his [*MS damaged*] but was obliged to go off by the Hanwell train.—Went to Miss [*MS damaged*] party and nothing could be more welcome to me after my worry. [*MS damaged*] that I should dine with him which I agreed to most willingly—[*MS damaged*] Penn, and one other guest whose name I did not hear [*MS damaged*] description of him as "the pen often cut but never [*MS damaged*] and [*MS damaged*] whether we have ever met in society since that well remembered night at Hampstead House when, after a great Ball there the male part of the company remained at supper for a good while after the Ladies had left us, and Penn who had got exceedingly drunk, was made the butt of the whole party. The door of the room had been locked to prevent him from escaping, and I have him now before my eyes, as he faced round upon us with that odd phyz of his—his hands in his breeches pockets & his cocked hat (which he had put on hind part foremost) flapping over his eyes, while the young Stanhopes kept shying oranges at him most profusely—The best part of the joke, however, (as Penn was then, and has been ever since, a great pretender to literature) was their lifting him onto a hackney coach, when he had fallen down insensible in the hall, and desiring the coachman to drive him to Lackington's, the Temple of the Muses in Fensbury Square—adding gravely that he was young Mr. Lackington, and that the coachman must deliver him safely into his father's hands.—What was the final result of this farcical joke, I know not, but it came strongly to my recollection as I sate looking at him during dinner.}

22 [Sunday]—Breakfasted at Rogers's, with a very amusing party, Milnes, Kenny {[*MS damaged*] fledged poet of Rogers's hatching whose name I forget,} and somebody else. {Rogers most kind at our parting—}Wrote a letter to Bessy and sent it as a parcel (this being Sunday) in order that she may have a little treat tomorrow—{Find the following in looking over my letter to her, which I have now before me.—"I write this at Brookes's in the midst of vociferous laughter caused by Kensington reading aloud some extraordinary instances of bets out of the old Club-betting book"—I thought it worth while to take down one or two of these bets ("nom nominanda inter Christianos,") as specimens of the wit and morality of those memorable Whig times. "Lord Cholmondely has given two guineas to Lord Derby, to receive five hundred guineas whenever his Lordship ――― a woman in a balloon one thousand miles from earth"—Mr. Fitzpatrick and Mr. Hanger have agreed that whenever either of them shall [*deletion unrecovered*] in King's ――― loudly, he shall pay ten guineas to the other, to his quietus. Witnesses, the Duke of Devonshire, Lord E. Bentinck and Charles

Fox." Met Lord St. Vincent who asked me to come to his daughter's (Mrs. Dy Sombre's) this evening, but I said it would be hardly possible for me as I must be home early to pack. "At all events" he said "You must contrive to call upon her in the course of the day." This, however, I was resolved *not* to do—For I should hate to see so nice a thing as she once was in the hands of such "a foul Egyptian" as I hear Mr. Dy Sombres is. Dined at Sir John Macdonals—the company Sir Kerr Porter (on leave of absence from his mission) Miss Porter, the Countess Kitty (Stephens that *was*) and her niece—home and packed—}

23 [Monday]—Off to the station at nine where I was met by Hume—{Had for our companion a great part of the way John Houlton—a good deal of talk with him about the pleasant old times at Farleigh, which is now let & he, in general a wanderer abroad—Arrived at Birkenhead in the evening & got to bed early having to be on board a packet between five & six in the morning. Most unchristian arrangement.

24 [Tuesday]—After a few hours of vain attempt at sleep—a tremendous storm of wind, thunder & *hail* had come on—I was roused up by Hume, but on seeing the state of the elements, both, after some conference thought it wisest to go to bed again—and so we had the long, dull day to pass at [Birkenhead] with the same operation (barring, we hoped, the thunder and hail) to go through on the morrow}

25 [Wednesday]—Had a good passage, with my favourite Commander, Townley, and got in early in the evening—a great crowd of spectators, as usual, on the Jetty, and my name having [*MS damaged*] forth, a good many cheers attended my progress—{A seat being vacant next me in that carriage, a very gentlemanlike young fellow jumped eagerly into it, but, not being *sure* evidently that I was the man, asked instantly of our opposite neighbour, pointing at the same time to me, and almost laying his hand on my arm "Is this Moore?" The other nodded assent and I saw that the young fellow was then a little ashamed of his empressement. I found him, however, during the few minutes' conversation I led him into to be very modest & gentlemanlike—had been to Naples &c. &c. Somebody told me his name, but it gave me no clue as to who he was.} Found my dear little Nell in readiness for me, and was installed in the same comfortable site as before.

{26 [Thursday]—Sallied forth & found myself known, but not to as many people as on my last début here—the old rail have died off or become indifferent, and to the young I am personally unknown—so that my *pro-*

gress here is not what it was in other days. There is a look of decline, too, in the streets & buildings themselves which added a little to the feeling of *change* that all I met impressed me with—Went out by the rail-way to call upon Lord Fortescue at Maretimo—found him at home, and was introduced by him to Lady Fortescue. He enquired most kindly after Bessy, and asked me to dine and sleep on Sunday next at Maretimo—showed me all round this beautiful place, and the various views it commands, which are now in their most sunny perfection—Went out with Nell to dine at the [*MS damaged*]—meant to have gone out with Nell to dine at Cuming's, but found that Crampton had made an engagement for me to dine at Sir Edward Blakeney's (the Commander in Chief) to meet Prince George who is here with his regiment—A very large party—a few of whom I knew but the majority of them strangers to me—a large addition to the party in the evening and most *strenuous* Italian singing by a young lady & gentleman unknown to me—many attempts made to get *me* to sing—but I knew better—

27 [Friday]—Forget what I did this morning, but my dinner was at Cuming's—a larger party than I bargained for, and none of them very charming—with the exception of the hostess herself, who is a nice good-humoured person. Sung for them in the evening, but with little success either in my own opinion or, I fear, in theirs. Glad to get home—My visit to Lord Fortescue was not yesterday I now recollect but this morning.—Went afterwards with Finlay to Donnybrook Fair and was much struck by the marvellous change that Father Mathew has worked.}

28 [Saturday]—Occupied myself for some time at the College Library—but with little success. The key of the MS. room was missing, and when, at last found, would not open the door. The MSS. therefore, I suspect have a very quiet time of it. Went to look for Johnny Napier, but could not make him out. Indulged myself with a solitary peep at two or three spots hallowed by old recollections from poor old Aungier St. House, and the lodgings of my dear Bess's mother in Suffolk St.—Dined with Norman Macdonald at his beautiful lodge (the Under Secretary's) in the Phoenix Park—the first time I have seen it, though often at the other Lodges—this the most agreeable of all, I think. {A small circle of beauties there, [*MS damaged*] Williams &c. to meet Prince George, who is any thing but a beauty. Was made to sing in the evening, but with little or no echo in my auditors—at least so I fancied.}

29th. [Sunday] Went to the Catholic Church in Marlborough St. and heard as usual some charming music, Peter Leigh (Ellen's friend) being my companion. We then set out for Kingstown together, and, on our way went into a new Chapel (in Merrion St. I think) to which the old establishment I used to frequent in my younger days (Townsend St. Chapel) has been removed. Was introduced to the chief Clergyman, who bids fair, as Leigh told me, to be archbishop, on Murray's death—and he told me that this establishment still retains the name of the "Irish Gentleman's Chapel" which was given to the other in consequence of my book "The Travels of an Irish Gentleman" &c.—This I was glad to hear. {Saw the Fortescues who asked me to come to luncheon but I had promised to go with Leigh to the Mearas.} Went afterwards to the Jetty, the great promenade of a Sunday, and was almost stared off my legs my companions being Leigh & Finlay. Shall not easily forget the hearty hug I got from an honest fellow who, on my dropping my umbrella, picked it up, and giving it to me, threw his arms about my neck, ejaculating, "My sweet fellow!" Find he is the proprietor of a great glass-shop in Dublin, and Finlay said that nothing would make him more happy than my leaving my card at his house—so resolved to do it. Went from the Jetty to Lord Fortescue's where I dined. After I had dressed sat looking out of the window at the beautiful bay and the solitary light on Howth and quite forgot how the time went, till the servant came to tell me that the company was not only all arrived but were then going in to dinner—found to my shame it was so. {Company, chiefly, if I recollect right, my Lord's staff and my Lady's family. Sat with him talking some time and then to bed. Part of our conversation was as to the person likely to succeed him [*MS damaged*] *not* Devon, he said, for he was too liberal.

30 [Monday]—At breakfast Lady Fortescue proposed to take me on a drive round Killiney, which kind offer I most gladly accepted—the day fine & the open phaeton very agreeable—was glad, too, of such an opportunity of studying a little her new ladyship and judging how far she would be able to stand a juxta-position with those noble dames of England among whom she is about to be introduced. Feeling a most sincere regard & respect for him I could not but rejoice in the result of my observation which was—that she will do exceedingly well. "Le premier principe d'un femme" (as some thorough woman, an actress, said to a critic who was prosing to her about the "first principle" of an actress) "le premier principe d'une femme c'est de parvître jolie" and this foundation of the sex's success Lady Fortescue is still possessed of. She is also quiet and gentle, which is another good ingredient, and in short I came to the conclusion, during a very delightful drive down Killiney Hill, past [*MS damaged*] and through a variety of green lanes once familiar to my eyes that she may take her place at Woburn, Chatsworth, Bowood, or any other such place not only with safety but with success. Dined with the Cramptons, (merely themselves & Hume) and went afterwards to the Opera to hear Grisi, Lablache &c. who to the credit of Dublin are exhibiting with great success here. Went first to the Commander-in-Chief's (Blakeney's box) and afterwards to Lady Fortescue's.}

31 [Tuesday]—Joined Nell and some of her friends at the Porto-Bello gardens to hear some very agreeable band music—had been for several hours before looking over, & transcribing from the MS. Annals of The Four Masters, at Hodges & Smith's—Forgot to mention that one of these days, finding that the Provost had returned to town, I called upon him. We were class-fellows, I think he said, in College which I had not before been aware of—Was very civil about the MSS. room but insisted to the poor Librarian that the difficulty about opening it was all owing to his not knowing how to apply the key and that he (the Provost) would show him the difference. Accordingly we all three proceeded together to the Library— but, lo, the key was just as refractory in the hand of the Provost, as in that of the inferior officer, and after various grave trials it was found that the locksmith must be the *dernière ressource* after all—so that my access to the MSS. was put off to another time—Dined alone with Nell and went to Lady Clarke's (whom I had called upon in the course of the day) that evening— No one there worth remembering with the exception of the fair Josephine herself, than whom there are few more accomplished persons—Sang for each other and I flatter myself to each other's contentment—This morning, as I was coming out the College, one of the Porters ran after me and begged I would inform him whether I had not graduated in that University—I told him I had, on which he thanked me with a face full of smiles and said there had been a wager on the subject.

{September 1 [Wednesday]—An interchange of notes with Lady Howth on the subject of a day which I had fixed for dining with her but which was interfered with by a musical party at Mrs. White's—Dined at Finlay's—a large party of men, ODwyer, Howth, Paddy Murphy &c. &c.

2 [Thursday]—The Bianchi & the [MS damaged] were the stirring parties at [MS damaged] but the three Bianche (the three Mrs. Whites) are the great people here, and I got into a scrape by one of them this day, or rather evening—The hour fixed by her & [MS damaged] being by mistake half past seven, (instead [MS damaged]) I returned [MS damaged] be a dinner and was bumped out to her [MS damaged] a distance of between 3 & 4 miles)—found [MS damaged] exclusion, and had nothing for it but to proceed two miles further to the [MS damaged] near Kingstown, where I had some fish & a pint of sherry, and then returned to my party which was all very grand & vice-regal and musical, the Lord Lieut. & Grisi & Lablache being there in full force—got home very late

3. [Friday] Forget what I did through the day—dined at Crampton's—no one besides themselves, except a beautiful daughter of [MS damaged] Camp-

bell's) who however has a most ungraceful impediment in her utterance—
Theatre in the evening—sate first for some time in a box with some Castle
people, and then joined Nell & the Meyler's in theirs—

5 [Sunday]—Went to Marlborough Street Chapel where the sacred singing
touched me far more than any I heard from Grisi &c. last night—A fine
rich female voice giving forth clearly & without ornament the solemn songs
of the Mass—then the full burst of the organ & choir—no Opera could
compare with it. It brought tears too which the music of last night *did* not.—
Could not. Went out to Kingstown for a promenade on the Jetty—met Lord
Fortescue, who asked me to luncheon but I had promised to dine with the
Mearas—returned to him and had some conversation after which I proceeded to the Jetty.—Scene pretty much as before—I have, indeed, confused, I find, the incidents of the two Sundays, from some inaccuracy in my
Memoranda—Dined [*MS damaged*] dress of the Lancers, Royal Barracks,
Forester being my inviter—Sate between the Commander-in-Chief and the
Colonel (Stawell) and had opposite to me Prince George—also a much
more agreeable face, that of my old acquaintance, Sir Andrew Barnard, just
arrived—The day odd, but hearty and new to me, particularly the scene in
the smoking room after dinner. Barnard and I came away together on an
open car, but liked it not & took to our legs.—Hume, who has hitherto been
in a hurry to return to England, seems now inclined to stay behind me
here—the illness of his brother is, I beleive, the cause of this change. I had
promised Boyse to take a run down to Bannow, if possible, to see his new
house—& had there been a rail-way, I should have done it & paid a visit to
the Arrans at the same time—but three or four days lost in coaching makes
all the difference in such cases.

6 [Monday]—Had a visit from an old correspondent of mine (though I had
never seen him before) the Priest, or Parson, I forget which he is, of Castle-
Town Delvin—one of the many brother-*poets* who try to make me also a
brother-*reader*.—Went to Hodges's & Smith's and finished my references to
Four Masters. This and the reading over Lee's Letter in the MS. Room of
the College (where I found also another paper for my purpose, but of no
great value) formed the whole of my acquisitions, in that line since I came.
Met at Hodges's, one day, Mr. Gale the author of the work on Irish
Corporations, which I have quoted, I think, in my History—Went out in a
Cab to call on D'Aguilar (or rather Mrs. D'Aguilar) but found they were
dressing for dinner—A grand dinner at home, Nell having made it a point
that I should keep myself disengaged one day for that purpose—The
Meylers, Finlay, Mrs. Lavelle, Kate Berrel &c.—had singing and dancing in
the evening "quorum pars magna fui," and a gay supper to finish.—I forget

whether I have mentioned in this Journal the death, some months since, of my brother-in-law John Scully, the only one of my kith or kin who had it in his power to leave me any money, and he has "died and left no sign," as far as I am concerned. But the worst of it is he has not done what he was bound by promise to his wife to do for my poor sister, Nell,—thus increasing my difficulties in that quarters. (Find I have made some mistake as to the dates of two or three days in this last week)}

7 [Tuesday]—This {is} my wind-up day, having settled to be off tomorrow—{Hume remaining behind for a few days more—Received a letter (sent on to me by Bessy) from Lord John asking me, by the Duchess of Bedford's desire to come to Woburn, and meet him and Lady John—The Lansdownes there at present, [*MS damaged*] a day or two—Resolved to manage this if I could, and found that there is a [*MS damaged*] Liverpool which would place me within six or seven miles of the Duke's.} Dined with the Cramptons—only themselves—and all went to the Opera together— strong symptoms of the rising spirit of Toryism in the House—Conservative names given out with cheers, and vollies of the Kent-Fire, which I now heard for the first time—Was glad to find, however, that *my* name formed a sort of neutral ground, and that "a cheer for Tom Moore," which they gave two or three times was well received.

{8 [Wednesday]—Sailed for Liverpool in a very crowded packet, Hume, OMeara, and a good many others having come to see me off—It is curious how frequently acquaintances of other times turn up in my path—The Mate, or Lieutenant of this packet, whom OMeara appealed to in my behalf for a comfortable berth proved to be an old shipmate of mine who belonged to the Phaeton when I went in her to America. He did as much as he could for me but that was little, as the packet was wretchedly crowded—}

9 [Thursday]—Arrived between four & five in Liverpool—{found on enquiring that I was not in time for the train I had counted upon for getting to Woburn. My stock of clean shirts too, had been so much reduced by my "last days of Pompeii," that I found I should be rather too much in the condition of my brother-poet, Tag, at Woburn, and thus gave up the visit—} Breakfasted and started by the train for Cheltenham—Two nice women with their brother my companions all the way—{struck up an intimacy with them as usual, and astonished them at parting by confiding to them who I was—}one of them a great singer, I found, of my songs.—Dined with honest Corry at Cheltenham—

10 [Friday]—Took a most delicious drive with Corry and Curran, who is staying here, to see the beautiful Valley of Evesham—the day most perfect for it—Dined, Curran and I, at Corry's—

11 [Saturday]—Off for Cirencester by the coach—Corry with me, on his way to town—found all right at home, thank God.

{11, 12, 13 &c. [Saturday, 11 September–Thursday, 30 September] Set to work and had quiet for some little time—At the latter end of the month had Vivash, Drury & one or two more to dinner.}

October {1, 2 &c [Friday, 1 October–Monday, 11 October]—The first week in this month Bessy & I to Bowood for two or three days—the party there an agreeable family one, consisting of Lord Ilchester, his son, Lord Stavordale, Lady Teresa Strangways, and Lady Elizabeth}

12 [Tuesday]—To Bowood—the party, Sir Stratford & Lady Canning, the Milmans, Twopenny, and a pretty girl, the daughter of Doctor Birbeck—Stratford Canning & myself got on very sociably together and he tried a good deal to persuade me to take a trip with him to Constantinople. If I were a little younger, and had less cares on my head, there are few things I should like better—{Sung in the evening some of Canning's old favourite songs

13 [Wednesday]—Remained at Bowood—Sung in the morning, at Mrs. Milman's request, for her poor invalid girl, who was carried down to the drawing-room to hear me.

14 [Thursday]—Walked home after breakfast—

15, 16 &c [Friday–Saturday]—Notes & messages from Lady L. entreating me to come to Bowood on Tuesday the 19th to meet Lord Clarendon—agreed at last to come on Thursday.

19th. [Tuesday] To Bowood—Lord Clarendon went yesterday—found (besides that eternal Twopenny) the Lysters, Hallam, the Miss Berrys, Lady

Gordon (Mrs. Austin's daughter) and two or three more.—Singing in the evening—Miss Berry full of delight at "Wit's celestial feather."[1] A good deal of conversation with Hallam, which I should like much to be able to record—but, alas, my memory, though still good for *work,* lets matters of conversation "sink through me like a leaky sieve," as becomes every day more & more apparent in the contents of this Journal. Lady Gordon told me at dinner that, wherever she went on the Continent (particularly in Germany) the first question generally asked of her was "whether she had seen OConnell?" and the second "whether she had seen Moore?" Query— do I feel much flattered by this juxtaposition? I fear not, though I suppose I *ought,* for OConnell has done great things. But then, the *manner* of doing them?

20 [Wednesday]—In walking alone, composed the following distich on Mr. Twopenny:

> Men differ in tastes; but I'm one of many
> Who wouldn't for Twopenny give one penny

21, 2, 3 &c. [Thursday, 21 October–Sunday, 31 October]—Nothing worth noting, except that at the end of this month or the beginning of the following one, I accompanied our new neighbour Vivash in his carriage to dine at the Hughes's in Devizes, company Archdeacon Macdonald, young Brabant & his wife, & her brother &c}

November 1, 2, 3, 4 &c. [Monday, 1 November–Tuesday, 9 November]— Began to work at the 4th Volume of my Irish History, and read & noted all there is about the reign of Elizabeth in the books I possess—having brought away with me from Bowood the Sidney Papers, Holinshed, &c. with the same view. Found, however, that I could not get on with any satisfaction without seeing as much at least as has been calendered of the papers of Elizabeth at the State Paper Office, and resolved therefore to run up to town—

{10 [Wednesday]—Started for Chippenham and so on by the rail-road to town, having been kindly permitted by Lady Elisabeth (and it is a *real* kindness) to fix myself at Sackville St. Found all very comfortable—called at Bryan's, with the view of offering myself for dinner, but they had already sat down, I found, and the servant not looking very *invitingly,* went and had a cutlet at Brookes's, and dullified myself with the newspapers afterwards—

11 [Thursday] Had brought up a squib with me three parts finished—
(Canto the Second of Corn-Law [*MS damaged*] and was in hopes I should be
able to dispatch the remainder of it in town—but nothing would come,
though I brooded over it several hours—so sallied forth in despair. Didn't
know, by the bye yesterday of the birth of a Prince till I heard of it in the
rail-carriage.[1] The same young fellow who mentioned it to me told me also
of his being in the habit of travelling with *large* sums of money in his care,
and not long since, travelled all night with no less than £70,000 in his
keeping—an uneasy charge. In the course of my perambulating to-day met
Bryan who rated me for not making my way up to the dining-room
yesterday, and asked me for to-day—Got into an awkward scrape soon
after, having met a young fellow, just as I was turning out of Brookes's, who
seized my hand most cordially, and expressed much pleasure in meeting
with me. I responded most heartily to this salutation (sicut meus est mos)
without knowing who the deuce my dear friend was, but still with a faint
notion that it was not very long since I last saw him—"By the bye," I said,
"where was it that we last met?" and rather a shade, as I thought, passed
over his brow, while he answered, "Why, twas in Dublin," and then we
parted—Before I had reached however the bottom of St. James's St, it all
flashed upon me that the young gentleman I had treated thus cavalierly was
no less a personage than Prince George of Cambridge,[2] who had taken
such pains to put on my cloak comfortably for me when I dined at the Mess
with him in Dublin. But I had got into quite another sort of *mess* with him,
and was very sorry for it, knowing that Royalty like his, lying on the *outskirts*,
as it were, is always the most touchy about its rights—Called upon Sir J.
Macdonald—told him of the *leze-majesté* I had just been guilty of & he
advised me to go immediately and write my name in the Prince's book,
which I did—Met Macauley and walked some time with him—Called at the
Privy Council to see Charles Greville, and while I was standing on the steps
Poole (Paul Pry) stopped to speak to me—"You see me" I said, "haunting
regions with which I have no longer any fellowship."—"A *bel* esprit, at *least*,"
he answered—Went to State Paper Office, and had some conversation with
Mr. Lechmere—"The papers of Elizabeth's reign alone (he said) would take
a life-time to do them justice."—A pleasant hearing for me—Fixed that I
would come and commence my studies here tomorrow. Called at Sir M.
Shee's, the first time for a long while, which I feel rather ashamed of—Saw
Shee himself & the ladies—asked me to dine with them Sunday, which I
most gladly agreed to do. When I first came to London, Shee's was one of
the very few dining places open to me and now though I have a plurality of
them I ought not to forget them—dined with Lady Holland (at South St)
company Lord & Lady Radnor, & son & daughter, Lord Russell, and
Luttrell—Had some conversation to-day with Lord Melbourne at
Brookes's—talked of Peter Burrowes who is just dead—his favourite oath
"Pon my honour and my God," an oath, as Luttrell says "at once civil &

ecclesiastical." This Lord L. had not heard before & it made him chuckle.} A note from Sydney asking me to breakfast with him tomorrow—"Dear Moore—I have a breakfast of philosophers tomorrow at ten *punctually*—Muffins and Metaphysics—Crumpets and Contradiction—Will you come?" Wrote him an excuse telling him of my engagement at the S. P. Office, and saying that though his breakfast would be very agreeable, it would "take a large slice of a reign out of me."—{(I have made a mistake here of a day, having dined one day with Bryan & his daughter)

13 [Saturday]—Breakfasted at home, and went afterwards to the S. P. Office—Found the Papers all laid out for me; and another gentleman there employed in a similar manner to myself—after some interval he introduced himself to me, though I ought not to have wanted this ceremony, as I had been made acquainted with him not very long since at Holland House. He kindly offered me all the assistance in his power towards my object, and very great use he can be of to me, having, as the world knows, laboured well & hard at this mine himself—While there, received a visit from Crofton Croker, who asked me to come & see his treasures in the Irish historical line, and placing them almost friendily at my disposal—Not to forget the Letter about the murder[1]—Staid about four hours at my task, & then to Brookes's—Met Lord Dacre who said he was going in the evening with Lady Dacre to hear Miss Kemble in Norma,[2] and, on my saying I should like much to do the same, asked me to dine with them & go—but, my dinner with Lady Holland being in the way, told him I should join them, if possible, in the evening—Company at dinner, Buller, the M. P., Stanley & Lady ———— Stanley (I forget how to designate either him or her), Lord Melbourne, and one or two more—Got away as soon as I could, but the opera was over & the Dacres vanished—sat in their box to see a stupid thing (the Wrong Man.)[3]

14 [Sunday]—Went to call upon Crofton Croker at his ridiculously named place, Rosamond's bower, and arriving there at about two o'clock, found himself and a party seated at *dinner*—good, primitive people! A Colonel, Sir Charles ODonell (whose card I found the other day left for me, together with another Colonel's, Sir Michael Creagh) being of the party—Talked of the name ODonell, and what a *foreign* name it has become. Told me of a little incident that happened him, once abroad when he & some other English were questioned as to their names at some douane or by some fellow-travellers; every other name was listened to either in silence, or with an exclamation of "Diable" at the sound, but when ODonell came to declare his, there was an instant smile of recognition, and his questioner exclaimed "Ah, vous êtes Chrétien donc!," meaning an Irishman and a Catholic—

Croker took me for a few minutes to his Cabinet and gave me a glimpse of the treasures he possesses connected with Irish History & Antiquities—said I should have the free use of them all. Returned in the omnibus with two of his guests. Dined at Shee's, only themselves, but making altogether, I think, not less than a dozen—In the evening had singing in plenty—the young male Shees & their sisters being able to get up duetts, trios, quintettes &c. in very good style. I was myself of course not allowed to be idle, and though my audience were Irish (I am thinking now of Dublin) had no lack of enthusiasm to complain of.—The three sons, I am told (the youngest being a slight dapper little fellow) are nick-named in society "He, *She* and *It*."

15 [Monday]—Met Hume by appointment at Brookes's & he accompanied me to the Paper Office, where I remained till 3 o'clock—made then some calls and went to Mrs. Gibbons's about my new set of shirts—Forgot to mention that the Shees talked a great deal about my squibs yesterday—it is apparent they watch every thing that has the least appearance of being mine in the Chronicle[1]—[The] Longmans, by the bye, have again shown a shirking shabbiness (at least [*MS damaged*] former doings) in reference to an advance I have asked for on the next Volume of my History—Had a visit from Tom Longman yesterday evening about it—}

16 [Tuesday]—To the Paper Office. Found, this day or the last a most curious letter of the Earl of Sussex to Elizabeth telling her with the utmost coolness, of a proposal he had made to a fellow to murder Phelim ONeill for a reward of 100 marks of land a year—Showed this to my fellow workman, Tytler, who indeed helped me to make out part of the writing— Sussex's hand being one of the most difficult to read—Tytler who has been well broken in to royal murders by his Scottish History (Cardinal Beaton's, for instance, and he is now ferretting out another) was not quite so shocked by this discovery as I was[1]—dined at Milman's, company, Hallam, Lockhart, Westmacott, and one or two more—very agreeable

17 [Wednesday]—State Paper Office for nearly four hours—Am getting into scrapes about dinners—{had promised Bailey (who [*MS damaged*] in offering us his house once) to dine with him to-day but afterwards re-collected that I had already promised the same to Murray, in case Lord Mahon who had expressed a wish to meet me could come—was forced to put off Bailey—}Company at Murray's Lord Mahon, Sir Francis Head & his daughter, Lockhart, &c—in the evening Miss Head sung, and very pret-tily—I was also, of course, called into play, & sung a good deal—Much surprised to find Sir Francis Head such a mild and quiet person and with so

little of the Bubbles of the Brunnen in either his look or manner—Murray sends by me to Bessy a copy of the beautiful Edition of Childe Harold he has just published. A letter from Bess full of sweet and good feeling about our poor Tom who has been very ill in that wretched place, Lower Scinde, but gives great comfort to her, and of course to me by the better feelings towards home and home associations which his whole letter breathes. He will, I trust in God, be yet a pride and blessing to us.—{Getting into scrapes as usual about my dinners—Was told by no less than 3 or 4 men yesterday at Brookes's that they were asked to meet me at Hastie's (the owner of Burns's punch-bowl) tomorrow, whereas my real place of dining is to be at Tom Longman's—Went to Rogers, who arrived yesterday evening from Paris, and whom I found full of kindness & good-humour—walked out with him and called on Mr. Grenville, who pursues his usual wise plan (for a man of 84 years of age)—that is, never to leave his own comfortable house during the winter months. But he gives dinners daily to a party of about six or eight people, and is himself as erect and blooming as a hale man of forty or fifty—asked us to join his party to-day—dined at Lady Holland's, but her intended expedition to Bowood—by the rail-way!—is now the great topic of conversation with her &, perforce, her guests—Napoleon setting out for Russia was nothing to it—she has had the roads surveyed—the baggage-waggons are all ready, and nothing is wanting but Brunel[1] himself to lead the van.}

18 [Thursday]—{Again all day at the State Paper Office, and find that the stooping for so many hours every day (so unlike my *home* work) does not at all agree with me—Sydney Smith has written a prayer for the Young Prince, which is not bad, nor yet very good—being intended more as a satire against George the Fourth than as any plea of aspiration in favour of any other Prince—Henry Webster showed me four not bad lines written [*MS damaged*] by some lady of his acquaintance—

> "There's a good deal of wit or pith,
> In the prayer of Smith
> But, by Jupiter and Mammon
> There's much more gammon"}

Dined at Tom Longman's in the Regents Park—Company, some of the Longmans, Dundas, and a few more—Mrs. Longman looking very pretty and sung very prettily also—

19 [Friday]—{A note from Lady Lansdowne, who having heard that I mean to start for home on Monday next, expresses a hope that I will let them intercept me on that day and asks at what hour she may send the

carriage for me to the railway—hopes that I will stay till Wednesday. This, with the cold & illness I feel coming on, is any thing but agreeable.} After returning from the Paper Office yesterday I was seized with a giddiness during which the room seemed to turn around with me—The cause of this, I have no doubt, is my having kept my head down over those papers for so many successive days & so many hours each day. This morning, however, I held the papers in my hand & sat upright. Dined at Mr. Grenville's—company, Lord & Lady Mahon, Rogers, & Mr. & Lady ——— somebody whom I now forget—all very agreeable.

{20 [Saturday]—Went to S. Paper Office—Called at Bryan's to offer myself for dinner to-day and was most readily & friendlily accepted—Had called on Lord Monteagle either in the morning or yesterday, to ask his interest with his son for some little favour I want done towards our friend Hughes's son Edward in the Custom-House—Poor Monteagle[1] (whom I found in his office, or den, beset with all the bustle and worry of his exchequer-bill-affair) admitted me immediately when announced and was all kindness as to my request—said my best plan was to go off to his son at the Custom House and I might depend on his doing all that was in his power for me—Having told the Bryans of my intended expedition, they offered to take me in their carriage, but I was too late at the Custom House, Young Rice having left it for his country house half an hour before—Performed several commissions, having made up my mind to start for home tomorrow—}

21 [Sunday]—Desperate day of wet—got off in the half-past ten train—{A Mr. Goldie (as I learned when parting with him) my companion & colloquist on the way—an intelligent man of business at Chippenham.} When we were about half-way on our road, a gentleman joined us, with somewhat of the foreigner in his mode of speaking, and on my asking him whether he was going any further than Chippenham, he answered "I am going to the Duke of Beaufort's." Upon which I said (hardly knowing why I said it, or what put it in my head)—"Pray, what's become of the Duke's friend, Mastuchievchz?" "*I* am Mastucievicz," he answered courteously, and then all flashed at once upon my mind—my meeting him once, and *but* once, many years ago, at dinner at the Duke of Beaufort's in London, and never having known any more of him since than seeing his name now & then in the newspapers—He seemed much pleased at our recontre, and we had a good deal of agreeable conversation together during the remainder of our journey. Such is life—at least, *my* life—for I hardly move a step without something odd or agreeable turning up in my path.—Got home, notwithstanding with a very bad cold which was neither agreeable nor odd—{the weather being most trying—Found my dear Bess pretty well & a note from Lady Lansdowne waiting me respecting tomorrow—So must

go—Forgot to mention, I think, Lord Dudley Stuart's being so glad when I said I would go to the Ball for the Poles, last week—When I found, however that it was so far off as Guildhall, and nobody to take me, my Liberalism cooled very much and I didn't go.—Next day at Brookes's, I had just written him a note and inclosed a sovereign for my ticket (one of the *very* few in my possession) when Pigou, who is a leading man in Polish concerns, and to whom I mentioned what I was doing, exclaimed, "Oh we don't want any money now—the Ball has made us rich, and you may keep your money for another time"—"Sic me servavit" Pigou [*MS damaged*] my sovereign from its envelope most gladly, and Pigou undertook to tell Lord Dudley that he prevented me from sending it. Little do the people I live with know what a hard-run poor devil I am.

22 [Monday]—To Bowood and found Lady Holland inshrined there, with her Bonza, Allen, on one side, and her page on the other—Bobus Smith also of the party, *always* agreeable—

23, 24 &c. [Tuesday–Wednesday]—On & off at Bowood, during the remainder of the month—Rogers walked home with me once or twice, coming expressly to see the Lady of the Cottage, to whom he is always kind—my efforts to work with all this constant interruption most annoying and make me often wish the whole party at their own homes again.—

24. [Wednesday] One of these days Lord John walked over with Rogers to see Bessy—anxious for me to join their party, but having got away to my workshop, shall stay there as long [*incomplete*]. I said a page or two back, that nothing was wanting but Brunel's superintendence to make Lady Holland's *progress* by steam perfect, and accordingly Brunel *was* made to lend his guardian presence to this "magnum opus," and he actually accompanied her to Bowood!

23, 24 [Tuesday–Wednesday][1]—One of these evenings Bobus read aloud to us a playful Epitre in verse of Voltaire's, and with very good French accent & point—sung a little the same evening to Lady Holland & him.

25, 26 [Tuesday–Wednesday]}

December {1, 2, 3 &c. [Wednesday–Friday]—The early part of this month I was left tolerably quiet, and [*MS damaged*] for the *first time* wrote a few pages of the fourth Volume of my Irish History—Whether I shall live to finish it, who knows?

4–&c. &c [Saturday, 4 December–Tuesday, 14 December]}

15, 16 [Wednesday–Thursday]—About the middle of the month the plot again began to thicken at Bowood, and I was again accordingly brought into play—but not having time to particularize, I can give only a summary retrospect of some of the persons and events—Rogers staid more than a week, still fresh in all his best faculties, and improved wonderfully in the only point where he was ever at all deficient—temper. He *now* gives the natural sweetness of his disposition fair play. He walked over to see Bessy one or two days through all the wretched mud of the Bowood lane & our own, making (to us and back again) at least six miles—Among the other successive guests were Doctor & Mrs. Fowler—A good story by the bye told by Fowler of a man selling a horse—The would-be purchaser enquiring as to his leaping powers, asks, "would he take timber?"—"He'd jump over *your* head," answers the other—"I don't know what you call *that*."—Macauley another of the guests and staid for some time—{he is losing & more every time I see him that jaunty and raree-showman-sort of manner in which he used to pour out his treasures, both of memory and original thought; and accordingly we now have the treasures with but little of this discount upon them—} He is a most wonderful man, and I rejoiced to learn that the world may expect from him a History of England taken up, I believe, from where Hume leaves off—Rogers directed my attention to the passage in his last Edinburgh Article where he describes Warren Hastings's Trial[1] and the remarkable assemblage of persons and circumstances which it brought together—Agreed perfectly with R. as to the false taste and over-gorgeousness of this part of the article—But the whole produces great effect and is every where the subject of conversation. Mrs. Butler (Fanny Kemble) was another of the visitors bringing with her her American husband & two little children & their stay was I think for near a fortnight. On one of the evenings she read out to us Much ado about Nothing with much skill and effect—She and I too sung on two successive evenings my Duett of "Oh come to me when daylight sets"[2]—{On the whole I was led to like her somewhat better than formerly—though her [*MS damaged*] exclamation to Romeo, during the death-scene "where the devil is the dagger?"—her speech to young Castlereagh "Those who mean nothing when they speak &c." and what Rogers tells of her saying when she saw the young men hurrying on shore after their long passage over the Atlantic "Curse my petticoats!"—All these and other such little traits of character rather prevent one from envying much Mr. Butler's good-fortune.} We had also Lord

John {and his nice new little wife—}he accompanied Rogers one day to Sloperton to see Bessy and is in high spirits for the approaching conflict—{reminding me, (as I told him aside) of our friend R. of whom somebody said "How well he is this year!—he's in full venom."—}Among the latest visitors of this month was Charles Greville who had never before been at Bowood and was enchanted with the great beauty of the house—{Mentioned to him an object I had with respect to the State Paper Office which now that the Tories had got in I almost despaired accomplishing particularly as Graham, its *chef,* had been one of those rather quizzed by me.—"Oh that doesn't matter at all" answered Greville—"it's what you were both made & born for—he to be quizzed and you to quiz him." He then added that he was quite sure Graham would be most happy to do what I wished, and if I would make a memorandum of my request he would send it to him—and so I did.—Received one of these days the following nice note from the Duchess of Beaufort.

"Dear Mr. Moore—Count Matusewitz having told me that you kindly enquired after us lately, and hearing from Charles Greville that you are now at Bowood encourages me to try and persuade you to come on here. Will it suit you to come here about Monday next? We shall be delighted to see you—Believe me, dear Mr. Moore yrs truly, Emily Beaufort."

Wrote to say that I was delighted to find myself so kindly remembered by her but that if I could find time to go any where, it must be to Woburn where I had promised Lord and Lady John to meet them, if possible. If to the guests already mentioned I add the Rotschilds—(Rotschild *fils,* and rather a handsome wife) I finish off as far as I have time to recollect, the series of our company in this month—}

Notes to 1841 Entries

7 January

1. The translation is of Moore's song, "The wreath you wove" (*Works*, 1:313), done by William Spencer; criticism by Gabriele P. G. Rossetti, father of Christina and Dante Gabriel Rossetti.

12 April

1. Moore placed the passage in square brackets at the end of the MS page, with asterisks indicating its location in the text.

15 April

1. Moore's brackets.

17 April

1. A reference to Dryden's play *The Kind Keeper, or Mr. Limberham* (1678). See entry for 13 June 1828 and its n. 1. Moore's brackets.

20 April

1. Moore placed the two passages in square brackets at the end of the MS page, with asterisks indicating their location in the text.

23 April

1. Moore placed the passage in square brackets at the end of the MS page, with asterisks indicating its location in the text.

26 April

1. Moore placed the passage in square brackets at the end of the MS page, with asterisks indicating its location in the text.

27 April

1. Moore placed the passage in square brackets at the end of the MS page, with asterisks indicating its location in the text.

29 April

1. Probably Henry Nelson Coleridge, nephew and literary executor of Samuel Taylor Coleridge. His edition of Coleridge's "Table Talk" was published by John Murray in 1835.

2. Moore placed the passage in square brackets at the end of the MS page, with asterisks indicating its location in the text.

1 May

1. Moore placed the passage in square brackets at the end of the MS page, with asterisks indicating its location in the text.

3 May

1. "The Song of the Old Time," *Works,* 5:201.

23 June

1. A reference to the battle fought at Worcester in 1651 in which the forces of Cromwell, supported by Lambert, defeated the Royalists, led by Charles II.

28–29 June

1. See n. 1 for 1–3 July.

1–3 July

1. A highly laudatory review of *The Poetical Works of Thomas Moore* (1841) appeared in the *Dublin Review* 10 (1841): 429–50.
2. A collection of Moore's *Gedichte,* translated by J. R. Schuller, was published in 1830, and another collection (translator not named) appeared in 1839.

8–10 July

1. *Works,* 2:xxv. Moore suspected that his invitation from Stockholm to become a Knight of the Order of St. Joachim was a "ponderous piece of pleasantry," and that in the name he detected a "low and irreverent pun of St. Jokehim."

19 October

1. "On the Shamrock," *Works,* 3:307–9.

11 November

1. Albert Edward (1841–1910), Edward VII, who reigned from 1901–10.
2. George, Duke of Cambridge (1819–1904), grandson of George III and cousin of Queen Victoria.

13 November

1. See n. 1 for 16 November 1841.
2. Bellini, *Norma* (1831).
3. Probably *The Wrong Master* (1839), author unknown.

15 November

1. Moore published the following squibs in the *Morning Chronicle* in 1841: "The Reign of the Wrongheads—A Dream" (4 August); "Corn-Law Visions" (2 November); and a sequel to the latter (2 December). On 23 February the *Chronicle* published "A Threnody on the Approaching Demise of Old Mother Corn-Law."

16 November

1. "Essex" in Russell. Thomas Radcliffe, 3d Earl of Sussex (1526?–83), Lord Deputy of Ireland (1556–64) attempted twice to arrange for the assassination of Shane (not Phelim) O'Neill (1530?–67). Patrick Frazer Tytler, *History of Scotland,* 9 vols. (1828–43).

17 November

1. Isambard Kingdom Brunel (1806–59) built most of the Great Western Railway.

20 November

1. Thomas Spring Rice (1790–1866) was Chancellor of the Exchequer from 1835–39 and was made first Baron Monteagle of Brandon in 1839. Monteagle was Comptroller of the Exchequer in 1841, when the great forgery of Exchequer Bills occurred. The forged bills were put in circulation by a man named Rapallo. See Greville's *Memoirs,* 2:50.

23–24 November

1. The confusion in dates indicates that Moore was writing from memory.

15–16 December

1. Macaulay's review of the *Memoirs of the Life of Warren Hastings . . . Compiled from Original Papers* by the Rev. G. R. Gleig, 3 vols. (1841), appeared in the *Edinburgh Review* 74 (1841): 160–255. The author notes that a contract must have been made whereby Hastings's representatives were bound to furnish papers and Gleig to furnish praise. Each party did its duty, resulting in "three big bad volumes, full of undigested correspondence and undiscerning panegyric." The trial of Warren Hastings is described on pp. 241 ff. Macaulay published his multivolume *History of England from the Ascension of James II* in 1849–62.
2. *Works,* 4:165.

1842

January—1842. About the first days of January went over to meet the Palmerstons, Lord & Lady Cottenham, Lord Duncannon and some of his nice family—never forgetting that charming person, Lady Kerry, who has now become a constant inhabitant of Bowood, and it could not have one more ornamental to it—I sung a good deal as usual, and even the matter-of-fact-looking, Ex-Lord Chancellor placed himself close to the piano-forte, and though it didn't quite amount to the "iron tears down Pluto's cheek"[1] seemed very much pleased. I *think* it was he who mentioned that the nickname they've now got in Dublin for Peel is "the veiled Prophet," alluding to those promised revelations respecting his future policy for which the world is waiting—{Forgot to mention a gay school-boy sort of party that Bessy & I went to at young Drury's, our curate, on the last evening of the new year—the Moneys, Schombergs &c. and all played at child's games—my dearest Bess, (though ill for several days before) being among the youngest of the young—In writing to Hume one of these days about my *friends*, and Longmans, I said with [*MS damaged*] much truth that certainly their ancient name-sake, Artaxerxes *Longimanus* could not have been a more grasping-fisted fellow than the *Co.* is—Had a good deal of talk with Lord Duncannon about Ireland and rejoiced to find him "Hibernis [*MS damaged*] hiberniorum"

Received a note from Lord Lansdowne asking me to come over to meet Lady Keith and her daughter, and telling me it would be their last dinner before the meeting of Parliament—Accordingly went on January 6th, and found there, besides Lady Keith and Madlle. de Flahaut (who is not *quite* so pretty as she used to be) Lady Stratford Canning, Zamoiski, & Messrs. Senior and Lewis. Sung a good deal the two evenings I staid, the ladies having, on the second evening come furnished with a list of the favourite songs of theirs which I had not sung for them before. Returned home on the}

8th. [Saturday] Most sad news for me after all my gaiety—our darling Russell had been dangerously ill; and though better when Lord Auckland (from whom the account comes) wrote his letter, cannot, the physicians say, remain in India with safety, and was therefore in two or three weeks to sail for England. This time twelve months—almost to the very day—the delay of a letter from him prevented my sweet Bess from partaking in the gaieties at Lacock, and now a far worse fear about him jars in with our festivities— Lord Auckland had met the poor boy, as he tells us, out driving, but looking much more fit for the sick bed, and with a kindness never to be forgotten by me, if I were to live years on years, had him brought to Government House and there watched over and attended to—God bless him for it. {The Hughes's of Buckhill all dined with us—Johnny, who has been lately ordained, having come over to preach at Bromham—They are happy in their children—}

10th [Monday]—A visit from Lady Lansdowne to whom Lord Auckland had also written an account of our poor Bussy's illness—Nothing could be more feeling and affectionate than her manner—kissed Bessy like a sister, on leaving us, and said to me, when I was putting her into her carriage, "she is a most marvellous person"—alluding of course to the deep but calm feeling with which my poor Bessy is making up her mind to the worst—

11, 12, 13 &c. [Tuesday–Thursday] We now find, in addition to our apprehensions about Russell, that Tom, too, if not actually embarked, is coming home upon sick leave—His accounts of himself from Lower Scinde were such as a good deal to prepare us for this—but to say nothing of the anxiety & grief caused by it, how on earth am I to meet the additional expences which the return of both boys will now entail while still I am in debt too for most of the money which their first outfit, passage &c. required. I am still willing, and thank God able to work, but the power comes slower, and the effort is therefore more wearing. If I could write, with the facility & variety which some people give me credit for, I *should* indeed be like Mrs. Malaprop's Cereberus, three gentlemen at once.[1] It was but a few months since, that I received two letters pretty nearly at the same time— one of them from Mr. Blewit a composer of Comic Songs and Country-Dances (who, by the bye, has turned most of the Melodies, both gay and serious into quadrilles) proposing an alliance between himself and me for the production of all sorts of musical comicalities,—while the other letter was from Mr. Bagshaw, on the part of the Dublin Review, begging that I would undertake an article, for that work, on the recent edition of Dodd's Ecclesiastical History!—He says, among other things, "A notice on this work, by Dr. Lingard, appeared in the Dublin Review, at the time of the appearance of the First Volume, and the great importance of the Work appears to the proprietors to justify troubling you with the present application; the more especially as the delicacy of the task (regards being had to many of the topics discussed, and their bearing upon the actual position and differences of opinion existing among members of the Catholic body) requires that none but a master hand should be relied on."—The juxtaposition here of such men and such subjects—Blewit and Lingard!—jigs and theology! is *impayable.*

13, 14 &c [Thursday–Friday]—A most joyful relief to us, one of these days—the 14th. I believe—in a letter from Miss Eden, telling of the rapid and (as it would appear) almost complete recovery of our dear Russell from his threatening attack of illness. He had become so well, she tells us, as to be able to join a large dinner-party they had the day before—It is still thought expedient, however, that he should avail himself of his sick leave, as encountering another hot summer might be dangerous. A second most welcome item of her intelligence is that Russell's passage is to be paid by the Company—so *that* burthen is also off my mind.

{14, 15, 16 &c. [Friday–Sunday]—Busied with [*MS damaged*] and alternately employed with them and my History

17, 18, 19 &c. [Monday–Wednesday]

21 [Friday]—Bessy and I to Bowood to dine and sleep—the party at dinner several neighbours, the Starkeys, Clutterbucks, Dr. Greenough, [*MS damaged*]—Before dinner Bessy paid some visits in the Lansdownes' carriage, her own equipage having been long [*unrecovered*] by the want of a poney.

22 [Saturday]—Returned home after luncheon—

23, 24 &c. [Sunday–Monday]

28 [Friday]—Bessy's nephew, young Murray (nephew also to Mrs. Henry Siddons) came to pass a few days with us previously to his departure for India.

I shall now give a few memorandums, extracts &c from some of the various & numerous communications which I almost daily receive to the no small waste and disturbance of my time—The first that comes to my hand is a letter from a Roman Catholic clergyman (an Irishman also) named Nicholson, and dated Palazzo Maresca, Sorrento Naples, Septr. 6th. 1841— The following are extracts from it:—

"To you to whom the fame and religion of our common country owe so much I need not apologize in calling your attention to a portion of its History published by you. I saw with delight in Paris that History translated in French, and my happiness was increased on finding it in German in the library of a distinguished Professor at Munich.[1] If there be any class of Irishmen to whom such an impartial History as yours can bring especial delight, that class, I think, must be the Catholic clergy. . . . Often have I made it the subject of my conversation among well-educated Italians. . . . While in Florence last year I became acquainted with one of its noble families who claimed our Leinster family as a descendant of his stock. An Article was published on that point and it refers to your account of the origin of that family &c. &c."—}

The following squib of mine having been left out of my general Edition (though published soon enough to have appeared in it) may as well be preserved here.

To The EDITOR Of The MORNING CHRONICLE

SIR—You have already, I doubt not, been made acquainted with the very old and curious Prophecy, called the Schism of the Isms, which has been for some time past circulating through various parts of the kingdom. As I have been lucky enough, however, to have lighted upon a more correct copy of this singular production than is generally to be met with, I venture to submit it to your editorial consideration; and have the honour to be

Your obedient servant, E. G.

THE SCHISM OF THE ISMS.

There shall come, in the latter days, a Schism
Unnamed in Bible or Catechism,
'Mong all such things as end in '*ism*,'
Whether Puseyism, or Newmanism,
Or, simply and solely, mountebankism.

Then, woe is me! not Gentilism,
Nor Judaism, nor scepticism,
E'er work'd such ill as that day of schism.
For all shall then be egoism,
And separatism, and cabalism;
And priests shall mix mock Romanism
With very indifferent Protestantism;
And drug the mess with th'unholy chrism
Of Pusey's once-dear Rationalism.

Then Bishops shall ape the nepotism
That drew on Popes such stigmatism;
And bring up their sons to sinecurism,
While rolling, themselves, in epicurism.
Then Ph——lp——tts, ready for any "ism,"
But liberalism and Christianism,
Shall show that, of all sectarianism,
His natural sect is con*trar*y-ism.
And S——l, too, upon Romanism,
Will sport his raree-showmanism;
Proving, by dint of sheer humbuggism,
That Tipperary swarms with Thuggism!

When these things happen, in synchronism,
Then, woe and alas for the Oxford schism!—
It hath reached its hour of fatalism,
It hath felt its last faint paroxysm.
And Puseyism and Newmanism,
And even long-winded Sewellism,
Shall all, for want of some better "ism,"
Be swamped in one gen'ral Cataclysm!

{The following note accompanied a present of the works of M. de Fondras (whoever that poet may be) which was sent me sometime since through the hands of Mr. Westmacott (the sculptor) his note being addressed I think, to a Mr. Hutchins,

"My dear Sir—On receiving the accompanying works from my much valued friend, Le Marquis de Fondras I had promised myself the enviable satisfaction of placing them personally in the hands of the distinguished poet to whom they are addressed &c. &c.

Mr. Westmacott concludes by expressing his regret that he had been deprived of an interview "with him who is looked upon both at home and abroad, as the sweetest poet of the age."

Am afraid I never acknowledged the receipt of the Marquis's Volumes.

Received a letter from the Editor of the Salopian Journal, asking me whether some verses he had met with and had "already set up for insertion in the S. Journal" were really mine—Wrote back that, if mine, they had quite escaped my memory; but that, from all the circumstances, I had little doubt that they *were*, though very incorrectly given—Here they are as "set up."

EXTEMPORE.

To *James Perry*, to whose interference I chiefly owe
the very liberal price given for the poem of Lalla Rookh.

When they shall tell, in future times,
Of thousands given for idle rhymes,
    Like these—the pastime of an hour,

They'll wonder at the lavish taste
That could, like tulip-fanciers, waste
   A little fortune on a flower!

Yet wilt not thou, whose friendship set
   Such value on the bard's renown,
Yet wilt thou not, my friend, regret   Thy heart, at
   The golden shower thy spell brought down;   least, will not
For thou dost love the free-born muse   regret
Whose flight no curbing chain pursues;
   And thou dost think the song that shrines
That image,—so adored by thee,
And spirits like thee, Liberty,
   Of price beyond all India's mines.

Received some time in October last a Proof copy of the Engraving of
Burns's Monument, from Mr. David Auld, of Doonbrae Cottage, accompanied by a very courteous note, as follows—"Sir—your well-known talent
of which I have long been an admirer, and the notice you have taken of our
National Bard in the 1st. Number of the Irish Melodies[2] prompts me to
believe that you will excuse the liberty I take in presenting you with &c. &c.
I have been most anxious to have a copy forwarded to you, but could never
find out a proper mode of getting it conveyed. I have at last fallen in with a
friend (Mr. Gilbert Burns, of Dublin, nephew of the Poet) &c. &c."—This
Dublin nephew of the Scotch Bard is quite new to me.
   Have had a good deal of correspondence lately, on Irish matters—viz—
Round Towers—the Melodies &c. of which I shall here make some memoranda and first and foremost must mention the translation of the Melodies
into Irish which (ignorant as I am of them in that shape) gives me great
pleasure. The letter I wrote to the gentleman who gave me the first
intimation of this work will be found in the newspaper excerpt given
below:[3]—

TRANSLATION OF THE "MELODIES" INTO IRISH

   The following letter was not, we understand, intended for publication by
either its celebrated writer or the gentleman to whom it is addressed; but as
it has got into the public press, by means of a copy given for private use to
O'CAVANAGH, the translator of the Irish Melodies, it has thus become
public property, and we, therefore, give it to our readers:—

                              "Sloperton, Devizes, Oct. 5th. 1841
   "DEAR SIR,—Absence from home alone prevented me from acknowledging, more speedily, your welcome and interesting letter. The results of
the Round Tower researches are both curious, and, as far as they go,
satisfactory; but, I must confess, the news which I, for the first time, receive

from your letter of an intended translation of the "Melodies" into Irish, by Mr. Eugene O'Cavanagh, touches me far more closely and deeply than all that even the late O'Brien himself could have found out, or fancied about the Round Towers. These songs have the good fortune to be *admitted* into most of the languages of Europe; but this will be like naturalizing them on their own land, bringing them home, in short; and I rejoice to learn from you that such a work is in progress.

"Over the property of the "Irish Melodies" I have, unluckily, no hold; but I cannot conceive that any objection will be made to such a use of them, particularly if it is not intended to print the original along with the translation.—This might, but ought not, produce opposition to such an undertaking.

"With many thanks for your communication,

I am, dear Sir, yours truly,
"THOMAS MOORE.
"John Windele, Esq., Sunday's Well, Cork."

On the day I received this letter a good many more reached me, and thinking it a woman's hand and not being able to make out the signature, I threw it aside under the impression that it was merely a ruse to get a letter from me on the subject of the Melodies, that which I wrote to Mr. Windele having very lately appeared. It struck me also as improbable that *two* translations of the Melodies should thus spring to life at the same moment. I therefore threw the letter aside among the heap that await their chance of being answered—On taking it up again, after the lapse of some days, I saw the little cross before the name and then discovered that my correspondent was no less a personage than John MacHale, the Catholic Archbishop of Tuam, whom I have, on two or three occasions, taken the liberty of quizzing—It was a most fortunate thing that I did not answer it on the day it reached me, as I should have most probably directed my letter to Mrs. or Miss Mac-Hale, Tuam, which would have been worse even than the squibs.—Answered him very civilly saying how flattered I was &c. &c. MacHale after all, though much too stilted in his style of writing, is a very clever fellow—I recollect Curran once saying of Lady Morgan "she writes very tall English for such a little woman," and Mac-Hales's prose is certainly of the gigantic stature—not, however, in his private letters, of which I shall here give another example—

I find I have not time to transcribe his other letter, which is, besides, chiefly occupied with the more mechanical part of his undertaking—Shall give, however, a scrap from a long political Epistle of his, printed lately in the Freeman's Journal—"Apostacy &c. &c."[4]

Have wafered in here as mere curiosities [*MS damaged*]} Among my letters lately was one from a zealous Teetotaller, who is about to publish a book on the subject; and, after saying that he does not recollect having ever seen any published opinions of mine on the subject, begs that I will favour him with a few sentences in favour of the cause. Wrote back to him to say that I thought no man had a right to preach what he does not practise, and that my own habits at table, though certainly not intemperate, extended to a freer use of wine than would authorize me with a grave face to recommend abstinence to others.—

February {1, 2, 3 &c [Tuesday, 1 February–Wednesday, 9 February]—We have had Bessy's nephew, young Murray, with us for about a week previously to his departure for India—Remarkably like his mother, and his visit was a great pleasure to Bessy—Took him on the 1st to Bath where he had never been—called upon the Napiers—poor Napier himself in bed with one of his violent attacks—Sate some time with him—this illness peculiarly hard upon him, just now, poor fellow, when a general promotion is taking place, and his friend Fitzroy Somerset has already proffered him a choice of good military commands—a command in Ireland among the rest. The Napier girls looking all very smiling and pretty, and little Pamela (as Bessy always predicted) grown the prettiest of them all.

10 [Thursday]—Another thunder-clap upon me in the way of money— have mentioned already I believe the relief it was to me to find that Russell's passage home was to be paid by the Company—I little knew (or at least thought of) the other et caeteras that were to follow. But this morning a bill drawn upon me by Russell for £100 at 30 days after [MS damaged] was presented [MS damaged] (the sum having been advanced to him by Lord Auckland [MS damaged] that were necessary. Of these his outfit formed a great [MS damaged] together with the payment of some moderate debts which he could have paid himself had he not fallen ill—

11, 12 &c [Friday–Saturday] A letter from Russell himself accompanied by one from Miss Eden both in every way satisfactory as to the necessity and reasonableness of this demand upon me—But how to meet it?—I am really "au bout de mon Latin," or (as in English slang one would say) my *Spanish*.

14, 15 [Monday–Tuesday]—Was taken by surprize, one of these days, by a visit from Moxon, the publisher. In writing to thank him the other day[1] for [MS damaged] lately of some of his new publications to Mrs. Moore and the [MS damaged] dear publishers, the Longmans) I happened to say, in a postscript that I was [MS damaged] undertaking to propose to me, that would require a Preface, and the [MS damaged] "to carry it through," and which might bring him and myself [MS damaged] money. Upon this hint it was that he started for Sloperton, and I hail it as a sign that my name is not quite unknown in the Book-market—In what I had said to him, in my note, I meant little more than a laughing allusion to the late job-works of Campbell in the editorial and prefatory line[2]—a track in which his success has not been such I believe as to tempt one to follow. During Moxon's short stay (for he merely lunched with me and then started on his journey to town) he told me a good deal about the authors of the day which I should love to have remembered sufficiently to set down. I had taken it into my head, I confess, that the numberless new editions which have appeared of Roger's works were not all the legitimate offspring of public sale and consumption, but that partly for the *éclat* of such success and partly for the pleasure of retouching and resyllabling, of which he is never weary, he had been himself, in his own study, the solitary consumer of many of these editions— But I find from Moxon that all of it is fair and bona-fide consumption (as the receipts both by Rogers himself and his publisher Moxon would show) that Rogers not only "le mieux renté de tous les beaux esprits," as [*MS damaged*] says [*MS damaged*] but also the best bought and read.—Moxon mentioned also what I have been long aware of, Campbell's excesses from time to time of drunkenness. Of Wordsworth he told me what I could hardly have supposed, that there never was a more hard, mean and grinding fellow than he is in making his bargains. This Moxon attributes a good deal, and I dare say justly to the very narrow means that Wordsworth was limited to for a great part of his life, £70 a year being all that his wife & he had to live on for a considerable period. His works of late have much [*MS damaged*] both in renown and sale. Have just stumbled upon the following verses of mine which, I *rather think,* have never appeared in print. It is odd they should *not*—but, if it be true that they are not published any where, it must have been owing to my having made acquaintance with Southey that I suppressed them.—

Epitaph[3]

Beneath these daisies buried deep
  The bones of Bob, the bard, lie hid,—
Peace to his manes—may he sleep,
  As soundly as his readers did.

Through ev'ry sort meand'ring
  Bob went, without a pitch or fall,
From Epic, Sapphic, Alexandrine
  To verse that—was no verse at all.

Till, thinking *fiction* quite enough
  To make a bard, how'er absurd,
And, wishing to have quantum suff.,
  He took to praising George the Third.

[*MS damaged*] brought him, in due time, the laurel;
[*MS damaged*] with [*MS damaged*] Day Odes alone,

All his works, [*MS damaged*] quarrel,
    Because, Dieu Merci! he wrote none.

In right, however, of his crown,
    Us hapless Whigs he doomed to slaughter,—
Like Donellan, of [high] renown,
    Pois'ning us all with *laurel* water.

Poor Bob—at first, some awkward qualms he
    [Felt] on deserting honour's track;
But Princes have been drown'd in Malmsey
    And how can bards be safe from Jack?

To all his tomes, prodigious writer,
    Death writes the final finis thus.—
Oh may the earth on him lie lighter
    Than did his quartos upon us!

The following scraps are also, I believe unpublished any where:

A Scotchman's purse, the wise aver,
May serve as a thermometer.
Though down to Zero, when at home
Let it a few miles southward come,
And you will see the *silver* rising
Within it—in a way surprising.

*   *   *   *   *   *   *

At first, a kilted sans-culotte,
    Over the hills he wander'd bare;
Then, all at once, to breeches got,
    And wore a most enormous pair!

A wag, who saw his novel plight,
    And knew the trim he's sported last,
Said, "Thus it is—your proselyte
    Is always an enthusiast!"

13, 14 &c. [Sunday–Monday]¹—Having at last completed the number of squibs for which Easthope made me the advance last year (£150) I was again obliged to make recourse to him for assistance and wrote to say I should be obliged by an advance of £75. A whole week having elapsed without any answer from him, I wrote to beg he would let me know whether the advance would be inconvenient to him as I had another string to my bow if this did not respond to the touch. By return of post, arrived a cheque for £75, with a very laconic note, saying "I inclose &c. &c." In acknowledging the remittance I said, kindly & cheerfully (but perhaps foolishly) that I saw in all this a delicate hint that he had had enough of my rhymes and would so take it, at the same time thanking him for the kindness of his conduct throughout our literary connection, and adding that I would repay as much of this advance in the prosaic form of *cash* as I could manage.[2] To return to the letters on Irish matters which I have received lately, I had one, about the middle of last month from a Mr. Connor Mac Sweeny—the first paragraph of which I shall here cite—

"Sir—I know not whether you have ever heard of or seen certain letters on the subject of Irish antiquities which appeared in the Limerick Chronicle with the signature below, and in the Cork Southern Reporter under that of Aegyptus—The writer of these lines is anxious to repair any wrong he may have done you by some passages which conveyed strictures on your History of Ireland and allusions to yourself which he now feels were unwarrantable. My apology is that they were written under excitement produced by sympathy with OBrien, whose general theory on the subject of the Round Towers I was asserting. I had participated fully in his enthusiasm, and had only been reading his essay for the first time, when some observations on the subject in the Limerick Chronicle produced a reply from me. At the moment of writing this article I had not the faintest hint that *you* had any share in the transactions which I have since learned hurried his life to its catastrophe."—This awful charge against me of having hurried Mr. O'Brien to his catastrophe is founded on an article of mine in the Ed. Review some years since upon that gentleman's book about the Round Towers.[3] I heard at the time that the poor man took it very much to heart, and even threatened personal vengeance for the liberty I had taken in laughing at him—but as to its having had any share in *killing* him, I don't believe a word of it. This gentleman himself (the writer of the letter) runs nearly as mad in Irish as poor OBrien did; witness, the few following specimens. After alluding to the Greek Phallus (which he learnedly castrates of one of its ls. spelling it phalus) he thus proceeds—"The word corresponding to this in the Irish language is *bud,* which like the Greek words means any one of the objects above named—i.e. a mast, a pole, a pillar &c.—Between this term and the Persian and Irish word Budh, Boo (this jump to Boo is excellent) OBrien perceived a coincidence of letters, but his limited knowledge of the Irish language did not enable him to perceive also that they were quite different words. In the one the final *D* is heard, in the other it is silent. The Persian Budh means a Lord, the Lord of Nature, God, as well as any earthly lord also, Na*bu*chodonosor, Ná-boo-chodonosor, the Lord Chodonosor, Nabopolassar, Na-Boo Polassar &c. &c. You are doubtless well aware to what history & country these names of Princes belong. It is also applied to the divinities of the Persians. Bel, Baal, is broken, Naboo is destroyed, that is, the Lord, the God of the Persians—It should be written, Na *Budh,* Irish *an* Boo, the Great One. Here was the ground of OBrien's error &c. &c." and so he learnedly goes on. This is all, to *my* uneducated notion as like what's called "saying *Boo* to a goose" as possible.—To return to the Irish translation of the Melodies,—I shall here give an extract from the letter of Mr. Windele of October 1841 (already referred to) which first informed me of the intention of Cavanagh to publish such a work—"I also take the liberty of enclosing you by particular desire, a prospectus of a translation into our venerable native tongue of your "Irish Melodies." OCavanagh who would aspire to be your interpreter to the Gaels is a capital Irish scholar—more solid, perhaps, than elegant or polished; and although I cannot assert that I *quite* like the new as well as *your* original costume, yet I must say from the specimens which I have seen that the intended version will not much lower your reputation or tarnish your lyre who yet speak and understand the fine old Vernacular of Ireland &c."

15, 16 &c [Tuesday, 15 February–Tuesday, 22 February]—Received the following letter some days since from Lord Francis Egerton, accompanied by a copy of his newly published Poem on Palestine—

"My dear Mr. Moore—As you have been strong so I have found you merciful on former occasions and one or two of my Irish friends & yours (Crampton and James Corry to wit) have so far encouraged me as to make me think the inclosed will not be unacceptable. It began as a sort of catalogue raisonnée to some sketches and crawled as such things will, into its present shape and volume. I am a great admirer of the Hebrew Melodies and I hope Lord Byron's friends will not consider my allusions to them impertinent—I have heard some curious details of the impression made by Palestine scenery and figures on poor Wilkie and I beleive he died of pleasurable excitement there produced. Beleive me &c. &c. F. Egerton."

23, 24 &c. [Wednesday–Thursday] It was on one of these days, I think, that I sent up the first of my new batch of squibs to the Morning Chronicle, having for its title "A Threnody on the approaching demise of old Mother Corn-Law"[1]—Answered the letter of the Catholic Priest who wrote to me lately from Ballinahinch Co. of Down inclosing specimens of a translation which he contemplates of some of the Hymns of the Roman Breviary, and asking my opinion as to his qualification for the task—Told him in my answer that, two or three years since, Doctor Baines (the Catholic Bishop at Bath) put into my hands the Preces Matutinae, expressing a wish that I should be induced to translate and set to music a few of them, but that, on looking over the collection, I found the task would be beyond my power— This I mentioned to him, I said, as one guidance in the course he himself should pursue—In a similar line is a letter I received not long since from a Mr. Liefchild, who dates from Russell Place, Fitzroy Square—"Sir—my father the Revd. J. Leifchild, D. D. is about to publish a Volume of Original Hymns for public worship, of a higher poetical character than is commonly attributable to such works,—the production of living poets. Among others which have been contributed, the accompanying one has been forwarded anonymously and the purpose of my letter is to request that you will do us the favour to inform us if it be one of your compositions, which the style of it leads us to suspect, although we cannot discover it in the new Edition of your Works. Perhaps it is not too much to expect the favour of one line in reply to a stranger's enquiry." He then comes to what is really the object of the letter—"It might be, however, too much to hope for, but a few verses from your pen to insert in our hymn-book, would be extremely acceptable, and most gratefully received—although certainly more than we have any right to request or expect."&c &c}

25 &c. [Friday]—The difficulty as to how I can raise the £100 to meet Russell's draught still haunts me most worryingly—there being, in addition to this the yet unpaid Bill for the outfits both of him and Tom. It redounds much to the honour of my kind Hume that, when I wrote to him the other day telling him of Russell's draught, he instantly answered, and enquired of me when the bill would become due, evidently meaning to help me through it. This, after all (in a world where money is the universal touch-stone) deserved eminently to be noted down as *true* friendship. Lord Bacon cites some ancient philosopher, who said that "gold was tried with the touch-stone, and men with gold" and the great chancellor, who was, him-self, perhaps (while at Gray's Inn) run hard sometimes for this "trier of spirits" seems to have felt deeply its truth.

March {1, 2 &c. [Tuesday–Wednesday] Have made up my mind, as some resource in my present difficulties, to dispose of the autographs of those letters of Byron which have been published—being constantly teazed by people applying for scraps of his writing, and having already given away far more than I ought, I must now see what they will fetch in the market for myself—Have been occupied with Bessy these two evenings past, looking over and sorting the letters—must also carefully expunge from the auto-graphs most of those passages for which I substituted *stars* in their present published form—In one or two instances perhaps I may venture to restore the original, where the objects of his satire have passed away from the scene—but these instances are few, if any and the attacks upon Rogers are *deadly*. I was in hopes I should be able to avail myself also of his Journals—but they can hardly ever, I think, meet the light—certainly never while any one connected with or interested in Lady Byron remains alive. They are therefore a worse than useless deposit with me.

3, 4 &c. [Thursday–Friday] Received yesterday or the day before a beau-tifully bound copy of a new German translation of Lalla Rookh, by Baron Pechlin, with the following Inscription prefixed;—spelling and all.

"Baron Pechlin asks lieve to present the accompanying translation of Lalla Rookh to Mr. Thomas Moore Esqre., its illustrious author—
Francfurter M. January 1842."[1]

Being about to expunge the *starry* parts from the original letters, I shall here preserve whatever I think *may* be safely preserved—at least safely in *manuscript.*

"You say nothing of * *—how is the old fellow? Has he written nothing more *posthumous* since Jacqueline?"

"Septr. 19, 1818—I should have preferred Medea to any woman that ever breathed. You may perhaps wonder that I don't in that case take to my wife. But she was a poor mawkish, mortal Clytemnestra (and no Medea) who likes to be vindictive according to law, and to hew me down as Samuel sawed Agag, religiously. I would have forgiven her the dagger or the bowl—any thing but the deliberate desolation she piled upon me when I stood alone upon my hearth with my Household Gods shivered around me"

"Three on the clock—I must "to bed—to bed" as Mother Siddons (that tragical friend of the mathematical Blue Devil, my wife) says."

Speaking of R. he says "The Countess Albrizzi showed me a head of him done by Denon at Paris—as like and large as death.—"

He calls Queen Caroline, the *Quim,* and has several coarse jests thereon.

The following postscript is appended to one of his letters—"P. S.—What do you think of "Manfred?" Considering *all things,* it must astonish *you.* But—always a but—I can't express myself, in writing—however you will understand me."

In a letter Feby. 2nd. 1818—after having said, "I have a great love for my little Ada," he adds "though perhaps she may torture me like the mathematical Medea, her mother, who thinks theorems and speaks problems; and has destroyed, as far as in her lay, her husband, by only shaking her head, like Lord Burleigh, in the Critic."

In speaking of Murray he says, it is hardly possible for tradesmen to continue long gentlemen. "They may start like a free-booter, into a sudden fit of grandeur, but they are sure to relapse"—In this there is but too much truth—

In one of his letters to me he talks of my having endured so long Rogers's "liver-complaint, or if you choose to latinize it, *livor.*" The great bulk indeed of the erasures I am obliged to make, are passages relating to Rogers, the deadly bitterness of which is sometimes frightful; and (making full allowance for all Rogers's former deserts in this way) tell far worse against the inflicter of such abuse than against its victim.

In speaking of the Ninth Canto, I think, of Don Juan, he says, "with much sarcasm on those butchers in large business, your mercenary soldiery, it affords also a good opportunity of gracing the Proem with that disgrace to his country, the pensioned imposter, Wellington."—In a letter from Pisa is the following passage respecting Hobhouse—"H. has been here, and is gone to Florence—do you remember your saying that you would rather *praise* him than *live* with him? For my part I say nothing."— The following is of Rogers, written in 1814—"Lately I have seen him much—with that chin of his like the Dew Drop—it never falls without some character hanging by it to dislocation. It is a good man—but they tell me he loveth me not. Whether he does or no, I make great efforts to like him. This says moreover he likes not the success of another.—Do you beleive in such things? I don't [*MS damaged*] I suppose it is what in time we shall all come to." In a letter of the year 1815 he says—"Sam [*MS damaged*] depend upon it—Who would dare to cut off his head, as [*MS damaged*] fellow [*MS damaged*] decapitated the Gorgon? I suppose you think it is rolling down the Bienta or Po, muttering the Pleasures of Mummery."—Having asked him on some occasion whether he knew any one who would undertake a review of Sismondi, he says, in his answer, "If I thought you meant it to me, I should swear you were not shamming, but *Sam*-ming me—comprenez vous?—i.e. trying to make me do a foolish thing for the pleasure of seeing a particular friend fail."—In one of his many tirades against Wordsworth, and the Lakers, he states Wordsworth "that pedlar-praising son of a bitch." Another of the erased passages about * * is as follows—"You may say what you please, but please *think* as I do about him.—damn him. I believe him to be [*MS damaged*] of unhappiness." The very day of his quitting Pisa, I heard of the death of [*MS damaged; two lines unrecovered*].[2]

9th [Wednesday] Having with the aid of the "neat-handed Bessy" [*MS damaged*] arranged and packeted all the letters, set off for town [*MS damaged*] merchandize "and muckle may it speed!" as the old Scotch song says—though, for every reason, it is with misgivings and regret I find myself driven to such a mode of raising the supplies—[*MS damaged*] Heneage for my companion on the way, his attendance being required at the division this evening.—Went to Sackville St.—Dined alone at Brookes's and whiled away the evening there having come for two ballots, Allen's & young DeClifford's, to each of whom I [*MS damaged*] white ball.

10 [Thursday]—Found that, while I was kicking my heels so unprofitably at Brookes's last night, there was an assembly going on at Lansdowne House which I knew nothing about, and which is always the most precious sort of *début* to a London visit, as putting one immediately *au courant* of all that is going on without the slow process of visiting tickets &c. &c.—Called upon Rogers, who took me in his carriage to make calls upon different people— Sate a short time with Mr. Grenville, who asked us to dine with him on

Wednesday next—Called at Lady W. Paulet's (Lord Lonsdale's daughter) where I lunched—then to Lady De Dunstanville's, to Lord Duncannon's &c and lastly to Lansdowne House, where I was called to account for not having known and attended the Assembly last night and was asked to dine with them to-day—Forgot to mention that when I went to Rogers's this morning, I found with him an elderly matron Rotschild (whether Baroness or not, I don't know), her son (a most dandyfied young Hebrew), and a pretty girl who is soon to become his wife—Madam Rotschild, when taking her leave, returned (evidently from a hint given her by the young lady) to say how happy she had been in meeting a gentleman of such talent, and that it would give her much pleasure to see me at her house.—Saw Moxon to-day about my autographs, having called upon Evans yesterday evening on the subject. Both thought they were sure to sell well—so much as four pounds has been sometimes given for a letter, and as these amount to 160 in number, an average of two pounds, or even one for each letter would more than suffice for my immediate exigency—

11. [Friday]—Went to the Horse-Guards to see Macdonald on the subject of young Meyler's commission, the young fellow having set off from Dublin, immediately on hearing I was about to visit London, to add to my many plagues. I was myself anxious to know about Tom's regiment and found that it is still in Lower Scinde.—Saw Hume to whom I explained the circumstances of Russell's draught upon me.

Dined at Lansdowne House—company, the Rotschilds (those we had at Bowood) Lord Marcus Hill, the Gibson Craigs, and four or five more—went for a short time to Brookes's, afterwards—and home.

11.[1] Went to the Horse-Guards to learn something about Tom's regiment—found that it is still in Lower Scinde—had breakfasted at Rogers's to meet Tom Campbell and his niece who lives with him—Before I left home Moxon had called upon me on the subject of the autographs—was going into the city, and would enquire, he said, among "the Americans" (who are great hunters of autographs) to see what could be done towards a *private* sale, which, though far less likely to bring much money, is what I now mean to confine myself to. Dined at Brookes's for the purpose of going to see poor Griffin's Tragedy of Giuseppus[2]—George Byng who was dining there with the same intent, asked me to join him in the Duke of Bedford's box which I did.}

12 [Saturday]—Had written to Hume to meet me at Brookes's this morning on the subject of Russell's Bill (£100) which was to fall due on the 15th and

which I trusted he would enable me, by some accommodation, to meet—
On explaining to him that I merely wanted his acceptance of a draft upon
him, to that amount, at a month's date, he most readily & kindly assented—
Went with him to his banker's—made the Bill for £120 to meet some other
little exigencies and wrote off to *my* bankers (at Devizes) to apprize them
that they should have provision for the Bill by Tuesday morning's post.—
Was delighted to have to tell my dear Bessy that all had been arranged so
comfortably—Couldn't help ruminating a little on the essential difference
there is between *useful* and merely *ornamental* friends—But one mustn't
grumble—both are good in their different ways—{Had called on Bryan
(yesterday, I think) and was asked by him to meet a large party, all Irish, at
dinner to-day—Among the number (15 or 16) there were some I was glad
to meet—viz Phil Dalton, Edward Moore, and I may add OConnel's
nephew (John), who is the most civilized specimen I have seen of that
race.—There were also two ladies, which, for Eliza's sake, I rejoiced to see.}

13 [Sunday]—Breakfasted with Rogers, company, Everett (the American
minister), Lord Mahon, Milnes, Luttrell, &c. &c. Talking of Lady Holland's
crowded dinners and her bidding people constantly "to make room,"
Luttrell said "it must certainly be *made*, for it does not *exist*." {Paid several
visits—}dined at Lady Holland's—Found in the hall, as I was going in, a
victim of *one* of her ways of making room, in the person of Gore, who was
putting on his great coat to take his departure, having been sent away by my
Lady for want of room—Company, Lord Melbourne, Lords Errol and
Kinnaird (if I recollect right) Lord Dalmeny and a good many more—So
great was the "pressure from without," that Allen, after he had performed
his carving part, retired to a small side-table to dine.—All was very agreeable, however, and I have seldom seen Lord Melbourne in such good
spirits—Rogers's theory is that the close packing of Lady Holland's dinners
is one of the secrets of their conversableness and agreeableness—and
perhaps he is right—{"Good measure (as St Luke says) shaken together
and flowing over."

14 [Monday]—Went to Evans, according to appointment after breakfast,
but some business which he had to attend to immediately, intervened, and
our autograph matters were deferred till next day—In the mean time, my
feelings on the subject, from maturer consideration, cannot better be told
than in the following note which I wrote on this day to my sweet Bess—"My
spirits, I confess, have a little sunk as to my prospects; for I greatly fear that
a public sale of the Autographs would, in the eyes of the world, be thought
not quite right; while a private one, while it would be almost as well known,
would not bring any thing like the same amount of money—In short I feel

any thing but comfortable on the subject, and (much as *you,* I fear will dislike the alternative) the very best thing I can do, under the circumstances, will be, I think, to accept the loan of Nell's money, pay her the same interest the Longmans do, and give her a right over these and others as her security. It will then be known only to our selves, *I* shall be saved from what in *this* world I dread most, any tarnish of my "fair fame," and poor Nell will, I know, feel all the happier on thus being made useful to those she loves. To all this I shall only add that *my* mind will be a hundred-fold the easier for getting over the difficulty in this manner. I mean to copy out what I have said above and send it to Nell[1]—Called upon the Burdetts—Miss Coutts asked me to dine with her & go to the French play which I was glad to be able to do—Perlat in full force.

15 [Tuesday]—Evans came and we looked over some of the autographs together—from what he said there seemed little doubt that it would not be difficult to get me £300 for them by private sale—but then one could not answer for their being kept private afterwards—Told him my determination to think no more at present of parting with them—dined with Standish—a most *recherché* affair as usual, and two very recherché ladies to partake of it, in the fair shapes of Mrs. Norton and the Comtesse D'Orsay—Ellis, also, the diplomate, one of the guests—The impression I have always had, even in her best days, of Mrs. Norton's coarseness, becomes the more confirmed every time I meet her.—She told some story to-day which I heard but imperfectly, of a prudish lady being shocked at an exhibition of the Nudo, in some Opera dancers, and another remarking that they ought to wear "Opera decencies"—her *manner* of telling the story was worse even than the matter—}

16 [Wednesday]—{Forgot to mention that I breakfasted with Lord John and his nice kind little wife, yesterday morning—his playful manner with the children, as usual, delightful—stayed with them after breakfast, while he sate, or rather stood, for a full-length drawing now making of him—Was with them again after breakfast this morning, as they wished me to suggest any change in the portrait that might occur to me.—the artist (whose name I did not make out) very anxious that *I* should submit myself to his pencil—but I knew better. Told him of the menagerie of monsters that had been already made of me, and that Mrs. Moore kept a cabinet collection of them to laugh at. "If Mrs. Moore," he said "does not approve of mine when finished, I shall most readily destroy it"—}Dined with Mr. Grenville—Company only Lady Francis Egerton, the Archbishop of York and his niece and Lord Harrowby—Choice Church-and-State companions for *me!* but all very kind and agreeable and the male portion, veterans of the first order—

Mr. Grenville himself being 86, the Archbishop, I suppose, little short of that age, and Lord Harrowby, as he told us, 80—no great deficiency visible in any of them, and Lord Harrowby let off some of his sarcastic jokes as livelily as ever—Sate a good while talking after dinner and then home. The Archbishop in the course of the day reminded me of the Ancient Music, and the little use I had made of my privilege of entrée to "the Preserve," and Lady Francis asked me to *her* music tomorrow evening—Had a note from Sydney this morning—I had met him, soon after my arrival in town, at Lady Holland's and he then told me that his list of dinners was full, both at home and abroad for ten days to come—Alluding to this, in the excuse I sent him, I added that most willingly would I have *fasted* for the chance of dining with him. The following was his reply.

"My dear Moore—I must explain why my invitation to you came so late. Before I knew you were in town my party was completed—but Lord Carlisle is ill, and I hastened to supply his place from the Aristocracy of Nature—Ever &c."

{17 [Thursday]—Breakfasted at Rogers's to meet Mrs. Shelley and some others—Have not mentioned, I beleive, that in addition to my other plagues [*MS damaged*] Meyler has come over from Dublin to get me to apply to the Horse-Guards about his commission—Went to Macdonald on the subject who was as usual very kind; but on [*MS damaged*] to the List it appeared that the young fellow's name had not been put down, and as he was now nearly twenty years of age, his case seemed [*MS damaged*] hopeless—On further enquiry, however, I found that young Meyler had actually received [*MS damaged*] Horse-Guards last year telling him that his name was down [*MS damaged*] and luckily brought that letter with him. This of course will settle the whole matter [*MS damaged*] not very creditable to the official accuracy of the Horse-Guards, as the young fellow [*MS damaged*] his commission [*MS damaged*]—Made some memorandums this morning for my speech at the Dinner—Had a call one of these days from Tom Longman on the subject of Lord Mahon's new Copy-Right Bill. Lord Mahon himself had written to me to Sloperton about it, and the following is an extract from his letter—"You are one of the persons who, [*MS damaged*] the great and, I doubt not, lasting popularity of the works you have produced are most [*MS damaged*] interested in this measure of justice for the extension of Copyright and I beg to assure you that any suggestions or recommendations which might occur to you during the progress of the Bill and which you might have the goodness to communicate to me will be very gratefully received and very respectfully considered"—Was much amused with a very characteristic trait of the *Row* which came out in Tom Longman's great anxiety from his great zeal for the bill—that publishers at least were well taken care of by it. I laughingly asked him "is there any good to come to *me* from it?" "Oh yes, there is," he eagerly replied. After a few more words between us I subscribed my signature to the List, when having gained his object, he with much composure said "The *good* is very *remote*."[1] This reservation of the real fact till his point had been gained was Row all over. "*Row*, brothers, *row*," as my boat-song says.[2] Called for by Hume at the appointed hour, and both proceeded to the Bishop of Derry's, who was to take us to the dinner—sat some time with the Vescova and her daughters, and then set off for the dinner, having looked at Mrs. Ponsonby with no common respect on recollecting her laconic despatch to a friend announcing her husband's promotion to a see—"Dick is Derry." The dinner but scantily attended—Lord Fortescue in the chair, supported by Lord Elliot, Lord Brabazon (I think) and one or two other Irish notables—Several of the Melodies sung by Broadhurst and others, and the plaudits and encores were most enthusiastic—My health, too, proposed most friendlily by Lord Fortescue, was received with such overwhelming cheers as nearly deprived me of all power of returning thanks for it—the consequence was that I forgot much of what I meant to say, and rather confused the rest—but this didn't make much difference—I was applauded as vociferously as if I had been Cicero or Dan himself, and two or three hearty Paddys left their seats at the bottom of the table and strode up the room to shake hands with me— Brought home by the Bishop—Meant to have gone to Lady Francis Egerton's music but felt that I wanted fresh toilette which would have taken time and trouble, so took to my bed instead—}

18 [Friday]—Went for a few hours to the State Paper Office to see how far they had got on with the Calendaring since I was last there—was sorry to find they had made but little progress—took some notes of what they had done—Dined at Mrs. Cunliffe's—company large enough, but (strange to say) quite a blank in my memory—whether through *their* faults or *mine*, I know not. I have heard of a "Tabula Rasa," but a whole dinner-table thus suddenly erased from one's memory is a new phenomenon. In one of Bessy's last letters she mentioned that a letter had arrived at Sloperton from Tom, dated Lower Scinde, and stated a few of the particulars contained in it. Something struck me that there was much held back by her through the fear of annoying me—

19 [Saturday]—Went to the Horse-Guards [*MS damaged*] {Meyler and [*MS damaged*] the regular officially signed letter which Meyler had received [*MS damaged*] commission. This, of course, set all right—but} Macdonald [*MS damaged*] put into my hand a letter or paper which revealed all that my poor Bessy had withheld from me. Tom has sold his commission, and is on his

way home! thus casting away all that I had managed to do for him with so much anxiety and self-denial, {and throwing himself upon the world without profession, means or, I fear ultimately, character. This is most distressing and embarrassing. To show me that I had companions in my misfortune Macdonald gave me a letter to read [which] he had just received from Lord William Somerset, whose son, (much younger I beleive than Tom), has just committed the same foolish and selfish act. People talk of the foolishness of old age—it is bad enough, but *young* selfishness beats it hollow. [Dined] at Sir Henry [*MS damaged*]—a small party most of them strangers to me [*MS damaged*] hostess great favourites of mine, though it is so long since we last met—Joined Bryan & his daughter a short time at the Opera, and went from thence to Lady Palmerston's where all the [*MS damaged*] was assembled—I saw nothing there so pretty as Headfort's daughter—was introduced by Hobhouse, at her own request, to another very pretty person whose name I didn't make out—Home.—}Forgot to mention that I breakfasted this morning with Milnes, to meet the American minister, Hallam, Macauley, &c. &c—{These two last the great talkers, and their outstanding voices made, I must say, (being seated next to them) no very agreeable music in my ears. Talking of music,} Macauley opened for us quite a new chamber of his marvellous memory which astonished as much as it amused me; and that was his acquaintance with the old Irish slang ballads, such as "The night before Larry was stretched" &c. many of which he repeated as glibly off as I could in my boy-hood. He certainly obeys most wonderfully Eloisa's injunction "Do all things but *forget*."[1]

20th. [Sunday]—Bd. with Rogers—{meant to have gone to the Catholic Chapel to hear the music but was fool enough to mind Eliza Bryan who told me it was not yet in full musical strength—so lost it, and heard afterwards how good it was.—}Made visits—called (this day, I beleive it was) on the Halls, the clever writers on Ireland, who live at Old Brompton, but did not find them at home—so had my long walk for nothing—Dined at Fonblan-que's,—a very large party in a small room—got luckily seated between Shiel and our host, so that I had the flower of the whole assemblage—{among the rest were D'Este, Sir George Wombell, &c. &c.—A large party in the evening and a regular set-in for music, commenced by the hostess herself in an Italian Trio, to which I paid but little attention, having my whole mind bent on escape—my retreat embarassed by the chaos of the cloak-room and the utter impossibility, as I feared, of ever finding my great coat—the Trio too on its last legs, and the Hue & Cry after me sure to commence at its close. This at least, was my imagination of the matter—but Apollo saved the intended victim and I got safe into a most pelting shower, having left my umbrella behind.

21 [Monday]—Despatched a messenger for my umbrella, with a note to Mrs. Fonblanque, lamenting and apologizing for my abrupt flight. Forgot to mention that Lover was one of the evening guests, and that I had an opportunity of telling him how doubly precious his portrait of our dear Russell had become to us since his departure for India—*Mems.*—Rio, the other morning, at breakfast, quoted the following good instructions of a Chouan chief to his troops—"Si j avance, suivez moi.—Si je recule, tuez moi.—Si je meurs, vengez moi."—Somebody told of [*MS damaged*] (Mrs. Norton's precious spouse) that on being asked by some lady why he had dyed his whiskers, he said 'twas {"to} please his wife"—"Oh," replied the lady, ["to] please *her,* you should have died yourself"—Forget [*MS damaged*] the rest of [*MS damaged*]}

22 [Tuesday]—Off for home by the half-past ten train, and in the next carriage to me was Jeffrey, Mrs. Jeffrey, Empson, Mrs. Empson and child. Jeffrey, I was sorry to find, not in good health, and going to Clifton for change of air. Asked him to pay us a visit at Sloperton, and said that if possible I would set him an example by coming to see him at Clifton—How comfortable even these glimpses are of old and dear friends. As I say, myself, in one of my songs

> "Ah, well may we hope, when this short life is gone,
>   To meet in some world of more permanent bliss;
> For, a smile or a grasp of the hand, hastening on,
>   Is all we enjoy of each other in this."[1]

This "hastening on" would seem to have been written with a prospective view to my meeting Jeffrey thus in full speed on a rail-road. Found my sweet Bessy pretty well, but, like myself, full of alarm and anxiety about our two boys—the one good & prosperous, but in ill health, the other,—but, alas, there's no use in dwelling upon what is so painful.

{23, 24 &c. &c. [Wednesday, 23 March–Thursday, 31 March] Forget whether I have mentioned that, on the day I went down to Birchin Lane to receive poor Nell's money (which was transmitted to me through a great bank there) I met Rotschild, who stared at me with some degree of wonder, while we shook hands—"This is not" I said, "a very accustomed haunt of mine." "No," he replied—"I was quite astonished to see you here" "Yes— and still more astonishing" I added—"twas to receive money I came." Whereat the rich man laughed. What a pair of extremes we were! and yet— would I change with him?—*No*—decidedly, *No.*}[1]

April 1, 2, 3 &c. [Friday–Sunday]

6 [Wednesday] We had been for some time daily expecting our dear Russell, and this morning a letter arrived from him, dated Hastings, and telling us we might expect him in the course of the day. Our ears and eyes were of course on the watch for every carriage that approached, and at last we heard his own voice telling the fly-man *not* to drive into the gate—Our feeling at this remembrance of his mother's neat garden & his thoughtful wish not to spoil the gravel was hardly expressed by us when we saw the poor fellow himself getting slowly out of the carriage and looking as if the next moment would be his very last. It seemed indeed, all but death. Both his mother and myself threw our arms around him and all three remained motionless for some time—the poor boy the only calm one of the three, and my feelings and fears being far more I confess about the mother than about him—It was very frightful nor shall I ever forget those few minutes at that gate.

7, 8, 9 &c. [Thursday–Saturday] Have had Brabant two or three times to see Russell, and he evidently thinks him in great danger—no ulceration yet in the lungs, but tubercules he thinks have formed

10, 11 [Sunday–Monday]—My poor Bessy day and night watching over her patient, to whom she has given up her own room, and at every cough she hears from him at night is by his bed-side. It is for *her,* I most fear

12, 13, 14 [Tuesday–Thursday]—Great appearances of amendment, and Brabant evidently begins to think him better.

15, 16, 17 &c. [Friday–Sunday] I shall now as some amusement to my mind, notice a few of the various communications I have been receiving lately— and, first & foremost the following scrap of one of my dear Bessy's letters while I was in town (the very letter which contained or rather suppressed the bad news about Tom) deserves well to be preserved—"The violets are getting ready to welcome you back, and I have had a number of little nothings done to keep us tidy, so that without expence we shall go on again looking tolerably decent. The wall is up and the honeysuckle arranged. Polly [Mary Hughes of Buckhill] and I worked hard at your face [A cast from Kirk's bust of me which stands in our drawing-room.] to wash it clean, and we succeeded in a degree. Remember to bring down Mr. Rogers." [A print of himself from Lawrence's picture, which he had promised to give to Bessy.][1]

18 [Monday] Received last month the following letter from Mrs. Hall, the writer of the inimitable Stories &c. about Ireland.—

Dear Sir—I venture to present you with a copy of my Sketches of Irish character, for though, being my first work it is crude and full of faults, yet, relating as it does to my native Bannow, and being inscribed to your old friend Thomas Boyse, I hope it may find favour in your eyes. I have long desired to present you with "my works!" I owe you in common with all those who can feel, so much gratitude, that even to be able to say "I am grateful," is a privilege—but had it not been for your kind note to my husband, I should not have presumed to address you, even now. I cannot avoid mentioning a little circumstance which afforded us both much pleasure. We were reading your History of Ireland, and found that you had immortalized a Poem on Jerpoint Abbey, by mentioning it with a few precious words of praise. That poem was written by my husband, when quite a youth; and long before he thought of exchanging his pen for a Barrister's gown. I am sure you would not regret your generous words, if you had witnessed *my pride* for him. I have the honour to be your most obliged & grateful.

A. Maria Hall

{A letter from my "Sunday's Well" friend, enclosing the result of further investigations on the Round Tower question. "The finding of *Urns*" he says, "is a sad poser to the 'Christians'; Cremation and Urn burial being unquestionably Pagan. As the find rather now holds out a hope, I trust that, in the course of the summer, I may have further confirmation of your views to transmit to you"—

Received a Poem "À Thomas Moore, sur la Poesie" from a M. Chevalier F. Chatelain—the following a specimen

> "Toi, dont la voix mélodieuse
> Des anges [?charma] les amours—
> [MS damaged] dont la lyre harmonie[use]
> [MS damaged] brillante [unrecovered]
> [MS damaged; rest of poem unrecovered]

[MS damaged] America—address, wording and all,—is worth preserving

"Athens, Greene Co. State of N.Y.
March 9th. 1842

"Honoured Sir—Though I have the honour of knowing you only through the media of your works am persuaded that I need not letters of commendation to you to introduce you to [*MS damaged*] which I am about to make. I am not exactly "the man that hath no music in himself," but am so near to it that, like Burns's father, my knowledge of tunes is confined to a very limited number indeed—But among those which I have a perfect knowledge of is "Let me in this ae night," which I spent some three or four months in learning, as it had a peculiar melody in my ears. Now the request which I have to make is that you will be so kind and condescending as to write me a Sacred Song to the above-mentioned tune, founded on the 25th, 2nd. of the Song of Solomon, in connexion with Rev. 3 and 20, together with such other passages of Scripture as *your Honour* may see fit to embody in the Song. The reason why I apply to you for the Song is that your poetry, unlike that of most moderns, possesses "the flash of the gem with its solidity too." You are therefore to consider this address, if agreeable to you, as one of the rewards of merit; and, if otherwise, as one of the inconveniences of eminence. However you shall receive it, I shall think it my duty to exalt your fame, and purchase your works, as they issue from the press.—I am, may it please your Honour, with sentiments of profound respect your humble

Servant

"Hon. Thomas Moore   C. A. Hollenbeck
      London
Great Britain"

Have not mentioned, I beleive, a request made of me by Rio while I was in town that I should write something for him illustrative of the Chouans & their wars & adventures, for a work on the subject which he is about to publish—He spoke to me in the midst of a crowded assembly, and I was not well able to make out his wishes or views on the matter—Have since received a long letter from him, as well as from Hayward, pressing me for the verses which they say I promised, and which Hayward wants for an article on the subject of the Chouans which he is preparing for the Quarterly Review—The following is Hayward's note—"At Rio's request I forward the sheets of his forthcoming work—Wordsworth and Mrs. Norton have promised him poems to be published with it, and I hope you have done the same—I am to be the critic and will give you the best possible reception."—Rio in his letter to me on the subject, says that while engaged [*MS damaged*] work he had read parts of it in different societies, both French & English [*MS damaged*] mes auditeurs il s'est trouvé des poëtes tellement [*MS damaged*] du [*MS damaged*] leur admiration en vers plus on moins beaux, mais &c. [*MS damaged*] à ma prose. Mon bonheur n'a pas été complet, [*MS damaged*] notre Poète Catholique dont la sympathie m'appartenoit [*MS damaged*] by mentioning the different contributions he had received for the work [*MS damaged*] besoin d'une epitaphe faite par un poète catholique [*MS damaged*] et enfans très au combat de Muzillac, et a quel poète [*MS damaged*] se nous en cherchons un du premier order—il n'y en a pas eu [*MS damaged*] Allemagne; il'y a Manzoni, en Italie et vous en Angleterre, ou [*MS damaged*] qui nous donne à nous Bretons plus de droits sur vous."—[*MS damaged*] of Hayward on this subject, he calls my attention to some verses in the Times [on] Wakley the coroner, for his late attack in the House upon Wordsworth. "If you have not read" he says "the verses on Wakley in yesterday's Times, do. They are by Mrs. Norton and well conceived though the execution is hasty.[1] But,—as we agreed yesterday, by common consent at a dinner-party—no one can do this sort of thing as it ought to be done but Moore."

The Chevalier Poet M. Chatelain, already mentioned, has shown me (if indeed such knowledge was wanting) what a fool one is to be civil to such people—at least, *over* civil. Having said something like praise, I suppose, of this gentleman's verses, he now has the face to ask me to translate them into French for a young lady, a friend of his, who *does not know that language.*— "Une Dame Anglaise qui ne comprend pas encore bien la langue Française a été pour moi l'inspiration de ces lignes—Je regarderais comme une fortune de lui en présenter une traduction qui seroit signée, Thomas Moore."}

May 1, 2, 3 &c. &c. [Sunday, 1 May–Monday, 9 May] Again disturbed from home and work, and obliged to run up to town on a fool's errand—namely, the acting as one of the stewards at the approaching Dinner of the Literary Fund—his Royal Highness Prince Albert having consented to take the Chair on the occasion. This is, indeed, meeting the spirit of the times more than half way—the King-Consort taking the chair at a Free-Mason-Tavern Dinner! {But it is all in the natural course of things—Ca ira.}

10 [Tuesday]—Started for town leaving our dear boy somewhat better— Found with my usual good luck, {an invitation awaiting me, just such as I would have most wished—}a note from Murray asking me to meet at dinner *to-day* the man of all others I wanted to shake hands with once more—Washington Irving. Called at Murray's, to say "Yes—yes" with all my heart—{Performed some of my commissions—Company at dinner, Lockhart, and two or three more whom I forget—In talking of Miss Crump, Murray mentioned not a bad blackguardism about her—a rump with a large C before it.}

11 [Wednesday]—{Went to Huffel about a new morning-coat, which I sadly want, but tremble at the expenditure—Huffel, as usual, full of surprise and admiration, at the neat preservation in which I keep my clothes, and at last,

taking a generous interest in my old coat, he exclaimed "I'll tell you what I'll do, Sir—I'll cut away this old lapel in front, the only part that looks at all seedy, and then the coat will look as good new"—Thanked him for this seasonable relief, which he seemed to have as much pleasure in affording as I had in receiving and left his door exclaiming like the hero in Foote's Tragi-comedy "Spoke like a trusty and a gallant Tailor!"[1]—} Went to the Literary Fund Chambers to see what were the arrangements & where I was to be seated—having in a note to Blewitt, the secretary, begged of him to place me near some of my own personal friends. Found that I was to be seated between Hallam and Washington Irving—all right. By the bye Irving had yesterday come to Murray's with the determination, as I found, not to go to the dinner and all begged me to use my influence with him to change this resolution. But he told me his mind was made up on the point—that the drinking his health & the speech he would have to make in return were more than he durst encounter—that he had broken down at the Dickens Dinner (of which he was Chairman) in America, and obliged to stop short in the middle of his oration, which made him resolve not to encounter another such accident. In vain did I represent to him that a few words would be quite sufficient in returning thanks—"That *Dickens* Dinner" which he always pronounced with strong emphasis hammering away, all the time, with his right arm, *more suo*—that "*Dickens* Dinner" still haunted his imagination, and I almost gave up all hope of persuading him—At last, I said to him—"Well, now, listen to me a moment—if you really wish to distinguish yourself, it is by saying the fewest possible words that you will effect it. The great fault of all the speakers—*myself* among the number—will be our saying too much. But, if you content yourself with merely saying that you feel most deeply the cordial reception you have met with and have great pleasure in drinking their health in return, the very simplicity of the address will be more effective, from such a man than all the stammered-out rigmaroles that the rest of the speechifiers will vent." This suggestion seemed to touch him; and so there I left it, feeling pretty sure that I had carried my point. It is very odd that while some of the shallowest fellows going are so glib and ready with the tongue, {that they could "speak a King's part off-hand,"} men whose minds are abounding with matter should find such difficulty in bringing it out. I found that Lockhart also had declined attending this dinner, under a similar apprehension, and only consented, on condition that his health shoud not be given. {On my arrival at the Free-Masons Tavern I found most of the great folks assembled, Prince Albert (whom I now saw for the first time), Lord Lansdowne &c. &c.—Had told Brabant, who wished me to help him to a good seat at the dinner that I should do my best for him, and his name being now brought to me I had to make my way through all the bustle of waiters, dishes &c. to find him and with much difficulty got back again, not being able after all to reach him—a most arrant fool's errand of mine—The Dinner & the

Speeches that followed—the hot comet and its tail—were insufferably long, and had I not been agreeably placed, between Washington and Sir Robert Ingles (the latter full of courtesy to me) I should have yawned outright. There had been some alarm as to Irving's coming, when I first arrived, from his not having yet made his appearance and I began to fear that after all my persuasion had failed—With respect to the Speeches, Prince Albert's new sentences, from time to time, were delivered with much grace and in what the ladies call "very pretty English" and Lord Lansdowne as acting Chairman, did his duty efficiently & eloquently. What amused me most, however, was that Washington Irving in returning thanks adhered almost *verbum verbo* to the formula of speech I had prescribed for his use—the only addition made by him being that he was "unused to public speaking." The reception given him was beyond that of any of the other performers—Poor Campbell made a most [*MS damaged*] exhibition having broken down from sheer tipsiness in the middle of his oration. He had been over cheered by those immediately round him through his first sentences and the same fellows, as it appeared to me were foremost in afterwards [*MS damaged*] & laughing him down. I have seldom witnessed any thing, of a public kind, that gave [so much] pain—"As Dugald Stewart says" was one of the first starting-posts for Campbell at which his hearers set off, and when, on being allowed to recommence, he again began "As Dugald Stewart says," nothing more was allowed to be heard and he found himself obliged to sit down. It was all, indeed, most lamentable and painful—As for myself, my health was given, by Lord Mahon, as "Thomas Moore & the Poets of England," a strange and wrong accouplement, especially when Campbell, so much more worthy a representative of the bards of the Empire was present. My reception by the company was most flattering and my speech, I beleive, did pretty well, though not very audible to the "Ultima Thule" of my listeners. It had one merit, that of being somewhat briefer than most of the other people's speeches.} The best thing of the evening, however (as far as *I* was concerned) occurred after the whole grand show was over. Irving and I came away together and we had hardly got into the street, when a most pelting shower came on, and cabs and umbrellas were in requisition in all directions. As we were provided with neither, our plight was becoming serious when a common cad ran up to me, and said "Shall I get you a cab, Mr. Moore? Sure, ain't *I* the man that patronizes your Melodies?" He then ran off in search of a vehicle, while Irving and I stood close up, like a pair of male caryatides, under the very narrow projection of a hall-door ledge, and thought at last that we were quite forgotten by my patron. But he came faithfully back, and, while putting me into the cab, (without minding at all the trifle I gave him for his trouble), he said confidentially in my ear, "Now, mind, whenever you want a cab, Misthur Moore, just call for Tim Flaherty, and I'm your man." Now, this I call *fame*, and of somewhat a more agreeable kind than that of Dante, when the women in the street found him out by the marks of hell-fire on his beard—(See Ginguené)—²

{12 [Thursday]—Breakfasted with Rogers, who asked me to dine to-day and tomorrow—promised for both days—Most agreeably surprised by a note from my friend Tom Boyse, who is in London with his sister—Called upon them & found to my disappointment they were to be off again so soon as tomorrow—Offered myself for dinner to-day though with the fear of Rogers before my eyes, to whom I wrote to announce my defection and its cause—Only the Boyses themselves, young Carew (Lord Carew's son) who *souped* with us, being obliged to set off immediately to the new Opera— A good deal of kind and cordial confab with my excellent friends the Bs. after which I hastened to Rogers's, and found there the party (rather a large one) he had had to dinner—the Gladstones, Lyttletons, &c.

13 [Friday]—Went, I *beleive,* to the State-Paper Office—but have been sadly remiss in my journalizing, this time, having so many people to see & so many things to do—Called at Lord John's about four o'clock—but found he was then at dinner in order to go to the Houses—begged I would wait till he could come to me, so I sate down & wrote a letter to Bessy, from which the following are scraps—"Miss Boyse was most charming yesterday. I promised, for *you,* that we should both, please God, pay them a visit at Bannow; and, who knows but our dear Bussy may make one of the party? Tell him this with my love—This is [*MS damaged*] an *ex* official pen I am writing with—but you have come in for a longer [*MS damaged*] by it than you would otherwise have had. I wish they had asked me [*MS damaged*] most furiously hungry"—I had hardly written this last sentence [*MS damaged*] came to say that my Lady hoped I would join them [*MS damaged*] did so most willingly and lunched prodigiously—Dined [*MS damaged*] at Rogers's—Company, a large one, but of which I can recollect only [*MS damaged*] (*not,* luckily for themselves, mere *canons*) the Archbishop of Canterbury and the Bishop of London—The latter I had never before seen, but Canterbury was an acquaintance of mine in "auld lang syne," and his gradual recognition of me, holding up his hand above his eyes as if to scrutinize me more accurately, not a little amusing. Having found me out, however, he was exceedingly courteous. The Bishop of London struck me as a bold, clever man of the world, fit for any thing—*every thing*—except being a Bishop.

14 [Saturday]—Breakfasted with Rogers—forget who were the party— Stories of Lady Alborough—her saying of women's dresses, "as thin as

bank-notes—one can see the water-mark." Story of Alvanley—his saying to some stingy Amphytrion he was going to dine with, "The little I drink is at dinner"—but, on seeing the other chuckle at this welcome intelligence, adding, "but the *great deal* I drink, is *after* dinner."—Dined again at Rogers's—another large party, Lady Howick, Miss Rogers, Lady Holland, Bobus Smith &c.—This dinner had been of Lady Holland's own proposing and the account Rogers gave me of the whole transaction was very amusing. At the beginning of the week she had written to him saying she should like to dine with him *quietly* on Friday—"a small, snug party"—and he good-naturedly wrote back that she should have just such a dinner—upon which apprehensive lest he should take her meaning too literally she despatched her page to say that she "wouldn't object to a party of fourteen or so."

15 [Sunday]—Met Otway Cave at Brookes's, and on my asking after the Burdetts', he told me they are out, at —— I forget the name of the place, three or four miles from town, —and that he was going out to dine with them—Seeing something in my face, I suppose, like a wish to be of the party, he proposed that I should accompany him, and said he would send to say we were coming—To this I readily agreed, and between six and seven o'clock, found myself seated among those nice girls, in a strange, solitary hotel, at —— where they had gone for a short sojourn—A good deal of talk in the evening about Mesmerism, of whose wonders Mrs. Travanion appears to be a believer, not even boggling, I think, at such achievements as reading with the back of one's neck &c. &c.—The only drawback on this agreeable *turn-up* was Sir G. Sinclair, one of those Tory toadies among whom poor Burdett has taken refuge. Did not go any where else.}

16 [Monday]—{Went to breakfast with Hallam and found I had made a mistake—it having been somewhere else I was invited—The materials of breakfast however, were got together again most promptly, and himself & his nice niece made my mistake a very agreeable one.—I forget whether I mentioned—for I at least *try* to forget all connected with this painful subject as much as possible—that Tom had suggested to me, in one of his rambling letters, whether I could not manage to get him into some foreign service, and the thought appeared to me altogether hopeless, till on talking over the subject, with Talbot, one night at Lacock, he said that the Prussian Service was that to which least objection could be made, on the score of possible hostilities that might arise between the two countries, and it appeared to him that the King of Prussia from his love of letters & literary patronage would not be unlikely to take a son of mine by the hand very assistingly. Though never very [*MS damaged*] to such claims on my part, I thought this hope was at least better than nothing, and having been introduced at the Literary Fund Dinner to Bunsen, the Prussian Minister, I called upon him,

and after a note or two passing between us I saw him at his house this morning—The amount of what he told me was that the King of Prussia [is] employed in entirely remodelling his army and that until that process is completed or at least much farther advanced there will be no openings for any [*MS damaged*] or promotions in the Prussian Service. So much for *that* hope. Went out to Richmond, taken by the Ords, to dine with the Lansdownes—the day beautiful and a fine sunset got up for us on our arrival— Only one or two besides ourselves at dinner—Returned to town at night.— Have been much pestered these two or three days by a little fairy-looking old woman about a large picture in worsted-work which she wants to exhibit or sell.—She way-lays me every where.} Forgot to mention that I went to the Rehearsal at the Ancient Music this morning, the Archbishop of York having good-naturedly called me to account the other day for never using my privilege of entrée to the Preserve; nothing certainly could be more gratifying than my reception now among them—Lord Cawdor who had been sitting beside the Archbishop when I entered, said laughingly "Let us place him next the Archbishop" and laying his hands on my shoulders, made me take his seat. Two old *stock* articles of mine "Fallen is thy Throne" and "Sound the Loud Timbrel"[1] happened to be among the selections for the day and every body was very flattering about them. The manner, however, in which "Fallen is thy Throne" was given worried me not a little, from its dull sameness, and I felt very much relieved when I found they stopped after the second verse—To have heard them *snore* out "Go" saith the Lord, ye conquerors" (into which I myself in singing it throw all the force and passion I can muster up) would have been rather {a little} trying. Nothing however could be agreeable than the whole séance—the nice people around me, Lady Lyttleton, Mrs. Gladstone, my old friend Lady Cawdor, and the Archbishop's good-humoured daughter—the beauty of some of the music, and the flattering reception given to my own old strains—all was very agreeable.

{17 [Tuesday]—Breakfasted at Murray's—nobody, besides their own family, except Harness—Called upon Count Pollon, the Bavarian minister (having met him at Rogers's at dinner the other day) to see if *he* could do any thing for me towards getting Tom into military service—But I was met *in limine* by an objection which I had not before thought of—that Tom is a Protestant, and all must be Catholic (doubly-distilled Catholic, I believe) in Bavaria. He suggested, however, that Austria was a quarter where something might be done, and, on my saying that I was unluckily unknown to the Austrian ambassador, he sate down and wrote a note introducing me to him. On my arrival with this at Nieumen's, I sent the note in by the servant, and when admitted found the ambassador all surprise at my thinking it necessary to have an introduction to *him* whom I had known so many years. It would not have been polite to tell him that I had forgot all about him, but such was the case till we now met face to face. The result of my conversation with him was in so far better than in the two other cases that there was at least an opening and chance if I were but able to avail myself of it—My son must first qualify himself by learning the German language, and the second qualification was my allowing him a hundred a year! "Cannot a man live upon his pay?" I asked—"Oh yes, there are some remarkable instances of an officer keeping within his pay—but it is hardly to be expected—Your son would get into debt and then the same difficulties and exposure would arise." I repeated to him that I feared it would be wholly out of my power (involved as my small means were already) to encounter such an expenditure—but asked whether, if I *did* make up my mind to this, I might count upon his assistance, and he said that he would do all in his power for me,—but, at the same time, advised that I should get Lord Fitzroy to [*MS damaged*] him (Niemen) on the subject. Thus I shall have fresh favours to ask, and [*MS damaged*] fear before my eyes—*first*, that they may be refused, and secondly that if granted they will be abused—Dined at Sir Benjamin Hall's, a large, grand dull dinner—except that luckily for me I got next to Mrs. Cunliffe's niece [*MS damaged*] little girl—at the other side of me was a most repellant personage, Lady Charlotte Fitzroy with whom I hardly exchanged a word—the only other acquaintance of mine among the guests were Lord & Lady James Hay—Dinner mortally long—home—Asked one of these days to dine with the Clanrickards, but could not manage it.

18 [Wednesday]—My State-Paper operations a good deal interrupted this week by the number of Holidays which Whitsuntide imposes—leaving me but three days for work—Forgot to mention that I yesterday went to Rogers after breakfast, and found Wordsworth with him—The great poet rather more "like folks of this world" than I have generally found him. In the course of our talk, Rogers bid me repeat to Wordsworth some lines from a squib (imputed to *me,* but *not* mine) about the Firm of the Row "Alas, for &c." and I was just beginning to do so when I recollected that this said verse begins with an allusion to Wordsworth himself. The following are the lines; and the easy gait at which all the partners trip along in the last line is very amusing:

> "Alas for *Simplicity's* Poet!
>   Alas for her tradesmen in town!
> And none have such good right to know it
>   As Longman, Hurst, Rees, Orme and Brown."

I got over the difficulty by saying "Alas for the poet—alas for his tradesmen &c. &c." Dined at Lady Holland's—a small party—have forgotten who they were—Went afterwards to the Ancient Music, where I arrived very late but met with a most cordial reception in the select circle where the Duchess of Kent was seated on a sort of tabouret (I suppose it was) and some of the Princesses on each side of her—she very graciously *smiled* me over to her and half rose from her seat when she shook hands with me, saying how long it had been since we last met. When she passed me, too, in going out, leaning on the Duke of Wellington, she again said how happy she was to see me. The great man's eyes, I am sorry to say, entirely overlooked me—N.B. I have made a transposition of the dinners of these last two days—it was on the 17th. I dined with Lady Holland, and my dinner to-day was with Sir B. Hall.

20 [Friday]—Breakfasted (Corry and I) at Lady Listowel's—Called in the course of the day at the Row—my first visit there this time—had some conversation about money-matters, and made a discovery—or rather was reminded of a mournful fact—that the sum of £60 which I give Ellen annually, and which I have gone on thinking was still the interest (6 per Cent) of the £1000 deposited in Longman's hands has been ever since 1838 paid out of my yearly means, and must of course so continue to be paid!— Bessy, who has a much more unencumbered memory for these matters than *I* have, told me when we last talked on the subject that I was deceiving myself in thinking *that* fund to be still in existence—as it had all gone towards the last settlement of my account with the Longmans, and such I now found to be the case—"a sad breaking of the talisman!"—Have been doubting whether I should go to the Duchess of Sutherland's Grand Fete this evening—not liking the operation [*MS damaged*] white neckcloth and "something tight below," which is now the least possible approach [*MS damaged*] on such occasions—Made up my mind at last *not* [*MS damaged*] If it [*MS damaged*] a "distinguished" thing (as every body seems to think) to go to such a [*MS damaged*] it is surely a more distinguished thing to be asked and stay away from it [*MS damaged*] I staid away—[*MS damaged*] who came up expressly for the Queen's Concert the other night [*MS damaged*] had at Bryan's—Was in hopes that kind old Corry would have been of the [*MS damaged*] under restrictions to dine quietly at his hotel [Went in the evening to Lady Holland's, knowing that I was *sure* to be welcomed there in such a dearth of visitors as would be caused by the Duchess's Fête. Found her accordingly almost entirely alone—there being no one but Luttrell, who was on his way to the Fête, and whose effort at full dress, poor fellow, showed me how wise I had been in not attempting the same. Was lucky, however in coming in for a good specimen (as far as *dress* went) of the Sutherland House party, in Lady Harriet Baring who came to show herself to Lady Holland]}[1]

21 [Saturday]—Breakfasted at Hallam's—A grand display of literati; and the poets particularly in great force—there being of the party Campbell,

Wordsworth, Rogers, and myself. What a scene for a Blue to peep in upon!—and yet the whole thing ordinary enough. {Forgot to mention that I had half promised Sir George Warrender to go down to him to Clifden to-day to meet the Bellhavens &c. and stay till Monday. But a note I found on my arrival in town from Lord Lansdowne asked me for to-day to Lansdowne House—"I hope" he said in his note "that if you stay so long in town you will dine with us on Saturday next, the 21st. when you will meet some agreeable Tories—rather a novelty chez moi"—The party to-day very much what he promised me—Tory and agreeable, there being the Cawdors, Westmorelands, Lords Mahon and Ossulston, a French general & his wife (whose names I forget) and the Archbishop of York and his daughter—sate next to the Archbishop and found the whole day very agreeable.

22 [Sunday]—Forget what I did with myself in the morning—the day being Sunday, I had no remembrancers of business to dwell in my mind—Dinner at Edward Moore's—an equally blank concern—or rather worse than blank, being filled up with his bouncing French mistress—poor man! at his age, too.

23 [Monday]—My time for return home fast approaching, whereat I rejoice—Lady Elisabeth thinks of going at the same time—lunched to-day at Bryan's who is in exceeding good humour with me—Dined with the Archbishop of York—Some very pretty Lady *Somebodys* there, between two of whom I sate at dinner, but have now forgotten their names—rather a large addition to the party in the evening, and for the purpose, I soon saw, of music, which I was resolved to escape. One of my pretty assessors at dinner sung two or three of my Melodies and very beautifully—one, in particular "I saw from the beach"[1] she sung with much feeling —particularly the lines "Give me back, give me back the wild freshness of morning" which she gave with a delicacy of passion seldom met with in singers—Asked her to give it again which she did—Much pressed by her and others to sing, but the company was not only too large, but too widely dispersed, so I took an opportunity of making my escape—Was told to-day by somebody that Lady Harriet's dress (which was more admired than most others at the Fete) was of a strangely mixed progeny. She went it seems as "a Primitive Christian" and the dress had been made out of a Chinese Mandarin's!

24. [Tuesday]—Made no memorandum of this day's dinner—had been by the State Paper Office in the morning and think I dined with Bryan.}

25 [Wednesday]—Went one of these mornings to the British Museum to look over works about Ireland—Panizzi and the Librarian most alert &

kind in their attentions—{Dined at Tom Longman's—a laggish party—Mrs. L. sung in the evening very prettily, but my speaking voice was quite enough to plead excuse for my not attempting to sing—a heavy cold having within these few days come on.—Asked to breakfast with Lord Mahon tomorrow—}

26 [Thursday]—Started for home. {Had but one companion almost the whole of the way—a nice lively young lady who was going (I suspect as Governess) to some family a short distance from Devizes—a good deal of conversation chiefly about music, all the way, and my own things often mentioned by her as favourites—Told her I should let her know who I was, before we parted, and the *dénouement* was very amusing—Instead of being at all awed at the discovery she whipped off her glove, seized my hand and shook it as cordially, as if we were two most dear friends, who had just that moment met—much to the surprise, I saw, of some gentlemen, who had joined us but a short time before, and had found us sitting beside each other as tamely as most fellow travellers do [*unrecovered*]. They must have been puzzled, I think, at such a sudden burst of inspiration, in the young lady.}—On arriving at home, found our dear Russell somewhat better than I had expected.

June {1, 2, 3, &c. &c. [Wednesday–Friday] Have not mentioned I think that when I saw Miss Boyse alone the morning I called upon them on my making allusion to my present difficulties &c in business she said in the kindest & most delicate manner that she knew nothing would give her brother more pleasure than in being allowed to be of service to me, and before I left them that day Boyse took me into his own room & saying that she had told him of our conversation—repeated the substance of what she had said, in the most friendly terms. I assured him that I felt their kindness most thoroughly and added that if I found myself reduced to such necessity he would be the first friend I should apply to—I might have added and perhaps *did* that he was the only one of my friends to whom it had occurred to make such an offer—}

4, 5, 6 &c. [Saturday–Monday]—This whole month has been passed quietly at home—if "quietly" I can call it with such pressing cares and anxieties on my mind. The dying state (for I fear it is no better) of our poor boy at home, and the still worse state (for death is after all not the worst evil) of the unlucky Tom now thrown upon the world without profession or means of subsistence make up altogether a prospect which (but for the courage, warm-heartedness and never-failing spirit and spirits of my admirable Bessy) I never should be able to sustain.—

{The following extract from a late article in the Literary Gazette has been sent me by Miss Costello,—herself the writer of it.[1]

Here, too, is another scrap from some late newspaper, which shows that Lalla is not yet entirely forgotten.}[2]

7, 8, 9, 10 &c. [Tuesday, 7 June–Thursday, 30 June] The remainder of this month, passed at home and hard at work—somewhat enlivened however by the following announcement of an agreeable honour lately conferred upon me by the King of Prussia:—

"Berlin—June 1st. 1842. His Majesty has been pleased to found a special Class of the Order "pour le Mérite," to be conferred on persons who have distinguished themselves in the sciences and arts. The number of the Members of the German nation is fixed at 30. To enhance the splendour of the order it will also be conferred on eminent foreigners, the number of whom is not fixed, but is never to exceed that of the German members. Among the foreign members in the class of science (including, it seems, the Belles Lettres) are Robert Faraday, Sir John Herschell, members of the Royal Society of London, and Mr. Thomas Moore." *Prussian State Gazette*

July 1, 2, 3, 4 &c. [Friday–Monday] Came to the resolution at last of accepting Boyse's friendly offer, as relieving me, at least, from one great source of anxiety, the want of means for small daily demands. Wrote to him to say that I would accept his kind offer of a loan of £200, and, almost by return of post, received from him a most friendly letter enclosing notes to that amount.

5, 6, 7 &c. &c. [Tuesday–Thursday] Working at my history, which must now be my whole & sole task—

{8, 9, 10 &c. [Friday–Sunday] The unfinished state in which I had left my applications for Tom when last in town, and the singular circumstance of his name [*MS damaged*] mentioned in the Gazette as connected with the 41st. Regiment [*MS damaged*] me think it expedient to run up to town for a few days to satisfy myself on both points.

15 [Friday]—Started for town—the train much crowded by the numbers coming from the great agricultural meeting at Bristol—had for companions Lord Torrington & a friend of his and got over the operation very agreeably—Had some conversation, at one of the stations with the Duke of

Beaufort (likewise coming from Bristol) who repeated very kindly his own wish & that of the Duchess that I would visit them at Badmington—Talbot being expected in Sackville St. I was thrown out of my *gite* there & took up my quarters at Cox's Hotel.

16, 17, 18 &c. &c [Saturday–Monday]—Have unluckily lost my little memorandum-book while in town, in which I had kept only the diary of my dinners &c. but (what was of much more importance) made a good many extracts from the State Papers of Elizabeth—I am left without any resource, except my memory & my short notes to Bessy to make out a journal of this visit to town.

15 [Friday]—(The day of my arrival)—Got rather late to town—called upon Rogers, whom I was lucky enough to find just setting out to dine with his sister in the Regent's Park—asked me to accompany him, which I did most willingly, "accoutred as I was"—and thus, with my usual good fortune (in such matters) found myself in for a very agreeable dinner. The company, Turner, the Artist, Krazinski, and another Pole, and in the evening, Eastlake—Turner, whom I sate next at dinner talked a good deal to me about the losses he had experienced on the score of the Epicurean—so many of the designs he had made for it being left on his hands &c. &c.[1]

16 [Saturday]—Breakfasted with Rogers—Went to the Horse-Guards to see Macdonald on the subject of Tom but did not meet with him—dined with the Burdetts—
    To day, in talking with Lady Elisabeth, I happened to say something respecting the state of my own feelings which struck her as so mournful that she burst out a crying and said "I cannot bear to hear you speak in that way."—Dined at Burdett's—Company, Lord St. Vincent, Penn and one or two others.}

17. [Sunday] Breakfasted with Rogers—went afterwards to Warwick St Chapel, and was lucky enough to come in for Mozart's Requiem—Dined at Lord Lansdowne's, having been my own inviter—I had heard, on arriving in town, that he was to have a "Dickens' dinner" (as Washington would call it) on this day and wrote to propose myself as a guest—Among the other diners besides Dickens, were Rogers, Luttrell, Sir Edward Head, and one or two more—Had a long séance to day with Macdonald at his own house, on the subject of Tom. Something that fell from Bryan yesterday gave me a faint glimpse of hope that *he* was a little inclined to interpose his aid in my

present emergency—"Wasn't it possible" he asked "that Tom might enter the army again as an Ensign—that rank being so much more easily purchasable?" I therefore questioned Macdonald on the subject—"Why, my dear fellow" he answered "an Ensigncy would cost £450 and the payment of £400 would preserve to your son his Lieutenancy." He also mentioned, what was most tantalizing under the circumstances that it was not, as I supposed their intention to continue Tom in his present regiment, (where there are near twenty lieutenants before him) but that they had a snug berth ready for him in a regiment which was now in England & would remain so for some time, and in which there would be but two or three between him and promotion. I forget now the number of this regiment but he showed it to me in the Army List. This is real and *essential* kindness, if I *could* but have availed myself of it.

{18 [Monday]—Forget which [*MS damaged*] dined with the Burdetts and accompanied Clara & one of [*MS damaged*] in the evening—Among the company at Burdett's were Sir Alan Macnab, and [*MS damaged*] whose names I forget. From the Institution I accompanied the Burdetts to [*MS damaged*] Dy Sombre's—the first time I have seen her since her fall. But I forgot even [*MS damaged*] "filthy bargain") when she began to sing, which she does more sweetly [*MS damaged*] when first I saw your face" was given by her [*MS damaged*] touching expression. But, alas, when I turned to the "face" that was among the lookers-on, it dissolved the whole vision.}

19 [Tuesday]—{The slight hope I had felt from what Bryan said was to-day put to flight. On my mentioning to him this morning what Macdonald had said as to the price of an Ensigncy, he passed carelessly on to some other subject—so that, Friday being the last day they could keep Tom's affair suspended, I was obliged to make my decision—N. B.} It was *this* day, I beleive—not yesterday—that I dined at Burdett's to meet Mac-Nab &c.— the loss of my memorandum book has allowed all that was *agreeable* to escape out of my mind—the *dis*agreeable is sure to remain—Called upon Macdonald & told him the utter hopelessness of my case; so, *there ends* the whole matter and, I fear, all my unfortunate boy's prospects. Sate a good while with Macdonald, while he was dressing for some levee and had an account from him of the small beginnings from which he rose to be what he is—all naturally, shrewdly and interestingly told.—{While waiting for the time appointed by Macdonald, I had called upon Lady Dover, and found her surrounded by her children, as gentle, nice, and womanly as ever— though acting, I understand the part of an Irish landlord, in a way to put Squire *Man* to the blush.

20, 21, &c. &c [Wednesday–Friday]—It is useless to affect the form of a Diary, having lost my Day-book—I shall therefore (to use a poetic phrase) *lump* my town transactions—Wishing to hear some account of my announced Prussian order, I called upon Bunsen, the Prussian minister, and found him at home. He had not, it appeared, received any further announcement of the honour that I had seen, myself, in the Gazette—I told him my impression was that I owed to *him* the selection of my humble self for this distinction, but he assured me that he had known nothing about it till he saw the public announcement. I said something of my surprise at being thus singled out, and added that if the King of Prussia had even *known* me during his stay in England, I should have been less astonished at such a kindness—"Known you!" exclaimed Bunsen, "he knew you long before he knew *me*—he has quantities of your poetry by heart." He then advised that I should write a short note to Baron Humboldt, saying that I had seen the announcement in the Gazette, but had not yet received any official communication on the subject.

21 [Thursday]—Called upon the Duke of Sussex—was shown in to the Duchess, who took me to the Duke's room through a part of his Library which I had not before seen, nor had I before known that his theological library consists of no less than 2000 different Editions of the Bible! The Duke himself confined to the house by a cold—asked me to dine with him to-day—but I had already (unluckily) engaged myself to a tete-a-tete dinner with Bryan. "Will you dine with me on Monday, then?" he asked. On that day, I told him, I should be obliged to leave town—but would [*MS damaged*] chance of being able to come, by allowing me to defer my answer, [*MS damaged*] "most willingly"—In talking of my Prussian honour, he said [*MS damaged*] of the prettiest" of all the European orders, and then [*MS damaged*] it, which, however, I now entirely forget. An amusing [*MS damaged*] of things I have to think of and look to, occurred one of these [*MS damaged*] for the period of Edward VI there was one respecting the [*MS damaged*] in which the letters H. G. occurred pretty often, [*MS damaged*] then made that this new form of Prayer was dictated by the Holy Ghost. In the same memorandum-book I had also scribbled a good deal about my visits, hours of appointment at the Horse-Guards, in [*MS damaged*] the same abbreviation H. G. and my puzzle between these two [*MS damaged*] subjects of reference was not a little amusing. Was much releived by learning that Bryan had got Wyse to meet me at dinner, which made quite another thing of it.}

22, 3 [Friday–Saturday]—{On one of these days called again at Bunsen's to learn more accurately Humboldt's address, in case I should think it expedient to write to him—Bunsen himself out but saw his secretary, a civil intelligent man, who in the course of our conversation said, after looking earnestly at me for a few seconds "You are too young to have been the Moore to whom Lord Byron addressed those beautiful verses "My boat is on the shore"?—"No, indeed," I answered laughing—"I am that very Moore"—"But Byron was older than you, surely?"—"Not so, either—he was a good many years my junior"—From what he said about the order, I was led to suspect that some difficulty as to its being acknowledged by the English court had delayed the formal intimation of it, and accordingly resolved not to take any steps in the matter—Called upon Lady Palmerston, from whom I had received a note asking me to dinner on Saturday next— in the course of conversation made her laugh by telling what the Prussian secretary had said about my young looks—"Well, you *do* look wonderfully young" she said, on which we both laughed still more. What poor Stevenson used to say when people flattered him in the same way is about the true state of the case—"What the devil's the use of a man *looking* young when he's *not* so?"—} Having now no other hope for Tom, I again turned my thoughts to the chance of the Austrian service for him—but the recommendatory note from Lord Fitzroy which Neimen required appeared to me rather a stumbling-block. As, however, he could *but* refuse I wrote him a letter on the subject, which he answered promptly and kindly, inclosing, at the same time, the required note for Neimen, and thus crowning the uniform course of his kindness to me—Lost no time in delivering the note to Neimen, who said that he would do all that he could towards favouring my object. {Forgot to mention that on the day I dined with Bryan, I had called upon Mrs. Story in the morning, the first time I had seen her for ages—She asked me to come to her in the evening, which I did, somebody having sent a carriage for me to Bryan's—Found at Mrs. Story's, Christine Villamil (daughter of our old Spanish friends) and her husband, whose name I do not now remember—She sung several Italian & Spanish things at the Piano-Forte, not so well as her mother, in "auld lang syne," but reminding me of her very agreeably—Called this morning to see the Doctor Johnson whom Brabant consulted upon Russell's case some time since—but it was past his time for receiving visitors}

23 [Saturday]—Went to Dr. Johnson's, who did not speak quite so encouragingly about Russell's case as he did to Brabant, who told us that in speaking of young men obliged to come home for this sort of disorder he said—"It is very, very tedious, but they all recover"—Dr. Johnson, however, mentioned a physician upon whom he had more reliance, in East Indian cases than himself and said he would procure & communicate to me his opinion on this subject. When I offered my fee, he very courteously

declined it.—[Met with another [*MS damaged*] very flattering as well as convenient liberality a few hours after, when, wishing to have [*MS damaged*] and having long resolved to give up Hutchins who has grown blind and [*MS damaged*] called at Cartwright's—(no—it was yesterday I called at Cartwright's), and before [*MS damaged*] I would come to-day—The great operator himself being just then occupied [*MS damaged*] into the hands of his nephew, who did for my purpose just as well. [*MS damaged*] the operation and given my fee, I said to him (being quite sure, from his exceeding courtesy to me that he knew who I was) something civil respecting Cartwright, and our having met once—I forgot where—Whatever it was I said the whole fact at once flashed upon him, and he instantly exclaimed how delighted he was &c. &c. adding "Good God, Sir, I cannot think of taking a fee from you," and at the same time whipping the sovereign out of his waistcoat-pocket and forcing it back into my hand. He then begged that I would let him inform Mr. Cartwright of my being there, and running off returned with the great operator himself, reeking from some patrician jaws (there being a coronet on the carriage at the door) and it turned out that we never *had* before met. A few seconds of hearty hand-shaking followed, and we then bade adieu—till I next want my teeth cleaned.—Went with Clara Burdett to the Panorama in Leicester Square and afterwards to the Chinese exhibition—the most interesting show I have ever seen—Dined at Lord Palmerston's—tried to be as late in arriving there as possible, but found I was still an hour too soon—I had been told that Lord & Lady Ponsonby were to dine there, and found a lady and gentleman already arrived who turned out to be them and, as I discovered afterwards, every [*MS damaged*] meet me as such, though I had quite forgot *them*. Among the rest of the company was Lord Melbourne. Had a good deal of conversation with Lord Ponsonby in the evening.

24 [Sunday]—Set off for home, by the two o'clock train—Happened on Edward Moore and his bouncing French mistress (the wife of a courier, I beleive) who were going pleasuring—it being Sunday—to Slough! There was also an odd fellow, a man who passed his whole life in trout-fishing all over the world, and who brought his tackle (rods, minows and all) into the carriage with him, after some opposition from the rail-way people to which he seemed well accustomed and got over it like an experienced traveller— He spoke French with Moore's Madame, like a native, and there seems hardly a trout-stream in Europe that he was not acquainted with.—When we were near parting with Edward Moore at Slough I saw Madame saying something, in a whisper to our piscatory friend and found afterwards that she had been officiously telling him who I was, for he now passed from fishing to rhyming & told me that he had translated into French verse

several of my poems. The best of it was, too, he took it into his head that Edward Moore was Sir Edward Bulwer, and I am sorry I did not leave him under so grand a mistake—Edward Moore a romance-writer!!

The above is from a Letter in one of the Orange newspapers of Dublin, against my friend Bishop Mac-Hale![1]

25, 26 &c. &c. [Monday–Sunday, 31st]—Found our dear boy, on my return, much the same, and the poor mother bearing up still most wonderfully under all her night-watching and anxiety—}

August {1, 2, 3 &c. [Monday–Wednesday]

6th. [Saturday] Went to Lacock for a couple of days, to meet a learned German Professor named Leipsius, who is about to proceed to Egypt on an antiquarian mission by order of the King of Prussia, and wishes to learn Talbot's art for the purpose of Photogenizing buildings, ruins &c.—a very intelligent man—our conversations "de omnibus rebus" highly amusing & agreeable—if I could remember them. Slept there.

7th [Sunday]—The German very anxious to have me [*MS damaged*] for one of those "formidable likenesses"—but I refused, as I have hitherto most stoutly—I say "hitherto," for on this occasion I at last gave in [*MS damaged*] and all being collected into a groupe of monstrosities which I could not refuse—[Sou]thron who came over to luncheon was forced also to contribute to the [*MS damaged*] beauties. What the picture settled into afterwards I know not—Day, same [*MS damaged*] quiet & agreeable.

8 [Monday]—After sauntering about the grounds & [*MS damaged*] for books through the Library went to dine at Southron's—my first time [*MS damaged*] invitations—Company Captain Rooke & family, the Drurys, the [*MS damaged*] two more—was to have slept there, but preferred a chaise home.}

8, 9, 10 &c. [Monday, 8 August–Monday, 15 August]—Hard at work at my history, which must now be my whole and sole task but when to be finished, God only knows.

16 [Tuesday]—Received a letter from Tom containing somewhat more comfortable glimpses of a Future for him than have for a long time opened upon me—A French gentleman whom he has got acquainted with through our friend Villamil, and who is a Member of the Chamber of Deputies, has invited him to pass some weeks with him at his country house at Eu, and has also suggested as a possible resource for him his entering into the Légion Etrangere of the French Army employed in Algiers,—the King being likely, he thinks, to give him a commission in that service—This is at least worthy of consideration—A very happy use was made by Peel the other day, in his clever answer to Lord Palmerston of some lines of mine from the Melodies. Alluding to the flight of Lord John & most of the other opposition-leaders from town leaving Palmerston to stand the brunt of the House alone, he compared him to

> The last Rose of Summer left blooming alone.—
> All his lovely companions were faded & gone.

{The Dandyism of Palmerston was as happily hit off in this simile as his lonely position.

11, 12, 13 &c. [Thursday–Saturday]—A letter also from our Spanish friend Villamil on the subject of Tom and the prospect of getting him into the Legion Etrangere—About the same time a letter from Tom himself asking me with the same view, to give him an introduction to Madame Adelaide— These letters reached me about the 16th.

16, 17, 18 &c. [Tuesday–Thursday]—Though much misliking the rather humiliating step of applying to Madame Adelaide (more especially after what happened relative to my Life of Lord Edward)[1] I thought it right not to leave such a chance untried, and accordingly enclosed to Tom the letter of introduction. How it will turn out, God knows.—}

19, 20 &c. [Friday–Saturday] An amusing instance of the spread of literature just now—one of Bessy's old women in the village sent her lately a letter from her son, in which was the following learned piece of criticism. "The following lines are written by Thomas Moore Esqr.—I consider them beautiful—very sarcastic upon the gentry." Then follow these lines from Lalla Rookh—

> A heav'n, too, ye must have, ye lords of dust,—
> A splendid paradise—pure souls, ye must.

> That prophet ill sustains his holy call,
> Who finds not heavens to suit the tastes of all.[1]—

This metamorphosis of my friend Mokanna into a lampooner of "the gentry" is excellent—a sort of Oriental Tom Brown the Younger.

21, 22 &c. &c. [Sunday, 21 August–Wednesday, 31 August] Work and worry, my daily portion.—Wrote to Lord Auckland to welcome him home—to tell him of poor Russell's continued illness & thank him as warmly as language *could* thank for his kindness to him—In his answer he says "You are very grateful for a very little—having a palace and {some} 400 servants, it was no great effort for me to give a bed to the son of so old a friend."

September 1, 2, 3 &c. [Thursday, 1 September–Sunday, 11 September] Received about the 10th. or 11 a letter from Tom which agreeably relieved me from the misgivings I have had about my letter to Madame Adelaide—I shall here transcribe all he says on the subject—"The following particulars which I trust will give you pleasure, I must state briefly, as time passes. On last Sunday morning I was presented at Court. His Majesty received me most graciously, conversing with me (in English, which he speaks perfectly) during five or six minutes. The same day I received an invitation to dine at the Palace when I was equally well received. On Tuesday I had an audience with Madame Adelaide, and the Princess was most kind. She received me alone and conversed for a considerable time; but did not open your letter while I was present—But yesterday evening I received the following note from the Lady in waiting—"Madame Adelaide désirerais parler demain à 11 heures à Monsieur T. Moore. La Comtesse de Montjoie s'empresse de l'en prevenir—Chateau d'Eu." Accordingly I waited upon Madame this morning who was really quite friendly both in her manner & in what she said. She told me that on reading your letter she spoke upon the subject to the King who immediately expressed himself most anxious to meet your wishes. His Majesty also recommended me strongly to Marechal Soult, to whom she, too, had spoken upon the subject. Madame then spoke to me very kindly concerning the badness of the climate and the severity of the duty in Africa; observing that after my health having already suffered in India, I should not think of venturing in Africa &c. &c. Madame concluded by telling me that she had settled every thing with Maréchal Soult who would receive me immediately and she added "Si voulez me suivre, je vais vous présenter moi-même a son aid-de-camp &c. &c." Maréchal Soult who *can* be a *Tiger,* is gentle enough where Kings are concerned; and, it was no doubt to the intervention of his Majesty and Madame that I owed the politeness of my reception. But here the first obstacle has arisen, in consequence of my not being in possession of the papers which I forwarded to England by your desire. The Marechal requires also a Certificate &c. &c. &c. . . . From all that the Marechal said to me I could see plainly that my request was a very difficult one for him to fulfill—but he expressed himself most ready to do every thing in his power as soon as he should receive my papers and find every thing satisfactory. . . . Therefore it is that I venture to ask you to obtain from Lord Fitz Roy the favour of a letter of recommendation to Marechal Soult—as a letter from him as our minister of War to Marechal Soult upon whom every thing depends would undoubtedly facilitate the affair &c. &c. Madame Adelaide bid me write to you to-day and assure you of the continued friendship for you which exists no less on her own part than on that of Louis Philippe; and she added that she intended writing to you herself and assuring you of her kindly dispositions, for, she added "Votre pere et moi nous avons toujours été de très bon amis."

There's a good deal more of the letter, but I have given only the most interesting parts. What will come of it all, heaven knows. But I see not much to hope—and, and in the mean time, it is but a continuation of that spoiling process to which poor Tom (as my son) has been from his childhood subjected. Let the result, however, be what it may the kindness of these Royal people is even more creditable to themselves than to me; and shows what injustice I did them in supposing the "tantaene animis coelestibus irae" to supply also to these earthly godheads. Their anger with me (if indeed they ever felt it) has all evidently passed away—It being the opinion both of Bessy and Ellen that I ought to run up to town and confer with my friends at the Horse-Guards on this matter, I started from home on the

12th. [Monday]—My companion a poor sick young clergyman who had been to try the air of Clifton for relief; and (as happens constantly with me) it chanced that in the course of our conversation, I touched a spring which brought us in *rapport* with each other. In speaking of the Charter-House where it appeared he had been educated, I said that a son of mine had been also brought up there whom he might have known, named Moore, upon which his poor pale face lighted up with smiles, and without saying a word he took off his hat to me. {These things come like glimpses of sunshine across one's path—Called at Rogers's and found he was (for a wonder) in town—the depopulation being now to an extent seldom before witnessed—Left word I would come breakfast with him in the morning—Dined at Brookes's and had side by side with me Lord Tavistock, who was by no means tongue-tied, as usual, but talked well and agreeably—Took him to task a little for living so much out of the world, and one of the reasons he gave for it (as well as for not continuing in Parliament) was that the late hours did not agree with him. I had found on arriving that Lady Mount-

Edgecumbe had come from the Continent with her boys and was at Thomas's Hotel—went there and found her in all the bustle of preparation for Windsor where she was to go in the morning to enter on her course of waiting—looking as kind and *almost* as pretty as ever—drank tea with her & then home

13 [Tuesday]—Breakfasted with Rogers—Mrs. Jamison of the party—R. produced Alfred Tenyson's new Volume of Poems[1] which led to a discussion of his merits—Mrs. J. praised very much that ballad of his with a strange burden, about the "wind being fresh in Hadon tree" (or some such line) and read it aloud to us. But Rogers took it to pieces, while I rather defended it; though never, I confess, well understanding what the writer means. He has found a critic, too, I see, in the last Quarterly who deals as largely in the unintelligible as himself.[2] For instance, the Reviewer says that Mr. Tennyson's work is "full of liquid intoxication and the language of *golden oneness.*" What does this mean? Had it been paper *one*ness, I should have thought it alluded to a one pound note. In summing up the poetical qualities of Mr. Tennyson, the [Reviewer *MS damaged*] his brain for him— "In his better and later works, the [*MS damaged*] brain, abounding in gold dust and diamond power, and [*MS damaged*] and hieroglyphic beasts, pours out its wealth and [*MS damaged*]"—This is rank Bedlamitism. Rogers talked of the [*MS damaged*] notes on the "Italy" relative to the remark made by an old Domine [*MS damaged*] the Last Supper, at Padua. This story was Wilkie's, and [*MS damaged*] monk made one observation which Rogers *coolly* [*MS damaged*] himself. It has been told in print, Rogers said, by four [*MS damaged*] Wordsworth being one of them, and his version, (which [*MS damaged*] of all. Went to the Horse-Guards—Lord Fitzroy [*MS damaged*] the case, gone away.—A good deal of talk with [*MS damaged*] who is of opinion that Lord Fitz Roy would *not* be disposed to give the letter of introduction to Soult which Tom wished for—Intimated, too, (what already of course had occurred to myself) that the new Commander in Chief would not be so easily manageable as the last one—Mentioned in the course of conversation the Duke's rage at the time of the occupation of Algiers by France—his expostulation, threats of war, &c.—the French ambassador writing home in alarm and the Minister of that day (query, who?) writing back in return, "Don't mind him—laugh at him—there is not a man in Europe who would be more unwilling to go to war than Wellington"—Called on Charles Kemble—his melancholy account of himself and his concerns—asked him to put me somewhere this evening to hear his daughter in the Somnambula—Dined at Brookes's—was seated in a nice private box at the Theatre, but found the whole performance most disagreeable—Rogers told me today that in a few months he will have reached his 80th year—A most marvellous man, I must say for him, both bodily and mentally—}

14 [Wednesday]—Breakfasted at Brookes's—Rogers, my grand dispenser of that meal having gone for some days to Lord Palmerston's—Wrote a long letter to Madame Adelaide, on the subject of Tom, Marshal Soult, Algiers &c. which was in every respect a most painful operation to me—Took it myself to the French ambassador's, with the hope that he had returned from Paris, and having a sort of notion that I am personally acquainted with him, in which case I would have tried to enlist him in the cause of {poor-devilish} Tom—but he had not yet returned. Being so near my old (or rather young) lodgings in George St. thought I would treat myself to another peep at them—the last time I saw them having been with my poor boy, Russell. But the "gentleman up two pair of stairs," was now unwell and I got no farther than the hall.—Met Lady Holland in her carriage in St. James's St.—a god-send (or to speak more gallantly) a goddess-send, at this time of the year in London.—Asked me of course to dinner, to-day, which I most gladly accepted—had already formed a sort of slip-knot with East-hope to dine out at his country-house—but he had luckily put me off till tomorrow. I had now dined two successive days at my own expence which, in London, is a sort of monstrosity—"Base is the slave that pays,"[1] says some one, and I feel deeply the truth of ths aphorism when paying for a dinner for myself in London—Company at Lady Holland's, (besides herself and Allen) Sir C. Hamet and Henry Bulwer—The conversation very agreeable, and my Lady read to us after dinner a letter from Sydney quite as piquant as any of her dishes.—Thought to have remembered some of it, but my knack at reporting, never very good, is now nearly gone. I remember, however that before dinner, Allen provoked me a little. That people shouldn't *read* my History is no blame to them, God knows; but that *without* that previous process, they should (before the author's face, too) profess to give an account of it and criticise it is rather too bad and shows that at least some of our Irish *brass* must have adhered to them. Allen gravely assured the company that the first Volume of my History was chiefly employed in supporting those fabulous claims to antiquity which my countrymen had set up; whereas I am the first real Irishman who has ever ventured to protest against our Milesian pedigree and relieve the real antiquities of the land from the incubus of that dull fable. So much was this the case, and so essentially had this stale nonsense come to be connected in the minds of Irishmen with their great national cause that I remember Lynch, the author of "Feudal Dignities"[2] (a man well versed in our *real* and ancient lore) writing to express to me his deep regret that I had adopted this view of the question and adding that he "foresaw in it future concessions to English prejudice" on my part. In the evening Lord Fitzgerald joined our party— Lady Holland very anxious that I should meet him at dinner tomorrow, and tried all her moods—the imperative, among the rest,—to make me say that I would come, but, without telling her where I was engaged, I declared it to be impossible.

15 [Thursday]—{Called early on Doctor Johnson to ask him about our poor Russell—but found his room filled thick and three fold. Met Bulwer (Sir Edward) at Brookes's and told him of the sort of *double* he had had in my companion, the other day, in the omnibus—"I dare say," replied Bulwer, "you were clever enough for *both* of us." His tone and manner in saying this,—combined with his ringlets "dropping odours" &c. fresh from Paris (whence he has just come) was all super-exquisite. In what queer heads Genius *se niche* sometimes!—rather like him, though.} Called for by Easthope at half past three—our companion a Mr. Doyle a young Irishman, lately added to the staff of the Chronicle, {and the writer (as Easthope confided to me) of the late articles against Lord Ellenborough[1]—} Easthope's place not far from Oatlands—none but his own family at dinner—three daughters and a son—Being asked to sing in the evening, was glad of the opportunity of again trying my voice, not having sung a note for months—and the last time I ventured having been before our poor dying boy, when after a note or two I broke irresistibly into a fit of sobbing most painful of course to us all—ever since then I had not ventured to touch the piano-forte till this evening, when, glad of the opportunity of another trial, I consented to sing and was rejoiced to find I could get so well through it—my voice being much the same as ever, and my audience evidently much touched and pleased.

{16 [Friday]—After breakfast Easthope proposed to drive me over to Oatlands which I was glad of the opportunity of seeing—returned to town after luncheon—Walked about for some hours, not like Diogenes, looking for an honest man, but looking for *any* man, honest or not, who would ask me to dine with him—but none such turned up, and I was obliged again to feed at my own expence. Was lucky enough, however, "sicut meus est mos," to fall in with an agreeable companion, William Ponsonby (Lord de Morley?) and our tables being laid alongside each other, and the coffee-room all to ourselves got along very conversibly and comfortably—Told me a great deal about Naples from whence he is just returned—}

17 [Saturday]{The following note from Lady Holland, dated last night, shows that I need not have dined alone yesterday, but for an accident—she had sent her servant (in every direction but the right one) to find me out. [*MS damaged*]—I am very much disappointed after all the trouble I have taken [*MS damaged*] dine with to-day—Pray, come tomorrow"—} Called again upon Dr. Johnson and had some talk with him—told him of our trial once or twice of the bath he had recommended, and of our leaving it off on account of the painful trouble it gave our poor boy and the opinion of our physician that it would do him but little good. He then suggested some

easier mode of applying the bath, and said that he should like to have it continued—Company at Lady Holland's (besides Rogers who took me) Sir James Kemp, Sir Stephen Hammeck, some foreign minister whose name I could not catch and one or two more. Some talk with Allen, during which I asked him whether he did not feel wearied sometimes by the sort of effort it must be to keep up conversation during these evenings, and he owned that it was frequently a most heavy task, and that if he had followed his own taste and wishes he would long since have given up that mode of life. For myself (as I beleive I told him) that Holland-House sort of existence, though by far the best specimen of its kind going would appear to me, for any continuance, the most wearisome of all forms of slavery, and the best result I find of my occasional visits to town is the real relish with which I return to my quiet garden and study, where, in the mute society of my own thoughts and books I am never either offended or wearied—{Left at home by Rogers—

18 [Sunday]—Breakfasted with Rogers, and started for home by the railroad at 2 o'clock—Found our poor boy still as I left him, and the anxious mother, though every minute almost by his bed-side, yet finding time to help cheerfully in packing for our dear Nell, who, to my great regret was to leave us on the morrow.

19, 20, 21 &c [Monday–Wednesday]}

23 [Friday]—Received Lord Fitzroy's answer to my letter—refusing, as I had anticipated, to give Tom the introduction to Soult, but full of most kind & considerate feeling—The following are extracts from his letter—"I have been considering your poor son's case most seriously, and I really do not feel at liberty to write to Marshal Soult in his behalf. I will confess to you moreover that, however unfortunate his position may be, I do not see the advantage of his entering "La Légion Etrangère" and I find this to be the opinion of a Gentleman of Authority,[1] in such matters whom I had the opportunity of consulting yesterday by the merest accident. I do not know what the precise object may be in having with the Corps d'Armee in Algiers a "Légion Etrangère." It can be from no want of men, of whom France possesses an abundance and whom she can place in the ranks at any moment by means of Conscription. But I conceive it to be from a natural desire to save the national troops from fatiguing and unhealthy services, & to have what must be done performed by those whose lives are less valuable to them. Nor do I know how officers in this corps are paid. It is presumed, however, that the duties to be discharged are such as to render imperative

on an English gentleman the possession of comforts which his mere pay alone cannot command; and that, after all, with all the exposure to disease and extraordinary fatigue, your son would not be better off in this respect with the Légion Etrangère than he would in the Austrian army.—It is difficult to advise when one has nothing to offer, if our advice should be followed—but I cannot help urging you to reconsider this matter in which your poor son's fate is involved, and to see if his admission to the Austrian army is really out of the question."

Nothing can be more kindly and considerate than this truly high-bred and soldierly letter, and his words "your poor son," went to my heart. It is indeed a bleak prospect for the unfortunate boy. {But he [*MS damaged*] suae ruinae artifex" and has accomplished it, I fear, but too effectively [*MS damaged*] only take care that the ruin does not extend to others far more valuable & more dear to me

22nd. [Thursday]—Were favoured with a visit (and a very kind one) [*MS damaged*] by Doctor Drummond, Lord Auckland's Indian physician, who had come lately on a visit to Bath and to whom Auckland wrote on the subject of our poor boy begging he would come and see him—Having had notice of his intended visit we appointed Kenrick to meet him, & the result of their consultation was "for the time, at least" comfortable and satisfactory.—He had known Russell in India.—Having staid two or three hours with us Doctor Drummond returned to Bath

23, 24 &c. &c. [Friday–Saturday] Have been looking over the curious farrago of things which I have thrown by in my drawer—the pick and cull of the odd communications which I received almost daily from strangers, male & female,—but find they have accumulated so much of late, that even to give extracts from them would be a task far beyond what I have now time for—I cannot help noticing, however, while it is in my memory, an odd sort of compliment I have lately received, namely, an Elegy on my own *death,* by a great admirer (as the poor man appears to be) of my life and writings. It appears, too, that while he was making thus free with *my* existence, he was rather in a fright about his *own*—The following is part of his letter—"The lines I have taken the liberty to forward to you were composed within the immediate prospect of death. I was given over in a decline, and under these circumstances I wrote them—a dying tribute to my Country's Bard, or rather, I should say, to his memory; as, strange to say, they were intended as a monody for the death of a man still living—and long may he live!—Why I should have written on such a subject, I cannot *now* say; But that the sentiments they exhibit are the true feelings I entertained, will not, I trust, be questioned; I shall hardly be accused of flattery, when the circumstances under which these [were com]posed and the event they anticipated are taken into consideration"—[*MS damaged*] there never *was* such a blundering between life and death as he [*MS damaged*] it; and it is only wonderful that I am still well and alive [*MS damaged*] here a few specimens of this Threnody—(or Monody, [*MS damaged*] it.)—

> "Let [*MS damaged*] once more be suspended
>   [*MS damaged*] born it had slumbered before,
> For he [*MS damaged*] with poesy blended,
>   No [*MS damaged*] touch shall wake it no more.
>
> Hark [*MS damaged*] the death-song of sorrow,
>   [*MS damaged*] music sorrowing sings;
> While [*MS damaged*] night which shall never see morrow,
>   [*MS damaged*] hopelessly over its strings.}

25, 26, 27 &c. [Sunday–Tuesday] Some correspondence has passed between me & *Dan* lately, in consequence of a letter I wrote to him respecting a statement made in more than one of his speeches of the hospitable reception given, in Dublin, to the English Protestants, who fled thither for safety in the reign of Queen Mary. He has frequently alluded to this circumstance in his speeches, and more than once quoted a long account from some book, giving in detail, an account of the demonstrations made of this liberal feeling by the Catholic Corporation of Dublin—Though pretty sure that the short notice we have in Ware, Harris &c.[1] is our only authority for so remarkable an event, I wrote to OConnel to beg he would assist me on the subject—His letter (which, being characteristic I shall give an extract from) tells me of course no more about the matter than I had already known from the authors above mentioned.

"My dear Moore—Do not be angry with me for not having sooner answered your letter. The fact is, I wanted to answer it satisfactorily, but have consumed the time in vain. . . . I remember distinctly having read the facts somewhere, though I cannot lay my hand upon the authority—I mean the facts relative to the Corporation of Dublin. Of this much there is no doubt that the Irish Catholics did not persecute any Protestants in the reign of Queen Mary; nay, more, it is quite certain that many Protestants fled from England to escape persecution, and received protection in Ireland from the Irish Catholics . . . &c. &c."—I have since found and unluckily lost again the extract from O'Connell's speech relating to this matter, wherein he enters into the details of the public proceedings of the Dublin Catholics on that occasion. I should be right glad that he had any such historical fact to adduce; but the *real* state of the case is, I believe, neither more nor less than what Ware thus states—"This year several of the Protestants of England fled over into Ireland, by reason Queen Mary began to persecute, &c. viz., John Harvey, Abel Ellis, John Edmonds & Henry Hough, all Cheshire men, who, bringing over their goods and chattels, lived in Dublin & became citizens of this city; *it not being known wherefore they came thither until after Queen Mary's death."*

28, 29, &c. &c. [Wednesday–Thursday] On looking again at O'Connell's letter, I see that he *does* mention those poetical facts which he had stated in the speech referred to—"I cannot bring" he says, "to my recollection where I found the fact of the hiring of seventy-two houses in Dublin for the Bristol Protestant Refugees, in Mary's reign—but find it I certainly did, and will not cease until I find it again."

October 1, 2, 3 &c. &c. [Saturday–Monday] The same melancholy course of life which has been our fate (or rather, the fate of my poor Bessy and her suffering invalid) for the last six or seven months—gleams of hope, now and then, but one after another vanishing, and at last Kenrick has told us we must prepare for the worst. One great consolation is that the poor fellow suffers but little pain—God send it may be so to the last—A night or two since he was singing over some of his favourite songs, and, indeed sung himself to sleep.

{4, 5, 6 &c. [Tuesday–Thursday] I have again found the newspaper scrap from OConnel's Speech & here it is.—

. . . in Sweden, in Denmark, and other countries by the vilest and most sanguinary persecution. Three times (said he) since the Reformation the Catholics were in power in Ireland, and they never persecuted. To be sure, Queen Mary, backed by English advisers, persecuted Protestants; but at the very time she was so employed, the Catholic corporation of Dublin opened no less than seventy houses for the support of the Catholics [*sic*] in Bristol who fled from Mary's persecution. Several hundred of these people were [*MS damaged*] clothed, and lodged for a period of two years when [*MS damaged*] were sent back fat and [*MS damaged*] The Irish. . . .

7, 8, 9, &c. [Friday–Sunday]—Have not mentioned, I beleive, a kind letter I received from Lord Auckland, since his return, in answer to one I wrote him expressing my gratitude for his great kindness to our poor Russell "You are very grateful" he says "for very little. Having a palace and 400 servants, I might well afford to give a bed to the son of an old friend."

10, 11, &c [Monday–Tuesday]—It is rather a comfort to find that *all* people don't write good poetry nowadays, and that there are still some followers of good old doggrel left. The following extract, for instance, from a tailor's advertisement, in to-day's paper, is quite refreshing

> Our last compare with what you've paid before;
> Then see the goods, you'll wonder more and more.
> And recollect the plan that we purs*ue*,—
> For what don't please, the money's return'd *you*.

12, 13, &c. [Wednesday, 12 October–Wednesday, 19 October] A letter, one of these days, from a young would-be author, whose notions of "merit" are rather amusing. "Sir—being about to publish a work, and conscious of the merit which your name will attach thereto, I most respectfully submit your subscription &c. &c"

20 [Thursday] A most [kind note] from Lady Lansdowne asking me to come & dine there [on Thursday] (the 20th) to meet Sydney Smith and stay till Monday. Knowing [*MS damaged*] not just now leave Mrs. Moore alone she makes an arrangement to [*MS damaged*] Mrs. Hughes to Sloperton on Saturday and likewise take [*MS damaged*]—could not of course say "No" [*MS damaged*] but ill-fitted for society just now. The sad scenes [*MS damaged*] still haunt me wherever I go. But my darling Bess, too, [*MS damaged*] some change, so I answered in the affirmative.

22nd. [Saturday] To Bowood [*MS damaged*]—Company, besides Sydney, Lady Elizabeth, Lady Mt Edgecomb and Horatia, Drury and his pupil, young Pierrespoint—Sydney's story of [*MS damaged*] whether he wasn't a Bishop?—"Yes, Ma'am" "But, where's your [*MS damaged*] gone to be let out."—His account of the confused state of [*MS damaged*] half asleep between the Thirty-Nine Articles and the Nine [*MS damaged*] which was which, or whether there were only Nine Articles [*MS damaged*] or the contrary.

23 [Sunday]—Sydney preached [*MS damaged*] "So use this world as not to abuse it"—a good plain matter-of-fact sermon and as little Sydney-Smithical as possible—Party at dinner the same as yesterday—minus Drury & pupil. Some Sacred things of Rossini's played charmingly in the evening by Lady Mt. E. and Horatia.}

24 [Monday]—{Home. Received letters, and both about the same time, from Tom and our Spanish friend Madame de Villamil, informing us of no less an event than a proposal of marriage having been made to Helen de

Villamil by Master Tom and, as it seems accepted by father and mother! What a drama (and a most Tragic-comical one) is this world of ours! Answered both—but have not time to say *how*—Great difficulties (as I anticipated) about Tom's military scheme—but no lack of kindness in any quarter. A most anxious letter from Chabot to Lady Lansdowne (as she told me) enquiring Tom's address.} Wrote a day or two since to Tom, asking him to come here as soon as he could to see poor Russell—It is strange—but some lines of my own, long forgotten, have lately turned up in my memory, which are sadly applicable to my poor Bessy's present affliction—All I remember of them is that they were written, at somebody's request, for some unhappy mother, who was suffering under the anguish they so poorly describe.—

There is no grief beneath the sun
   Like that with which the mother sighs,
Who sees her first, her only one,
   Withering away before her eyes.

And if that One be loved as well
   As thou art, darling child, by me,—
Ah, parents' hearts alone can tell,
   How deep thy parent's misery!

{25, 26 &c [Tuesday–Wednesday]—Received while at Bowood a communication from that Man of Latin, Archdeacon Wrangham, who seems really to live, move & have his being in Latin. A most polite note, in English accompanies the exercises he sends me, beginning as follows "Archdeacon Wrangham with [*MS damaged*] compliments ventures to obtrude on Mr. Moore, whose recondite learning he has often had occasion to admire, a copy of some humble translations [*MS damaged*]

27 &c. [Thursday] Not a bad story—somebody saying to [*MS damaged*] didn't believe in the Athanasian Creed—"Why, [*MS damaged*] "Ah, the Archbishop has fifteen thousand a year [*MS damaged*] the same rate, if I was as well paid for it."}

November 1, 2 &c. [Tuesday–Wednesday]—A visit from Lord Auckland and Miss Eden;—neither of them much changed in appearance. Their friend, poor Russell, being unable to receive Lord A. in his bed-room, but will I trust when they next come, as he now seems really to have made a rally—took a long walk with Lord A. across the Spy-Park fields, in order to put him in his way to Lacock. He has got grey and grave—a sad alliteration.

3, 4 &c [Thursday–Friday]—Received an amusing little book about "Whist," with the following note from the anonymous author—"The author of the accompanying trifle has been so frequently and so highly amused delighted and astonished with Mr. Moore's works that he has requested his publishers to forward the volume with this note." A most anxious and urgent note from Lady Lansdowne asked me to come for two or three days during the stay of the Clarendons, John Russells &c. and proposing an arrangement by which her carriage should bring Mrs. Hughes to stay with Bessy during my absence and then take her back again. Though not very well myself and with a mind any thing but comfortable, could not refuse such kind importunity. Nothing indeed could be more truly affectionate than Lady Lansdowne has been to my poor Bess during the whole of this sad trial—no sister could be more kind.

5[Saturday]—To Bowood—the carriage having brought Mrs. Hughes—but I preferred walking thither—Company at dinner—the Aucklands, John Russells, Clarendons, Strangways, Lady Kerry & one or two more.

6 [Sunday]—Read & worked a little during the day—In the evening, volunteered to sing, seeing that Lady Lansdowne felt delicate about asking me—was glad to be able to make the effort, and got on much better than I expected—all seemed greatly pleased

7 [Monday]—Meant to have closed my visit this morning, but Lady Lansdowne & indeed the whole party urged so anxiously my staying over to-day, that I agreed to return, if, on seeing how all was at home, I could do so with comfort—Lord John, too, offered to walk with me to Sloperton, both to see Mrs. Moore and to bring me back. Our walk very agreeable, and after sitting for some time with Bessy, he returned to Bowood alone, taking along with him my promise to come to dinner—The same company as yesterday with the addition only of Paulet Scroope—In the evening, Lord John begged of me to begin my singing (if I *did* sing) a little earlier, in order that Lady John who is obliged to go early to-bed, might hear me—having missed it last night. Did so, of course—{In a nice letter Lady Lansdowne has from Mrs. Napier there is the following passage—"Norah (her youngest daughter) is tolerably well and strong and grown beautiful—There was a Fancy Ball here lately, and her sisters contrived a dress for her that suited her particularly—Alethe in the Epicurean. She had a soft white muslin dress, with a blue girdle covered with stars, a tiny looking-glass on her shoulder, her hair hanging down and a number of Brazilian beetle wings threaded into the flowing hair, and one lotus flower on the side of her

head. There could not have been a prettier personification of Alethe, her air & style suited [*MS damaged*] and Mr. Moore would have liked to have seen her."

8, 9, &c. [Tuesday–Wednesday] Among [*MS damaged*] letters is one from Lord Howden from Paris asking me to decide a question which [*MS damaged*] there among some of his friends, whether Lord Byron was ever at [*MS damaged*] to me he says "I assure you I have not done it with [*MS damaged*] say with misgivings, for that would be to doubt your [*MS damaged*] and am I not a brother-Irishman? but to have any communication [*MS damaged*] time" is an epoch in my life not unaccompanied with [*MS damaged*] following is from another letter lately received—"Sir—Having [*MS damaged*] of Maclise's beautiful picture of the Origin of the Harp taken [*MS damaged*] may I ask the favour of you to give me your opinion [*MS damaged*] which he has succeeded in embodying your ideas &c. &c. &c. [*MS damaged*]

10, 11 &c [Thursday–Friday]—Forgot [*MS damaged*] another application I have had lately from a lady named Jane Janning for some autographs of mine to help [*MS damaged*] liberating [*MS damaged*] slaves!—From a printed account she gave me of the last Bazaar held for this [*MS damaged*] America, it appears that the autographs which have brought the best prices are Father Mathew's, OConells and mine. "I beg to draw your attention (the lady says) to how highly prized your autographs have been. If you would give me six, a friend would paint a wreath round the name, and the novelty of this would encrease their value."—What a project! emancipating American slaves with Irish autographs!}

13, 14 &c. [Sunday–Monday] {Having received a letter not long since from Mrs. Banim, widow of the Irish author, begging me to use my influence in her behalf with the Literary Fund Society, I wrote to them on the subject, and was glad to learn by a letter from them to-day that they have in consequence of my application given her fifty pounds}—The Aucklands called in their way from Bowood (which they have left to go to Lord Grosvenor's) having promised to make another effort to see Russell—but the poor fellow was asleep and we did not like to disturb him—

{15, 16, 17 [Tuesday–Thursday]—Day after day passed in anxious efforts to work, but with little success, my fastidiousness and slowness growing the more obstinate as the necessity of despatch increases—have had a great shock, too, in the news of the loss of the Reliance, the ship in which Russell went out to India, and the mate of which (poor Walsh now lost) was so truly kind to him. The ghastly look and hysterical cry of our poor boy on hearing the news (I know not how it came to be told to him) was quite frightful. To Bessy, too, it has been a severe shock for her heart was full of gratitude to Walsh. But so this life goes on—or rather *off*—on every side of us!}

December [Thursday, 1 December–Saturday, 31 December]—I have not had the heart to return to this Journal for some weeks past—All is over— our dear boy expired on the 23rd. of last month, and the calmness, sweetness, and manliness of his last moments was such as to leave even in the mother's heart not only comfort but also pleasure. He suffered but little indeed of actual pain throughout the whole illness, nor was it till two or three days before his death that he became aware of his danger. His mother then, I think, suggested his taking the Sacrament, but he declined or at least deferred doing so—On the morning of the 23rd, he asked his mother to bring pen and ink, and make memorandums of some little gifts he wished to leave. After inquiring about a bequest of £100 left by Betty Starkey which was to fall at some distant period, he said "Very well" and thus proceeded— "Mrs. Hughes may have my chain; she will like that." "And your seal ring" asked his mother—"there's your Papa." "Papa won't wear it." "But he will use it." "Yes—my ring, then, to Papa." "Your dressing case; shall Tom have your dressing-case?"—"He wouldn't like it. Let Herbert Brabant have my dressing case." He then proceeded—"I should like to give something to Annie" (the daughter of our neighbour Mrs. Schomberg with whom the poor fellow, before he went to India was rather in love). Let Annie have the little seal." "What for Ellen? Would you like her to have the little lip-salve box, and Rogers's Italy?" "Yes—send my hunting-whip to Mr. Schomberg— Polly Hughes, my blue purse—Mr. Hughes, of Buckhill would like my pencil"—"And what for Tom?" asked his mother again—"I have nothing to leave that he would like—give him my dying love and Campbell's Poems." He then stopped, as if to rest. "You haven't said any thing for Mr. Starkey?"—to this he made no reply. Turning to Ruth, our good-natured housemaid, he thanked her for her kind attention to him during his illness, adding "I suppose you'll soon be married, Ruth?"—(the girl being, he knew engaged) "Yes, Sir, please God, some time." He then spoke of his clothes, and desired that such as his brother Tom did not like should be sold or given to the poor. After he had rested a little while, his mother asked whether she could do any thing to make him comfortable? "Read to me," he replied—"What shall it be?"—"Read to me about the Communion." After she had read some time, he said "I think I shall take it." His mother read a little more, and then said "Should you like Mr. Drury sent for?" "Yes—but not now." The poor mother then read on until her feelings became too much for her, and she was obliged to stop. After an interval, she asked "Would you like to see Mr. Drury to-day?"—"Yes." He became then composed, and his mother, as usual, washed him, brushed his hair & teeth, and scented his pocket-handkerchief. Drury came and after having talked with him for a short time, said that he did not hesitate to give him the Sacrament as soon as he liked,—"Now or tomorrow?"—"Now" answered the dear boy, and turning to the mother, asked, "Will you take it too?"—"Yes." "Very good." He then attentively watched Drury's preparations for the Communion; and, having before said that he feared Drury would find the room rather offensive, held out his handkerchief for him to smell to. He swallowed the consecrated bread with much difficulty, but when the ceremony was over, Bessy asked him how he felt and he said "Better and more comfortable." "Should you like Mr. Drury to come again tomorrow?" said his mother. "Yes—if I'm alive."

All this, which I have taken down from the poor mother's lips (not being able, myself, to stand the scene) took place on the morning of the 23rd. about eleven o'clock; and within three hours after our beloved child was a corpse.

It is with some reluctance that I enter on this 11th. Volume of my Journal. I *ought* to have finished the year 1842 in the preceding Vol.—but I could not bear to return to its pages after my last melancholy record—If any thing could heal such a sorrow as my dear Bessy's it would be the warm, the affectionate interest taken by all those—but I forbear to say any thing more on the sad subject, and I shall now pass to ordinary matters.

On the 5th. of December, Bessy and I went to Bowood to luncheon— Lady Lansdowne had most kindly pressed us to come there immediately after the funeral and stay some time—telling Bessy that she should have apartments entirely to herself where nobody else should come till she chose it. Nothing, indeed, could be more affectionate & sisterly than her whole manner and conduct towards my poor wife.

{I shall now turn over such odd letters, verses &c. as I have lately received (and *not* thrown into the fire) to see whether there is any thing in them worth recording.

By the enclosed note from Philip Crampton to Mrs. Tom Hume (whose husband's nick-name with his friends is Barney) I perceive that Philip supposes the old Epigram "A knife, dear girl, cuts love some say" to be mine. The answer to the Epigram (which I take for granted is Mrs. Tom Hume's?) is exceedingly good. Have received several letters from a young literary gentleman, in Dublin, who favours me with his opinion of my different works, in the following strain—"If you had written nothing but Little's Poems, your name would be immortal—you would have been known to the latest ages as "purissimae impuritatis auctor" &c. &c. "I have often thought why it is that the Irish Melodies have so great an effect upon me. It is no doubt partly owing to &c. &c. In Lalla Rookh most people prefer the Fire-Worshippers, and some the Veiled Prophet but the Light of the Haram for *me* &c. &c." The following sent to me by somebody, as a curious specimen of impudence, is certainly matchless in its way. But the thief *ought* to have stolen better, while he was about it—for it is one of the worst of all the Melodies that he has laid his hands upon.

[*Clipping missing*]

A Mr. Downes having lately sent me a Volume of his entitled "Temperance Melodies" I wrote him a civil answer marked *"Private,"* and accordingly find it to-day (Decr. 28th.) in the Times newspaper, as follows.[1]

"TEMPERANCE MELODIES."—The *Limerick Chronicle* says, "We feel pleasure in publishing the annexed letter from Mr. Thomas Moore, 'the poet of all nations and the idol of his own,' to Mr. W. M. Downes, the patriotic young bard, whose recent verses in praise of temperance have most deservedly elicited the praise and patronage of the Rev. Theobald Mathew and of all the societies in Ireland enlisted in the same glorious cause:—

"'Sloperton, Dec. 10, 1842.

"'Dear Sir,—I have been prevented by painful circumstances from sooner acknowledging and thanking you for your kind present, as well as the cordial and welcome letter which accompanied it. Your excellent friend, Father Mathew, has, among the millions that look up to him, no greater admirer (albeit an unworthy disciple) than myself, and few things have flattered me more than hearing from a country-woman of ours the other day, that not long since, at a bazaar held somewhere in America for the relief of the black slaves, the autographs that bought the best prices were O'Connell's, Father Mathew's, and those of my humble self. I have not yet had time to look through your book of songs, but I have read enough to satisfy me that they are not (like your subject) *spiritless,* but, on the contrary, considering the theme, very lively indeed. Wishing them and yourself every success,

"'I am, dear Sir, yours faithfully,
"THOMAS MOORE.

"'William M. Downes, Esq.'"

Apropos of Father Mathew, I find connected with his name (in another newspaper scrap) a tune called after myself, of which I never before heard.

[*Clipping missing*]

December 26 [Monday]—Went to Bowood—Company, Lord Duncannon, his son-in-law Ponsonby & wife (Lady Kerry)[1] Twopenny (whom I get to like much better than formerly) a young German, named Kohl, who has published Travels in Russia, and is now just come from *doing* Ireland in the space of six weeks—Miss Fox—

27 [Tuesday]—Tried to work, but was seized by the ladies & set down to the Piano-Forte—sung most abundantly—Additions to the party at dinner— Mr. & Mrs. Shuttleworth, Senior, & Macauley—Again made to sing, and sung till I was quite hoarse—Reminded Macauley of my triumph in having puzzled even *his* omniscience by my song of the crystal-hunters[1]—such hunters having never before been heard of by him—M. Kohl, by the bye, told me of his having been much struck by some Improvisatori (in Irish) he met in the north of Ireland.}

31 [Saturday]—A letter from Tom, which affected Bessy most sadly, telling us that he cannot come to us, before his departure for Algiers—Bessy had counted upon seeing him most sanguinely—though (foreboding the difficulties that might arise) I endeavoured to prepare her for such a disappointment. The reasons he assigns for not applying for a furlough under the circumstances in which he is placed seem all right and prudent, but, not the less for that, disappointing—and saddening—A most kind letter from Lady Lansdowne to Bessy on this subject—

{Received one of these days a letter which lets one into a scene of domestic life rather amusing and dramatic—the eldest son, (a sort of mock-heroic personage) having an air of profound mystery round all his pursuits and movements and so far mystifying the rest of the family as to lead them to think he must be something very great. The part, which I play in this domestic drama is not a little amusing—

"Dear Sir—The following circumstances I trust may be some excuse for the liberty I take in trespassing on you. My only brother, George Gibbon, for many years previous to his decease, which took place some few months since, had been engaged in writing for the press, but in what time and under what name, my father and myself, the only surviving members of the family, have been as yet unable to discover. In a casual conversation that took place a short time before his death, he mentioned something about his having been the author of the lines on the death of the Duke of York, entitled "The Slave" which appeared in one of the London papers (the Morning Chronicle, I believe) a few days after the Duke's death. These lines have very generally been attributed to *you;* and I may also state that at the time of the conversation respecting them, my brother also said that he had had some communication with you on the subject of them. Previous to his death he sealed up almost all his papers, with an injunction that they should not be opened for some time to come, so that from them we are unable to trace any knowledge of his publications. . . . He lived a very retired life & although very communicative with his family on all other subjects, he never let them know any thing of his pursuits. From time to time he used to leave this country, & be absent for weeks, but never on his return let his family know where he had been." The letter which is signed H. Gibbon concludes with a request that I would, if in my power, solve this mysterious gentleman for them. Received under the date Novr. 7th. a most enthusiastic letter from a young Irish linen draper, asking for my autograph. The following scrap describing the effect that the written name will have on him is rich in its way—and there's just room for it here:—

And that in after years I might feel as I looked upon that signature (proudly as did Franklin when he gazed on the conductor of Electricity from the clouds) the latent feelings of the soul roused by the magic of that name—as I said within myself [it] is this, this alone (foolish though it may seem) that [*MS damaged*] me to request, not the formality of a reply but simply your signature—that will suffice—

Should it not be your wish to comply may I beg you will pardon my importunity. And believe me that nothing but an infatuated admiration of your genius and sentiments would have induced me so far to overstep the line of "etiquette" in addressing you as a *Stranger* and on as it may seem to you a frivolous matter—for which in ex-[*incomplete*]]}

Notes to 1842 Entries

1 January

1. Milton, "Il Penseroso," l. 107. The "ex-Lord Chancellor" is Lord Monteagle.

11–13 January

1. *The Rivals,* 4. ii.

28 January

1. There were two French translations of Moore's work *(Histoire d'Irlande)* in 1835 and one in 1836. Moore's *History* appeared in a one-vol. German translation *(Geschichte von Irland)* in 1835, 1836.

2. *Works,* 4: 113 ("Advertisement to the First and Third Numbers"). "If Burns had been an Irishman (and I would willingly give up all our claims upon Ossian for him), his heart would have been proud of such music, and his genius would have made it immortal."

3. The article in the newspaper is an overly enthusiastic tribute to Moore. Moore's covering letter is left as part of this entry, though the remainder of the article is omitted.

4. Moore did not include this item in the text.

14–15 February

1. Dowden, *Letters,* 2:871, in which Moore thanks Moxon for his gift to Bessy.

2. *The Dramatic Works of Shakespeare,* with remarks by T. Campbell (1838, 1843, 1848) and *The Life of Petrarch,* 2 vols. (1841).

3. This poem, entitled "Epitaph on a Well Known Poet," is to be found in *The Poetical Works of Thomas Moore* (Philadelphia, 1831), pp. 394–95. The printed version differs from this one in the last three stanzas.

13–14 February

1. There is a confusion in the dating of the MS at this point, Moore having placed the entries for 14–15 February before those for 13–14.

2. See Dowden, *Letters,* 2:874, where Moore repays the £75 in cash.

3. *Edinburgh Review* 59 (1834): 143–54. See Dowden, *Letters,* 2:779 and 781. In the *Edinburgh Review* article, Moore objected to O'Brien's theory, set forth in *The Round Towers of Ireland,* that the towers are "Buddhistic remains." O'Brien was found dead in bed at the home of a friend on 28 June 1835, aged 27.

23–24 February

1. See 15 Nov. 1841 and its n.1.

3–4 March

1. Baron Pechlin sent Moore his translation of Moore's *Gedichte* (1842). See Dowden, *Letters,* 2 : 872.
2. The excerpts from Byron's letters to Moore contained in this entry are included in Marchand, *LJ,* 11: 196–98.

11 March

1. Moore made two entries under date 11 March.
2. Gerald Griffin, *Gisippus* (1842).

14 March

1. Moore's punctuation creates an ambiguity. It is unclear whether the last sentence was addressed to Bessy or merely included in the Journal.

17 March

1. The Copyright Act of 1842 provided copyright for 42 years from the date of publication, or until seven years after the author's death, whichever came first.
2. "Canadian Boat Song," *Works,* 2 : 322–24.

19 March

1. Alexander Pope, "Eloisa to Abelard," l.200.

22 March

1. "And Doth Not a Meeting Like This Make Amends," *Works,* 6:62.

23–24 March

1. At this point, under dates 25 and 26 March, Russell quotes an undated newspaper article, pasted in the MS, concerning a translation of Moore's *Melodies* into Irish.

15–17 April

1. Moore placed the passages in square brackets at the end of the MS page, with asterisks indicating their location in the text.

18 April

1. A squib signed "P. S.," entitled "The Wooling of Wakley to become a Poet" appeared in the *Times* for 11 April 1842. Wakley, a physician and M.P., had spoken against the Copyright Act and attacked Wordsworth, saying "I could write a bushel of such things; I could write 'em by the mile." The last stanza is a tribute to Wordsworth, "the gray old man of Rydal-Mount," as well as a satire on Wakley.

11 May

1. *The Tailors,* [attributed to Samuel Foote, although he denied authorship] (London: 1778), 1, i.
2. See P. L. Ginguené, *Histoire littéraire d'Italie,* 14 vols. 1811–35), 1: 502 (note to p. 456).

16 May

1. *Works,* 4:257–69.

20 May

1. Moore placed the passage in square brackets at the end of the MS page, with asterisks indicating their location in the text.

23 May

1. *Works,* 3:349.

4–6 June

1. Moore tipped into the MS a newspaper clipping in which a French poem entitled "Reboul" by M. Dumas was quoted. This clipping was followed by Moore's poem "This World is All a Fleeting Show," *Works,* 4:262.
2. Moore included an account of a soirée at the home of the Duchess of Gloucester attended by the Queen, the Prince Consort and the King and Queen of the Belgians at which Moore's *Lalla Rookh* was presented as a tableau.

15 July

1. J. M. W. Turner illustrated the 1839 edition of Moore's *Epicurean.*

24 July

1. The clipping deplores the fact that John of Tuam "hurled" anathemas against the National Board; that "not one national school for the teaching of God's word now stands in the diocese of Tuam"; and that the work of translating Moore's melodies on which the "doctor is busily engaged" will "teach resignation to the starving men of Tuam infinitely better than the Bible."

16–18 August

1. See entry for 15 December 1831. In his biography of Lord Edward Fitzgerald, Moore mentions the claim of Lady Edward "to the near relationship she is supposed to have borne to the family of Orleans." The King denied this claim, and he and his sister Madame Adelaide requested that Moore set the matter right in a future edition.

19–20 August

1. "The Veiled Prophet of Khorassan," *Lalla Rookh,* in *Works,* 6:48–49.

13 September

1. Tennyson, *Poems,* 2 vols. (1842).
2. "Poems by Alfred Tennyson" appeared in the *Quarterly Review* 70 (1842): 385–416.

14 September

1. *King Henry V,* 2. i. 92.
2. William Lynch, *A View of the Legal Institutions, Honorary Hereditary Offices, and Feudal Baronies Established in Ireland during the Reign of Henry II* (1830).

15 September

1. Edward Law, Earl of Ellenborough (1790–1871) was appointed governor-general of India in 1841. He enlisted the services of Sir Charles Napier in a war with the amirs of Sind. Napier conquered the entire country, and the Sind was annexed on 26 August 1842. The campaign was generally condemned as a war of aggression prompted by territorial greed. Andrew Doyle, the author of the articles against Ellenborough, was editor of the *MC* 1843–48.

23 September

1. "I have little doubt, from the wording of this passage—from the capital letters, and from the pains taken to state that it was 'by the merest accident' the opportunity of consulting was afforded, that this Gentleman of Authority was no other than the Duke of Wellington." (Moore's note.)

25, 26, 27 September

1. For Moore's account of Irish religious tolerance of Protestants during the reign of Queen Mary, see his *History of Ireland,* 4: 14–19. His source is Sir James Ware, *Complete Works,* translated by Walter Harris, 2 vols. (1764).

1–31 December

1. The clipping is left as part of this entry because the letter it contains is the only extant copy of the letter known.

26 December

1. Lady Kerry was Augusta, second daughter of John Ponsonby, Baron Duncannon of Bessborough. She married William Thomas, Earl of Kerry (Lord Lansdowne's son), who died in 1836; she did not remarry until 1845. Moore was mistaken in naming Lord Duncannon's "son-in-law Ponsonby" as being of the dinner party.

27 December

1. "The Crystal Hunters," *Works,* 4: 193–94.

Index

This index includes only names of people closely associated with Moore or prominent during the period covered in this volume. A comprehensive index will appear in Volume 6.